Taboo Pushkin

Publications of the Wisconsin Center for Pushkin Studies

Series Editors

David M. Bethea
Alexander Dolinin

Taboo Pushkin

Topics, Texts, Interpretations

EDITED BY

Alyssa Dinega Gillespie

THE UNIVERSITY OF WISCONSIN PRESS

Publication of this book was made possible through support from the Department of Slavic Studies and Literature at the University of Wisconsin–Madison, and from the Nanovic Institute for European Studies and the Institute for Scholarship in the Liberal Arts, College of Arts and Letters, at the University of Notre Dame.

The University of Wisconsin Press
1930 Monroe Street, 3rd Floor
Madison, Wisconsin 53711-2059
uwpress.wisc.edu

3 Henrietta Street
London WC2E 8LU, England
eurospanbookstore.com

Printed in the United States of America

Library of Congress Cataloging-in-Publication Data
Taboo Pushkin : topics, texts, interpretations / edited by Alyssa Dinega Gillespie.
p. cm.—(Publications of the Wisconsin Center for Pushkin Studies)
Includes bibliographical references and index.
ISBN 978-0-299-28704-7 (pbk.: alk. paper)
ISBN 978-0-299-28703-0 (e-book)
1. Pushkin, Aleksandr Sergeevich, 1799–1837—Criticism and interpretation. 2. Pushkin, Aleksandr Sergeevich, 1799–1837—Appreciation—Russia. 3. Pushkin, Aleksandr Sergeevich, 1799–1837. I. Dinega, Alyssa W. II. Series: Publications of the Wisconsin Center for Pushkin Studies.
PG3355.5.T33 2012
891.71′3—dc23
2011042002

I gratefully dedicate this book to my teachers, mentors, and colleagues far and wide, whose example inspires, challenges, and sustains me.

Бойтесь пушкинистов.

Владимир Маяковский

[Pushkin scholars are to be feared.]

Vladimir Maiakovsky

Contents

Foreword

The Power of the Word and the Turn to Taboo

CARYL EMERSON

In his chapter on *The Captain's Daughter* (*Kapitanskaia dochka*) for this volume, David Bethea asks what is surely a central question about Pushkin's handling of the forbidden: "Taboos by definition set boundaries; how does one experiment at those boundaries without becoming tainted?"

The question has relevance both to the poet and to those who study him, for, as artist, Pushkin seems not to taint. To be sure, the behavior of "Pushkin the man" has been subject to withering criticism, stretching from Lev Tolstoi in the nineteenth century to the Soviet literary censor Pavel Lebedev-Poliansky in the twentieth (see Carol Any in this volume). But the texts, as aesthetic artifacts, invariably resist. One of the startling things about this poet—a trait he shares with Shakespeare and Nabokov—is the degree to which lewdness and bawdiness, graphic violence and a wholly unsentimental relation to the body, can coexist with a "chasteness" sensed everywhere in his writing: a lack of embarrassment, a directness of expression, balance, dignity, a sense of honor. Thus, one might argue, in watching Pushkin "experiment" at the edges of taboo we can indulge our own salaciousness while being somehow magically elevated out of it. We feel ourselves purer when experiencing this poet.

Bethea develops the theme of forbidden boundaries mythopoetically and politically in connection with Pushkin's foray into the realm of Catherine the Great's corrupt matriarchy. In that world, it is only Petr Grinev's innate nobility and his ability to push the envelope of permissible intimacy with rebels and outlaws that allow him to preserve his honor in his *own* way, not in the way of his fathers. And thus he survives. Other chapters in this volume emphasize sexual taboos, religious and chauvinistic transgressions, bureaucratic and censorship humiliations. But all are subsumed under Bethea's observation, which was also Iurii Lotman's on the poet's crisis-ridden life. Whenever Pushkin tests boundaries (those he himself provokes, or those that emerge to trap him, or the constraints he was born to and feels honor-bound to address), he transforms the horrific, the disillusioning, the unfree, and the forbidden into a new aesthetic landscape that seems—for all its crude dark matter—sunswept and clean. The power of Pushkin's word derives in part from his radiant play on the boundary of what cannot be said.

This preface speculates on the intrinsic force of such taboo themes in Pushkin's life and works. One framework, drawn on fruitfully by Bethea, Gillespie, and other contributors is Sigmund Freud's 1913 treatise *Totem and Taboo*. Several assumptions made by Freud in that book might be noted here. First, tabooed objects are always ambivalent (that is, part sacred and part unclean). Second, the person who breaks the taboo becomes, in turn, taboo for others within the same community. And finally, according to Freud, three categories of person—each possessing dread powers that must be appeased, tamed, or won over—are maximally liable to be tabooed by other members of the community: enemies, rebel or chiefs, and the dead. All three categories would be relevant to a rebellious, martyred poet from a culture accustomed to revering its writers as (in Solzhenitsyn's phrase) a "second government." But a second government will produce a second rival set of rulers and leaders. The number of inviolate boundaries doubles; the sense of danger rises. For to question or be curious about possible sources or reasons for the prohibition is itself taboo.

Are the taboos that have surrounded Pushkin—as cultural icon, rebel, chief—more intense because he was "martyred"? In 1837, hard upon the fatal duel, Mikhail Lermontov insisted that Pushkin is not just a deceased poet but a murdered poet, an enemy of the tsarist state done to death through the negligence, perhaps even the complicity, of that state's highest authorities. For half a century the image of Pushkin wavered between courtier and dissident, a toady to tsarist power and a victim of it. By the twentieth century, the Russian state had dropped the poet-as-outlaw epithet and embraced Pushkin as its foundational writer. Freud was fascinated by those savage tribes in Borneo that would kill an enemy with extreme cruelty and then thrust dainty morsels into the dead mouth of his decapitated head—on the logic of *first kill it, then get it over to your side*. Victorious warriors (that is, murderers) had to undergo elaborate purification and isolation procedures to atone for their victory, to "win back the body." What a wonderful motto for the Pushkin jubilee of 1937.

In Freud's view, this complicated ritual imposed by society on victorious "murderers" is matched by a similarly massive network of restrictions laid down by society on the rulers themselves. When applied to a Russian context, such reciprocal unfreedom is intriguing. In the arena of poet versus tsar, who is the more powerful ruler? Surely the poet. In a poem from her 1931 cycle *Verses to Pushkin* (*Stikhi k Pushkinu*), Marina Tsvetaeva defined Tsar Nicholas I as a "pitiable gendarme of Pushkin's glory" (Pushkinskoi slavy / Zhalkii zhandarm)—a minor bureaucrat in the age of Pushkin. But Freud would say: no matter who is judged the greater ruler in such a context, each party must continually be both "guarded, and guarded against." Such caution is required because chiefs, kings, and priests are "vehicles of a mysterious and dangerous magical power, which is transmitted by contact like an electrical charge and brings death and ruin to anyone who is not protected by a similar charge."[1]

In tsarist and Soviet Russian culture, these two equally powerful electrical charges, poet and tyrant, primary creator and punitive censor, constantly sought each other out to test their potency against each other. They had to affirm, and reaffirm, that they were "protected [from each other] by a similar charge." Examples of this provocation in Pushkin's life are legion, as they are in the lives of later great poets like Osip Mandel'shtam (who lost the wager) and Boris Pasternak (who miraculously survived it). What is the result of this potent dynamic? The authoritative, even authoritarian, aura of both legacies, poetic and tsarist, continues to grow—and must be placed under taboo. Such a "tribal" (or neurotic) treatment of murderers and their victims is of vital, morbid interest to the politics of Pushkin reception, as several chapters in this volume attest. But other chapters in this book deal not with the politics of reception but with acts of creation, and these require other angles of approach.

A writer (and especially our poet) may place some dark thing under taboo out of superstition. Or alternatively, he may avoid it out of fear of getting a thing going that cannot be stopped. One mark of a true poet is an inborn instinct for patterning, for "situational rhymes" as well as sound and rhythm repetitions. Once set up, these patterns work themselves out in life—because, the poet would insist, lives properly lived *are* like poems. Set up the first half of a rhyme, and inevitably it will come around to trap you; the thought, the contour, will not be complete until it snaps shut on itself. Adopt a rhythmic scheme and you will be pulled into its mesmerizing flow; a radically new metric (or suddenly no metric at all) will fail to satisfy. For Pushkin, this combination of form and content came to rest in his special sense of a "poet's fate"—fixed but in no sense passively realized. The poet must actively struggle to realize his fate in the right way. This struggle was risk laden, dangerous, intuitive, because for Pushkin there were not only pitfalls to be avoided and trials to be undergone but exorcisms to be carried out. And here a second text might be brought to bear on the enticements of taboo, one written by a practicing poet: Ilya Kutik's 2005 study *Writing as Exorcism: The Personal Codes of Pushkin, Lermontov, and Gogol.*

By "personal code" Kutik has in mind a type of poetic shorthand that contains a message *in* code, embedded far below the surface. Exorcism refers to the activity that "writers perform while fighting on paper with their inner demons, fears, and even fate and death."[2] The act of writing can exorcise the fear, shaping self-expression through a "psychological dominant" that Kutik calls an "extra." The subjects of his study each began as poets in the romantic era. They took for granted the transfiguring power of words. Of the three, Kutik reminds us, Pushkin was the most deeply, openly superstitious, fond of creating fictional characters who shared this vulnerability and nourished it through folk taboos and auguries. But at the same time Pushkin, with his neoclassical tastes and intellect, warmed to the challenge of exorcizing superstition with irony.

Kutik notes the various forms this irony could assume in the course of the poet's efforts to find psychic relief: a fixation on numbers, bad omens, fortune-telling, prophecy, which can leak out onto the page to become the anxious poet's recognizable signature. "This type of creative process is fully *conscious*," Kutik notes. "The author knows precisely that *which* he exorcizes, the writer does not suppress or repress his secret fears or wishes, but, on the contrary, splashes them out on paper and thus struggles with them."[3] Kutik is a non-Freudian. He declines to understand creative energy as a product—or byproduct—of a writer in the grip of a neurosis or crippled by unconscious prohibitions. Creativity cannot be understood as some involuntary discharge; its dynamics, more likely, are fueled by tabooed material that the poet consciously reroutes to the surface and forces to assume the form of words. In that realm the poet knows he will win, because the Word is the poet's primary and invincible weapon against every dark force. Key for Kutik is the insistence that "exorcism is not a literary device but a dimension of the creative process and one of its results."[4]

Sigmund Freud would love to deliver a postmortem on the chapters in the present volume. He might say: from what I can tell, your Russian poet is a ruler. And quoting his own *Totem and Taboo,* he would note that "rulers are allowed great privileges"; they may do or enjoy precisely what other people are forbidden by taboo.[5] "As against this freedom," Freud nevertheless cautions us, "we find that [rulers] are restricted by other taboos from which common people [that is, the non-poets, the scholars, those writing for this book] are exempt."[6] Since "contacts with the King" are "healing and protective" as well as dangerous, Freud would fully understand why we crave these contacts with the beloved dead.[7] We fear the power of the ghost even as we worship it. Chances are small that we will improve the perfection of the ruler by meddling in his substance, but to approach his boundary without the risk of being tainted is an irresistible pleasure. Once drawn into his world, we feel that whatever taint came with us has become, for the moment, lighter and less compromising. We borrow a bit of Pushkin's magic by prying into the world that was his secret.

Notes

1. Sigmund Freud, *Totem and Taboo: Some Points of Agreement Between the Mental Lives of Savages and Neurotics,* trans. James Strachey (New York: Norton, 1950), 41.
2. Ilya Kutik, *Writing as Exorcism: The Personal Codes of Pushkin, Lermontov, and Gogol* (Evanston: Northwestern University Press, 2005), 3.
3. Ibid., 5.
4. Ibid., 121.
5. Freud, *Totem and Taboo,* 47.
6. Ibid., 48.
7. Ibid.

Acknowledgments

This book is the end result of a genuinely collaborative effort, having been first conceptualized in the context of a three-day international conference that was held in January 2009 on the campus of the University of Notre Dame. Without the generous financial support of the Nanovic Institute for European Studies, the Institute for Scholarship in the Liberal Arts, and the Graduate School, and the capable assistance of Harriet Baldwin, director of academic conferences for the College of Arts and Letters—all at the University of Notre Dame—such a major undertaking would have been impossible. Particular thanks are due to Jim McAdams, director of the Nanovic Institute, and Anthony Monta, associate director, for their faith in this project from its inception to its final stages. The book's publication is made possible, once again, by support from the Nanovic Institute and the Institute for Scholarship in the Liberal Arts, as well as from the Wisconsin Center for Pushkin Studies book series, whose editor, David M. Bethea, first provided me with the opportunity to challenge received wisdom about Pushkin's life and works (in the context of a graduate seminar on Pushkin in spring 1992) and who has remained a stimulating conversation partner and esteemed mentor to me ever since. I would also like to express my thanks to Gwen Walker, acquisitions editor at the University of Wisconsin Press, for her initial faith in this project and her continuing goodwill even as the manuscript's word count began to creep up and up, far beyond the originally forecast length; to MJ Devaney for her careful and judicious work as copyeditor; to editor Sheila McMahon for her expert assistance with the book's final stages; to Laura Paulini for her striking cover design; as well as to the other excellent personnel at the press with whom I have had occasion to work in bringing this project to completion. Thanks, too, to Margie Towery for creating a thoughtful, comprehensive index. The two readers for the press, Stephanie Sandler and Angela Brintlinger, provided careful, detailed readings of the lengthy manuscript and astute suggestions for revision, and my sincere thanks go out to them as well. Additionally, I am grateful to Katya Hokanson for her assistance with this project in its early stages; she was a welcome interlocutor and a constant source of encouragement and input, and indeed it was her panel proposal on taboo approaches to Russian literature for the AAASS National Convention in 2007 that first formed the kernel of my idea for the book. A generous supported research leave from the University of Notre Dame in 2010–11 allowed me the much-needed time to carry this project to completion. Finally, I must express my tremendous gratitude to all of the book's contributing authors for their wisdom, patience, fortitude, graciousness, and unflagging enthusiasm for our joint undertaking. I have not only learned a great deal in the process of our work together but have derived much pleasure from it.

Note on Transliteration and Translation

The transliterations in this book follow both the Library of Congress system and conventions used in nonspecialist publications. A few first names have been anglicized (Aleksandr has become Alexander, Mariia is Maria, and the apostrophes have been omitted from names such as Natalia and Tatiana). Many last names have been rendered in the form most familiar to western readers (Gogol rather than Gogol', Meyerhold instead of Meierhol'd, Gorky not Gor'kii), and in general the -skii ending in surnames has been spelled -sky throughout. A few Russian nouns commonly used in English have also been spelled according to usual conventions (guberniya, not guberniia), while the Russian spelling of some names has been retained for the sake of consistency (Maksim not Maxim, Lev not Leo, Tolstoi not Tolstoy). Spellings in bibliographic citations all adhere to the Library of Congress system. Translations are the author's unless otherwise indicated.

Taboo Pushkin

Introduction

Beyond Pushkin as Dogma

Alyssa Dinega Gillespie

Russian poet Alexander Pushkin (1799–1837) was a man deeply of his own country and era, but he has come to be seen as a figure outside place and time. Though he was reared on the Enlightenment ideals of the eighteenth century, his playful artistic methods and sensibilities endeared him to the modernists and postmodernists of the twentieth century and continue to make him attractive to writers of the twenty-first century. Twice exiled from Russia's capital cities and viewed with suspicion by both government authorities and his own associates, he was the unlikely progenitor of Russia's national literary and cultural tradition. Yet his art was founded on the creative pilfering, imitation, and assimilation of other nations' literary forms and ideas; his literary genius emerges from a principle of lively artistic syncretism that runs counter to the general Russian tendency toward conservatism and monologic construction of truth and, thus, stands in a paradoxical—and often anxiety-producing—relation to the status he has been accorded as the most perfect exemplar of Russia's unique national spirit. Indeed, the fact that he has been continually forced into this heavily demanding role (which has, at certain periods, burgeoned in scope and significance beyond all reasonable human expectation), combined with the pathos of his early death, has contributed to the sense that he is a sort of messenger from another dimension: "Pushkin himself lived on a sort of uninhabited island, but his manuscripts, sealed in the bottle of time, floated on the waves into the future and are still out there."[1]

This book represents a collective effort to recover some of the messages that have remained sealed in the bottle of time, whether because of overt political and social prohibitions on reading and discussing them, because of scholars' own squeamishness at venturing into uncharted and often uncomfortable realms, or because the very existence of the messages has simply remained unknown and undetected until now. Forays into Pushkin's own writings lie at the center of our project, and these are flanked by investigations into the two kinds of context that form an essential framework for our understanding of the substance and reception of his literary work: the biographic and the scholarly. But before we open the bottle, let us survey the shoals of taboo that litter the ocean in which it has been floating.

Pushkin as Taboo

In Freud's foundational work *Totem and Taboo*, the concept of "taboo" is linked on the one hand with the sacred and the extraordinary and on the other hand with the uncanny, the dangerous, the forbidden, and the unclean.[2] The ambivalence surrounding the taboo reflects both its desirability and the risk of imitation—and thus contagion—inherent in its violation; as a result, the principle of the taboo is, in Freud's terms, "not a neurosis but a social institution," a "cultural creation" whose transgression "would quickly lead to the dissolution of the community" and that therefore may be understood to lie at the very foundation of the social order.[3] The contemporary French-born philosopher René Girard makes a very similar argument in the context of his theory of mimetic desire when he writes that the sacred and the forbidden share a social purpose: "Prohibitions serve a basic function. They maintain a sort of sanctuary at the heart of the community."[4]

Whether or not one is generally inclined to a Freudian-Girardian interpretation of human behavior, it must be acknowledged that these thinkers provide a basic definition of taboo that is both insightful and useful in an empirical context. Their understanding of taboo as an ambivalent, titillating yet toxic, principle that serves as the cornerstone of a given community and thus must be zealously guarded—a principle potentially linked with both the sacred and the demonic, both the magic of transcendence and the curse of transgression—is a productive starting point for a discussion of the problem of taboos in Pushkin studies. Indeed, the grounding of taboo in the enforcement of societal conformity and, mutatis mutandis, in the codification of a communal identity turns out to be key to understanding the ways in which Pushkin's works and image have been both exploited and regulated by successive Russian regimes. Nevertheless, despite a few excellent studies that have begun pointing in this direction, the workings of taboo have hardly been explored in relation to Pushkin's afterlife in Russian culture and society: the very topic of taboo in connection with Pushkin has been itself taboo.

And yet what has been interpreted by scholars in recent years as the history of the making of the official "Pushkin myth" could just as well be read in the inverse manner: as the history of a serial accumulation of taboos surrounding Pushkin's biography, works, and reception.[5] For the taboo functions as the photographic negative of the myth: it is the unmentionable category that (though usually undetected) always silently, relentlessly accompanies the category of the obligatory, the catechistic, the formulaic, the dogmatic. The taboo is the inscrutable underside of the shining cultural icon into which Pushkin has been fashioned, the enticing umbra of the "sun of Russian poetry." Just as there can be no understanding of light without an appreciation of darkness, so it is precisely the accompanying presence of taboo that lends the myth of Pushkin as Russia's quintessential national poet its binding, even terrifying, force, "to the point of passion, infatuation, sectarianism. . . . Don't touch our holiest of holies!"[6] This canonization or "consecration" of Pushkin, his elevation to the realm of the holy and untouchable, occurred, perhaps surprisingly, even in the atheistic society of Soviet Russia, though it was couched in overtly secular, patriotic terms.[7]

Beginning soon after his death and continuing to the present day, Pushkin has been served up in officially sanctioned editions, biographies, edicts, and celebrations as charismatic "pretext, symbol, cloak" (these words of the nineteenth-century populist thinker Nikolai Mikhailovsky point toward the tabooed unspeakable hidden in the sign) legitimizing the Russian state's power over the Russian populace.[8] In the process, a series of officially mandated "Pushkins" has been created, transforming the poet from a champion of autocracy in the tsarist era, to a proto-Soviet patriot and promoter of the *narod* (common people) in the Soviet era, to a deeply devout Orthodox Christian in post-Soviet times.[9] Sergei Davydov has aptly dubbed this unlikely series of political appropriations of Pushkin's image "ideological 'body snatching.'"[10] During the Soviet period in particular, a rigid system of literary institutions, publications, and prestige grew up around the ideological imperative to mold and control the Pushkin myth; the remnants of this system still survive today, despite altered ideological circumstances. In the Russian diaspora, too, Pushkin was pressed into service as "the embodiment of what was most profoundly Russian"—an "anchor" of religious, philosophical, and cultural identity standing in opposition to "Sovietness" that was upheld by a vigorous international network of "Pushkin Committees"; the post-Soviet Orthodox Pushkin can be seen in large part as an outgrowth of this émigré Pushkin.[11] Yet irrespective of changing bureaucratic institutions and the wildly lurching vicissitudes of Russian history, in every era Pushkin's status as a quasi saint has been inseparably linked with his purported embodiment of the ineffable essence of "Russianness" or what has been called "the Russian idea."[12] Thus, one contemporary Pushkin scholar (Irina Surat) even goes so far as to claim that Pushkin is totally inaccessible to non-Russians, that he is "tabooed for other nations [*tabuirovan dlia drugikh narodov*], just as a national or religious sacred object may be tabooed."[13]

The proclaimed "father of Russian literature" and originator of the graceful, capacious Russian literary language from which the self-identity of the modern Russian nation originates, Pushkin can thus be seen as the apical ancestor of the clan writ large. He is a powerful totem both worshipped and tabooed, whose dominion over literate society has been vigorously maintained and promoted by the reigning political elite.[14] In this context, the ecstatic dictum of nineteenth-century literary critic and poet Apollon Grigor'ev that "Pushkin is our all" (Pushkin—nashe vse), which has often been pressed into ideological service, takes on an ominous tone. In every era, indeed, Pushkin's image has been used to define the limits of all and nothingness, of us and them, of loyalty to and betrayal of an ideal, a government, a people, a language, a culture, a nation. And it is precisely the lurking presence of taboo that has given these limits their form and their bite.[15] As a result, critics who would propose interpretations that deviate from the ideologically sanctioned veneration of the poet's image have been so completely relegated to the margins by the proponents of the official Pushkin myth that they dare not speak except in hints and whispers; explicitly dissenting views have been construed as tantamount to hooliganism, profanation, or even treachery. Yet, despite the dangers, Pushkin's enforced sanctity has not always remained intact.

Taboo Uses of the Pushkin Idea

Poet Vladimir Maiakovsky begins his 1924 "Jubilee Poem" ("Iubileinoe") by introducing himself informally to Pushkin, his addressee, and sets off on a loose verbal ramble in which he bemoans the state of Soviet poetry and fantasizes about working together with Pushkin on *agitki* (propaganda posters), all the while chatting with his imaginary dead poet-comrade as an equal. He ends with the admission that he loves Pushkin "but alive, not mummified" (no zhivogo, / a ne mumiiu) and dreams of dynamiting the Pushkin monument on Tverskoi Boulevard in Moscow. The wistful comment early in the poem that sometimes one feels alienated from life and then, suddenly, "through all the nonsense you understand something big" (bol'shoe / ponimaesh' / cherez erundu) is perhaps the central idea of Maiakovsky's address to Pushkin. At the same time, it is the core of his challenge to the official Pushkin myth, which shuns nonsense, informality, the uncontrolled verbal ramble, alienation from the enforced ideal, and thus life itself—privileging instead seriousness, death, mummification, and unhesitating fealty to immovable monuments.

The informality and alienation that underlie Maiakovsky's poetic address to Pushkin comprise an appropriate challenge to the power of the Pushkin taboo, insofar as they contravene his totemic status, based as it is on the necessity of an oxymoronic combination of formalized, awed distance and clan affiliation. Reimagining Pushkin back into a living, breathing, touchable, fallible human being is thus a highly transgressive act. Given that Maiakovsky performed it in the 1920s, however, before the Soviet Pushkin had been codified and while such irreverent fantasies could still be aligned with the laudable revolutionary mode that was engaged in breaking down the idols of the tsarist past, the act was still admissible. Early Soviet humorists such as Daniil Kharms and Mikhail Zoshchenko likewise used informality and alienation to poke fun at the Pushkin myth. Their good-natured satire, however, was directed more at the foibles of their compatriots and at contemporary social problems than at Pushkin himself. For example, in one of Kharms's anecdotes, Pushkin's famed indolence (coded as a tendency toward "dreamy contemplation" [mechtatel'noe sozertsanie]) is contrasted with novelist Ivan Turgenev's vaguely ridiculous revolutionary bustle in purely Soviet terms and language: "First he'd drop in to sign a petition, then it was off to the nihilists' meeting or some civil funeral rite" (To zabezhit petitsiiu podpisat', to k nigilistam na zasedanie, to na grazhdanskuiu panikhidu). Kharms thus gently mocks the ethos of his own society; Pushkin is the means rather than the target.

Such an oblique strategy was apparently more acceptable to the reigning powers than a direct assault on the poet's cultural status would have been.[16] Other writers in the 1920s and 1930s, both those living in Soviet Russia and those in emigration (including the poets Valerii Briusov, Vladislav Khodasevich, Marina Tsvetaeva, and Anna Akhmatova), formulated their own personal Pushkin ideal ("my Pushkin" [moi Pushkin]) that stood outside the officially mandated one ("our Pushkin" [nash Pushkin]) without ever directly challenging the authority of the latter.[17] In some cases the moral authority of the official Pushkin was even co-opted by the individual, becoming an implicit sign of continuing humanity in the face of a tyrannical and inhuman regime, as when Evgeniia Ginzburg recites the entirety of *Eugene Onegin* (*Evgenii Onegin*) from memory on a transport train to the Gulag—to the amazement of the guards, who are themselves restored to a semblance of humanity by Pushkin's words.[18]

The qualities of alienation and informality, standing in for the humanity of the unruly "alive, not mummified" Pushkin and thus a potential source of cultural renewal and reinvention, have remained a hallmark of individuals' creative dissent from the official myth of the poet. It is no accident, then, that the most controversial iconoclastic response to the Soviet Pushkin cliché was, like Maiakovsky's poem, founded on the conceit of an informal ramble (in this case, both verbal *and* peripatetic)—a ramble that estranges the reader from the official Pushkin even as it brings the dead poet miraculously back to life. The generically unclassifiable *Strolls with Pushkin* (*Progulki s Pushkinym*) by Abram Tertz (the pen name of Andrei Siniavsky) was surreptitiously written in the form of letters to his wife during his imprisonment in a labor camp in the late 1960s and published in the West in 1975 and then in Russia in brief excerpt in the journal *October* (*Oktiabr'*) and in full in the 1990 issues of *Questions of Literature* (*Voprosy literatury*) that appeared in 1991, unleashing a furious backlash that continues even today. Writing under a Jewish pseudonym, Tertz portrays Pushkin as a quintessential outsider, by turns female, Jew, and vampire. Stephanie Sandler has perceptively discussed the ways in which "the woman, the other, the explicitly and dangerously sexual, facilitates a seemingly non-erotic, nation-defining drama between men" in this work.[19]

Yet one could go even further in analyzing why it was that Tertz's playfully irreverent work resulted in furious accusations that he was a "'russophobe' who had 'defiled Russia's national treasure.'" Not only does his essay "violate official borders and . . . [trespass] on forbidden territory, . . . rambling over boundaries and treading on space traditionally held sacred in Russian culture" but it also subverts the very basis of the official Pushkin formula from within.[20] It does so by daring to exaggerate the already highly exaggerated official dogma of Pushkin's supposedly universalizing "protean nature" to proclaim, in effect, that what is known as "Pushkin" is an empty signifier, a vessel into which any expedient contents can be poured: "Emptiness was Pushkin's content. Without it he wouldn't have been full, he couldn't have existed, just as there can be no fire without air, no inhalation without exhalation. It more than anything else ensured the poet's receptivity, which yielded to the fascination of every caprice. . . . He all the more industriously and truthfully devours the souls of others because he doesn't have enough stuffing of his own, because for him impersonation is a way of life and subsistence."[21] Although these words have greatly discomfited those who insist on a narrowly worshipful attitude toward the poet, they in fact comprise an attack not on Pushkin himself but on the proclivity of tyrannical regimes (and the conservative Pushkinists that serve them) to plug the floating-point variable of the dead poet into their inflexible ideological algorithms.

In essence, what Tertz has done here is to reveal that the emperor has no body under his new clothes: as Mikhailovsky had suggested a century before, "Pushkin" is a scarecrow, a pretext, an artificial construct, ideologically manipulated and engineered. The taboo, then, exists only for the sake of social control; the totem it supposedly protects is nonexistent, a cynical fiction. It is not so much the transgression of particular taboos surrounding Pushkin's image as the annihilation of their very basis for existence that renders Tertz's ramblings anathema in the hearing of his conservative, nationalistic detractors (for if there is no such thing as Pushkin, then there is no such thing as Russia!). In this sense, Tertz's work can also be read as a sophisticated metaliterary meditation on the constructedness of the very category of the author. What we have come to know as "Pushkin," in short, is a politically expedient fiction lacking intrinsic spiritual reality, a carefully engineered phenomenon rather than a noumenon.

In the glasnost period and beyond, artistic unmaskings (or what Liudmila Zubova terms "deconstructions") of the official Pushkin have multiplied.[22] To cite just a few examples, in works such as Iurii Mamin's satirical film *Sideburns* (*Bakenbardy* [1990]), Timur Kibirov's epistolary poem "To Serezha Gandlevsky on Several Aspects of Today's Sociocultural Situation" ("Serezhe Gandlevskomu o nekotorykh aspektakh nyneshnei sotsiokul'turnoi situatsii" [1990]), and Tatyana Tolstaya's dystopian novel *The Slynx* (*Kys'* [2000]), the two axes of formality/informality and affiliation/alienation that shaped earlier works of creative dissent from the Pushkin myth continue in force, although they function differently in each of the given works.

Rather than emphasize alienation from the myth, *Sideburns* adopts the opposite tactic, taking affiliation and formality to a preposterous extreme as the Pushkin cliché replaces the now-shabby Lenin cliché and subsumes a town full of aimless, brawny, highly sexed late-Soviet youth. It transforms them into a strictly regimented army of neofascist "pushkinists" (pushkintsy) who are ready to kill in the name of maintaining the social order but who eventually devolve into chaos and are destroyed by the civil authorities. By casting Pushkin in the unlikely role of leader of a new, violent personality cult, Mamin suggests the proclivity of the Russian psyche toward totalitarianism. By the same token, he reveals that the exploitation of this national characteristic is inherent in the construction of Pushkin as idol.

Kibirov's long poem, on the other hand, revolves around a different sort of cultural substitution. The poem is infused with a profound sense of double alienation from the late Soviet "sociocultural situation," in which the familiar, though empty, political slogans are replaced with even emptier signs of capitalism ("where before there gleamed 'Glory to the Communist Party,' now 'Coca-Cola' shines" [gde siiala ran'she "Slava / KPSS," tam "Coca-Cola" / Gorit]). In a state of self-ironizing nostalgia, Kibirov counters this commercialization of daily life with a poetic antidote: he absorbs scattered fragments from Pushkin's best-known verse into his own lines with irreverent but fond informality, even as he marks his own and his society's bittersweet estrangement from the mawkishly reductive official Pushkin cliché: "He is squeezed into an epigraph, / rammed in, defiled, sold on the black market, / not a hybrid of monkey and tiger / but a mixture of Samoilov with Rubtsov" (On uzhimaetsia v epigraf, / zabit, zamyzgan, zafartsovan, / ne pomes' obez'iany s tigrom, / a smes' Samoilova s Rubtsovym).[23]

Tolstaya's unsettling novel takes place two hundred years after a catastrophic Blast (Vzryv) has destroyed Soviet (and perhaps world) civilization—an event that parodically signifies the dissolution of the Soviet Union yet at the same time recalls Nikolai Gogol's oft-quoted statement that "Pushkin is an extraordinary occurrence and, perhaps, a singular occurrence of the Russian spirit: this is the Russian man in his development as he will appear, perhaps, two hundred years from now."[24] The inhabitants of what was once Moscow are debased mutants, barely human, who sport strange bestial appendages such as cockscombs, tails, and claws and subsist on a diet of mice, worms, and weeds; they live in a highly regimented but morally corrupt society that at once evokes both the Stalinist "glory days" and post-Soviet Russia.[25]

In this gruesome context, Tolstaya takes a different approach to the debunking of the official Pushkin: her two central characters, a new-age mutant youth with artistic inclinations and an elderly member of the old Soviet intelligentsia who survived the Blast, carve Pushkin in wood—an idol, a totem pole. They thereby reify the Soviet Pushkin cliché, all the while ironically invoking yet another totemic model, the Alexander column from Pushkin's poem "I built myself a monument not made by human hands" ("Ia pamiatnik sebe vozdvig nerukotvornyi"), which has entered their fractured (and often nonsensical) language as a formulaic and thus essentially meaningless verbal trope: "Old pushkin-mushkin probably didn't want to get married either. . . . His proud head rose higher than the Alexander column. He rode in sleighs. Was bothered by mice. Ran around with girls, got his rocks off. He was famous: now we're carving a Pinocchio of him . . . Pushkin is our be all and end all [*Pushkin—nashe vse*]—the starry sky above and the law in our heart!"[26] These ramblings do not possess the dangerously iconoclastic insouciance of Tertz's creative debunking of the Pushkin myth but are rather an instance of the sanctioned and highly codified familiarity that the myth itself allows, according to which Pushkin becomes a household name, a beneficent household deity, the unquestioned law of existence.[27] And indeed, the totem that the two characters produce is not only strictly faithful to the formula of the official Pushkin monument ("the bowed head and the arm, . . . a curly head, a straight nose, and a thoughtful face, . . . [s]ideburns, . . . the shoulders, arms, hands, the arms are the most important. Understood? Bend the elbow") but also ominously reveals its ideological origins in the fact that it is carved out of a type of wood that bears the name of the head of the secret police ("dubel't" in the original Russian, rendered as "beriawood" in English translation).[28]

In effect, Tolstaya, not unlike Iurii Mamin in *Sideburns*, debunks the Pushkin myth not by countering its force or estranging her characters from it but rather by causing them to embrace it to the fullest extent possible, in the process revealing and actualizing the taboos that delimit the myth and so give it substance. But whereas Mamin's emphasis is on societal taboos, with Pushkin serving as menacing inhibitor of anarchy and a cynical political ordering principle, Tolstaya's emphasis rather is on emotional and spiritual taboos, with Pushkin serving as inhibitor of human self-expression. Thus, "the pushkin," as they refer to the totem carved out of beriawood, has six fingers. This accidental deformity is an allusion to the six-winged seraph of Pushkin's poem "The Prophet" ("Prorok") and so a satirical embodiment of Pushkin's supposed spiritual superiority, but at the same time, it is a projection of Tolstaya's characters' own mutant semihumanity. They are absurdly unable to bring themselves to cut off the extra finger ("But . . . [h]ow could he, so to speak, dare to have the Freethinking temerity to blasphemously hack off the poet's hands at his own caprice? A tail was one thing, but this is a hand!!!"), demonstrating that formalized Pushkin worship serves as a proscription against freedom of thought and thus prevents both them and Pushkin from attaining a fully human status.[29]

Moreover, the pushkin's inviolability also results in its lack of a bodily nether region: "And the pushkin didn't have any legs, they decided not to bother with legs. They didn't have time. Only the trunk, just down to the sash around his shirt. After that it was like a stump, all smooth."[30] This smooth stump that replaces groin and legs is reminiscent of the unmentionable missing genitalia of the princesses in Pushkin's own *Tsar Nikita and His Forty Daughters* (*Tsar' Nikita i sorok ego docherei* [1822])—an absence that serves a satirical purpose in Pushkin's poem and in *The Slynx* ingeniously incarnates the principle of taboo inherent in Pushkin's idolization. (Incidentally, the eponymous "slynx" [kys'] is a mythical, unseen creature that is itself a figment of taboo and a fear tactic, a tool for societal control.) Pushkin is superhuman; hence Pushkin's genitalia are unspeakable to the point of nonexistence. Fittingly, Tolstaya's totemic pushkin, like the Pushkin of the official myth, ultimately becomes a scapegoat: it is incinerated, cynically burned at the stake by the new regime in the name of the preservation of art.[31]

Pushkin in Today's Russia

Literary scholar and theorist Iurii Lotman notes that "ethical maximalism is deeply rooted in the very foundations of Russian culture."[32] In his meditation on Russia's historical patterns, he observes the persistence of a Russian tendency toward explosion or catastrophe over the gradual, evolutionary progression that is typical of the Western historical process. Russia, unlike the West, thinks in binary categories, according to Lotman, and rather than retaining and modifying cultural values as society evolves, Russia holds to the binary ideal of "complete annihilation of everything that existed formerly as if it were contaminated by incurable defects."[33] Furthermore, whereas the trinary Western system "strives to adapt an ideal to reality, the binary one attempts to realize an unrealizable ideal in practice."[34] Although this radical approach is at first inspired by the poetic promise of the "instantaneous construction of a 'new earth and new sky,'" it inescapably leads eventually to yet another cycle of disillusionment, decay, and catastrophe.[35] Writing in the early 1990s shortly before his death, Lotman voiced these reflections on the Russian preference for cataclysm over gradual change in the context of the situation in his country at that time and his fear that Russia would once again give in to its destructive habits rather than embrace the chance to build constructively on past experiences and thereby move closer to the West. Pushkin's official status now, twenty years later, can serve as an indicator of the extent to which Lotman's worst fears have since been realized.

In his 1987 book *Perestroika: New Thinking for Our Country and the World* (*Perestroika: Novoe myshlenie dlia nashei strany i dlia vsego mira*), Mikhail Gorbachev called for a new world vision compatible with Lotman's in which Russia would be fully incorporated into a "common European home." A decade later, in the wake of NATO expansion and renewed tensions between Russia and the West, this vision of Russia's future became untenable, and Boris Yeltsin established a Kremlin committee to search for a Russian "national idea" to replace the lost ideology of communism. The effort produced nothing save "a digest, a catalogue, an inventory of the opinions published in Russian mass media, a digest that was not even accompanied by an analytical commentary."[36] In the mid-1990s, the communist past served Russians as a common, negational point of reference, but no positive, affirmational vision could be constructed in the void of history. As one scholar put the matter in an article published in 1994: "Denied a recognized place on a recognizable spectrum of political forces, political subjects migrate toward that grand cenotaph, Russia. There, attempts at self-validation in terms of some greater concept of nation seem to confuse matters further, as pragmatic orientations are overwhelmed by mythic notions retrieved from the past."[37] The dilemma continues to the present day, as witnessed, for example, in a recent editorial in the *Literary Gazette* (*Literaturnaia gazeta*), whose author bemoans the fact that twenty years after the revolutionary removal of the iconic statue of Felix Dzerzhinsky (the first Bolshevik secret police chief) from the center of Moscow, nothing has replaced the monument: "The empty hole—both on Lubianka Square and in the consciousness of the people, as well as in the politics of our government—still gapes; one might even say it triumphs."[38]

In other words, post-Soviet Russia has found itself in a paradoxical situation. On the one hand, Russian culture is trapped in what Serguei Oushakine has termed a nostalgic state of "aphasic regression" in which "the major part of the population" is "'locked' within the old frame of symbolic (e.g., Soviet) references."[39] On the other hand, Russian politicians and intellectuals display a compulsion to discredit, vehemently and unequivocally, every facet of the Soviet experience (recalling thereby Lotman's commentary on Russia's fidelity to a self-destructive binary ideal). In the years since Vladimir Putin's rise to power, this paradox has led to a perplexing practice of simultaneous regurgitation and demonization of Soviet-era mythic constructs, a practice that has become entrenched and routinized in the general cultural discourse. This ailment is nowhere more apparent than in the episode of the "Name Russia" ("Imia Rossiia") television contest devoted to Pushkin, which was broadcast by Rossiia 1 television channel on 17 December 2008.

The "Name Russia" contest was dedicated to the selection of the historical figure judged to be "the most valued, notable, and symbolic [*tsenimyi, primetnyi, i simvolichnyi*] personality of Russian history"; this project was thus, in some sense, the natural successor to the Kremlin's "national idea" committee of a decade prior. The contest began in spring 2008 with a long list of five hundred names supplied by the Institute of Russian History of the Russian Academy of Sciences, which was trimmed down to fifty names and then to a shortlist of twelve. Each of the final twelve contenders was presented to viewers in a separate hour-long dedicated television episode; these were broadcast throughout fall 2008. The final outcome of the popular vote was Alexander

Nevsky in first place, Petr Stolypin in second, Joseph Stalin in third, and Pushkin in fourth; in the judges' vote, Nevsky and Pushkin tied for first place, with Alexander Suvorov in second and Stolypin in third (Stalin occupied tenth place).[40]

From a Western perspective, the relevance of a mass-media spectacle such as the "Name Russia" television contest to the niceties of scholarly research on Pushkin is likely not immediately apparent. Yet in the world of post-Soviet Russia, constraints on the media (television in particular) and on academic freedom are closely related. Since the late 1990s, the Russian mass media have ceased to be independent and have become, instead, a tightly controlled mouthpiece for politicians—in particular, for Putin's efforts in the 2000s to reshape the symbolic image of the nation into a new "Great Russia" characterized by meek forbearance in the face of challenges, patriotic unity, a heritage of Russian Orthodoxy, and a shared national devotion to combating perceived internal and external foes.[41] The state-owned Rossiia 1 channel (previously known as RTR or Channel 2) on which the "Name Russia" contest aired supported Putin faithfully in the 2000 presidential election and therefore, following the election, enjoyed preferential access to the president and to major news events.[42] This channel also served as "a sort of assembly shop for the symbolic reality of Russia in 1999, a prototype for the 'Great Russia' that the commentators, the politicians, the army and the government finally succeeded in building at the end of a decade of chaos and power struggles"—indeed, both Putin's rise to power and the rise of the new "Great Russia" image were, at base, television constructs.[43] Rossiia 1 is second in popularity only to ORT (Channel 1), and in 2008 (the year of the "Name Russia" contest) it boasted 75 percent of the urban weekly audience; according to the channel's website, it is now viewed by 98.5 percent of the Russian population.[44] Hosting the "Name Russia" contest in such a venue ensured an enormously wide captive audience for the government, which was intent on shaping a renewed popular conception of Russian heroism.

The line between journalistic freedom and academic freedom is almost impossible to draw in the contemporary Russian context. Academics critical of the government are not only reportedly barred from television news and political talk shows but are even sometimes digitally erased from such broadcasts before they are aired, and at a recent convention of the Russian Academy of Sciences, journals and newspapers were summarily banned.[45] Even more disturbingly, in May 2009 (just six months after the "Name Russia" contest concluded), Putin's hand-picked successor as president, Dmitrii Medvedev, signed a decree establishing a commission to detect and combat attempts to "falsify history to the detriment of Russia's interests," particularly in regard to World War II and its aftermath as well as the atrocities of the Stalinist period, which the current regime has chosen to downplay in its own quest for authoritarian legitimacy.[46] The penalties for such "falsifications" range from three years' imprisonment for the average citizen to five years for a journalist or public figure (a category which, presumably, includes academics).[47]

In such a political climate, it is perhaps unsurprising that the scholarly portfolio of the Russian Academy of Sciences' Institute of Russian History features such didactically inclined projects as "Russia's Historico-Cultural Heritage and Spiritual Values," a government-run program titled "The Patriotic Formation of Citizens of the Russian Federation," and, perhaps most tellingly of all, "The Renascence of Russia" ("Vozrozhdenie Rossii"), a wide-ranging and ambitious (in both ideological and scholarly terms) initiative spanning the years 2008–11. The ruling United Russia Party's announcement in June 2010 that it was forming a commission to draft a new textbook that would present a party-approved, patriotism-inducing version of Russian history that would then become the uniform standard in school curricula fits squarely within this pattern of governmental meddling—supported by the efforts of carefully selected, like-minded (or opportunistic) academics—in the world of scholarship, particularly in fields concerned with Russia's history and cultural heritage.[48]

Thus, the same controlling and tabooing political forces are at work in contemporary Russia in the spheres of both the mass media and scholarly discourse; it is significant that the "Name Russia" contest was cosponsored by Rossiia 1 and the Russian Academy of Sciences' Institute of Russian History and also that the broadcast episode devoted to Pushkin called on the expertise of a highly placed, elder Pushkin scholar as a means of conferring the stamp of venerable academic authority on the televised proceedings. In such a climate, where both the media and the academy are necessarily (or must appear to be) in cahoots with the ruling political elite and their ideological priorities, an examination of the way Pushkin was presented in the "Name Russia" mass-media extravaganza can reveal the underlying constraints and directives imposed on scholarly study of Russia's foremost poet as well.[49]

The hour-long television episode in support of Pushkin's candidacy in the "Name Russia" contest began with the screening of a brief documentary film before roundtable panelists and their studio audience.

This film provides baldly unambiguous documentation of the Putin-era rendition of "official Pushkin," which, oddly enough, parallels the Soviet "official Pushkin" in its compulsoriness and zealous predictability, even as it departs radically from the substance of the Soviet Pushkin on almost every point. Narrated by a deep, guttural, male voice that almost seems to growl and that evokes associations with the villain of a horror movie, the film begins with a critique of past generations' failure to bring Russia to the state of greatness for which she is destined and ends with an accusation against a post-Soviet Russian public (a vaguely defined yet barbed "we" [my]) that has proven unable or unwilling to rise to the level their guardian poet demands of them. The eerily unsettling background music at the beginning and agitated music at the end of the film deepen the subliminal sense of fear, urgency, and danger that the narrator's message conveys. The entire film is framed within a context of taboo and is overtly and unashamedly didactic, propagandistic, menacing.

This film's ideological contents can be argued to encapsulate neatly the three core principles of today's Pushkin myth. First, Pushkin both represents and justifies Russia's aggressive certitude in the greatness of her international destiny. Second, Pushkin is capable of unifying all rifts in the national fabric—in particular, the rift between the post-communist present and the tsarist past. And third, Pushkin is a deeply Christian figure whose name is synonymous with Russian Orthodoxy and who is even responsible for Russia's reawakening to religion—a reawakening that, it is strongly intimated, was the cause of the Soviet Union's downfall (!). As the narrator explains, in a tone of mockery modulating into triumph, "The Bolsheviks hoped that Pushkin would illuminate their illegitimate [*samozvancheskii*] power, write them into the book of eternity [*propishet v vechnosti*], and guarantee their mythological right to run the country. But he, conquering the formulas of the dead textbook, returned to the people who had been infected with the plague [of communism] [*zachumlennye liudi*] the sensation of a free [*vol'naia*] life, the ideal of human dignity, and to some, also, religious faith." The echoes of Pushkin's own themes and vocabulary—the illegitimate ruler (samozvanets), eternity (vechnost'), plague (chuma), liberty (volia)—in this passage are far from accidental; these echoes represent a strategic attempt to harness the subconscious "Pushkinian" stratum of viewers' moral sensibilities.

Throughout the documentary film, the three principles of the new Pushkin myth are articulated in a hyperbolic and often jarring manner. For instance, the principle of Pushkin as the healer of historical rifts is invoked when, in a single breath, the poet is given credit not only for his usual achievements according to the well-worn cliché—he "linked two ages, gave to our culture a common language"—but also for having "drained the blood from communism [*obeskrovil kommunizm*]"! How he might have anachronistically accomplished this monumental (and, one might add, following Tertz's lead, vampiric) task is left entirely to the imagination. At the other ideological extreme, Pushkin is reimagined as a sort of new "great leader" who makes vast masses of the Russian population dispensable—a chilling suggestion in light of historical memory: "It turns out that Pushkin does not so much stand together with Russia's politicians, intelligentsia, and citizens but rather stands in place of them [*kak by vmesto nikh*]; he has substituted himself [*zamestil soboiu*] for millions of spiritual good-for-nothings." The jagged propagandistic language, tone of admonishment, and subliminal message of warning and threat that are used throughout the film illustrate its bizarre aim of using Soviet linguistic, rhetorical, mythopoetic, and political strategies to nullify Soviet ideologies in the ideological vacuum created by the collapse of the Soviet ideal.

A good example of this strategy of simultaneous substitution and nullification is found toward the end of the short film, when a passage from Pushkin's poetry is quoted out of context. It is thereby forcibly melded with political meanings wholly foreign to the original text and to Pushkin himself (Boris Tomashevsky once decried this practice of "dogmatizing and quotation-mongering" in post–World War II Pushkiniana[50]). The passage in question is six lines from the unfinished 1836 poem "There was a time: our young holiday" ("Byla pora: nash prazdnik molodoi")—the last, wistful example of Pushkin's poetry dedicated to his friends at the lyceum, in which he reflects on the innocence of their youth and their failure to intuit the coming storms of history (the conflict with Napoleon of 1812 and, implicitly, the Decembrist revolt of 1825):

Чему, чему свидетели мы были!
Игралища таинственной игры,
Металися смущенные народы;
И высились и падали цари;
И кровь людей то Славы, то Свободы,
То Гордости багрила алтари.

[What, what have we witnessed! The playthings of a mysterious game, the confused peoples rushed about; and tsars were elevated and fell; and the blood of people crimsoned the altars in turn of Glory, Freedom, Pride.]

Pushkin's mode in these lines is philosophical rather than political; he is commenting on the capriciousness of history's muse and on the futility and ephemerality (as well as self-centeredness) of any political ideology. Yet when quoted in the context of the post-Soviet "we" of the "Name Russia" documentary film, Pushkin's words ("What, what have we witnessed!") come to refer to the sufferings and privations of the Soviet period and its traumatic aftermath and thus take on the opposite inflection, a purely political tonality in which "Glory, Freedom, Pride" are elevated to a paranoid, jingoistic slogan. Simultaneously, Pushkin's abstract and symbolic "altars" are accorded a newly literal, religious meaning, and the cue to wallow momentarily in a collective mood of disillusionment is intended to sublimate the potential for anarchic rage and impotent vengefulness that might otherwise break through to the surface. (Any viewers who could recall from memory the poem's final lines might also have subconsciously linked Pushkin's portrait of Tsar Nicholas I as "the new tsar, severe and mighty, [who] placed himself briskly against Europe's border" [novyi tsar', surovyi i moguchii, / Na rubezhe Evropy bodro stal], with the figure of Vladimir Putin.) This bait-and-switch quotation tactic is worthy of the formulaic twisting and tweaking of Pushkin's words at Soviet Pushkin jubilees—which, however, the narrator is careful to malign expressly, calling them "jubilee attacks of obscurant Pushkin-mongering [*pushkinobesie*]." It is telling that this phrase is the strongest, most vitriolic language in the entire course of the film's narration. Clearly, the similarities between the Soviet-era mass spectacles dedicated to promoting the official Pushkin and this post-Soviet reenactment, complete with cued applause, are too close for comfort.

The screening of the documentary film at the beginning of the 17 December 2008 television episode was followed by a brief presentation in support of Pushkin's candidacy and then a roundtable discussion by a panel of venerable political and cultural figures (all of them, incidentally, male), which was conducted before a live studio audience amid a game show atmosphere. In the course of this discussion, the three components of the new Pushkin cliché (Pushkin as a symbol of nationalistic pride and aggression; his ability to repair the cultural, temporal, and geographical rifts that beset post-Soviet Russia; and his status as the incarnation of the Russian soul and true faith) were everywhere apparent, as were the regions of taboo implied by these officially mandated interpretations. Metropolitan Kirill, the head of the Russian Orthodox Church, charted one domain of taboo surrounding the poet's figure when (via prerecorded video feed) he pointedly omitted any judgment against Pushkin's personal (especially sexual) foibles, instead absolving him of moral wrongdoing through the circuitous argument that the deeply Christian and conservative Fedor Dostoevsky would never have been what he was without Pushkin. The patriarch also indicated in no uncertain terms the chief religious and political taboos governing the post-Soviet image of Pushkin in his emphatic denial that the poet had ever been a freethinker (i.e., atheist) or a revolutionary (these, of course, were the two linchpins of the Soviet Pushkin cliché).

Pushkin's purportedly aggressive patriotic stance and his status as an apologist for Russian imperialism were confirmed by the patriarch's quotation from the poem "To the Slanderers of Russia" ("Klevetnikam Rossii"), a reactionary invective written in response to the 1831 Polish insurrection that was republished on the front page of the newspaper *Soviet Russia* (*Sovetskaia Rossiia*) in 1992.[51] Quotations from a number of other Pushkin works in praise of tsars and empire, as well as several off-handed comments by roundtable participants (on the recent Russian-Georgian conflict, and on the Ukrainian capital Kyiv as a "Russian" city, for example), confirmed Pushkin's new function as a code word for Russian chauvinism and rampant nationalistic ambitions. Pushkin was said (and made) to be "absolutely contemporary" (kraine sovremenen), the "primary carrier of what we call 'Russianness' [*russkost'*]." Such comments mask discomfort with the tabooed matter of Pushkin's racial heritage. Although racial innuendo was not lacking in the discussion, this uncomfortable topic was quickly dispatched with the outrageously unfounded—but presumably ideologically reassuring (from the point of view of international power symmetries) and thus compensatory—assertion that Pushkin and U.S. president Barack Obama have shared bloodlines.

The leading academic who, as mentioned earlier, independently confirmed Pushkin's elite stature was also included in the television broadcast via prerecorded video (presumably it would have been unseemly for this ultra-earnest Pushkinist, as for the patriarch, to sully himself by descending in person into the live television arena). Valentin Nepomniashchy of the Russian Academy of Sciences' Maksim Gorky Institute for World Literature in Moscow—whom Svetlana Evdokimova and Vladimir Golstein credit with having given birth to a new discipline they term "Orthodox philology" and with having accomplished a new form of ideological "mummification of Pushkin"—proclaimed Pushkin's paramount spiritual role in today's Russia, voicing the inflated (Dostoevskian-style) idea that Pushkin "is simply indispensable for the salvation of our culture."[52] Russia must think about the human soul, in contrast to the West, which, according to Nepomniashchy, thinks only of material comfort and is therefore tumbling into a moral abyss. Indeed, in a 2005 interview published under the revealing title "Pushkin as a Question of National Security" ("Pushkin kak vopros natsional'noi bezopasnosti"), Nepomniashchy lashes out against the West and its "propaganda of tolerance," arguing that the Western-induced normalization of Push-kin's occasional lapses into obscenity is a threat to the very DNA of the Russian character:

> Pushkin, it would seem, had always been the unshakable pillar and center of the Russian world. Even now he is called none other than "our all" [*nashe vse*]. But what is our all? . . . Only specialists know what attacks are now being launched against academic Pushkin studies. The goal [of the attackers], in the best case, is to adapt Pushkin to the accomplishment of some sort of private aims and, in the worst case, to excuse through the intercession of a genius the unworthy and, frankly, shameful [sensibility] that they are attempting to legitimize in our consciousness as the norm. . . . Geneticists have directly stated that a once-tabooed lexicon [when released from taboo] destroys the foundations of the human, his genetic code.[53]

Nepomniashchy spectacularly moves on from this stunning announcement to a reading of *Eugene Onegin* as a parable of Russian moral resistance to the "grasping instinct" (khvatatel'nyi instinkt) that post-Soviet Russia has learned from the capitalist West and then to a declaration that the American cartoon version of *Winnie the Pooh* is a cultural "catastrophe"! At base, his key point is that Pushkin represents the unifying soul of Russia, its "shared spiritual space" (obshchee dukhovnoe prostranstvo) that stands firmly against the corrupting influence of creeping capitalism and the moral relativism with which it goes hand-in-hand, both of which are motivated by the West's "inexorable egotism and passion for self-satisfaction," in contrast with Russia's "self-sacrifice, . . . self-denial, feats of heroism, and suffering." Nepomniashchy's religious vocabulary reflects the dominant scholarly approach to Pushkin in contemporary Russian Pushkin studies: as Irina Surat observes in an article on the 1999 post-Soviet Pushkin jubilee: "Both Pushkin and his future fate are . . . a matter of faith."[54]

Indeed, many comments proffered during the "Name Russia" broadcast were compulsory declarations of Pushkin's essentially messiah-like status and salvational powers: "We need [his ability to voice the high ideals of holy Rus'] today as we need air"; "Faster: we need Pushkin today as never before!"; "The name of Pushkin is a holy name"; "His genius lies outside of time"; "He will never leave us, he is always with us, everywhere in all places." One additional profession of faith displaces Russia's previous cultural saint through a parodic play on an old Soviet formula: "Pushkin always has been, is, and will be with us!" echoes Vladimir Maiakovsky's slogan "Lenin lived, Lenin lives, Lenin will live!" (from the 1924 poem "Komsomol Song" ["Komsomolskaia"]). Perhaps even more significantly, this statement also echoes the famous spiritual ode "God" ("Bog" [1784]) by eighteenth-century poet Gavrila Derzhavin: "Thou wert, thou art, thou wilt be ever!" (Ty byl, ty est', ty budesh' vvek!).

Those scholars who have dared to subvert this dominant "Orthodox philological," nationalistic approach to Pushkin's biography and works in recent years have been vilified. Although the "Name Russia" contest was a phenomenon of mass culture, it clearly encapsulated, albeit in simplified form, the primary currents of today's officially sanctioned Pushkin myth. It also clearly (even threateningly) sent the message as to which areas of potential inquiry (relating to sex, race, politics, religion, language) are now off-limits. As one of the roundtable participants said, "In essence there is nothing to add [to our current knowledge of Pushkin]," while another offered the conspicuous corrective, reminiscent of a Soviet-era "social demand" (sotsial'nyi zakaz), that Pushkin's "iron will, which championed Russia's national interests," is, however, still not sufficiently studied.[55] The limits of allowable scholarly latitude are clear.

Although it is difficult to ascertain to what extent the new Pushkin cliché served up during the "Name Russia" broadcast reflects the directives of the highest political authorities, Metropolitan Kirill's participation indicates at least some degree of governmental "interest" if not involvement, given the close ties between the Putin regime and the Russian Orthodox Church. As Irina Surat notes, already at the time of the 1999 jubilee, the promotion of Pushkin's status was seen as a matter of post-Soviet political expediency and an antidote to Russia's general "inferiority complex," which had reached a crisis point due to NATO's bombing of Yugoslavia the previous spring.[56] However, the Pushkin portrayed during the 1999 festivities—a jolly, carnival version of the poet ("cheerful, domestic, vivacious, well-dressed, superfluous, persistent, slightly banal")—was markedly different from the 2008 Pushkin of the "Name Russia" contest; he was a sort of endearing Yeltsin-Pushkin by contrast with today's stern Putin-Pushkin.[57] The past decade has witnessed a noticeable tightening of the ideological reins.[58]

Taboo Pushkin

During the glasnost era, in both the media and the fine arts, newly permitted freedom of expression largely came to mean the possibility of critiquing negative aspects of Russian society. This widespread indulgence in demoralizing *chernukha* (blackishness, unrelenting pessimism) bred a distasteful association between civic freedoms and denunciatory rhetoric in the popular mind, which soon grew weary of both.[59] Thus, a survey conducted in the winter of 2003–4 found that 76 percent of the Russian population favored restoring censorship over the mass media.[60] Indeed, popular opinion in Russia over the past decade has come increasingly to value "order" over freedom, a preference that Pushkin—who was himself constantly drawn to exploring the dynamic interaction between these two complementary principles, in his life as in his art—could not have countenanced. Yet this post-Soviet preference for *poriadok* (order), often couched in terms of moral respectability (poriadochnost') and amounting to "toeing the official line," carries over, as well, into the domain of scholarship, particularly scholarship on Pushkin. Scholarly approaches, topics of study, and methods of argumentation that do not conform to accepted standards are subjected to strong judgmentalism and stigmatized, as in the pejorative phrase "alternative Pushkin studies" (al'ternativnaia Pushkiniana) that is sometimes attached to them.[61]

Nor are the current restrictions on Pushkin scholarship—or attempts to break free of them—anything new. During Russia's Silver Age (the early years of the twentieth century), in particular, modernist writers attempted to escape the stultifying utilitarian constraints of critical realism by turning their attention back to Pushkin and romantic writers generally. As Greta Slobin has shown, their "appropriation of the irreverent Pushkin" became a key ingredient of their creative rebellion and of the new modernist aesthetics: "For this purpose they undertook to restore the authentic image of Pushkin from the varnish of 'misreading' arising from his position in the official cultural-literary canon."[62] Slobin argues that "irreverence" came to supplant "adoration" in the modernist attitude toward Pushkin, even as the practice of *bran'* (invective) in addressing Pushkin replaced customary protestations of love.[63] The rediscovery of Pushkin's incendiary narrative poem *The Gabrieliad*

(*Gavriiliada*) and its incorporation into the Pushkin canon, first championed by symbolist poet Valerii Briusov and later by the leading Soviet Pushkin scholar Mikhail P. Alekseev, represented a first step toward the overcoming of religious and sexual taboos that had distorted (and still do distort) readers' understanding of Pushkin's oeuvre and creative path.[64]

The Soviet experiment, however, largely put an end to such risky scholarly innovations—the towering achievements of Soviet Pushkin studies in the comparatively safer arenas of textological, linguistic, and biographical analysis notwithstanding. Among the Russian émigré community, too, Pushkin has been treated mostly as an untouchable, revered talisman of the Russia that was lost, an inviolable repository of the cultural values assaulted by the Bolsheviks. It is only in the last decade or so—with the onset of soul searching that has accompanied the end of the previous era's ideological command structure and the beginnings of scholarly attention to the mythologizing processes to which Pushkin has been subjected across past historical eras—that a new phase of recalibrating Pushkin's image has begun. The critics of this post-Soviet project have dubbed its motivation "demythologization"—a dirty word akin to *chernukha* for many contemporary Russian academics. Nikolai Pertsov's lament in the context of a July 2008 polemic with émigré scholar Alexander Zholkovsky makes this attitude plain: "The demythologizer is bent upon the mockery and debasement of [his] subject, on turning it topsy-turvy. . . . The immorality and irresponsibility rampant in many aspects of Russian life . . . are fully conducive to a mood of general cynicism in the sphere of culture too."[65] For Pertsov, any critique of the official Pushkin myth is anathema.[66]

In his response to Pertsov's accusations, Zholkovsky attempts to tame his opponent's language, noting reasonably that "the business of demythologization . . . is the fundamental imperative of contemporary poetic study. . . . [W]here there are myths, there should be demythologization, which does not at all imply the overthrow of the author, but rather an adequate search for the meaning of the author's mythology."[67] In a recent conference paper Tatiana G. Shemetova similarly defines "demythologization" in such a way as to remove all pejorative connotation from the term: "The task of a demythologizer is to revivify the object by means of a defamiliarized reading, as if one were reading a previously unknown author."[68] While the substance of these remarks may strike one as self-evident, the fact that scholars like Zholkovsky and Shemetova have found it necessary to voice them at all is revealing of the current state of academic discourse around Pushkin.

Against this highly charged cultural background, we offer the present volume. Our contributions are heterodox in their themes, approaches, findings. Taken together, the chapters of this book strive to bring into being a more fully realized Pushkin and demonstrate how potent a challenge the unofficial, tabooed, "alternative" Pushkin has proven to be across the centuries, not only for the Russian political establishment but for the literary establishment too. This patchwork does not pretend to constitute a complete panorama, but by revealing to the gaze at least a few select fragments in all their fascinating and complex detail, we hope to contribute to a more robust appreciation of the poet's restless, all-encompassing genius and to stimulate further such efforts in the future.[69]

It is important to note that the taboos surrounding Pushkin have never been static but have evolved alongside the Pushkin myth; what was permissible in the Bolshevik 1920s was out of the question in the Stalinist 1940s, while what was taboo in the 1920s might well seem quite tame by the standards of today. It is hard, if not impossible, to talk *in theory* or *in general* about the taboo on Pushkin, to define what it is, where it is, since by its very nature it is the inverse of *what is* and *what may be* at a particular cultural moment: the unspoken, unknown, uncontemplated. However, *in practice* it is possible to demonstrate the workings of taboo-in-action in specified, carefully drawn contexts and to use the tools of responsible scholarly inquiry to go beyond taboo in order to discover the worlds of unexplored, explosive meaning that lie within. This is the project on which the authors of this book have collectively embarked. As Vladimir Novikov has observed, any new approach to Pushkin is fraught with dangers: "This territory in the course of two hundred years has become completely littered with the mines of myths: at any point one could explode."[70] But along with these risks come great rewards.

Many taboo-breaking stunts of the young Pushkin are well known but not well studied. Nor has the enduringly transgressive nature of his personality and poetic gift been subjected to close scholarly scrutiny. Past attempts at artistic and scholarly approaches to Pushkin that boldly disregard or circumvent taboos or, alternatively, activate submerged taboo potentials in Pushkin's life and writing have been suppressed or neglected in official Pushkin studies. Indeed, to this day, some of Pushkin's own words and works are omitted from even the most authoritative academic editions. These general regions of cultural and scholarly blind spots, then, have led to the three major divisions of our collection: "Taboos in Context," "Taboo Writings," and "Taboo Readings."

The chapters in the opening section, titled "Taboos in Context," cover a broad set of topics related to Pushkin's own life and the society in which he lived, ranging from his government service career to his relations with the Decembrists, early poetic influences, and religious freethinking. The book's second part, "Taboo Writings," begins with an illuminating case history of the scholarly tabooing of what is indisputably Pushkin's most "undesirable" poetic work, *The Shade of Barkov* (*Ten' Barkova*). The following chapters in this section analyze the sexual, religious, social, linguistic, and political taboos that Pushkin himself explores in various texts—some of which are canonical and receive prominent place in Pushkin scholarship, and others that are mostly ignored or quarantined. The third and final part of the book, "Taboo Readings," illustrates the evolution of taboo-laced or taboo-skirting interpretations in accordance with the changes in cultural, intellectual, and political sensibilities over time. This section begins with a contemporary reading of *The Captain's Daughter* (*Kapitanskaia dochka*) as a proto-Freudian master-narrative of the internal "family dynamics" of the Russian nation, in which taboo plays a central role; the remaining chapters dip back into the Soviet past to examine tabooed critical and creative interpretations of Pushkin's works from various historical vantage points. As our book draws to a close, it becomes clear that Pushkin's richly ambiguous works—which can be interpreted in new contexts in ever new ways (a hermeneutic versatility that was perhaps born of the censorship of his own era)—proved to be fertile source material for the Aesopian subterfuge in which Stalinist-era writers and scholars in particular were compelled to engage. The theatricality both of Pushkin's own life and works and of the scholarly practice of officially sanctioned Pushkin studies is inescapable. "Pushkin," ultimately, becomes a performance of authenticity of one kind or another—whether subversive or legitimizing.

The Pushkin myth requires a heroic Pushkin at its center, and heroism in turn requires the kind of binary maximalism that Lotman posits as characteristic of Russian culture: a Russian hero must be all good, all bright, all pure. Yet in studying certain tabooed nodes of Pushkin's biographical story, our authors present a much more complex picture, in the process returning Pushkin from heroism to basic humanity. The central arguments of two chapters from our book's first section that address, respectively, the two poles of Pushkin's biography—the mundane and the spiritual—can serve as illustrations of how this restoration comes about.

In the opening chapter of the present volume, Irina Reyfman recovers the "repressed memory" of Pushkin's career in government service, contradicting as she does so the received wisdom that he entered such service only under duress and suggesting that, at times, he may in fact have striven to cooperate with the government. She likewise overturns the notion that Pushkin was justified in viewing his appointment as a court *kammerjunker* (junior chamberlain) later in life as demeaning and unreasonable, thus suggesting that his own resentment at the title was itself unreasonable and made him the (until now unrecognized) butt of other writers' irreverent satires. In sum, the mythic separation of Pushkin the poet from Pushkin the government functionary, Reyfman concludes, is unjustified: in life Pushkin was as much one as he was the other, and it is only our belated historical gaze and our commitment to the mythical vision of Pushkin as martyr that finds this coincidence improper.

Oleg Proskurin addresses a different sort of inaccuracy of the belated historical gaze. In his chapter, he takes on the post-Soviet hagiographic approach to Pushkin's biography through the prism of the poet's multi-staged interchange with Metropolitan Philaret, who was canonized by the Russian Orthodox Church in 1994. Proskurin challenges the recent construal of Pushkin as an Orthodox Christian poet, dissecting the several texts that Pushkin addressed to Philaret (whether openly or in camouflage) to argue that what has been read as Pushkin's sincere "conversion" and thus Christian salvation thanks to Philaret's intervention was, in fact, a tactical play with genre conventions. Rather than confessing his deepest religious convictions to Philaret (as scholars of the "Orthodox philological" persuasion have argued he does), Pushkin instead transposes the terms of the discussion from the treacherous terrain of faith/disbelief to the theme dearest to him: the sanctity of poetry and the poet. Pushkin emerges in the process as neither an unrepentant atheist nor a humbled saint, neither an overt rebel nor a yielding subject. Rather, he is a poet playing the subversive game of poetry—which is what he cares most about—within the rules and confines of his society.

As these two representative examples show, in our collection the heroic, mythic Pushkin is replaced by a multifaceted, ambiguous Pushkin—one much more difficult to encapsulate in simple binaries and thus more interesting but also more dangerous from the myth-enforcing point of view, which relies on the assumption that reality can always be unequivocally bisected. In fact, if any common refrain can be gleaned from the diversity of the studies that comprise our taboo-analyzing and taboo-breaking project, it is the idea that what is most toxic, most dangerous, most taboo about Pushkin is his proximity to the very essence of taboo: his ambiguity, his double-voicedness, his tendency toward the blurring or pollution of boundaries—social, racial, sexual, generic, gender, linguistic, stylistic, national, political—in particular, the boundaries between the figurative and the literal, art and life, word and deed, the sacred and the profane. For the deepest function of taboo is to make and to keep such separations inviolable. One should not boil fish and meat in the same pot (Rybu i miaso v odnom kotle ne variat), as the Russian saying goes. In the context of the highly regimented culture and society in which Pushkin lived (and lives on), these transgressions (or the potential for such transgressions) could not but engender a strong reaction on the part of the authorities: a word that may become deed has an explosive and fearful power.[71] In the context of Russian society today, in which meanings are once again strictly circumscribed, the threat of the Pushkinian word released from the silencing, binding power of taboo retains its potency.

And yet, as both Freud and Girard well understood, the taboo is rooted in desire. Desire is at the core of human existence, experience, and institutions. Without desire, there is no humanity. All the more so is desire at the core of poetry. And thus, in its craving to transcend the mundane in the guise of the prosaic and to channel infinity through music and magic, poetry is inherently taboo. Indeed, thinkers as diverse as Plato and Sir Philip Sidney have recognized that poetry is a dangerous, disorderly, and exciting business. Without desire or danger, without the ability to shock, startle, condemn, arouse, there is no poetry, and all of human experience is flattened out or, worse, controlled and tyrannized.

Pushkin's work, perhaps more so than that of any other Russian poet, is shot through with desire. In large part, it is a metaphysical desire that collapses all antimonies and transcends all limitations—the most dangerous kind. In Abram Tertz's eloquent formulation, "It is the very readiness of Pushkin's restless eroticism to touch everything on the face of the earth, sometimes eclipsing this world and sometimes returning its light, that deprives this very eroticism of distinct boundaries and helps it pour itself out into thoughts that at first glance have no relation to it and seem uncharacteristic of it, but which in fact demonstrate its force and tensile strength."[72] The aim of this book's contributors has been to convey the relentlessly desiring eroticism of Pushkin's writing, to shiver and thrill at his genius, his daring, his naughtiness, his spiritual thirst, and to follow him wherever he goes. At the same time, we have had to free Pushkin, and ourselves, from the grip of ideological taboos, unexamined assumptions, and critical inertia in hopes of seeing the poet clearly and reading his works with open and receptive minds.

Notes

My thanks go to Oleg Proskurin and Igor Pilshchikov for their highly informative presentations at the Pushkin conference at the University of Notre Dame in January 2009; their insights helped to shape my thinking about the role of Pushkin in contemporary Russian society. I am also grateful to Caryl Emerson, David Bethea, Oleg Proskurin, David Humbert, and the University of Wisconsin Press's manuscript readers for their helpful comments on an earlier version of this introduction.

1. Tatyana Tolstaya, *Pushkin's Children: Writings on Russia and Russians*, trans. Jamey Gambrell (New York: Houghton Mifflin, 2003), 82.

2. Sigmund Freud, *Totem and Taboo: Some Points of Agreement Between the Mental Lives of Savages and Neurotics*, trans. James Strachey (New York: Norton, 1950), 18, 22.

3. Ibid., 71, 32–33.

4. René Girard, *Violence and the Sacred*, trans. Patrick Gregory (Baltimore: Johns Hopkins University Press, 1979), 221. Mary Douglas likewise analyzes the relationship between primitive ideas of contagion and the role of ethics in modern societies, finding that the danger of "pollution tends to support moral values," which have a "socially useful function" (*Purity and Danger: An Analysis of Concepts of Pollution and Taboo* [London: Routledge and Kegan Paul, 1966], 135, 131).

5. On the formation and evolution of the Pushkin myth see, for example, Marcus C. Levitt, *Russian Literary Politics and the Pushkin Celebration of 1880* (Ithaca: Cornell University Press, 1989); Boris Gasparov, Robert P. Hughes, and Irina Paperno, eds., *Cultural Mythologies of Russian Modernism: From the Golden Age to the Silver Age* (Berkeley: University of California Press, 1992); Paul Debreczeny, "Zhitie Aleksandra Boldinskogo: Pushkin's Elevation to Sainthood in Soviet Culture," in *Late Soviet Culture from Perestroika to Novostroika*, ed. Thomas Lahusen with Gene Kuperman (Durham: Duke University Press, 1993), 47–68; Mariia N. Virolainen, ed., *Legendy i mify o Pushkine* (St. Petersburg: Akademicheskii proekt, 1999); Angela Brintlinger, *Writing a Usable Past: Russian Literary Culture, 1917–1937* (Evanston: Northwestern University Press, 2000); Stephanie Sandler, *Commemorating Pushkin: Russia's Myth of a National Poet* (Stanford: Stanford University Press, 2004); and Evgeny Dobrenko, "Pushkin in Soviet and Post-Soviet Culture," in *The Cambridge Companion to Pushkin*, ed. Andrew Kahn (Cambridge: Cambridge University Press, 2006), 202–20.

6. Andrei Bitov, *Pushkin House* (*Pushkinskii Dom*), quoted in Levitt, *Russian*

Literary Politics, 174. Svetlana Evdokimova and Vladimir Golstein's metaphor of Pushkin as the "lightning rod . . . of polemics on the greater issues of national identity and ideology" implicitly addresses Pushkin's taboo status as simultaneous life giver and death giver, the untouchable source of unbearable light and darkness ("Pushkiniana as an Encyclopedia of Contemporary Literary Criticism," in *The Pushkin Handbook*, ed. David M. Bethea [Madison: University of Wisconsin Press, 2005], 611). It should be acknowledged that my use of the term "taboo" in a pejorative sense—that is, as an equivalent for ideological manipulation and prohibition—departs from the principle upheld by thinkers like Freud and Girard that the taboo is a beneficial and necessary regulator of human relations. In my application of the term, the taboo protects not the health of society broadly speaking but the narrow, self-serving interests of a ruling elite and a privileged political ideology. A similar disclaimer could be given in regard to my pejorative use of the word "myth" to denote not a fertile cultural foundation in the sense that Mircea Eliade (for example) has used the term but a set of strictly prescribed precepts that brook no heterodoxy (see Eliade, *Myth and Reality* [London: George Allen and Unwin, 1964]).

7. Paul Debreczeny argues that the myth of Pushkin as "saintly sufferer" had deep roots in Russian popular culture, going back to saints' lives such as those of Boris and Gleb (the first Russian political martyrs), and that, immediately after his death, "attributes of the sacred began to attach themselves to his name." According to Debreczeny, Soviet public ritual, particularly during the Stalinist years, lacked "richness of resonance and multivalence of symbolism"; the hagiographic Pushkin myth was the only such phenomenon that retained a degree of spontaneity and popular appeal, and the Soviet government thus tried to expropriate it for its own ideological purposes: "Unlike Lenin's, the cult of Pushkin has been able to loosen social attitudes as well as bind the nation" ("Zhitie Aleksandra Boldinskogo," 52, 58–59, 64).

8. Quoted in Levitt, *Russian Literary Politics*, 11.

9. Official jubilee celebrations of the poet's life and death (in 1880, 1899, 1921, 1924, 1937, 1949, and 1999) served to codify and publicize each new stage in his mythic transformation; arguably, the 2008 "Name Russia" television contest could be added to the list of significant turning points in the evolution of the Pushkin myth. On the jubilee celebrations, see Sandler, *Commemorating Pushkin*.

10. Sergei Davydov, "The Evolution of Pushkin's Political Thought," in Bethea, *The Pushkin Handbook*, 283.

11. Robert P. Hughes, "Pushkin and Russia Abroad," in Kahn, *The Cambridge Companion to Pushkin*, 183. Hughes notes that by January 1937, there were eighty-five local Pushkin Committees in thirty-seven countries on five continents all planning jubilee celebrations (178); the Central Pushkin Committee had been formed in Paris in February 1935 to oversee jubilee celebration plans. For a history of the Central Pushkin Committee and its members, as well as a compilation of

their writings on Pushkin, see *Tsentral'nyi Pushkinskii Komitet v Parizhe (1935–1937)*, 2 vols. (Moscow: Ellis Luck, 2000).

12. Tim McDaniel defines the "Russian idea" broadly as the idea that Russian culture and history are unique and thus guarantee for the Russian nation a special and higher destiny (*The Agony of the Russian Idea* [Princeton: Princeton University Press, 1996], 11). He goes on to explain that what is, in fact, distinctive about the process of social change that has taken place in Russia over the past two hundred years is the way in which this idea of Russia's uniqueness has been "yok[ed] together" with a despotic state and the commitment to rapid modernization; the result has been a succession of hypocritical regimes "constructed on a foundation of mendacity" in which word and deed, belief and practice, are so fully out of alignment with one another that the social order comes to seem surreal, leading to the point of societal and political crisis and collapse (14–15).

13. Irina Surat, "Pushkinskii iubilei kak zaklinanie istorii," *Novyi mir* 6 (June 2000): 186. Vissarion Belinsky's statement that "literature must necessarily be an expression and a symbol of the inner life of a nation [*narod*]" in his 1834 essay "Literary Dreams (An Elegy in Prose)" ("Literaturnye mechtaniia (Elegiia v proze)") has sometimes been taken out of context to rationalize the ideological regulation of Pushkin as national treasure (for example, in Valery Serdyuchenko's "Pushkin as the Mainstay of Russian Civilization," which was published in the unashamedly propagandistic journal *Diplomat* that is distributed monthly to foreign embassies, media bureaus, and other foreign organizations throughout Moscow).

14. Freud cites James Frazer's explanation that the "clan totem is reverenced by a body of men and women who call themselves by the name of the totem, believe themselves to be of one blood, descendants of a common ancestor, and are bound together by common obligations to each other and by a common faith in the totem. Totemism is thus both a religious and a social system"; Freud adds that "any violation of the taboos that protect the totem are automatically punished by severe illness or death" (*Totem and Taboo*, 103–4).

15. For an excellent study of the influence of Pushkin and his works on social realities, see Paul Debreczeny, *Social Functions of Literature: Alexander Pushkin and Russian Culture* (Stanford: Stanford University Press, 1997). Debreczeny concludes that Pushkin's potent role in this respect is unique in all of world literature.

16. See Daniil Kharms's "Anecdotes from the Life of Pushkin" ("Anekdoty iz zhizni Pushkina" [1939]) and such stories by Mikhail Zoshchenko as "Pushkin" (1927) and "On the Pushkin Days" ("V pushkinskie dni" [1937]).

17. See Stephanie Sandler, "The Pushkin Myth in Russia," in Bethea, *The Pushkin Handbook*, 403.

18. Eugenia Semyonovna Ginzburg, *Journey into the Whirlwind* (San Diego: Harcourt Brace, 1995), 295–96.

19. Stephanie Sandler, "Sex, Death and Nation in the *Strolls with Pushkin* Controversy," *Slavic Review* 51.2 (1992): 294.

20. Catharine Theimer Nepomnyashchy, introduction, in Abram Tertz [Andrei Sinyavsky], *Strolls with Pushkin*, trans. Catharine Theimer Nepomnyashchy and Slava I. Yastremski (New Haven: Yale University Press, 1993), 1, 6.

21. Tertz, *Strolls with Pushkin*, 82–83.

22. See Liudmila Zubova's excellent "Dekonstruirovannyi Pushkin (Pushkin v poezii postmodernizma)," *Pushkinskie chteniia v Tartu* 2 (2000): 364–84, for numerous examples of such postmodernist deconstructions. Zubova sees the root of this late twentieth-century innovation in Pushkin's own poetics: "Postmodernism can be considered a development and often a completion of that which was first laid out (or mastered) by Pushkin. This includes playful behavior, parodic yet serious intertextuality, mockery of literary clichés, anti-romanticism, the overcoming of the text's genre and stylistic homogeneity, imitation of nonartistic speech, the shocking (to contemporaries) introduction into the text of 'unpoetic' elements, compositional openness, multiple points of view, catalogs of everyday details, and information about its own structure" (365). Additional examples of postmodernist deconstructions of Pushkin can be found in Dobrenko, "Pushkin in Soviet and Post-Soviet Culture," 216–18.

23. Kibirov's poem, whose very title ironically inhabits the Pushkinian genre of the friendly epistle (druzheskoe poslanie), was published in his collection *Santimenty: Vosem' knig* (Belgorod: Izdatel'stvo Risk, 1994). The phrase "hybrid of monkey and tiger" originates in Voltaire's characterization of the moral nature of the typical Frenchman as a "tigre-singe"; "tiger-monkey," along with "Frantsuz" (Frenchy), was one of Pushkin's nicknames during his time at the lyceum at Tsarskoe Selo (see Iurii M. Lotman, "Smes' obez'iany s tigrom," in his *Pushkin: Biografiia pisatel'ia; Stat'i i zametki, 1960–1990; "Evgenii Onegin," Kommentarii* [St. Petersburg: Iskusstvo-SPB, 1995], 329–32). Evgenii Samoilov was a decorated Soviet film actor who was named a People's Artist of the USSR in 1974; Nikolai Rubtsov was a third-rate Soviet poet who died in a drunken brawl at the hands of his fiancée.

24. Nikolai V. Gogol', "Neskol'ko slov o Pushkine," in his *Polnoe sobranie sochinenii*, 14 vols. (Moscow: AN SSSR, 1937–52), 8:50–55.

25. These strange beings update and incarnate Valentin Nepomniashchy's observation that Soviet-era Pushkin speeches reveal "a spectacle of radical, historically instantaneous deflation of the level of culture, some sort of mutation of the consciousness and spirit" ("Da ukrepimsia," in *Rechi o Pushkine: 1880–1960-e gody*, ed. Valentin S. Nepomniashchii and Mikhail D. Filin [Moscow: Tekst, 1999], 378).

26. Tatyana Tolstaya, *The Slynx*, trans. Jamey Gambrell (Boston: Houghton Mifflin, 2003), 137–38. My interpretation of Pushkin's ambivalent function in this novel differs from the nostalgic reading given by Sof'ia Malen'kikh; she sees Pushkin as "a shard of a vanished culture, the gleam of lost perfection"

("Pushkinskii mif kak tekst," *Virtual'nyi seminar Professora S. A. Goncharova*, http://www.aseminar.narod.ru/malenkih.htm [accessed 31 July 2010]).

27. "Pushkin is a sort of domestic god, always handy for scolding a misbehaver. Therefore, a Russian's first encounter with Pushkin is likely to be as a child: 'Who is going to close the door after you—Pushkin?!'" (Alexander Zholkovsky, "Pushkin Under Our Skin," in *Alexander Pushkin: A Celebration of Russia's Best-Loved Writer*, ed. A. D. P. Briggs [London: Hazar, 1999], 189.

28. Tolstaya, *The Slynx*, 120, 121. Leontii Vasil'evich Dubel't, one of the most reactionary members of Tsar Nicholas I's administration, was the chief of staff of the Corps of Gendarmes and a member of the censorship board in Pushkin's last years; he served as dreaded head of the Third Section (secret police) from 1839 until 1856. Lavrentii Beria, Stalin's chief henchman, is presumably better known to English speakers.

29. Ibid., 150.

30. Ibid.

31. This outcome reveals the unmentionable vampiric/sacrificial underpinning of Pushkin's canonization, as others have also noted. For instance, in the 1999 film *Bronze Pushkin* (*Mednyi Pushkin*), the writer Andrei Bitov calls the whole historical sequence of Pushkin jubilee festivities a "ceaseless murdering, ceaseless crucifixion" (quoted in Surat, "Pushkinskii iubilei," 181). Stephanie Sandler notes that Pushkin "*became* Pushkin when he died in a duel" and suggests that "the Russian belief that 'Pushkin lives!'" has been "premised on the fact of his death" ("The Pushkin Myth in Russia," 403–4). The conflagration that ends Tolstaya's novel ironically reenacts the genesis of the myth of Pushkin's immortality: "The Oldeners bent their knees, held hands, and began to rise in the air. . . . 'Why didn't you burn up?' 'Didn't feel like it! Just didn't feeeeel like it!' 'So you mean you didn't die? Huh? Or did you?' 'Figure it out as best you can!'" (275). Viacheslav Desiatov discusses the fantasy of a contemporary, revivified ("cloned") Pushkin in contemporary Russian fiction in "Klon Pushkina, ili russkii chelovek cherez dvesti let," *Zvezda* 2 (2000): 198–202.

32. Iurii M. Lotman, *Kul'tura i vzryv* (Moscow: Gnozis, 1992), 265. This work has recently become available in an English translation: Juri Lotman, *Culture and Explosion*, trans. Wilma Clark, ed. Marina Grishakova (Berlin: Mouton de Gruyter, 2009).

33. Ibid., 258.

34. Ibid.

35. Ibid.

36. Serguei Oushakine, "In the State of Post-Soviet Aphasia: Symbolic Development in Contemporary Russia," *Europe-Asia Studies* 52.6 (2000): 1003–4. After the Russian National Football Team's unexpected 3–2 victory over France at the Stade de France in June 1999, the radio station Echo of Moscow (Ekho Moskvy) suggested that football should be declared Russia's national idea (see Surat, "Pushkinskii iubilei," 185).

37. Michael Urban, "The Politics of Identity in Russia's Postcommunist Transition: The Nation against Itself," *Slavic Review* 53.3 (1994): 737.

38. Igor' Serkov, "Ziiaiushchie niziny," *Literaturnaia gazeta*, 6–12 April 2011, 1–2.

39. Oushakine, "In the State of Post-Soviet Aphasia," 1003.

40. The complete rankings and full information about the contest can be found on the project's website at http://www.nameofrussia.ru; the quoted passage is from the "About the Choice" ("O vybore") page. The video of the Pushkin episode can be viewed at http://www.nameofrussia.ru/video.html?id=4026, and a summary of the episode can be found at http://www.nameofrussia.ru/doc.html?id=4026 (accessed 2 August 2010). For a discussion of the contest's outcome and competing claims of vote rigging, see Tom Parfitt, "Medieval Warrior Overcomes Stalin in Poll to Name Greatest Russian," *Guardian*, 29 December 2008, http://www.guardian.co.uk/world/2008/dec/29/stalin-name-of-russia (accessed 24 April 2011).

41. For more on Putin's "perestroika" of Russia's "media-political system," see Ivan Zassoursky, *Media and Power in Post-Soviet Russia* (New York: M. E. Sharpe, 2004), especially chap. 6, 189–228.

42. See Laura Belin, "The Russian Media in the 1990s," in *Russia After Communism*, ed. Rick Fawn and Stephen White (London: Frank Cass, 2002), 149.

43. Zassoursky, *Media and Power in Post-Soviet Russia*, 114, 147. Zassoursky notes that the idea of "Great Russia" is all about visual image and spectacle and has nothing to do with intellectual understanding; among other symbols making up "Great Russia" are the "cultural codes and events that figure in a common cultural memory," including "'the great Russian literature,' which is still taught intensively in schools," beloved Soviet films, and holidays (157–58).

44. Alexei Bessudnov, "Media Map," *Index on Censorship* 37.1 (2008): 183–89, 184; "O telekanale Rossiia," http://www.rutv.ru/section.html?cid=16&d=0 (accessed 20 April 2011).

45. Clifford J. Levy, "It Isn't Magic: Putin Opponents Vanish from TV," *New York Times*, 3 June 2008, http://www.nytimes.com/2008/06/03/world/europe/03russia.html (accessed 20 April 2011); "Svoboda slova po-akademicheski: Na Obshchem sobranii RAN zapreshcheno rasprostranenie gazet i zhurnalov," *Polit.ru*, 15 December 2009, http://www.polit.ru/science/2009/12/15/freedom_of_smi.html (accessed 20 April 2011).

46. "Medvedev Says No to False History," *Russia Today*, 24 May 2009, http://rt.com/politics/medvedev-says-no-to-false-history (accessed 20 April 2011). The twenty-eight-member commission responsible for passing judgment is made up primarily of high-ranking government officials and army and intelligence personnel; it includes only three, relatively unknown, academics. On Russia's complex strategy vis-à-vis its Stalinist past, see the discussion in the fascinating and chilling Russian WikiLeaks document "Predstavliaet li dukh

Stalina ugrozu akademicheskoi svobode?," 21 December 2010, http://ruleaks.net/1059 (accessed 2 August 2011).

47. These threats evoke an unpleasant sense of déjà vu and remind one of the Soviet practice of imprisoning writers and intellectuals whom the government viewed as troublesome (traitors, parasites, enemies of the state). An editorial in the *Guardian* points to the similarity between the new mandate to create an "official history" and Soviet methods of codifying official "truths" and usefully identifies the potent chauvinistic undertones of the seemingly neutral term "heritage": "The moment the informed debate stops and one version is proclaimed to be 'the truth,' history dies, and what emerges in its place is either ideology or 'heritage,' or both" (Irina Filatova, "Medvedev's New Russian Orthodoxy," *Guardian*, 21 May 2009, http://www.guardian.co.uk/commentisfree/2009/may/21/russia-medvedev-history [accessed 20 April 2011]). According to the December 2010 Russian WikiLeaks document, less than a month after President Medvedev signed the new decree, Valerii A. Tishkov, director of the Institute of Ethnology and Anthropology of the Russian Academy of Sciences, sent an email to the heads of all subdivisions under his purview "politely" requesting information about sources containing potential "falsifications" in the recipient's sphere of scholarly expertise, including student activities that "encourage 'falsification' or 'ideas that could harm Russia's interests'" ("Predstavliaet li dukh Stalina ugrozu akademicheskoi svobode?," section 3).

48. See Miriam Elder, "Ruling Russian Party Wants 'United' History Textbooks for Schools," *Guardian*, 17 June 2010, http://www.miriamelder.com/?p=256 (accessed 21 April 2011).

49. I do not, of course, intend to suggest that all of Russian academia acquiesces to these ideological pressures—or even that the cultural priorities in question are always necessarily objectionable—but simply to point out the pressures that do exist.

50. Boris Tomashevskii, *Pushkin: Kniga vtoraia (1824–1837)* (Moscow: AN SSSR, 1961), 474, quoted in Levitt, *Russian Literary Politics*, 170.

51. See Wendy Slater, "The Patriots' Pushkin," *Slavic Review* 58.2 (1999): 426. Slater points out that the privileging of this text beginning in the early 1990s was related to the xenophobic contention that Pushkin died as a result of a foreign Masonic plot, a version of Pushkin's death that accorded well with the "classic Russian myth of the national martyr." In Slater's view, in the 1990s this trope of martyrdom came to serve as the new "Russian national idea" that the country was so sorely lacking.

52. Evdokimova and Golstein, "Pushkiniana as an Encyclopedia of Contemporary Literary Criticism," 618–19. In their very useful brief survey of both Russian and Western contemporary scholarship on Pushkin, the authors suggest that Pushkin studies constitutes "an important historical document illuminating the history of criticism and unveiling its underlying ideological assumptions" (610).

53. Valentin Nepomniashchii, "Pushkin kak vopros natsional'noi bezopasnosti," *Relga: Nauchno-kul'turologicheskii zhurnal*, 16 September 2005, http://www.relga.ru/Environ/WebObjects/tgu-www.woa/wa/Main?textid=612&level1=main&level2=articles (accessed 24 April 2011). Nepomniashchy's shockingly negative use of the term "propaganda" in connection with Western tolerance of differing sensibilities and points of view is counterbalanced by the shockingly positive use of the same term by a member of the Russian Duma, who complained to the Interfax news agency that "Russia lacks an institute in charge of historical propaganda—and this is why we are losing the war against the falsification of Russian history" ("Predstavliaet li dukh Stalina ugrozu akademicheskoi svobode?," section 8).

54. Surat, "Pushkinskii iubilei," 186.

55. The suggestion that there is nothing new to say about Pushkin echoes the rationale of Kremlin officials and political talk show hosts for excluding dissenting viewpoints from television broadcasts: "People hostile to the Kremlin do not appear on TV simply because their views are not newsworthy"; "No one supports them. They have nothing to say" (Levy, "It Isn't Magic"). Clearly, the current Russian government has succeeded in making its likes and dislikes known and instigating an insidious form of cynical self-censorship without having had to resort to overt censorship. This pressure is not absolute and can be resisted by those who choose to do so by "using the force of inertia and passive sabotage" (WikiLeaks, "Predstavliaet li dukh Stalina ugrozu akademicheskoi svobode?," section 9), yet its implications for the health of the culture are dire, as historian Natalia Lebedeva points out: "A totalitarian society is not one ruled by despotic leaders, but a society which has a single ideology, a single set of ideas and feelings" (Elder, "Ruling Russian Party Wants 'Unified' History Textbook").

56. See Surat, "Pushkinskii iubilei," 185.

57. Andrei Zorin, "Den' rozhdeniia Aleksandra Sergeevicha," *Neprikosnovennyi zapas* 5.7 (1999): 59.

58. Nevertheless, the groundwork for today's conservative Pushkin myth, which rests on a dual foundation of Russian nationalistic paranoia and the traditions of Russian Orthodoxy, was already being laid in the 1990s, as Wendy Slater demonstrates in "The Patriots' Pushkin."

59. See Olga Shevelenko, *Crisis and the Everyday in Postsocialist Moscow* (Bloomington: University of Indiana Press, 2009), 36.

60. Cited in Richard Pipes, "Flight from Freedom: What Russians Think and Want," *Foreign Affairs* 83.3 (2004): 11. Beginning in the 1990s, the dizzying increase in the range of published materials available "drove the Soviet Russian population from a feeling of claustrophobia into a state of what one might call agoraphobia, with an accompanying desire for old-style certainties, limits, predictability and security"; the resurgence of the Russian Orthodox Church was also "conducive to a widespread feeling that freedom had gone too far and

that restraints such as censorship would, on balance, be beneficial to society" (Martin Dewhirst, "Censorship in Russia, 1991 and 2001," in Fawn and White, *Russia After Communism*, 31).

61. See, for example, Surat's use of the term in "Pushkinskii iubilei," 178ff.

62. Greta N. Slobin, "Appropriating the Irreverent Pushkin," in Gasparov, Hughes, and Paperno, *Cultural Mythologies of Russian Modernism*, 217.

63. However, in the present day, needless to say, love once again is on the ascendancy: Surat mournfully notes that "one could hardly expect deep and intelligent [*osmyslennyi*] love for Pushkin" in the context of the contemporary cultural decline ("Pushkinskii iubilei," 184), while Nikolai Pertsov bemoans the current state of Russian philology by pointing to the etymology of that word: "After all philology is love for the word, and not abasement [*unizhenie*] of the word" ("O fenomene demifologizatsii klassikov v sovremennoi kul'ture (v sviazi s 'detskoi rezvost'iu' dvukh pochtennykh professorov)," *Russkii zhurnal*, 23 July 2008, http://www.russ.ru/layout/set/print/pole/O-fenomene-demifologizacii-klassikov-v-sovremennoj-kul-ture [accessed 21 April 2011]).

64. For a discussion of how Briusov rediscovered Pushkin through a combination of documentary evidence and poetic intuition, see Joan Delaney Grossman, "'Moi Pushkin: Briusov's Search for the *Real* Aleksandr Sergeevich," in Gasparov, Hughes, and Paperno, *Cultural Mythologies of Russian Modernism*, 73–87.

65. Pertsov, "O fenomene demifologizatsii klassikov v sovremennoi kul'ture (v sviazi s 'detskoi rezvost'iu' dvukh pochtennykh professorov)."

66. Interestingly, in one of his earliest poems, the 1816 "To Zhukovsky" ("K Zhukovskomu"), Pushkin already intuits these ideological constraints: "He who boldly whistled forth a humorous satire, who expresses himself in the language of truth and does not want to humble himself before Russian Stupidity! . . . He is the enemy of the Fatherland, the sower of depravity!" (Kto smelo prosvistal shutlivoiu satiroi, / Kto vyrazhaetsia pravdivym iazykom, / I russkoi Gluposti ne khochet bit' chelom! . . . / On vrag Otechestva, on seiatel' razvrata!). In this passage Pushkin could just as well be describing the ideological situation of a post-Soviet "demythologizer" of his own reputation as the dire situation of the poet in early nineteenth-century Russia.

67. Aleksandr Zholkovskii, "Ostorozhno, trenozhnik! (Otvet opponentu)," *Russkii zhurnal*, 30 July 2008, http://www.russ.ru/layout/set/print/pole/Ostorozhno-trenozhnik! (accessed 21 April 2011). Zholkovsky concludes that the conservatism that rules the Russian academy can be attributed partly to the fact that Russia did not experience the Renaissance and therefore was a latecomer to "the culture of laughter, principles of pluralism, relativism, ambivalence, openness to the other."

68. Tat'iana G. Shemetova, "Ramochnye komponenty v opytakh po demifologizatsii klassiki (A. Siniavskii, Iu. Karabchievskii, A. Zholkovskii)," paper delivered at the "Phenomenon of the Title" conference of the Russian State

Humanities University, 2007, http://science.rggu.ru/article.html?id=66075 (accessed 2 August 2010).

69. One area of potential study that our collection does not address at all, for example, is the taboos affecting modes of portrayal of Pushkin in visual arts such as painting and film; we also, regrettably, omit consideration of Pushkin's racial heritage, which has, however, received outstanding and varied treatment in the anthology *Under the Sky of My Africa: Alexander Pushkin and Blackness*, ed. Catharine Theimer Nepomnyashchy, Nicole Svobodny, and Ludmilla A. Trigos (Evanston: Northwestern University Press, 2006).

70. Vladimir Novikov, "Dvadtsat' dva mifa o Pushkine," *Vremia i my* 143 (1999): 179. Novikov's categorization of Pushkin myths in binary pairs, which follows his introductory comments, is both useful and revealing.

71. Two excellent studies that address the all-encompassing regimentation of noble Russian society in Pushkin's time are the following: Irina Reyfman, *Ritualized Violence Russian Style: The Duel in Russian Culture and Literature* (Stanford: Stanford University Press, 1999); and Iurii M. Lotman, "The Decembrist in Daily Life (Everyday Behavior as a Historical-Psychological Category)," in *The Semiotics of Russian Cultural History*, ed. Alexander D. Nakhimovsky and Alice Stone Nakhimovsky (Ithaca: Cornell University Press, 1985), 95–149. Maria Virolainen distinguishes the historical epochs of the "canon" and the "paradigm" in the Russian cultural cosmos: the "canonical" period is one of intuitive, unstated, and inherited cultural forms, as in folklore; the "paradigmatic" period, on the other hand, is characterized by the explicit formulation of normative models, a shift from anonymous production to authorship, and an organizational and didactic imperative. In Virolainen's view, the shift from the canonical to the paradigmatic historical phase, which had been taking shape for decades, was ultimately realized by Pushkin during his time at the lyceum. See Mariia Virolainen, "Struktura kul'turnogo kosmosa russkoi istorii," in her *Rech' i molchanie: Siuzhety i mify russkoi slovesnosti* (St. Petersburg: Amfora, 2003), 15–68.

72. Tertz, *Strolls with Pushkin*, 60.

Part 1

Taboos in Context

Pushkin the Titular Councilor

Irina Reyfman

In addition to being a great writer, Pushkin also was a man of a particular time and a member of a particular estate, namely, the service nobility. As such, he participated in the Russian service hierarchy; that is, he was in imperial service and had a rank. While to us Pushkin's service may seem the least important aspect of his life, it was not so for Pushkin himself and for his contemporaries. Furthermore, his service career was perhaps important in many different ways and invites various questions. Did Pushkin's participation in imperial service affect his sense of authorial self? Did it figure in the way he modeled his behavior (such modeling, as we know, was a highly creative activity for him)?[1] Is Pushkin's participation in the service hierarchy reflected in his literary works?[2] Did his contemporaries—especially fellow writers—pay attention to Pushkin's service career or comment on it in their works?

I want to begin mapping approaches to the discussion of Pushkin's service career by considering our apparent reluctance to engage with this topic. Why is it a virtual taboo for Pushkinists, something to gloss over as superfluous to Pushkin's "real" biography or to represent as a nuisance distracting the great poet from writing poetry or to portray as a tool used by an oppressive government to control the unruly genius? Do we avoid it simply because, to us, only his literary production is important, and service seems to be something secondary, something almost beside the point? Or is it our ambivalence about the greatest Russian poet's participation in the infamous Russian bureaucracy that discourages us? Could it be that Pushkin's serving the state, at times with enthusiasm, interferes with our desire to concentrate on his conflicts with that state, which can be interpreted in a heroic way? Or do we, perhaps, ignore Pushkin's service career because it was so unsuccessful?

In order to glean some explanations, I offer a brief overview of Pushkin's service career and document some common opinions about it—opinions that are, in some cases, debatable. I suggest that certain established interpretations of Pushkin's biography may interfere with our examining Pushkin's service career and with our considering its significance for him and people around him. I then demonstrate that Pushkin's contemporaries were, indeed, not indifferent to it. Finally, I consider two works of literature, Osip Senkovsky's "A Poetic Journey through the Wide World" ("Poeticheskoe puteshestvie po belu svetu") and, briefly, Nikolai Gogol's "Notes of a Madman" ("Zapiski sumasshedshego"), in both of which, I propose, the authors make reference to Pushkin's service career.

In comparison with the multitudes of volumes dedicated to Pushkin's literary works and other aspects of his life, his service has been surprisingly neglected. A good example of such neglect by Soviet scholars is the 1931 *Guide to Pushkin* (*Putevoditel' po Pushkinu*), a dictionary of names and subjects commenting on all aspects of Pushkin's life and works, which nonetheless lacks entries explaining his collegiate secretary and titular councilor ranks (whereas some ranks held by other people are explained).[3] In today's Russia the attitude has not changed much: volume 5 of the 2007 biographical dictionary *Russian Writers, 1800–1917* (*Russkie pisateli: Biograficheskii slovar', 1800–1917*) devotes only one and one-third out of roughly sixty-four columns of text (excluding illustrations) to Pushkin's service career.[4] Western scholars follow suit: the entry on Pushkin in Victor Terras's *Handbook of Russian Literature* mentions Pushkin's "status on the margin of two social and cultural positions—'gentleman' and 'author'"—but does not address the question of whether his service rank played a role in this marginality.[5] To be sure, publications documenting Pushkin's service career do exist (and I cite them in this chapter), but, with few exceptions, they concentrate on presenting facts, not interpreting them.[6]

If biographies of Pushkin refer to his service career at all, as a rule they pay different amounts of attention to its different stages. His entering the Ministry of Foreign Affairs after graduation from the Imperial

Lyceum is usually mentioned, although not examined in any serious way: as Natalia E. Miasoedova notes, the topic "Pushkin the diplomat" "has not been realized to this day, nor has the question even been posed."[7] Pushkin's return to service in the early 1830s receives far less attention: it is either disregarded or briefly explained by his need to have access to the imperial archives in order to work on his history of Peter the Great.[8] The only episode of Pushkin's late service that is commonly commented on is his investiture with the title of *kammerjunker* (junior chamberlain)—apparently both because Pushkin himself repeatedly wrote about this event in his diary and letters and because it conveniently lends itself to being interpreted as an offensive action by the tsar against the great poet.[9]

When putting together a record of Pushkin's service career, we have to face the fact that it is short and not particularly glamorous. He served from 1817 to 1824 and then again from 1831 to 1837. Upon graduating from the Imperial Lyceum fourth from the bottom of his class (fourteenth out of seventeen graduates), Pushkin received the rank of collegiate secretary (tenth class). In comparison, his classmates whose class standing was higher received the rank of titular councilor (ninth class). Both ranks were high, given the age of the recipients, and opened paths to good service careers. The difference, however, was felt by some: Fedor Matiushkin, Pushkin's fellow collegiate secretary, wrote to a friend: "I have been graduated with the rank of collegiate secretary. You certainly will congratulate me on a felicitous beginning of service. Without having done anything, to be of the tenth class, is, of course, a lot. But we judge by comparison: some of us have been graduated as titular councilors."[10]

Pushkin did not complain about his rank, but reportedly he was not overjoyed to be appointed to the civil service: he had wanted to join the military. However, his father was not prepared to pay for his equipment as was required, and so Pushkin joined the Ministry of Foreign Affairs, a diplomatic career being the most prestigious among all the civil service careers available to a young nobleman.[11] He took oath on 15 June 1817.[12] In May 1820, after three years in St. Petersburg—years in which Pushkin earned recognition as a poet but did not advance in rank—he was transferred to Ekaterinoslav to serve under Ivan Inzov, the head of a chancellery that supervised foreign colonists.[13] At the same time, Inzov was made the acting governor general of Novorossiia and vice regent (namestnik) of Bessarabia, and Pushkin moved with his chancellery to Kishinev, where he served until the summer of 1823. He then transferred to Odessa, to serve under Mikhail S. Vorontsov, who replaced Inzov as governor general and *namestnik*. In June of 1824, amid worsening relations with Vorontsov and after a series of missteps (such as his refusing to fulfill Vorontsov's order to inspect damage inflicted by locusts in the Kherson guberniya and sending by imperial post a letter in which he discussed his atheism—a letter that was opened by the police), Pushkin handed in his resignation notice, citing poor health as his reason for resigning. The petition was readily granted, and Pushkin was retired without, as was customary, having been promoted to the next rank, which clearly indicated imperial displeasure with his service and behavior. He was ordered to reside in Mikhailovskoe under police surveillance.

Two generally accepted opinions dominate interpretations of Pushkin's early service career: that between 1817 and 1824 Pushkin was not very serious about his service duties, and that he was exiled to the south as a punishment for writing antigovernment poetry. Both opinions need to be reexamined.

The position that Pushkin held upon graduation was supernumerary (his salary of 700 rubles a year came from the state treasury, not the ministry) and thus perhaps could be considered a sinecure that required little work. Contemporary memoirs and later biographers seem to agree that Pushkin took advantage of this situation.[14] If he did, his behavior was extraordinary: many of his classmates were appointed to similar positions, and, judging by their careers, they did not neglect their duties.[15] Furthermore, evidence exists that Pushkin was not as completely idle as the sources suggest. His position required regular presence at the office and fulfillment of certain duties, such as being on call to receive diplomatic mail, and there are no indications that he neglected them.[16] Furthermore, Vadim E. Vatsuro cites Vladimir Sollogub's record of a story Pushkin once told, in which he mentioned his being on call: "Pushkin recounted that, when he served at the Ministry of Foreign Affairs, he once was on duty together with one very old clerk."[17] Pushkin also worked as a translator; this is how he is referred to in a letter written by the head of the ministry, Count Ioann Kapodistria, at the time of Pushkin's transfer to Ekaterinoslav: "Yesterday the Emperor ordered the ministry to give Mr. Pushkin, translator, 1,000 rubles for travel expenses."[18] We know that in Kishinev Pushkin continued to work as a translator. In his letter to Kapodistria of 28 April 1821, Inzov reports that he has given the poet the task of "translating Moldavian laws written in French into Russian." Likewise, he writes to Petr M. Volkonsky on 1 December 1821: "Mr. Pushkin, who is attached to my office, is well-behaved. I occupy him with correspondence in French and with translations from Russian to French, because, given his lack of experience, I cannot trust him with other paperwork."[19] In his 1981 article "Pushkin the Translator at the Ministry of Foreign Affairs," I. P. Medvedev argues that Pushkin's supervisors were reasonably content with his efforts.[20]

The scarcity of documents concerning Pushkin's early service, both in St. Petersburg and in the south, makes it difficult to decide how involved in his service Pushkin actually was. While all the formal aspects of his early career are documented, the only extant evidence of the particular service duties Pushkin performed is the documents that I have cited. Perhaps he did not take advantage of the career opportunities he was given—unlike some of his classmates or, for example, Alexander S. Griboedov, who was appointed to the ministry at the same time but with a lower rank (provincial secretary, twelfth class) and yet by the time of his death in 1829 had attained the rank of state councilor (fifth class).[21]

In her commentary on the collection of records documenting Pushkin's life from 1811 to 1829, S. V. Berezkina states: "At present, the absence of any business paperwork that came from Pushkin's quill from 1817 to 1820 can be confirmed."[22] However, the very absence of a paper trail may be suspicious. At the time of his service in Petersburg and Kishinev, Pushkin belonged to a circle of people, many of them in diplomatic service themselves, who, according to Maria Maiofis's reconstruction of their activities, participated in Count Kapodistria's Russian modernization project, in which major reforms were proposed including the gradual introduction of a constitution and the abolition of serfdom.[23] Kapodistria's plans were initially supported by the tsar, but the count failed to retain that support, and in 1822 he left his post at the ministry and went abroad, never to return to Russia. He officially resigned the post in 1827. Maiofis writes about the conspicuous absence from the appropriate archives of many documents concerning Kapodistria and his circle; she suggests that documents related to Kapodistria's project were actively destroyed throughout the 1820s.[24] It is not inconceivable that Pushkin's service documents were among them.

Pushkin formally served under Kapodistria from the moment he took oath until Kapodistria left Russia. Furthermore, Kapodistria's young associates were the poet's close friends and benefactors: all of them, including Kapodistria, were members of Arzamas, a literary association founded by Sergei S. Uvarov, the infamous minister of public education under Nicholas I but at the time an ambitious statesman of liberal persuasion. Among the members of Arzamas were several diplomats (Dmitrii N. Bludov, Dmitrii V. Dashkov) as well as poets (Petr A. Viazemsky, Vasilii A. Zhukovsky, Konstantin N. Batiushkov). Kapodistria was elected an honorary member in March of 1816. Pushkin joined on 7 April 1818, at the last official meeting of the association.[25] As Maiofis argues, the members of Arzamas, striving to make Russia a truly European nation, considered "demonstrating the great success of Russian literature and enlightenment" instrumental to this task.[26] Their encouragement of Pushkin's literary talent should be seen in this context. Furthermore, it was no coincidence that the poetry that supposedly inflamed the tsar was in line with Kapodistria's and his associates' modernization plans—and was, arguably, not far removed from the tsar's own ideas at the time.

In his essay "Washing Away the Sad Lines," Igor Nemirovsky argues that in May 1820 Pushkin was not so much exiled from Petersburg for writing radical poetry as he was removed from the capital to stop his defiant and provocative behavior (including widely circulating his unpublished and thus uncensored poems)—behavior that Nemirovsky interprets as the poet's response to the rumor that he had been flogged by the police.[27] The removal was supposed to be temporary and was represented as a service reassignment: not only was Pushkin given 1,000 rubles for travel expenses (a surprisingly large sum) but he also served as a courier, bringing Inzov his letter of appointment as acting governor general and vice regent. Furthermore, the lengthy trip to the Caucasus and Crimea that Pushkin undertook right after his arrival in Ekaterinoslav was likely sanctioned in advance.[28]

To be sure, Alexander was not amused by Pushkin's provocative behavior, and several older friends had to intercede on his behalf, Kapodistria among them.[29] It was in fact Kapodistria who arranged with the tsar the details of Pushkin's reassignment to the south, as is evident from the rough draft of his letter to Inzov, approved by Alexander.[30] The letter gives a mostly positive characterization of Pushkin, citing his "unusual talent" and intellect (but also his absence of moral fortitude) and expressing the conviction that it was possible "to make out of him an excellent servant of the state or, at least, a first-rate writer." It also seems to imply that Kapodistria expected to take Pushkin under his wing upon his return to St. Petersburg: "Mr. Pushkin, it seems, wants to choose a diplomatic career and to begin it in [my] department. There is nothing I wish more than to give him a position close to me, but he will receive this favor only through you, when you tell me that he deserves it."[31] It is significant in this context that Pushkin's duties under Inzov were connected with Kapodistria's pet project: providing laws for the newly acquired province.

Nemirovsky argues that Pushkin began to view his temporary reassignment as an exile in the spring of 1821, a year after his departure from Petersburg: it was then, according to Nemirovsky, that he began to model his authorial image not on Byron but on Ovid, and Alexander became a "sly Augustus" in his eyes.[32] However, it appears that Pushkin's status did not in fact change unequivocally until after Kapodistria's fall in May 1822. In May 1823, Inzov was also dismissed as vice regent, and Vorontsov appointed in his stead.[33] Pushkin's friends (especially Alexander I. Turgenev and Zhukovsky) had a high opinion of Vorontsov and urged Pushkin to transfer to his office in Odessa, which he did.[34] As we know, this was a fatal mistake: the two did not get along. Furthermore, while Kapodistria had valued Pushkin's poetic gift, Vorontsov did not. He wrote to Pavel D. Kiselev on 6 March 1824: "I am not a great admirer of his gift: one cannot be a true poet without constantly working on expanding one's knowledge, and his is not sufficient."[35] In response to Vorontsov's exacting treatment of him, Pushkin flaunted his lack of ability as a bureaucrat and refused to fulfill his duties. The poet's insubordination in the locust affair, his caustic epigrams directed at the *namestnik* (whose wife he was reportedly courting), and, finally, the letter about atheism that the police read led to his dismissal from service.

Whether Pushkin was a participant in Kapodistria's modernization project, a happy-go-lucky, good-for-nothing playboy, or (as he wrote at the height of his conflict with Vorontsov in an unsent letter to one of his supervisors), a poet who had chosen "a different destiny" and therefore "for seven years had not engaged in service, had not written a single paper, and had not had any relations with a single supervisor [*nachal'nik*]," or even all three combined, one fact is certain: he was not promoted during his years of service and remained in the rank of collegiate secretary throughout his forced retirement.[36] It is also clear that he was increasingly unhappy about it. On 16 April 1830, soon after his engagement to Natalia N. Goncharova, Pushkin wrote to Alexander Kh. Benkendorf expressing his discontent with his service status: "I was dismissed from service in 1824, and this stain still remains. Having finished the Lyceum in 1817 with the rank of the tenth class, I never received the two ranks that were mine by right, because my superiors passed me over when it was time to recommend me [for promotion], and I did not find it necessary to remind [them] about myself."[37] Concerned primarily with removing the stigma of his forced retirement to mollify his future in-laws, Pushkin did not ask to return to service at that time, citing his literary activities as his main occupation and source of income. A little more than a year later, in July 1831, he repeated his complaints in another letter to Benkendorf: "My present rank (the very same with which I graduated from the lyceum) unfortunately impedes me in my service career. I was listed [*schitalsia*] at the Ministry of Foreign Affairs from 1817 to 1824. For time in grade [*za vyslugu let*], I should have been promoted twice, that is, to the ranks of titular [councilor] and collegiate assessor, but my former supervisors kept forgetting to nominate me. I do not know whether I can still receive what I was entitled to."[38] In this letter, Pushkin offers his services to the tsar. On 14 November 1831, he was reinstated at the ministry at the rank of collegiate secretary and on 6 December promoted to the rank of titular councilor (ninth class).[39] Pushkin's new service position brought him a yearly income of 5,000 rubles and access to the imperial archives. On 31 December 1833, Pushkin was granted the title of *kammerjunker*, and his official service designation became "titular councilor with the title of *kammerjunker*." He never advanced any further.[40]

The usual explanation by scholars and biographers that Pushkin returned to service only because he wanted access to the imperial archives is challenged by his remarks to Benkendorf. In his letter, Pushkin notes his readiness to serve the emperor as a journalist: "If my lord emperor wishes to use my quill, I will strive to fulfill his will with exactitude and zeal, and I am ready to serve him to the best of my abilities. . . . I would happily undertake editing a *political and literary journal*, that is, the kind of journal that would publish political and foreign news. I would unite gifted writers around it and thus would draw closer to the government useful people who now still shy away from it, thinking it to be hostile to enlightenment."[41] The desire to serve the government that Pushkin expresses here needs to be taken seriously: not long before he wrote to Benkendorf, offering his services, he jotted down a program for a periodical, concluding with the following two points: "I offer my journal to the government, as an instrument of its influence on the general opinion. Officialism [*ofitsial'nost'*]."[42] Maiofis points out the program's similarity to that of the Arzamas group in the late 1810s and draws attention to the fact that at the time Pushkin wrote the letter to Benkendorf and sketched out this program he was in touch with two former Arzamasians, Filipp F. Vigel and Uvarov. Notably, in July 1831, Vigel wrote to Pushkin expressing his and Uvarov's support for the project. Vigel suggested that Uvarov could help obtain permission to publish the journal.[43] The project failed, but Pushkin's collaborative relations with Uvarov continued until 1834.

In his letter to Pushkin urging him to reconnect with Uvarov, Vigel writes: "You, as a poet, do not have to serve, but why shouldn't you become a courtier? If a laurel wreath adorns the head of Apollo's son, why can't the chamberlain's key adorn the behind of the scion of an ancient noble family?"[44] Vigel suggests that with Uvarov's help, Pushkin could obtain the title of chamberlain. Uvarov did facilitate Pushkin's election to the Russian Academy on 7 January 1833, but the poet was never appointed chamberlain.[45]

Instead, in December 1833, Pushkin was made a *kammerjunker*. Pushkin's diaries and letters indicate that he was extremely unhappy with this title, considering it to be beneath what he deserved given his status and age. According to several sources, he complained not only privately but also publicly. Pavel Nashchokin described Pushkin's agitation to the poet's early biographer Petr Bartenev in strong terms (he was "beside himself, having flared up, with his face aglow") and claimed that Pushkin's friends had to pour cold water on him to calm him down.[46] Likewise, Lev Pushkin reported that his brother cursed and foamed at the mouth upon receiving the news.[47] However, the extent of Pushkin's public protestation is questioned by his friend Sergei A. Sobolevsky, who attached a comment to Bartenev's record of Nashchokin's comments: "Nonsense. Pushkin was too well-mannered [for this]."[48] Bartenev also remarked: "Soon (as can be seen from his letter to Nashchokin) he realized that the tsar did not want to offend him and calmed down."[49] Indeed, in the letter mentioned by Bartenev, written in March 1834, Pushkin notes: "Certainly, having made me a *kammerjunker*, the tsar was thinking of my rank and not of my age—surely, he did not want to pique me."[50] The sincerity of this acknowledgment can be suspected, however: Pushkin's mood remained noticeably depressed throughout the summer of 1834, and on 25 June he attempted to resign from service, asking the tsar only not to suspend his archival privileges. The resignation was accepted, his archival privileges were revoked, and Pushkin was able to remain in service only thanks to Zhukovsky's active intercession.[51]

A few words on the history of the *kammerjunker* title can help clarify the matter. Beginning in 1809, *kammerjunker*, hitherto a rank of the ninth class in court service (that is, formally the same as titular councilor in civil service), ceased to be a rank and became an honorary title (zvanie). From then on, every *kammerjunker* had to be in the military or civil service. At first, there was no consistent correspondence between this title and rank, but in 1836, about three years after Pushkin was made a *kammerjunker*, the correspondence was established, and the title could be granted only to persons of ninth to fourth class. For chamberlains the corresponding ranks were fifth to third class.[52] Pushkin's fellow *kammerjunkers* (161 persons) included people from the fourteenth (one person) to the fifth (two persons) classes. Forty-two *kammerjunkers* in this group had the rank of titular councilor, and twenty-one had the rank of collegiate assessor (eighth class).[53] From Nicholas's point of view, the title of *kammerjunker* corresponded to Pushkin's service rank.[54]

With respect to Pushkin's age as well, Nicholas seems to be not entirely off the mark. According to Reiser, who succeeded in finding dates of birth for 86 percent of Pushkin's fellow *kammerjunkers*, thirteen were born between 1791 and 1799; and twenty-three between 1801 and 1812. Of these younger *kammerjunkers*, only nine were born after 1805—that is, were significantly younger than Pushkin.[55] At the same time, Pushkin was not the oldest in the group: some of his fellow *kammerjunkers* were over forty. Pushkin may have been upset because the majority became *kammerjunkers* at a younger age: according to Reiser's calculations, one usually became a *kammerjunker* between sixteen and thirty-nine, most receiving the title between twenty and twenty-five.[56]

Such is the tentative (and, at times, blurry) history of Pushkin's service. It is tentative not only because we lack relevant documentation but also because our biases interfere. We want to see Pushkin in a heroic light, consistently opposing what we regard as an oppressive government. At times Pushkin obliged, but at least twice in his life (at the turn of the 1810s and in the early 1830s) he may have seriously striven to cooperate with this government. If he did, both times he did so while he was employed in the state service. What was an accepted behavior in Pushkin's time may seem improper to us, and this sense of impropriety makes it more difficult for us to see Pushkin's service career as it was. In addition, our biased sense of justice may make us resent Pushkin's apparent lack of service success.

Pushkin's contemporaries looked at his service career through a different lens, in some respects a more distorting lens than ours but in others, perhaps, more accurate. Most importantly, they did not regard

Pushkin's service career and rank as something irrelevant. Two examples illustrate this point. One is Uvarov's alleged indignation over Vladmir F. Odoevsky's obituary for Pushkin, in which Odoevsky famously called him "the sun of our poetry." The obituary was published by Andrei A. Kraevsky in the supplement to the *Russian Invalid* (*Russkii invalid*) that he edited at the time. The next day Kraevsky was summoned to the Ministry of Public Education and dressed down by an official:

> I have to pass on to you . . . that the minister is very, very cross with you. Why this publication about Pushkin? Why this black frame around the news of the death of a person of low rank, without any real position in the state service? Well, that would still be not too bad! But what kind of expressions did you use?! "Sun of poetry!!" For pity's sake, why such an honor? "Pushkin died half-way through his great career!" What kind of career? Sergei Semenovich has rightly pointed out: was Pushkin a military leader, a commander, a minister, a statesman? Finally, he died at almost forty. To write little verses [*stishki*] does not mean, as Sergei Semenovich has put it, to have a great career! The Minister has authorized me to admonish you and to remind you that, as a clerk at the Ministry of Public Education, you in particular should refrain from such publications.[57]

Granted, by the time of Pushkin's death, Uvarov had developed so passionate a hatred for the poet that it alone can explain his rage over what he perceived as an overwrought obituary. But Uvarov was not alone in considering Pushkin's achievements as a writer insufficient to offset his low service rank. Nashchokin's wife recounts a high-ranking military officer's reaction to the news of Pushkin's widow's impending marriage to Petr P. Lanskoi: "After Natalia Nikolaevna's engagement, General Vrangel, the commander of the Moscow artillery, dropped by. I asked him: 'Have you heard the news?'—'What news?' he asked. 'Pushkina is going to marry.'—'Whom?'—'General Lanskoi.' 'Good for her! At least he is a general, not some Pushkin or other, a man without a name and status.'"[58]

It was not only high-ranking officials who paid attention to Pushkin's lack of service success: even contemporaries who knew his worth as a writer also noticed his low service rank. Both Senkovsky and Gogol, I maintain, poked fun at Pushkin the servitor in their fiction. As it would take me too far afield of my topic, I do not consider *why* they evoke Pushkin's service career; I merely demonstrate that references to it are present.[59]

Senkovsky's "Poetic Journey through the Wide World," the second chapter in his *Fantastic Travels of Baron Brambeus* (*Fantasticheskie puteshestviia Barona Brambeusa* [1833]), is the story of a collegiate secretary who has remained in this rank for five years and is desperate for promotion. The story is narrated in his voice: "I felt that I was created for higher ranks and higher sensations, but some magical, invisible force fettered my existence to the tenth class with a heavy chain; it seemed to me that I would never get out of it [*iz nego ne vylezu*], that when all of humanity was promoted to the rank of titular councilor, I alone on the entire globe would remain a collegiate secretary."[60] Angry and frustrated, the narrator becomes "an awful freethinker," stops "going to the office," and begins "going to [his] supervisor's wife instead in order to turn" his supervisor's attention to himself.[61]

The narrator's situation is complicated by the fact that in his soul he is not a bureaucrat but a poet: "My soul could not fit the narrow confines of the tenth class anymore. . . . I was born a poet, a romantic, and my soul required strong sensations."[62] The narrator reads new romantic literature, dreams of horrifying adventures and awful misfortunes that would make his life more exciting, and, since "all great poets gamble," he gambles. Fleeing the wrath of two collegiate registrars who lost 50,000 rubles to him, the narrator moves to Moscow, then goes to Ukraine, Novorossia, and, finally, to Odessa. Eventually he ends up in Constantinople, where he experiences a passionate love, a series of humiliating frustrations, and a near-mortal illness. As a result, he loses his romantic disposition and becomes a scholar. (I omit many twists of the plot not directly relevant to the task at hand.)

At first glance, the story of a collegiate secretary with the soul of a poet waiting for years to become a titular councilor looks too generic to be referring to Pushkin. No doubt there were many collegiate secretaries who did not get promoted; some of them were likely to become freethinkers, many considered themselves poets, and some of them gambled; yet others had love affairs with the wives of their superiors; some of them could have ended up serving in Odessa; and some perhaps were thinking of running off to Constantinople. However, if taken together, these traits begin to coalesce into a grotesque portrait of someone resembling Pushkin: a freethinking collegiate secretary, a poet and a gambler, traveling to the south of Russia and ending up in Odessa where he had (or was rumored to have had) a love affair with the wife of his superior. Pushkin's sympathies with the Greeks in their battle to overthrow Ottoman rule are well known, and, according to his letter to Lev, he considered running off to Constantinople.[63] The romantic poems written by Pushkin during his stay in the south add another relevant connection. Finally, it was shortly before Senkovsky wrote

"Poetic Journey through the Wide World" that Pushkin was promoted to the rank of titular councilor. His longish stint as a collegiate secretary could have attracted attention at that point.

Even more important is the fact that the story contains references to Pushkin's works. It begins with two lines of dots with a question mark at the end. This is a feature of the romantic fragment in general, but it is also a feature of Pushkin's *Eugene Onegin* (*Evgenii Onegin*), with its omitted stanzas replaced by dots. More references to *Eugene Onegin* follow. Arriving in Moscow, Senkovsky's narrator characterizes it thus: "No, it is boring in Moscow. What can I see there? The ruins of ancient boyar pride, over which bridegroom-profiteers [*zhenikhi-spekulianty*] languidly find their way in rented carriages. Piles made up of the debris of estates freed from mortgage obligations, upon which brides sit, dressed in fine clothes [*razodetye v pukh*], twiddling their thumbs and counting the stars on the chests of those who come from Petersburg!"[64] Compare chapter 7 of *Eugene Onegin*, in which Tatiana is taken to Moscow to "the marriage market" and is chosen by the "haughty general" to be his wife. Also compare Pushkin's portrayal of Moscow as a ruined seat of ancient boyars in his essay "A Journey from Moscow to Petersburg" ("Puteshestvie iz Moskvy v Peterburg"). Written in 1833–35 and not published in Pushkin's lifetime, it contains his views on the status of the Russian nobility as they took shape in the late 1820s and the early 1830s. It is not improbable that Pushkin shared his views with his fellow literati, and they could have been known to Senkovsky.

Another reference to *Eugene Onegin*, or, rather, to "Onegin's Journey" ("Puteshestvie Onegina"), is the scene of the narrator's arrival in Odessa. After his carriage gets stuck in the middle of a huge mud puddle, his coachman promptly drowns in the mud and the narrator is prevented from leaving the carriage until morning, when he is removed from it by locals. Compare "Onegin's Journey":

В Одессе пыльной, я сказал.
Я б мог сказать: в Одессе грязной—
И тут бы, право, не солгал.
В году недель пять-шесть Одесса,
По воле бурного Зевеса,
Потоплена, запружена,
В густой грязи погружена.
Все домы на аршин загрязнут,
Лишь на ходулях пешеход

По улице дерзает вброд;
Кареты, люди тонут, вязнут.[65]

[I said, "In dusty Odessa." I could have said, "In muddy Odessa," and, honestly, I wouldn't have been lying. Five or six weeks a year, at the pleasure of stormy Zeus, Odessa is flooded, inundated, submerged in thick mud. All the houses are sunk in two feet of mud, and only on stilts do pedestrians dare to walk down the street. Carriages and people drown, get stuck.]

Finally, the narrator provides a direct reference to *Eugene Onegin*: "If I return to Petersburg at some point in time, I will compose a novel in verse, that is a poem, in which I will paint in mud the grandiose picture of my wanderings and my sensations."[66] My contention is that in his "Poetic Journey" Senkovsky is mocking Pushkin's service career and marks his mockery with references to Pushkin's life and, especially, works.

My other case is Gogol. Gogol, of course, liked to refer to Pushkin directly, by name, and indirectly, citing or paraphrasing his works. One such reference is found in "Notes of a Madman." Poprishchin reads Nikolai Nikolev's poem and comments: "Looks like Pushkin's composition."[67] However, I believe this is not the only way Pushkin is present in the story: Gogol also seems to evoke Pushkin's service career.

Written in the summer of 1834, that is, about six months after titular councilor Pushkin received the ostensibly humiliating title of *kammerjunker*, Gogol's story culminates in an imaginary clash between Poprishchin, a titular councilor, and Teplov, a *kammerjunker*, in which the lowly titular councilor goes mad and perishes. What drives Poprishchin mad is the supposedly insuperable difference—a vertical rift—between the service status of a titular councilor and the service status of a *kammerjunker*: Poprishchin blames his failure in love on Teplov's considerably superior rank. It is unlikely, however, that Teplov's rank is superior. Poprishchin is clearly off the mark when he compares Teplov's title to the rank of general ("everything that is good in this world goes to *kammerjunkers* or generals"): generals belonged to the first four classes.[68]

Poprishchin's mistake is a reversal of the misreading of the worth of the title of *kammerjunker* reflected in Pushkin's reportedly violent reaction to the news of receiving it: while Poprishchin believes that the title of *kammerjunker* is significantly above his rank of titular councilor, Pushkin considered it significantly beneath his own status. The reaction, however, is similar: Pushkin's contemporaries, as we remember, described his response to the news of receiving the title as that of a person gone mad: he was "beside himself, having flared up, with his face aglow," "foaming at the mouth." The medicine is also similar: Poprishchin's madness is treated with water poured on his head, as was Pushkin's rage, according to the account Nashchokin supplied.

Senkovsky ties his narrator to Pushkin by repeatedly referring to his works, and yet scholars have so thoroughly repressed the memory of Pushkin's service career that they fail to connect the dots and see the great poet in the laughable collegiate secretary striving to become a titular councilor. Granted, Senkovsky's works are not widely read, and his references to Pushkin could simply have been overlooked, but Gogol's story is a universally acknowledged classic and therefore provides an even better illustration of how our inattention to Pushkin's service career makes us blind to what seems to be a rather obvious reference to it. The taboo that persists in regard to the topic of Pushkin the servitor prevents us not only from adequately reconstructing Pushkin's life but also from reading correctly some of the best-known masterpieces of Russian literature.

Notes

1. For an analysis of Pushkin's modeling his behavior in the late 1810s and early 1820s, see Igor' V. Nemirovskii, "Smyvaia pechal'nye stroki," in his *Tvorchestvo Pushkina i problema publichnogo povedeniia poeta* (St. Petersburg: Giperion, 2002), 19–73. While Nemirovsky offers a convincing interpretation of Pushkin's attempts to create his public image as a poet, he does not take into account the fact that these attempts were undertaken by a person whose behavior was constrained by his participation in imperial service.

2. I address this question in "Prose Fiction," in *The Cambridge Companion to Pushkin*, ed. Andrew Kahn (Cambridge: Cambridge University Press, 2006), 96–101.

3. *Putevoditel' po Pushkinu* (Moscow: Goslitizdat, 1931).

4. *Russkie pisateli: Biograficheskii slovar', 1800–1917* (Moscow: Nauchnoe izdatel'stvo "Bol'shaia Rossiiskaia entsiklopediia," 2007), 5:189–216.

5. *Handbook of Russian Literature*, ed. Victor Terras (New Haven: Yale University Press, 1985), 357.

6. One good example is Timothy J. Binyon's *Pushkin: A Biography* (New York: Vintage Books, 2004), which provides an outline of Pushkin's service career,

without, however, giving it a thorough interpretation in the contemporary context or considering its impact on him as a writer.

7. Natalia E. Miasoedova, *Pushkinskie zamysly: Opyt rekonstruktsii* (St. Petersburg: SpetsLit, 2002), 4.

8. Notably, Iurii M. Lotman, who in his biography of Pushkin is usually attentive to all details of his life (and does note his anxiety, in the early 1820s, over his low standing in the service hierarchy), mentions that Pushkin was granted access to archives and a yearly salary but does not tell the reader that to gain these favors Pushkin had to return to service. See his *Aleksandr Sergeevich Pushkin: Biografiia pisatelia* (Leningrad: Prosveshchenie, 1981), 86–87 (on anxiety), 196 (on access to archives).

9. See ibid., 212. It is the only fact concerning Pushkin's service career that is mentioned in Victor Terras's *A History of Russian Literature* (New Haven: Yale University Press, 1991), 205.

10. *Aleksandr Sergeevich Pushkin: Dokumenty k biografii*, vol. 1, *1799–1829*, ed. Vadim P. Stark et al. (St. Petersburg: Iskusstvo-SPB, 2007), 282, commentary to document no. 174 (hereafter *Dokumenty, 1799–1829*). Matiushkin's situation was particularly annoying: he was first on the list of collegiate secretaries.

11. See Lotman, *Aleksandr Sergeevich Pushkin*, 32–33. Pushkin apparently continued to entertain plans to transfer to the military; see Sergei A. Sobolevskii, "Iz stat'i 'Tainstvennye primety v zhizni Pushkina,'" in *Pushkin v vospominaniiakh sovremennikov*, 2 vols. (Moscow: Khudozhestvennaia literatura, 1985), 2:11; and Aleksandr I. Turgenev to Petr A. Viazemskii, 12 March 1819, in *Ostaf'evskii arkhiv kniazei Viazemskikh*, vol. 1 of *Perepiska kniazia P. A. Viazemskogo s A. I. Turgenevym, 1812–1819* (St. Petersburg: Izdanie grafa S. D. Sheremeteva, 1899), 202.

12. *Dokumenty, 1799–1829*, 572, document no. 362.

13. For a discussion of some of Pushkin's activities in St. Petersburg from 1817 to 1820, see the chapter by Joe Peschio in the present volume.

14. See Filipp F. Vigel', "Iz 'Zapisok,'" in *Pushkin v vospominaniiakh sovremennikov*, 1:222; Lotman, *Aleksandr Sergeevich Pushkin*, 33. Nikolai I. Turgenev's reproaching words to Pushkin for his idleness are quoted in Aleksandr I. Zaozerskii, "Vtoraia opravdatel'naia zapiska N. I. Turgeneva," in *Pamiati dekabristov: Sbornik materialov*, vol. 2 (Leningrad: AN SSSR, 1926), 122. It is noteworthy that the often-quoted letter by Egor A. Engel'gardt to Aleksandr M. Gorchakov of 10 December 1817 mentioning Pushkin's idleness presents it as an anomaly, the consequence of his illness: "Pushkin does nothing at the ministry; he doesn't even show up there. I have been told that he is ill now" (see Egor A. Engel'gardt, "Pis'mo Gorchakovu A.M., 18 ianvaria 1818 g., Tsarskoe Selo," *Literaturnoe nasledstvo* 52 [1952]: 34n2, original in French).

15. See *Dokumenty, 1799–1829*, 284, 294–95, document nos. 177, 181. On Pushkin's classmates' careers, see ibid., 299, commentary to document no. 182.

16. See ibid., 296, commentary to document no. 181.

17. Vadim E. Vatsuro, "Iz razyskanii o Pushkine," in *Vremennik Pushkinskoi komissii, 1972* (Leningrad: Nauka, 1974), 100 (in Sollogub's text, an anecdote about Paul I follows).

18. *Dokumenty, 1799–1829*, 343, document no. 212.

19. Ibid., 366, 385, document nos. 226 and 239.

20. I. P. Medvedev, "Pushkin—Perevodchik Kollegii inostrannykh del," in *Vremennik Pushkinskoi komissii, 1978* (Leningrad: Nauka, 1981), 105–6.

21. See Nikolai K. Piksanov, *Letopis' zhizni i tvorchestva A. S. Griboedova, 1791–1829* (Moscow: Nasledie, 2000), 15, 122, 129.

22. *Dokumenty, 1799–1829*, 301, commentary to document no. 183.

23. See Mariia Maiofis, *Vozzvanie k Evrope: Literaturnoe obshchestvo "Arzamas" i rossiiskii modernizatsionnyi proekt 1815–1818 godov* (Moscow: Novoe literaturnoe obozrenie, 2008), 24–27, and esp. chap. 5.

24. Ibid., 41–44.

25. Ibid., 44. In her dating of Pushkin's admission, Maiofis follows Oleg Proskurin, "Kogda zhe Pushkin vstupil v Arzamasskoe obshchestvo? (Iz zametok k teme 'Pushkin i Arzamas')," *Toronto Slavic Quarterly* 15, http://www.utoronto.ca/tsq/14/proskurin14.shtml (accessed 5 February 2011).

26. Maiofis, *Vozzvanie k Evrope*, 37–38.

27. Nemirovskii, "Smyvaia pechal'nye stroki," 22–31.

28. Ibid., 30.

29. See Lazar' A. Chereiskii, *Pushkin i ego okruzhenie*, 2nd ed. (Leningrad: Nauka, 1989), 181; Igor' V. Nemirovskii, "Smyvaia pechal'nye stroki," 31; *Dokumenty, 1799–1829*, 339, commentaries to document no. 210.

30. *Dokumenty, 1799–1829*, 336–38, document no. 210.

31. Ibid., original in French.

32. Nemirovskii, "Smyvaia pechal'nye stroki," 19–21, 36–37. For Pushkin's presentation of Alexander as Augustus, see "Iz pis'ma k Gnedichu," in Aleksandr S. Pushkin, *Polnoe sobranie sochinenii*, 10 vols., ed. Boris V. Tomashevskii (Leningrad: Nauka, 1977–79), 2:33.

33. *Dokumenty, 1799–1829*, 408, commentaries to document no. 263.

34. Ibid.

35. Ibid., 416, commentary to document no. 270, original in French.

36. Ibid., 421, document no. 272. This letter was obviously written in a state of fury, which explains Pushkin's overstatement of his disengagement from service.

37. Aleksandr S. Pushkin to Aleksandr Kh. Benkendorf, 16 April 1830, in Pushkin, *Polnoe sobranie sochinenii*, 10 vols., 10:219, original in French.

38. Ibid., [no later than 21] July 1831, 10:499.

39. See *Aleksandr Sergeevich Pushkin: Dokumenty k biografii*, vol. 2, *1830–1837*, ed. S. V. Berezkina et al. (St. Petersburg: Izdatel'stvo Pushkinskii Dom, 2010), 173, document no. 732 and 179–180, document no. 738, respectively (hereafter *Dokumenty, 1830–1837*).

40. Ibid., 349, document no. 914. For a summary of Pushkin's service, see Dmitrii Iakubovich, "Posluzhnoi spisok Pushkina 1834 g.," in *Pushkin: 1834 god* (Leningrad: Pushkinskoe obshchestvo, 1934), 141–44.

41. Pushkin to Benkendorf, [no later than 21] July 1831, in Pushkin, *Polnoe sobranie sochinenii*, 10 vols., 10:499, emphasis in the original.

42. Aleksandr S. Pushkin, "Materialy i zametki, sviazannye s izdaniem gazety 'Dnevnik,'" in Pushkin, *Sobranie sochinenii*, 10 vols., ed. Dmitrii D. Blagoi (Moscow: Izdatel'stvo khudozhestvennoi literatury, 1962), 6:373.

43. Maiofis, *Vozzvanie k Evrope*, 657–59; Filipp F. Vigel to Aleksandr S. Pushkin, June–July 1831, in Pushkin, *Polnoe sobranie sochinenii*, 17 vols., ed. Vladimir D. Bonch-Bruevich et al. (Moscow: AN SSSR, 1937–49), 14:202, original in French.

44. Vigel to Pushkin, June–July 1831, 14:202.

45. About Pushkin's election to the Russian Academy, see *Dokumenty, 1830–1837*, 284–85, document no. 856.

46. Petr Bartenev, interview of Pavel Nashchokin and Vera Nashchokina, 1851–53, "P. V. i V. A. Nashchokiny: Rasskazy o Pushkine, zapisannye P. I. Bartenevym," in *Pushkin v vospominaniiakh sovremennikov*, 2:231.

47. Iakov Polonskii, interview of Lev Pushkin, n.d., "Rasskazy L. S. Pushkina v zapisi Ia. P. Polonskogo," in *Pushkin v vospominaniiakh sovremennikov*, 1:57.

48. For Sobolevsky's remark, see P. I. Bartenev, *O Pushkine: Stranitsy zhizni poeta: Vospominaniia sovremennikov* (Moscow: Sovetskaia Rossia, 1992), 358n**.

49. Bartenev, "P. V. i V. A. Nashchokiny," in *Pushkin v vospominaniiakh sovremennikov*, 2:231.

50. Aleksandr S. Pushkin to Pavel Nashchokin, mid-March 1834, in Pushkin, *Polnoe sobranie sochinenii*, 10 vols., 10:364.

51. For the documents pertaining to the episode, see *Dokumenty, 1830–1837*, 428, document no. 982 (Pushkin's letter of resignation), 432–33, document no. 986 (Benkendorf's letter informing Pushkin that his resignation is accepted by Nicholas but access to archives is denied), and 436–40, document nos. 989, 990, and 991 (Pushkin's letters to Benkendorf withdrawing his resignation). For an analysis of the episode, see Boris Gasparov, "Pushkin's Year of Frustration," *Ulbandus* 12 (2009–10): 49–50.

52. Leonid E. Shepelev, *Otmenennye istoriei: Chiny, zvaniia i tituly v rossiiskoi imperii* (Leningrad: Nauka, 1977), 121.

53. Solomon A. Reiser, "Tri stroki dnevnika Pushkina," in *Vremennik Pushkinskoi komissii, 1981* (Leningrad: Nauka, 1985), 148.

54. Boris Gasparov rightly points out that there was no malice on Nicholas's part in making this appointment, just "his obsession with laws and rules." See his "Pushkin's Year of Frustration," 47.

55. Reiser, "Tri stroki dnevnika Pushkina," 149.

56. Ibid., 150.

57. Petr A. Efremov, "Aleksandr Sergeevich Pushkin, 1799–1837," *Russkaia starina* 28 (1880): 536–37. Uvarov also wrote to Sergei G. Stroganov, the trustee of Moscow School District, instructing him to observe moderation in published responses to Pushkin's death; see *Dokumenty, 1830–1837*, 801–2, document no. 1318. Stroganov, in his turn, forbade the use of black borders around obituaries for the poet; see ibid., 850, document no. 1372.

58. Petr Bartenev, interview of Vera Nashchokina, "P. V. i V. A. Nashchokiny: Rasskazy o Pushkine, zapisannye P. I. Bartenevym," in *Pushkin v vospominaniiakh sovremennikov*, 2:247.

59. For a detailed discussion of Pushkin's presence in "Notes of a Madman" and of Gogol's reasons for referring to him, see my "Kammerjunker in 'Notes of a Madman': Gogol's View of Pushkin," in my collection *Rank and Style: Russians in State Service, Life, and Literature* (Brighton, MA: Academic Studies Press, 2011).

60. Osip I. Senkovskii, "Poeticheskoe puteshestvie po belu svetu," in his *Sochineniia barona Brambeusa* (Moscow: Sovetskaia Rossiia, 1989), 38–39.

61. Ibid., 39.

62. Ibid.

63. For an overview of Pushkin's attitude to the insurgency, see Miasoedova, *Pushkinskie zamysly*, 106–16; Aleksandr S. Pushkin to Lev Pushkin, January–early February 1824, in Pushkin, *Polnoe sobranie sochinenii*, 10 vols., 10:65.

64. Senkovskii, "Poeticheskoe puteshestvie po belu svetu," 41.

65. Pushkin, "Puteshestvie Onegina," in his *Polnoe sobranie sochinenii*, 10 vols., 5:176.

66. Senkovskii, "Poeticheskoe puteshestvie po belu svetu," 43.

67. Nikolai V. Gogol', "Zapiski sumasshedshego," in his *Peterburgskie povesti*, ed. Ol'ga G. Dilaktorskaia (St. Petersburg: Nauka, 1995), 113.

68. Gogol', "Zapiski sumasshedshego," 119.

Why Pushkin Did Not Become a Decembrist

IGOR NEMIROVSKY

The opinion of Decembrist and member of the United Slavs Ivan I. Gorbachevsky (1800–69) about Pushkin is perhaps the most scathing and tabooed contemporary appraisal of the personality of the poet in Pushkin studies. Contained in a letter from Gorbachevsky to another Decembrist, Mikhail A. Bestuzhev (1800–71), Gorbachevsky's impression of Pushkin so embarrassed the Pushkinist Mikhail I. Semevsky that he excluded it from the first publication of the letter, explaining his action, unorthodox for an historian, by stating that Gorbachevky's views could not be published because they were "extremely harsh about the personal character of a great poet, and unsubstantiated."[1]

In a scholarly about-face, Gorbachevsky's opinion was admitted into scholarship not long before the 1917 revolution, when the authority of Pushkin began to cede prominence to that of the Decembrists as the initiators of the Russian revolutionary movement. Pavel E. Shchegolev, the publisher of Gorbachevsky's appraisal of Pushkin, was not only an impressive Pushkinist and historian but also a professional revolutionary. Therefore Gorbachevsky's letter appeared in full for the first time on the pages of the revolutionary (Menshevik) newspaper *Day* (*Den'*), and only after that was it published in a separate edition of

Gorbachevsky's notes and letters.[2] It was not accidental that this publication occurred in the hundredth-anniversary year of the Decembrist uprising in 1925. Furthermore, as late as 1963, in the next academic (that is to say, would-be complete) edition of Gorbachevsky's notes and letters, the Decembrist's assessment of Pushkin was published with a cut. I quote it here in full:

> I cannot forget that pamphlet that I read to you—that essay by our own Iv[an] Iv[anovich] Pushchin about his lyceum upbringing and about his Pushkin, about whom he wrote a lot. Poor Pushchin doesn't even know that we were in fact forbidden by the Supreme Duma to become acquainted with the poet Alexander Sergeevich Pushkin when he lived in the south. And why this was was stated directly: that because of his character and cowardliness, because of his dissipated lifestyle, he would immediately make a denunciation to the authorities about the existence of the Secret Society. And now I am completely convinced that it is so; he himself near his death confirmed it to Zhukovsky: "Tell him [Emperor Nicholas I] that if not for this, I would have been completely his." What does this mean? And this was said by the National Poet, the name by which all the aristocrats and toadies call him. Read carefully about their upbringing in the lyceum; is that really the soil from which grow national poets, republicans, and patriots? Was our youthful life like theirs? Did they suffer through those wants, those humiliations, those deprivations, like hunger and cold, that we suffered through? And look at them from the perspective of morality. Murav'ev-Apostol and Bestuzhev-Riumin told such stories about Pushkin's escapades in the south that even now I blush to my very ears.[3]

Gorbachevsky wrote this after reading "Notes about Pushkin" ("Zapiski o Pushkine"), written by Ivan I. Pushchin (1798–1859), the poet's lyceum friend, Decembrist, and member of the Northern Society.

The Soviet publishers of Gorbachevsky, Shchegolev and Boris E. Syroechkovsky, hastened to explain the harshness of this appraisal and the shocking character of the facts Gorbachevsky asserted as the result of errors in his memory.[4] They considered the main mistaken memory to be Gorbachevsky's assertion that the Southern Society was banned from making the acquaintance of Pushkin and hypothesized that in September 1825, when the contact between Gorbachevsky, Bestuzhev-Riumin, and Murav'ev-Apostol took place (Bestuzhev-Riumin and Murav'ev-Apostol were responsible for the communication between the Supreme Duma of the Southern Society and the Society of United Slavs), there was no need for such a ban, since Pushkin had already left the south of Russia and was in exile in Mikhailovskoe. But of course this circumstance alone is not enough to refute Gorbachevsky's assertion and serve as evidence for his having misremembered it. In fact, in September 1825 Pushkin's exile in Mikhailovskoe could not yet seem an insurmountable obstacle to contact between him and a member of the Southern Society. At that time no one could yet suppose that in December of that very year the uprising would take place, and that after it a meeting of the poet with the Decembrists would become impossible. Therefore, if the Supreme Duma of the Southern Society truly had as its goal the cutting off of contact between Pushkin and its members, in September 1825 such a ban might still have been in force, even if it had been instituted earlier, during Pushkin's time in the south.

Vadim S. Parsamov, a researcher of Decembrism, has put forward an interesting analysis of Gorbachevsky's critique of Pushkin. Parsamov believes that the harshness of Gorbachevsky's opinion reflects only his individual position and not that of a particular portion of the Decembrist society—it is the position of a *raznochinets* (member of the middle classes) rather than the viewpoint of someone of noble descent and outlook: "For Gorbachevsky, Pushkin embodies the noble, loyal culture and noble mode of behavior. Not only did Gorbachevsky's distrust of the nobility not fade away during the ensuing years; it grew apace and reached its apogee in the years of the peasant reforms, which he evaluated from a revolutionary-democratic position."[5] Parsamov goes on: "Thus, Gorbachevsky's opinion reflects the circumstances not so much of 1825 [when the Decembrist briefly but passionately socialized with Bestuzhev-Riumin and Murav'ev-Apostol], but rather the ideological situation at the beginning of the 1860s."[6]

One can agree with Parsamov at least about the fact that Gorbachevsky represents the most "leftist," most democratic wing of the Decembrist movement. The scathing quality of his evaluation of Pushkin truly divides him from other Decembrists. Yet it is interesting that a contemporary of Gorbachevsky who knew him well, Vladmir A. Obruchev, the revolutionary "man of the sixties" and friend of Nikolai Chernyshevsky, does not confirm the democratic sympathies of Gorbachevsky asserted by Parsamov. In 1862, Obruchev lived in a settlement in Petrovskii Zavod, where the Decembrists spent their time in hard labor in Siberia and where, after having being freed, Gorbachevsky stayed to live. In his memoirs about that year Obruchev wrote:

Ivan Ivanovich was then sixty-three years old. He was a broad man, a little bit taller than average height, with a powerful, barely grayed head, coiffed or rather tousled in the manner of generals of Alexander's day, but with a fluffy mustache and sideburns. Judging by his appearance, he would have been at home only as a corps commander. And his speech was that of important elders, lordly [*barskii*], rich, pure Russian, without the least trace of his Ukrainian origins or Siberian experience. His gaze, likewise, was lordly, always benevolent. In everything he was a gentleman [*barin*].[7]

What it is impossible to agree with Parsamov about is the idea that Gorbachevsky's insistence that the Supreme Duma had issued a ban on associating with Pushkin was determined by the circumstances of the 1860s. Because if this is not a mistake of memory and not a fact from the history of Decembrism but a circumstance mediated by the ideological imagination, then one could not call it anything but slander. As an aside, both Gorbachevsky's contemporaries who knew him and scholars are agreed that Gorbachevsky was incapable of slander. Furthermore, among the Decembrists Gorbachevsky had the reputation of a reliable and trustworthy memoirist. His memoiristic *Notes* (*Zapiski*) to this day provides the most precise and thorough evidence about the Society of United Slavs and the uprising of the Chernigov regiment. It follows therefore that the ban he mentions must have existed in some form.

Natan Ia. Eidel'man was the first of the Soviet historians to acknowledge the truth of Gorbachevsky's statement about the existence of a ban against being acquainted with Pushkin for the members of the Southern Society.[8] In addition, Eidel'man explained the decree of the Supreme Duma as the result of a chance circumstance—namely, slanderous information about Pushkin that had come to the attention of Bestuzhev and Murav'ev-Apostol through an Odessa acquaintance of the poet, Alexander Nikolaevich Raevsky.[9] As evidence indicating that Raevsky slandered the poet, Eidel'man cites the poem by Pushkin titled "Perfidy" ("Kovarnost'" [1824]), pointing out that the lines "He himself was an invisible echo of despicable slander" (Sam prezrennoi klevety / . . . nevidimym byl ekhom") refer to Raevsky.

Much has already been written about the complex role of Alexander Raevsky in Pushkin's Odessa period. Eidel'man was not the first to suggest that Pushkin had Raevsky in mind in "Perfidy." The scholar who first made this hypothesis was Tatiana G. Tsiavlovskaia, and the kindest thing one can say about it is that it has not become widely accepted.[10] Hence, layering hypothesis upon hypothesis, Eidel'man compromises his usual scholarly objectivity, explaining the Southern

Society's decree against Pushkin as the result of chance circumstances. The scholar was but one step away from giving Gorbachevsky's evaluation a deep historical explanation. But he did not take this step because he wanted to avoid making a sharp division between Pushkin and the Decembrists. From his point of view, Pushkin and the Decembrists belonged to the same ideological camp, and disagreements between them, if there were any at all, were not of a principled nature and were founded merely on chance confluences of circumstances. Meanwhile, Pushkin's behavior in Odessa was sufficiently scandalous that there is no necessity to search for additional circumstances that could have led to the ban. One diverting and nonessential but extremely telling parallel is that the parents of seventeen-year-old Count Mikhail D. Buturlin, having discovered that he had become friends with Pushkin, forbade the young man any further contact with the poet.[11] No insinuations were required to provoke this reaction; the reputation that the poet had acquired sufficed.

It must be noted that there was an important circumstance that could have shed a negative light on Pushkin's reputation: the formal reason for his exile was an accusation of atheism. Therefore the poet was exiled to Mikhailovskoe under spiritual ("church") surveillance.[12] Although it is not quite clear when exactly the wider public found out about this accusation (probably it happened after Pushkin's departure from Odessa), it is obvious that Pushkin's atheism ruined his reputation in the eyes of the Decembrists no less than in the eyes of his other contemporaries. Thus, there are weighty reasons to suppose that the ban on acquaintanceship with Pushkin that applied to members of the Southern Society was determined not by happenstance but was in fact a consequence of Pushkin's "social reputation" that had formed by that time.

The concept of "social reputation," which was first developed in the context of Russian literary scholarship by Vadim E. Vatsuro, has great significance for our investigation, and it is worth citing his definition in its entirety:

> In all times a social reputation accompanies a historical personage. Alongside the real person there lives, like a shadow that has detached itself from him, his image as created by his contemporaries, an impression of his personality and his social role. If this image sharply contradicts the objective meaning of his accomplishments, then the task of restoring historical justice falls to his descendants. The social reputation of Pushkin was created by various people operating

from various motives, both through honest mistakes and intentionally, because beginning in 1826 he found himself within the sphere of political and literary battle.[13]

Continuing Vatsuro's comparison between the social reputation of the poet (Pushkin) with the "shadow that has detached itself from him," I note that no matter how independent this reputation was, like a real shadow, it reflected to a significant extent certain real qualities of Pushkin's personality and creative works. As a matter of fact, Gorbachevsky's evaluation elicited resistance from Pushkinists, verging on complete denial, precisely because it so harshly and unambiguously linked the ban on associating with Pushkin to specific behaviors of the poet himself: "And why this was was stated directly: that because of his character and cowardliness, because of his dissipated lifestyle, he would immediately make a denunciation to the authorities about the existence of the Secret Society." It might be possible to consider such an evaluation to be the private opinion of a less than well-educated person, if we had not come to understand during the past several decades that this opinion really does reflect Pushkin's "social reputation."

The goal of the present chapter is to reconstruct what the Decembrists said among themselves in private, out of earshot of the court of public opinion, which was then absorbed into Gorbachevsky's negative appraisal of Pushkin.

Among those with whom Gorbachevsky socialized during his years of hard labor and exile, many were personally acquainted with Pushkin, but most likely the opinions of four men, Sergei G. Volkonsky, Ivan D. Iakushkin, Vasilii L. Davydov, and Pushchin, affected his views on Pushkin to the greatest extent. Firstly, this was because all four knew Pushkin well, and Pushchin, as we know, was one of the poet's closest friends. Secondly, all these Decembrists, like Gorbachevsky himself, having been given the most severe punishment—the death penalty, which was commuted to twenty years of hard labor—had by 1830 gathered in Petrovskii Zavod: such was the name of the small settlement where they carried out their sentence. Gorbachevsky spent years in close contact with the four others and maintained friendly relations with them even after he was freed. Significantly, the "public" story of the relations between Pushkin and each of the four Decembrists includes a narrative about how Pushkin was very nearly accepted into the secret society but at the last moment was not.

Sergei Grigor'evich Volkonsky

Volkonsky is the only one of the four Decembrists who gave an explicit reason for not accepting Pushkin into the secret society. His son, Mikhail Sergeevich Volkonsky, tells the story as follows:

> I don't know whether I told you that my father was instructed to accept him into the Society and that my father did not fulfill the order. "How could I have taken that upon myself," he told me more than once, "when the executioner's block could have threatened him; but now that they have killed him, I am sorry about it. He would have been alive, and in Siberia his poetry would have taken a new path." And truly, imagine Pushkin in the mines, in Chita, in Petrovskii Zavod, and in the settlement—what he would have composed there.[14]

The time during which Pushkin and Volkonsky associated can be divided into two relatively brief periods; the first lasting from May 1820 until February 1821 and the second during the first half of June 1824. If Volkonsky had intended to accept Pushkin into the secret society, then it is more likely that this would have happened not during the first period of their acquaintance but during the second. In 1820 Volkonsky himself was a freshly inducted member of the Union of Welfare, but by 1823 he had become one of the leading actors of the Southern Society, the head of its Kamenetskaia branch, and therefore he had the necessary authority to induct Pushkin. Moreover, Mikhail Volkonsky would not have implied that participation in the somewhat openly known Union of Welfare invited the threat of the executioner's block, whereas the Southern Society was another matter entirely. None of its members escaped punishment. Clearly, then, Mikhail Volkonsky's letter must refer to the second period of his father's acquaintance with Pushkin.

The only letter that has come down to us from Volkonsky to the poet was written during the second period of Pushkin's friendship with the Decembrist. Written soon after Pushkin's expulsion from Odessa, it contains not only hackneyed expressions of regret related to that event but also informal expressions of friendship, which apparently must have had a special significance in the context of the scandalous events surrounding the expulsion. Volkonsky refers directly to the "gossip that the Moscow featherbrains cooked up about you" (spletn, koi moskovskie vertushki vam nastriapali), by which he throws doubt on the idea that Raevsky had authored these rumors. Further on he characterizes his future relative (in that same year, 1824, Volkonsky married Raevsky's sister Maria) as follows: "You were incorrect about Melmoth when you said that his nature was such that he *gave his blessing to nothing;* previously I agreed with you, but from experience I know that he has feelings of friendship, noble and not changed by circumstances."[15] The narrow circle of those "demonically" inclined Odessa friends of Pushkin called Alexander Raevsky "Melmoth" after the hero of the novel by Charles Maturin, *Melmoth the Wanderer*. The woman with whom Pushkin was then in love, Karolina Sobańska, belonged to that circle and was at the same time the lover and political agent of General Ivan O. Witt.[16] General Witt occupied the post of commander of the military settlements, and, as the official documentation of the investigation of the Decembrist affair notes, "having found out about the existence of the secret society and by permission of the late emperor, he indicated his wish to become a member, intending by this means to reveal the details of the conspiracy."[17] Volkonsky attached himself to Pushkin's and Raevsky's circle in order to observe Witt and, as the documents attest, "recommended rejecting Count Witt's proposal to join the society."[18]

Together with the letter from Volkonsky, Pushkin received a letter from Alexander Raevsky. This letter conveys the impression of having been written not so much for Pushkin as for the letter's potential censors:

> You write that you fear compromising me by my correspondence with you. Such an apprehension is childish in many respects, and furthermore there are circumstances when one should not take such matters into consideration. And what could be compromising in our correspondence anyway? *I have never had a conversation with you about politics; you know that I don't have a very high opinion about the politics of poets, and if there is anything for which I can reproach you, it is only for your insufficient respect for religion—remember this well, for it is not the first time I am speaking with you about it.*"[19]

Raevsky's letter shows that he knew that Pushkin had been exiled owing to an accusation of atheism and that the poet's correspondence was being censored. It is very likely that Pushkin did not trust that it was his friend's sincere wish to explain himself to *him* and considered what he wrote to be addressed to the censors. In any case, it was on the very day when the letters from Volkonsky and Raevsky arrived, 18 October 1824, that Pushkin wrote the poem "Perfidy."

Volkonsky's letter included aesthetic advice for Pushkin: "The nearness and memories of Velikii Novgorod, of the veche bell and the siege of Pskov, will be for you the subject of poetic activity, while for your compatriots your work will be a monument to the glory of their ancestors—and their contemporary."[20] The somewhat muffled style of this advice indicates that its author is more of an infantry brigade commander than a subtle connoisseur of literature. The patriotic character of the advice might serve as oblique testimony to the fact that as a Decembrist leader of the middle tier, Volkonsky was thinking about how to steer Pushkin's creativity in the "correct" direction. But of course, by itself it cannot serve as even oblique testimony to his intention to accept Pushkin into the membership of the Southern Society. It does, though, very likely bear witness to the fact that, in Volkonsky's opinion, Pushkin's work was not on the "path" that was considered necessary.

The memoirs of the Decembrists and, above all, the documents of the investigation into the Decembrist uprising do not give evidence of Volkonsky's intention (and even less so, of orders given to him by someone else) to accept Pushkin into the Southern Society. Furthermore, in the final document of the investigation, the so-called *Alphabet of Decembrists* (*Alfavit dekabristov*) compiled by Alexander D. Borovkov in 1826–27 by order of Tsar Nicholas I, it is specially noted that "despite the fact that [Volkonsky] was the leader of the Kamenetskaia branch, he was not involved either in attracting new members to the society, nor in preparing those under him toward that goal. In his answers he was sincere."[21]

In his later years, Petr A. Viazemsky did not believe that the Decembrists had failed to accept Pushkin into the secret society out of fear for his talent, and he wrote about this explicitly:

> Many of them [the Decembrists] were his friends, but they did not find in him a ready, like-minded thinker, and happily for him and for Russia, they left him in peace, left him on the outside. Pushkin's having been spared from the wreck of 1825 can be attributed more to these considerations and calculations of theirs than to their wish, as many assume, to preserve his gift and the future literary glory of Russia. After all, Ryleev and Alexander Bestuzhev most likely saw themselves as just such investors in the treasure house of future Russian literature as Pushkin, but that did not stop them from self-confidently staking all of this literature on only one card, on the card of a political "to be or not to be."[22]

Ivan Dmitrievich Iakushkin

The period of Pushkin's close association with Iakushkin was in November 1820, when the poet was living at Kamenka, the estate of the Davydov brothers. Here in November and December of 1820 Pushkin was at the epicenter of a discussion that was continued in January 1821 at the Moscow congress of the Union of Welfare. The question that was being discussed at Kamenka—whether a secret society could be useful to Russia—was also the central question in Moscow, where, just as at Kamenka, the opinions of the Decembrists were divided; some derided the usefulness of the idea, while others, among them Iakushkin and Vasilii Davydov, considered that in Russia a secret society was absolutely necessary.

From Iakushkin's memoirs we learn of the famous argument that took place in Kamenka. According to Iakushkin, Mikhail F. Orlov "posed the question of how useful it would be to set up a Secret Society in Russia"; Iakushkin's position was that such a society would have no use, but Raevsky jokingly tried to show that it could indeed be useful

> and enumerated all the occasions on which a Secret Society might operate with success and effectiveness; as an answer to his prank I told him, "It wouldn't be difficult for me to prove to you that you are joking; I propose this question to you: if a Secret Society already existed now, you most likely would not join it, would you?" "On the contrary, I probably would," he answered. "In that case, give me your hand," I said to him. And he held out his hand to me, after which I burst out laughing, saying to Raevsky: "It goes without saying that all this is merely a joke."
>
> The others also laughed, except for A. L. [Alexander Davydov], "the majestic cuckold," who was dozing, and Pushkin, who was very agitated; he had become convinced that a Secret Society either existed or would at this very moment come into being, and that he would be a member of it; but when he saw that only a joke had resulted, he stood up, blushing, and said with tears in his eyes, "I never was as unhappy as I am now; I already saw my life ennobled and an elevated goal before me, and all of it was merely a wicked joke." At that moment he was truly beautiful.[23]

This episode is one of the most famous in Pushkin's biography. It is usually brought out as evidence of Pushkin's nearness to the Decembrists. And to a certain extent that is true, because the argument at Kamenka was not a mere hoax after all, but the beginning of heated debates that were continued by its participants, Orlov, Iakushkin, and Konstantin A. Okhotnikov, in Moscow at the last congress of the Union of Welfare, less than a month after the discussion at Kamenka. Pushkin's participation in this discussion is an important indicator that he came very close to the conspiracy.

At the same time, however, this is a story about how Pushkin, having approached the conspiracy, nonetheless was not drawn into it. Iakushkin does not give a direct explanation for this circumstance but "makes" Pushkin explain it, putting words into the poet's mouth which he most likely never pronounced. Iakushkin writes that in 1827 when Pushkin "came to say goodbye to A. G. Murav'eva, who was leaving for Siberia to join her husband Nikita, he said to her, 'I understand very well why these gentlemen did not want to admit me into their society; I was not worthy of that honor.'"[24] Then again, remembering his meeting with Pushkin in 1820, Iakushkin lets slip the following: "Sometimes he [Pushkin] played the daredevil [*korchil likhacha*], probably remembering Kaverin and his other hussar friends at Tsarskoe Selo; at the same time he recounted the most desperate [*otchaiannye*] anecdotes about himself, and altogether it turned out to be rather vulgar."[25]

This mention of "other friends" of Pushkin, who represented norms of behavior foreign to Iakushkin, betrays the real reason why Iakushkin did not want to cross the border separating the poet from the secret society in his relations with Pushkin. One must note that Pushkin's flirtation with the twenty-year-old daughter of Davydov had earned him the particular disapproval of the high-principled Iakushkin. To this one may add that Pushkin's romance with Davydov's wife, Aglaia, unfolded before the eyes of everyone at Kamenka.

Vasilii L'vovich Davydov

Pushkin's relationship with Vasilii Davydov turned out to be deeper and more dramatic than his relationship with Iakushkin. Davydov was among those who did not recognize the decision of the Moscow congress of the Union of Welfare to dissolve the organization, and he took a very active part in the creation of a new secret society. Pushkin accompanied Davydov on his trips to Tul'chin and Kiev. It was in these very places that discussions took place similar to the one that Iakushkin described, and out of these discussions the Southern Society was born.

There is no direct evidence that Davydov was planning to accept Pushkin into the secret society but then changed his mind, yet Pushkin was never closer to the conspiracy than he was in the period January through March 1821. Then suddenly, and without obvious reason, relations between the poet and the Decembrist were cut off. This happened shortly after Easter, in March 1821. One can suppose that the initiator of the break was Davydov. This conclusion is supported by a note

Gorbachevsky made in the margins of his letter to Bestuzhev: "Davydov drove him [Pushkin] away [*prognal ot sebia*]."[26] The most likely reason for the break would appear to be Pushkin's composition of a verse epistle to Davydov in the spirit of libertinage, "To V. L. Davydov" ("V. L. Davydovu"), which was written immediately after Easter week 1821. I have analyzed this poem elsewhere, but it must be noted here that the poem linked political liberalism with religious freethinking (vol'nomyslie) of a provocatively blasphemous type.[27] The epistle, which was consistent with the spirit of French prerevolutionary libertinage, together with the blasphemous behavior of Pushkin himself in the same spirit on Easter Day in 1819 when he used praying as a pretext for picking up young women, were hardly likely to be to the taste of Davydov, whom contemporaries characterized as a person of patriotic and even folksy sentiments.[28] Others expressed a similar distaste for Pushkin: "I didn't like him as a person," testified the Decembrist Nikolai V. Basargin, who became acquainted with Pushkin during this period. According to Basargin, Pushkin had "some sort of swashbuckling quality, smugness, and a desire to mock and pique others. At that time many who knew him said that sooner or later he would die in a duel."[29]

Ivan Ivanovich Pushchin

Gorbachevsky's negative appraisal of Pushkin was, as noted, a polemical reaction to Pushchin's "Notes about Pushkin." While Pushchin's article is, on the whole, benevolent in regard to Pushkin, it nevertheless contains several highly critical assessments of his behavior. For example:

> Meanwhile the very same Pushkin, liberal in his views, had some sort of unfortunate habit of betraying his noble character and often made me angry and in general made all of us angry insofar as he loved, for example, to hang around the orchestra with Orlov, Chernyshev, Kiselev and others; with patronizing smiles they would listen to his jokes and witticisms. It would happen that they would give him a sign from their seats, and he would immediately run over to them. You would say to him, "What do you get, dear friend, out of spending time with those people? Not a single one of them would share your sympathies," and so on. He would patiently listen, would begin to tickle and hug, which he usually did when he got a little flustered. Then, you'd see—Pushkin was again with those lions of old! (An anachronism: this nickname for aristocrats did not yet exist then. Pardon me!)[30]

This assessment of Pushkin sounds especially severe because the company in which Pushchin situates his friend is marked by its "special" relationship to the Decembrists and the Decembrists to it. Thus, the Orlov mentioned, Aleksei Fedorovich Orlov (1786–1861), actively took part in putting down the uprising of the Decembrists and from 1844 on was the chief of the corps of gendarmes and the head of the Third Section (secret police). Chernyshev was Alexander Ivanovich Chernyshev (1785–1859), a member of the Supreme Criminal Court in the trial of the Decembrists and from 1832 the minister of war. The sentences he recommended for the Decembrists were distinguished by their extreme severity. Kiselev was Pavel Dmitrievich Kiselev (1788–1872). His reputation was significantly more complex. He became friends with many Decembrists and at the same time initiated the shadowing of the Decembrists in the Second Army, which he himself essentially headed. Under Nicholas I he became the minister of government property. The exiled Decembrists, who had been stripped of their noble status and reclassified as "state peasants" (gosudarstvennye krest'iane), were under his authority.

The fact that Pushchin situates his lyceum friend Pushkin in such dubious company testifies to the fact that he judged him no less severely than did Gorbachevsky. Furthermore, Pushchin does not limit himself to recounting just one episode when Pushkin "betray[ed] his noble character" but recalls at least one other:

> Soon it so happened that I met Sergei L'vovich [Pushkin's father] on Nevsky Prospekt. "How are you, Sergei L'vovich? How's our Alexander?"
>
> "When did you see him?"
>
> "A few days ago at Turgenev's place."
>
> I noticed that Sergei L'vovich was somehow morose.
>
> [*In French.*] "I have nothing better to do than to bend over backward to reestablish the reputation of my dear son. [*In Russian.*] Obviously you do not know his latest mischief [*prokaza*]." Here he told me about something that had happened, though it's true, I don't recall precisely what, and I don't care to remember.
>
> "Forget that nonsense, venerable Sergei L'vovich! You know that one can forgive Alexander much; he compensates his pranks [*shalosti*] with inalienable virtues that one cannot but love."
>
> The father pressed my hand and continued on his way. I fell into thought, and I confess, this chance encounter created a strong impression: the thought of accepting Pushkin [into the secret society] disappeared completely from my head.[31]

It is characteristic that Pushchin, like Iakushkin and Gorbachevsky, does not speak directly about what it is in Pushkin's behavior that is so provocatively amoral. Gorbachevsky alludes to the stories of his older comrades ("Murav'ev-Apostol and Bestuzhev-Riumin told such stories about Pushkin's escapades in the south that even now I blush to my very ears").

Pushchin in his "Notes" is no more specific. In attempting to understand what it was that had so profoundly shocked Pushkin's father, who was accustomed to much bad behavior from his son, and what it was that Pushchin kept quiet about in his memoir, one can assert that it was almost certainly not Pushkin's adventures in love that were at issue. Pushchin recalls these without any reproach, even with pleasure:

> Our relations with one another were not without mischief. It would happen that he would come to my place. Instead of saying "Hello," I would ask, "From her to me or from me to her?" I should explain the meaning of this to you, since I have begun to chatter.
>
> In my neighborhood on the Moika lived one Angelika, a charming Pole!
>
> Upon the rest there is a veil! [*Na prochee—zavesa*]![32]

At the same time Pushchin's "Notes" gives the key, not explicitly, but clearly enough, to understanding what it was that he considered particularly reprehensible in the behavior of his friend. This key is contained in the following confession by Pushchin:

> Don't conclude, please, on the basis of this grumbling, that I was once a Spartan, some kind of Cato; I was far from all that: I always made mischief, fooled around and caroused with my good friend. Pushkin himself immortalized our doings in the verses he dedicated to me, but in spite of all my readiness to partake in revelry with him, I wished that he would not overstep certain boundaries and not profane himself, if one might express it that way, by becoming close to people who, because of their position in society, might willy-nilly cast certain aspersions on him.[33]

Hence, it is not simply revelry but some sort of particular, profanatory revelry, which was defined by Pushkin's social relations with certain dubious people, that Pushchin censures in his friend's behavior.

Pushchin's "Notes" allows a rather precise dating of whatever it was Pushkin did and with whom he did it that so upset his father and that simultaneously became an obstacle to his acceptance into the secret society: "Pushkin's most urgent entreaty to me in regard to the secret society was when he met with me at N. I. Turgenev's place, where all who wished to participate in the proposed publication of a political journal were then meeting."[34] We can definitively date this meeting to May 1819. That was precisely when the something happened that would so upset Sergei L'vovich Pushkin; we may suppose that this something happened in the company of those with whom, as Pushchin thought, Pushkin was "overstep[ping] certain boundaries" and "profan[ing] himself." I have already noted Pushchin's opinion that Pushkin humiliated himself by striving to associate with Orlov, Chernyshev, and Kiselev—people whose social position was higher than his own—but of course, it was not with them that the poet overstepped boundaries and profaned himself.

Then with whom?

Pushkin's active participation in the meetings of the Green Lamp, a friendly literary society founded by Nikita V. Vsevolozhsky, began in March 1819. And here it is worth remarking that the first biographers of Pushkin, Pavel Annenkov and Petr Bartenev, considered the Green Lamp to be, irrefutably, an orgiastic society.[35] Shchegolev just as irrefutably declared the Green Lamp to be an affiliate of the Union of Welfare on the grounds that several of its members took part in the meetings and banquets of that society.[36] Boris M. Tomashevsky mainly agrees with Shchegolev that the Green Lamp was an affiliate of the Union of Welfare but supplements his position as follows:

> All the rumors about the merry [*veselyi*] character of the meetings at Vsevolozhsky's house have as their source the fact that they mix up the meetings of the Green Lamp with Vsevolozhsky's merry evening parties, at which the host truly did not stint on champagne. It was these same parties, and not the Green Lamp at all, that Pushkin was reminiscing about in his 1824 letter to Vsevolozhsky, where he declared himself faithful to Vsevolozhsky's *Saturdays*. In fact it was the Saturdays at Vsevolozhsky's with which all the rumors about orgies were associated, rumors that are probably highly exaggerated. But we have already seen that not a single meeting of the Green Lamp took place on a Saturday. This is understandable: there were no plays on Saturdays.[37]

One can agree only partially with Tomashevsky's logic, taking into account the fact that the circle of persons who were present at the sedate meetings of the Green Lamp on weekdays coincided to a great extent with the circle of participants in the "orgiastic" Saturdays. Revealing the identities of both sets of individuals is not difficult, insofar as the archive of the Green Lamp has come down to us and contains the names of those who visited Vsevolozhsky's house on weekdays, whereas Pushkin's correspondence and his poetic epistles name those who made merry there on Saturdays.

On the basis of the archive of the Green Lamp, it is clear that the members of the society were Sergei P. Trubetskoi, Fedor N. Glinka,

Iakov N. Tolstoi, Alexander A. Tokarev, Pushkin, Anton A. Del'vig, Nikolai I. Gnedich, Alexander D. Ulybyshev, Dmitrii N. Barkov, Dmitrii I. Dolgorukov, Arkadii G. Rodzianko, Fedor F. Iur'ev, Ivan E. Zhadovsky, Pavel B. Mansurov, and Vsevolozhsky. Those who were present at Vsevolozhsky's house on Saturdays were Mansurov, Nikolai I. Krivtsov, Fedor Iur'ev, Vasilii V. Engel'gardt, the Vsevolozhsky brothers (Nikita himself and brother Alexander), and Rodzianko. Probably Del'vig and Tolstoi also came to the merry Saturdays. And we should remember that both these and "other" cultural events took place in one and the same house, that of Vsevolozhsky. Here on weekdays the members of the society gathered so as to discuss theatrical reviews and political news and to read their creative work to one another, and on Saturdays they came for the sake of other pursuits, which linked forms of traditional depravity with activities of a distinctly blasphemous character. Thus, for example, while acting out scenes titled "The Expulsion of Adam and Eve from Paradise," one of the members of the society called himself "a citizen of Sodom."[38]

Pushkin was an active participant in at least three official meetings of the Green Lamp and a significant number of the "orgiastic" ones. These orgiastic gatherings often took place in public places, which, naturally, made them particularly scandalous. On Easter in 1819, Pushkin and possibly also Nikita Vsevolozhsky headed into the church at the Theater School, as if to fast and pray before confession, in order to court the young female pupils.[39] This happened not long before the meeting of Pushkin and Pushchin at Nikolai Turgenev's house in May of that year, and it was apparently this event that angered Pushkin's father and explained why Ivan Pushchin changed his mind about letting his friend in on his plans regarding the secret society (although it is possible that this event happened instead on Easter in 1820, and that the poet's father was upset about a different event from his son's life). In any case, in May 1819 Pushkin already had a firm reputation as a libertine, upon which Alexander I. Turgenev passed judgment in a letter to Viazemsky. Reproaching Viazemsky for comparing himself with Christ, Turgenev finds that this comparison is "godless and worse [*i bezbozhno, i khuzhe etogo*], in the vein of young Pushkin."[40]

Pushkin's Libertinism

To Boris Tomashevsky belongs the point of view that has become widespread in Pushkin studies, namely that "it was not only biographical circumstances that incited Pushkin to protest: the merry blasphemy [*veseloe koshchunstvo*] to which Pushkin was given was not merely a reaction to the compulsory exercise of religious rituals. A mystical tone ruled at that time in high government circles."[41] Tomashevsky termed Pushkin's narrative poem *The Gabrieliad* (*Gavriiliada*) an instance of "merry blasphemy," and it was precisely this poem that he considered to be a reaction against the mysticism of Tsar Alexander's court. However, the poem was written during the Easter and pre-Easter weeks in 1821 in Kishinev, whereas the main location of governmental mysticism was St. Petersburg, and the time period of its most active propagation was Pushkin's Petersburg years of 1818–20. The blasphemous behavior of the poet during those years was indeed a reaction against the governmental policy of establishing in Russia an inflexible set of religious-moral norms in the form of an "evangelical government."[42] The center of this large-scale spiritual project was the Department of Spiritual Affairs of the Ministry of Education, headed by Alexander Turgenev. A similar task was simultaneously being undertaken by the Bible Society, where Turgenev also played one of the most important roles. Turgenev's reaction to Pushkin's blasphemous behavior was particularly acute precisely for this reason: at one and the same time, he was the person from the older generation who was closest to Pushkin and one of those most active in steering the government's course.

From Turgenev's letter to Viazemsky it is clear that he saw in Pushkin's behavior not just "merry blasphemy" but a form of libertine behavior, insofar as he reproached Pushkin not merely for "godless[ness]" but for something that was "worse." What is worse than atheism is libertinage, which not only disavows the existing system of religious values but also offers a particular alternative to it. The efforts of the government to uphold the moral and ethical norms of society were not the only such efforts. Another norm-enforcing hub with regard to civic behavior in 1818–20 was the Union of Welfare; in fact the general orientation of codifying efforts by the government and the Union of Welfare coincided in many respects, and the two could be distinguished from each other in only one area, although it was of course a very substantial one: the government upheld religious freedom in the country and supported a certain equality among the various Christian confessions, whereas the Decembrists attempted to assert the priority of the national principle in their civic ethics and in religious life and thus privileged Orthodoxy exclusively. Therefore, Pushkin's "merry blasphemy" was received as hostile not only by the government but also by the Decembrists, insofar as the poet's libertinage did not particularly distinguish the government's propagation of mysticism from the moralizing efforts undertaken by members of the Union of Welfare, and especially because this libertinage carried a certain anti-Masonic nuance (just as the Saturday gatherings, that is, the revelrous ones, of the Green Lamp had at their foundation an element of parodying Masonic meetings).

One can definitely assert that in the eyes of his contemporaries between 1818 and 1820, the eroticism of Pushkin's poetry and his blasphemous behavior outweighed his no less definitely demonstrated tendency toward political freethinking. Meanwhile, for the poet himself, all three component parts of his artistic worldview were important—namely, the aforesaid eroticism, religious freedom, and political liberalism. In just this combination Pushkin expressed his credo in a series of programmatic poems of 1819 and 1820: "To N. N." ("N. N.") ("N. N." is Vasilii Engel'gardt), "A Merry Feast" ("Veselyi pir"), "To Vsevolozhsky" ("Vsevolozhskomu"), "Epistle to Prince Gorchakov" ("Poslanie k kn. Gorchakovu"), all from 1819, and the 1820 "To Iur'ev" ("Iur'evu"). All of these works except the "Epistle to Prince Gorchakov" are addressed to members of the Green Lamp. The trinity of eroticism (the cult of pleasure), political liberalism, and religious freethinking is expressed in the poetic formulas by means of which the poet characterizes his friends. Hence he addresses Engel'gardt as "the true son of Freedom and Bacchus, / The devout worshiper of Venus / And the ruler of pleasures!" (svobody, Vakkha vernyi syn, / Venery nabozhnyi poklonnik / I naslazhdenii vlastelin!). Pushkin was prepared to chat with Engel'gardt "about the inveterate groveler, / About the tsar of heaven / And sometimes about the earthly one" (naschet kholopa zapisnogo, / Naschet nebesnogo tsaria, / A inogda naschet zemnogo).[43] Nikita Vsevolozhsky was called a "happy son of feasts, / Spoiled child of Freedom! (schastlivyi syn pirov, / Balovannyi ditia Svobody!).[44] The poetic formulas I have cited here are topoi of Pushkin's poetry of this period; they are not very individualized and could be applied to any of the poet's merry, freedom-loving friends from the Green Lamp.

Pushkin's self-descriptions, by contrast, are significantly more individualized, particularly in the poem "To Iur'ev":

А я, повеса вечно-праздный,
Потомок негров безобразный,
Взрощенный в дикой простоте,

Любви не ведая страданий,
Я нравлюсь юной красоте
Бесстыдным бешенством желаний.[45]

[But I, a scapegrace always idle, / Descendent of ugly Negroes, / Brought up in wild simplicity, / Not knowing love's suffering, / I am pleasing to young beauty / In the shameless madness of my desires.]

Here the "shameless madness of desires," which can be explained by the author's African heritage, should have reminded the reader of another poet of African heritage, one whose erotic poetry determined the major features of the Russian love lyric of the Pushkin period. This poet was Evariste Désiré de Forges, vicomte de Parny (1753–1814).[46] The importance of Parny's poetry for Pushkin in the period we are examining and, in particular, in the year when he composed the epistle "To Iur'ev" has been noted by previous scholars.[47] However, Pushkin's accentuation of his African heritage has never been examined in connection with the name of Parny.

The African heritage of the French poet was important for his contemporaries. Thus, René Chateaubriand recalled about Parny: "I never knew a writer who so resembled his works: a poet and a Creole, he required very little—the sky of India, a freshwater spring, a palm tree, and a woman."[48] Russian writers knew Parny as the author of *Chansons Madécasses* (*Songs of Madagascar* [1787]), in which the "Negro" theme is central. The "Eighth Song" in a translation by Konstantin Batiushkov (1811) was especially popular in Russia. However, the erotic character of the original was weakened in Batiushkov's translation. And this was typical for Parny's poetry in Russian translation. As Vatsuro has shown, the Russian translators of Parny omitted from their translations everything that would offend decency.[49] The concept of "sensuality," which was key to Parny's poetry, was subjected to especially strong transformation on Russian soil. Thus, in Batiushkov's versions, according to Vatsuro, "sensuality [*sladostrastie*] appears as a synonym of 'spiritual pleasure' [*dukhovnoe naslazhdenie*]."[50] Pushkin's "shameless madness of desires" together with the accentuation of his own African heritage should have restored the image of Parny that was lost in Russian translations, that of "a Creole . . . [who] possessed from birth a receptivity to music and the sensitivity of a southerner"—thus was Parny described by one of the most perceptive literary critics of his time, Charles Augustin Sainte-Beuve.[51]

Parny was interesting to Pushkin not only as the author of love lyrics but also as a poet who was open to political themes. It was not by accident that Petr O. Morozov saw the influence of Parny in Pushkin's most pointed political poem of 1819, "The Countryside" ("Derevnia").[52] And finally, Parny's anticlerical works were extremely important for Pushkin, most of all the 1799 *La guerre des dieux anciens et modernes* (*The War of the Ancient and Modern Gods*). True, this aspect of Parny's work was not reflected in Pushkin's poetry until somewhat later, in *The Gabrieliad* and in the epistle "To V. L. Davydov" in 1821. Taking into account Pushkin's strong interest in Parny, one may boldly suppose that he knew well the biography of the French poet and thus knew of his participation in the French Revolution and his opposition to Napoleon's despotism in the years of the empire.

Pushkin's self-identification with Parny should have given his readers the key to a synthetic perception of Pushkin himself in the role of the "Russian Parny" and should have rendered the eroticism, libertinage, and liberalism that were characteristic of his poetry into a unified creative image, perhaps as a counterweight to Batiushkov's version of Parny. As we know, this did not happen. Pushkin's contemporaries failed to spot the links with Parny in his works of the Green Lamp period. Yet Batiushkov's reaction to Pushkin's verse epistle "To Iur'ev" is telling: as Annenkov notes, Batiushkov "feverishly squeezed in his hands a piece of paper and uttered: 'Oh! how that villain has begun to write!'"[53] It is possible that Batiushkov was the only one to perceive in the epistle "To Iur'ev" Pushkin's aspiration to the role of the "Russian Parny" and feared the rivalry.

"To Iur'ev" was printed by Iur'ev himself not later than 1821 in a limited number of copies without any indication of the place and year of publication, but the poem was not disseminated among the future Decembrists.[54] One can explain this by reference to the fact that the circle of people among whom the poem made its rounds did not intersect with that of the Decembrists. Pushkin's poetic epistles to other members of the Green Lamp also were not widely disseminated in Decembrist circles. The only poems of the poet that became popular in the Decembrist milieu were ones in which political radicalism was intermixed with strict morality, primarily "To Chaadaev" ("K Chedaevu"), "The Dagger" ("Kinzhal"), and "Liberty" ("Vol'nost'"). For the Decembrists a mixture of libertine and liberal discourses was not permitted, either in life or in poetry.[55] Pushkin personified the opposite principle, according to which political freedom not only could but was simply *required* to combine with a wide spectrum of other of life's pleasures.

This distinction marks a significant division not only between Pushkin and the Decembrists but also between the Decembrists and the friendly literary society the Green Lamp. It now appears that it is at last possible to bring a long-standing polemic to conclusion and answer the question as to whether or not the Green Lamp was a Decembrist organization in the negative. This is the explanation for why Pushkin himself, despite his friendships with many members of the secret society and his sympathy for their important goals, should not be considered a Decembrist. His combination of erotic, libertine, and liberal discourses was irritating and unacceptable to both the government and the Decembrists. Therefore, at approximately the same time, the government sent the poet into exile under spiritual surveillance and the Supreme Duma of the Southern Society placed a ban on acquaintanceship with him.[56]

Thus, although in its manner of expression, Gorbachevsky's appraisal of Pushkin sounds more scathing than the judgments of his other contemporaries, in essence it coincides with several of them and reflects what Vatsuro terms Pushkin's "social reputation." By way of comparison with Gorbachevsky's opinion, consider the way the Decembrist Dmitrii I. Zavalishin expresses his opinion of Pushkin: "With all his might he attempted to gain membership in the Secret Society, but it was ordered that he not be accepted, given his extreme changeability—and the better we knew him, the more certain we were of this extreme shortcoming of his, having witnessed many instances of his swift transitions from one extreme to another, and thus having a good reason not to trust him not to penetrate into high society and court circles in order to ingratiate himself there, a tendency that we always noticed in him."[57] Gorbachevsky, however, expresses his opinion with democratic directness, thereby breaking the taboos to which the Decembrists adhered in their public evaluations of Pushkin. In this frankness lies the main reason why Gorbachevsky's opinion, in its turn, became tabooed in Pushkin studies.

NOTES

Translated by Katya Hokanson. Translator's note: I would like to thank Alyssa Gillespie for her careful revision and improvement of this translation and my other for the present volume, Oleg Proskurin's "Pushkin and Metropolitan Philaret: Rethinking the Problem." She went over each translation in great detail, correcting mistakes and suggesting many more felicitous turns of phrase that enhanced their readability in English, and in general she could not have been a more attentive editor both in terms of the translations and the volume as a whole. I would also like to thank Igor Nemirovsky and Oleg Proskurin for the opportunity to translate their fascinating and thought-provoking articles.

1. Mikhail I. Semevskii, "Aleksandr Sergeevich Pushkin: 1799–1837," *Russkaia starina* 1 (1880): 130.

2. *Den'* 6–10 (1913); Ivan I. Gorbachevskii, *Zapiski i pis'ma*, 2nd ed., ed. Boris E. Syroechkovskii (Moscow: Sovremennye problemy N. A. Stolliar, 1925), 359–60.

3. Cited in Natan Ia. Eidel'man, *Pushkin i dekabristy* (Moscow: Khudozhestvennaia literatura, 1979), 147–48. The manuscript of Gorbachevsky's opinion is archived in the Manuscripts Department of the Russian National Library, St. Petersburg.

4. Pavel E. Shchegolev, *Iz zhizni i tvorchestva Pushkina* (Moscow: Gosudarstvennoe Izdatel'stvo, 1931), 293–96; Ivan I. Gorbachevskii, *Zapiski, pis'ma*, ed. Boris E. Syroechkovskii et al. (Moscow: AN SSSR, 1963), 337.

5. Vadim S. Parsamov, "A. S. Pushkin v otsenke dekabrista I. I. Gorbachevskogo (Iz kommentariev k pis'mu I. I. Gorbachevskogo M.A. Bestuzhevu ot 12 iunia 1861 goda)," *Istoriograficheskii sbornik Saratovskogo gosudarstvennogo universiteta* 17 (1998): 108–14.

6. Parsamov, "A. S. Pushkin v otsenke dekabrista I. I. Gorbachevskogo," 112, 114.

7. Vladimir A. Obruchev, "Iz perezhitogo," quoted in Gorbachevskii, *Zapiski, pis'ma*, 245.

8. Natan Ia. Eidel'man, "'Ia ne mogu zabyt' . . . ' (Dekabrist Gorbachevskii o Pushkine)," in his *Pushkin i dekabristy*, 143–68.

9. Ibid., 158.

10. See Tat'iana G. Tsiavlovskaia, "Khrani menia moi talisman," *Prometei (Almanakh)* 10 (1974): 46.

11. Mikhail D. Buturlin, "Zapiski," *Russkii arkhiv* 5 (1897): 15.

12. See in this regard Mikhail I. Semevskii, "K biografii Pushkina," *Russkii vestnik* 11(1869): 77–78. About the fact that Pushkin may have been subjected to an *epitimia* (special penance imposed by a priest in the Orthodox Church), see Petr I. Bartenev, *O Pushkine: Stranitsy zhizni poeta. Vospominaniia sovremennikov* (Moscow: Sovetskaia Rossia, 1992), 298; and Svetlana V. Berezkina, "Pushkin v Mikhailovskom: O dukhovnom nadzore nad poetom (1824–1826)," *Russkaia starina* 1 (2000): 3–20.

13. Vadim E. Vatsuro, "Pushkin v soznanii sovremennikov," in *Pushkin v vospominaniiakh sovremennikov*, 2 vols., ed. Vadim E. Vatsuro and Elena O. Larionova (St. Petersburg: Akademicheskii proekt, 1998), 1:13.

14. Quoted in Militsa V. Nechkina, "Novoe o Pushkine i dekabristakh," *Literaturnoe nasledstvo* 58 (1952): 163.

15. Sergei G. Volkonskii to Aleksandr S. Pushkin, 18 October 1824, in Pushkin, *Polnoe sobranie sochinenii*, 17 vols., ed. Vladimir D. Bonch-Bruevich et al. (Moscow: AN SSSR, 1937–59), 13:112.

16. See Iurii Lotman, *Aleksandr Sergeevich Pushkin: Biografiia pisatelia* (St. Petersburg: Iskusstvo, 1995), 90–91.

17. *Dekabristy: Biograficheskii spravochnik*, ed. Sergei V. Mironenko (Moscow: Nauka, 1988), 252.

18. Ibid., 240.

19. Aleksandr Raevskii to Aleksandr S. Pushkin, 18 October 1824, in Pushkin, *Polnoe sobranie sochinenii*, 17 vols., 13:529, original in French.

20. Volkonskii to Pushkin, 18 October 1824, in Pushkin, *Polnoe sobranie sochinenii*, 17 vols., 13:112.

21. *Dekabristy: Biograficheskii spravochnik*, 240.

22. Petr A. Viazemskii, postscript to the article "Tsygany: Poema Pushkina," in *Pushkin v vospominaniiakh sovremennikov*, 1:119.

23. Ivan D. Iakushkin, "Iz 'Zapisok,'" in *Pushkin v vospominaniiakh sovremennikov*, 1:356.

24. Ibid., 1:358.

25. Ibid., 1:357.

26. Quoted in Eidel'man, *Pushkin i dekabristy*, 148.

27. See Igor' V. Nemirovskii, *Tvorchestvo Pushkina i problema publichnogo povedeniia poeta* (St. Petersburg: Giperion, 2003), 45–73.

28. See Vladimir P. Gorchakov, "Vyderzhki iz dnevnika ob A. S. Pushkine," in *Pushkin v vospominaniiakh sovremennikov*, 1:231.

29. Nikolai V. Basargin, *Zapiski* (Petrograd: Ogni, 1917), 24.

30. Ivan I. Pushchin, "Zapiski o Pushkine," in *Pushkin v vospominaniiakh sovremennikov*, 1:86.

31. Ibid., 88.

32. Ibid., 86. The final line is a quotation from Pushkin's 1814 poem "Carousing Students" ("Piruiushchie studenty").

33. Ibid., 88.

34. Ibid.

35. Pavel V. Annenkov, *A. S. Pushkin v Aleksandrovskuiu epokhu* (St. Petersburg: Izdatel'stvo Stas'iulevicha, 1874), 63.

36. Pavel E. Shchegolev, *Iz zhizni i tvorchestva Pushkina* (Moscow: Gosudarstvennoe Izdatel'stvo, 1931).

37. Boris V. Tomashevskii, *Pushkin*, 2 vols. (Leningrad: AN SSSR, 1956–61), 1:205, emphasis in the original.

38. Pavel V. Annenkov, *A. S. Pushkin v Aleksandrovskuiu epokhu*, 63.

39. Aleksandr S. Pushkin to Nikita V. Vsevolozhskii, October 1824, in Pushkin, *Polnoe sobranie sochinenii*, 17 vols., 13:115.

40. Aleksandr I. Turgenev to Petr A. Viazemskii, in *Ostaf'evskii arkhiv kniazei Viazemskikh*, vol. 1 of *Perepiska kniazia P. A. Viazemskogo s A. I. Turgenevym, 1812–1819* (St. Petersburg: Izdanie grafa S. D. Sheremeteva, 1899), 228.

41. Boris V. Tomashevskii, *Pushkin*, 1:427–28.

42. See Elena A. Vishlenkova, *Religioznaia politika: Ofitsial'nyi kurs i "obshchee mnenie" Rossii Aleksandrovskoi epokhi* (Kazan: Izdatel'stvo Kazanskogo universiteta, 1997), 108–9.

43. Aleksandr S. Pushkin, "N. N.," in his *Polnoe sobranie sochinenii*, 17 vols., 2:83.

44. Aleksandr S. Pushkin, "Vsevolozhskomu," in his *Polnoe sobranie sochinenii*, 17 vols., 2:101.

45. Aleksandr S. Pushkin, "Iur'evu," in his *Polnoe sobranie sochinenii*, 17 vols., 2:139–40.

46. On Pushkin and Parny see Vadim E. Vatsuro, *Lirika pushkinskoi pory* (St. Petersburg: Nauka, 1994), and Boris V. Tomashevskii and Larisa I. Vol'pert, "Parni," in *Pushkin: Issledovaniia i materialy*, vol. 18 (St. Petersburg: Nauka, 2004), 233–35.

47. Efim G. Etkind writes that "Parny was Pushkin's favorite foreign poet in 1819" (*Poeziia Evarista Parni* [Leningrad: Nauka, 1970], 190); see also Petr O. Morozov, "Pushkin i Parni," in *A. S. Pushkin* (St. Petersburg: Izdatel'stvo RAN, 1907), 2:390.

48. Quoted in Etkind, *Poeziia Evarista Parni*, 199.

49. Vatsuro, *Lirika pushkinskoi pory*, 104.

50. Ibid., 97.

51. Ibid., 87.

52. Morozov, "Pushkin i Parni," 2:390.

53. See Pavel V. Annenkov, *Materialy k biografii Pushkina* (St. Petersburg: Izdanie Imperatorskoi Akademii nauk, 1855), 55.

54. Pushkin, "Iur'evu," 2:1077.

55. See Iurii M. Lotman, "Dekabrist v povsednevnoi zhizni," in *Literaturnoe nasledie dekabristov* (Leningrad: Nauka, 1975), 60–61.

56. See the letter from Mikhail S. Vorontsov to Dmitrii Gur'ev of 24 July 1824: "The sovereign emperor has deigned to discern from the many pieces of intelligence His Majesty has received, that not only has the collegiate secretary Pushkin unfortunately not changed the behaviors and bad principles that have marked the first steps of his life in society, but that he even spreads in his letters reprehensible and harmful opinions" (*Aleksandr Sergeevich Pushkin: Dokumenty k biografii: 1799–1829*, ed. Vadim P. Stark [St. Petersburg: Iskusstvo, 2007], 446).

57. *Pisateli-dekabristy v vospominaniiakh sovremennikov*, 2 vols., ed. Vadim E. Vatsuro (Moscow: Khudozhestvennaia literatura, 1980), 2:247–48.

Lighting the Green Lamp

Unpublished and Unknown Poems

Joe Peschio

Pushkin's Petersburg period (1817–20) is one of the most problematic periods of his literary biography. The Soviet Pushkin industry and, before it, prerevolutionary progressive Pushkinists, were exceedingly anxious to paint this juncture in the national poet's biography as its defining political moment, one linking him to the revolutionary movements of his day. As a result, our literary-historical picture of the Petersburg period is somewhat skewed. Pushkin did of course have close ties to many prominent figures of the secret societies during this period, and that fact is of no small importance. However, the single-minded pursuit of that one simple, golden piece of evidence that would overtly and incontrovertibly tie Pushkin to the revolutionary secret society the Union of Welfare (Soiuz blagodenstviia) has all too often blinded scholars to details that might enrich our picture of the Petersburg period. Worse yet, this ideologizing imperative has on occasion even led scholars to conceal primary materials such as the obscene ballad *The Shade of Barkov* (*Ten' Barkova*) from colleagues and the public.[1]

Pushkin's involvement in the Green Lamp (Zelenaia lampa), a secret literary society active in 1819–20, is a case in point. There seems to be general agreement among the generations of Pushkinists who have studied the group that the Green Lamp is key to understanding Pushkin's Petersburg period. The progressive Pushkinist Pavel Shchegolev, for example, wrote in 1908 that "it has even a cardinal significance. Any resolution of the question [of the Green Lamp] is the angle from which one must view Pushkin's works of 1818–20, the development of his worldview."[2] The "question" Shchegolev refers to is the question of what, exactly, the Green Lamp was. There have been various answers, and they trace the kind of arc that would bring a smile to the face of any postprocessualist archaeologist.

Nineteenth-century Pushkinists, particularly Pavel Annenkov, concluded on the basis of interviews and some very limited documentary evidence that the Green Lamp was an "orgiastic" circle that, as Boris Modzalevsky put it in 1899, "gathered primarily for merrymaking but also had a literary bent."[3] They, like the gendarmes who investigated the Green Lamp in 1821 and 1826, found no reason to characterize it as a political formation. As more documents came available, first from the Third Section (secret police) and later from the archive of the Green Lamp itself, another thesis emerged, according to which the Green Lamp was a branch charter of the Union of Welfare and little more than a propaganda arm of the early Decembrist movement. For a variety of reasons, many of which remain unclear, this "anti-orgiastic" thesis gained currency over the course of the twentieth century and remains firmly entrenched to this day in both scholarly literature and the popular imagination.[4] It is repeated in popular biographies of Pushkin, taught in schools and universities, reiterated at museums, and proliferated in print and online reference works.[5] Yet this case is exceedingly difficult to make without acknowledging that the imperial Pushkinists were at least partly right: the direct evidence (a single report from one police informant) that the Green Lamp was part of the Union of Welfare is scant and unreliable, but there is ample evidence that libertinage and a "light"—that is, non-Decembrist—literary aesthetic reigned in the Green Lamp. Perhaps for this reason, the Pushkinists making the "anti-orgiastic" case are extremely categorical in rejecting the "orgiastic" thesis and often engage in sharp, personal attacks on their predecessors.[6]

Scholarly interest in the Green Lamp gained momentum in the 1860s, and there was a flurry of publications around the turn of the twentieth century, but little has been written on the Green Lamp for the last hundred years. Since 1908, only three works of original, fundamental research have been published—by Shchegolev, Modzalevsky, and Boris Tomashevsky—and none since 1956. All three works are concerned to a degree (Modzalevsky much less so than the others) with the possible links between the Green Lamp and the Union of Welfare. In their effort to "legitimize" the Green Lamp and Pushkin's involvement in it by painting the group in the somber tones of early Decembrism (as it was understood in Soviet literary history), these venerable Pushkinists neglect many texts and much evidence: almost everything that does not embody the aesthetic program outlined in the Union of Welfare's charter, the famous "Green Book," is excluded from consideration.[7] In this, the Pushkinists fall prey to the false premise that liberalism and libertinism in their many forms were mutually exclusive in this period, when they were in fact often connected.[8] Libertinism in Russia, as elsewhere, was a combination of freethinking with a disregard for behavioral and moral convention.[9] Even more often, these two modes of deviant behavior were concomitant and conflated, as in the Green Lamp. That is to say, demonstrative violations of propriety and libertine bravado were often an expression of political dissent and vice versa. Iurii Lotman notes that "in the scholarly literature, the notion of the Green Lamp as simply a legal branch of the Union of Welfare has gained currency. . . . But this notion oversimplifies things. . . . The Green Lamp combined freethinking and serious interests with a playful atmosphere, wild merriment, and a demonstrative challenge to the 'serious' world."[10] This correction, suggested by Lotman (in 1981) and even by Viktor Zhirmunsky (in 1937), has yet to be fully made.[11]

This chapter is devoted to explicating some of the neglected primary materials that point to the more complex behavioral picture of the Green Lamp suggested by Lotman. In particular, I focus on poems from the Green Lamp archive that remain unpublished, little studied, or both. In the textology of these poems, in the literary tastes and affinities announced by their reminiscences and allusions, in the range of referents, and in their publication histories, we can uncover a more complete picture of the Green Lamp. The Green Lamp is the first and only literary society of which Pushkin was a founding member and an active participant. It was his post-lyceum training ground, and he continued his education here not only in the mechanics and methods of versification but also in editing and critique, literary collaboration, and the construction of literary institutions. All his subsequent literary collaborations and literary-institutional activities, up to and including the creation of

Sovremennik (*The Contemporary*) in 1836, bear the mark of his experience in the Green Lamp.

Taking a positivistic approach to the Green Lamp is a uniquely difficult task for one simple reason: the Green Lamp was a secret society. The conspiratorial imperative does not brook any proliferation of reliable evidence and often leads to the creation of code languages.[12] And, at nearly two hundred years' distance, literary historians are miserably ill-equipped gendarmes. As a result, scholars are faced with an extreme paucity of primary materials. The Green Lamp archive consists of a grand total of forty-four original works—poems, historical essays and anecdotes, theater criticism—authored by various members and presented at Green Lamp meetings. Only twenty-three of them have ever been published, and only sixteen of them in the last hundred years. Twenty-one remain unpublished. This meager collection is complemented by the most problematic sorts of secondary materials. There are only three eyewitness accounts, and two of these were extracted from Lampists with Decembrist ties during the 1826 investigation of the Decembrist uprising. The Commission of Inquiry collected further testimony and information on the Green Lamp, but only two brief summaries of its findings have been preserved. The Green Lamp is also described in three Pushkin poems and in his famous letter to fellow Lampist Boris Mansurov.[13] Beyond that, we have a smattering of second- and third-hand accounts, including one official denunciation, and the findings of the first Pushkinists Petr Bartenev, Pavel Annenkov, and Mikhail Longinov, who interviewed surviving contemporaries of the Lampists.

Certainly, the materials are scant and problematic, but some basic facts about the Green Lamp have been established. Before proceeding, I should provide a review of the few undisputed details. There were at least sixteen members of the Green Lamp. These included well-known writers like Pushkin, Anton Del'vig, Iakov Tolstoi, Fedor Glinka, Nikolai Gnedich, and Arkadii Rodzianko. Most meetings were held at the home of the brothers Nikita and Alexander Vsevolozhsky, ostentatiously wealthy young bon vivants. Other members included the prominent Decembrists Sergei Trubetskoi and Alexander Tokarev. Most Lampists were military men; almost half were veterans of 1812 like the guardsmen Fedor Iur'ev, Dmitrii Barkov, Pavel Mansurov, and Ivan Zhadovsky, a retired colonel. Many Lampists later had distinguished careers like Dmitrii Dolgorukov, who became a senator, and Alexander Ulybyshev, who was the editor-in-chief of the French-language *Journal of St. Petersburg* (*Journal de St.-Pétersbourg*) for eighteen years. Besides these sixteen, there likely were more members (Tolstoi says "upward of twenty" in his 1826 letter to the tsar), but they left no trace in the Green Lamp archive, and their membership is not attested in any other documents.[14] The Green Lamp held at least twenty-two meetings between March 1819 and late fall of 1820, most of them at the home of Nikita Vsevolozhsky, where Children's Clinic no. 27 at 35 Prospekt Rimskogo-Korsakova now stands, across the street from the Nikola Church Square.

The Green Lamp had formal rules, but we know very little about them. We do not even know, for example, whether the group had a written charter or not. None such has been preserved. Petr Efremov examined the Green Lamp archive in the 1890s, when it was in the possession of the historian Mikhail Semevsky, and reported on various occasions that the archive included protocols (minutes) and other organizational documents.[15] Semevsky, for his part, makes no mention of a charter or protocols in his writing on the Green Lamp.[16] Unfortunately, these documents, whatever they were, assuming they even ever existed, were lost: when the archive resurfaced in the 1920s, there were no protocols—only a few bits of marginalia survived.[17] Other sources provide some information on the rules of the Green Lamp but not very much. Two Lampists, Tolstoi and Trubetskoi, submitted descriptions of the Green Lamp to the authorities in 1826.[18] Drawing from these documents (if we are to believe them), we can reconstruct some of the rules: members were admitted to the society only on the basis of a unanimous vote. They were sworn to secrecy. They were required to present any new works to the Green Lamp before publishing them. The presidency of the society was an elected and rotating office. Members were required to have a ring with the Green Lamp insignia. There was also a "statute" that called on the members to write and speak freely. Finally, there was a rule according to which Vsevolozhsky's Kalmyk servant boy was to salute any member who let fall an indecent expression (poshloe slovtso) at table. Beyond these few and disparate points, there is no evidence to suggest whether a charter existed or if it did, what it prescribed and prohibited.

The Green Lamp archive documents some of the society's activities. We can say for certain that members presented works of four types at Green Lamp meetings: poems, historical works (essays and anecdotes, historical-educational projects and outlines), journalism, and theater criticism. Reading and discussing poetry was, according to almost all reports, the Green Lamp's main raison d'être. The archive bears this out. Of the forty-four works preserved in the Green Lamp archive, the bulk—twenty-five—are poems. Twelve of the sixteen known members are represented in the archive. Of these, ten contributed poems. Thus, poetry was the primary form of contribution. With one exception, the distribution of the poems' authorship is fairly even among contributors. Of the twenty-five poems, two are as yet unattributed, and the remainder are by Pushkin (two poems), Iakov Tolstoi (nine poems), Arkadii Rodzianko (one poem), Fedor Glinka (two poems), Anton Del'vig (three poems), Alexander Tokarev (two poems), Dmitrii Barkov (two poems), Dmitrii Dolgorukov (two poems). In all likelihood, a lot more poems were read, recited, and discussed at Green Lamp meetings, especially if members obeyed the rules, which required them to present all work to the society before publishing. Pushkin, Rodzianko, Glinka, and Del'vig published quite a bit in 1819–20, and if they adhered to the rules, then at least twenty more poems can be added to this list, including Pushkin's commercial and critical coming-out, *Ruslan and Liudmila* (*Ruslan i Liudmila* [1820]).

Only eleven of the twenty-five poems in the archive were deemed publishable in the 1820s. Seven were included in Tolstoi's 1821 poetry collection, *My Idle Time; or, A Collection of Some of Ia. N. Tolstoi's Works* (*Moe prazdnoe vremia, ili sobranie nekotorykh sochinenii Ia. N. Tolstogo*); Pushkin included one Lampist poem, "To Vsevolozhsky" ("Vsevolozhskomu"), in his 1826 collection; Glinka published one poem, "A Charade" ("Sharrada" [1820]); and Del'vig published two of his three poems in the archive. It appears that none of the other Lampists ever planned to publish the works they brought to meetings—or at least not those works that have been preserved in the archive. As such, the Green Lamp was an authentic embodiment of, to borrow Boris Eikhenbaum's term, "literary domesticity" and not a constructed one.[19] The intimacy of this cloistered readership that the Lampists extol in their poems is not just a trope but also reflects a social reality that did indeed exist.

According to Pushkin House records, only four scholars, myself included, have requested materials from the Green Lamp *opis'* since 1972, and the other three (Vadim Vatsuro, Sergei Fomichev, and one other scholar whose identity is uncertain) requested only two poems, both of which had already been published. Despite the lack of recent fundamental research on the subject and all the uncertainties that remain, references to the Green Lamp abound in both scholarly and popular literature of the last forty years, and it remains a topic of great interest. With all the interest in the Green Lamp and its apparent relevance to Russian culture and society, why, then, has there been no serious research on the group in over fifty years? This is partly a matter of scholarly squeamishness. Since the nineteenth century, when the project of constructing a national canon commenced, Russian literary history has always been loath to reveal anything "unseemly" that might compromise the integrity of that canon. As in the case of Pushkin's *The Shade of Barkov*, it is also a matter of cultural politics and institutional inertia. To this day, getting the institutions entrusted with guarding Pushkin's legacy to admit that he had a libertine streak is an iffy proposition. The assertion that, at the age of twenty, Pushkin was probably just as interested in champagne, actresses, and Piron as he was in radical politics meets with resistance in these quarters, where it is perceived as a challenge to his worthiness as an object of national veneration.

Though it is clear that poetry was the main focus of the Green Lamp, we still lack a description of the shared aesthetic values that make the Lampist poetry a distinct and cohesive corpus. This lack is, in large part, due to the fact that Tomashevsky and other Soviet Pushkinists made only selective use of the archive. And their selectiveness was motivated primarily by ideology and practical exigency, not philology. We have no direct proof of any official prohibition on the discussion of themes, texts, and topics that were "frivolous" from the point of view of Soviet morality: such proof cannot exist in a society in which anything not explicitly permitted is forbidden. Nonetheless, the consistent pattern of ignoring and concealing the frivolous in Soviet literary history provides ample circumstantial evidence that there was a taboo on literary libertinism of any kind except anticlericalism.

It is possible to develop some notion of the collective aesthetic of Green Lamp poetry even by looking only at what has already been published. Indeed, Lotman writes that, in examining these materials, "we immediately see in them a certain unity," the "combination of manifest and unequivocal political liberalism with a cult of joy, sensual love, blasphemy, and a certain Libertine bravado."[20] But to complete this picture, we must look at all the Green Lamp poetry in the archive. Toward this end, I offer the following survey, organized by author, of the Green Lamp poems that are unknown, unpublished, and/or little understood. This survey reveals that the society was a poets' workshop, one where Pushkin learned how to be part of a literary collective.

Pushkin's "I know battle" and "To Vsevolozhsky"

Though he produced a whole cycle of verse epistles addressed to his fellow Lampists, only two poems that Pushkin presented at meetings of the Green Lamp were preserved in its archive: "To Vsevolozhsky" ("Vsevolozhskomu"), composed in 1819 and published in 1826, and "I know battle" ("Mne boi znakom"), composed around 1820.[21] Pushkin published only "To Vsevolozhsky." "I know battle" was not suitable for publication, presumably because it focuses on the "warrior for freedom"—a collocation most likely not looked on kindly by the St. Petersburg Censorship Committee in 1819–20. The poem remained practically unknown until its first publication forty years later, but it gained a place in the Pushkin canon and was even put to music by the composer Boris Liatoshinsky for the 1937 jubilee.[22] Later, it was taken up as an example of Pushkin's supposed Petersburg-period radicalism and was linked to the Spanish Revolution of 1819.[23] "I know battle" is of a piece with another martial poem in the Green Lamp archive, Iakov Tolstoi's "To Veteran X" ("K veteranu ***"), composed in 1819, which remains unpublished. It is also closely connected to *Ruslan and Liudmila*, in which the same idea of martial prowess as a prerequisite for sexual access provides the central structural conceit.

The second Pushkin poem in the Green Lamp archive, "To Vsevolozhsky," is of particular interest because Pushkin altered it significantly before publishing it in his 1826 collection. Here we can see the difference between the insular world of the Green Lamp and the broad, public stage of published literature with particular clarity. Pushkin changed the opening lines of the poem before publishing it. Whether he was instructed to do so by the censor, we do not know. It may well have been self-censorship. Whatever its motivation, this change fundamentally altered the poem. The Green Lamp version of the poem opens:

Прости, счастливый сын пиров,
Балованный дитя свободы!
Итак, от наших берегов,
От мертвой области рабов,
Капральства, прихотей и моды
Ты скачешь в мирную Москву.[24]

[Farewell, fortunate son of feasts, / The pampered child of freedom! / And so, from our shores, / From our dead region of slaves, / Military brutishness, caprice, and fashion / You are galloping to peaceful Moscow.]

In the published version of the poem, these lines are cut and replaced with lines of a more measured tone and lexicon:

Любимец муз, поклонник моды
И Терпсихоры и стихов!
Ты в жизни любишь перемену:
Ты скачешь в мирную Москву.[25]

[The muses' favorite, a worshipper of fashion / And Terpsichore and verse! / In your life you love change: / You are galloping to peaceful Moscow.]

There are at least two constraints in play here. First, the lexicon of free-thinking (freedom, slaves, the brutality of military life, the vague but charged idea of "change") is not suitable for publication. Second, the portrayal of the profligate Vsevolozhsky, that "son of feasts," is not suitable for public consumption and is replaced with an emphasis on Vsevolozhsky's dedication to fashion, the theater, and poetry. In the Green Lamp redaction of the poem, the collocation of libertinage and what might be called "fashionable liberalism" ("The pampered child of freedom") is set up in the very first line. Most importantly, while this collocation of freethinking and "feasts" was not publishable, it was not only permissible but encouraged in the context of the Green Lamp. Furthermore, by dissociating Vsevolozhsky from the excesses of the Moscow feasts described later in the poem, Pushkin makes it possible to read the rest of it as a condemnation of such profligacy—which many Soviet scholars did—and that, presumably, would have made it more palatable to the censors.

Iakov Tostoi's "To Veteran X" and "The Cockroach Rhetorician"

Iakov Tolstoi was already an established poet and playwright when the Green Lamp formed and became, as Tomashevky puts it, the society's "poet in residence" (prisiazhnyi poet).[26] Along with Sergei Trubetskoi and Fedor Glinka, he was also a highly placed member of the Union of Welfare. More than any other Lampist, Tolstoi put the Green Lamp at the very center of his public poetic biography (so much so that it almost seems a breach of the Lampists' vow of secrecy). His 1821 poetry collection, *My Idle Time*, includes seven of the nine poems he is known to have presented at the Green Lamp, nearly a third of the book's twenty-three poems. Its title page even features the symbols of the Green Lamp—the lamp, the lyre, the anchor (a symbol of hope, like the color green)—which, though known to few, immediately announce the volume's affinities.[27] Tolstoi had close ties to Pushkin, both of a personal and business nature, and Tolstoi's early verse and literary-political biography have thus been amply described.[28] Over the course of 1819–22, the two exchanged epistles, and it was in reply to Tolstoi's epistle "To A. S. Pushkin" ("K A. S. Pushkinu"), composed in 1819 and revised and published in 1821, that Pushkin penned his most well-known poem about the Green Lamp, "Are you burning, our icon lamp" ("Gorish' li ty, lampada nasha"), composed in 1822, an epistle he included in a business letter to Tolstoi.[29] In this reply, Pushkin, still unaware that the society had disbanded the previous year, casts the shadow of exile and nostalgia on the exchange, deflating the joyful-hedonistic tone of Tolstoi's epistle. Tolstoi's epistle, in turn, was an obliging reply to Pushkin's "Stanzas for Tolstoi" ("Stansy Tolstomu"), composed in 1819 and published in 1826, in which Pushkin chastises him for abandoning the goblet of Horace for the lamp of Epictetus.

Of Tolstoi's nine poems preserved in the archive, he decided not to publish only two, "To Veteran X" and "The Cockroach Rhetorician" ("Tarakan-ritor"), composed in 1819. Both remain unpublished and therefore require some description.[30] The epistle "To Veteran X" sings the praises of its addressee in martial terms, describing his (and Tolstoi's own) exploits between 1812 and 1814. The addressee is a great man worthy of admiration purely owing to his prowess and experience on the battlefield: "O you! whose head grayed in battle, / Hero covered with wounds! / In the war, my brave teacher!" (O ty! vo brani posedelyi, / Pokrytyi ranami Geroi! / Moi, na voine, uchitel' smelyi!).[31] This celebration of battlefield experience, which "To Veteran X" of course has in common with Pushkin's "I know battle," likely found a receptive audience at the Green Lamp, which consisted mostly of military men, including a few celebrated veterans (a fact not taken into consideration by Gukovsky and Tomashevsky, who stress the revolutionary tones of "I know battle"). Tolstoi's addressee has now retired to "the fields," a choice for which his lyric subject professes admiration. But the subject himself cannot do the same and turns to his addressee as someone who understands "How difficult it is to abandon the craft, / In which I grew up and was raised" (Skol' trudno kinut' remeslo, / V kotorom vzros i vospitalsia). He offers an apologia for his inability to do so, stressing notions of glory, honor, the splendor of battle, and so forth. The addressee, however, has soured on all this and is having none of it. In a long soliloquy, he recounts the more gruesome sights of war, questioning whether glory is worth the rivers of blood spilled for it. He discounts laurels and medals: "For what purpose are both Glory and Ranks? . . . The path to the grave is the same for everyone!" (K chemu i Slava, i Chiny? . . . Ko grobu vsem edinyi put'!). It follows that military service in peacetime is foolhardy and even dishonorable. Yet he is no happier in his new civilian life. He bares his chest to show his scars and cries "Ah! It would have been better to fall on the battlefield . . . Than to live, as I do now, in suffering!" (Akh! Lucheb pal na ratnom pole . . . Chem zhit', kak nynche ia, stradaia!). In the end, though, Tolstoi's lyrical subject is unmoved by the veteran's soliloquy: "I am agreed that there is truth in your words; / But I lack the strength to change my mind, / And I can see that your efforts are in vain; / Forgive me!—I still want to serve!" (Ia vpravde slov tvoikh soglasen; / No mysl' ne v silakh premenit', / I vizhu, chto tvoi trud naprasen; / Prosti!—Khochu eshche sluzhit'!).

It is difficult to find anything in this poem that would have given the censors pause. But, as Tomashevsky points out, it was subject to the Green Lamp's own "in-house" censorship.[32] Four lines describing Alexander I at the conclusion of the 1813 campaign in a positive light were crossed out by another Lampist (the script and the ink are not Tolstoi's) and replaced with the lines "How glory rewards adversity, / My spirit seethed with merriness!" (Kak slava trudnost' nagrazhdaet, / Moi dukh veseliem kipel!). Clearly, Tolstoi's praise of the tsar was deemed inappropriate. Yet, this fact cannot be taken merely as evidence that the Green Lamp was acting in accordance with the imperatives of the Union of Welfare.

Though we can only speculate on what the censors' response to this poem might have been, the textology makes the Lampists' response absolutely clear: except for the four lines about Alexander I, the poem "passed." Why, then, did Tolstoi not publish "To Veteran X," choosing instead to fill *My Idle Time* with verse celebrating its author's capacity for champagne and devotion to pure, blowsy friendship? The poem is, in some respects, a serviceable expression of Decembrist values like selfless devotion and the rejection of careerism. If the Green Lamp was indeed an instrument for promulgating Decembrist ideas, then wouldn't Tolstoi be obliged to publish such a poem? It is easy enough to explain why Soviet Pushkinists did not publish the poem or comment on it in any substantive way: the lyrical subject's profession of ardor for military service complicates their case for the Green Lamp as a branch charter of the Union of Welfare. But Tolstoi's own reasons for not publishing it remain unclear.

His reason for not publishing the second poem, "The Cockroach Rhetorician," is much easier to divine: it is a literary-polemical fable, and literary polemic was not much valued in the Green Lamp. In this allegorical poem, Tolstoi describes an insect funeral for three flies that drowned in a forgotten glass of wine. In the course of his eulogy, the cockroach rhetorician angers two spiders in attendance, who then eat him. It concludes:

Как часто рифмачи подобны таракану;
Похвальну песнь поют из денег, перстенька,
Достойному хвалы и вместе с тем тирану;
Но жаль, что нет для них лихаго паука![33]

[How often rhymesters are like the cockroach; / They sing a song of praise for money, a ring, / To one deserving of praise and to a tyrant alike; / But it is a pity that there is no intrepid spider to take care of them!]

Only three of the twenty-five poems in the Green Lamp archive are pronouncedly polemical: "The Cockroach Rhetorician," Barkov's "A Death Sentence for the Letter Ъ" ("Prigovor bukve Ъ"), composed around 1818, and Tolstoi's "To Emel'ianovka" ("K Emel'ianovke"), composed in 1819 and published in 1821. Only the last was published, and only with major revisions, including the removal of a lengthy ad hominem polemical attack (on whom exactly, I am not yet sure). Unlike Arzamas, an earlier familiar literary society (druzheskoe literaturnoe obshchestvo) of which Pushkin was also a member and which was in some respects its model, the Green Lamp avoided literary polemic in general and in published form in particular. Even within Arzamas, there was some fierce debate over whether members should be permitted to engage publicly in literary polemic.[34] This was a point of contention from the very beginning of the Arzamasians' efforts to consolidate a collective, years before the first meeting convened in 1815. For example, Petr Viazemsky condemned Dmitrii Dashkov's famous "encomium" for Count Dmitrii Khvostov in 1812 (a pointed piece of polemical performance art), saying, "But a piece like this piece of Dashkov's, whom you all worship so, might have an effect on your minds, and not for the better. And then you'll all run out into the streets to flash your bare arses at the passersby."[35] By 1819, literary polemic was thoroughly unfashionable. Though an inveterate and furious polemicist, even Pushkin often feigned disdain for public literary polemic during his Petersburg period. While a Lampist, for example, he penned the second canto of *Ruslan and Liudmila*, where we read in lines 9–13: "You, knights of the Parnassian mountains, / Try not to make the public laugh, / With your immodest disputes; / Argue—but carefully" (Vy, rytsari parnasskikh gor, / Staraites' ne smeshit' naroda / Neskromnym shumom vashikh ssor; / Branites'—tol'ko ostorozhno).

Arkadii Rodzianko's "To Ligurinus"

Arkadii Rodzianko was one of the Green Lamp's actively publishing poets, but only one of his poems was preserved in the society's archive: "To Ligurinus" ("K Ligurinusu"), composed in 1816.[36] Presumably, he presented more of the forty-seven poems he is known to have composed by 1821, but we have no concrete evidence that he did. Rodzianko himself never published this poem, though he did present it to at least two literary societies—the Free Society of Lovers of Literature, the Sciences, and the Arts in 1818 and the Green Lamp in 1819 or 1820.

Modzalevsky discovered a redaction of "To Ligurinus" in the archive of the Green Lamp and published it in his 1928 article on the archive. The Green Lamp text is unsigned, and Modzalevsky expresses his vexation at the fact that he could not attribute what was, in his opinion, a fine poem. He links it to Ovid's *Metamorphoses* 10:184—the myth of Apollo's love for Hyacinth, which is the primary subtext of the poem.[37] Vadim Vatsuro later discovered another text of "To Ligurinus" in a manuscript collection of Rodzianko's verse that was preserved in the papers of Avram Norov at the Russian State Library, a find that served as the first documentary proof that Rodzianko was a member of the Green Lamp. Vatsuro describes "To Ligurinus" as a translation of ode 10 in book 5 of Horace's *Odes*.[38] In fact, though, "To Ligurinus" bears little relation to Horace's famous Ligurinus odes (odes 1 and 10 in book

4). The name Ligurinus does of course originate with these odes, and Horace was, at the least, on the Lampists' minds: the Russian master of the "Horatian ode," Del'vig, contributed three exempla to Green Lamp meetings. Yet it is more likely that Rodzianko got the name from Voltaire than Horace. In the entry "Amour nommé Socratique" in his *Dictionnaire philosophique,* Voltaire writes, "The love of boys was so common in Rome that it was impossible to punish this turpitude, into which almost everyone was rushing headlong. Octavius Augustus, that debauched murderer and coward who exiled Ovid, thought it fitting that Virgil sing the charms of Alexis; Horace, his other favorite, created small odes to Ligurinus. Horace, who praised Augustus for reforming morals, speaks in his satires of boys and girls in the same way."[39] Voltaire's association of Horace with homoeroticism was taken up by many of his Russian adepts, and Rodzianko's reputation for homoeroticism was based, in no small part, on his appropriation of the Horatian name Ligurinus. In any case, Voltaire's entry in the *Dictionnaire* was firmly connected with Rodzianko in the minds of his contemporaries. For example, in his 13 June 1823 letter to Alexander A. Bestuzhev, Pushkin borrows Voltaire's term, calling Rodzianko "the bard of Socratic love."

Rodzianko's reputation as a homoerotic poet is something that Pushkinists could not quite come to terms with. Vatsuro, for example, does not even mention the poems in the Russian State Library collection that substantiate this reputation in the two publications of his that include poems by Rodzianko, though he knew them well.[40] In any case, there has been, without a doubt, a certain amount of philological squeamishness when it comes to Rodzianko, and this has clouded our picture of his work, his often problematic friendship with Pushkin—whom he ridiculed in an 1822 satire, "Two Ages" ("Dva veka"), and with whom he competed for the attentions of Anna Kern—and his involvement in the Green Lamp.[41]

While there is much of interest in "To Ligurinus," one hitherto unremarked aspect of its textology is most germane here. The Russian State Library text is, in a sense, both earlier and later than the Green Lamp text: it is dated 1816, but the Russian State Library Avram Norov collection that contains the manuscript itself was created only in 1848. However, the pattern of variations and corrections in the first two stanzas of this text shows that the Russian State Library text was an earlier redaction and the Green Lamp version a later one.[42] Thus, it was most likely the Russian State Library redaction that Rodzianko presented to the Free Society of Lovers of Letters, Sciences, and the Arts on

18 August 1818.[43] (Incidentally, this session of the Free Society is the first documented meeting of Rodzianko with the Lampists Fedor Glinka, Anton Del'vig, and Pushkin, though there is some reason to believe they might have met earlier.[44]) Roughly three years after he first drafted it, Rodzianko presented a new, revised version of the poem at a meeting of the Green Lamp. We can only assume that these revisions put the poem more in line with the tastes of the group. One revision is particularly striking. Rodzianko, so to speak, changed the sexual orientation of the third stanza before bringing the poem to the Green Lamp:

Russian State Library version	Green Lamp version
Во взорах женщины прекрасной	Во взорах отроков прекрасных
Иль полногрудых дев младых	Иль полногрудых дев младых
Грозит равно бог неги страстной	Грозит равно бог чувствий страстных
Жестоким жалом стрел своих;	Жестоким жалом стрел своих;
И Нимфе, близ тебя дрожащей,	И Нимфе, близ тебя дрожащей,
Урок любови первый дать	Урок любови первый дать
Прелестней, чем рукой горящей	Равно прелестно, как горящий
Мальчишку друга обнимать.	Цвет друга юного сорвать!

[Russian State Library version: In the gazes of a beautiful woman / And of busty young maidens / The god of passionate languor threatens equally / With the cruel sting of his arrows; / And to give a first lesson in love / To the Nymph trembling next to you / Is more delightful than with a burning arm / To embrace a young boy friend.]

[Green Lamp version: In the gazes of beautiful boys / And of busty young maidens / The god of passionate sensations threatens equally / With the cruel sting of his arrows; / And to give a first lesson in love / To the Nymph trembling next to you / Is equally delightful / As it is to pluck the burning flower of a young [male] friend.]

Thus, in the semi-public context of Izmailov's Free Society (the Russian State Library text), Rodzianko's lyrical subject gives sexual preference to women over boys, whereas in the context of the Green Lamp, he finds both "equally delightful." In the manuscript collection of Rodzianko's works from which the Russian State Library text comes, we find other "Horatian odes" from the same period, two of which are frankly homoerotic.[45] That Rodzianko did not seek to publish any of these poems serves as good evidence that this was, for him, very much a private subgenre—but one of interest to his fellow Lampists. Apparently, Soviet literary historians were in agreement that these poems were not for publication. The 1972 edition of the famous anthology *Poets of the 1820s and 1830s* (*Poety 1820-kh i 1830-kh godov*) devotes eighteen pages to Rodzianko but includes none of the hedonistic or homoerotic verse that comprises the bulk of his oeuvre and that served as the basis for his literary and social reputations of the late 1810s and early 1820s, when he was known to contemporaries as the "bard of Socratic love," the "bard of merriment and love," and the "Piron of the Ukraine."

Anton Del'vig's "To Fanny"

Though Anton Del'vig, along with Pushkin and Glinka, was one of the Green Lamp's best-known poets in 1819, scholars have tended to downplay his participation in the society. Three Del'vig texts are preserved in the Green Lamp archive: "To Fanny" ("Fanni"), probably composed between 1814 and 1817 but not published until 1922, "To a Boy" ("K mal'chiku" [1819]), and "Daphne" ("Dafna" [1814]). All three poems are devoted to decidedly un-Decembrist, sensualist, Horatian themes.

Del'vig habitually worked on poems for ten years or more, and the textological history of these three poems is the richest source of evidence that the Green Lamp's poets, and Del'vig in particular, were quite serious about using the society as a projected audience, a forum for discussion of technique, and a source of feedback on their work. Del'vig revised all three of these poems extensively in 1819, and these revisions are to varying degrees connected with the Green Lamp. Together with Pushkin and his roommate, Evgenii Boratynsky, Del'vig completely rewrote "Daphne," a translation from Matthias Claudius and one of Del'vig's first published works. He published the new redaction with a new title, "First Meeting" ("Pervaia vstrecha"), in 1820, after first presenting it to the Green Lamp, and he reworked it once more before including it in his 1829 collection.

Like the other poems, Del'vig first composed the poem "To a Boy" while at the lyceum. He revised it in early 1819 and published it in *The Well-Intentioned* (*Blagonamerennyi*) in February 1819, shortly before the

Green Lamp convened. However, the society exerted an influence on this poem nonetheless: the redaction preserved in the Green Lamp archive differs significantly from the version in *The Well-Intentioned*, but it is identical to the final, definitive text that Del'vig published in 1829, including one correction in Pushkin's hand that was evidently made during a Green Lamp meeting. Thus, Del'vig arrived at the final version with the help of his fellow Lampists.

Finally, we come to "To Fanny," which is the most significant of the three poems for understanding the Green Lamp. Because of its frank treatment of sex with prostitutes, "To Fanny" could not be published and was almost completely unknown for a century after Del'vig presented it to the Green Lamp. But "publishability" had little bearing on the amount of care Del'vig devoted to the poem: he revised "To Fanny" at least once before presenting it to the Green Lamp and once soon afterward. Though well known to scholars since its publication by Modest Gofman in 1922, "To Fanny" remains rather mysterious.[46] Given the textological timeline and the provenance of the known texts of "To Fanny," there can be little doubt that this is very much a "Green Lamp text"—a poem shot through with the ethos and the aesthetic of the Green Lamp, and part of the group's literary production, not merely a schoolboy poem that Del'vig dug up for a laugh. Moreover, the poem subsequently became part of the Green Lamp's cloistered lingua franca. For example, in his epistle to Mikhail Shcherbinin, Pushkin predicts, "At the door to the grave, I will say to you / 'Do you remember Fanny, my dear man?'— / And we will both quietly smile." Some years later, Pushkin quoted the poem in the fourth stanza of the excluded passage of *Eugene Onegin* (*Evgenii Onegin*) known as "Women" ("Zhenshchiny")—a quotation that remained a complete mystery to all readers except the Lampists until Gofman found the source nearly a hundred years later.[47]

"To Fanny" was such an important poem to the Lampists because it plays on a set of subtexts and referents peculiar to their milieu. What is most intriguing here is that the addressee, Fanny, appears to have been a real person who may well have read the poem. According to Iurii Shcherbachev, the grandson of two "suspected" Lampists, Mikhail Shcherbinin and Pavel Kaverin, Fanny was an entertainer who performed only for the most exclusive elites. She also moonlighted as a highly sought-after consort for gentlemen of the highest rank. Naturally, it is hard to imagine Del'vig, the adolescent lyceum ward, having access to a star like Fanny. As Shcherbachev tells it, Pushkin could not have afforded to enjoy her company, and by mentioning her in his epistle to Shcherbinin, he sought to place himself in the small circle of men who could (apparently including Shcherbachev's grandfather).[48]

The characteronym "Fanny" already had a developed set of conventional associations in 1819. There are Fannies in the works of writers the Lampists are known to have read: Denis Diderot, Alphonse Karr, Benoît-Louis Prevost, Friedrich Gottlieb Klopstock, Auguste von La-Fontaine, André Chénier, and Claude Joseph Dorat. Without exception, these Fannies are the objects of sexual desire, and most are consorts or prostitutes. Thus, Del'vig links the realia of St. Petersburg nightlife to a well-defined onomastic vein of European literature—one that later took root in Russia, where the name Fanny continued to bear the same connotations throughout the late nineteenth century.

Two redactions of "To Fanny" are subtitled "A Horatian Ode." This generic designation has more to do with the local semantics of Del'vig's immediate milieu than with Horace. Horace was the mask Del'vig donned as a poet. Just as Pushkin was the "new Juvenal" and Rodzianko the "Piron of the Ukraine," so too Del'vig was the new, Russian Horace before he even graduated from the lyceum. Del'vig's early poems were perceived as imitations of Horace. Del'vig's schoolmate and first biographer, Pushkin, wrote, "His first attempts at versification were imitations of Horace."[49] In mid-1819, Boratynsky opened an epistle to Del'vig with "So, my dear Horace" (Tak, liubeznyi moi Goratsii).[50] Almost immediately, Del'vig published a reply to Boratynsky that lays out the associations of Epicureanism, friendship, lassitude, and sexual license that the appellation conveyed:

За то ль, Евгений, я Гораций,
Что пьяный, в миртовом венке,
Пою вино, любовь и граций,
Как он, от шума вдалеке,
И что друзей люблю—старинных,
А жриц Венеры—молодых.[51]

[Am I Horace, Evgenii, / Because while drunk, in a myrtle garland, / I sing of wine, love, and the Graces, / Like him, far from the bustle, / And because I like my friends old, / And my priestesses of Venus young?]

In short, the Horatian ode was an Epicurean catchall, a designated form for frank sensualism that found an eager audience in the Green Lamp. Rodzianko's "To Ligurinus" is, of course, a prime example. In fact, Rodzianko and Del'vig both make use of an interesting "Horatian" trope: the comparison of different kinds of sexual pleasure. Del'vig asks if it is not sweeter to take a lesson in sex from the experienced Fanny than to suffer the sighs and feigned sleep of a younger girl, and Rodzianko ponders the relative sexual merits of women, girls, and young boys.

Fedor Glinka's "The Glimmer of Her Eyes"

When the Green Lamp formed, Fedor Glinka was by far the most distinguished and widely published author among the membership. Nonetheless, only two of his poems were preserved in the Green Lamp archive. One, "A Charade" ("Sharrada" [1820]), he published shortly after presenting it. The other, "The Glimmer of Her Eyes" ("Blesk ochei"), was published in a different redaction in 1818, a year before the Green Lamp convened (a fact that previous studies of the Green Lamp have missed). "A Charade" is the single, solitary poem in the Green Lamp archive that can be without qualification called a political poem.[52] It is a verse riddle, the solution to which is "the Throne." "The Glimmer of Her Eyes" is a relatively straightforward love lyric subtitled "A Free Translation from the Polish." I have yet to discover a possible Polish source for this poem, which consists of variations on the title theme: "But my friend! My angel! To me the *glimmer of your eyes* / Is dearer than the pink sunset and the young moons" (No drug moi! Angel moi! Mne *blesk tvoikh ochei* / I rozovoi zari i lun mladykh milei). Needless to say, such a poem does not fit in with Soviet literary history's image of Fedor Glinka as the humorless and unemotional revolutionary, though it does, in part, put to rest the bemusement of Lotman, who writes, "It is difficult to imagine what F. Glinka did at meetings of the Green Lamp."[53] Now we know: Glinka contributed, it turns out, not only political verse and news from Governor-General Miloradovich's office but also light love lyrics.

Dmitrii Dolgorukov's "Thoughts on the Death of Mr. B"

Dmitrii Dolgorukov was the son of the well-known poet Ivan Mikhailovich Dolgorukov. The two poems he left in the Green Lamp archive are the earliest known works of this lifelong poet-dilettante. One, a *romans*, was published by Modzalevsky, who characterizes Dolgorukov's poetry as a throwback to the 1790s. The other, "Thoughts upon the Death of Mr. B" ("Razmyshleniia pri smerti g-na B-va"), possibly composed in 1819, remains unpublished. This poem, half lament and half meditation on death, does indeed evoke turn-of-the-century sentimentalist verse, and it is littered with stylistic and linguistic anachronisms. Yet it has some edge to it as well. For example: "Dress up your chest in diamond stars / If your soul is quiet looking upon this corpse / In the embrace of false hope / Time will destroy you, too" (Riadite grud' v almazny zvezdy / Kol' zria sei trup dusha molchit / V ob"iatiiakh lozhnyia nadezhdy / Vas takzhe vremia sokrushit).[54] The text of "Thoughts upon the Death of Mr. B" in the Green Lamp archive is a very rough copy with several corrections (in Dolgorukov's hand but apparently with a different ink), so much so that it is difficult to transcribe. No doubt, Dolgorukov brought it to the Green Lamp soon after completing a first redaction and received there some suggestions. Thus, we again see evidence of the Green Lamp as poets' workshop, a social formation dedicated not solely to antics, libertinage, and politics, but also—and perhaps even primarily—to craft.

Alexander Tokarev's Burlesque

We know relatively little about Tokarev, except that he was a member of the Union of Welfare and, shortly before his death that same year, one of the initiators of the new societies in 1821. He died young and wrote little, which is a shame because he was one of the Green Lamp's deftest versifiers. Tokarev's two poems in the Green Lamp archive were both published by Modzalevsky and are interesting primarily for what they tell us about the society's idiosyncratic literary canon. One of the poems, "A Sonnet on the Impermanence of Earthly Things" ("Sonet na tlennost' zemnykh veshchei" [1819]), is a loose translation of French poet Paul Scarron's famous burlesque sonnet about the Coliseum.[55] The second poem, an untitled comic ode to tobacco, is in essence an exercise in Scarron's burlesque: Tokarev deflates the pathos of the Pindaric ode by addressing it to a low subject, just as Scarron "lowers" both the sonnet and the Coliseum by comparing the latter's ephemerality to "a nasty black doublet" that has worn out at the elbow.

Tokarev's ode also has a more local generic affiliation: Barkoviana. One of the central subgenres of Barkoviana is the high-flown Pindaric ode to a low addressee: "To the Victorious Heroine, the Cunt" ("Pobedonosnoi geroine pizde"), "To the Fist Fighter" ("Kulashnomu boitsu"), and so forth.[56] This is a generic transposition of the mock-heroic epic's central conceit from the narrative poem to the ode. While the travesty employs heroic diction for a low fiction, the Barkovian ode employs a strange mix of Pindaric and vulgar diction to sing the praises of a low addressee. Thus, Tokarev's Green Lamp poems are a most interesting case: the national specificity of Barkoviana intertwines with the poet's direct knowledge of its European and classical sources. Pushkin and Del'vig could, of course, also claim the same sort of broad knowledge of and facility with the burlesque tradition, both foreign and domestic, from Scarron down to Maikov. No doubt, conversations with Tokarev and other Lampists were part of this education.

Adaptations, Translations, Sources

The European and Russian poets whose influence is evident in the poems of the Green Lamp—sometimes in the direct form of adaptations and translations, sometimes in the more oblique form of subtext—are a motley group but point to what might be called the society's "synchronic canon." Even if we stick solely to those poets explicitly referenced in Lampist poetry, we can still get a picture of the vein of literary history in which they sought to cast their work and which they worked together toward emulating. For example, the fact that the Lampists knew Scarron well enough to discuss Tokarev's translation and that they liked Scarron well enough to do so shows they had a developed and literary-historically informed taste for burlesque.

Almost without exception, the literary models explicitly invoked by the Lampists are "light" poets known in Golden Age Russia for their sensual and/or comical verse. Horace, of course, tops the list: there are three Horatian odes in the archive, and Horace figures in several other Lampist poems as well (for example, Pushkin's "Stanzas for Tolstoi"). Another writer important to the Lampists was Claude Joseph Dorat, the eighteenth-century jack of all literary trades most well known for his light verse and erotic prose. His epistolary novel *The Woes of Inconstancy* (1772) is a probable subtext for Del'vig's "To Fanny." Tolstoi, in fact, includes a quotation from Dorat on the frontispiece of his 1821 collection *My Idle Time*, just below the symbols of the Green Lamp. The quotation, which Tolstoi no doubt found fitting for the Green Lamp, reads: "Far from me is the bitterness of a prickly Critic / I speak to friendship, I have the right to say anything / If one must weigh one's words and measure one's play / To remain free and glad, I renounce the art of writing."

Evariste Désiré de Forges, vicomte de Parny, is a prominent presence in the Green Lamp, though one has to wonder whether he might not have been the same sort of generic catchall for the Lampists that Horace was—that is, whether "Parny" might have signified, simply, "light, mannered erotica." That said, Parny was also a concrete source for one poem: Tolstoi's most erotic poem in the Green Lamp archive, "To a Young Beauty" ("K iunoi krasavitse" [1821]), subtitled "An Imitation of Parny," is actually a fairly faithful translation of Parny's "A Eléonore."

Their taste for light verse is especially evident when Lampists evoke poets whose works are a mixture of the light and the grave. For example, Del'vig translated Claudius's "Daphne," choosing it from among his other works, many of which are gloomy, Klopstockian exercises in pietism. I hardly need mention that, for the Lampists, "Horace" is wine, sex, revelry—and not other, equally important Horatian themes like empire, freedom, mortality. In any case, we find nary a civic poet in the Green Lamp's canon. The Lampists aimed to float down a rather different literary current, and the long-standing characterization of their literary activities as the recitation of "republican" poems is a distortion and a mistruth.

Pushkin and the Poetry of the Green Lamp

Taking an honest look at the poetry of the Green Lamp yields some important findings for Pushkin scholarship. First, we now know beyond all doubt that the regnant depiction of the group as a somber cell of the Union of Welfare is far from the whole truth. The Lampists were concerned with craft, and they prized levity over civic discourses, which explains why Pushkin's most politically charged poems of the Petersburg period (e.g., the 1817 "Liberty" ["Vol'nost'"], the 1819 "The Countryside" ["Derevnia"]) date not to the time after the Green Lamp convened but to the period before. Thus, contrary to the conventional scholarly wisdom, the Green Lamp was not a school in political radicalism for the young Pushkin. The poetry of the Green Lamp and its textology provide ample evidence that the Green Lamp was also a rollicking and tipsy literary training ground. Pushkin found here a family of poets and litterateurs like those of Arzamas, a society he longed to join throughout his early adolescence; he did so only after it had mostly disintegrated.[57]

That the Lampists clearly saw no disjunction between light verse and radical politics is perhaps the most important finding here, and one that forces us to recalibrate our understanding of the most important work of Pushkin's Petersburg period, *Ruslan and Liudmila*. The collocation of radical politics and libertine verse points to a behavioral poetics in which writing and reading playful verse and erotica are themselves an act of dissent. It was precisely the breeziness and levity of *Ruslan and Liudmila* that made it the single most controversial work of the early 1820s, and for good reason: levity presented a "demonstrative challenge to the 'serious' world."[58] Pushkin developed this poetic stance of flippant challenge in the Green Lamp, where he had his only substantial experience with the familiar literary societies that were a cornerstone of literary evolution in the early part of the century. He continued to cultivate this stance for years after his exile and the disbanding of the group.

NOTES

Research for this chapter was supported by the Fulbright-Hays Program and by the University of Wisconsin–Milwaukee Graduate School's Research Committee. Tatiana Krasnoborodko and her colleagues at Pushkin House provided invaluable help with the Green Lamp manuscripts, and I am very grateful for their extraordinary generosity. Thanks are also due to Professor Lorena Terando of the University of Wisconsin–Milwaukee, who assisted me with the translations from French.

1. On *The Shade of Barkov* and the effort to keep it hidden, see Igor Pilshchikov's article in the present volume.

2. Pavel E. Shchegolev, "Zelenaia lampa," *Pushkin i ego sovremenniki* 8 (1908): 19–50, http://feb-web.ru/feb/pushkin/serial/ps7/ps720412.htm?cmd=0 (accessed 14 August 2011).

3. Boris L. Modzalevskii, "Iakov Nikolaevich Tolstoi: Biograficheskii ocherk," pt. 1, *Russkii arkhiv* 9 (1899): 589. See also Pavel V. Annenkov, *Pushkin v Aleksandrovskuiu epokhu* (Minsk: Limarius, 1998), 56–58.

4. Boris Tomashevsky's work on the Green Lamp, published in 1956, is the most carefully researched work in the "anti-orgiastic" camp and has been the last word on the subject since its publication. See Boris V. Tomashevskii, *Pushkin*, 2 vols. (Moscow: Khudozhestvennaia literatura, 1990), 1:173–209.

5. A few examples: academician Militsa Nechkina, a principal architect of the official Soviet history of Decembrism, asserted on numerous occasions that the Green Lamp was "a branch charter of the Union of Welfare" (*Dekabristy* [Moscow: Nauka, 1975], 35.) On the website of the city of Orel, hometown to the Lampist Alexander Tokarev, we find the very same language (http://www.oryol.ru/material.php?id=4479). The Russian Wikipedia article on Decembrism repeats it, as do several term papers for sale on the Internet to high school and university students.

6. Of Annenkov's account of the Green Lamp Tomashevsky says that "every word . . . is untrue" (*Pushkin*, 1:182), a crude blanket statement that is itself untrue. And Shchegolev accuses Annenkov of desecrating Pushkin manuscripts out of the same prudishness and puritanical zeal that supposedly blinded him to the real truth of the Green Lamp ("Zelenaia lampa," 33).

7. With many notable exceptions, Soviet literary historians portray the Decembrists as an exceedingly somber lot, and their movement as one with no room for levity. The Decembrists were to be clean-living, earnest proto-Bolsheviks. As a result, some writers with links to Decembrism have been misconstrued as civic poets. For a detailed critique of one such misrepresentation—Vadim Vatsuro's construction of Arkadii Rodzianko as a civic poet—see my article "Once More about Arkadii Rodzianko and Pushkin," *Pushkin Review* 8–9 (2005–6): 77–93.

8. See Igor Nemirovsky's article in the present volume for a broader discussion of the connection between libertinism and liberalism.

9. The Russian libertine tradition is as yet little studied, primarily because of implicit prohibitions against the study of anything "frivolous" in Soviet academe. For an overview of Russian libertinism's French models, as well as recent scholarship on French libertinism, see Catherine Cusset, "The Lesson of Libertinage," in "Libertinism and Modernity," ed. Catherine Cusset, special issue, *Yale French Studies* 94 (1998): 1–14. On British libertinism, see David Foxon's classic book *Libertine Literature in England 1660–1745* (New Hyde, NY: University Books, 1965).

10. Iurii M. Lotman, *Pushkin: Biografiia pisatelia; Stat'i i zametki, 1960–1990; "Evgenii Onegin," Kommentarii* (St. Petersburg: Iskusstvo-SPB, 1995), 52.

11. Viktor M. Zhirmunskii, "Pushkin i zapadnye literatury," in *Vremennik Pushkinskoi komissii*, vol. 3 (Moscow: AN SSSR, 1937), 69.

12. On "conspiratorial" language, see Iurii M. Lotman's "K funktsii ustnoi rechi v kul'turnom bytu pushkinskoi epokhi," in his *Izbrannye stat'i*, 3 vols. (Tallin: Aleksandra, 1992–93), 3:430–38.

13. What some have described as Pushkin's "Green Lamp cycle" includes the poems "Stanzas for Tolstoi" ("Stansy Tolstomu"), "To Iur'ev" ("Iur'evu"), "To Shcherbinin" ("Shcherbininu"), "To Engel'gardt" ("Engel'gardtu"), and "To Vsevolozhsky" ("Vsevolozhskomu").

14. For the text of this letter and other relevant documents, see Shchegolev, "Zelenaia lampa." Modzalevsky asserts that Pavel Kaverin, Mikhail Shcherbinin, Alexander Iakubovich, and Vasilii Engel'gardt were among these "suspected" members. Earlier Pushkinists also included Ivan Iakushkin.

15. See Boris L. Modzalevskii, "K istorii 'Zelenoi lampy,'" in his *Pushkin i ego sovremenniki: Izbrannye stat'i (1898–1928)* (St. Petersburg: Iskusstvo-SPB, 1999), 10–11.

16. See Mikhail Semevskii, "Ocherki iz istorii politicheskikh i obshchestvennykh idei Dekabristov," *Russkoe bogatstvo* 4 (1908): 55–98, esp. 73–78.

17. The Green Lamp's papers turned up in the archive of the journal *Russian Archive* (*Russkii arkhiv*), which ended up at Pushkin House after the 1917 revolution.

18. See Shchegolev, "Zelenaia lampa," for the full text of Tolstoi's letters to the tsar and Trubetskoi's testimony.

19. Boris M. Eikhenbaum, "Literaturnaia domashnost'," in *Moi vremennik; Slovesnost'; Nauka; Kritika; Smes'* (Leningrad: Izdatel'stvo pisatelei v Leningrade, 1929), 82–88.

20. Iurii M. Lotman, "Dekabrist v povsednevnoi zhizni," in his *Besedy o russkoi kul'ture* (St. Petersburg: Iskusstvo-SPB, 1994), 361.

21. Neither of these poems was still in the archive when Modzalevsky discovered it in the 1920s, but Pushkinistic tradition holds that they were both read at a Green Lamp meeting and that they were both initially preserved in the Green Lamp archive. This provenance is repeated in all the commentaries of the Academy's critical editions. Examination of Pushkin House records reveals nothing that either confirms or refutes it. In his commentary, Tomashevsky further adds that this version of "I know battle" had been lost (nyne utracheno) (Aleksandr S. Pushkin, *Polnoe sobranie sochinenii,* 10 vols., ed. Boris V. Tomashevskii [Leningrad: Nauka, 1977–79], 1:461).

22. A. Aleksandrov [possibly a pseudonym], "Podgotovka i provedenie pushkinskogo iubileia v SSSR," in *Pushkin: Vremennik Pushkinskoi komissii,* 3:516.

23. Gukovsky uses this poem as an example of Pushkin's martial poetry: "Pushkin's martial poems of 1820–21 sounded, no doubt, radical-political and were Decembrist poems" (*Pushkin i russkie romantiki* [Moscow: Khudozhestvennaia literatura, 1965], 205).

24. Pushkin, *Polnoe sobranie sochinenii,* 10 vols., 1:326.

25. Ibid., 1:458.

26. For Tolstoi's biography, see historian Petr P. Cherkasov's fascinating study *Russkii agent vo Frantsii: Iakov Nikolaevich Tolstoi* (Moscow: Scientific Press, 2008).

27. On the symbolism of the title page, see Modzalevskii, "K istorii 'Zelenoi lampy,'" 35n1. Modzalevsky's interpretation is corroborated by the lines "For us, young allies, / The lamp of hope has been lit!" (Dlia nas, soiuzniki mladye, / Nadezhdy lampa zazhzhena!) from Pushkin's epistle to the Lampist Fedor Iur'ev.

28. Pushkin, for example, had promised the rights to his first collection of lyric poems to Tolstoi; their friendship ended when Tolstoi was informed that Pushkin had sold the rights to Gnedich. The most complete treatment of this friendship is in Modzalevsky's two-part literary biography of Tolstoi: "Iakov Nikolaevich Tolstoi: Biograficheskii ocherk," pt. 1, *Russkii arkhiv* 9 (1899): 587–614; and "Iakov Nikolaevich Tolstoi: Biograficheskii ocherk," pt. 2, *Russkii arkhiv* 10 (1899): 175–99.

29. See Iakov N. Tolstoi, *Moe prazdnoe vremia* (St. Petersburg: Tipografiia Karla Kraiia, 1821), 48–51. The poem was most recently published in Modzalevskii, "Iakov Nikolaevich Tolstoi: Biograficheskii ocherk," 593–96.

30. Manuscripts Department, Pushkin House, St. Petersburg, f. 244, op. 36, ed. khr. 37, l. 28. Tomashevsky insists that Tolstoi is not the author of "The Cockroach Rhetorician," but offers no substantive argument for calling Modzalevsky's attribution into doubt (*Pushkin*, 1:188). Both of these poems are written in Tolstoi's hand.

31. Manuscripts Department, Pushkin House, f. 244, op. 36, ed. khr. 37, l. 1.

32. Tomashevskii, *Pushkin*, 1:188–89.

33. Manuscripts Department, Pushkin House, f. 244, op. 36, ed. khr. 28, l. 1 (ob.).

34. On the formation of Arzamas and the Arzamasians' internal debates over the proper mode for enacting their political, linguistic, and literary agenda, see Mariia Maiofis's superb book *Vozzvanie k Evrope: Literaturnoe obshchestvo "Arzamas" i rossiiskii modernizatsionnyi proekt 1815–18 gg.* (Moscow: Novoe literaturnoe obozrenie, 2008).

35. Petr A. Viazemsky to Konstantin N. Batiushkov, 12 April 1812 (*Arzamas: Sbornik*, 2 vols., ed. Vadim Vatsuro [Moscow: Khudozhestvennaia literatura, 1994], 1:189).

36. Quoted here from the Green Lamp version. The Green Lamp version can be found in the Manuscripts Department, Pushkin House, St. Petersburg, f. 244, op. 36, ed. khr. 40, l. 1, and the Russian State Library version in Arkadii Rodzianko's manuscript collection "Stikhotvoreniia, 1812–1840" ("Poems, 1812–1840"), found in the personal fond of Avram S. Norov, Manuscripts Department, Russian State Library, Moscow, f. 201, no. 7.

37. Modzalevskii, "K istorii 'Zelenoi lampy,'" 41.

38. Vadim Vatsuro, "Pushkin i Arkadii Rodzianka (iz istorii grazhdanskoi poezii 1820-xx gg.)," in *Vremennik Pushkinskoi komissii, 1969* (Leningrad: AN SSSR, 1971), 48.

39. Voltaire, *Dictionnaire philosophique*, ed. Béatric Didier (Paris: Imprimerie Nationale, 1994), 79.

40. Besides the analysis in his article "Pushkin i Arkadii Rodzianko," Vatsuro also anthologized Rodzianko in *Poety 1820-kh i 1830-kh godov*, 2 vols., ed. Lidiia Ia. Ginzburg, Vadim E. Vatsuro and Vasilii S. Kiselev-Sergenin (Leningrad: Sovetskii pisatel', 1972), 1:153–171.

41. Rodzianko, "Dva veka (otryvok)," in *Poety 1820-kh i 1830-kh godov*, 162–66.

42. I discuss the textology of "K Ligurinusu" at length in chapter 3 of my forthcoming *The Poetics of Impudence and Intimacy in the Age of Pushkin* (Madison: University of Wisconsin Press, 2012). In short, the Russian State Library text has several corrections. In all cases, these corrections (some of them metrical, some of them corrections of incorrect classical references) reinstate variants from the Green Lamp text. Thus, Rodzianko's scribe worked from an earlier redaction, and Rodzianko (or perhaps Avram Norov) inserted all the corrections from the later Green Lamp redaction. The only variant from the Green Lamp text that was not reinstated is the third stanza, which was left uncorrected.

43. St. Petersburg State University's library has published the Free Society's protocols online. See http://www.lib.pu.ru/rus/Volsnx/prot/prot18.html.

44. On the dating of Pushkin's acquaintance with Rodzianko, see my "Once More about Arkadii Rodzianko and Pushkin," 83–86.

45. "To a [Male] Friend: An Imitation of Horace" ("K drugu: Podrazhanie Goratsiiu" [1814]), in Rodzianko, "Stikhotvoreniia, 1812–1840," 104–7; "Epistle on Friendship and Love to Avram Sergeevich Norov" ("Poslanie o druzhbe i liubvi Avramu Sergeevichu Norovu" [1818]), in Rodzianko, "Stikhotvoreniia, 1812–1840," 132–40.

46. Anton A. Del'vig, *Neizdannye stikhotvoreniia*, ed. Modest L. Gofman (St. Petersburg: Trudy Pushkinskogo doma pri Rossiiskoi akademii nauk, 1922), 50, 125.

47. On "To Fanny" as an example of "circle poetics," see Joe Peschio and Igor Pil'shchikov, "The Proliferation of Elite Readerships and Circle Poetics in Pushkin and Baratynskii," in *The Space of the Book: Print Culture in the Russian Social Imagination*, ed. Miranda Remnek (Toronto: University of Toronto Press, 2011), 82–107.

48. Iurii. N. Shcherbachev, *Priiateli Pushkina M. A. Shcherbinin i P. P. Kaverin* (Moscow: Izd. Imp. Ob-va istorii i drevnostei rossiiskikh pri Moskovskom universitete, 1913), 15, 16, 182.

49. Aleksandr S. Pushkin, "Del'vig," in his *Polnoe sobranie sochinenii*, 17 vols., ed. Vladimir D. Bonch-Bruevich et al. (Moscow: AN SSSR, 1937–59), 11:274.

50. Evgenii Boratynskii, "Del'vigu," in his *Polnoe sobranie stikhotvorenii*, 2 vols. (Leningrad: Sovetskii pisatel', 1936), 100–101.

51. Anton A. Del'vig, "K Evgeniiu," in his *Polnoe sobranie stikhotvorenii* (Leningrad: Sovetskii pisatel', 1959), 129.

52. Tomashevsky published the poem with his commentary in *Pushkin*, 1:187.

53. Lotman, "Dekabrist v povsednevnoi zhizni," 365.

54. Manuscripts Department, Pushkin House, f. 244, op. 36, ed. khr. 13.

55. Paul Scarron, *Poesies diverses* (Paris: Didier, 1947), 496–97. For an interesting take on this poem, see Francesco Orlando, *Obsolete Objects in the Literary*

Imagination: Ruins, Relics, Rarities, Rubbish, Uninhabited Places, and Hidden Treasures, trans. Gabriel Pihas (New Haven: Yale University Press, 2006), 74–76.

56. See *Devich'ia igrushka, ili Sochineniia gospodina Barkova*, ed. Aleksandr Zorin and Nikita Sapov (Moscow: Ladomir, 1992), 41–45, 78–85.

57. On the tricky question of when Pushkin was initiated into Arzamas, see Oleg Proskurin, "Kogda zhe Pushkin vstupil v Arzamasskoe obshchestvo? (Iz zametok k teme 'Pushkin i Arzamas')," *Toronto Slavic Quarterly* 14 (Fall 2005), http://www.utoronto.ca/tsq/14/proskurin14.shtml (accessed 14 August 2011).

58. Lotman, *Pushkin*, 52.

Pushkin and Metropolitan Philaret

Rethinking the Problem

Oleg Proskurin

The Holy Monk and the Repentant Sinner

The topic of Pushkin's relations with Metropolitan Philaret cannot in itself be considered taboo: during the last two decades in Russia (as well as beyond her borders) more publications have been dedicated to this subject than during the entire former history of Pushkin scholarship.[1] But for all that, in recent times a certain approach to the topic that can be called, without much exaggeration, *hagiographic* has become dominant (and, in relation to post-Soviet Russia, one may even say "canonical"). According to this approach, the relationship between Pushkin and Philaret is made to conform to the paradigm of the life of a saint who miraculously saves a wayward sinner.

The attention of the authors of this interpretation turns out to be concentrated exclusively on one episode in Pushkin's relations with Philaret—the so-called poetic dialogue that took place between the poet and the metropolitan in 1830. In brief, the gist of the events that transpired consists in the following: in the spring of 1828 Pushkin wrote the pessimistic "A vain gift, a chance gift" ("Dar naprasnyi, dar sluchainyi"), placing its date of composition, 26 May 1828, at its beginning (this was Pushkin's date of birth according to the Julian calendar). At the beginning of 1830 Elizaveta Khitrovo, the daughter of the famous commander Mikhail Kutuzov and a passionate admirer of Pushkin, made this poem known to a prominent Russian Orthodox Church official, Philaret (Drozdov [1782–1867]), the Moscow and Kolomna metropolitan. The metropolitan unexpectedly responded to Pushkin's poem with his own verses. Using the structure of Pushkin's poem, he replaced Pushkin's message with a canonical Orthodox explanation of the reasons for the depression and hopelessness that may engulf a human being and indicated that the only path to overcoming pessimism is to turn to God for help. Elizaveta Khitrovo gave the metropolitan's verses to Pushkin, who in his turn replied in verse to the metropolitan's answer (during Pushkin's lifetime this poem was printed under the title "Stanzas" ["Stantsy"]; now it is published without a title and is identified by its first line: "In times of leisure or idle boredom" ["V chasy zabav il' prazdnoi skuki"]).[2]

Before the Russian Revolution, literary scholars did not attach any special meaning to this "poetic correspondence" and occupied themselves very little with the subject of Pushkin's relations with Philaret. More often this topic was addressed by right-wing publicists and ecclesiastical writers. They interpreted it in a conservative-panegyric and bluntly biographical manner, as seen for example in this text written by an archpriest:

> Metropolitan Philaret . . . wrote in answer a poem that was profound and truly Christian. . . . Pushkin, with the grandeur of repentant feeling, wrote to the Archbishop: "I shed streams of unexpected tears." . . . And now he no longer beckons death unto him: his soul is full of ideas for new creations in which the poet's enlightened spirit, having rejected the "gloom of earthly vanity," will reveal itself.[3]

In Soviet times, too, little was written about Pushkin and Philaret. What little Soviet scholarship there is on this topic dates from the 1920s; then, as atheist ideology and anticlerical propaganda intensified, almost everyone stopped writing about the topic altogether.

This situation changed in the last years of the Soviet Union, during Gorbachev's perestroika and the general liberalization of the country's religious climate. In 1989, riding a wave of interest in topics related to church and religion that had been forbidden until only recently, there appeared in the journal *New World* (*Novyi mir*) a long article by Valentin Nepomniashchy, a dissident man of letters, titled "The Gift" ("Dar"), which was to have great influence on later interpretations of Pushkin's relations with Philaret.[4] Subsequently, Nepomniashchy's concept was filled out in his 1999 book *Pushkin: A Russian Picture of the World* (*Pushkin: Russkaia kartina mira*), but the essence of his argument did not change.

Under the influence of the "religious-philosophical criticism" of the beginning of the twentieth century, which had begun to come back into fashion once again toward the beginning of the twenty-first, Nepomniashchy examines all of Pushkin's creative work as a path to the true Christian (i.e., Orthodox) understanding of the mission of art. Along the way Pushkin experienced both sublime revelations (the poem "The Prophet" ["Prorok"]) and abysmal failures. Nepomniashchy declared the poem "A vain gift, a chance gift" to be one such failure; from his point of view, it was blasphemous, full of audacious reproaches to God. However, according to Nepomniashchy, after reading the poem, Metropolitan Philaret did not "grind Pushkin into dust" but, realizing Pushkin's importance for Russia, instead addressed the fallen poet in a language accessible to him—which is to say the language of poetry—with words of exhortation and support.[5] The deeply shaken Pushkin realized the depth of his own degradation, repented, and from that time on firmly established himself on the path of Christian art. Nepomniashchy's interpretation differs from the speeches of the Orthodox pastors of the late nineteenth century by dint of its more radical reading of the poem as "spiritual suicide" and also by the fact that he construes Pushkin's correspondence with Philaret not just as one of many instructive examples of the beneficial influence of the church on a doubting layperson but as the *central event of Pushkin's spiritual biography*.

In 1994 the Russian Orthodox Church canonized Metropolitan Philaret. The canonization of Philaret led to his relationship to Pushkin being examined in a new light as well. At this time the well-known icon painter Archimandrite Zinon painted the icon *The Life of Saint Philaret of Moscow*, where Philaret's dialogue with Pushkin is represented not metaphorically but completely literally as an episode in the life of the new saint. In the same year, panegyric publications on the theme of "Pushkin and Philaret" also began to appear, to one or another degree repeating the writings of the pastors of the end of the nineteenth century and/or Nepomniashchy's thesis.[6]

The "epoch of Putin" (i.e., the years 2000 to the present) has seen new inflections in the treatment of this topic. During this time the authorities began to regard the Russian Orthodox Church as the ideological

Archimandrite Zinon (Theodor), *Pushkin and Metropolitan Philaret* (after 1994).

foundation of the Russian government and the Russian national consciousness (although laws about religious equality and the separation of church and state are formally still in place).[7] In the Putin years, the view of Pushkin as a Christian—and even a specifically Orthodox Christian—poet became more and more widespread. The basis for such an interpretation is found in the writings of the early twentieth-century conservative Russian philosopher Ivan Il'in (Vladimir Putin's favorite thinker): "Pushkin taught Russia to see God and through this vision to affirm and strengthen her innermost, God-given national-spiritual powers."[8] It is not surprising that in the twenty-first century the "hagiographic" interpretation of the correspondence of Pushkin and Philaret—which in the 1990s was disseminated mainly among the educated clergy and the churchgoing intelligentsia—has received almost official status and has begun to be widely disseminated in academia, the media, and school curricula.[9]

Symptomatic of this trend is the fact that Nepomniashchy's *Pushkin: A Russian Picture of the World* was favored with the highest official prize, the State Prize, awarded in the Kremlin on 12 June 2001. A second edition of the book came out that same year. At the same time, the ideas of Nepomniashchy, who had become the chairman of the Pushkin Commission of the Maksim Gorky Institute for World Literature (Moscow), began to be popularized—naturally, in a simplified and vulgarized form, both in the government press and in school teaching.[10] The reduction of the relationship between Pushkin and Metropolitan Philaret to that of a sinner and the saint who had saved him became generally accepted. Isolated attempts to correct the picture, to attribute to it a less "iconographic" appearance, have had no substantial resonance in Russia: the hagiographic treatment of this subject has turned out to be to a great extent in harmony not only with the ideological requirements and goals of the authorities but also with the emotional and intellectual mood of post-Soviet society.[11]

The goal of the present chapter is to move the topic from a hagiographical into a historical space. I try to examine the relationship between Pushkin and Philaret not in terms of the paradigm of a saint's life but in relation to its concrete historical context.

"Flocks of jackdaws on the crosses": Did Philaret Lodge a Complaint against Pushkin?

The first known evidence of Metropolitan Philaret's attention to Pushkin's work dates to the time when Pushkin had returned from his exile at Mikhailovskoe after being "forgiven" by Emperor Nicholas I. At that time the heightened attention of society was riveted on the poet. Nor did the Moscow metropolitan remain on the sidelines of this trend. In a letter sent to Paris in the first half of October 1828, the well-known man of letters Prince Viazemsky related to Alexander I. Turgenev, his correspondent of many years, the content of a conversation Philaret had had with the poet Evgenii A. Boratynsky (who had recently visited the metropolitan together with his father-in-law, Senator Lev N. Engel'gardt):

> [Boratynsky] says that Philaret and in general our monks of exalted rank always remind him of something feminine: their robes are like skirts, and in their manner there is some sort of coquettishness, the playing of a conventional role, and so on. It seems to me that this observation is exceedingly true. Philaret criticized the scene depicting Father Pimen's cell in *Boris Godunov*, in which Grishka Otrep'ev lies on the floor, first, because in monasteries monks don't sleep in pairs; let us suppose this were true, he goes on, but furthermore: why make Otrep'ev loll about on the floor? "Go into any monastery," he says, "into any cell: you will find that every monk has a little bed of some kind, not richly appointed but at least clean." Is that how it seems to you, Mr. Philophilaret? And didn't I guess the truth in my noël, when I had him say:
>
> И что я в умники попал
> Нечаянно случилось!
>
> [And I accidentally landed
> among the ranks of clever men!][12]

Viazemsky's addressee, Turgenev (who at one time had been director of the Department of Religious Affairs of Foreign Confessions in the Ministry of Public Education and Religious Affairs, and also the secretary of the Bible Society, in which Philaret played a visible role), was a longtime friend of Philaret and regarded him sympathetically. This explains the provocative tone of the caustic Viazemsky.[13]

According to Viazemsky's account, the metropolitan demonstrated a surprisingly retentive memory: the scene he touched on from Pushkin's tragedy *Boris Godunov*, "A Cell in the Chudov Monastery" ("Kel'ia v Chudovom monastyre"), had been published in the first issue of the *Moscow Herald* (*Moskovskii vestnik*) for 1827, which is to say more than a year and a half before his conversation with Boratynsky. Philaret's objections might appear surprisingly trifling (Viazemsky waxed ironic about their absurd pettiness by casting doubt on the metropolitan's intelligence), but in their own way they are appropriate: Philaret, an adherent of the institution of monasticism, interpreted with especial sensitivity any statement that was likely to throw a disadvantageous light on monastery life.

However, by all accounts Philaret's private conversation with Boratynsky in 1828 was not the first time he had expressed an unfavorable opinion of Pushkin. On 16 March 1834 the censor Alexander Nikitenko, a well-known man of letters and professor at St. Petersburg University, noted in his diary an anecdote that he had heard from the philosopher, scholar, and clergyman Nikolai Sidonsky:

> Sidonsky told me about the persecution he was subjected to by the monks (meaning Filaret) on account of his book *Introduction to Philosophy*. I also heard an amusing anecdote from him about how Filaret complained to Benkendorf about a line in Pushkin's *Onegin*. Describing Moscow, Pushkin says: "and a flock of jackdaws on the crosses." Filaret found this insulting to things holy. The censor, who was summoned for an explanation, said that jackdaws, as far as he knew, really did perch on the crosses of Moscow churches, but that in his opinion it was not the poet and the censor who were guilty here but rather the Moscow Chief of Police, for permitting this. Benkendorf replied to Filaret politely, saying that this matter wasn't worthy of the intervention of such a respectable clerical personage. {"What is written, is written" [*ezhe pisakh, pisakh*].}[14]

This colorful anecdote has been eagerly cited by scholars, but never has it been subjected to careful analysis.[15] The lack of such analysis gave Natalia Mikhailova, assistant director of the Alexander S. Pushkin State Museum and organizer of the sensational exhibit "Pushkin and Metropolitan Philaret" (2000–2001), an opening to raise questions about the credibility of Sidonsky's story: "This is all merely an anecdote. . . . The trustworthiness of this story has not been verified by anyone in any way."[16] How well-founded are such doubts?

It is certainly true that when one looks closely at the story recorded by Nikitenko, one discovers things that are strange and contradictory. Above all, it is unclear when Philaret lodged his complaint. Most scholars have never touched on this question. Felix Raskolnikov (apparently basing his information on the date of Nikitenko's diary entry) dates the complaint to 1834.[17] This would seem to agree with the fact that the first complete edition of *Eugene Onegin* (*Evgenii Onegin*) was published in March 1833. However, the problem is that this edition of the novel (just like the separate edition of its seventh chapter, which came out in March 1830) was stamped "With the permission of the authorities." This meant that these two publications *were not subjected to the regular censorship*: instead, Pushkin received permission for publication from Tsar Nicholas through his intermediary, the chief of the Third Section, Count Alexander Kh. Benkendorf. Philaret, therefore, would have had to lodge a complaint with Benkendorf against the sovereign emperor or against Benkendorf himself. There was no other censor who could possibly have been "summoned for an explanation." Consequently, at first glance, there are rather weighty reasons to pronounce this popular anecdote untrustworthy, despite the fact that Sidonsky's uncommonly upstanding personality is unlikely to support the suspicion of his being the hawker of unreliable rumors.[18]

But a rush to such a conclusion would also be mistaken. Although the separate editions of *Eugene Onegin* were published with the personal sanction of the emperor, several stanzas of the novel's seventh chapter containing a description of Moscow (including the notorious "flock of jackdaws on the crosses") were published twice *before* the appearance of the separate editions in periodicals that had to pass through the regular censorship. The first such excerpt was published in January 1828 in the journal *Moscow Herald*, and a corrected version was published in February of the same year in the St. Petersburg newspaper the *Northern Bee* (*Severnaia pchela*).[19] This fact removes the main doubts aroused by Sidonsky's story and solves many related puzzles—in particular, it makes clear why Philaret became indignant about the trifling "jackdaws on the crosses," while he makes no comment about those parts of the novel that were more subversive from the perspective of the Orthodox Church (beginning with the novel's very first stanza, where the hero expresses the blasphemous wish that his dying relative be quickly taken away by the devil!). Philaret had not read *Eugene Onegin* in its entirety; he had read only a few *excerpts* of the novel in one of the periodical publications that he happened to glance at.

But in which of the two publications? The *Moscow Herald* was edited by Mikhail P. Pogodin, a great admirer of Philaret, who knew of this admiration.[20] Philaret might have expressed his discontent with Pushkin's publications in the *Moscow Herald* in a private manner, but to lodge a complaint with the secret police against his own fans and followers would have been completely pointless.[21] Thus, the *Northern Bee* can, with great likelihood, be assumed to have been the source of Philaret's acquaintance with the excerpt from *Eugene Onegin*. This fact may also explain why Philaret's complaint did not achieve any traction with the authorities and did not lead to any serious repercussions for either the publisher or the author. For Faddei Bulgarin, the publisher and editor of the *Northern Bee*, was a secret agent of the Third Section, which is to say a member of the same agency to whose chief Philaret's complaint was directed.[22] It was not in Benkendorf's interest to see his associate suffer. (If Philaret had complained about the *Moscow Herald*, on the other hand, then his complaint would most likely have been examined with all seriousness: in the Third Section the *Moscow Herald* was regarded with extreme ill will, mostly thanks to Bulgarin, who wrote political denunciations of his literary rivals without disdaining the use of unverified rumor and outright slander).[23] Instead, the matter ended with the censor's oral explanation, in accordance with Sidonsky's story. The censor of the *Northern Bee* in February 1828 was Vasilii Nikolaevich Semenov, who had distinguished himself with qualities rare for a censor: an independent character, bravery, and wit. The scathing answer about the Moscow jackdaws and the Moscow chief of police is completely in the spirit of analogous elucidations by Semenov.[24] This resourceful answer allowed the matter to be closed without further consequences.

Thus, we have every reason to conclude that the story told by Sidonsky (and retold by Nikitenko) *is truthful in its foundation*. However, it does not date to 1833, but to a significantly earlier time—most likely to February 1828. Most likely, the complaint lodged with the Third Section was the *first* time Metropolitan Philaret voiced an opinion about Pushkin.

To all appearances, Pushkin himself found out about Philaret's complaint fairly quickly. The most probable source of information about this incident was the censor Semenov, who was made to answer for it: he, like Pushkin, had graduated from the Tsarskoe Selo Lyceum in 1820 (that is to say, the next class after Pushkin's). The biographer of Semenov writes, "Thus, in the course of three years (1814–17), Semenov was a witness to the lyceum period of Pushkin's life and was on close, friendly terms with him (they addressed each other using the familiar *ty* [thou]), even though they were not in the same graduating class."[25] During the course of the 1820s and 1830s Pushkin met with Semenov more than once, so that theoretically he might have found out about the incident when it was still fresh, in the spring of 1828.[26] But it is more likely that their conversation on this topic did not take place until the following year. The fact is that, soon after the appearance of the issue of the *Northern Bee* with Pushkin's verses, Semenov, who had come to find the duties of a censor burdensome, received leave "for the improvement of his health" and by the beginning of March had already left for the mineral waters of the Caucasus, where he stayed until November

1828.[27] When Semenov returned to St. Petersburg, Pushkin was gone: he was absent from the capital from 20 October 1828 until 18 January 1829. Around 10 March 1829 Pushkin left St. Petersburg, headed for Moscow, and from there, to the Caucasus and Arzrum.[28] Thus, Pushkin most likely met with Semenov in the interval between the end of January and the beginning of March 1829 (a meeting before a journey to the Caucasus with a person who had just returned from there would have been completely natural), and that was when he found out about the incident that had arisen from the publication of the excerpts from *Eugene Onegin* in the *Northern Bee*. Pushkin replied to the metropolitan's complaint quickly and in an original manner.[29]

Ecclesiastical Readers of Secular Books

At the time of his travels to Arzrum Pushkin began to compose the entries that became his *Travel Notes* (*Putevye zapiski*); these served as the basis for the narrative *Journey to Arzrum* (*Puteshestvie v Arzrum*), but *Travel Notes* does not coincide with *Journey to Arzrum* completely. Pushkin wrote his notes in the so-called first Arzrum notebook, which he took along with him for the trip.[30] One of the lengthiest and most important entries in this notebook, dated 22 May 1829 (and annotated "Vladikavkaz"), is dedicated to the state of the affairs of the Russian Empire in the Northern Caucasus. Pushkin, in analyzing the geopolitical situation in the region, comes to the conclusion that subduing the Caucasian mountaineers through armed conflict is impossible. Therefore he suggests two alternative paths for their "pacification" and integration into the Russian Empire. The first is the dissemination in the Caucasus of the "blessings" (i.e., luxuries) of European civilization. The second is the dissemination of Christianity in the Caucasus through a significant increase in missionary activity. But on this path certain difficulties crop up.

Pushkin's judgments about this question in the preserved manuscript (as opposed to the Academy of Russian Sciences edition of his complete works) appear as follows:[31]

There is after all a means that is more powerful, more moral—more in conformity with the enlightenment of our era {but until now Russia has neglected this means: the preaching of the Gospel}. Patience by itself is a very good thing—but is proselytizing really incompatible with it? Is truth really given only to be kept from the light of day? We are surrounded by peoples [*narody*] crawling around in the darkness of primitive delusions—and as yet not one of us has thought to gird himself up and go with peace and the cross to the poor {tribes} fellows who until now have been bereft of the true light. It is easier for our cold laziness, in place of the living word, to churn out {Tatar} dead letters [*bukvy*] and send mute books to people who do not know how to read.—It is difficult for us to travel among them, undergoing hardships and dangers according to the example of the {ancient Apostles} and the new Rom[an] Cath[olic] missionaries. Hypocrites [*litsemery*]! Is this how you carry out the duty of Christianity—are you Christians?—You should hang your heads and keep silent in contrition and repentance [*s sokrusheniem raskaianiia*]. . . .

. . . Who among you is a man of Faith and Humility, who has become like the holy monks who wander the deserts of Africa, Asia, and America, without shoes, in rags, often without shelter or food—but animated by warm zeal and humble wisdom[.]—What kind of reward awaits them? The salutation of an aged fisherman or a nomadic family of savages, poverty—sometimes hunger—a martyr's death.—We are able {in magnificent cathedrals} {from the quiet pulpit} to sparkle serenely with {wily} magniloquence, {vainly [*tshcheslavno*]} become drunk on the praises of the {secular} audience—We read books and pompously find blameworthy [*predosuditel'nyi*] {places} {words} {utt[erances]} expressions in {secular [*svetskie*]} ephemeral compositions [*suetnye proizvedeniia*].[32]

This entire fragment is endowed with acute topical meaning. The problem of christianization of the Caucasus had acquired particular urgency during the Russo-Turkish War of 1828–29. At the same time, pagan and semipagan peoples of the Caucasus were being actively islamicized, in an effort that was supported in every possible way by the Turks: Islam provided an additional—religious—stimulus for the struggle of the peoples of the Caucasus against the Russian Empire and for rapprochement with the Ottoman Porte.[33] Thus, the christianization of the Caucasian mountaineers was linked to hopes of weakening Turkish influence in the region and of a gradual rapprochement of the Caucasus with Russia. Meanwhile the only Caucasian people among whom Christian missionary work had borne some fruit was the Ossetians. According to the official version, the christianization of the Ossetians had achieved considerable success by the mid-1820s (almost the entire population of Ossetia was considered to have converted to Christianity); in fact, however, the success was modest at best.[34] The majority of the Ossetians were only nominally Christian: in everyday life they preserved pagan beliefs, customs, and religious rites (Pushkin witnessed the archaic Ossetian funeral rite during his journey, and his impressions of this funeral were reflected in his *Travel Notes*, the unfinished narrative poem "Tazit" ["Tazit"], and *Journey to Arzrum*). There was a catastrophic lack of prayer books and competent priests, especially Russian ones: mainly Georgians preached the divine Word to the Ossetians. Worship services in the few Ossetian churches were also conducted in the Georgian language. Among the other peoples of the Northern Caucasus, cases of Christian conversion (even in name only) were literally isolated instances; moreover, these conversions were performed almost exclusively by *Protestant* missionaries—in part, by members of the Scottish mission, which had been founded in the Caucasus by John Paterson, a member of the British Bible Society.

Such is the real-life political and religious background to Pushkin's fragment. Vasilii L. Komarovich has demonstrated that several motifs of this important excerpt are linked with both Pushkin's literary impressions and the historical realia of his epoch: for example, François-René de Chateaubriand's praise of Roman Catholic missionaries and the activities of the Scottish Protestant mission in the Northern Caucasus.[35] However, the central topic of the fragment remains completely unstudied: namely, the topic of Orthodoxy and Orthodox missionary work (or, more accurately, the lack of such work).[36]

Yet there is no doubt that the addressee of Pushkin's invective ("we," the pronoun substituted for the formal "you" of an earlier draft) is the Orthodox clergy, indeed the upper clergy, which determines the politics of the Orthodox Church and serves as its representative. It is precisely the highest-ranking church officials to whom Pushkin addresses his reproach about their evasion of the most important mission standing before the Orthodox Church—the preaching of Christianity amongst the "savages" on the borders of the Russian Empire. Furthermore, the fragment is constructed in such a way that failure to carry out this urgent and important *political* task is interpreted as a shirking of *religious* duty, the duty of a true Christian. The negligent pastors are termed "hypocrites" ("Hypocrites! Is this how you carry out the duty of Christianity?"). This term is a reference to the accusatory words of Jesus Christ in the twenty-third chapter of the Gospel of St. Matthew, which are directed against scribes and Pharisees ("But woe unto you, scribes and Pharisees, hypocrites!"[37]). In enumerating those characteristics that make the priests subject to reproach, Pushkin uses not the general topoi of anticlerical criticism, but very specific, almost portrait-like allusions. Without much difficulty one can discern that the main addressee of Pushkin's accusation here is none other than Metropolitan Philaret. Let us examine these "portrait-like" details, moving from the most easily recognizable (those that lie on the surface of the discourse, so to speak) to the more intimate ones, attesting to Pushkin's close knowledge of the metropolitan's biography.

"We are able {in magnificent cathedrals} {from the quiet pulpit} to sparkle serenely with {wily} magniloquence, {vainly} become drunk on the praises of the {secular} audience." This sentence must have immediately conjured up the image of Metropolitan Philaret in readers' imaginations. Philaret was the most famous church orator of his time. Even at the end of the nineteenth century the sermons (or "words") of Philaret, which had already been published in several editions during Pushkin's life, were regarded as a consummate model. In a standard high school textbook of the time, the following was written about them: "In the words and speeches of Metropolitan Philaret, the language of the sermon displayed a new, unprecedented strength that constitutes the highest level of development of this genre of literature."[38] Philaret's sermons were also valued exceptionally highly in the first third of the nineteenth century. Philaret was the creator of a new style of preaching. He moved away from the scholastic oratory of previous eras and brought the church sermon closer to the language and understanding of the secular "good society." The new sermon style thus brought Philaret success with the secular, as well as the religious, audience. This secular success, as many noted (Viazemsky, as we recall, scathingly), in its turn facilitated his dazzling church career. It is Philaret's qualities as a preacher and the dependence of his position in the church at the time on his *secular* success that Pushkin's lines hint at.

Pushkin's fragment makes other allusions to episodes from Philaret's biography that are not so widely known, but are, perhaps, more painful for him personally: "Not one of us has thought to gird himself up and go with peace and the cross to the poor {tribes} fellows who until now have been bereft of the true light. . . . It is difficult for us to travel among them, undergoing hardships and dangers according to the example of the {ancient Apostles} and the new Rom[an] Cath[olic] missionaries." At first glance, these reproaches do not have a direct relationship to the *Moscow* metropolitan. But only at first glance. By the beginning of the 1820s the position of Philaret in the Russian church seemed to be quite solid. He held the post of archbishop of Moscow and Kolomensk, was the vice president of the Moscow chapter of the Russian Bible Society, and had compiled the catechism of the Russian Orthodox Church, which all literate Russians were supposed to use to study the foundations of the Orthodox religion.

However, in 1824 his position changed abruptly: his patron Prince Aleksei Golitsyn, the minister of public education and religious affairs, was dismissed; work on translating the Bible, which was being conducted with Philaret's active assistance, was stopped, and the catechism Philaret had compiled was forbidden (in part because the sacred texts it contained were written not in Old Church Slavonic but in Russian).[39] Philaret's position was suddenly on shaky ground. His enemies in the Holy Synod went into action. In order to deprive him of his influence in the highest ecclesiastical circles, they suggested that he be removed as far away as possible from both capitals. "The enviers of the Moscow pastor set to work on getting him removed from Moscow to Georgia," the well-informed Nikolai Sushkov explains in his memoirs.[40] A transfer to Georgia in the capacity of exarch of Caucasian Iberia and Imeretia, who had his residence in Tiflis, would have formally been considered a promotion (from the rank of "archbishop" to that of "metropolitan"). But in practical terms, such a move would have been akin to exile and would have meant Philaret's complete loss of influence in the Holy Synod. Therefore Philaret, while outwardly expressing submission to his fate and God's will ("a monk is like a soldier," he subsequently told Sushkov), activated all of his connections and diplomatic talents so as not to end up in the "realm of St. Nina."[41] In particular, he succeeded in enlisting the support of the head of the synod, Metropolitan Seraphim of St. Petersburg and Novgorod, whose relations with Philaret were extraordinarily complex.[42] The bishop of Revel' Grigorii (Postnikov), a student and friend of Philaret, informed him from St. Petersburg on 3 July 1824 that "after all this I'd venture to say that they won't point you the way to Georgia unless they stop obeying the Master" (that is, Seraphim).[43] In any case, Philaret succeeded in keeping his position in Moscow.

Meanwhile, it just so happened that the Ossetian commission, which was charged with the mission of christianizing the Ossetians and other mountain peoples of the Caucasus, was located under the authority of the Iberian (Georgian) exarch. Thus, when he escaped being transferred to Georgia, Philaret also refused the opportunity to carry the "true light" to his "poor fellows" living on the periphery of the Russian Empire. Pushkin's fragment alludes to this circumstance.

Pushkin opposes "the living word" to "dead letters": "It is easier for our cold laziness, in place of the living word, to churn out dead letters and send mute books to people who do not know how to read." This passage is also directly relevant to Philaret. In the Moscow chapter of the Bible Society (where Philaret was the vice president), translations of Holy Writ were published in the languages of the peoples of the Russian Empire. At the time when Philaret managed to escape a transfer to the Caucasus, he was busy preparing for publication an edition of the Bible in Ossetian. On 7 November 1824 Grigorii Postnikov conveyed to Philaret the instructions of Metropolitan Seraphim (who was obliged to serve as the president of the Bible Society, although he considered it harmful): "The Patriarch has ordered me to write to you that he has ordered only six hundred copies of the Ossetian Bible to be printed and that you should not compile any Bible collections."[44] The translation into Ossetian was made from the Georgian language and was to have been printed using the Georgian alphabet (the Ossetians did not have their own writing system). The fate of this Ossetian Bible is unclear; it is not even known whether it was ultimately printed.[45] But in the mid-1820s—also under the aegis of the Moscow Bible Society and of Archbishop Philaret personally—several prayer books were printed in Ossetian, likewise using "Georgian letters," and sent to the Caucasus.[46]

This undertaking was unsuccessful. While conducting an inspection of Ossetia in 1847, Vladimir S. Tolstoi reported that "the church service proceeded in Georgian. An attempt had been made to print an Ossetian translation using the Georgian alphabet, but it resulted in sounds that no one could understand."[47] In speaking of "dead letters" sent to people who could not read, Pushkin most likely had in mind either the ill-fated Ossetian translation of the Bible or the Ossetian prayer books that had been published by the Moscow printing press under Philaret's supervision. The correction Pushkin made to his text is noteworthy: first he wrote "Tatar letters," then corrected "Tatar" to "dead." Probably this change was made not only for the sake of an effective antithetical construction ("the living word—dead letters") but also to correct a mistake: the Ossetian prayer books were printed not in Tatar letters, but Georgian ones.

How could Pushkin have known these obscure biographical details about Philaret, including the circumstances of his would-be career in the Caucasus? Pushkin could have found competent informants in both St. Petersburg and Moscow. However, he might have already learned several important pieces of information during the period of his Mikhailovskoe exile. In May and September 1825 Pushkin visited the archbishop of Pskov, Evgenii (Kazantsev), several times.[48] Archbishop Evgenii had a gift for literature and was a longtime friend of Philaret;

he was also a great enthusiast of the Bible Society and of translating the Bible into new languages. Conversations between Pushkin and Evgenii (who met the poet cordially) could not have avoided touching on the current situation in the Orthodox Church, a situation that worried the archbishop deeply. Indeed, this topic, which occupied the minds of all educated members of society at the time, was of particular personal interest to Pushkin himself: his exile to Mikhailovskoe had been prompted by an incautious remark about atheism in a private letter. His fate in many ways would depend on the future course of church politics. Evgenii would have been unable to reassure Pushkin in this respect (he himself abandoned the Pskov diocese at the end of 1825 and left for Siberia so as to distance himself from the troubles in the church), but he could have informed the poet of certain details of the dramatic events that were transpiring, including details related to the intrigue against Philaret.

We have come to the sentence that crowns Pushkin's denunciation of hypocritical clergymen, the key to the entire passage: "We read books and pompously find blameworthy expressions in ephemeral compositions." In Pushkin scholarship until now, this statement has not received a coherent interpretation—more precisely, it has received no attention at all. And this is unsurprising, since the historical context of the statement remained unknown. But now we do know that context: it is the complaint Philaret lodged against Pushkin with the authorities in February 1828. And the phrase "blameworthy expressions in ephemeral compositions" (Pushkin, as is evident from the original manuscript, sought the needed words for a long time) refers to the notorious jackdaws on the crosses in the seventh chapter of *Eugene Onegin*. Incidentally, the formulation that Pushkin settled upon in the end ("blameworthy expressions") allows one to reconstruct Philaret's complaint with a certain level of confidence: the metropolitan, ostensibly, was disturbed not by Pushkin's accurate reflection of the Moscow landscape but precisely by his *expression*, which profanely united the sacred symbol of salvation with base, filthy creatures on a single semantic plane.

The formula "*ephemeral* compositions" (which replaced the original phrase "*secular* compositions," apparently to avoid an overly transparent allusion to the recent occurrence) is also significant. This is because in 1828 two sets of regulations were confirmed practically at the same moment—the new Censorship Statute (one of the most liberal in the history of Russia; great hopes were pinned on it at that time) and the Ecclesiastical Censorship Statute. These laws clearly delineated the functions of the civil ("secular") and ecclesiastical censorship: the latter oversaw only ecclesiastical literature and works by secular authors that were devoted to specifically religious (i.e., eternal) and church-related topics. *Eugene Onegin* obviously did not belong to this category. In using the phrase "ephemeral compositions," Pushkin rather transparently pointed to the fact that his ecclesiastical critic, having taken on himself the function of a voluntary literary censor, had exceeded the authority accorded to him by the law.

Meanwhile the archpriest-censor, having dodged missionary work in the Caucasus that was necessary to Russia's interests and having narrowly avoided donning a martyr's crown, should have found it incumbent on himself to refrain from judging jackdaws in ephemeral works by secular writers and instead should have "hung his head and kept silent in contrition and repentence." Such was the meaning of Pushkin's first answer to Metropolitan Philaret, composed in May 1829.

On the Path to Print

Pushkin conceived of his 1829 *Travel Notes* not as a private diary but as a text intended for publication (the complex narrative structure and intensive stylistic revisions attest to this fact). Likewise, its printing was intended as a response to Philaret, though it masqueraded as reflections on missionary work and the Orthodox clergy in general. Pushkin's desire to publish his answer to Philaret can be explained first of all by his ongoing battle to preserve his special literary status. Already at his first meeting with Pushkin in September 1826, Nicholas I had promised to become his personal censor.[49] Pushkin (like the majority of his contemporaries) regarded the tsar's promise as a privilege. The tsar had no higher authority over himself and therefore had no reason to forbid one or another work out of fear of repercussions from those authorities. Moreover, Pushkin reckoned that general awareness of his extraordinary relationship with the tsar would help his "minor" works (which he published in newspapers and journals) pass through the regular censorship more easily.[50] For a relatively long time, Pushkin supposed—mistakenly, as it later became clear—that he was not required to submit these minor works to the tsar for preliminary approval but could send them directly to the press according to the normal procedure. Pushkin must have regarded the complaint of Metropolitan Philaret as an attempt by the church to appear in the role of yet another controlling body, operating alongside both the regular censorship and the special censorship of the tsar. Pushkin could not have evaluated this attempt as anything other than an encroachment on the—already extremely narrow—zone of literary freedom allowed to him. His answer was supposed to teach the metropolitan a lesson and, if possible, prevent the church from making any further incursions into the literary arena.

The political atmosphere of the first five years of Nicholas's reign (that is to say the second half of the 1820s) justified Pushkin's belief that his sharp criticism of the clergy was in accordance with the aims of the highest governmental authorities. During this time, the emperor was bent on suppressing the claims of the church hierarchs to an independent role in society and in government; in fact, in an effort to circumvent their achieving their goals, he attempted to establish rigid government control over the church. Thus, between 1826 and 1829, the role of the civil servant in the Holy Synod, the chief procurator, was dramatically strengthened: ministerial powers were attached to the procurator's position by a great number of special resolutions. Meanwhile, the position of the ecclesiastical members of the synod, that is of the highest church officials, was significantly weakened.[51]

Finally, Nicholas I had not forgotten that the members of the Decembrist secret society had planned to include Philaret in the interim revolutionary government that they would establish after their seizure of power. In the report by the Commission of Inquiry it was noted that one of the ideologues of the conspiracy, Gavriil Baten'kov, "intended to designate as members of this government *one ecclesiastical personage*, himself, and, after some time, a third—Prince Sergei Trubetskoi."[52] The "ecclesiastical personage" in question was Philaret. The secret supplement to the report that was submitted to Nicholas indicated further plans to invite Nikolai Mordvinov, Mikhail Speransky, and several other figures into the revolutionary government, but the printed text of the report included only the allusion to Philaret—a fairly transparent allusion, since no other high ecclesiastical official aspired to a governmental role. These facts are indicative of the emperor's particular guardedness with respect to the Moscow metropolitan. For Nicholas it was unimportant whether or not Philaret had been let into the conspiracy (in fact, he had not); more important was the very fact of the conspirators' selection of him: this meant that they viewed him as an ambitious man whose potential willingness to take part in the government that would oust the tsar was beyond a doubt.

The recently created Third Section, the highest organ of police surveillance, was closely attuned to (and, to a certain extent, stimulated by) the disposition of Nicholas. This organ also mediated Pushkin's access to the tsar. In those years there was a kind of rivalry between the

Third Section and the church for the right of primary control over public morality and, accordingly, for influence over the tsar. Therefore the secret police strove to arouse in Nicholas a guarded distrust of the clergy. In the first ever annual analysis of Russians' political views, *A Brief Survey of Public Opinion for 1827* (presented by the Third Section to Nicholas at the very beginning of 1828), one of the reasons for the public's goodwill toward the new emperor was declared to be "the removal of women and priests from any harmful influence on the affairs and fate of individual persons."[53] (This was an obvious allusion to the late Alexander I; it was generally believed that his policies had been harmfully influenced first by the mystically inclined Baroness Kriudener, then by members of the Bible Society, and finally by the fanatical Orthodox archimandrite Photius). In the same *Brief Survey* the clergy as a whole was portrayed as an extremely disloyal and even dangerous estate: "The clergy in general governs itself poorly and is pervaded by a harmful spirit [*vrednyi dukh*]. In most cases priests spread bad news and disseminate ideas of freedom among the people."[54] Society was well aware of the authorities' negative disposition toward the clergy, and Pushkin could not have failed to know of it as well.

Moreover, by the very structure of his text, Pushkin had insured himself against possible new denunciations by Philaret. For in order to lodge an official complaint with the appropriate body, the Moscow metropolitan would be obliged to indicate *exactly which* features of Pushkin's depiction of a hypocritical clergyman had evoked his displeasure and thus struck him as *personally* insulting. In other words, Philaret would have to verify the accuracy of Pushkin's unflattering literary portrait of himself. Clever Philaret would never fall into such a trap. Instead, he would have to endure silently the offense to his pride and, in future, refrain from pestering Pushkin over trifles so as to avoid any further unpleasant incidents. At least this is how Pushkin himself must have viewed the matter.

At the beginning of January 1830 Pushkin began to prepare a large excerpt of his *Travel Notes* for a new edition of Baron Anton Del'vig's *Literary Gazette* (*Literaturnaia gazeta*), in which he was intimately involved. The fragment about the Caucasus containing Pushkin's sharp critique of the Orthodox clergy was chosen for inclusion (it would appear in print under the title "Georgian Military Road" ["Voennaia gruzinskaia doroga"]). Before rewriting the text and sending it to the censor, however, Pushkin had revised it in his Arzrum notebook. Ianina Levkovich has given the following precise description of this earlier editorial work: "When working on the article 'Georgian Military Road' in 1829, Pushkin used his diary as a foundation. Several words, phrases, and paragraphs that he considered inadmissible in the article were crossed out in the diary. He indicated his removal of these segments in most cases uniformly, with a few slanted strokes that were sometimes almost perpendicular to the line of text. In this way he preserved unspoiled the initial textual variant, which in the given instance he did not have need of. He also reformulated a few places in the text from scratch."[55] In the fragment dedicated to the task of christianizing the Caucasus, Pushkin made two significant cuts. First, he crossed out the entire sentence about the fact that Russia does not carry out any missionary work among its "poor fellows" (from "We are surrounded by peoples" to "who until now have been bereft of the true light"): this assertion contradicted too obviously the official declaration of a successful christianization of the Caucasus. Second, he crossed out the sentence in which active Catholic missionaries are contrasted with lazy Orthodox clergymen: at the end of the 1820s the anti-Catholic tendencies in Nicholas's church policies had intensified.[56] In this atmosphere, setting up Catholics as an example to the Orthodox was, of course, out of place.

Pushkin's revisions during the first stage of preparation of the text for publication were mainly limited to these two significant changes. Hence the final version of the article that he eventually submitted to the censor appears all the more unexpected: in it, the entire discussion of prospects for christianizing the Caucasus had been replaced with just *two sentences*: "The Caucasus awaits Christian missionaries. But it is easier for us in our laziness, in place of the living word, to churn out dead letters and send mute books to people who do not know how to read!" The accusations against the Russian clergy present in the earlier version of the text had been omitted. In order to understand what it was that led Pushkin to so radically alter his text, it is necessary to keep in mind that it was precisely during the short interval of time between his revision of the manuscript in the Arzrum notebook and his preparation of the article for the censorship that Pushkin became acquainted with Metropolitan Philaret's response to his poem "A vain gift, a chance gift." This circumstance played a decisive role in the events that followed.

What Did Philaret Read in Pushkin's Poem?

Elizaveta Khitrovo made Philaret aware of Pushkin's poem, judging by everything we know, at the very beginning of January 1830.[57] There is practically no doubt that she showed (and perhaps even gave) Philaret not Pushkin's manuscript but the almanac *Northern Flowers for 1830* (*Severnye tsvety na 1830 god*), published by Del'vig; in it Pushkin's poem was published for the first time. (This almanac, having received the censor's approval on 20 December 1829, appeared in print at the very end of December.) On page 98 of *Northern Flowers* Philaret read the following:

Дар напрасный, дар случайной,
Жизнь, зачем ты мне дана?
Иль зачем судьбою тайной
Ты на казнь осуждена?

Кто меня враждебной властью
Из ничтожества воззвал,
Душу мне наполнил страстью,
Ум сомненьем взволновал? . . .

Цели нет передо мною:
Сердце пусто, празден ум,
И томит меня тоскою
Однозвучный жизни шум.

[A vain gift, a chance gift, life, for what purpose have you been given to me? Or for what purpose has a secret destiny condemned you to torture? Who has summoned me from nothingness with inimical power, has filled my soul with passion, has disturbed my mind with doubt? . . . There is no goal before me: my heart is empty, my mind is idle, and the monotonous hubbub of life wearies me with its melancholy.]

According to Nepomniashchy, Philaret detected in these lines something horrifying: the poem "is an attempt at spiritual suicide"; by "inimical power" Pushkin means the power of the Creator; the verses of Pushkin are "mutinous and blasphemous"; "the poem anticipates the mutiny of Ivan Karamazov, who returns his 'ticket' to God."[58] Nepomniashchy's epigones, naturally, share his opinion.

Mark Al'tshuller, an American author of Russian extraction, has given a different but in essence even more radical interpretation of Pushkin's poem: "The poet expresses doubt about the existence of God.

Life is not a divine gift to man, but a chance, perhaps even meaningless phenomenon of being. The second stanza is pierced through with agnosticism. To the question of *who* created the soul and mind of man, and why is man mortal (condemned to torture), the poet has no answer. From this follows the rejection of a teleological approach to the world, and of the idea of the divine predestination of humanity."[59]

In his recent book on Pushkin's lyric poetry, Andrew Kahn does not associate himself completely with any of the widespread interpretations of "A vain gift, a chance gift," but he does perceive in Pushkin's poem a serious retreat from the Orthodox conception of the world: "Whether or not line 6 (and specifically the word *nichtozhestvo*) is deliberately meant to echo Voltaire's deist discussion of the creation of matter from the nothing ('le néant'), or atheistic usage, the effect is the same. . . . The position suggests skepticism if not outright atheism."[60]

If one is to accept such interpretations as accurate, then one can only wonder why Philaret, who had been affronted by the lack of a proper bed in a seventeenth-century monastery cell and by the mention of jackdaws on the crosses of Moscow churches, displayed in this case a surprising tolerance: not only did he not "grind Pushkin into dust" (although, in the opinion of Nepomniashchy, he might have done so!), but he even entered into a poetic correspondence with him. Although Nepomniashchy explains the metropolitan's mild reaction to Pushkin's blasphemous verses by way of reference to the exceptional spiritual sagacity of the prelate and his deep understanding of Pushkin's importance for Russia, it seems that everything can in fact be explained far more simply: Philaret did not find—and could not have found—in Pushkin's verses all those dangerous meanings that have been detected in them by Pushkinists of the twentieth and early twenty-first century.

Recent and current scholars, who have focused on close analysis of the poem, have been unintentionally diverted from its historical context. Nevertheless, it is impossible to imagine that Pushkin, having barely escaped exile to Siberia (or at least believing he could be exiled) as a result of his blasphemous narrative poem *The Gabrieliad* (*Gavriiliada*), would have decided to publish either a theomachistic or an atheistic work. And it is even harder to imagine that such a blasphemous composition would have been approved by the censor (the poem had to pass through the regular censorship, along with the other materials in the almanac). Yet the poem not only successfully passed the censorship but was later reprinted in the third part of *Poems of Alexander Pushkin* (*Stikhotvoreniia Aleksandra Pushkina* [1832])—this was *after* Philaret composed his answer—and was even included in all posthumous collections of Pushkin's works, including those that were published during the periods of harshest censorship![61]

What then was Pushkin's poem really about, and what did Metropolitan Philaret see in it? Above all, the metropolitan understood correctly to whom the poem's main questions and reproaches were addressed—that is, he understood the identity of the one who had "summoned [the poet] from nothingness" (iz nechtozhestva vozzval). But what does "nothingness" mean here? Nepomniashchy, Al'tshuller, Kahn, and Vadim Liapunov all presume that the word is used in the sense of "nonexistence."[62] Only God can call forth life from nonbeing; hence, in these scholars' view, the poem's addressee is God himself.

The word "nothingness" (nichtozhestvo) in the sense of "nonexistence, nonbeing" does of course occur in Pushkin's works.[63] But this is far from the only meaning of this word in Pushkin's poetic lexicon. At around the same time he wrote "A vain gift, a chance gift," Pushkin was also working on his novel *The Blackamoor of Peter the Great* (*Arap Petra Velikogo*). This novel (which he left unfinished) is based on historical material but it also indisputably contains autobiographical projections: the fate of Pushkin's ancestor Abram Gannibal is made to correspond in many respects to the fate of Alexander Pushkin himself. In the first chapter of the novel, Gannibal, a young Negro, finding himself in Parisian society by the will of fate, suffers from the fact that the Parisians are attracted only to his "otherness," his dissimilarity to the people around him: "He felt that for them he was a species of some kind of rare beast [*zver'*], a creature [*tvoren'e*] that was special [*osobennyi*], foreign [*chuzhoi*], accidentally brought over into their society although he had nothing in common with them. He even envied people whom no one noticed and considered their nothingness [*nichtozhestvo*] to be a sign of their well-being."[64] Here the word "nothingness" is used in the sense of "total unremarkableness, insignificance, mediocrity." The word is used twice with a similar meaning in the 1827 "The Poet" ("Poet"). Until Apollo has called the poet to serve, he may lead a life that is in every way unremarkable, ordinary, mediocre, remaining indistinguishable from the masses: "And among the insignificant children of the world, perhaps he was the most insignificant of all" (I sred' detei *nichtozhnykh* mira / Byt' mozhet, vsekh *nichtozhnei* on).[65]

In these contexts, the word "nothingness" is not used to mean "nonbeing" but rather "insignificance," which is how it is used in "A vain gift, a chance gift." Consequently, the poem's reproaches are addressed not to the one who gave life to the lyric hero of the poem but to the one who distinguished this life from an "ordinary" life, filled it with passions, doubts, and, as a result, sufferings. And this "somebody," of course, cannot be God. The late Mikhail F. Mur'ianov was one of the few scholars who correctly identified the addressee of Pushkin's reproaches (although unfortunately his observation has gone unnoticed by the majority of Pushkinists): "Let us turn our attention to one detail that has escaped the attention of literary historians who have written about this poem: the 'who' under question in the second stanza is not the biblical God, but his antipode; only the power of the latter is *inimical* [*vrazhdebnyi*]; it was he that created the first *doubt* [*somnenie*], the cause of original sin."[66] It is impossible not to agree with this observation. And thus, not God, but infernal, demonic forces appear in Pushkin's poem as the cause of his "torture" (kazn')—that agonizing state in which the lyric subject abides. And therefore, the main question is this: how does a person come to find himself at the mercy of secret infernal, demonic powers?

The theme of a destructive, demonic principle present in the life of modern man had first appeared in Pushkin's work in 1823, in the poem "The Demon" ("Demon").[67] "A vain gift, a chance gift" is closely connected to this work, as Faddei Bulgarin perceptively pointed out in a review of *Northern Flowers for 1830*: "This last piece is a brilliant inspiration, similar to the one that goes by the title 'The Demon.' First rate!"[68] But even after "A vain gift, a chance gift," Pushkin did not leave this theme behind: he went on to compose several more poems with similar thematic motifs: these include the 1829–30 "The Devils" ("Besy") and the 1830 "Verses Written at Night during Insomnia" ("Stikhi, sochinennye noch'iu vo vremia bessonitsy"). These texts are connected to "A vain gift, a chance gift" along various parameters (ranging from the poems' system of images and motif structure to their meter); thus, there is a basis for examining these three works as a kind of lyric cycle.[69]

Philaret, doubtless, did not detect in Pushkin's poem either atheism or theomachy. He saw something else: a lack of trust in God and his providence, a lack of faith in his constant care for humanity. And the metropolitan answered the questions posed by Pushkin in accordance with the Orthodox Church's teachings on such matters. Here is Philaret's poem, as it was published in the almanac *Little Star* (*Zvezdochka*):

Не напрасно, не случайно
Жизнь от Бога мне дана;
Не без воли Бога тайной
И на казнь осуждена.

Сам я своенравной властью
Зло из темных бездн воззвал,
Душу сам наполнил страстью,
Ум сомненьем взволновал.

Вспомнись мне, Забытый мною!
Просияй сквозь мрачных дум!
И созиждется Тобою
Сердце чисто, правый ум![70]

[Not vainly, not by chance is life given to me by God; nor is it condemned to torture outside God's secret will. I myself with capricious power summoned evil from the dark abyss, I myself filled my soul with passion, disturbed my mind with doubt. Remember yourself to me, One Forgotten by me! Shine through gloomy thoughts! And by You will be created a pure heart, a righteous mind!]

Philaret's poem is written from Pushkin's point of view, but this is the viewpoint of a "corrected" Pushkin, who has come to understand the deep reasons for his confusion and pessimism and has finally found a way out from the blind alley. The metropolitan himself called his answer a "parody of Pushkin's verses" (much like the Russian formalists, he did not link the concept of "parody" with comical content). In his poem to Pushkin, Philaret did not resort to sophisticated theological arguments. His answer imparts the basic principles of the Christian catechism—the elementary introduction to the Orthodox lessons of faith.

According to the catechism, among the thirteen sins against the First Commandment (including the most serious sin, atheism, which Philaret did not find in Pushkin's poem) is lack of faith in God (neverie): "when men, who admit the existence of God, disbelieve his providence and his revelation."[71] The complete and final stage of "lack of faith" is deism: that is, religion minus the principle of divine grace. However, as attested to in many of Philaret's own writings, between true faith and deism there is an intermediate stage—skepticism (maloverie). There are two paths away from this sin: one leads to deism (and even atheism), the other to true faith. In order to go along the second, correct path, one must rid oneself of another sin, "trusting in man" (chelovekonadeianie): "when anyone trusts in his own means and strength, or in the means and strength of others, and not in the mercy and help of God."[72]

Philaret had already had the occasion to express similar ideas in conversations with laymen. Nikolai Sushkov's story is notable in this regard; this man of letters, fairly well known in his time and a friend of Pushkin, had told of his soul-saving conversations with Philaret in the fall of 1828 (for taking part in a duel in which a man was killed, Sushkov had been sentenced to a two-year church penance). The themes and arguments that Philaret developed in these conversations coincided in many ways with the verses he addressed to Pushkin. A person's suffering is not the result of his abandonment by God but of pride and excessive confidence in himself. God sends humans trials precisely as a consequence of this extreme self-reliance: "The Omniscient God has no need of trials, but trials are necessary strictly and only for us. They reveal to us our insignificance [*nichtozhestvo*], humble our pride, restrain our passions, teach us patience, lead us to humility and obedience to the divine will" (compare this statement with Philaret's lines "Nor is it [life] condemned to torture outside God's secret will" [Ne bez voli Boga tainoi / I na kazn' obrechena]). God permits humans to become lost, to believe boldly in their own strength, but behind this permission a higher design is always hidden: "God's permissiveness grants our own free will to us. It is here that we discover, often via bitter experience, that it is dangerous to give ourselves over to our will" (again, compare Philaret's lines "I myself with capricious power summoned evil from the dark abyss" [Sam ia svoenravnoi vlast'iu / Zlo iz temnykh bezdn vozzval]). Human beings who have become receptive to the good as a result of their trials must recognize their own weakness and turn to God for help: "In everything it is best to depend on the will of God"; the desire to overcome temptation is given to "everyone who, not relying on himself, searches for it in prayer, patiently, humbly and wisely" (compare "Remember yourself to me, One Forgotten by me!" [Vspomnis' mne, Zabytyi mnoiu!]).[73] What Philaret said to Pushkin, he might have said to any secular person of weak faith.

To Whom Was Pushkin Speaking in His Answer to Philaret?

Philaret's poem became known to Pushkin in the first half of January 1830 through the offices, once again, of Elizaveta Khitrovo.[74] It prompted Pushkin to take several important steps.

Most importantly, Philaret's verses created a completely new context for the passage about the clergy in Pushkin's article "Georgian Military

Road," which he had prepared for publication in the *Literary Gazette*. The appearance of Philaret's verses gave the "anticlerical" fragment of this article a totally new meaning that drastically diverged from Pushkin's original intention. The poet could not fail to realize that now his criticism of hypocritical ecclesiastical figures who read secular books and find in them "blameworthy expressions" would be linked not with the little-publicized incident that had occurred two years earlier in regard to the jackdaws on crosses, *but with Philaret's just-published poem*. Pushkin's criticism would unavoidably be read, both by the public and by the metropolitan himself, as a response to Philaret's poem. This outcome would be unfavorable for Pushkin to the highest degree: it would appear that Pushkin had responded to Philaret's summons to seek God's help for the salvation of his soul by recommending that the metropolitan not butt in with his sermons but instead mind his own business: preaching the divine Word to savage peoples. Under the circumstances, even if the censor were to approve Pushkin's text, there would be no need for Philaret to lodge another complaint against Pushkin with the Third Section. Beyond a doubt, the opinions of both society and the authorities would be on the side of the metropolitan, and everyone would see cynical freethinking (vol'nodumstvo) in Pushkin's behavior. This turn of events would have had lamentable consequences for the poet's future.

Therefore, Pushkin made a decision that was unavoidable but natural under the circumstances: he simply excluded from his already revised article the attack on the clergy that contained allusions to Philaret. This was done, judging by the available evidence, around the middle of January; the manuscript of Pushkin's article, in which the segment in question *was already absent*, reached the hands of the censor Serbinovich on 17 January 1830.[75] The article "Georgian Military Road" was printed in the eighth number of the *Literary Gazette* on 5 February. But Pushkin did not limit himself to this one gesture.

Philaret's poem, which was most likely intended benevolently, was not unthreatening for Pushkin in the situation in which he found himself at the beginning of 1830. Not long before, in 1828, the dangerous *Gabrieliad* affair had run its course. To the best of our knowledge, in a confidential letter to the tsar, the poet had admitted his authorship of the blasphemous poem but had provided a false date of composition—1817. It was important that he relegate all of his sins and "blasphemies" to the distant past.[76] He strove to assure the authorities that between Pushkin of the *present day* and Pushkin of the *past* there was absolutely nothing in common. Pushkin wanted to avoid appearing before the authorities not only as an atheist but even as a "skeptic" (malover): what another person might have easily gotten away with could seriously harm Pushkin, whose behavior was watched with heightened attention. Besides, Pushkin could not be completely sure that the metropolitan would limit himself to composing poetry and would not resort to the genre of denunciation that he had sampled once already. In a word, it was in Pushkin's best interest to ensure that Philaret's poem did not cause any damage. Pushkin escaped from this predicament with great poetic wit.

No sooner had Pushkin submitted the manuscript of his article "Georgian Military Road" to the censor than he wrote a poetic answer to Metropolitan Philaret, which appeared in the twelfth number of the very same *Literary Gazette* on 25 February under the title "Stanzas" ("Stantsy"):

В часы забав иль праздной скуки,
Бывало, лире я моей
Вверял изнеженные звуки
Безумства, лени и страстей.

Но и тогда струны лукавой
Невольно звон я прерывал,
Когда твой голос величавый
Меня внезапно поражал.

Я лил потоки слез нежданных,
И ранам совести моей
Твоих речей благоуханных
Отраден чистый был елей.

И ныне с высоты духовной
Мне руку простираешь ты,
И силой кроткой и любовной
Смиряешь буйные мечты.

Твоим огнем душа палима
Отвергла мрак земных сует,
И внемлет арфе серафима
В священном ужасе поэт.

[In times of leisure or idle boredom, it would happen that I would confide the delicate sounds of madness, indolence, and passion to my lyre. But even then I would interrupt the sound of the sly string involuntarily, when your majestic voice would suddenly strike me. I poured out streams of unexpected tears, and the pure balm of your fragrant speeches soothed the wounds of my conscience. And now from a spiritual height you extend your hand to me, and with a gentle and loving strength you quiet my stormy fantasies. Scorched by your fire, my soul has rejected the gloom of earthly vanities, and the poet harkens to the harp of the seraph in sacred terror.]

If one assumes that the addressee of these verses ("you" [ty]) is Metropolitan Philaret (which indeed most critics do), then a series of puzzles arises. All of these elevated images—the pure balm of fragrant speeches; streams of unexpected tears; the hand stretched out from a spiritual height; the soul scorched by fire—are too powerful to be used in relation to any mortal. Even in Pushkin's 1826 poem "Stanzas" ("In the hope of glory and goodness") ("Stansy" ["V nadezhde slavy i dobra"]), addressed to Emperor Nicholas, there had been nothing of this kind. Furthermore, if one takes into account the fact that, only recently, Pushkin had voiced an opinion about this same personage that was far less flattering, then one would have to recognize the poem as some sort of monument to hypocrisy that fulfilled, at best, purely tactical objectives. Yet Pushkin himself had a completely different perspective on this poem: it was not by chance that he included it in a collection of his poetry and later planned to include it in his complete works. On the other hand, all these paradoxes can be avoided if one recognizes the much more reasonable explanation that this poem, which was *inspired* by the verses of Metropolitan Philaret, in fact has another addressee. That addressee is God.[77]

In his explanation of the genesis of "Stanzas" ("In times of leisure"), Petr A. Viazemsky wrote that Pushkin "was savaged [*byl zadran*] by the verses of His Grace."[78] The correct interpretation of this comment is that Pushkin felt *provoked*. In other words, he decided to enter into a poetic contest with Philaret in that same poetic form that Philaret himself had dictated. Philaret, who loved to write poetry and had been good at it since his youth, had converted the romantic elegiac reflection of Pushkin's original into a semblance of a neoclassical spiritual ode in praise of God's wisdom. His poem ended, in accordance with the genre conventions of the spiritual ode, with a direct address to God. Pushkin accepted this literary challenge. In his rejoinder to the metropolitan, he too used the conventions of the spiritual ode.

The attributes of God accompany the very first appearance of the addressee ("you") in the poem: "But even then I would interrupt the sound of the sly string involuntarily, when your majestic voice would suddenly strike me." Scholars sometimes relate the phrase "your majestic voice" directly to Metropolitan Philaret (and even attempt to explain which particular sermons Pushkin has in mind), but these words could hardly refer to the metropolitan; all his contemporaries unanimously attest that Philaret had not a majestic (velichavyi) voice but a quiet and weak one. For example: "Anyone who has ever heard Philaret of Moscow, whether performing a Liturgy, preaching in church, or conversing somewhere or other, will affirm that he always, since his youth and even from the pulpit of the Ecclesiastical Academy, spoke not with a loud voice but quietly and, at the same time, very precisely. Indeed he did not like noisy talk or loud conversation at all."[79] No, the "majestic voice" is not the voice of Philaret but that of God, as described, for example, in the book of Job: "Hear attentively the noise of his voice, and the sound [that] goeth out of his mouth. . . . After it a voice roareth: he thundereth with the voice of his excellency; and he will not stay them when his voice is heard" (37:4). The Old Church Slavonic text of this biblical passage reveals an especially close lexical link with Pushkin's phrasing: "After it a voice roareth, he thundereth in the *voice* of his *majesty*" (Vsled ego vozopiet glasom, vozgremit *glasom velichiia* svoego) (emphasis added).

In the poem's third stanza allusions to the New Testament have begun to predominate: "And the pure balm of your fragrant speeches soothed the wounds of my conscience." God as the healer of spiritual wounds is a common topos of both church sermons and religious poetry (compare the address to God in Fedor Glinka's poem "Repentance" ["Raskaian'e"]: "Send me happiness from Your heavens and heal the wounds of my heart" [Poshli s Tvoikh nebes mne radost' / I rany serdtsa zazhivi]). "Pure balm" is an allusion to Christ's parable about the Good Samaritan (Luke 10:30–37). According to the church fathers, the Samaritan who relieves suffering with balm is an image of Christ himself. Therefore, the "speeches" in Pushkin's poem, like the soothing "balm," are Jesus's words that are captured in the Gospels. Such an interpretation of these lines in Pushkin's text is supported by his much later characterization of the Gospel as a sweet "book" in his article on the Italian poet Silvio Pellico (1836): "And such is its eternal delight, that if we, surfeited by the world or dragged down by despair, happen to open it, then we have not the strength to resist its sweet attraction, and we plunge our souls into its divine oratory."[80] The unusual formulation "fragrant speeches" most likely has its source in Francis of Assisi's "Second Letter to the Faithful." In it this same epithet is applied to the words of Jesus Christ: "Since I am the servant of all, I am obliged to serve all and to administer to them *the fragrant words of my Lord*."[81]

The semantic culmination of the poem is found in the fourth stanza: "And now from a spiritual height you extend your hand to me, and with a gentle and loving strength you quiet my stormy fantasies." This stanza contains several levels of biblical and liturgical allusion. The first allusion is to Psalm 143 (Psalm 144 in the Western tradition), which has been rewritten in verse form by many Russian poets: "Send thine hand from above; rid me, and deliver me out of great waters" (Posli ruku tvoiu s vysoty, izmi mia i izbavi mia ot vod mnogikh [Psalms 144:7]). The second allusion (especially important in the given context), is to the Gospel story about Jesus walking on water as if it were dry land, saving Peter and quieting the storm:

> And in the fourth watch of the night Jesus went unto them, walking on the sea. And when the disciples saw him walking on the sea, they were troubled, saying, "It is a spirit"; and they cried out for fear. But straightaway Jesus spake unto them, saying, "Be of good cheer; it is I; be not afraid." And Peter answered him and said, "Lord, if it be thou, bid me come unto thee on the water." And he said, "Come." And when Peter was come down out of the ship, he walked on the water, to go to Jesus. But when he saw the wind boisterous, he was afraid; and beginning to sink, he cried, saying, "Lord, save me." And immediately Jesus stretched forth his hand [*I abie Iusus" proster" ruku*] and caught him, and said unto him, "O thou of little faith, wherefore didst thou doubt?" And when they were come into the ship, the wind ceased. (Matthew 14:25–32)

The third allusion is liturgical. In a prayer that was read at the worship service at the beginning of the Lenten fast, the priest asked God to forgive his "servants who are repenting of their sins, known and unknown, intended and unintended." This request was illustrated by a relevant image from the Gospel: "*Stretch forth Thy right hand*, and receive them, *as Thou didst receive him who was drowning in the sea*, and strengthen them against the agitation of demons: cleanse their souls and bodies of all filth."[82] It is possible that there is also a fourth allusion to several statements of Metropolitan Philaret himself. Nikolai Sushkov, in his memoirs about his conversations with Metropolitan Philaret, includes a characteristic dialogue that addresses the meaning of the trials sent to humans by God:

PHILARET: Even the Apostles underwent trials. Peter would have drowned in the sea, *if the Lord had not stretched forth his hand to him*; several of the disciples took fright at the storm.
SUSHKOV: What's miraculous in the fact that they took fright? And what does this prove?
PHILARET: It proves that their faith was still not firm. The trial prevented them from the sin of dangerous self-assurance.[83]

There is a very high probability that the metropolitan might also have used this explanatory allusion to the Gospel episode in his conversation with Elizaveta Khitrovo about Pushkin's poem.

And thus, it is God himself (and not Philaret!) who, with his "gentle and loving strength" quiets the poet's "stormy fantasies"—that is to say, his destructive delusions—just as Christ once quieted the blustering waves.[84] And it is his outstretched hand that extracts the poet from the waves of delusion, just as he saved the Apostle Peter. God's attributes are displayed, at last, in the poem's concluding stanza: "Scorched by your fire, my soul has rejected the gloom of earthly vanities." The image of divine fire that scorches the soul refers back to the Old Testament, and also to the Gospels and the Epistles of the Apostles: "Is not My word like as a fire?" (Jeremiah 23:29); "I am come to send fire on the earth; and what will I, if it be already kindled?" (Luke 12:49); "For our God is a consuming fire" (Hebrews 12:29).

It stands to reason that Pushkin's poem cannot serve as a biographical document. To draw the conclusion that Pushkin was experiencing "penitential feelings" on the basis of this poetic text would be the same as using verses from his "Imitations of the Koran" ("Podrazhaniia Koranu")—"The earth is motionless; the vaults of heaven, O Creator, were placed by Thee" (Zemlia nedvizhna; neba svody, / Tvorets, postavleny toboi)—to form an idea of the poet's understanding of cosmogony in the mid-1820s. On the contrary, Pushkin's poem functioned as the solution to an important tactical problem. In it, Pushkin demonstrated to Philaret that, first of all, he had never forgotten about God, and secondly, that the metropolitan's poem had given the poet occasion once again to marvel at the wisdom, omniscience, and mercy of the Lord, which had been revealed through his servant (the seraph in the poem—a heavenly envoy who reveals the divine truth to mortals—is an elegant allusion to the metropolitan). In this way, Pushkin shifted the poetic dialogue away from the slippery theme of faith and lack of faith to that of the constant presence of the Deity in the life of the poet: that is, to the theme of the poet's *divine election.*

Philaret's verses thus served as the basis for Pushkin's creation of a new poetic text that was organically linked with one of the central themes of his poetry in the second half of the 1820s: the sacred nature of poetry, the poet's higher calling.[85] This theme is present in a number of poems of that period, including the 1826 "The Prophet" (the link between this poem and "In times of leisure" has been remarked by scholars more than once), the 1827 "The Poet," the 1828 "The Poet and the Crowd" ("Poet i tolpa"), and the 1830 "The Adolescent" ("Otrok"). In these poems the system of images from the Old Testament, Christianity, paganism (antiquity), and even Islam (the Koran) are widely used. This very diversity and variation in Pushkin's use of religious symbolism indirectly attests to the fact that for Pushkin, all religious symbols carried a conventional and relative significance: they were necessary only insofar as they helped to manifest his message about the sacredness of poetry—a sacredness that could not be accommodated within any canonical religious creed.[86]

Epilogue

The historical approach to the study of Pushkin's relationship with Metropolitan Philaret has allowed us to reexamine commonly accepted interpretations, uncover new facts, and look at well-known facts in a new way. We may now boldly assert that the famous "correspondence" of the metropolitan and the poet was not a miracle of divine revelation but just one link in the history of the complex relations between the two men (and, more broadly, between Pushkin and the Orthodox Church). But the subject of the "poetic correspondence" does not conclude the history of Pushkin's relationship with Philaret.

On 22 December 1834, Pushkin made an ironic entry in his diary: "Censor Nikitenko is at police headquarters under arrest, and this is why: Delarue printed in Smirdin's *Library* [*for Reading*] [*Biblioteka dlia chteniia*] a translation of an ode by Victor Hugo that contains the following deep thought: if I were God, then I would give up my heaven and my angels for the kiss of Milena or Chloe. The metropolitan (who is pleased to read our ravings in his leisure) complained to the Emperor, requesting him to defend Orthodoxy from the attacks of Delarue and

Smirdin. Hence the storm."[87] Pushkin's parenthetical phrase, in this case addressed not to Philaret but to Seraphim, nevertheless contains the very same thought that was expressed in his 1829 *Travel Notes* (and which, through self-censorship, he excluded from his article "Georgian Military Road"): the highest Orthodox priests have the regrettable habit of meddling in literary matters instead of going about their own affairs. This statement acquires additional significance if one knows that in high society there were rumors that the instigator of the "storm" was not Metropolitan Seraphim, but Metropolitan Philaret. Philaret himself wrote in this regard to Andrei N. Murav'ev from Moscow on 4 February 1835: "The publisher of the *Telescope* [*Teleskop*] here has complained about Delarue's verses, saying I had denounced them. Not having known them until this complaint and having read them when I heard, I found that the complaint is not offensive to me, although it is unjust. They deserved a denunciation, and blessed is he who turned upon them his impartial gaze."[88]

In the draft of a letter to Chaadaev of 19 October 1836, Pushkin linked the behavior of the clergy with its cultural marginalization—a result of the halfway reforms of Peter the First: "As to the clergy, it is outside society, it is still bearded. One sees no part of it either in the salons or in literature; it is not of good society. It is not above the people, it does not want to be the people. Our sovereigns have found it convenient to leave it where they found it." Pushkin formulated with aphoristic acuity the results of the clergy's marginal position: "Like eunuchs, they have no passion but power. So they are dreaded." He strengthened this maxim with a real-life example: "And [I know] someone [who] despite all of his energy has submitted to them in one important matter—[Which in its time enraged me]."[89] Pushkin alludes here to the story of the removal of the archpriest Gerasim Pavsky from the position of instructor of divine law to the heir to the throne, Grand Prince Alexander Nikolaevich; he tells the story in his diary in a laconic manner: "Philaret made a denunciation of Pavsky, saying that he was a Lutheran.—Pavsky was dismissed from the Grand Prince. The Metropolitan and the Synod upheld Philaret's opinion. The Sov[ereign] said that in spiritual matters he is not the judge but gently bid Pavsky farewell. I pity the intelligent, learned, and kind priest!"[90] In this diary entry the behavior of the emperor Nicholas is implicitly opposed to the behavior of the clergy: the emperor acknowledges himself to be incompetent "in spiritual matters" and therefore, despite his personal liking for Pavsky, submits to the decision of the synod. What a contrast and what a moral lesson to the clergy, who wished to have power not only in their own sphere but also beyond its borders!

Pushkin was mistaken, however. A few days after he had begun to write his letter to Chaadaev, the tireless metropolitan of St. Petersburg and Novgorod, Seraphim, sent a letter to Benkendorf. This letter began as follows: "Your Excellency! In January 1835, Your Excellency informed me personally of His Majesty the Emperor's highest wish, that in those cases when, in literary compositions published for general use, I might discover opinions or ill intentions that go contrary to faith, morality, and the social order, I should convey my observations to Your Excellency so that they may be brought to the Emperor's attention."[91] Seraphim's letter gave impetus to the "Chaadaev affair," as a result of which the Moscow philosopher was officially pronounced insane, the censor who had approved publication of his "First Philosophical Letter" in the *Telescope* was removed from his position, and the journal publisher was exiled. Seraphim's communication shows with great clarity that the clergy's control and surveillance of secular literature in the 1830s was *not* the initiative of the clergy themselves, as Pushkin thought. Instead, this surveillance was a government initiative. Beginning in 1834, "Orthodoxy" became one of the cornerstones of a new government ideology. Accordingly, everything that was suspicious from the point of view of Orthodoxy was now treated as dangerous to the social order as well. Now the church was obligated to investigate "opinions that go contrary to faith" in the name of government interests. "The thirst for power" characteristic of the clergy was now harnessed to government service.

The winner of the competition between Pushkin and Metropolitan Philaret that began at the end of the 1820s was neither the poet nor the priest but a third power—the Russian Empire. This power had no need of an independent literature or an independent church. Both one and the other were necessary to it only as components of the vast governmental machine.

Notes

Translated by Katya Hokanson. See the unnumbered translator's note (80–81) in Igor Nemirovsky's "Why Pushkin Did Not Become a Decembrist."

1. In the 2000s two major museum exhibitions were organized that were dedicated to the theme of "Pushkin and Metropolitan Philaret." The first exhibition opened on 20 December 2000 at the State Pushkin Museum in Moscow, while the ceremonial opening of the second, at the Church-Historical

Museum in Samara, took place on 21 January 2006. A catalog of the Moscow exhibition was published under the title *Pushkin i Filaret, Mitropolit Moskovskii i Kolomenskii* (Moscow: Moskovskie uchebniki i Kartolitografiia, 2003); the materials of a conference titled "A. S. Pushkin and the Spiritual Culture of His Time" were published as an addendum to this catalog.

2. For a factual account of these events see Vadim Liapunov, "Not in Vain and Not by Chance: Pushkin and Philaret (Drozdov), Metropolitan of Moscow," in *Philaret, Metropolitan of Moscow 1782–1867: Perspectives on the Man, His Works, and His Times*, ed. Vladimir Tsurikov (Jordanville, NY: Variable Press, 2003), 36–40. The spelling of the poem's original title, "Stantsy," was patterned on the Italian form of the word rather than the more common "Stansy," patterned on the French (see Liapunov, "Not in Vain and Not by Chance," 40n9).

3. Ioann Vostorgov, "Pamiati A. S. Pushkina: Vechnoe v tvorchestve poeta" (1899), in *A. S. Pushkin: Put' k pravoslaviiu* (Moscow: Otchii dom, 1996), 231–32.

4. Valentin S. Nepomniashchii, "Dar: Zametki o dukhovnoi biografii Pushkina," *Novyi mir* 6 (1989): 241–60. One should keep in mind that these were the last years of a "literature-centric" culture in the Soviet Union; in order to gain a sense of how broadly Nepomniashchy's article resonated, let us recall that the issue of the journal *Novyi mir* in which his article was printed had a print run of 1,629,000 copies.

5. This phrase also makes an appearance in later versions of Nepomniashchy's article. See Valentin S. Nepomniashchii, *Pushkin: Izbrannye raboty, 1960-kh–1990-kh gg.*, 2 vols. (Moscow: Moskovskie uchebniki, 2001), 2:208.

6. See Elena B. Dobrovol'skaia, "Bozhestvennyi glagol," *Pushkinskaia epokha i khristianskaia kul'tura* 6 (1994): 16–28; and Ioann Malinin, "K literaturnoi perepiske mitropolita Filareta i A. S. Pushkina," *Pushkinskaia epokha i khristianskaia kul'tura* 6 (1994): 37–42. Similar publications appeared in the following years. See, for example, M. I. Lepikhov, "'Ne naprasno, ne sluchaino . . . ': K istorii odnogo stikhotvoreniia," *Russkaia slovesnost'* 5 (1997): 19–22.

7. See Zoe Knox's richly informative *Russian Society and the Orthodox Church: Religion in Russia after Communism* (London: RoutledgeCurzon, 2005). For a short but significant survey of the situation see also Yuri Zarakhovich, "Putin's Reunited Russian Church," *Time*, 17 May 2007, http://www.time.com/time/world/article/0,8599,1622544,00.html (accessed 15 August 2010).

8. Ivan Il'in, "Prorocheskoe prizvanie Pushkina," in *Pushkin v russkoi filosofskoi kritike: Konets XIX–pervaia polovina XX v.*, ed. Renata A. Gal'tseva (Moscow: Kniga, 1990), 354.

9. For a discussion of the ideological basis and particularities of this process, see the section "Pushkin in Today's Russia" in Alyssa Gillespie's introduction to the present volume.

10. A good example of this vulgarization in the government press is an article by Maria Gorodova, published shortly before yet another anniversary

of Pushkin's birth: "The poem 'A Vain Gift, a Chance Gift' was a challenge. A challenge tossed into the heavens. The Metropolitan of Moscow Philaret answered that challenge. . . . Read carefully—what tactfulness there is toward one who has called the power of God inimical. Not an angry reproof, but a soft reproach" ("Dar sluchainyi? Chem stikhotvornaia perepiska poeta i mitropolita interesna nam segodnia," *Rossiiskaia gazeta-Nedelia*, 5 June 2008, http://www.rg.ru/2008/06/05/pushkin.html [accessed 15 August 2010]). (Incidentally, the *Russian Gazette* [*Rossiiskaia gazeta*] is the official organ of the Federal Assembly of the Russian Federation, the supreme body of Russian legislative authority.) An example of the vulgarization of Nepomniashchy's interpretation in the context of pedagogy can be found in a model lesson for government schools on the theme of Pushkin and religion published on the website of the publishing house First of September (Pervoe sentiabria), which specializes in pedagogical literature: "A mood of depression leads Pushkin to struggle with God. . . . The priest directs the poet's gaze to the true source of his dire condition. . . . [Pushkin] valued the letter of the Metropolitan not as private correspondence, but as a divine message" and so on. See http://festival.1september.ru/articles/416599/ (accessed 4 November 2011).

11. For one of these few attempts, see the late Russian émigré Pushkin scholar Feliks Raskol'nikov's "Pushkin i religiia," *Voprosy literatury* 3 (2004): 81–112. The article has been translated into English; see Felix Raskolnikov, "Pushkin and Religion," *Russian Studies in Literature* 42.1 (2005–6): 7–35.

12. Petr A. Viazemskii to Aleksandr I. Turgenev, October 1828, in *Ostaf'evskii arkhiv kniazei Viazemskikh*, vol. 3, part 1 of *Perepiska kniazia P. A. Viazemskogo s A. I. Turgenevym, 1824–1836* (St. Petersburg: Tipografiia Mikhaila M. Stasiulevicha, 1899), 180.

13. The couplet quoted in the letter is from Viazemsky's 1814 "Noël" ("Noel'"), which uses the form of French Christmas songs for political and literary satire. The following is said about Philaret in "Noël": "A new orator, Philaret, approaches Christ: 'I am at your service, I the Bossuet of the Neva! I never, it's true, dreamt of being a clever man, but this one whispered, the other one spoke aloud, and I accidentally landed among the ranks of clever men!'" (K Khristu orator novyi / Podkhodit, Filaret: / "K uslugam vam gotovyi, / Az nevskii Bossiuet! / Mne, pravo, nikogda byt' umnikom ne snilos', / No tot shepnul, drugoi skazal, / I chto ia v umniki popal— / Nechaianno sluchilos'!") (Petr A. Viazemskii, *Sochineniia*, 2 vols. [Moscow: Khudozhestvennaia literatura, 1982], 1:50). Jacques-Bénigne Bossuet was a French orator and theologian renowned for his sermons.

14. Aleksandr Nikitenko, *The Diary of a Russian Censor*, abr., ed., and trans. Helen Saltz Jacobson (Amherst: University of Massachusetts Press, 1975), 47. The ending of the entry, given here in curly brackets, is left out of the abridged translation. See http://az.lib.ru/n/nikitenko_a_w/text_0030.shtml for the Russian text (accessed 17 August 2010).

15. See, for example, Vadim E. Vatsuro and Maksim I. Gillel'son, *Skvoz' umstvennye plotiny*, 2nd ed. (Moscow: Kniga, 1986), 229–31; Iurii M. Lotman, *Pushkin: Biografiia pisatelia; Stat'i i zametki, 1960–1990; "Evgenii Onegin," Kommentarii* (St. Petersburg: Iskusstvo-STB, 1995), 697.

16. Natal'ia I. Mikhailova, "Pushkin i sviatitel' Filaret (O vystavke v Gosudarstvennom muzee A. S. Pushkina)," *Russkoe vozrozhdenie* 80 (2002): 32–33, http://pagez.ru/philaret/about024.php (accessed 15 August 2010).

17. Raskolnikov, "Pushkin and Religion," 11.

18. Gustav Shpet in his "Ocherk razvitiia russkoi filosofii"—a scathing survey of Russian intellectual life in the eighteenth and first half of the nineteenth centuries—changes his tone when he analyzes Sidonsky's 1833 *Introduction to Philosophy*, that is, the very same book that brought about Philaret's persecution: he calls it "positively the best book about philosophy of those having appeared in Russia up to that point" (*Sochineniia* [Moscow: Pravda, 1989], 158). For a more in-depth and recent look at Sidonsky, see Irina A. Poliakova, *Fedor Fedorovich Sidonskii (1805–1873): Pravo na biografiiu* (Moscow: Izdatel'stvo Russkoi Khristianskoi gumanitarnoi akademii, 2009).

19. The issues in question were *Moskovskii vestnik* 1, published in January 1828 (the number was issued after 9 January and not later than 18 January) and *Severnaia pchela* 17, published on 9 February 1828.

20. Pogodin's diary at the beginning of the 1820s contains many enraptured notes about Philaret, his sermons, and his catechism; see Nikolai Barsukov, *Zhizn' i trudy M. P. Pogodina*, vol. 1 (St. Petersburg: Tipografiia Mikhaila M. Stasiulevicha, 1888), 128, 218, 220, 234, 306.

21. It is significant that neither in Pogodin's extensive correspondence nor in his diary is there any mention of, nor even any hint at, the metropolitan's having lodged a complaint. The same can be said about the no less extensive correspondence and well-known memoirs of the censor of the *Moscow Herald*, Sergei T. Aksakov.

22. See Abram I. Reitblat, "Bulgarin i III Otdelenie," in *Vidok Figliarin: Pis'ma i agenturnye zapiski F. V. Bulgarina v III otdelenie*, ed. Abram I. Reitblat (Moscow: Novoe literaturnoe obozrenie, 1998), 5–40.

23. Natan Ia. Eidel'man, *Pushkin: Iz biografii i tvorchestva (1826–1837)* (Moscow: Khudozhestvennaia literatura, 1987), 68–79; on Bulgarin's denunciations of Pogodin and his colleagues at the *Moscow Herald* see *Vidok Figliarin*, 88–89, 232, 289.

24. Compare Semenov's 1830 explanation of why he had approved for publication a quatrain (in French) that had been written by Casimir Delavigne for a Parisian monument to the victims of the July Revolution (Vladimir V. Stasov, "Tsenzura v tsarstvovanie imperatora Nikolaia I," *Russkaia starina* 107.8 [1901]: 662).

25. Konstantin Ia. Grot, "Vasilii Nikolaevich Semenov, literator i tsenzor: K literaturnoi istorii 1830-kh godov," *Pushkin i ego sovremenniki* 37 (1928): 155.

26. For a summary of the facts of Pushkin's acquaintance with Semenov, see Lazar' A. Chereiskii, *Pushkin i ego okruzhenie*, 2nd ed. (Leningrad: Nauka, 1989), 392–93.

27. Grot, "Vasilii Nikolaevich Semenov, literator i tsenzor," 163.

28. Mstislav A. Tsiavlovskii and Nikolai A. Tarkhov, comps., *Letopis' zhizni i tvorchestva Aleksandra Pushkina*, 4 vols., ed. Ianina L. Levkovich (Moscow: Slovo, 1999), 2:427, 3:11, 26.

29. It is worth adding that at this time Pushkin also had many opportunities to find out about Philaret's other unfavorable "critical review" regarding his incorrect depiction of monastery life in *Boris Godunov*. The account of Philaret's opinion, as already noted, goes back to Boratynsky. Pushkin actively socialized with Boratynsky in Moscow at the end of 1828 and the spring of 1829 (he was there from 6 December 1828 until 7 January 1829 and then from 14 March until 1 May 1829). See Aleksei M. Peskov, "Pushkin i Baratynskii: Materialy k istorii literaturnykh otnoshenii," in *Novye bezdelki: Sbornik statei k 60-letiiu V. E. Vatsuro*, ed. Sergei I. Panov (Moscow: Novoe literaturnoe obozrenie, 1995–96), 253–54.

30. Pervaia arzrumskaia, Manuscripts Department, Pushkin House, St. Petersburg, PD 841.

31. The 1937–59 Academy of Russian Sciences seventeen-volume *Polnoe sobranie sochinenii* treats the *latest* version of this text as canonical, whereas I am interested in its *earliest* variant, written in 1829. As much as possible I try here to show the *dynamics* of Pushkin's work on the text in its beginning stage, noting the changes made. Crossed-out words are indicated in curly brackets.

32. Pervaia arzrumskaia, Manuscripts Department, Pushkin House, St. Petersburg, PD 841, fol. 10r, fol. 10v (reproduced in facsimile in *Rabochaia tetrad' PD 841 (Pervaia arzrumskaia); Rabochaia tetrad' PD 842, Vtoraia arzrumskaia*, in Aleksandr S. Pushkin, *Rabochie tetradi*, 8 vols. [St. Petersburg: Institut Russkoi literatury, 1997], 7). Compare with the version in Aleksandr S. Pushkin, *Polnoe sobranie sochinenii*, 17 vols., ed. Vladimir D. Bonch-Bruevich et al. (Moscow: AN SSSR, 1937–1959), 8:1035–36.

33. On the role of Islam in the eighteenth and nineteenth centuries as a religious and ideological basis for resistance by the peoples of the northern Caucasus to the expansion of the Russian Empire, see the following valuable works: Anna Zelkina, *In Quest for God and Freedom: The Sufi Response to the Russian Advance in the North Caucasus* (New York: New York University Press, 2000); and *Russian-Muslim Confrontation in the Caucasus: Alternative Visions of the Conflict Between Imam Shamil and the Russians, 1830–1859*, ed. and trans. Thomas Sanders, Ernest Tucker, and Gary M. Hamburg (London: RoutledgeCurzon, 2004).

34. See the section "Ob uspekhakh Osetinskoi Dukhovnoi Kommissii," in *Istoriia gruzinskoi ierarkhii, s prisovokupleniem obrashcheniia v Khristianstvo Osetin i drugikh gorskikh narodov, po 1-e Genvaria, 1825 goda* (Moscow: Sinodal'naia tipografiia, 1826), 77–96. This book was published on the orders of the Holy Synod.

35. Vasilii L. Komarovich, "K voprosu o zhanre 'Puteshestviia v Arzrum,'" in *Pushkin: Vremennik Pushkinskoi komissii*, vol. 3 (Moscow: AN SSSR, 1937), 333–35; Vasilii L. Komarovich, "Vtoraia kavkazskaia poema Pushkina," in *Pushkin: Vremennik Pushkinskoi komissii*, vol. 6 (Moscow: AN SSSR, 1941), 230–34.

36. This question is not discussed at all in the most recent work dedicated to Pushkin's *Travel Notes*; see Ian M. Helfant, "Sculpting a Persona: The Path from Pushkin's Caucasian Journal to *Puteshestvie v Arzrum*," *Russian Review* 56.3 (1997): 366–82.

37. All English-language citations from the Bible in this chapter are from the King James version, which, thanks to its archaic language and elevated style, is closest to the Old Church Slavonic version used in the Russian Orthodox Church.

38. Aleksei D. Galakhov, *Ot Karamzina do Pushkina*, vol. 2 of *Istoriia russkoi slovesnosti, drevnei i novoi*, 2 vols., 3rd ed. (Moscow: Izdatel'stvo V. V. Dumnova, 1894), 2:388. For a recent work on this theme, see Mark Arndt, "Mitropolit Moskovskii Philaret (Drozdov) i ego mesto v kontekste russkoi propovedi, " in *Philaret, Metropolitan of Moscow, 1782–1867*, 52–104.

39. Regarding Golitsyn's fall, the ban on Philaret's catechism, and the destruction of the Bible Society, see Judith Cohen Zacek, "The Russian Bible Society and the Russian Orthodox Church," in *Church History* 35.4 (1966): 427–35; and Allen McConnell, *Tsar Alexander I, Paternalistic Reformer* (Arlington Heights, IL.: Harlan Davidson, 1970), 172–74. Philaret's catechism was published in revised form in 1828.

40. Nikolai V. Sushkov, *Zapiski o zhizni i vremeni sviatitelia Filareta, mitropolita Moskovskogo* (Moscow: Tipografiia A. I. Mamontova, 1868), 106.

41. Ibid. St. Nina, who introduced Christianity to Georgia in the fourth century CE, is one of the most revered saints of the Georgian Orthodox Church.

42. Although he presented himself in his letters to Philaret as a sincere supporter, in fact Seraphim not infrequently took the side of Philaret's enemies when deciding the most important questions of the day. See Illarion A. Chistovich, *Rukovodiashchie deiateli dukhovnogo prosveshcheniia v Rossii v pervoi polovine tekushchego stoletiia* (St. Petersburg; Sinodal'naia tipografiia, 1894), 242, 252, 260.

43. Apollinarii N. L'vov, ed., "Pis'ma dukhovnykh i svetskikh lits k mitropolitu moskovskomu Filaretu (s 1812 po 1867 gg.)," pt. 3, "Pis'ma mitropolita Novogorodskogo i S.-Peterburgskogo Grigoriia," *Khristianskoe chtenie* 3 (1898): 408.

44. Mikhail I. Sukhomlinov, "Iz bumag v boze pochivshego mitropolita Moskovskogo Filareta," *Zhurnal ministerstva narodnogo prosveshcheniia* 137 (1868): 20.

45. See Aleksandr N. Pypin, *Religioznye dvizheniia pri Aleksandre I* (St. Petersburg: Akademicheskii proekt, 2000), 253. Alexander S. Shishkov, the new minister of education and persecutor of the Bible Society, would be the next

opponent of translations of Holy Writ into new languages in general and "barbaric" languages in particular.

46. *Istoriia gruzinskoi ierarkhii, s prisovokupleniem obrashcheniia v Khristianstvo Osetin i drugikh gorskikh narodov, po 1-e Genvaria, 1825 goda*, 90–93.

47. Vladimir S. Tolstoi, "Iz sluzhebnykh vospominanii V. S. Tolstogo: Poezdka v Osetiiu v 1847 godu," *Russkii arkhiv* 6 (1875): 267.

48. A. I. Davydov, "Pushkin i arkhiepiskop Evgenii (Kazantsev)," in *Pushkin i ego sovremenniki* 40.1 (1999): 275–80.

49. On this topic, see Eidel'man, *Pushkin: Iz biografii i tvorchestva*, 48–50.

50. Thus, on 9 April 1829, on the eve of his departure from Moscow to Arzrum, Pushkin, being dissatisfied with the censorship's delay of his composition for the *Moscow Telegraph* (*Moskovskii telegraf*), wrote to the censor Ivan Snegirov: "It is necessary for me that it be published, and in the case of a refusal I will find myself obliged to appeal to the highest authorities, together with a complaint about the partiality shown to whom, I do not know" (Pushkin, *Polnoe sobranie sochinenii*, 17 vols., 14:41).

51. See Fedor V. Blagovidov, *Ober-prokurory Sviateishego Sinoda v XVIII i v pervoi polovine XIX st.* (Kazan: Tipo-litografiia Imperatorskogo universiteta, 1899), 369–73; and David W. Edwards, "The System of Nicholas I in Church-State Relations," in *Russian Orthodoxy under the Old Regime*, ed. Robert L. Nichols and Theofanis George Stavrou (Minneapolis: University of Minnesota Press, 1978), 158.

52. Report of the Commission of Inquiry, in *Gosudarstvennye prestupleniia v Rossii v XIX veke: Sbornik izvlechennykh iz ofitsial'nykh izdanii pravitel'stvennykh postanovlenii*, ed. B. Bazilevskii [Vasilii Yakovlev], vol. 1 (St. Petersburg: Russkaia skoropechatnia, 1906), 36.

53. *Rossiia pod nadzorom: Otchety III Otdeleniia, 1827–1869*, comp. Marina V. Sidorova and Ekaterina I. Shcherbakov (Moscow: Rossiiskii fond kul'tury; Rossiiskii arkhiv, 2006), 20.

54. Ibid., 25.

55. Ianina L. Levkovich, *Avtobiograficheskaia proza i pis'ma Pushkina* (Leningrad: Nauka, 1988), 134. Pushkin's later editorial changes are easy to distinguish from corrections he made in the early stages of writing: revisions for the article were made in an ink that differs in color from the original text of the *Travel Notes*.

56. In 1828 a new policy had been implemented in the western territories of the Russian Empire in relation to the Uniate (Greek Catholic Church), with the goal of uniting it with the Orthodox Church.

57. Metropolitan Philaret was in St. Petersburg from fall 1829 until spring 1830 at a session of the Holy Synod.

58. Valentin S. Nepomniashchii, *Pushkin*, 2:188–89, 203, 210.

59. Mark G. Al'tshuller, "Diptikh Pushkina i psevdopalinodiia mitropolita Filareta," in his *Mezhdu dvukh tsarei: Pushkin 1824–1836* (St. Petersburg: Akademicheskii proekt, 2003), 237.

60. Andrew Kahn, *Pushkin's Lyric Intelligence* (Oxford: Oxford University Press, 2008), 291.

61. It is true that during the censorship process of the almanac *Northern Flowers*, several complications arose. The censor Konstantin Serbinovich "found it difficult" (zatrudnilsia) to approve the poem for publication, having discerned in it a "doubtfulness of expression" (somnitel'nost' vyrazhenii), and passed the matter on to the St. Petersburg Censorship Committee for resolution. At the meeting of that committee on 3 December 1829, Serbinovich's misgivings were seconded by the censor Pavel Gaevsky, who announced that "this piece cannot be allowed into print." However, the other members of the Censorship Committee, including its chairman, "basing their decision on paragraph 13 of the Censorship Statute"—which stipulated that the strict precision required in descriptions of elevated subjects and in exalted compositions was not required in belles lettres and fiction—"decided to grant permission to publish the aforementioned piece" (*Aleksandr Sergeevich Pushkin: Dokumenty k biografii, 1799–1829*, ed. Vadim P. Stark [St. Petersburg: Iskusstvo-SPB, 2007], 907).

62. Vadim Liapunov offers the following linguistic commentary: "*Vozzval* [*summoned*] here is a Slavonic form of 'vyzval' [*called out*], and *nichtozhestvo* is an early translation of Latin *nihilum* or French *néant*—'nichto, nebytie' [*nothingness, nonexistence*]" ("Not in Vain and Not by Chance," 47n19).

63. *Slovar' iazyka Pushkina*, 4 vols, ed. Viktor V. Vinogradov, Sergei I. Bernshtein, and Anna D. Grigor'eva (Moscow: Gosudarstvennoe izdatel'stvo inostrannykh i natsional'nykh slovarei, 1956–61), 2:869.

64. Aleksandr S. Pushkin, *Arap Petra Velikogo*, in his *Polnoe sobranie sochinenii*, 17 vols., 8:5.

65. Ibid., 3.1:65.

66. Mikhail F. Mur'ianov, "Pushkin i Pesn' pesnei," in *Vremennik Pushkinskoi komissii, 1972* (Leningrad: Nauka, 1974), 59.

67. About this poem and its place in Pushkin's poetry see Pamela Davidson, "The Muse and the Demon in the Poetry of Pushkin, Lermontov, and Blok," in *Russian Literature and Its Demons*, ed. Pamela Davidson (New York: Berghahn Books, 2000), 170–72.

68. *Northern Bee for 1830*, 11 January 1830. Reprinted in *Pushkin v prizhiznennoi kritike, 1828–1830*, ed. Ekaterina O. Larionova (St. Petersburg: Gosudarstvennyi Pushkinskii Teatral'nyi Tsentr, 2001), 216. Vasilii V. Gippius detected in Bulgarin's review a veiled denunciation with political overtones ("Pushkin v bor'be s Bulgarinym v 1830–1831 gg.," in *Pushkin: Vremennik Pushkinskoi komissii*, 6:236–37). But Gippius was mistaken: several weeks still remained until Bulgarin's final break with the Del'vig-Pushkin circle. His evaluation is entirely complimentary and highly accurate.

69. David M. Bethea, *Realizing Metaphors: Alexander Pushkin and the Life of the Poet* (Madison: University of Wisconsin Press, 1998), 98.

70. *Zvezdochka: Zhurnal dlia detei starshego vozrasta* 28 (1848): 16. The metropolitan's poem has been published in a number of variant forms, based on

different written copies and in different editorial versions, which diverge rather significantly from one another. Mark Al'tshuller has proposed that the text published in Sushkov's book should be considered the most "authentic" ("Diptikh Pushkina," 240). This proposal, however, is flawed: Sushkov himself explains that Philaret was recalling his poem many years after its composition while reading a defective copy. It is not surprising that in recalling his verses, he might have left some of the mistakes in the copy intact and unintentionally "edited" the old text in other places. Furthermore, the final line of Sushkov's version reads: "And by You will be created a pure heart, a bright mind!" (I sozizhdetsia toboiu / Serdtse chisto, svetlyi um). Yet Vadim Liapunov has justly remarked that the version in *Zvezdochka* ("And by You will be created a pure heart, a righteous [*pravyi*] mind!") allows one to find in this poem a paraphrase of the fiftieth (the so-called penitential) psalm (Psalm 51 in the Western tradition): "Create in me a pure heart, O God; and renew a righteous spirit within me" (Serdtse chisto sozizhdi vo mne, Bozhe, i dukh prav obnovi vo utrobe moei). Unfortunately, this observation has not prevented Liapunov from relying on the Sushkov version of the text in his analysis (Liapunov, "Not in Vain and Not by Chance," 48).

71. "The Longer Catechism of the Orthodox, Catholic, Eastern Church," trans. Richard W. Blackmore, in *The Creeds of Christendom*, 3 vols., ed. Philip Schaff (New York: Harper and Brothers, 1877), 2:525.

72. Ibid.

73. Sushkov, *Zapiski o zhizni i vremeni sviatitelia Filareta, mitropolita Moskovskogo*, 4–5.

74. Pushkin's note to Khitrovo, in French, has been preserved. It was written in answer to her invitation to visit her (not preserved) so that he might become acquainted as quickly as possible with Philaret's poem (see *The Letters of Alexander Pushkin*, trans. and ed. J. Thomas Shaw [Madison: University of Wisconsin Press, 1967], 372). Pushkin's note dates to the first half of January 1830.

75. On 17 January Serbinovich wrote in his diary: "I am reading censorship papers: *Journey to Arzrum*, articles for the *Slav* [*Slavianin*], the *Literary Gazette*" ("Pushkin v dnevnike K. S. Serbinovicha," ed. Vera S. Nechaeva, in *Pushkin, Lermontov, Gogol'*, vol. 58 of *Literaturnoe nasledstvo* [Moscow: AN SSSR, 1952]: 259).

76. See Vasilii P. Gur'ianov, "Pis'mo Pushkina o 'Gavriliiade,'" in *Pushkin: Issledovaniia i materialy*, vol. 8 (Leningrad: Nauka, 1978), 284–92.

77. Vadim Liapunov has expressed a similar idea, though the nuance is somewhat different: "Philaret is present here as as a highly authoritative representative of the standpoint of Christian faith (as he was, in fact, historically), but what Pushkin has ultimately in view is his relationship with what Philaret represents—with Christian faith, and not his relationship with Philaret. . . . I see nothing surprising, therefore, in the fact that for some readers the 'thou' ('ty') of the poem is Christ" ("Not in Vain and Not by Chance," 50.)

78. Petr A. Viazemsky to Aleksandr I. Turgenev, 25 April 1830, in *Ostaf'evskii arkhiv kniazei Viazemskikh*, 192.

79. Nikolai V. Sushkov, "Zametka na zametku," *Chteniia v Imperatorskom obshchestve istorii i drevnostei rossiiskikh* 2 (April–June 1868): 211. Additional evidence can be found: "It was impossible to make out the voice of Philaret. He spoke so quietly that even those who were surrounding the throne told me that they could not hear anything" (Anna F. Tiutcheva, *Pri dvore dvukh imperatorov*, vol. 2, *Dnevnik, 1855–1882*, 2 vols. [Moscow: Izdatel'stvo Sabashnikovykh, 1929], 120); "His voice is weak, barely audible" (Sergei D. Sheremetev, *Moskovskie vospominaniia shestidesiatykh godov* [Moscow: Tipo-litografiia N.I. Kumanina, 1900], 20).

80. Aleksandr S. Pushkin, "Ob obiazannostiakh cheloveka: Sochinenie Sil'vio Pelliko," in his *Polnoe sobranie sochinenii*, 17 vols., 12:99–100.

81. *Francis of Assisi: Early Documents*, vol. 1, ed. Regis J. Armstrong, J. A. Wayne Hellmann, William J. Short (New York: New City Press, 1999), 45, emphasis added. The question of the influence of Francis of Assisi on Pushkin, first remarked on by Dmitrii Merezhkovsky, has been insufficiently studied, but see Archimandrite Augustin [Dmitrii E. Nikitin], "Pushkin i Frantsisk Assizskii: Frantsiskanskie motivy v russkoi poezii," *Stranitsy* 3.2 (1998): 239–55. Pushkin most likely became acquainted with the works of Francis of Assissi in 1823–24 in Odessa, where he had the opportunity to use the rich library of Count Vorontsov.

82. *Trebnik* (Moscow: Sinodal'naia Tipografiia, 1882), 382, emphasis added.

83. Sushkov, *Zapiski o zhizni i vremeni sviatitelia Filareta, mitropolita Moskovskogo*, 3–4, emphasis added.

84. The double sense of this image derives from the fact that Pushkin often uses the epithet *buinyi* (stormy) in a dual meaning: both to denote savage, uncontrolled, ungovernable passions and those who experience them (e.g., "buinye ego sotovarishchi" [his wild companions], "buinyi strelets" [a fierce soldier]) and also to characterize a strong wind ("I buinyi vikhor' vyl unylo" [And a turbulent whirlwind howled dejectedly]) or destructive storms of wind and water, as in the Gospel scene ("Neva vsiu noch' / Rvalas' k moriu protiv buri, / Ne odolev ikh buinoi duri" [The Neva all night strained against the storm toward the sea but could not overcome its violent bluster]). It should be noted here that the formula "with gentle strength" (siloi krotkoi) contains a direct parallel to Fedor Glinka's "Psalm 62," which had been published in the same almanac as "A vain gift, a chance gift": "But with a *gentle, fatherly* hand / Thou leadest those who are suffering to peace" (No *krotkoi, otcheskoi* rukoiu / Vedesh' Ty strazhdushchikh k pokoiu) (*Severnye Tsvety na 1830 god* [St. Petersburg: Tipografiia Departamenta narodnogo prosveshcheniia, 1829], 55, emphasis added).

85. For a discussion of how Pushkin's views on this matter correlate with the views of his contemporaries (particularly those who were members of the literary circle surrounding *The Moscow Herald*), see Natal'ia N. Mazur, "Pushkin

i 'moskovskie iunoshi': Vokrug problemy geniia," in *Pushkinskaia konferentsiia v Stenforde, 1999: Materialy i issledovaniia*, ed. David M. Bethea et al. (Moscow: OGI, 2001), 54–105.

86. See Alyssa Gillespie's analysis of "The Prophet" in her article "Bawdy and Soul" in the present volume. Although one might wonder whether an allegorical connection can be made between the seraph in "The Prophet" and Metropolitan Seraphim, implying the pointedly ironic suggestion that Philaret is just the "mouthpiece" of Metropolitan Seraphim and does his bidding, there is insufficient evidence for such a reading. In all of Pushkin's notes in both his diaries and his letters, Philaret is presented as a fully autonomous figure.

87. Aleksandr S. Pushkin, diary entry, 22 December 1834, in his *Polnoe sobranie sochinenii*, 17 vols., 12:335. For a detailed discussion of this "storm" see Nikitenko, diary entry, 1 January 1835, in *The Diary of a Russian Censor*, 54–56.

88. Metropolitan Philaret to Andrei N. Murav'ev, 4 February 1835, in *Pis'ma mitropolita moskovskogo Filareta k A. N. M[urav'evu], 1832–1867* (Kiev: Tipografiia I. i A. Davidenko, 1869), 16.

89. Aleksandr S. Pushkin to Petr Ia. Chaadaev, 19 October 1836, in his *Polnoe sobranie sochinenii*, 17 vols., 16:261, original in French.

90. Aleksandr S. Pushkin, diary entry, February [*sic*] 1835, in his *Polnoe sobranie sochinenii*, 17 vols., 12:336–37.

91. Metropolitan Seraphim to Aleksandr Kh. Benkendorf, 27 October 1836, in Petr Ia. Chaadaev, *Sochineniia*, ed. Vera Iu. Proskurina (Moscow: Pravda, 1989), 531.

Part 2

Taboo Writings

If Only Pushkin Had Not Written This Filth

The Shade of Barkov *and Philological Cover-Ups*

IGOR PILSHCHIKOV

Mikhail Gasparov (1935–2005), a great scholar and a man of wit, noticed several times that the Russians' preference for a particular work of Pushkin's had always been of an ideological rather than a scholarly or purely aesthetic nature. "Twenty years ago we honored Pushkin for his ode 'Liberty,' but now we seem to honor him for 'Hermit fathers and chaste wives' or *The Shade of Barkov*"—and this is what we call 'ideology.'" Such an approach is opposed to a scholarly research approach, argued Gasparov, and philology (that is, linguistic and literary studies) should withstand it.[1] The 2008 TV contest "Name Russia" ("Imia Rossiia") added a fourth key text to the three noted by Gasparov: "To the Slanderers of Russia" ("Klevetnikam Rossii" [1829]).[2] This is a new turn of ideologization: if the ode "Liberty" ("Vol'nost'" [1817]) symbolized the left-wing Pushkin, then "To the Slanderers of Russia" shows Pushkin as a right-wing poet. The opposition of "Hermit fathers and chaste wives" ("Ottsy pustynniki i zheny neporochny"), composed in 1836, to *The*

Shade of Barkov (*Ten' Barkova*), composed in 1814–15, shows two other cultural processes besides ideologization at work, namely mythologization and demythologization. The point is that "Hermit fathers and chaste wives" represents Pushkin the Orthodox writer, while *The Shade of Barkov* stands for Pushkin's libertinism (even though it was written before its author had the chance to become a libertine).

Ivan Barkov (1732–68) was the most notorious Russian poet, famous for his obscene odes (including an imitation of Alexis Piron's "Ode to Priapus" ["Ode à Priape"]), and Pushkin's poem in the style of Barkov, with his name in the title, points too explicitly to an "unpleasant" aspect of Pushkin, the "symbol of Russia." The proponents of Pushkin the religious thinker (like Valentin Nepomniashchy and his followers) tend to mythologize the poet as an emanation of the divine and reject too frivolous works of his as well as his earthly—sometimes too earthly—behavior, while the demythologizers (Abram Tertz and his imitators) seem to overestimate the usually underestimated erotic and libertine aspect of Pushkin.[3] From this point of view, demythologization may become just another version of mythologization; at the same time mythologization always goes hand in hand with ideologization.

To be cleared from all these exaggerations, all four of these key works, including the disreputable *The Shade of Barkov*, require a historical and philological rather than ideological or neomythological approach. The case is particularly difficult with *The Shade of Barkov*: it is still absolutely taboo in the eyes of the majority of Russian academicians. Considered either an authentic or dubious work of Pushkin, it has nevertheless not been included in any academic edition of Pushkin's work, even the *dubia* section.

An obscene ballad by Pushkin titled *The Shade of Barkov* was first mentioned by Viktor Gaevsky (1826–88) in his article on Pushkin's poems of the lyceum period published in Nikolai Nekrasov's *The Contemporary* (*Sovremennik*) in 1863. In this same article, Gaevsky also published fragments from Pushkin's poem. In his attribution of the ballad, he relied on the testimonies of Pushkin's classmates (first and foremost, Mikhail Iakovlev [1798–1868]). In 1880, Petr Efremov (1830–1907) included the fragments from *The Shade of Barkov* (from Gaevsky's article) in the first volume of his edition of Pushkin's works, but under the pressure of the censor Nikolai Ratynsky (1821–87) he had to excise the piece from the bound printed copies and replace it with the following note: "Here we placed the fragments from a ballad. In the meantime, it turned out that this ballad does not belong to Pushkin, and this is why it was excluded."

In 1903 and 1905 Efremov published two contradictory stories in which he told how he had come to change his view, what Ratynsky had told him (Ratynsky thought the ballad was Alexander Polezhaev's, but Efremov disputed this attribution), and how Gaevsky had allegedly agreed to Efremov's counterarguments (a suspicious claim that Efremov had never mentioned before and impossible to prove seventeen years after Gaevsky's death). Later Mstislav Tsiavlovsky characterized Efremov's conjectures as "unfounded" and even "absurd."[4]

The ballad attracted additional interest after 1928 when Pushkin's manuscript of his narrative poem *The Monk* (*Monakh* [1813]) was discovered in the archive of his former classmate, the state chancellor Prince Alexander Gorchakov (1798–1883); Gaevsky had also reported the existence of this poem, and the reliability of his information was thus confirmed. Such eminent scholars as Pavel Shchegolev (1877–1931) and Nikolai Lerner (1877–1934) spoke without reservation in favor of Pushkin's authorship of *The Shade of Barkov*.[5] In the 1930s Tsiavlovsky offered his reconstruction of the authentic text of the ballad and furnished it with an extensive commentary. However, this work would remain unpublished for more than half a century.

The significance of Tsiavlovsky (1883–1947) for the study of Pushkin's poetry of the lyceum period is difficult to exaggerate. Together with his wife, Tatiana Zenger-Tsiavlovskaia (1897–1978), he edited the first volume of the seventeen-volume ("big academic") edition of Pushkin's complete works and prepared a historical-literary and textual commentary on the poems of the 1813–17 period. However, in accordance with Stalin's personal instructions, all the detailed commentaries were excluded from the academic edition. Six decades later, Tsiavlovsky's commentary on the lyceum poems was used as a basis for the first volume of the new academic Pushkin.[6] The fate of his work on *The Shade of Barkov* was, however, rather different.

The bawdy ballad presents a particular problem in the preparation of the corpus of Pushkin's early writings. Pushkin's manuscript of *The Shade of Barkov* (as well as the manuscripts of many of his other libertine and antigovernmental pieces) did not come down to us; neither do we have a manuscript copy descending from his inner circle of friends. Only a few publishable fragments of the ballad appeared in print in the nineteenth century (all of them go back to Gaevsky's publication). As Shchegolev argued, "The unavailability of the full text of the ballad in printed form hampers the work of researchers, and one wishes the text would be published, even if only for private use, however small the print run." Tsiavlovsky completed the main part of his research in 1931. In the list of the scholar's unpublished works (compiled by his widow after his death), we find: "Pushkin's *The Shade of Barkov*. Special supplement to volume 1 of the Academic edition of Pushkin . . . not for sale . . . Typeset and composed, but not printed."[7] Obviously, such a work was unprintable under the Soviet as well as the tsarist censorship, except in a restricted number of copies distributed among a few chosen people.

The publishing house of the Russian Academy of Sciences, to which Tsiavlovsky submitted his manuscript, completed the typesetting by February 1937; proofreading was ongoing for several months but was never finished. *The Shade of Barkov*, which became a kind of governmental secret, was prepared for press in absolute secrecy at the printing house of the NKVD (People's Commissariat for Internal Affairs, the forerunner of the KGB). Despite all the safeguards, the page proofs of the ballad with Tsiavlovsky's commentary and part of Tsiavlovsky's manuscript disappeared and seemed to have perished: according to one version, the building of the NKVD printing house caught fire; according to another version, the page proofs of the book were requested by Sergei Ingulov, the head of Glavlit (Main Administration for Literary and Publishing Affairs), the highest censorial organ in the USSR. In November 1937, a "purge" in Glavlit started, Ingulov was arrested and then shot, and nobody dared to inquire about the fate of his papers in the swirl of the Great Terror. However, in 1940 the page proofs suddenly came to light at the Writers' Bookstore (Knizhnaia lavka pisatelei), a second-hand bookseller's, in Moscow, and in 1943, by a mere chance, Tsiavlovsky got back the missing portion of his manuscript.[8]

These documents were preserved within the family until the death of Tsiavlovskaia (30 May 1978), and then they, together with other materials intended for the first volume of the "big academic" edition, were handed over to the archive of the academic edition at the Manuscripts Department of Pushkin House in Leningrad.[9] This holding has not yet been inventoried (so it is rather difficult to retrieve a particular document from the collection). Meanwhile, another version of Tsiavlovsky's commentary on *The Shade of Barkov* is extant: when the manuscript of the commentary was at the publishing house or the printing house, somebody copied it, and this typewritten copy is preserved at the Alexander S. Pushkin State Museum in Moscow.

It is now important to summarize the main problems that were raised and solved by Tsiavlovsky, because today's scholars express varying opinions on his achievements in this regard (as always happens, there are two tendencies: to underestimate and overestimate his results). First and foremost, on the basis of six anonymous manuscript copies dating from the mid-nineteenth to the early twentieth centuries—which were available to him and which are reproduced in his commentary—as well as the fragments published by Gaevsky in 1863, Tsiavlovsky made the first attempt to reconstruct the full text of the poem. Whatever the shortcomings of his reconstruction may be, a new work of Pushkin thus came to light and became an object of further research.[10]

Tsiavlovsky's analysis of "the history of *The Shade of Barkov* in Pushkin scholarship" proved that Efremov, who claimed the ballad to be apocryphal, did not in fact demonstrate any strong "evidence against Pushkin's authorship," and therefore, Tsiavlovsky concluded, we "have nothing to oppose" to the testimonies of the poet's classmates that backed up Gaevsky's attribution of *The Shade of Barkov* to Pushkin. In addition, following Fedor Korsh (who was the first to touch upon this problem in 1899), Tsiavlovsky raised the question of obscene language in Pushkin; he revealed that the shocking style of the ballad is based on a "deliberate . . . 'heightening'" of the role of obscene swear words, which are "on the whole fairly common in both the poet's literary works and his letters." This statement is not as trivial as it may seem. Before Tsiavlovsky examined this rich material, it was not studied nor even published uncut. The only exceptions are the three volumes of Pushkin's correspondence prepared between 1906 and 1911 by Vladimir Saitov, aided by Boris Modzalevsky, for members of the Academy of Sciences only. Modzalevsky's own edition of Pushkin's letters leaves Pushkin's spelling intact but has all the "appropriate" censorial cuts. This also applies to the Soviet seventeen-volume academic edition (and, of course, to other editions of the Soviet era). Despite all the recent cultural changes, obscene language in Pushkin still remains a taboo for Russian scholars: the post-Soviet academic editions of his works contain the same editorial cuts as the publications of the previous epochs (sometimes, by tradition, rather innocent expressions are also excised; as a result, such texts look more indecent than they really are). Since Tsiavlovsky, Pushkin's interest in vulgar and obscene vocabulary has not been studied until recently. The topic did not even merit a section in Viktor Vinogradov's seminal studies of Pushkin's language.[11] For most Russian scholars, obscenity in folklore or in the works of a modern author is less insulting and thus more acceptable than in Pushkin's works: apparently, their symbolic potential cannot be compared to that of "the sun of Russian poetry."

Tsiavlovsky also compiled a list of "lexical and phraseological coincidences between . . . the ballad and Pushkin's other works of the early lyceum period." At the time when Gaevsky published *The Shade of Barkov*, many of these works were unknown or considered nonextant; if *The Shade of Barkov* was composed by somebody else, that somebody clearly knew Pushkin's early poetry as profoundly as Pushkin knew it himself. Of course, not all of these parallels are equally important; but we need to examine the exhaustive list of parallels to make a determination. Here are some good examples: "Accursed by Apollo" (Prokliaty Apollonom), said about poets, in *The Shade of Barkov* (line 100) and "And you, a poet accursed by Apollo" (A ty, poet, prokliatyi Apollonom) in *The Monk* (l. 17); "The aged virgin . . . grown gray under the penis" (Devitsu prestarelu // . . . Pod khuem posedelu) in *The Shade of Barkov* (ll. 186–88) and "Or the aged pug grown gray in the pillows" (Il' mos'ku prestarelu, / V podushkakh posedelu) in "To My Sister" ("K sestre"), composed in 1814; "To senseless poets" (Bessmyslennym poetam) in *The Shade of Barkov* (l. 102) and "We'll find senseless poets" (Naidem bessmyslennykh poetov) in "To Batiushkov" ("K Batiushkovu" [1814]); "He shouts everywhere: 'Great is Barkov!'" (Vezde glasit: "Velik Barkov!") in *The Shade of Barkov* (l. 123) and "They shout from generation to generation: 'Great, great is Svistov!'" (Glasiat iz roda v rody: / "Velik, velik—Svistov!"), meaning Barkov, in "A Small Town" ("Gorodok"), composed in 1815, and so on.[12]

Tsiavlovsky's commentary presents the first serious efforts to establish the literary context for *The Shade of Barkov* and its relations with the French and Russian burlesque ode, the Russian mock epic, as well as the lyrical-epic poems of Vasilii Zhukovsky (1783–1852) and their parodies. Having pointed out the significance of the lyceum "parodiomania" for Pushkin's early work, Tsiavlovsky then supported, with facts, Gaevsky's statement that *The Shade of Barkov* parodies a ballad by Zhukovsky called *Gromoboi* (*Gromoboi*), composed in 1810; he also discovered other important sources for Pushkin's poem—in particular, Zhukovsky's *Bard in the Camp of the Russian Warriors* (*Pevets vo stane russkikh voinov*), composed in 1812, and its parodic variation in Konstantin Batiushkov's (1787–1855) *Bard in the Colloquy of Lovers of the Russian Word* (*Pevets v Besede liubitelei russkogo slova*), composed in 1813. Lastly, Tsiavlovsky showed that Pushkin learned how "to rework parodically sublime literary works" from Paul Scarron and Alexis Piron, as well as from their Russian followers Vasilii Maikov (1728–78) and Barkov himself.[13]

Tsiavlovsky's results gave him every right to appraise the young Pushkin's ballad as "a work of great skill" and a "matchless" "oeuvre in the style of Barkov." At the same time, the scholar was not happy about his discovery. In a note addressed to a friend, Tsiavlovsky wrote, "Enclosed you will find . . . a new opus of Pushkin, but, honestly speaking, I am not radiant with joy. If only Pushkin had not written this filth [*Luchshe by Pushkin ne pisal etoi pakhabi*]."[14]

Convinced by Tsiavlovsky's results (which he started to communicate privately starting in the early 1930s), most prewar Pushkinists spoke in favor of Pushkin's authorship of the ballad, among them Vladimir Orlov (in his anthology of nineteenth-century epigrams and satires), Lev Modzalevsky (in his works on Pushkin's *The Shade of Fonvizin* [*Ten' Fon-Vizina*], composed in 1815), Iurii Tynianov (in his novel *Pushkin*), Georgii Chulkov (in *The Life of Pushkin* [*Zhizn' Pushkina*]), and Leonid Grossman (in his biography of Pushkin).[15] Many other scholars are known to have been familiar with Tsiavlovsky's investigations, but not one of them discounted or doubted Pushkin's authorship. This is why they unanimously decided to publish the ballad as a special supplement to the first volume of the "big academic" edition.

After World War II, Tsiavlovsky's commentary became known to a restricted circle of Moscow and Leningrad scholars. *The Shade of Barkov* was mentioned in 1950 in Dmitrii Blagoi's *The Artistic Development of Pushkin, 1813–1826* (*Tvorcheskii put' Pushkina, 1813–1826*). (However notorious Blagoi's name may be, his book—which was awarded a Stalin Prize of the second degree—remains one of the best studies of the early Pushkin.) Leonid Grossman in his 1955 article on Pushkin's *Ruslan and Liudmila* (*Ruslan i Liudmila*), composed between 1817 and 1820, gave an account of Tsiavlovsky's study and supported his conclusions.[16] Another book, which possibly is *the* best study of the early Pushkin—Boris Tomashevsky's 1956 monograph *Pushkin*—describes *The Shade of Barkov* as indisputably Pushkin's. Tellingly enough, Tomashevsky speaks of the ballad without explicit mention of its title: "Among the poems which are absent from Pushkin's *Collected Works* yet another poem should be added. Pushkin himself called it *The Shade of Korablev* [*Ten' Korableva*], considering the name of its hero itself (Barkov) to sound indecent."[17]

Then there was a long silence until the 1980s, when Valentin Nepomniashchy (in his book *Poetry and Destiny* [*Poeziia i sud'ba*]) and Iurii Lotman (in his article on Pushkin written for *History of World Literature* [*Istoriia vsemirnoi literatury*] published by the Maksim Gorky Institute for World Literature of the Russian Academy of Sciences) recalled *The Shade of Barkov* among Pushkin's works of the lyceum period.[18] This universal silence was determined by the sanctimonious atmosphere of the Khrushchev and Brezhnev periods (a curious and eloquent fact is that Khrushchev's "thaw" in no way affected society's attitude to the bawdy works of Russian classics). This atmosphere is well described in Lotman's letter to Vladimir Toporov (19 July 1983): "For me, to go there [Pushkin House] is now the same as to go down to the cesspool (excuse this unappetizing comparison!). In spring I needed a manuscript of Pushkin's *The Shade of Barkov* . . . They did not give it to me! And even gave me a lecture about how high one has to hold the honor of our classics and so on and so forth."[19] The "socialist culture" of the stagnation period was supposed to acquire and appropriate "the very best" of national and world cultures, and classics were proclaimed to have only positive—revolutionary, progressive, and highly moral—qualities (as opposed to negative—counterrevolutionary, reactionary, and amoral ones). The classic authors could have been "historically restricted," but they could not have been "immoral"; thus, aspects like anti-Semitism, adultery, or use of prostitutes were cut from their texts and were treated as if they were nonexistent. *The Shade of Barkov* was "nonexistent" in the same way, although it could be mentioned in passing in a specialized periodical, such as *Proceedings of the Pushkin Commission* (*Vremennik Pushkinskoi komissii*).[20]

The early 1990s were marked by the first appearance of *The Shade of Barkov* in print. The very first publication saw the light of day abroad: in 1990 Cesare De Michelis published the Russian text side by side with the Italian translation. His version of the ballad was based on Tsiavlovsky's reconstruction, Nikolai Lerner's (unnecessary) amendments taken from his 1929 article, and an enigmatic typewritten text of the ballad that turned out to be an inaccurate copy from the manuscript almanac *Flora*, dating from 1824 and preserved at the Russian State Library. In 1991, with the collapse of the Soviet Union, the public atmosphere in Russia drastically changed; censorship ceased to exist. Erotica and even pornography became legalized de facto, and the use of vulgar and even obscene language began to expand in the public sphere, including in the arts, documentaries, and the humanities (that is, obscenity became an object of study). Tsiavlovsky's reconstruction of *The Shade of Barkov* was published that same year, in the celebrated eleventh issue of the *Literary Review* (*Literaturnoe obozrenie*), which was devoted to the "erotic tradition in Russian literature." This publication demonstrated that "the honor of our classics" from Pushkin to Chekhov is a myth based on ideological manipulation.[21]

In 1992 two texts of *The Shade of Barkov* saw the light of day: a not particularly accurate version of the *Flora* text was published by its discoverer Alexander Iliushin, who did not mention its source, and one of the most inaccurate versions of *The Shade of Barkov* (from the manuscript *Fucking-Emblematic and Scabrous Almanac* [*Eblematichesko-skabreznyi al'manakh*], dating from 1865) was published by Valerii Sazhin as the supposedly earliest and most accurate copy of the ballad. This publication, protested by Maksim Shapir (1962–2006) in the *Literary Gazette* (*Literaturnaia gazeta*), gave ammunition to the argument that *The Shade of Barkov* is so poorly written that it cannot be Pushkin's. Shapir's objections were supported by Stefano Garzonio, who reviewed these editions of Pushkin's ballad in the first volume of the new Italian Russianist journal *Russica romana*.[22]

In 1993 the first post-Tsiavlovsky extensive study of *The Shade of Barkov*—Shapir's "From the History of Russian 'Ballad Verse'" ("Iz istorii russkogo 'balladnogo stikha'")—was published in the international journal *Russian Linguistics* and, in 1996 and 2000, republished in Russia with different amendments and under different titles. It is interesting to note that the 1996 publication appeared in the collection *The Anti-World of Russian Culture* (*Anti-mir russkoi kul'tury*) in the book series Russian Concealed Literature (Russkaia potaennaia literatura), which was promoted by the Ladomir publishing house. In 1995 this series was criticized by the official periodical the *Russian Gazette* (*Rossiiskaia gazeta*), after whose intervention an unsuccessful attempt was made (one of the last in post-Soviet Russia thus far) to prosecute the publishing house as a disseminator of pornography. Mikhail Gasparov, as a member of the Academy of Sciences and a State Prize winner, had to make a statement in support of the series; he argued that the expansion of interest in erotica and obscenities is a historically determined "pancultural shift" (obshchekul'turnyi sdvig) and that we have to study its course and its roots rather than fight against it.[23]

Shapir's study was devoted to the evolution of the semantic aura of so-called parodic ballad verse (Grigorii Vinokur's term, referring to a twelve-line stanza that alternates between iambic tetrameter and iambic trimeter) and its role in the polemics surrounding the "old and new styles" in the early nineteenth century. Shapir demonstrated that in their struggle against the "Slavophiles," the younger Karamzinists (first and foremost, Batiushkov and the early Pushkin) drew on the obscene burlesque poetry of the eighteenth century. At the same time, *The Shade of Barkov* was a double parody: Pushkin's parody of Batiushkov's parody of Zhukovsky. In his *Bard in the Colloquy of Lovers of the Russian Word*, Batiushkov had parodied Zhukovsky's *Bard in the Camp of the Russian Warriors* and elements of Zhukovsky's *Gromoboi*; in his *The Shade of Barkov*, Pushkin parodied *Gromoboi* and elements of *Bard in the Camp of the Russian Warriors*, and he also took Batiushkov's parody into account. This gave Shapir the right to say that Pushkin's parody is a travesty of Batiushkov's parody as well as a parody of Zhukovsky. One of the most apparent manifestations of Batiushkov's influence on *The Shade of Barkov* is the correspondence (already noted by Tsiavlovsky) between Batiushkov's description of the shade of Vasilii Trediakovsky and Pushkin's description of the shade of Barkov. Here is Batiushkov:

Чья тень парит под потолком
  Над нашими главами?
За ней, пред ней . . . о, страх!—кругом
  Поэты со стихами!
Се Тредьяковский в парике
  Засаленном, с кудрями,
С Телемахидою в руке,
  С Ролленем за плечами!

[Whose shade is hovering under the ceiling / above our heads? / Behind it, in front of it . . . o holy terror!—around us / there are poets with their verses! / Here is Trediakovsky in a wig, / curly and greasy, / with his *Telemakhida* in his hand, / with Rollin on his shoulders!][24]

And here is Pushkin:

Он видит—в ветхом сертуке,
  С спущенными штанами,
С хуиной толстою в руке,
  С отвислыми мудами
Явилась тень—идет к нему
  Дрожащими стопами,
Сияя сквозь ночную тьму
  Огнистыми очами.

[He sees—in a threadbare frock-coat, / with trousers pulled down, / With his thick penis in his hand, / With loose-hanging testicles, / The shade appeared: it is coming to him / with trembling steps, / its fiery eyes / shining through the nocturnal darkness.]

Note Pushkin's continuous "-ami" rhyme that, like Batiushkov's, embraces two quatrains (rather than one quatrain, as in Zhukovsky) and the straightforward correspondence between Batiushkov's "With his *Telemakhida* in his hand" (S Telemakhidoiu v ruke) and Pushkin's "With his thick penis in his hand" (S khuinoi tolstoiu v ruke). These correspondences do not have any equivalent in the sections of Zhukovsky's texts that are parodied (*Bard in the Camp of the Russian Warriors* [ll. 31–32] and *Gromoboi* [ll. 29–32]), which makes them even more valuable as a demonstration that Pushkin borrowed directly from Batiushkov.[25]

The first publications of *The Shade of Barkov* were accompanied by polemics on the pages of the Paris journal *Sintaksis* between the poet and journalist Andrei Chernov, who attacked Tsiavlovsky and Pushkin's authorship, and the lawyer and amateur Pushkinist Evgenii Shal'man, who spoke in support of them.[26] Chernov argued that "*The Shade of Barkov* was not written by a young boy but by an . . . old lecher, an extremely exhausted and experienced impotent who hates women and worships only his own phallus." Chernov believed that this old impotent was the poet Alexander Voeikov (1779–1839), a friend of Zhukovsky, who supposedly wrote the ballad in 1834–35 (which has now been disproved by the existence of manuscript copies from 1816–24).[27] It should be added that Shal'man was executor of Tatiana Tsiavlovskaia's will and possessed photocopies of documents concerning *The Shade of Barkov*, including a photocopy of the page proofs of the ballad that had been excised from the academic edition of Pushkin's work.

Shal'man prepared excerpts from Tsiavlovsky's commentary for publication in the same "erotic" issue of the *Literary Review* in which the text of *The Shade of Barkov* appeared, but in the end he changed his mind. In 1992, fragments from Tsiavlovsky's work were published by Alexander Iliushin and Konstantin Krasukhin. And only in 1996 did the journal *Philologica* (edited by Maksim Shapir and myself) publish the complete text of Tsiavlovsky's commentary based on Shal'man's photocopy of the page proofs and the Pushkin Museum typescript copy. This text was amended in the edition of *The Shade of Barkov* with comments and excursus edited by Maksim Shapir and myself, which saw the light of day in 2002.[28]

We pursued several goals in our edition. First of all, we attempted to reconstruct the text of the ballad on the basis of newly found sources (the 1821 copy and the 1824 *Flora* copy) and a critical analysis of the sources used by Tsiavlovsky. As a result, our version differs from Tsiavlovsky's by 25 percent (73 lines). For example, we restored the verb "eroshit'" (to dishevel) found in line 28 in the majority of the manuscripts: "I volosy eroshit!" (And dishevels his hair!). Tsiavlovsky rejected this reading (and replaced the verb "eroshit" with the impossible "klokochet" found in only one manuscript) for the simple reason that he disliked the inexact feminine rhyme "drochit—eroshit"; we demonstrated, however, that this rhyme type (when an affricate in one word corresponds to a spirant in the other) is common in the early Pushkin: it is found in *The Monk*, "A Small Town," and other poems from 1813 to 1815. In lines 118 and 261 we restored the expression "bagrova plesh'" (scarlet glans), which Tsiavlovsky had replaced with "Barkova plesh'" (Barkov's glans) in line 118 and with "I zharko plesh' [ognem gorit]" (And his glans [is burning] hot) in line 261. The variant "bagrova plesh'" is represented in the oldest manuscripts and supported by the vocabulary of the eighteenth-century Barkoviana (where we often find "plesh' bagriana" [scarlet glans]). In line 171 all the sources available to Tsiavlovsky gave distorted or meaningless phrasing, while the manuscripts from the 1820s give a coherent reading: "I ved'me strazhdushchei veshchal" (And he told the suffering witch); and so on.[29]

Second, we tried to find new arguments in support of the traditional attribution of the ballad to Pushkin. In particular, we revealed many points of contact between the poetics and imagery of *The Shade of Barkov*, on the one hand, and those of Pushkin the lyceist, on the other, such as the poet's persona as monk as well as identification of the lyceum as cloister and a dream of escaping out of it, found in *The Monk*, *The Shade of Barkov*, and "To My Sister." We also multiplied the parallels between the ballad and other poems of Pushkin.[30] It comes as no surprise that Tsiavlovsky missed quite a few impressive parallels: he did not have at his disposal either *The Dictionary of Pushkin's Language* (*Slovar' iazyka Pushkina*) or Thomas Shaw's concordance to Pushkin's poetry, not to mention modern digital libraries with full-text search.

Third, we identified Pushkin's two poems with which *The Shade of Barkov* has the most in common in terms of poetic phraseology and to which it is closest in genre: the mock epic *The Monk* and the romantic narrative poem (or verse romance) *Ruslan and Liudmila*, which Pushkin began writing immediately after he left the lyceum. Compare, for instance:

"Just follow my example" (Posledui lish' primeru moemu), says Barkov in *The Monk* (canto 1, line 23); "Just follow, mother-fucker, / my good advice" (Posledui lish', ebena mat' / Moim blagim sovetam), says the shade of Barkov in *The Shade of Barkov* (ll. 103–4); "Follow my advice" (Posledui moemu sovetu), says Naina in *Ruslan and Liudmila* (c. 2, l. 113).[31]

Finally, we show that the rhythm and rhyme of *The Shade of Barkov* is considerably closer to Pushkin's prosody than to the prosody of Zhukovsky and Batiushkov, who provided the metric pattern for the ballad. Thus, according to Shapir's calculations, in *The Shade of Barkov*, just as in Pushkin's "Carousing Students" ("Piruiushchie studenty" [1814]), written using the same "parodic ballad verse," the iambic tetrameters with pyrrhic (unstressed) third foot predominate (51.5 percent) over the fully stressed iambic tetrameters (36 percent), while in Zhukovsky and Batiushkov's texts fully stressed iambic tetrameter is more frequent by 10 to 15 percent than partially stressed iambic tetrameter. In early Pushkin (including *The Shade of Barkov*), the third foot of the iambic tetrameter is stressed in fewer than half of all lines, while in Zhukovsky and Batiushkov it is stressed in more than 60 percent of the lines.[32]

After 1996, when Tsiavlovsky's study was finally published, the number of skeptical voices increased. In 1994, Vadim Vatsuro (1935–2000), the editor of the "pilot" volume of the new academic edition of Pushkin's works, had identified the obscene ballad as a poem by Pushkin and promised "to publish it separately as a supplement in a limited number of printed copies." However, in 1999, in the final version of this volume, he justified the exclusion of the ballad by the "complexity of the problem of its text and its authorship."[33] No arguments against Pushkin's authorship were presented; moreover, the commentary to this volume (based on Tsiavlovsky!) always mentions *The Shade of Barkov* as a work of Pushkin's. Unlike Efremov or Tsiavlovsky, Vatsuro was not under censorial pressure, and one can only guess at his reasons for exclusion of the ballad from the volume (and even from its *dubia* section), apart from the trivial fact that the textological problem of *The Shade of Barkov* turned out to be too sophisticated and was not solved in time.

In 2000 the first volume of a collection of Pushkin's works arranged in chronological order (rather than by genre) was published under the editorship of Valentin Nepomniashchy by the Maksim Gorky Institute for World Literature. Here Nepomniashchy says that the ballad "could have been placed in the *dubia* section, if only its text had been suitable for print." The next year, in the fourth edition of his book *Poetry and Destiny*, the scholar once again called *The Shade of Barkov* a "splendid ribaldry" by Pushkin. In his article of 1992, Nepomniashchy had maintained that, even in the obscene ballad, "the young Pushkin is Pushkin, whatever A[ndrei] Chernov may think of it." This article was republished in 1999 as part of his *Pushkin: A Russian Picture of the World* (*Pushkin: Russkaia kartina mira*). Thus, in 1999 and 2001 Nepomniashchy considered *The Shade of Barkov* an authentic work, and in 2000 he called it dubious. Later, however, in 2005, Nepomniashchy declared that Pushkin's authorship of *The Shade of Barkov* is "more than evidently hypothetical," and alleged that all the prewar Pushkinists agreed about Pushkin's authorship of *The Shade of Barkov* simply because they were all politically engaged: they supposedly wanted to oppose a new "postrevolutionary" Pushkin to the imperial Pushkin. One might think that Nepomniashchy extrapolates from his own experience and his own ideological evolution: he, who was the author of the Pushkin entry in the third edition of *The Great Soviet Encyclopedia* (*Bol'shaia sovetskaia entsiklopediia*), which had to represent the official Soviet view of the universe, became the main partisan of the religious reinterpretation of Pushkin when the times and the political atmosphere changed.[34]

After Vatsuro's and Nepomniashchy's disavowals, the statements of the ballad's dubious character multiplied—first and foremost, they came from Moscow and St. Petersburg "academic" Pushkinists (this does not mean, of course, that every scholar at the Institute for World Literature and Pushkin House shares this point of view). In 2001 Vatsuro's colleague Sergei Fomichev wrote: "No one has so far seriously proved Pushkin's authorship of the poem *The Shade of Barkov* (of lyceum origins). . . . Doubts about it are rightful, first of all, in view of the pure weakness of the versification [*chisto versifikatsionnoi slabosti*] of this work, which is unlikely to be found even in the early Pushkin (see, for example, his 1814 poem *The Monk*)." We need hardly mention that, on the basis of the evolution of Pushkin's handwriting in his early manuscripts, *The Monk* is generally considered to have been composed in June or July 1813 (this fact is important for the chronology of Pushkin's early works), while the "weakness of the versification" may characterize the inaccurate copy of *The Shade of Barkov* published by Sazhin rather than the text of the ballad itself, and therefore this "characteristic" cannot help us in attribution. At the same time, Fomichev is ready to acknowledge *The Shade of Barkov* as a collective work of the lyceists (apparently, all together they were less moral and less skillful than Pushkin alone).[35]

Ekaterina Larionova of Pushkin House, in her review of our book on *The Shade of Barkov*, stated that Pushkin's authorship of this work "cannot be either factually proved or categorically refuted." Her colleague Vadim Rak, in his section of the same review, called the ballad "scabrous verses of very dubious descent." In our reply we pointed out that the reviewers and their colleagues did not present any decisive counter-evidence. The main counterarguments are always of an aesthetic and ethical nature: this fact was confirmed in their semi-informal interviews with Joe Peschio.[36] As in the time of Brezhnev, Pushkin scholars of the twenty-first century are reminiscent of political instructors guarding the sacred texts, who cannot allow any sullying of the poet's public image. Yes, indeed, "if only Pushkin had not written this filth!"

The next and, so far, the last champion of Pushkin's chastity was the amateur poet and philological dilettante Viktor Vogman, who publishes under the nickname Viktor Esipov (he now holds a position at the Institute for World Literature under the guidance of Nepomniashchy). In 2003 and 2005 he published two versions of his forty-page-long article against *The Shade of Barkov* and its editors (i.e., Shapir and myself) and later included this article in a collection of his papers printed (at his own expense) in 2006. In his *anticritica* he tries to reveal what he thinks to be glaring contradictions between *The Shade of Barkov* and the language norm of the early nineteenth century (as he understands it). Unfortunately, most examples reveal the critic's ignorance of the history of the Russian language. For instance, he qualifies the accentual form "dybóm" (instead of "dýbom") as "irregular," although this stress may easily be found in Ivan Nordstet's dictionary (1780–82). Another supposed mistake is found in the line "And having filled the glass with vodka" (I vodkoiu naliv bokal): Esipov assumes that Pushkin and his friends could not pour vodka into "bokaly" (today, wineglasses or goblets) but should rather have used "riumki" (small wineglasses) or "stakany" (tumblers or beakers). However, Vladimir Dal' (1801–72), who was only three years younger than Pushkin and thus belonged to the same generation, writes in his celebrated dictionary that "bokal" is a "big *stakan*" or "big *riumka*." In Pushkin's time *bokal* and *stakan* were synonyms, and this is why, in a lyceum collective poem published in the very first issue of the journal the *Lyceum Sage* (*Litseiskii Mudrets*), the sound of a *stakan* is at the same time called "the ring of a *bokal*" (zvon bokal'nyi).[37]

To respond to these challenges, Maksim Shapir and I published both an abridged and an extended version of a paper on the authorship of

The Shade of Barkov. Both versions appeared in 2005: in the Literature and Language series of the *Bulletin of the Russian Academy of Sciences* and in the yearbook *Anthropology of Culture* (*Antropologiia kul'tury*) published by Moscow State University, respectively. The *Anthropology of Culture* publication is titled "Textology vs. Axiology (Once More about Pushkin's Ballad *The Shade of Barkov*)" ("Tekstologiia vs aksiologiia: Eshche raz ob avtorstve ballady Pushkina *Ten' Barkova*"). In its title, "textology" stands for "philology," and "axiology" for "ideology."[38]

This 2005 article provides a detailed analysis of all the arguments for and against attributing the obscene ballad *The Shade of Barkov* to Pushkin. After clarifying and analyzing all the biographical, provenance, linguistic, poetic, literary-historical, and socio-psychological issues involved, we conclude that there is no doubt that Pushkin wrote the ballad. We stress once again that the versification, poetics, and imagery of *The Shade of Barkov* are considerably closer to Pushkin's poetry than anybody else's, and we point to eloquent phraseological and rhythmic parallels between the ballad and other works of early Pushkin—including works of the early post-lyceum period—such as "And his heart was throbbing strongly" (I serdtse sil'no bilos') in *The Shade of Barkov* (l. 230) and "I am trembling, and my heart is throbbing strongly" (Ia trepeshchu, i serdtse sil'no b'etsia) in *The Monk* (c. 1, l. 153); "And dishevels his hair!" (I volosy eroshit!) in *The Shade of Barkov* (l. 28) and "I dishevel my hair in tufts" (Eroshu volosy klokami) in "To My Aristarchus" ("Moemu Aristarkhu" [l. 31], composed 1815); "The guy's soul stood still in him" (Dusha v detine zamerla) in *The Shade of Barkov* (l. 237) and "And Ruslan's soul stood still in him" (I zamerla dusha v Ruslane) in *Ruslan and Liudmila* (c. 1, l. 121); "He fucks for hours on end" (Ebet po tselym on chasam) in *The Shade of Barkov* (l. 199) and "He watched for hours on end" (Smotrel po tselym on chasam) in *The Captive of the Caucasus* (*Kavkazskii plennik* [c. 1, l. 232], composed between 1820 and 1821), and so forth. Thus, Pushkin's authorship cannot be rejected on the basis of stylistic, lexical, or phraseological considerations: at the sight of hundreds of parallels between the text under consideration and those works wholly accepted as being the authentic works of Pushkin, we have no warrant for saying that the obscene ballad cannot be Pushkin's. At the same time, no such parallels are found between *The Shade of Barkov* and the works of other lyceum poets.[39]

The following year (2006), we published "The Evolution of Styles in Russian Poetry from Lomonosov to Pushkin." In this article, we offer a new global model of the evolution of Russian poetic styles that emphasizes the special role played by the burlesque and the mock epic in the Russian poetic tradition. We trace throughout the history of Russian poetic styles an evolutionary "rhythm" of swinging back and forth between two types of stylistic organization, the homogeneous and the heterogeneous. Styles of the homogeneous type are based on the combination of elements of the same stylistic register, while heterogeneous styles emerge from stylistic contrasts effected through the combination of elements from disparate registers. The first homogeneous style, the sublime style, was formalized by Mikhail Lomonosov (1711–65) in his odes; an alternative to sublime style, the so-called middle style, was being developed at the same time by Alexander Sumarokov (1717–77) in his lyric poetry. The first heterogeneous style was realized in Barkov's obscene burlesque, which was followed by the "official" burlesque of Gavrila Derzhavin (1743–1816), who managed to combine the heterogeneous Barkovian style with Lomonosov's sublimity. Nikolai Karamzin (1766–1826) and his followers sought to bring Sumarokov's stylistic program to its logical conclusion (a new homogeneity).

Yet it was two of his adherents, Batiushkov and Pushkin, who brought about the next turn in the literary reception of Barkov (a new heterogeneity) in their burlesque attacks on the literary society Colloquy of Lovers of the Russian Word. Pushkin developed a number of minor genres in the framework of the homogeneous Karamzinian stylistic tradition, but in the grand genres he did quite the opposite, and a heterogeneous burlesque vein runs throughout, from the mock-heroic *The Monk* and the obscene burlesque *The Shade of Barkov* to *Ruslan and Liudmila* and further—to *Eugene Onegin* (*Evgenii Onegin*), with its parody of the classical epic, and the self-parodic *Little House in Kolomna* (*Domik v Kolomne*), composed in 1830. In *Little House in Kolomna* the elements of style have no autonomous semantics: one and the same word, one and the same expression, one and the same theme can be offered up as both high and low, serious and comic, elegiac and burlesque. The objective stylistic unity of Lomonosov and Sumarokov, on the one hand, and the objective stylistic dissonances of Barkov and Derzhavin, on the other hand, are supplanted by Pushkin's subjective unity of style, which depends primarily on intonation and context. This is where *The Monk* and *The Shade of Barkov* eventually led Pushkin.[40]

Today the scholar who is studying *The Shade of Barkov* most actively is Leonid Bessmertnykh, a well-known expert in Russian "concealed literature." He spent several years compiling a catalog of the collection of erotic literature and art that belonged to Nikolai Skorodumov

(1887–1947), former deputy director of the Moscow State University Library, and that now forms part of the erotica archive at the Russian State Library. In the 1920s and 1930s Tsiavlovsky, like other prewar scholars, used Skorodumov's collection, and that is where he found two copies of *The Shade of Barkov*. After Skorodumov's death, his heirs allegedly tried to sell his collection in the United States or Japan; under this pretext it was confiscated by the NKVD and placed in the Special Custody Department (Otdel spetsial'nogo khraneniia, or "spetskhran") of the Lenin Library. Because the collection was not inventoried until 1968, it was not usable even by those select few who had access to it. Between 1991 and 1993, the "spetskhran" was reorganized, and since 2000 the corresponding part of the archive has been called the Collection of Literature for Restricted Use (Fond literatury dlia sluzhebnogo pol'zovaniia, or DSP); its materials are still not accessible to the majority of general visitors.[41]

Bessmertnykh has revised Tsiavlovsky's readings of the copies of *The Shade of Barkov* from Skorodumov's collection. He has also reconstructed the history of all available manuscript copies and discovered two new copies of Pushkin's ballad dating from 1816 and 1820. We can assert that the newly found copies throw fresh light on several unclarities in the text of the ballad and urge us to amend the reconstruction. For instance, Tsiavlovsky thought line 264 should read "And a hairy *kerch'* is blazing!" (I pyshet kerch' mokhnatyi!). The word "kerch'" is not known to historians of the Russian language, so our colleague Igor Dobrodomov suggested that "kerch'" had replaced the word "kher" (prick), which, in its turn, could have replaced the original obscene word "khui" (also meaning "prick" but more indecent than the euphemism "kher") found in several manuscripts. However, now we know that "kerch'" was a misreading of "korn'," a desyllabified variant of "koren'" (root).[42]

At the same time, Bessmertnykh plans to suggest a few changes in the traditional view of *The Shade of Barkov* that appear dubitable to me. First and foremost, Bessmertnykh stands up for 1813 as the date of the ballad's composition. He admits that, from the point of view of genre, phraseology, and imagery, *The Shade of Barkov* is nearest to *The Monk*, but he wants to interpret this relationship in the opposite direction: he thinks *The Shade of Barkov* was written before *The Monk* and is, in fact, the very first poem Pushkin wrote. To support such a chronological shift, he is ready to suppose that Pushkin was not familiar with Batiushkov's parody of Zhukovsky when he was composing *The Shade of Barkov*. Although Batiushkov's *Bard in the Colloquy of Lovers of the Russian Word* was composed in March 1813, even his close friends complained that they had not obtained a copy of the parody as late as July and October 1813. The lyceists knew this poem from Alexander Gorchakov's manuscript copy, which was written on paper watermarked 1814.[43] Thus, in my opinion, *The Shade of Barkov* could not have been composed earlier than mid-1814. (In the career of Pushkin the lyceist, one year makes a big difference.) Besides Bessmertnykh, the only scholar who has assumed that *The Shade of Barkov* was composed before *The Monk* (that is, in spring or early summer 1813) was Grossman, but in the 1950s he changed his view after he became acquainted with Tsiavlovsky's commentary.[44]

To appreciate and appraise the new facts and arguments in full, we have to wait until Bessmertnykh's book on *The Shade of Barkov* comes off the press. It is forthcoming from Ladomir in the Russian Concealed Literature book series in 2012. I hope further discussions will demonstrate who is right and who is wrong on different issues and why. I also hope that the time has come to debate scholarly questions rather than ideological, axiological, and neomythological conjectures.

Notes

1. Mikhail L. Gasparov, *Zapisi i vypiski* (Moscow: Novoe literaturnoe obozrenie, 2000), 87; see also Mikhail L. Gasparov, "Iu. M. Lotman: Nauka i ideologiia," in his *Izbrannye trudy*, vol. 2 (Moscow: Iazyki russkoi kul'tury, 1997), 490.

2. *Imia Rossiia: Istoricheskii vybor 2008*, http://www.nameofrussia.ru (accessed 12 August 2009).

3. Abram Tertz [Andrei Siniavsky], *Strolls with Pushkin*, trans. Catharine Theimer Nepomnyashchy and Slava I. Yastremski (New Haven: Yale University Press, 1993). On demythologization and eroticism, see Sergei Panov's review of Aleksandr Aleksandrov's *Pushkin: Chastnaia zhizn'* (Moscow: Zakharov, 2000) in *Novaia russkaia kniga* 8 (2001): 9–10. On Valentin Nepomniashchy's interpretations of Pushkin, see Sergei Bocharov, "O chtenii Pushkina," *Novyi mir* 6 (1994): 238–45, Benedikt M. Sarnov, "'. . . I gde opustish' ty kopyta?'" *Voprosy literatury* 4 (1994): 38–101; and Feliks Raskol'nikov, "Pushkin i religiia," *Voprosy literatury* 3 (2004): 81–112.

4. Viktor P. Gaevskii, "Pushkin v litsee i litseiskie ego stikhotvoreniia," *Sovremennik* 97.1 (1863): 155–57; Aleksandr S. Pushkin, *Sochineniia*, 3rd ed., 6 vols., ed. Petr A. Efremov (St. Petersburg: Iakov A. Isakov, 1880–81), 1:55–57 (at least three uncut copies of this volume are preserved in Moscow and St.

Petersburg libraries); Petr A. Efremov, *Mnimyi Pushkin v stikhakh, proze i izobrazheniiakh* (St. Petersburg: Aleksei S. Suvorin, 1903), 6–7; Aleksandr S. Pushkin, *Sochineniia*, 8 vols., ed. Petr A. Efremov (St. Petersburg: A. S. Suvorin, 1903–5), 8:18; Mstislav A. Tsiavlovskii, "Kommentarii (k ballade A. Pushkina 'Ten' Barkova')," ed. Evgenii S. Shal'man and Igor' A. Pil'shchikov, *Philologica* 3.5–7 (1996): 163, 166. It is worth noting that when *The Shade of Barkov* was composed, Alexander Polezhaev (1804/6–38) was between eight and ten years old. On the Efremov controversy see Leonid V. Bessmertnykh, *"Ten' Barkova" A. S. Pushkina: Pervoe krupnoe proizvedenie poeta, sozdannoe v mae 1813 g. do poemy "Monakh," im zhe osuzhdennoe i unichtozhennoe po sovetu kniazia A. M. Gorchakova (po dvum novonaidennym spiskam 1816 i 1820 godov)* (Moscow: Ladomir, forthcoming), chap. 1.

5. Pavel Shchegolev, "Poema A. S. Pushkina 'Monakh,'" *Krasnyi arkhiv* 31 (1928): 167–72; Nikolai O. Lerner, "Neizvestnaia ballada A. S. Pushkina 'Ten' Barkova,'" *Ogonek*, 3 February 1929, 8–9.

6. Aleksandr S. Pushkin, *Polnoe sobranie sochinenii*, 17 vols., ed. Vladimir D. Bonch-Bruevich et al. (Moscow: AN SSSR, 1937–59); Aleksandr S. Pushkin, *Stikhotvoreniia litseiskikh let, 1813–1817*, ed. Vadim E. Vatsuro (St. Petersburg: Nauka, 1994); Aleksandr S. Pushkin, *Polnoe sobranie sochinenii*, 20 vols., ed. Vadim E. Vatsuro et al. (St. Petersburg: Nauka, 1999–). On Stalin's interference in the preparation of the "big academic" edition, see Sergei Bondi, "Ob akademicheskom izdanii sochinenii Pushkina," *Voprosy literatury* 2 (1963): 125–27; Ludwig L. Domgerr, "Sovetskoe akademicheskoe izdanie Pushkina," *Novyi zhurnal* 167 (1987): 237–42; and Andrei L. Grishunin, "Problemy pushkinskoi tekstologii v otsenke Iu. G. Oksmana," *Izvestiia Rossiiskoi akademii nauk: Seriia literatury i iazyka* 58.3 (1999): 4–5. On the Tsiavlovskys, see Mstislav A. Tsiavlovskii and Tat'iana G. Tsiavlovskaia, *Vokrug Pushkina*, ed. Kseniia P. Bogaevskaia and Sergei I. Panov (Moscow: Novoe literaturnoe obozrenie, 2000).

7. Pavel Shchegolev, "Poema 'Monakh,'" in his *Pushkin: Issledovaniia, stat'i i materialy*, vol. 2, 3rd ed. (Moscow: Gosudarstvennoe izdatel'stvo khudozhestvennoi literatury, 1931), 31; Tat'iana G. Tsiavlovskaia, "Bibliografiia trudov M. A. Tsiavlovskogo," in Mstislav A. Tsiavlovskii, *Stat'i o Pushkine*, ed. Tat'iana G. Tsiavlovskaia (Moscow: AN SSSR, 1962), 418.

8. Tsiavlovskaia told this story to Evgenii Shal'man; see his introductory note to Aleksandr S. Pushkin, "'Ten' Barkova' (Kontaminirovannaia redaktsiia M. A. Tsiavlovskogo v sopostavlenii s novonaidennym spiskom 1821 g.)," ed. Igor' A. Pil'shchikov, *Philologica* 3.5–7 (1996): 133–35. Another version of the story was told by the Pushkin scholar Il'ia Feinberg; see this fragment from his memoirs: "Istoriia nesostoiavsheisia publikatsii," ed. Mael' Feinberg, *LG-Dos'e* (June 1990): 26. There are factual inaccuracies in both publications; they have been corrected by Bessmertnykh in his *"Ten' Barkova" A. S. Pushkina*, chap. 3.

9. The deed of conveyance was published by Shal'man in his preface to Pushkin, "'Ten' Barkova' (Kontaminirovannaia redaktsiia)," 155–56. For the

archival materials see Manuscripts Department, Pushkin House, St. Petersburg, f. 373; and Izol'd A. Polonskii Collection, Alexander S. Pushkin State Museum, Moscow, KP 8057/SP174.

10. Pushkin, "'Ten' Barkova' (Kontaminirovannaia redaktsiia)," 136–53; Tsiavlovskii, "Kommentarii," 171–98. Most of the manuscript copies Tsiavlovsky used are now preserved in archives (Russian State Archive for Literature and Art, Moscow; Manuscripts Department, Russian State Library, Moscow; Custody Department, Russian State Library, Moscow; Manuscripts Department, Russian National Library, St. Petersburg; Pushkin House, St. Petersburg). For their descriptions, see Tsiavlovskii, "Kommentarii," 167–71; Aleksandr S. Pushkin, *"Ten' Barkova": Teksty, Kommentarii, Ekskursy*, ed. Igor' A. Pil'shchikov and Maksim I. Shapir (Moscow: Iazyki slavianskoi kul'tury, 2002), 176–81, 302–4; and Bessmertnykh, *"Ten' Barkova" A. S. Pushkina*, chap. 2. It should be pointed out again that none of these copies represents the authentic text of Pushkin's poem: all of them are copies from other copies, and they contain numerous distortions; none of them is privileged, but each of them reflects the original in a different way.

11. Tsiavlovskii, "Kommentarii," 162–67, 198–213; see also Fedor E. Korsh, "Razbor voprosa ob okonchanii 'Rusalki' Pushkina po zapisi D. P. Zueva," pt. 1, *Izvestiia Otdeleniia russkogo iazyka i slovesnosti Imperatorskoi Akademii Nauk* 3 (1898): 634–785, Fedor E. Korsh, "Razbor voprosa ob okonchanii 'Rusalki' Pushkina po zapisi D. P. Zueva," pts. 2 and 3, *Izvestiia Otdeleniia russkogo iazyka i slovesnosti Imperatorskoi Akademii nauk* 4 (1899): 1–100 and 476–588, esp. 483–501; Aleksandr S. Pushkin, *Sochineniia: Perepiska*, 3 vols., ed. Vladimir I. Saitov (St. Petersburg: Imperatorskaia Akademiia nauk, 1906–11); Aleksandr S. Pushkin, *Pis'ma*, vols. 1 and 2, ed. Boris L. Modzalevskii (Moscow: Gosudarstvennoe izdatel'stvo, 1926–28); and Aleksandr S. Pushkin, *Pis'ma*, vol. 3, ed. Lev B. Modzalevskii (Moscow: Academia, 1935). See also Viktor V. Vinogradov, *Iazyk Pushkina: Pushkin i istoriia russkogo literaturnogo iazyka* (Moscow: Academia, 1935); and Viktor V. Vinogradov, *Stil' Pushkina* (Moscow: Gosudarstvennoe izdatel'stvo khudozhestvennoi literatury, 1941). Korsh's article is rather unfortunate; despite numerous useful observations, he wrongly concludes that the last part of Pushkin's play-in-verse *The Water Nymph* (*Rusalka*), composed between 1829 and 1832, was an authentic work of Pushkin's, when in fact it was fabricated by a certain Dmitrii P. Zuev. This is why this article (which spoiled Korsh's reputation in the eyes of later generations of Pushkinists) is very rarely mentioned in the scholarship and is not mentioned by Tsiavlovsky either.

12. Tsiavlovskii, "Kommentarii," 218–28. The first scholar who noticed some of these correspondences was Lerner, whom Tsiavlovsky disliked personally and did not cite as his predecessor in this respect. "Prokliaty[i] Apollonom" in both poems is, in effect, a quotation from Voltaire's *La pucelle d'Orléans* ("maudit par Apollon" [c. 1, l. 21]) and reflects Pushkin's early interest in *La pucelle*; see also Shchegolev, "Poema A. S. Pushkina 'Monakh,'" 168–69; and Shchegolev,

"Poema 'Monakh,'" 27–28. On Pushkin's rhymes with "posedelyi," see Vladislav F. Khodasevich, *Poeticheskoe khoziaistvo Pushkina: Kniga pervaia* (Leningrad: Mysl', 1924), 11–12.

13. Tsiavlovskii, "Kommentarii," 217–20, 230–38. Batiushkov's *Bard in the Colloquy of Lovers of the Russian Word* was coauthored with the poet Alexander Izmailov (who wrote only a couple of stanzas).

14. Tsiavlovskii, "Kommentarii," 265; for a facsimile of Tsiavlovsky's letter, see Evgenii S. Shal'man, "A vse-taki eto Pushkin! . . . (Otvet A. Chernovu)," *Sintaksis* 31 (1991): 116.

15. *Epigramma i satira: Iz istorii literaturnoi bor'by XIX-go veka*, 2 vols., ed. Vladimir N. Orlov (Moscow: Academia, 1931), 1:146; Lev B. Modzalevskii, "'Ten' Fonvizina': Neizdannaia satiricheskaia poema Pushkina," *Literaturnoe nasledstvo* 16–18 (1934): 815–17, 822; "'Ten' Fon-Vizina," ed. Lev B. Modzalevskii, in *Pushkin: Vremennik Pushkinskoi komissii*, vol. 1 (Moscow: AN SSSR, 1936), 13–15, 17, 22; Iurii N. Tynianov, *Pushkin* (Leningrad: Khudozhestvennaia literatura, 1936), 1–2, 538, 546; Georgii Chulkov, *Zhizn' Pushkina* (Moscow: Gosudarstvennoe izdatel'stvo khudozhestvennoi literatury, 1938), 39; Leonid P. Grossman, *Pushkin* (Moscow: Molodaia gvardiia, 1939), 101–2.

16. Dmitrii D. Blagoi, *Tvorcheskii put' Pushkina, 1813–1826* (Moscow: AN SSSR, 1950), 120, 548; Leonid P. Grossman, "Stil' i zhanr poemy 'Ruslan i Liudmila,'" *Uchenye zapiski Moskovskogo gorodskogo pedagogicheskogo instituta imeni V. P. Potemkina* 48 (1955): 153, 156–57. *The Shade of Barkov* is also mentioned in the second and the third editions of Grossman's biography of Pushkin published in 1958 and 1960, respectively.

17. Boris V. Tomashevskii, *Pushkin*, 2 vols. (Moscow: AN SSSR, 1956–61), 1:39. The story about Pushkin's having called the ballad *The Shade of Korablev* was reported by Gaevsky; in replacing Barkov for Korablev, Pushkin played upon the synonymy of the terms "barka" (barge) and "korabl'" (ship).

18. Valentin S. Nepomniashchii, *Poeziia i sud'ba: Stat'i i zametki o Pushkine* (Moscow: Sovetskii pisatel', 1983), 302; Iurii M. Lotman, "Pushkin," in *Istoriia vsemirnoi literatury*, 9 vols. (Moscow: Nauka, 1983–94), 6:322; Iurii M. Lotman, "Pushkin: Etapy tvorchestva," in his *V shkole poeticheskogo slova: Pushkin; Lermontov; Gogol'* (Moscow: Prosveshchenie, 1988), 9.

19. Iurii M. Lotman, *Pis'ma: 1940–1993*, ed. Boris F. Egorov (Moscow: Shkola "Iazyki russkoi kul'tury," 1997), 686.

20. See Lev S. Sidiakov, "'Ten' Fonvizina,'" in *Vremennik Pushkinskoi komissii*, vol. 23 (Leningrad: Nauka, 1989), 91 (with reference to Lev B. Modzalevsky).

21. Aleksandr Pushkin, *L'ombra di Barkòv: Ballata*, ed. Cesare G. De Michelis (Venice: Marsilio, 1990); Manuscripts Department, Russian State Library, Moscow, f. 178, op. 1, ed. khr. 1024, fol. 109–17v.; Aleksandr S. Pushkin, "Ten' Barkova," *Literaturnoe obozrenie* 11 (1991): 26–27. On cultural changes in Russia in the early 1990s, see in particular Nikolai A. Bogomolov, "Ot sostavitelia," in *Anti-mir russkoi kul'tury: Iazyk, Fol'klor, Literatura* (Moscow: Ladomir, 1996), 5–6; Andrei Zorin, "Legalizatsiia obstsennoi leksiki i ee kul'turnye posledstviia," in

Anti-mir russkoi kul'tury, 121–39; Paul W. Goldschmidt, "Article 242: Past, Present, and Future," in *Eros and Pornography in Russian Culture*, ed. Marcus C. Levitt and Andrei L. Toporkov (Moscow: Ladomir, 1999), 459–538; Igor' S. Kon, "Erotika i pornografiia v rossiiskikh politicheskikh debatakh," in *Eros and Pornography in Russian Culture*, 539–52; Gasan Guseinov, *DSP: Sovetskie ideologemy v russkom diskurse 1990-kh* (Moscow: Tri kvadrata, 2003).

22. *Tri veka poezii russkogo Erosa: Publikatsii i issledovaniia*, ed. Aleksandr A. Iliushin and Aleksandr N. Shchuplov (Moscow: Izdatel'skii tsentr teatra "Piat' vecherov," 1992), 62–67; Ivan Barkov et al., *Devich'ia igrushka*, ed. V. Sazhin (St. Petersburg: Biblioteka Zvezdy, 1992), 137–52; Manuscripts Department, Russian National Library, St. Petersburg, f. 905, op. 2, ed. khr. Q.769, fol. 43–53; Maksim I. Shapir, "'Khudozhestvenno-unikal'noe izdanie,' ili 'Devich'i shalosti' publikatora," *Literaturnaia gazeta*, 14 October 1992, 4; Stefano Garzonio, "Ob izdatel'skoi sud'be ballady *Ten' Barkova*: Kriticheskii obzor," *Russica romana* 1 (1994): 209–18.

23. Maksim I. Shapir, "Iz istorii russkogo 'balladnogo stikha': 'Perom vladeet kak eldoi,'" *Russian Linguistics* 17.1 (1993): 57–84; Andrei Shcherbakov, "'Ty ne zhmi menia k bereze,' ili Pokhabshchina po-nauchnomu," *Rossiiskaia gazeta*, 23 May 1995, 16; Maksim I. Shapir, "Iz istorii 'parodicheskogo balladnogo stikha': 'Perom vladeet kak eldoi,'" in *Anti-mir russkoi kul'tury*, 232–66; Mikhail L. Gasparov, "O serii 'Russkaia potaennaia literatura' izdatel'stva 'Ladomir,'" in *Anti-mir russkoi kul'tury*, 406–8; Maksim I. Shapir, "K semantike 'parodicheskogo balladnogo stikha' ('Ten' Barkova' v kontekste polemiki o starom i novom sloge')," in his *Universum versus: Iazyk, stikh, smysl v russkoi poezii XVIII–XX vekov* (Moscow: Iazyki russkoi kul'tury, 2000), 1:192–223. The term "Russkaia potaennaia literatura" (Russian concealed literature) belongs to Nikolai Ogarev, who published an anthology under this title in emigration in 1861.

24. Besides the infamous *Telemakhida*, which was a verse translation of François Fénelon's prose novel *Les aventures de Télémaque*, Trediakovsky also translated Charles Rollin's voluminous *Histoire ancienne* (1730–38) and *Histoire romaine* (1738–48).

25. Tsiavlovskii, "Kommentarii," 219–20, 277–78; Shapir, "Iz istorii russkogo 'balladnogo stikha,'" 57–60; Shapir, "K semantike 'parodicheskogo balladnogo stikha,'" 192–96; Pushkin, *"Ten' Barkova": Teksty, Kommentarii, Ekskursy*, 240–41, 316.

26. Andrei Iu. Chernov, "'Ten' Barkova', ili eshche o pushkinskikh eroticheskikh nozhkakh," *Sintaksis* 30 (1991): 129–64; Shal'man, "A vse-taki eto Pushkin!" 110–18. For another critique of Chernov, see Aleksandr A. Latsis, "V poiskakh utrachennogo smysla," in *Tri veka poezii russkogo Erosa*, 120–24.

27. Chernov, "'Ten' Barkova,' ili eshche o pushkinskikh eroticheskikh nozhkakh," 160, 162–64.

28. Evgenii S. Shal'man, "Vokrug 'Teni Barkova,'" *Nezavisimaia gazeta*, 14 January 1992, 8; Aleksandr A. Iliushin and Konstantin G. Krasukhin, eds., *"Letite, grusti i pechali . . .": Nepodtsenzurnaia russkaia poeziia XVIII–XIX vv.* (Moscow:

Littera, 1992), 144–222; Tsiavlovskii, "Kommentarii," 159–286; Pushkin, *"Ten' Barkova": Teksty, Kommentarii, Ekskursy*, 164–348.

29. Pushkin, *"Ten' Barkova": Teksty, Kommentarii, Ekskursy*, 25–154. The 1821 copy is preserved at the Russian State Archive for Literature and Art, Moscow, f. 74, op. 1, ed. khr. 13, fol. 17v.–22; it was first published in Pushkin, "'Ten' Barkova' (Kontaminirovannaia redaktsiia)," 136–53.

30. Pushkin, *"Ten' Barkova": Teksty, Kommentarii, Ekskursy*, 7–17, 317–26. On Pushkin the lyceist as "monk," see Khodasevich, *Poeticheskoe khoziaistvo Pushkina*, 13–14.

31. Pushkin, *"Ten' Barkova": Teksty, Kommentarii, Ekskursy*, 326–27.

32. Ibid., 108–14. On the problems of textology and attribution in connection with *The Shade of Barkov*, see also Manfred Schruba's review of our book in *Izvestiia Rossiiskoi akademii nauk: Seriia literatury i iazyka* 62.5 (2003): 62–64; Dmitrii P. Ivinskii's review, "'Novaia tekstologicheskaia programma' i 'Ten' Barkova'," *Novoe literaturnoe obozrenie* 60 (2003): 357–60; and my reply to Ivinsky in "Poriadok polemiki: (O fantome 'novoi tekstologicheskoi programmy')," *Voprosy literatury* 5 (2004): 324–41.

33. Pushkin, *Stikhotvoreniia litseiskikh let*, 511; Pushkin, *Polnoe sobranie sochinenii*, 20 vols., 1:564.

34. Aleksandr S. Pushkin, *Sobranie sochinenii: Khudozhestvennye proizvedeniia, kriticheskie i publitsisticheskie trudy, pis'ma, risunki, pomety i delovye bumagi, razmeshchennye v khronologicheskom poriadke*, ed. Valentin S. Nepomniashchii (Moscow: Nasledie, 2000–), 1:13–14; Valentin S. Nepomniashchii, *Pushkin: Izbrannye raboty 1960-kh–1990-kh gg.*, 2 vols. (Moscow: Zhizn' i mysl', 2001), 1:415; Valentin S. Nepomniashchii, "S veselym prizrakom svobody: Iz dnevnika pushkinista: Zametki mezhdu delom," *Kontinent* 73 (1992): 275; Valentin S. Nepomniashchii, *Pushkin: Russkaia kartina mira* (Moscow: Nasledie, 1999), 388; Valentin S. Nepomniashchii, "Ot redaktsii," *Moskovskii pushkinist* 11 (2005): 7; Valentin S. Nepomniashchii, "Pushkin, Aleksandr Sergeevich," in *Bol'shaia sovetskaia entsiklopediia*, vol. 21 (Moscow: Sovetskaia entsiklopediia, 1975), 246–50.

35. Sergei A. Fomichev, *Sluzhen'e muz: O lirike Pushkina* (St. Petersburg: Akademicheskii proekt, 2001), 170. The chronology of Pushkin's poems from the lyceum period was established by Mstislav and Tatiana Tsiavlovsky; their dating of *The Monk* was accepted for the new academic edition prepared by Pushkin House scholars. See Mstislav A. Tsiavlovskii, "Khronologiia litseiskikh stikhotvorenii," in *Stat'i o Pushkine*, 82–84; Pushkin, *Polnoe sobranie sochinenii*, 20 vols., 1:572.

36. Ekaterina Larionova and Vadim Rak, review of Pushkin, *"Ten' Barkova": Teksty, Kommentarii, Ekskursy*, *Novaia russkaia kniga* 13 (2002): 52, 55; Igor' A. Pil'shchikov and Maksim I. Shapir, "'Kogda partnery vashi—shulera' ('Ten' Barkova' i ee akademicheskie retsenzenty)," *Kriticheskaia massa* 2 (2003): 139–44; Joe Peschio, "'The Shade of Barkov' and the Struggle for Pushkin's 'Morality' in

Today's Russia," paper presented at the thirty-ninth National Convention of the American Association for the Advancement of Slavic Studies, New Orleans, Louisiana, 15–18 November 2007.

37. Viktor M. Esipov, "'Net, net, Barkov! skrypitsy ne voz'mu . . . ' (Razmyshleniia po povodu ballady 'Ten' Barkova')," *Voprosy literatury* 6 (2003): 63, 67; Viktor M. Esipov, "Okolo 'Teni Barkova'," *Moskovskii pushkinist* 11 (2005): 33; Viktor M. Esipov, *Pushkin v zerkale mifov* (Moscow: Iazyki slavianskoi kul'tury, 2006), 300–60; Ivan Nordstet, *Rossiiskii, s nemetskim i frantsuzskim perevodami, slovar'*, 2 vols. (St. Petersburg: Iogann Karl Shnor, 1780–82), 1:183; Vladimir I. Dal', *Tolkovyi slovar' zhivogo velikorusskogo iazyka*, 4 vols. (Moscow: Obshchestvo liubitelei rossiiskoi slovesnosti, uchrezhdennoe pri Imperatorskom Moskovskom universitete, 1863), 1:97. On the *Lyceum Sage* see Konstantin Ia. Grot, *Pushkinskii litsei (1811–1817): Bumagi I-go kursa, sobrannye akademikom Ia. K. Grotom* (St. Petersburg: Tipografiia Ministerstva putei soobshcheniia, 1911), 260.

38. Igor' A. Pil'shchikov and Maksim I. Shapir, "Eshche raz ob avtorstve ballady Pushkina 'Ten' Barkova,'" *Izvestiia Rossiiskoi akademii nauk: Seriia literatury i iazyka* 64.3 (2005): 41–52; Igor' A. Pil'shchikov and Maksim I. Shapir, "Tekstologiia vs aksiologiia: Eshche raz ob avtorstve ballady Pushkina *Ten' Barkova*," *Antropologiia kul'tury* 3 (2005): 219–48.

39. Unfortunately, our paper is not mentioned in Alexander Dubrovsky's PhD dissertation "The Poetic Pseudo-Pushkiniana"; he agrees with Esipov's critique, which we had already disproved in our article. See Aleksandr V. Dubrovskii, "Stikhotvornaia psevdopushkiniana (Issledovanie tekstov, pripisyvaemykh A. S. Pushkinu)" (PhD diss., Pushkin House, St. Petersburg, 2007); see also Aleksandr V. Dubrovskii, "'Mnimyi Pushkin' (Prizhiznennye spiski eroticheskikh stikhotvorenii i ekspromtov, pripisyvavshikhsia Pushkinu)," in *Vremennik Pushkinskoi komissii*, vol. 30 (St. Petersburg: Nauka, 2005), 311–17.

40. Igor' A. Pil'shchikov and Maksim I. Shapir, "Evoliutsiia stilei v russkoi poezii ot Lomonosova do Pushkina (Nabrosok kontseptsii)," in *Stikh, iazyk, poeziia: Pamiati Mikhaila Leonovicha Gasparova* (Moscow: Rossiiskii gosudarstvennyi gumanitarnyi universitet, 2006), 510–46. See also Alyssa Gillespie's observations in her chapter in the present volume.

41. Leonid V. Bessmertnykh, "O nekotorykh izdaniiakh eroticheskikh proizvedenii A. S. Pushkina i M. Iu. Lermontova," *Novoe literaturnoe obozrenie* 6 (1993–94): 293; "Svedeniia o fondakh i katalogakh," Custody Department, Russian State Library, Moscow, http://www.rsl.ru/r_tot7_271.htm (accessed and downloaded 11 July 2003; not available for the last few years).

42. See Bessmertnykh, *"Ten' Barkova" A. S. Pushkina*, chap. 2; Tsiavlovskii, "Kommentarii," 281; and Pushkin, *"Ten' Barkova": Teksty, Kommentarii, Ekskursy*, 329. The form "korn'" is found in the works of Sumarokov, Mikhail Murav'ev, and some other Russian poets of the eighteenth century. This reading is supported by the 1816 and 1820 manuscript copies of *The Shade of Barkov* as

well as one of the copies from Skorodumov's collection that was misread by Tsiavlovsky.

43. See Pil'shchikov and Shapir, "Eshche raz ob avtorstve ballady Pushkina 'Ten' Barkova,'" 48; and Pil'shchikov and Shapir, "Tekstologiia vs aksiologiia," 232–33. Gorchakov's copy is preserved at the Russian Federation State Archive, Moscow, f. 828, op. 1, ed. khr. 87.

44. See Grossman, *Pushkin*, 101–2; and Leonid P. Grossman, *Pushkin*, 2nd ed. (Moscow: Molodaia gvardiia, 1958), 83.

Bawdy and Soul

Pushkin's Poetics of Obscenity

Alyssa Dinega Gillespie

Despite the tomes and tomes of scholarship that have been penned about virtually every aspect of Pushkin's writing, his poetics of the obscene remains an almost untouched and untouchable field of inquiry. True, some excellent studies can be listed that treat individual works by Pushkin that may be counted in the category of the obscene or the bawdy, such as Mstislav Tsiavlovsky's commentary on *The Shade of Barkov* (*Ten' Barkova*) and two recent analyses of *Tsar Nikita and His Forty Daughters* (*Tsar' Nikita i sorok ego docherei*). Other relevant studies investigate the general phenomenon of bawdy thematics and/or obscene language in Pushkin's works, including key works by Anthony Cross and Maksim Shapir, and several anthologies present compilations of Pushkin's erotic productions in different media.[1] Yet even scholarship that touches on the racier emanations of Pushkin's pen tends to focus on particular instances of obscenity in Pushkin's writings, to remain rather conservative in methodology and outlook, and to sidestep consideration of the importance of obscenity for Pushkin's poetics as a whole.[2]

Thus, Tsiavlovsky, who was one of the first scholars to recognize the literary brilliance of *The Shade of Barkov*, nevertheless very delicately limits himself in his extraordinarily useful commentary on this work of gleeful poetic ribaldry to the standard textological methods, including source work and linguistic analysis, rather than approach its effusive sexual content too closely; he considers the poem's "'juvenile' origins" ("mal'chisheskoe" proiskhozhdenie) to be the explanation for its overabundance of scurrilous linguistic material.[3] Vocabulary denoting genitalia and other categories of obscenity has, wherever possible, simply been expunged from Pushkin's poems and letters in the fastidious Academy of Sciences editions of his works in the Soviet and, now, post-Soviet periods, by the substitution of a row of dashes in place of the offending terms—or, more seriously, by the omission of entire works. Surprisingly, even Sergei Denisenko's recent anthology of Pushkin's erotic writings omits *The Shade of Barkov*, with the excuse that it has already been published elsewhere; as Denisenko explains, this poem is not welcome in his volume, as it might shock readers "by reason of its extraordinarily strong obscenity."[4] This punctilious concern for readers' puritanical squeamishness implicitly goes hand in hand with the delineation of an imaginary boundary between the erotic and the pornographic in Pushkin's oeuvre.[5] While Pushkin's erotic sensibilities, in Russia's current climate of superficial sexual openness, may be celebrated, the suggestion of anything pornographic in the works of the Great Poet must at all costs be suppressed, and the traditional means of doing so is erasure, silence, and denial. It goes without saying that latent genital imagery sometimes present in Pushkin's less explicitly sexual texts in the form of metaphor or linguistic double entendres has been left deliberately unremarked and unstudied.

Yet the definition of pornography is in itself problematic, even as the phenomenon of pornography is fraught with cultural and historical specificity. Where does the love lyric end, and erotica begin? When does the erotic become pornographic? William Hopkins, author of a dissertation on the development of pornographic literature in Russia, points out that many cultural arbiters tend to link the definition of pornography to low literary and aesthetic quality, although they may actually lack the expertise to make this determination; he himself opts to sidestep the question entirely by devising the term "genital semantic function" to encapsulate all works that include such material, irrespective of cultural value judgments.[6] Marcus Levitt, on the other hand, makes a very useful distinction between the "highly literary barkoviana" of the eighteenth and early nineteenth centuries and later pornographic prose, while pointing out that the very concept of pornography arises in the context of "the regulatory discourse that defines it, as something to be disciplined and punished."[7] Eliot Borenstein, in a review article on post-Soviet pornography, similarly locates the origins of Russian pornography in relation to political, social, and literary prohibition: "What . . . can be more intriguing than that which we know has been hidden or excised? Censorship facilitates an extremely erotic, if not fetishistic, relation between the reader and the text."[8]

In this broadest sense outlined by Borenstein, any literature on any topic at all that flirts with the boundaries of the unprintable in the context of a censorship regime can be considered pornographic. This understanding appears to accord with Pushkin's own; in his "Epistle to the Censor" ("Poslanie tsenzoru") of 1822, he equates his purported addressee (the poem necessarily went unpublished during his lifetime) with a blade-happy castrate with blunted sensibilities who takes offense at even the tiniest hint at the illicit: "O barbarian! Who among us masters of the Russian lyre / Has not cursed your destructive hatchet? / You roam amidst the Muses like a tiresome eunuch" (O varvar! kto iz nas, vladel'tsev russkoi liry, / Ne proklinal tvoei gubitel'noi sekiry? / Dokuchnym evnukhom ty brodish' mezhdu Muz).[9] The overt link in this passage between poetic and sexual repression is revealing of a broader conceptual association in Pushkin's early works between the poetic and the sexual drives, inspiration and lust, creative and orgasmic fulfillment—attesting that Pushkin was interested in the pornographic as a sphere of artistic resistance. Most flagrantly, in his obscene ballad *The Shade of Barkov*, the sexual organ becomes a potent symbol of the transcendental sway of poetry itself, as it dares to resist the repressive taboos of the censorship and other forms of societal duress and thereby to displace the stifling authority of both state and church. In the analysis that follows, I first explore the functioning of this poetics of the obscene in *The Shade of Barkov* and then examine its continuing influence—heretofore undetected and unthinkable—in Pushkin's creative imagination, focusing on one of the most mysterious yet best-known mature lyric poems of the glorious Pushkin canon. Given the enormous disparity between "low" and "high" culture in Russia, my fundamental goal in arguing that Pushkin's most taboo and most celebrated works in fact emerge from and conform to one and the same poetics is to reunite the "low" Pushkin with the "high" Pushkin into a single integral being, thereby demonstrating the unity of his artistic vision.

The Shade of Barkov, to Write Is to Fuck, and the Polemic against the Archaists

The Shade of Barkov was written during Pushkin's years at the lyceum, probably in 1814 or 1815. The authorship of this unabashed feast of linguistic obscenity in the style of the talented eighteenth-century pornographic poet Ivan Barkov (1732–68) was long disputed; the manuscript was lost for many years, then reconstructed by Tsiavlovksy, and only recently, in 2002, published in a scholarly edition by Igor Pilshchikov and the late Maksim Shapir.[10] The ballad, written in a composite style that freely mixes the highest and lowest linguistic registers to hilarious effect, tells the story of a defrocked priest with the unseemly name of Ebakov (Fuckman), who visits a bordello with his companions and distinguishes himself as the fucker of greatest endurance, when he is suddenly beset by a tragedy of epic proportions: like a battle-weary warrior, his valiant member refuses to stand up. There ensues a fateful visitation by the shade of Barkov, who appears to Ebakov in the guise of the pagan fertility god Priapus, holding his preternaturally long penis in his hands, and makes a Faustian bargain the priest can't refuse in this pre-Viagra era: the little god with the giant prick will return Ebakov's sexual prowess with a vengeance, if only he will promise to memorialize Barkov in verse.[11]

Needless to say, Ebakov agrees, thereby accepting the dubious mantle of the pornographic poet, and other sexual adventures ensue. At the culmination of the narrative, he finds himself in a female monastery beset by a sexually voracious mother superior, who keeps him as her sex slave until all his virility is once again depleted, at which point she plans to castrate him in thanks for his services. The shade of Barkov, grateful for Ebakov's manifold verses in his honor, once again comes to the priest's rescue as the mother superior wields her sharpened knife, and the poor nun, confronted by Ebakov's miraculous erection, is so shocked that she soils herself and drops dead. After this triumph of grotesque slapstick, the ballad ends with a pat moral about good deeds being rewarded in kind and comes to a speedy, almost orgasmic, conclusion (not unlike the abrupt ending of the later *Tsar Nikita and His Forty Daughters* and, much later, the tongue-in-cheek parody of a moral that ends *Little House in Kolomna* [*Domik v Kolomne* (1830)]).

Defiance of social and linguistic taboo lies at the very foundation of *The Shade of Barkov*. The poem is chock-full to excess of rollicking bad language. Practically every line contains at least one verbal obscenity, many of them connoting some feature of the male or female genitalia: "khui" (prick), "eldak" (cock), "plesh'" (penile glans), "mude" (balls) and related forms thirty-seven times; "pizda" (cunt), "prorekha" (tear/ pussy), "sekelek" (clit), "shchel'" (crevice/vagina) eleven times; and others associated with the acts of coitus ("drochit'[sia]" [to jerk off], "ebat'/et'" [to fuck], "eblia" [act of fucking], "zaebina" [cum] sixteen times) or defecation ("obosrat'sia" [to shit oneself]).[12] Yet in spite of the horror and disgust that this material has evoked in most of its readers, who find themselves at a great remove from Pushkin's own linguistic and literary sensibilities, the ballad should in fact be seen as a carefully crafted work inspired by the burlesque tradition of the eighteenth century.

Indeed, as Maksim Shapir has shown, *The Shade of Barkov* cannot be fully understood and appreciated unless it is situated within the context of the stylistic debates of Pushkin's time and the strict eighteenth-century system of neoclassical genres within which Barkov himself worked.[13] Barkov did not create free-form literary smut simply for the sake of sexual titillation in the sense that we understand pornography today; on the contrary, his works and those of his followers (collectively termed Barkoviana) are, in essence, works of skilled literary parody in all the classical genres—ode, epistle, elegy, fable, epigram, inscription, epitaph, sonnet, riddle, song, mock epic, tragedy, and so on.[14] These unprintable (netsenzurnye) parodies comment implicitly both on the artificiality of the official literary genres as they are policed by the poetic elite (Sumarokov, Lomonosov, Trediakovsky, et al.) and on the external constraints and inhibitions imposed on poetry by the censorship. Thus, Barkoviana—which is produced by male writers for male consumers—provides a delicately calibrated psychological release and serves as a kind of poetic "shadow economy" alongside the triumphal products of officially sanctioned literature.[15] In other words, the titillation produced by Barkoviana is of a primarily literary rather than a sexual variety.

The question remains as to why Pushkin turned to the Barkovian model in one of his earliest poetic works. According to Shapir, Pushkin's great poetic forerunner Gavrila Derzhavin himself had learned the poetic craft through an encounter with Barkov: Derzhavin, in a sense, apprenticed himself to the pornographic poet by rewriting Barkov's illicit works using acceptable language. In this way, a process of double parody took place: Barkov first parodied works of high literature, turning them into pornography, and Derzhavin then parodied these obscene works, thereby turning them back into high literature (this transformation is in keeping with Tynianov's observation that "the parody of a comedy may be a tragedy"[16]). Through this reverse parodic process of moral cleansing and linguistic purification, Barkoviana—which was itself shaped by the official literature—at the same time came to have an influence over that literature, particularly through Derzhavin's work.[17] As Shapir explains: "This totality of the burlesque contained a threat that the reverse action of the literary 'underground' could have an effect beyond the boundaries of the comic genres and spread to all registers of official literature. And that is just what happened: even the highest genres of Derzhavin's poetry succumbed to the 'allure' of the obscene-pornographic burlesque."[18] Thus, even many of Derzhavin's most famous, most spiritually elevated poetic masterpieces are, paradoxically, shot through with pornographic reminiscences: for example, Derzhavin speaks about divinity in his meditative ode "God" ("Bog" [1784]) using the very same vocabulary ("Source of life, giver of blessings" [Istochnik zhizni, blag podatel']) that Barkov uses in his pornographic "Ode to the Prick" ("Oda khuiu"): "You, the source of all blessings—the prick!" (Toboi, vsekh blag istochnik—khui!).[19] For Derzhavin, the high and the low interpenetrate one another: both his comic and his serious poetic works are infiltrated with duplicity and (in Shapir's eloquent formulation) "balance on the thin edge between solemnity and the joke, varying only in their proportions."[20]

Given Pushkin's keen poetic ear and his receptivity to poetic echoes, it is very probable that he learned this thrilling balancing act from his reading of Derzhavin, in whose language he surely perceived the prurient traces of Barkov. Whereas Derzhavin's appropriation of Barkov may well have been subconscious (and therefore not blasphemous), as Shapir thinks, Pushkin's parodic appropriation of Barkov in his own ballad, inasmuch as it returned to a frankly, even exaggeratedly, pornographic idiom, was obviously fully conscious and intentional: a pointed poetic experiment and, at the same time, a preemptive strike against the opposing (Shishkovite) literary camp, which insisted on maintaining the eighteenth century's sterile stylistic hierarchy.[21] Thus Pushkin, in following Derzhavin's lead, in a sense makes Derzhavin's double parody triple. At the same time, *The Shade of Barkov* sets out the young Pushkin's aesthetic credo through yet another double parody of works by Zhukovsky and Batiushkov, which has been analyzed in detail by Shapir.[22] Through this multilayered parodic strategy, Pushkin at once gives winking homage to his poetic elders and charts a future path for poetry informed by a spirit of playfulness and linguistic license. In other words, writing in a Barkovian mode allows Pushkin to stake out his own poetic territory "on the thin edge between solemnity and the joke."[23] This is a venture in which Derzhavin is an unnamed yet immanent presence and one in which the younger poet, not without significant anxiety, dares to go well beyond the older poet's lead—not (as Derzhavin did) by adapting the structures and cadences of obscene poetry to higher poetic purposes but rather by identifying the very substance of his poetic calling with a pornographic urge.

This identification rests, fundamentally, upon a proto-Freudian equation between pen and penis. The equation is made explicit in stanza 11 of Pushkin's ballad, immediately following Ebakov's first salvific visitation by Barkov's shade, as a heady mixture of sexual arousal and poetic afflatus sets in:

И стал трудиться Ебаков,
Ебет да припевает;
Везде гласит: «Велик Барков!»
Попа сам Феб венчает.
Пером владеет как елдой,
Певцов он всех славнее . . . .
И стал ходить из края в край
С гудком, смычком, мудами,
И на Руси вкушает рай
Бумагой и пиздами.[24]

[And Ebakov began to work, / He fucks and he hums; / Everywhere he proclaims: 'Barkov be praised!' / Apollo himself crowns him poet. / He's master of the pen as of the prick, / He's the most famous poet of all . . . . / And he began to wander from land to land / With a fiddle, a fiddlestick, his balls, / And all through Rus' he samples paradise / On paper and in cunts.]

While cruder in its manner of expression than the majority of Pushkin's poetry, this passage echoes many other such instances in his personal letters to friends and fellow poets, such as Petr Viazemsky and Anton Del'vig, with whom he feels free to express his experiences of poetic inspiration and creative blockage in frankly sexual terms, even in later years. One example is his complaint to Del'vig in mid-November 1828 that it is "just as hard for [him] to break through to a madrigal as to break through a virgin." Another example is his letter to fellow poet and Green Lamp participant Arkadii Rodzianko on 8 December 1824, in which he discusses the diverse ethnicities of the heroines of a number of recent romantic poems, including his own *The Gypsies* (*Tsygany*), and closes with a joyful exclamation that these maidens are all the same in their capacity to inspire the poet: "I can imagine Apollo looking at them and crying out: *Why are you bringing me this one?* And what kind of girl do you require, damned Phoebus? A Greek? An Italian? In what way is a Finn or a Gypsy inferior to them? All cunts are the same—fuck her! Which is to say, bring her to life with a ray of inspiration and glory [*Pizda odna—ebi! t.e. ozhivi luchem vdokhnoveniia i slavy*]."[25] In all these examples, the penis is equated with poetic potency, the vagina with the sheet of blank paper that waits for the poet to write on it, and the paradise of sexual intercourse with the transport of poetic inspiration: each thrust is a line of poetry.

The inverse relation holds true in *The Shade of Barkov* as well: sexual impotence is equivalent to the feeble and clumsy attempts of an ungifted poetic hack, as is made clear when the prostitute's attempts to revive Ebakov's limp and unresponsive member are hilariously compared to the compositional blunders of Count Dmitrii Khvostov, later the butt of Arzamasian jokes, who thrusts his flaccid rhyme insistently but unsuccessfully into the frigid lines of his talentless odes: "And sideways, and slantwise, and straight on / He takes the resonant word, moaning, / And stabs it into his stubborn verse" (I vkriv', i vkos', i priamo / On slovo zvuchnoe, krekhtia, / Lomaet v stikh upriamoi).[26] This is a key passage, insofar as it makes explicit the literary polemic between archaists and innovators that is allegorized in the plot of *The Shade of Barkov* and urges a metaliterary interpretation of the ballad. Shapir explores this polemic at length and argues that its central question of whether one ought to speak as one writes (the archaists' position) or to write as one speaks (the innovators' position) by the time of Pushkin's composition of *The Shade of Barkov* had come—largely through Batiushkov's intervention—to be translated into a purely sexual idiom: should one "fuck with the pen" (ebat' perom) or "write with the penis" (pisat' khuem); which is to say, should one "fuck as one writes" (i.e., fuck gracefully, as in Barkov's poems) or "write as one fucks" (i.e., write with ease, in accordance with Pushkin's own erotic sensibility)?[27]

In light of this synonymy, the ebullient profusion of genital imagery and activity in *The Shade of Barkov* is not, as might seem to be the case, antithetical to poetry's transcendent aims. On the contrary, Ebakov's poetic ascendancy is charted as the very function of his erectile superstardom. In the course of baring so much unaccustomed private flesh, Pushkin bares the device as well: the metaphor of poetic pleasure loses its metaphoricity and becomes literalized in the most baldly physiological manner possible. Genitalia in *The Shade of Barkov* become the very engine of poetic pleasure, while orgasm is rendered a new synonym for the poetic sublime. At the same time, the dark side of this potential yet sometimes elusive bliss looms large: intense poetic performance anxiety (the anxiety of a young poet speaking in a male-to-male idiom and following irreverently in the footsteps of multiple past masters, Derzhavin foremost among them) is encoded as the ever-present specter of impotence (not only Khvostov's but also Ebakov's—and, by extension, Pushkin's own) and, even worse, castration.[28]

Enter the pagan figure of Barkov's shade, the savior who delivers the poet from these psychosexual dangers. The shade is an inspirational force: a stand-in for the muse and Ebakov's guardian angel, in whom the pagan gods of fertility and poetry, Priapus and Apollo, merge and become indistinguishable. As Hopkins perceptively observes: "The figure of Barkov becomes a symbol. It represents more than superhuman sexual prowess. This image becomes an objective correlative for prowess in creative literary endeavor. . . . [T]he genital semantic function realized by vulgar lexical items and descriptions of sexual behavior almost totally ceases to contain a genital semantic function. In other words the whole imagistic system of the poem which derives from that content becomes something other than itself, namely, a metaphor for the strength, power and dynamism of poetic inspiration and creative élan."[29] Indeed, the shade of Barkov overtly proclaims himself to be Ebakov's muse, declaring "Your friend! your Muse! I am Barkov" (Tvoi drug! tvoi Genii! Ia Barkov).[30]

But alongside this pagan function, the Christian nuances of Barkov's shade cannot be ignored—particularly in light of the fact that the sexually rapacious Ebakov, latterly turned pornographic panegyric poet, is a defrocked priest, while his even more sexually rapacious near-nemesis is the mother superior of a female monastery.[31] Like a divinity, Barkov's shade can perform miracles reminiscent of Christ's healing ministries in the Gospels, curing his minion instantly of his affliction, as the ballad's narrator ecstatically reports: "O miracle! His vigorous prick / Arises, blood boils in his huge balls / And his raging rod protrudes!" (O chudo! Khui iadrenyi / Vstaet, kipit v mudishchakh krov' / I kol torchit vz"iarennyi!).[32] Through this conflation of the heroic poetic manner with graphic depictions of Ebakov's miraculously restored genital apparatus, prayer is displaced from the sphere of Christianity to the sphere of poetry. M. H. Abrams has shown in his book *Natural Supernaturalism* that romanticism in general tends away from a worldview rooted in an embrace of the supernatural and in traditional religion, preferring instead a naturalistic understanding of the world; Pushkin's parodic transformation of the transcendent into the erotic in the figure of Barkov's shade follows much the same principle.[33] Nor is this conflation unique to Pushkin; as Igor Pilshchikov points out, the "intertranslatability of erotic and sacral/metaphysical languages" is also found in the works of John Donne and the other English metaphysical poets, as well as having been typical of the Russian romantics generally.[34]

Yet Pushkin, as he often does, goes farther and deeper. In an article on what he terms Pushkin's "religious erotica," Mikhail Vaiskopf convincingly argues that, unlike other Russian romantic poets who only flirt with the boundary between the carnal and the spiritual, Pushkin fully completes this heretical shift, thereby literalizing the romantic idiom that equates prayer with poetry, the eucharist and liturgy with anachreontic verse, and unity in the body of Christ with the union of coitus.[35] Vaiskopf discusses works ranging from *The Gabrieliad* (*Gavriiliada*) to *Eugene Onegin* (*Evgenii Onegin*) in demonstration of his thesis, but, although he omits mention of it, *The Shade of Barkov* is clearly the first of Pushkin's experiments in the sacralization of the profane.[36] Pushkin's playful parody of genres and linguistic registers in his pornographic ballad amounts to a poetics of obscenity that signifies what was and would remain always his most sacred value: the imaginative freedom of the poet.[37]

Quite literally, *The Shade of Barkov* is one of the first works Pushkin ever wrote. Clearly, the ballad narrates not only the tale of Ebakov's poetic awakening but of Pushkin's own poetic nascence too. Pushkin's humorously self-contradictory protestation to the deceased Barkov in the 1815 lyric "A Small Town" ("Gorodok") that "I'll never write / As you did, mother fucker" (Kak ty, ebena mat', / Ne stanu ia pisat') willy-nilly instantiates his assertion just a few lines earlier that "Svistov [i.e., Barkov] must be praised / In Svistovian [Barkovian] style" (Svistovskim dolzhno slogom / Svistova vospevat').[38] "A Small Town," like *The Shade of Barkov*, contains the self-conflicted religious thematics that characterize much of Pushkin's juvenilia: it ends with the dissolute lyric speaker going off to pray with the village priests. Similarly, a sexually crazed monk is the lyric speaker of the lyceum poems *The Monk* (*Monakh* [1813]), "To Natalia" ("K Natal'e" [1813]), and "To My Sister" ("K sestre" [1814]). The defrocked monk, aspiring poet, and fucker-extraordinaire Ebakov is, we can presume, a fitting alter ego for the teenaged Pushkin—who appears to have been beset by raging hormones, sexual fantasies and insecurities, and a not insignificant dose of moral confusion and guilt. Thus, it is quite appropriate to read *The Shade of Barkov* as Pushkin's celebration of the recognition that his poetic passion to create takes its origin in a heady mixture of sexual craving and the thrill of imaginative trespass into the forbidden realm of the taboo.

At the center of this narrative of origins is the trope of the young, living poet meeting with a dead poet's shade in the wilderness (pustynia).[39] This trope is present, too, in the lyceum poems "A Small Town" and *The Shade of Fonvizin* (*Ten' Fon-Vizina* [1815]), and, as Boris Gasparov has shown, it later became a constant in Pushkin's poetic mythology, as, for example, in the lyrics "To Ovid" ("K Ovidiiu" [1821–22]) and "André Chénier" ("Andrei Shen'e" [1825]).[40] The meeting, in each case, orchestrates a primal scene of poetic engendering. David Bethea has explored at length the mythopoetic use Pushkin made throughout his life of his famous meeting with Derzhavin at the lyceum, when Pushkin read his poem "Reminiscences at Tsarskoe Selo" ("Vospominaniia v Tsarskom Sele") to the admiration of the elder poet-statesman.[41] Incidentally, given the strong shadow presence of Derzhavin in *The Shade of Barkov* (with Ebakov parodically doubling for Pushkin and Barkov for Derzhavin), it seems logical to surmise that there is a very strong possibility that Pushkin's erotic ballad was composed *after* (and under the influence of) his encounter with Derzhavin in the flesh—in other words, no earlier than 8 January 1815. The foregoing analysis thus serves to narrow down the poem's probable window of composition (given by Pilshchikov and Shapir as 1814–15).

In summary, despite the apparent frivolity of this very adolescent text, it evidently encoded for Pushkin an entire package of fundamental anxieties that would never leave him: anxieties regarding the mystique of his poetic calling, his debt to his poetic forerunners (both licit and illicit), his manhood and ability to preserve it, his penchant for joking about matters of the utmost solemnity, his reverence for beauty and horror at its potential for corruption, and the Faustian trade-offs and dangers that loomed ahead of him (and, eventually, behind him too).

These strains were woven together in various patterns in differing literary contexts over the years, yielding a sort of idiosyncratic, highly personal poetic myth.

"The Prophet," Secret Burlesque, and Pushkin's Poetics of Obscenity

Fast-forward more than a decade, and we come to a poem that, to all appearances, could not be further from *The Shade of Barkov* in its themes, language, style, and sensibilities. Pushkin's poem "The Prophet" ("Prorok"), written in 1826 and published in 1828, is one of his most powerful yet most ambiguous investigations into the nature of poetic inspiration and a celebration of its stark pleasures and repercussions in an austerely minor key. This poem has played a key role in the formation of the Pushkin myth; in Andrew Kahn's apt formulation, "The exaltation of the poet as a visionary genius [in "The Prophet"] has become inseparable from Pushkin's own image. . . . [The] vision of the poet as a seer capable of self-renovation and the moral renovation of others has become a cultural archetype in Russia."[42] Yet if we leave behind our preconceived notions, we cannot help but notice a marked similarity between the basic plot scenario of this mature lyric poem and that of Pushkin's juvenile obscene ballad: in a moment of spiritual and physical crisis, the nameless hero of "The Prophet" encounters a supernatural being (a six-winged seraph) in the wilderness who, muselike, invests him with prophetic vision and poetic voice. The poem can thus be read as a mythopoetic narrative of poetic genesis and a successor to *The Shade of Barkov* in Pushkin's personal poetic mythology.[43]

Admittedly, most Pushkin scholars would regard such a suggestion as utterly preposterous. On the contrary, the scholarly tradition surrounding "The Prophet" has accorded it an exalted position at the pinnacle of Pushkin's most chastely spiritual accomplishments. This tradition was built largely on an 1842 assessment of the poem by Polish poet Adam Mickiewicz, who saw it as indicative of a moral turning point in Pushkin's own spiritual and personal life and asserted that it occupied "a completely unique, truly elevated place" in his oeuvre.[44] These comments gave rise to a mystical interpretation of "The Prophet" that put an emphasis on its autobiographical significance, which was dominant throughout the Silver Age and early Soviet period, as evinced in essays by Mikhail Gershenzon, Sergei Bulgakov, Semen Frank, and others.[45] Later Soviet scholars replaced the pathos of the religio-mystical reading with the pathos of an areligious civic reading that foregrounds the poem's commitment to the Decembrist cause and the Decembrist tradition of socially committed poetry, emphasizing its "didactic and disciplinary power" above all.[46] In the post-Soviet period, yet again, scholars such as Irina Surat have resolved the ideological/poetic divide in the reception of "The Prophet" in favor of a deeply autobiographical reading that interprets the poem as an exercise in the "privatization" of biblical events as facts of the poet's own fate, and sees the poem's composition as stemming from a crossroads in Pushkin's life that is at once both political and spiritual.[47]

Certain textological mysteries have also added to this poem's mystique, particularly since no manuscript versions of it survive. Thus, many recent scholarly publications focus on the question of whether the dubious quatrain that begins "Arise, arise, O prophet of Russia" (Vosstan', vosstan', prorok Rossii), reported in the memoirs of several of Pushkin's contemporaries as having formed the original ending of "The Prophet," should be considered to have been authored by Pushkin or not and, if authored by Pushkin, whether it is part of an early draft of "The Prophet" or a fragment of a separate, unrealized poem.[48] Scholars also touch on the significance of Pushkin's notation of "The Prophet" in an 1827 list of poems by means of its first line in an altered form: not "Tormented by a spiritual thirst" (Dukhovnoi zhazhdoiu tomim), as in the poem's canonical version, but "Tormented by a great grief" (Velikoi skorbiiu tomim).[49] Many commentators have thought this to be an earlier version of the poem's opening line and have linked its content with Pushkin's shock and mourning over the fate of the Decembrist conspirators, which he learned about on 24 July 1826, most likely immediately prior to his composition of "The Prophet."

Surat terms "The Prophet" a "double-bottomed" work, yet she may not in fact realize the full extent to which this observation is true.[50] It is my contention that, although "The Prophet" might seem to be the unlikeliest successor to *The Shade of Barkov*, this elevated lyric poem is in fact thoroughly imbued with a reminiscence of all aspects of the erotic ballad's language, imagery, themes, and mythopoetic and metaliterary concerns. Perhaps this unexpected "twinning" of the two poetic texts, one chaste and the other profane, should not be so surprising after all. As Boris Gasparov has shown, there are both continuities and discontinuities in the evolution of Pushkin's poetic vision, and the "plastic unity of Pushkin's creative world" stretches across enormous temporal distances.[51] For instance, Gasparov explores Pushkin's two versions of a response to Gnedich's translation of *The Iliad,* one in the form of a celebratory panegyric, the other in the form of a scornful and insulting epigram, and argues that the two, though diametrically opposed, require one another to express their full meaning: "Such duality and at the same time mutual complementariness of the image is typical for Pushkin; this [duality] lies behind many 'parodoxes' of Pushkin's work and behavior."[52] Similarly, Georgii Levinton and Nikita Okhotin show in the course of their analysis of *Tsar Nikita and His Forty Daughters* that Pushkin often explores one and the same creative problem in starkly contrasting works both synchronically and diachronically. Thus, for example, both *Count Zero* (*Graf Nulin*) and *Boris Godunov* are, at base, meditations on the problem of history, whereas the fragmentary *Vadim* (*Vadim*) and *Tsar Nikita* are both attempts to solve the problem of the Russian national *poema* (narrative poem).[53] Likewise both *The Shade of Barkov* and "The Prophet" may be understood as two mutually complementary attempts to address the problem of the poet's *body*—that is, the problem of the poet's corporeality and, more specifically, his sexuality in light of his spiritual calling.

The parodical context already established for *The Shade of Barkov* is highly pertinent to my analysis. Pushkin, as Tsiavlovsky and others have shown, is a parodic thinker (Tsiavlovsky refers to the "parodiomania" that was prevalent during Pushkin's lyceum years).[54] As I will argue here, "The Prophet" validates Tynianov's assertion that "the parody of a comedy may be a tragedy," for in it, the parody of an obscene mock ballad turns out to be a profound lyric testament to the highest spiritual and poetic values.[55] The context in which Pushkin composed "The Prophet" in 1826 indeed recapitulates the context in which he wrote *The Shade of Barkov* in a way that must have brought not only the obscene ballad itself but also its parodic and metaliterary dimensions vividly back to mind for him. David Bethea has usefully laid out the poem's compositional history and context. In 1822 Pushkin's former lyceum classmate Vil'gel'm Kiukhel'beker had composed a poem titled "Prophecy" ("Prorochestvo") that declared his allegiance to Derzhavin's mode of writing civic odes in praise of great national heroes using archaist, high-style (Old Church Slavonic-infested) vocabulary. Pushkin interpreted this poem, as well as Kiukhel'beker's 1825 essay trumpeting the need for a return to a Derzhavinian odic rapture (vostorg), as a betrayal. Perhaps in response, Pushkin resolved to reread all of Derzhavin's poetry and also wrote the mock "Ode to His Excellency

Count Dm. Iv. Khvostov" ("Oda ego Siiat. Dm. Iv. Khvostovu" [1825])—the very same Khvostov whom he had already subjected to ridicule in *The Shade of Barkov*.

In Bethea's interpretation, "The Prophet" must be seen as the "poetic residue" of Pushkin's meditations on Kiukhel'beker, the civic ode, Derzhavin, and the sacred role of the poet.[56] Additionally, Gasparov observes that, through Viazemsky's quotation of a passage from a Derzhavin poem in a letter to Pushkin about *The Gypsies*, purely by chance (given the letter's timing), "Derzhavin's verse entered the orbit of Pushkin's work on the theme of the prophet. . . . Derzhavin's words, addressed (via Viazemsky as intermediary) to Pushkin . . . were transformed into a divine command directed to the Prophet"—a command that Pushkin presumably may have chafed against, given his ambivalent attitude toward Derzhavin and the odic mode at the time.[57] Harsha Ram likewise sees Pushkin's composition of "The Prophet" as a critical response to Kiukhel'beker and an expression of his own ironic sense that "odic rapture" and the ceremonial ode had run their course and that all that was still possible in his era was a sort of diminished "'odic style,' one that retained select rhetorical and thematic features of the odic sublime in a form that was radically truncated and often juxtaposed alongside the distinguishing markers of other genres"—which is to say, an odic style that took the form of burlesque parody. Ram's assessment of "The Prophet" as "strangely equivocal" and characterized by "essential ambivalence" is astute.[58] Evidently, the very same set of metaliterary issues regarding the Derzhavinian model and the poetic shade/"father-figure" of Derzhavin himself, the eighteenth-century system of high and low genres, and the debates between linguistic archaists and innovators that set the scene for *The Shade of Barkov* also provide the backdrop for "The Prophet."

If Gasparov is correct that Viazemsky's epistolary quotation from Derzhavin's poem "Gypsy Dance" ("Tsyganskaia pliaska" [1805]) in his letter to Pushkin of August 1825 was an important source for the final line of "The Prophet," then a consideration of "Gypsy Dance" is a good place to begin our reading of Pushkin's poem.[59] The lines Viazemsky chose to quote were the poem's repeated refrain, addressed to the gypsy girl who is its subject: "Scorch souls, cast fire into hearts / From your swarthy face" (Zhgi dushi, ogn' brosai v serdtsa / Ot smuglogo littsa); the final line of "The Prophet," of course, is "Scorch the hearts of people with [the/my] w/Word" (Glagolom zhgi serdtsa liudei, l. 30).

In Gasparov's interpretation, the voice of Derzhavin becomes the voice of God calling Pushkin to prophesy—yet Gasparov ignores the original, hotly erotic context of Derzhavin's poem, which evokes the gypsy girl's "voluptuous ardor" (sladostrastnyi zhar) and "sensuality" (slastoliubie) and ends with the wish that her wild passions might be tamed within the comparatively more controlled dance ("gracefully, grandly, nobly" [plavno, vazhno, blagorodno]) of a Russian maiden and in the heart of a "tender bard" (nezhnyi pevets). Derzhavin's poem, in other words, is about harnessing erotic desire within a subdued, aesthetically disciplined poetic form. It is quite possible that Pushkin in "The Prophet" was responding to this particular challenge from his predecessor's pen as much as to Derzhavin's implied prophetic imperative.

Indeed, the metaphorical and lexical patterning of "The Prophet" strongly points to a sexual substratum in the poem's meaning.[60] This substratum is indicated, in part, by the pronounced duality of the physical landscape in which the lyric persona abides after he is touched by the seraph: suddenly the neutral emptiness of the "gloomy wilderness" (pustynia mrachnaia, l. 2) is replaced by a binary universe consisting only of the highest heights ("heaven" [nebo, l. 11], "the celestial flight of angels" [gornii angelov polet, l. 12]), and the deepest depths ("sea reptiles' underwater crawl" [gad morskikh podvodnyi khod, l. 13], "the vegetation of the valley stem/vine" [dol'nei lozy proziaban'e, l. 14]). This bifurcation hints at a bifurcation in the meaning of the poem as a whole, with soaring angels striving toward heaven on the lofty surface of the text and lurking, shameful depths hidden deep within. Moreover, the images of the sea reptiles and the vegetating stem ("loza" is also sometimes translated, even more suggestively, as "rod") can both be read as phallic. The metaphoric usage of landscape and spatial imagery to express sexual meanings is common in Barkov's poetry; for example, in the invocation to "Ode to the Cunt" ("Oda pizde"), the poet says, "Descend, O Muse, from the heights into the valley / And raise the hem of your skirt to the navel, / I am touching now upon the cunt / And wish anon to sing her praises" (Soidi, o Muza, sverkhu v dol / I na pup zalupi podol, / Ia nyne do pizdy kasaius', / Vospet' teper' eia khochu), while the entire short poem "The Miller and the Maiden" ("Mel'nik i devka") is based on the grotesquely realized conceit of a sexual landscape: "'There in front a stream sometimes flows, / And behind, although no large rivers pass, / A mighty wind gusts from a crevice' / . . . 'Where is that place, pray tell, so that I too will know.' / 'If you please,' said she, 'here between my legs'" (Tam speredi techet po vremeni ruchei, / A szadi khot' i net bol'shikh rechnykh kliuchei, / Da iz ushcheliny presil'nyi veter duet / . . . —Gde zh mesto, ukazhi, chtoby i ia znat' mog. / —Izvol',—skazala ta,—vot u menia mezh nog).[61]

The lyric persona of "The Prophet," beginning with its opening line, is "tormented by desire" (zhazhdoiu tomim), and although this desire is qualified as being of the spiritual rather than the sexual variety, highly sexual language and even the suggestion of genital imagery abound throughout the poem. This language and imagery may not be immediately apparent (nor indisputable), but reading the poem in the context of the tradition of Barkoviana, *The Shade of Barkov*, and Pushkin's other erotic works reveals the possible sexual plane of its meaning. For example, when the seraph first touches the persona "with the fingers light as fantasy" (perstami legkimi kak son, l. 5), these fingers are reminiscent of the titillating yet mystical "light finger" with which Satan touches Mary's genitals in *The Gabrieliad*: "He steals hastily beneath her raiments, / And his light finger playfully touches / Her sweet secret parts" ([On] kradetsia pod rizy toroplivo, / I legkii perst kasaetsia igrivo / Do milykh tain).[62] There follows a ubiquitous pre-orgasmic "shuddering" (sodrogan'e) that the lyric hero of "The Prophet" shares with the vastness of the universe all around him, and at the same time his ears are filled with the resonant "roar and ringing" (shum i zvon) of extreme sexual arousal. Terms such as "shuddering" (drozhanie) and "to shudder" (drozhat') are commonly found in Barkov's poems, connoting sexual excitement and orgasm.

The similarity here to *The Gabrieliad* (in which the Virgin Mary is seduced/sexually assaulted by three male supernatural beings in quick succession) is not accidental: the hero of "The Prophet" in fact does fill the vulnerable, passive, archetypally "female" role in his encounter with the seraph. It is not insignificant that his "prophetic eyes" fly open at the angel's touch "like those of a frightened she-eagle" (kak u ispugannoi orlitsy, l. 8). Furthermore, the fact that the first couplet rhyme in each of the second and third quatrains (ll. 5–6 and 9–10) ends with (and incorporates) the resonant pronoun "he" (on) ("son/on . . . on/zvon" [fantasy/he . . . he/ringing])—referring not to the poem's lyric speaker but to the seraph who assaults him—emphasizes the seraph's *maleness* and thus implicitly shunts the lyric persona into the female role. The imagery of mutilation that forms the poem's center also places the lyric speaker in the vulnerable female role: the seraph first replaces his tongue with the phallic "stinger of a wise serpent" (zhalo mudryia zmei, l. 18), "sheath[ing]" (vlozhil, l. 20) it between the hero's "frigid lips" (usta zamershie, l. 19) "with a bloody fist" (desnitseiu krovavoi, l. 20) and then "cleave[s] [his] breast with a sword" (grud' rassek mechom, l. 21), removing his "trembling heart" (serdtse trepetnoe, l. 22) and "insert[ing]" (vodvinul, l. 24) a "coal flaming with fire" (ugl', pylaiushchii ognem, l. 23) into his "gaping breast" (grud' otverstuiu, l. 24) in a metaphoric act of double rape. These images serve as a flagrant illustration of the stigma (pechat') or mutilation (uvech'e) that Gasparov notes as a corporeal sign of the prophetic mission; at the same time, they both realize and sexualize Ram's observation that "bodily ravishment will come to typify the prophetic topos."[63]

Each of these key images has strong roots in the tradition of Barkoviana and/or in Pushkin's own erotic works. The serpent, of course, is a prime actor in the biblical narrative of the Fall from Eden as well as in *The Gabrieliad,* in which Satan recapitulates the tale of the Fall in a revisionist vein. The serpent is also phallic in form, and this perhaps explains why it makes an appearance in an early draft of Pushkin's work *Little House in Kolomna* as a highly sexualized metaphor for poetry—precisely in the context of a rumination on the relative desirability of iambic tetrameter, a "low meter" and implicitly the vehicle of "jokes," versus the impossible hexameter and the threateningly, repulsively, dangerously carnal alexandrine (of course, Pushkin himself had written in all these meters):[64]

Но возвратиться всё ж я не хочу
К четырестопным ямбам, мере низкой.
С гекзаметром . . . о, с ним я не шучу:
Он мне невмочь. А стих александрийский? . . .
Уж не его ль себе я залучу?
Извивистый, проворный, длинный, склизкий
И с жалом даже—точная змия;
Мне кажется, что с ним управлюсь я.[65]

[But all the same, I don't wish to return / To the iambic tetrameter, a low meter. / With hexameter . . . O, with it I do not joke: / I cannot master it. And what of alexandrine verse? . . . / Why not lure it to me? / Slithery, agile, long, slimy / And with a stinger even—a real serpent; / It seems to me that I can get the better of it.]

The fact that *Little House in Kolomna* deals with an unnamed sexual visitor ("Mavrusha" is only his pseudonym) who disappears as unexpectedly as he arrives and with the shifting of masculine/feminine boundaries in both the poetic and the gender sense likewise aligns it with "The Prophet."[66] Nikolai Stepanov is quite right to point out that the "stinger" of the serpent in "The Prophet" brings to the poem's speaker not moral purity but *wisdom*, which is something very different and far more complex and ambiguous. At the same time, it is worth noting that the word "zhalo" (stinger) is used by Barkov as a synonym for the phallus—for example, in the elegy "Feklista" ("Feklista"): "Since that time your pussy torments my stinger" (S togo chasa shentia moe trevozhit zhalo).[67]

The remaining images in the double rape sequence in "The Prophet" strongly echo the language and images of Barkov's poetry. The "frigid lips" can of course be understood as a sexual image in their own right; similarly, in the second stanza of Barkov's "Ode to Priapus" ("I despise the Parnassian maidens" ("Oda Priapu" ["Parnasskikh devok preziraiu"]) and other works, the word "guby" (lips) is used in its sexual meaning: "And the lips of the tender pussies are rosy" (I guby nezhnykh pizd rumiany), while Barkov's "Ode to the Cunt" refers to the "cunt's mouth" (pizdii rot). Likewise, in "Ode to Priapus" ("Priapus, ruler of cunts and pricks") ("Oda Priapu" ["Priap, pravitel' pizd, khuev"]), we find mention of "the very narrowest cunts, / That clench their lips" (samym uzen'kim pizdam, / Kotory guby uzhimaiut).[68]

The "bloody fist" likewise bears strong traces of the Barkovian tradition, in which blood is often a sign of violated virginity—for example, in a triumphal stanza from "Ode to Priapus" ("Priapus, ruler of cunts and pricks"), in which Priapus is overjoyed because "all the virgins fuck before him. / Here every prick stands bathed in blood" (Vse tselki pered nim ebutsia. / Tut kazhdyi khui v krovi stoit), as well as in a key passage from "Ode to the Prick," where Barkov spells out Pushkin's suggestive sexual-textual metaphor beyond a doubt: "Dip yourself into the cunt's stream, / But do not extinguish your flame, / Wet yourself in the blood of victory / And with your glans, prick, write verses" (V istochnik pizdei okunisia, / No plamen' svoi ne utushi, / V krovi pobedy omochisia / I plesh'iu, khui, stikhi pishi). The use of the Old Slavonic term "desnitsa" for "right hand/fist" is attested in "Ode to the Cunt," where Phoebus Apollo ushers in the sunrise while riding in a scarlet (bloody?) chariot and "holding his balls in his mighty fist" (derzha ego mude v desnitse).[69]

The use of a sword (mech) as a phallic image is also fully in keeping with the tradition of Barkoviana, in which sharp pointed objects often are used as representations of the male organ (note the example of the "pen-prick" in the line "And with your glans, prick, write verses"; the riddle poem "The Miller and the Maiden," in which the windmill stands in for the penis, provides another relevant instance of such usage). In fact, the specific use of a sword as phallic image can be found in Barkov's epigram "Venus's Weapon" ("Venerino oruzhie"), where Venus first admires Mars's helmet, sword, and spear, only to be told condescendingly by Priapus "but for your hands a prick is the best weapon" (Dlia vashikh vit' ruk khui lutche ruzh'e).[70]

Not only does the "trembling heart" that the seraph removes from the future prophet's chest suggest the possibility of a romantic or erotic interpretation; the image of the heart (which recurs again, markedly, in the final line of "The Prophet") also makes an appearance in a purely sexual meaning in Barkov's "Ode to Priapus" ("Priapus, ruler of cunts and pricks"): "But the very narrowest cunts . . . / Foretell a great misfortune, / That a thick prick will fuck them, / And reach its length all the way to the heart" (No samym uzen'kim pizdam . . . / Bedy zh veliki predveshchaiut, / Chto tolstyi khui ikh budet et', / Dlinnoi do serdtsa ikh dostanet). Trembling, too, is often a code for sexual arousal, as in the same ode: "All the veins/sinews in me were trembling" (Vo mne vse zhily trepetali) and in the *poema* "The Battle between the Prick and the Cunt for First Place" ("Srazhenie mezhdu khuem i pizdoiu o pervenstve"): "And the prick, having laid eyes on the cunt, immediately began to tremble" (A khui, uzrev pizdu, totchas vostrepetal).[71]

The somewhat redundant and, thus, doubly resplendent image of the "coal flaming with fire," along with the command to the prophet at the poem's end to "scorch the hearts of people," evokes a rich tradition within Barkoviana of using an accumulation of the lexicon of heat, fire, burning, flame, and so on as a code for sexual desire and sexual contact, intercourse in particular (although it goes without saying that Pushkin's seemingly chaste lexicon, here as elsewhere in "The Prophet," is quite the opposite of Barkov's explicitly sexual wording). Numerous examples of such usage could be cited, but two passages will suffice. The first is from "Ode to Priapus" ("Priapus, ruler of cunts and pricks"): "Her face burned like a coal, / All her limbs trembled from the heat, / I myself, gazing upon her, smouldered, / . . . that narrow channel was visible / Which so captivated and scorched me" (Litse eia kak ugl' gorel, / Vse chleny s zharu v nei drozhali, / Ia, gliadia na nee, sam tlel, / . . . byl viden put' sei tesnyi, / Chto stol' menia plenil i zhog). An even more vivid illustration of this metaphoric vocabulary can be found in Barkov's riddle poem "The Fire" ("Pozhar"), in which a young man runs into the street yelling "Fire!" and is met by a priest, who asks where the fire is burning. The youth responds: "My rags are burning, / And so is your old woman's cunt. / It isn't possible, Father, to put out this blaze with water, / A fire like lightning . . . / Permit me to immerse my prick in your old woman's cunt, / Then my cock will release its rain into the cunt, / Her cunt will instantly drench my cock. / I'll put out the fire in my prick, and she in her cunt" (Gorit moia shmatina, / A takzhe u tvoei u matushki v pizde. / Ne mozhno, batiushka, zalit' sei zhar vodoiu, / Podobno molnii ogon' . . . / Veli spustit' moi khui ty s matkinoi pizdoi, / To pustit dozhd' v pizdu elda, / Eldu zh obmochit vmig pizda. / Ia khui svoi zatushu, a matushka pizdu).[72] Pushkin follows this Barkovian semantic tradition in *The Shade of Barkov*, too: Ebakov's powerful phallus is described at the outset of his adventures as "burning like a crimson pillar" (goria kak stolb bagrianyi); after being restored at the ballad's end, it becomes once again, in a marked reprise of its former glory, a "crimson glans" that "burns with fire" (bagrova plesh' ognem gorit).[73]

To complete the discussion of the Barkovian resonance of the vocabulary used to describe the seraph's rape-like mutilation of the prophet's body, we come at last to the final image of the "open breast" (grud' otverstaia). This image echoes the image of the she-eagle's "prophetic eyes" (veshchie zenitsy) that suddenly sprang open (otverzlis') at the angel's very first touch (l. 7). Thus, the persona's double rape by the seraph is framed on either side by an opening, and these openings point to one another—the first seeming to urge the reader to open his/her eyes to what is *really* being said beneath the surface of the text and the second making of the poet's breast, in which his soul is lodged, a sexual orifice. (Incidentally, the fact that the poet's tongue sins precisely by "idle talk" or, loosely, "profanity" [prazdnoslovie] and "cunning" [lukavstvo], l. 17, may also be read as a pointed hint to the reader to *read carefully* in order to glimpse the poem's unexpectedly obscene hidden content.)

This sexual layer of meaning is further enhanced by the other verbs describing the seraph's actions in relation to the prophet, with the repetition of verbs of insertion (vlozhil, vodvinul) alternating with verbs of extraction (vyrval, vynul) pointing to the rhythms of coital penetration. Lines 21–25 of "The Prophet" in particular lend themselves to strong Barkovian associations:[74]

И он мне грудь рассек мечом,
И сердце трепетное вынул,
И угль, пылающий огнем,
Во грудь отверстую водвинул.

[And he cleaved my breast with his sword / And removed my trembling heart / And inserted a coal flaming with fire / Into my gaping breast.]

Here the cloven breast (grud′ rassek) can be seen as doubling for the female sexual organ "shchel′" (crevice), while the invasive sword and flaming coal replace the male organ with which they are associated in the Barkovian lexicon. The grammatical structure of these lines also contributes to their sexual suggestiveness, with the grammatically feminine "grud′" (breast) appearing twice in the accusative case, as the object of aggression, and the grammatically masculine "mech" (sword) and "ogon′" (fire) both occurring in the instrumental case. The fact that these two nouns share a rare stressed instrumental-case ending adds to their phallic associations, as the pair "mechom/ognem" (with his sword/with fire) brings to mind the similarly stressed obscene rhyme "eldakom" (with his cock).

These sexual substitutions, though perhaps shocking, are not as fantastical as they might at first appear. Indeed, Pushkin himself substitutes acceptable rhyming words for obscene epithets in letters to his brother Lev and to Viazemsky of 1824: the pair "naiti/puti" (to find/paths) points to the unstated "eti" (to fuck) in the first case, while "Ol′dekop" points to "eb" (the interjection "Fuck!," pronounced "yop") in the second.[75] As Shapir explains, there is a tradition in Russian poetry of making erotic suggestions through expected but unrealized rhymes of the variety "pet′/et′" (sing/fuck): "The violation of the expected rhyme (similarly to obscene puns of the type 'KrePI ZDArov′e[,] daragaia')"—the capitalized portions of the first two words of this phrase meaning "Be well, dear" come together to form the hidden word "pizda" (cunt)—"is a *locus communis* of all obscene poetry."[76] Pushkin is fully aware of and subscribes to this tradition. In fact, it might be argued that there are several more unrealized obscene rhymes in "The Prophet" in addition to the "mechom/ognem/eldakom" triplet: "vlachilsia/iavilsia" (languished/appeared) in the poem's first quatrain brings to mind the common Barkovian verb (also present in *The Shade of Barkov*) "drochilsia" (jerked off, masturbated), while the rhyme "sodrogan'e/proziaban'e" (shuddering/vegetating) roughly at the poem's center suggests the sexual pair "lobzan'e/pod"eban'e" (sensual kissing/[female] responsive fucking). Thus, the shadow of an obscene lexical subtext haunts the poem's highly elevated language (through imagery, linguistic echoes, and unrealized rhymes) at its beginning, middle, and end.[77] This outrageous sexual contamination demonstrates the full truth of Andrew Kahn's observation that "the images of the 'The Prophet' violate the rules of good taste and expression that had been the legacy of La Harpe and Marmontel to Pushkin's poetics." Kahn characterizes the poem as "strikingly violent and even ugly," its persona as "faceless" and "repulsive," and its poetic epiphany as "deliberately repellent."[78]

Thus far, my analysis has mainly emphasized the heretofore unnoticed subterranean, Barkovian linguistic stratum of "The Prophet," which reveals the presence of a parodic component latent within the poem's complex and enigmatic set of meanings. In closing this discussion, I would like to return to *The Shade of Barkov*—which, like "The Prophet," enacts a narrative of poetic genesis through supernatural visitations and bodily transformations—to argue that the climactic ending of "The Prophet" seems to have been carefully crafted by Pushkin as an intentional echo of his early erotic ballad. Here are the familiar final lines of "The Prophet"; the hero, abandoned now by the seraph and spent from his ordeal, lies as if dead in the wilderness until he is suddenly resurrected by the voice of God:

Как труп в пустыне я лежал,
И бога глас ко мне воззвал:
«Восстань, пророк, и виждь и внемли,
Исполнись волею моей,
И обходя моря и земли,
Глаголом жги сердца людей.» (ll. 25–30)

[Like a corpse in the wilderness I lay, / And the voice of God summoned me: / "Arise, prophet, and behold and hearken, / Fill yourself with my will, / And traversing seas and lands, / Scorch the hearts of people with [the/my] w/Word."]

This passage, for all its high solemnity and seeming verbal purity, in fact reprises Ebakov's first miraculous encounter with Barkov in the wilderness of the bordello:

И страхом пораженный поп
Не смог сказать ни слова;
Свалился на пол будто сноп
К портищам он Баркова.
«Восстань, любезный Ебаков!
Восстань! повелеваю!
Всю ярость праведных хуев
Тебе я возвращаю.—
Поди еби Малашку вновь!»[79]

[And the priest struck with fear / Could not utter a single word. / He fell to the floor like a sheaf of grain / At the hem of Barkov's trousers. / "Arise, good Ebakov! / Arise! I command you! / All the ardor of righteous pricks / I herewith return to you.— / Go forth and fuck Malashka once again!"]

The similarities between these two passages are nothing short of astounding. Both segments narrate the poetic genesis of a figure who is visited by a divine presence precisely at the moment when he has been humbled and struck down: the defrocked priest Ebakov falls to the floor "like a sheaf of grain" (budto snop), while the future prophet lies on the ground "like a corpse" (kak trup). The two heroes' similarly prone positions, the similar phrasing using a word for "like" (kak/budto), and the phonetic similarity between the monosyllables "snop" (sheaf) and "trup" (corpse) all draw attention to the broader thematic parallels between the two poems.

Likewise, the two primary agents in both passages are the same. The first is the will of a higher being. "Fill yourself with my will [*voleiu*]," says God to his newly minted prophet; "I command you [*povelevaiu*]," says Barkov's shade to his newly hatched epigone: the noun "volia" (will) and verb "povelevat'" (to command, to will) are etymologically related. The second agent is the ambiguously poetic or prophetic word, revived from silence: the priest in *The Shade of Barkov* at first "could not utter a single word"; the prophet, too, lies speechless, having lost his tongue, until the voice of God infests him with the word/his Word. In both poems, powerful words are willed by supernatural entities; it is no accident that the poetic word and the motif of free will versus fate are perhaps *the* two central pillars of Pushkin's inquiring poetic worldview.[80] It remains an open question to what extent the poet's word in both poems (particularly in "The Prophet") will remain obedient to the constraints of a transcendental will in the longer term; an underlying ambiguity in the divine messages delivered in the two passages underlines this uncertainty. For these injunctions not only share the imperative mood but they also begin with one and the same word—"vosstan'" (arise)—as each respective godly intercessor enjoins each newly formed poet to unleash his gift upon the world in forceful acts of (pro)creativity that will verge on violence and thereby replicate the trauma of poetic genesis. The apparently chaste and triumphal verb "vosstat'" (to arise) in fact has covert, secondary meanings that evoke both erection and rebellion—and these subversive nuances themselves rise to the surface as the sexual and political taboos Pushkin traverses in the two seemingly incommensurate poems are twinned.[81]

The outcome of the miraculous resurrections in both poems is similar: the hero, now endowed with powerful poetic/prophetic voice and the sexual/(m)oral potency that comes with it, embarks on a proselytizing journey. In *The Shade of Barkov*, as we have already seen, Ebakov spreads both the good news of Barkov's greatness and his own sexual prolificness far and wide across Russia, increasing his personal wealth in the process: "And he began to wander from land to land / With a fiddle, a fiddlestick, his balls, / And all through Rus' he samples paradise / On paper and in cunts" (I stal khodit' iz kraia v krai / S gudkom, smychkom, mudami, / I na Rusi vkushaet rai / Bumagoi i pizdami).[82] In "The Prophet," likewise, the lyric persona will presumably obey God's command to "wander over seas and lands" (obkhod[it'] moria i zemli, l. 29), employing his newly attained powers of perception ("and behold and harken" [i vizhd', i vnemli, l. 27]) and burning the hearts of his listeners with his newly attained power of speech.[83] Some commentators on "The Prophet" have seen the poem as open ended: the reader sees only the persona's transformation, they argue, but never hears what he has to say in the aftermath.[84] However, if we recognize that the poem (which is narrated in the first person, in the past tense) is situated in a narrative moment that occurs of necessity *after* the transformation told within it, then we may in fact understand the text of the poem as the substance of the lyric persona's prophetic utterance. In other words, this powerful autobiographical narrative of the poet's own *agonia* in which the spiritual and the sexual, passion and torture are profoundly intertwined *becomes in itself the very message of his prophecy.*

On the Thin Edge between Sacred and Profane

If *The Shade of Barkov* brings about a sacralization of the sexual impulse in the name of poetry, then "The Prophet" can be seen as its inverse, a brutally sexual reenactment of spiritual asceticism. In both cases, the traumatic yet exhilarating sexual couplings described transform the poet irreversibly, although it is a transformation that is described in different (comic vs. serious) keys. The sexual crisis in *The Shade of Barkov* is the threat of impotence and castration; the "crossroads" (pereput'e, l. 4) at which the poet finds himself at the beginning of "The Prophet" is as much a metaphor for broken virginity as it is for spiritual crisis. On the deepest level, this poem is about the loss of innocence and the recognition that the making of poems is not a superficial activity but a serious existential choice that demands of the poet a willingness to submit body and soul to utter ravishment by the force of poetic inspiration and to accept the consequences and responsibilities of that decision. By the time he composes "The Prophet," Pushkin's earlier adolescent construal of virility (poetic and sexual) in terms of a boastful machismo has been replaced by his sober awareness of this stark ethical reality.

In the course of his process of maturation, Pushkin has shifted the stylistic polemic that formed the backdrop of *The Shade of Barkov* forward to the personal sphere: in his liberal, almost excessive use of high-style, archaic grammatical forms and biblical Slavonicisms throughout the text of "The Prophet" (e.g., "persty" [fingers], "zenitsy" [eyes], "otverzlis'" [opened], "mudryia" [wise], "desnitsa" [right hand], "otverstyi" [open], "glas" [voice], "vizhd'" [see], "vnemli" [hearken], "glagol" [word], and others), he parodies the language of Derzhavin's celebratory odes and of devout Decembrist poetry—not to mock it, but in order to make it his own. This achievement requires us to augment Ram's observation that "the prophetic topos in Russian verse is tied as much to a poetic reconceptualization of imperial history as to religious or aesthetic experience": for Pushkin in "The Prophet," the prophetic topos is tied to a reconceptualization of *sexual* experience as well.[85] Indeed, in this poem Pushkin recapitulates Derzhavin's own practice of merging high and low subject matter; perhaps this appropriation of his predecessor's powerful and dynamic poetics into his own spiritual and bodily experience—his own soul, his own vocal chords—can be understood as one source of the violence he undergoes. Sybil-like, he endures the torture of Derzhavin's voice speaking through him.

This inkling of the deeply personal nature of "The Prophet" sheds new light on the alternate first line of the poem: "Tormented by a great grief" (Velikoi skorbiiu tomim). This line has mystified scholars, who have generally assumed it to be a remnant of an early draft of the poem and have interpreted it in a political vein: as a reference to Pushkin's mourning over the fate of the five hanged Decembrist conspirators and his belief in the prophetic imperative thrust on him owing to his own miraculous survival.[86] However, "velikaia skorb'" can also be understood as "Great Tribulation" and can thus be interpreted as referring to the seven-year period of the Apocalypse during which those Christians who have turned away from God will be punished. My reading of "The Prophet," which recognizes the presence of an obscene underlayer throughout this seemingly chaste poem, suggests that the line "Velikoi skorbiiu tomim" was not part of an early draft (after all, the list of poems in which it appears was written in 1827, after "The Prophet" was finished, as far as we know) but rather an ironizing self-commentary written after the fact—that is, yet another layer of coded self-parody that reflects Pushkin's private admission to himself of the "sinful" origins of his poetic voice. In the end, he appears to regard his feat of secret burlesque—the subtle merging of sublimity and profanity—in "The Prophet" with a mix of satisfaction and chagrin.

As Gasparov has shown, for Pushkin the serious and the comical merge, and sacred texts and images (e.g., the Koran, Apollo) may take on demonic characteristics; similarly, Oleg Proskurin argues in "Pushkin and Metropolitan Philaret" in the present volume that for Pushkin, "all religious symbols carried a conventional and relative significance: they were necessary only insofar as they helped to manifest his message about the sacredness of poetry."[87] Different Pushkinian heroes and different Pushkinian texts situate themselves differently with respect to the sacred-profane divide, that "thin edge between solemnity and the joke" (we recall Tatiana's impassioned question to Onegin, "Who are you, are you my guardian angel, / Or an insidious seducer?" [Kto ty, moi angel li khranitel', / Ili kovarnyi iskusitel']: that is, is her beloved formed in the mold of the seraph or Barkov's shade?).[88] But they are never purely one or the other; instead, they behave in accordance with the phenomenon of Arzamasian obscene wordplays described by Shapir: "From behind the decent meaning, now and then, the indecent one shows through. Sometimes the secret meaning becomes almost manifest."[89] This multivalent linguistic, imagistic, and symbolic potency is evident, most of all, in Pushkin's poem "The Prophet," if only we are unafraid to look.

As we have seen, the equivalency between the poetic and sexual drives becomes more subtle and double voiced in Pushkin's later works. Yet I would suggest that this equivalency is present, albeit somewhat muted, throughout his creative oeuvre. Bethea sees the hanging of the

Decembrists and the composition of "The Prophet" as a watershed in Pushkin's creative life: "The closer the post-1825 Pushkin gets to the sacred space of myth or religious sensibility, the less apt he is to use that 'access' for any ulterior purpose"; "Although humor, scabrousness, and an unwillingness to moralize directly will be features of Pushkin's work right into the 1830s, there is not a shred of the strictly 'Voltairean' element, i.e., the 'atheistic' mocking of religious sensibilities, after 1826."[90] Nothing in my analysis should be construed as contradicting these observations. "The Prophet" is, indeed, about the "high calling of the poet" (Bethea's term); yet it harnesses the poetics of obscenity, not for the purpose of mockery but rather as an illustration of Pushkin's awareness (perhaps even subconscious awareness) of the fact that the low and the high are humanly inseparable. Far from contradicting the ethical principles that guide Pushkin's poetry, his use of sexual imagery and even verbal obscenity is a shorthand that gestures, with maximum vigor and efficiency, at the power of art to transgress, transcend, and transform. Neither the repressive power of the censorship nor the conservative strictures of society and the church can suppress the yearning for poetic freedom, however fraught with danger and suffering. Like sex, poetry lives everywhere and will continue to live, even if unpublished and in secret.

When Pushkin's acquaintance Alexandra Osipovna Smirnova-Rosset once remarked that Pushkin was "a lover of vulgarity" (liubitel' nepristoinogo), another Pushkin acquaintance, the diplomat Nikolai Kiselev, answered, greatly perplexed, that he himself had "never been able to comprehend [Pushkin's] antithetical habit of shifting back and forth between the obscene and the sublime."[91] The foregoing analysis of the poetics of obscenity in Pushkin's art might be construed as a belated response to Kiselev's consternation. As I have shown, for Pushkin there is no absolute separation between obscenity and sublimity but only the arbitrary boundary imposed by the censorship and social convention. The most brazenly sexual-textual capers are synonymous with the most powerful inspirational climax, the greatest antidogmatic challenge, and the most concentrated spiritual risk and release. Therefore, we should view Pushkin's obscene and risqué works, including *The Shade of Barkov*—as well as those such as "The Prophet" that embrace obscenity alongside the most elevated spiritual values—as comprising a boldly humanistic project that puts poetry and poetic values at its core. Both obscenity and sublimity involve the transcendence of mundane verbal formulas and meaningless clichés and both, therefore, serve

Pushkin's uplifting poetic purpose of liberating human thought and self-expression.

Notes

I am grateful to Igor Pilshchikov for his invaluable comments and suggestions. J. Douglas Clayton and Caryl Emerson also provided helpful feedback, and I thank them as well.

1. For a detailed history of Mstislav A. Tsiavlovsky's reconstruction of the text of *The Shade of Barkov* and its reception, see Igor Pilshchikov's chapter in the present volume. Tsiavlovsky's commentary to the poem is published, along with an extensive editorial commentary, in Aleksandr S. Pushkin, *"Ten' Barkova": Teksty, Kommentarii, Ekskursy*, ed. Igor' A. Pil'shchikov and Maksim I. Shapir (Moscow: Iazyki slavianskoi kul'tury, 2002), 164–348. Joe Peschio also discusses the reception history in his *The Poetics of Impudence and Intimacy in the Age of Pushkin* (Madison: University of Wisconsin Press, 2012). The other works I refer to include Georgii A. Levinton and Nikita G. Okhotin, "'Chto za delo im—khochu . . .': O literaturnykh i fol'klornykh istochnikakh skazki A. S. Pushkina 'Tsar' Nikita i 40 ego docherei,'" *Literaturnoe obozrenie* 11 (1991): 28–35, Igor' A. Pil'shchikov, "'Nichego il' ochen' malo . . .' (Skazka Pushkina 'Tsar' Nikita i 40 ego docherei': Dopolneniia k kommentariiu," in Pushkin, *"Ten' Barkova": Teksty, Kommentarii, Ekskursy*, 466–79; Anthony Cross, "Pushkin's Bawdy; or, Notes from the Literary Underground," *Russian Literature Triquarterly* 10 (1974): 203–36; Maksim I. Shapir, "Iz istorii russkogo 'balladnogo stikha': 'Perom vladeet kak eldoi,'" *Russian Linguistics* 17.1 (1993): 57–84; Aleksandr S. Pushkin, *Chas nevinnogo dosuga*, ed. Sergei V. Denisenko (St. Petersburg: Azbuka-Klassika, 2004); and Sergei V. Denisenko, *Eroticheskie risunki Pushkina* (Moscow: Nezavisimaia gazeta, 1997). The chapters in the present volume by J. Douglas Clayton and Natalia Vesselova on *Tsar Nikita* and Andrew Kahn on *The Gabrieliad* (*Gavriiliada*) also provide a welcome addition to the scholarly literature on Pushkin's erotically themed writings.

2. As sociologist Igor' Kon points out, "the contrast between the official 'high' culture, sanctified by the church and antisexual by its very nature, and the 'low,' everyday culture of the common people, in which sexuality was accorded a positive value," was much greater in Russia than it was in the West. Therefore, in Russia, "sexual dissidence was seen as a form of political opposition" and "obscenity was a direct challenge to authority," both secular and clerical. (See Igor S. Kon, *The Sexual Revolution in Russia: From the Age of the Czars to Today*, trans. James Riordan [New York: Free Press, 1995], 12–13, 26. The Russian text, which differs from the English version in some respects, is *Seksual'naia kul'tura v Rossii: Klubnichka na berezke* [Moscow: OGI, 1997].)

3. Tsiavlovskii, "Kommentarii," 212. In this chapter I do not question Pushkin's authorship of *The Shade of Barkov*, which appears to me to have been

proven beyond a reasonable doubt. Indeed, my analysis adds additional support to the likelihood of Pushkin's authorship of this sometime hotly disputed text. Pushkin's salacious mock-epic *The Gabrieliad* has undergone a similar fate in the scholarship, which has often dismissed the poem out of hand as a youthful prank (mal'chisheskoe balovstvo) or, at best, has speculated on its literary sources in Parny and others (see Sergei V. Denisenko, "'Ot vozderzhan'ia muza chakhnet . . .': Erotika Pushkina," in Pushkin, *Chas nevinnogo dosuga*, 11–12; Denisenko also characterizes *Tsar Nikita* as "yet another Kishinev prank" [15]).

4. Denisenko, "'Ot vozderzhan'ia muza chakhnet . . . ,'" 12.

5. Laura Wilhelm discusses the remarkable parallels between the lives of Pushkin and Aesop, arguing that Pushkin's (and Aesop's) eroticism is *redefined as pornography* by a chauvinistic regime: the voice "is the human attribute most feared by the pornographic imagination" ("Pornography and the Politics of Oppression in the Russian Aesopian Tradition," in *Eros and Pornography in Russian Culture*, ed. Marcus C. Levitt and Andrei L. Toporkov [Moscow: Ladomir, 1999], 266–67).

6. William Hugh Hopkins, "The Development of 'Pornographic' Literature in Eighteenth- and Early Nineteenth-Century Russia" (PhD diss., University of Michigan, 1977), 24. Hopkins wrote his dissertation with only a partial version of *The Shade of Barkov* at his disposal, resulting in occasional mistakes and misinterpretations of the text: primarily, he fails to realize that Ebakov the poet and the defrocked priest mentioned in the poem's opening stanza are in fact one and the same person.

7. Marcus C. Levitt, "*Barkoviana* and Russian Classicism," in *Eros and Pornography in Russian Culture*, 220, 232. See also Manfred Schruba, who makes a distinction in the Russian context between pornographic poetry and pornographic prose ("'Porno' v epokhu Prosveshcheniia: K spetsifike barkoviany na fone frantsuzskoi pornografii," in *Eros and Pornography in Russian Culture*, 201, 204). The use of the term "pornography" (pornografiia) is not attested in Russia until 1869 (see Natal'ia L. Pushkareva, "Russkie lubochnye kartinki XVII–XX vv: Nachalo pornografii ili otrazhenie narodnykh eroticheskikh vozzrenii?" in *Eros and Pornography in Russian Culture*, 43). For a useful commentary on the origins of pornography and the relationship between traditional popular culture and traditional ecclesiastical culture in Russia, see Eve Levin, "Pornography before Pornography," in *Eros and Pornography in Russian Culture*, 87–93.

8. Eliot Borenstein, "Slavophilia: The Incitement to Russian Sexual Discourse," *Slavic and East European Journal* 40.1 (1996): 147.

9. Aleksandr S. Pushkin, "Poslanie tsenzoru," in his *Polnoe sobranie sochinenii*, 10 vols., ed. Boris V. Tomashevskii (Leningrad: Nauka, 1977–79), 2:112.

10. The text of Pushkin's obscene ballad is published in Pushkin, *"Ten' Barkova": Teksty, Kommentarii, Ekskursy*, 33–41.

11. See Levitt for a brief discussion of the iconography of Priapus and the Priapian odic tradition as practiced by the ancient Roman poets as well as by

eighteenth-century French and Russian classicists, including Barkov himself ("*Barkoviana* and Russian Classicism," 221–23). It is conceivable that *The Shade of Barkov* intentionally plays with the Faust legend, which, according to Mikhail P. Alekseev, Pushkin likely knew from a publication found in his library, *Bibliothèque universelle des romans* from the year 1776, which included a French translation of excerpts from the late-sixteenth-century version of the German legend, in the section of the journal devoted to "comical, satirical, and lowbrow works." The excerpts are preceded by a brief introduction, which links the legendary Faust to the historical Jean Fust or Faust of Mainz, owner of one of the first commercial print shops, and concludes by characterizing the Faust legend as a moralistic allegory. It remains uncertain when precisely Pushkin first encountered this publication; for more on Pushkin's knowledge of various sources related to the Faust theme, including the one discussed here, see Alekseev, "Pushkin i frantsuzskaia narodnaia kniga o Fauste," in *Vremennik Pushkinskoi komissii, 1976* (Leningrad: Nauka, 1979), 97–109. Given the fact that the *Bibliothèque universelle des romans* publication highlights a historical Faust's possible literary vocation and situates the tale in the realm of the comical-satirical, Pushkin may have had the Faust legend and its trope of the demonic bargain in mind when conceiving *The Shade of Barkov*. The plot of Zhukovsky's ballad *Gromoboi*, which was published in 1811 and which Pushkin clearly knew when composing *The Shade of Barkov*, also revolves around a bargain with the devil. Tsiavlovsky appears not to appreciate this deep typological parallel between the two works when he writes that Pushkin does not parody Zhukovsky's plot but only borrows its meter and stanzaic form (Tsiavlovskii, "Kommentarii," 257).

12. See Tsiavlovskii, "Kommentarii," 212–13.

13. See especially Shapir's wonderful article "Iz istorii russkogo 'balladnogo stikha,'" as well as his highly informative "Barkov i Derzhavin: Iz istorii russkogo burleska," in Pushkin, *"Ten' Barkova": Teksty, Kommentarii, Ekskursy*, 379–457.

14. On this point see Maksim Shapir, who notes that these parodies, following the French poet Piron's "Ode to Priapus" ("Ode à Priape" [1710]), exactly reproduce the formal and stylistic features of the target genre (e.g., metrics, stanzaic form, rhyme patterns) as well as its typical rhetorical features and clichés ("Barkov i Derzhavin," 397–98). The first-ever scholarly collection of Barkov's works was published only in the late twentieth century: *Devich'ia igrushka, ili Sochineniia gospodina Barkova*, ed. Andrei Zorin and Nikita Sapov (Moscow: Ladomir, 1992). Lynn Hunt defines pornography as we understand it today as "the explicit depiction of sexual organs and sexual practices with the aim of arousing sexual feelings" (*The Invention of Pornography: Obscenity and the Origins of Modernity, 1500–1800* [New York: Zone Books, 1993], 10).

15. Igor Pilshchikov notes that in the Russian tradition, obscene poetry, along with blasphemous poetry, "belongs to the 'masculine-masculine' type of

communication," whereas, given an ounce of courage on the part of the poet, non-obscene erotic poetry in the early nineteenth century sometimes moved into the sphere of the "'masculine-feminine' communicative situation" ("Coitus as a Cross-Genre Motif in Brodsky's Poetry," *Russian Literature* 37.2–3 [1995]: 340), a shift that Pushkin plays with, for instance, in his poetic preface to *The Gabrieliad*. In contrast to the classical tradition, which was androcentric, sentimentalism gave the female reader precedence: "The ideal author for the Karamzinians was the one 'read by the ladies'" (Shapir, "Iz istorii russkogo 'balladnogo stikha,'" 65), the one who wrote "as women spoke." One result of this development was a growing awareness of gender as imitative, an awareness that was sometimes manifested in performances of literary dandyism—a practice (characteristic of Pushkin himself) that accords well with the Barkovian parody of classical literary forms: "Much of the new women's and 'women's' writing was characterized by a spirit of lightness, play, artifice, and artificiality as well as a domesticated and often parodic reversal of the Classical hegemonies . . . laying bare the fact that both are cultural constructs" (Gitta Hammarberg, "Gender Ambivalence and Genre Anomalies in Late 18th-Early 19th-Century Russian Literature," *Russian Literature* 52.1–3 [2002]: 313). For both the Karamzinians and the Barkovians more broadly, then, culture creation is synonymous with imitation or parody (see Shapir, "Barkov i Derzhavin," 426, on the legitimacy of imitation or "copying" in eighteenth-century Russian literary culture).

16. Iurii N. Tynianov, *Dostoevskii i Gogol' (K teorii parodii)* (Petrograd: Opoiaz, 1921), 9, http://feb-web.ru/feb/classics/critics/tynianov/t77/t77-198-.htm (accessed 16 February 2011).

17. See Shapir, "Barkov i Derzhavin," 417–19, 421–25.

18. Ibid., 427–28.

19. Ibid., 431.

20. Ibid., 439. See also Anthony Cross's discussion of the folk roots of the Russian joke in "Pushkin's Bawdy," 220.

21. Shapir, "Barkov i Derzhavin," 431.

22. Namely, Pushkin parodies Konstantin Batiushkov and Alexander Izmailov's "balladic-epic-lyric-comic-episodic hymn" *Bard in the Colloquy of Lovers of the Russian Word* (*Pevets v Besede liubitelei russkogo slova* [1813]), which is itself a parody of Zhukovsky's patriotic poem *Bard in the Camp of the Russian Warriors* (*Pevets vo stane russkikh voinov* [1812]) and also contains several parodic allusions to Zhukovsky's ballad *Gromoboi*. See Shapir, "Iz istorii russkogo 'balladnogo stikha,'" 57–61, along with Igor Pilshchikov's discussion in the present volume.

23. Indeed, *The Shade of Barkov* deploys its foul language not toward any shameful purpose but in the service of a good-natured literary joke, with the poetry of the archaist Shishkovites as its butt. In an important statement contained within his unfinished article "Refutation of Criticisms" ("Oproverzhenie

na kritiki"), written in Boldino in 1830, Pushkin clarifies his understanding of the boundary between morality and immorality in literature: "An immoral work is one whose goal or result is to shatter the rules on which the social good and human dignity are founded. A poem whose goal is to inflame [*goriachit'*] the imagination with lascivious [*liubostrastnyi*] descriptions degrades [*unizhaet*] poetry, turning her divine nectar into an inflammatory potion [*vospalitel'nyi sostav*], and the muse into a repulsive Canidia. But a joke [*shutka*] inspired by heartfelt joy [*serdechnaia veselost'*] and the momentary play of the imagination could only seem immoral to those who have either a childish or a hazy understanding of morality and who confuse morality [*nravstvennost'*] with moralizing [*nravouchenie*] and see in literature only a pedagogical activity" (Pushkin, *Polnoe sobranie sochinenii*, 10 vols., 7:131). Tsiavlovsky, probably erroneously, reads this passage as an expression of Pushkin's later regret at having written a shameful work like *The Shade of Barkov* and thus as the only written hint at Pushkin's authorship of the ballad; yet Tsiavlovsky himself admits that despite the poem's obscenity, irreverence, and pornographic content, it lacks any hint of cynicism or viciousness ("Kommentarii," 251–52, 212). In his first "Epistle to the Censor" of 1822, Pushkin would deplore the suspicion-driven, closed-minded censorship that saw "poetry as depravity, / the voice of truth as insurrection" (poeziiu razvratom, / Glas pravdy miatezhom), and he would go on boastfully to deny the censor's very efficacy, since both Barkov's "joking odes" (shutlivye ody) and Pushkin's own objectionable verses were able to bypass the censorship machine entirely and wander the world freely, though unpublished.

24. Pushkin, *"Ten' Barkova": Teksty, Kommentarii, Ekskursy*, 36.

25. Quoted in Tsiavslovskii, "Kommentarii," 223, 215. The obscenities and sexual content are expunged from the versions of these letters that are published in official editions of Pushkin's correspondence and collected works (see, for example, Pushkin, *Polnoe sobranie sochinenii*, 10 vols., 10:197, 91).

26. The final line quoted here is given as "stabs it *stubbornly* into his verse" (lomaet v stikh *upriamo*) in Pushkin, *"Ten' Barkova": Teksty, Kommentarii, Ekskursy*, 34, but "upriamo" has been corrected to "upriamoi" by Pilshchikov and Shapir in their "Tekstologiia vs aksiologiia: Eshche raz ob avtorstve ballady Pushkina *Ten' Barkova*," in Maksim I. Shapir, *Stat'i o Pushkine*, ed. I. A. Pil'shchikov (Moscow: Iazyki slavianskikh kul'tur, 2009), 343. See the commentary by Tsiavlovsky for some background on Khvostov and the role he plays in Pushkin's works ("Kommentarii," 233–36).

27. Shapir, "Iz istorii russkogo 'balladnogo stikha,'" 70, 67.

28. See Igor' P. Smirnov, "Kastratsionnyi kompleks v lirike Pushkina (Metodologicheskie zametki)," *Russian Literature* 29.2 (1991): 205–28, for a very far-fetched and peculiar yet occasionally insightful meditation on the pervasive presence of a "castration complex" in Pushkin's works. Smirnov focuses primarily on the lyric poems and thus fails to mention *The Shade of Barkov, Tsar*

Nikita and His Forty Daughters, or *The Tale of the Golden Cockerel* (*Skazka o zolotom petushke* [1834]), in all of which the theme of castration features prominently. For an excellent discussion of the metapoetic significance of castration and impotence in Pushkin's writing, see Clayton and Vesselova's "Resexing Literature" in the present volume, especially pages 229–32.

29. Hopkins, "The Development of 'Pornographic' Literature," 279–80.

30. Pushkin, *"Ten' Barkova": Teksty, Kommentarii, Ekskursy*, 35. Pushkin uses the word *genii* in his poetry both in the meaning of "muse" and in the more general meaning of "guardian spirit" (see *Slovar' iazyka Pushkina*, 4 vols., ed. Viktor V. Vinogradov, Sergei I. Bernshtein, and Anna D. Grigor'eva [Moscow: Azbukovnik, 2000], 1:470–71).

31. These two anti-Christian figures are purely satirical constructs reminiscent of Muscovite ecclesiastical representations of corrupt Roman Catholic and Protestant clergy. See Levin, "Pornography before Pornography," 90.

32. Pushkin, *"Ten' Barkova": Teksty, Kommentarii, Ekskursy*, 35.

33. M. H. Abrams, *Natural Supernaturalism: Tradition and Revolution in Romantic Literature* (New York: Norton, 1971).

34. Pilshchikov, "Coitus as a Cross-Genre Motif," 340–41.

35. Mikhail Vaiskopf, "'Vot evkharistiia drugaia . . .': Religioznaia erotika v tvorchestve Pushkina," *Novoe literaturnoe obozrenie* 37 (1999): 129–43. Vaiskopf traces the romantic phenomenon of religious erotica in the Russian context in part to the Catholic tradition of *imitatio Christi* as presented in the widely popular book ascribed to Thomas à Kempis, *O podrazhanii Khristu: Bogoslovie v kul'ture srednevekov'ia* (see Vaiskopf, "'Vot evkharistiia drugaia,'" 133 and 143n6).

36. On a purely linguistic level, Pushkin turns the tables and casts his transgressive project vis-à-vis traditional Christianity in restorative terms in a letter he wrote to Viazemsky in December 1823: "I would like to retain a certain biblical obscenity in the Russian language. I don't like to see in our primeval language traces of European affectation and French refinement" (Pushkin, *Polnoe sobranie sochinenii*, 10 vols., 10:62).

37. In this regard, the comment Pushkin reportedly made to Viazemsky's son Pavel that Barkov's works would be the first to be issued in a complete, unexpurgated edition in some imaginary utopian Russia of the future that would be liberated entirely from the censorship makes a great deal of sense (quoted in Vikentii V. Veresaev, *Pushkin v zhizni* [Moscow: Sovetskii pisatel', 1936], 297).

38. Quoted in Tsiavlovskii, "Kommentarii," 218. These lines are printed in the official editions of Pushkin's works in the following expurgated version: "I'll never write / As you did, I'm glad to swear it" (Kak ty, v tom kliast'sia rad, / Ne stanu ia pisat') (Pushkin, *Polnoe sobranie sochinenii*, 10 vols., 1:88).

39. In the case of *The Shade of Barkov*, the "wilderness" is realized first in the form of the bordello and later as the female monastery; the implied synonymy of the two spheres is significant here, as is the fact that one term for "monastery" in Russian is *pustyn'* (although this word does not explicitly appear in the text of Pushkin's ballad).

40. Boris Gasparov traces this trope in Pushkin's writing back to Dante's meeting with Virgil in *The Inferno* ("Funktsii reministsentsii iz Dante v poezii Pushkina," *Russian Literature* 14.4 [1983]: 317–50). Many of the ideas in this article later find their way, in a context largely divorced from reference to Dante, into Gasparov's English-language article "Encounter of Two Poets in the Desert: Pushkin's Myth," in *Myth in Literature*, ed. Andrej Kodjak, Krystyna Pomorska, and Stephen Rudy (Columbus, Ohio: Slavica, 1985), 124–53, as well as Gasparov's richly argued book *Poeticheskii iazyk Pushkina kak fakt istorii russkogo literaturnogo iazyka* (St. Petersburg: Akademicheskii proekt, 1999), first published in 1992 in *Wiener Slawistischer Almanach*.

41. Bethea provides an extensive and insightful analysis of Pushkin's meetings, first in life and later posthumously, with the poet Gavrila Derzhavin in his *Realizing Metaphors: Alexander Pushkin and the Life of the Poet* (Madison: University of Wisconsin Press, 1998), esp. pages 173–234.

42. Andrew Kahn, *Pushkin's Lyric Intelligence* (Oxford: Oxford University Press, 2008), 201. Kahn's reading of "The Prophet" bypasses the mythic status that the poem has accrued over time and analyzes its significance as one in a series of poems written in the late 1820s in which Pushkin puzzles through different aspects of the question of poetic authority in light of his professional and commercial ambitions.

43. Aleksandr S. Pushkin, "Prorok," in his *Polnoe sobranie sochinenii*, 10 vols., 2:304. Tsiavlovsky, and later Pilshchikov and Shapir, carefully trace a large number of linguistic and phraseological echoes between Pushkin's lyceum-era lyrics, his correspondence, and *The Shade of Barkov*; these have helped to establish the ballad's authorship beyond a doubt (see Pushkin, *"Ten' Barkova": Teksty, Kommentarii, Ekskursy*, 241–51, and Pilshchikov's chapter in this volume). My extension of this cross-textual comparison to the level of deep, archetypal plot and psychological parallels between the ballad and a major work of Pushkin's mature period represents the logical next stage in the process of scholarly assimilation of *The Shade of Barkov* into the Pushkin canon.

44. For further discussion of Mickiewicz's comments see Svetlana V. Berezkina, "'Prorok' Pushkina: Sovremennye problemy izucheniia," *Russkaia literatura* 2 (1999): 27–42.

45. These interpretations can be found in the following essays: Mikhail O. Gershenzon, "Mudrost' Pushkina" (1917); Sergei N. Bulgakov, "Zhrebii Pushkina" (1938); and Semen L. Frank, "Religioznost' Pushkina" (1933) and "Svetlaia pechal'," (1949).

46. See, for example, Nikolai L. Stepanov, *Lirika Pushkina: Ocherki i Etiudy* (Moscow: Khudozhestvennaia literatura, 1974), 313.

47. Irina Surat, "'Ia veruiu v prorochestva piitov . . . ,'" in her *Pushkin: Biografiia i lirika* (Moscow: Nasledie, 1999), 217–24; Irina Surat, "Bibleiskoe i lichnoe v tekstakh Pushkina," *Moskovskii pushkinist* 7 (2000): 87.

48. This variant of the poem's final four lines is given in Aleksandr S. Pushkin, *Polnoe sobranie sochinenii*, 17 vols., ed. Vladimir D. Bonch-Bruevich

et al. (Moscow: AN SSSR, 1937–1959), 3:461. Scholars who have supported the hypothesis that the fragment was authored by Pushkin include Nikolai O. Lerner, Dmitrii Blagoi, Mikhail V. Stroganov, Mstislav A. Tsiavlovsky, and, more recently, Svetlana V. Berezkina and Irina Surat; scholars who have doubted Pushkin's authorship include Tatiana G. Tsiavlovskaia, Alexander M. Slonimsky, Petr O. Morozov, Boris V. Tomashevsky, Vadim E. Vatsuro, and, again recently, Igor Nemirovsky, who proposes the fascinating hypothesis that the quatrain was in fact written in a satirical vein by members of the Moscow Wisdom Lovers circle with whom Pushkin had formerly been on close terms, as a harsh critique of his perceived betrayal of his patriotic ideals following the failure of the Decembrist revolt and of what they saw as his ambitious and self-serving attempts to "cozy up" to the new tsar (see Igor' Nemirovskii, "O 'Proroke' i proroke," *Russkaia literatura* 3 [2001]: 10).

49. The variant is given in Pushkin, *Polnoe sobranie sochinenii*, 17 vols., 3:578.

50. Surat, "'Ia veruiu v prorochestva piitov,'" 222.

51. Gasparov, *Poeticheskii iazyk Pushkina kak fakt istorii russkogo literaturnogo iazyka*, 245, 252.

52. Ibid., 253–54.

53. Levinton and Okhotin, "'Chto za delo im—khochu,'" 32–33. In their chapter in the present volume, J. Douglas Clayton and Natalia Vesselova analyze a similar twinning of profane and sacred texts, *Tsar Nikita* and the lyric poem "The Little Bird" ("Ptichka" [1823]).

54. See Tsiavlovskii, "Kommentarii," esp. 256–64.

55. Maksim Shapir has traced a similarly intriguing and unlikely chain of parodies and self-parodies in his article "O nerovnosti ravnogo: Poslanie Pushkina 'Kalmychke' na fone makroevoliutsii russkogo poeticheskogo iazyka," in *Tekst i kommentarii: Kruglyi stol k 75-letiiu Viacheslava Vsevolodovicha Ivanova* (Moscow: Nauka, 2006), 403–17. Shapir observes that Pushkin parodically follows up on themes from Derzhavin's ode "Felicia" ("Felitsa" [1781])—which, itself, is already a burlesque combination of high- and low-style odes by Lomonosov and Barkov, respectively—in the epilogue to his narrative poem *The Gypsies* (1824) and in his romantic elegy "To the Sea" ("K moriu" [1824]), then develops the parodic echoes even further in his joking epistle "To a Kalmyk Girl" ("Kalmychke" [1829]) until, finally, turning the parodic chain back toward a more somber register in Onegin's letter to Tatiana in *Eugene Onegin*. Roman Jakobson has similarly attested to the seemingly unlikely strong linguistic and thematic parallels between Pushkin's highly sexual, intimate lyric "No, I don't value the passionate enjoyment" ("Net, ia ne dorozhu miatezhnym naslazhden'em" [1830]) and his maximally chaste sonnet on the poet's independence and dignity "To the Poet" ("Poet, value not the people's love") ("Poetu" ["Poet, ne dorozhi liuboviiu narodnoi"] [1830]) ("Stikhi Pushkina o deve-statue, vakkhanke i smirennitse," in *Alexander Puškin: A Symposium on the 175th Anniversary of His Birth*, ed. Andrej Kodjak and Kiril

Taranovsky [New York: New York University Press, 1976], 25). It might be noted that both these poems are, at base, about the poet's right to privacy and spiritual independence.

56. For this enlightening discussion, see Bethea, *Realizing Metaphors*, 183–88. According to Bethea, Del'vig is also implicated in Pushkin's "polemical return to Lyceum-period semantics" and his "break with Derzhavinian *vostorg* [rapture]" (182).

57. Gasparov, *Poeticheskii iazyk Pushkina kak fakt istorii russkogo literaturnogo iazyka*, 243.

58. Harsha Ram, *The Imperial Sublime: A Russian Poetics of Empire* (Madison: University of Wisconsin Press, 2003), 163–64.

59. The full text of Derzhavin's poem can be found in his *Sochineniia*, 4 vols. (St. Petersburg: Izdanie N. F. Merttsa, 1895), 2:123–24.

60. This substratum seems to have gone wholly unrecognized by scholars. Even Brett Cooke, despite his psychoanalytic approach, misses the element of sexual fantasy in "The Prophet" entirely, claiming that Pushkin's "most overt expressions of male genital and scatological fantasies are found either in familiar letters and in second-rate literary works, or they are given ironic treatment in texts like *Eugene Onegin*. . . . With few, usually well-disguised exceptions, they do not appear in works that are generally regarded to be his best." Cooke sees the seraph's voice in "The Prophet" as a merely *metaphoric* "organ of insemination, one so subtle as to 'touch' the ear" (*Pushkin and the Creative Process* [Gainesville: University Press of Florida, 1998], 96–97).

61. Barkov, *Devich'ia igrushka*, 46, 190.

62. Aleksandr S. Pushkin, *Gavriiliada*, in his *Polnoe sobranie sochinenii*, 10 vols., 4:114.This is not the only possible association with the image of the "light fingers" in "The Prophet"; Gasparov notes that this image is also an attribute of the poet in antiquity (e.g., in Homer's works) (*Poeticheskii iazyk Pushkina kak fakt istorii russkogo literaturnogo iazyka*, 246).

63. Gasparov, *Poeticheskii iazyk Pushkina kak fakt istorii russkogo literaturnogo iazyka*, 250–51; Ram, *The Imperial Sublime*, 173.

64. Iambic tetrameter, ironically, is the meter not only of the Russian burlesque (as Pushkin alludes to here) but also of "The Prophet"—indeed, it is Pushkin's favorite meter, in which he wrote such lyric poems as "Preserve me, my talisman" ("Khrani menia, moi talisman") and "I remember a miraculous moment" ("Ia pomniu chudnoe mgnoven'e") as well as *Eugene Onegin*. For a discussion of the use of iambic tetrameter in the Russian burlesque, see Maksim I. Shapir, "' . . . Khot' pozdno, a vstuplen'e est'' ('Evgenii Onegin' i poetika burleska)," in his *Universum Versus*, 245.

65. This early variant of the eighth stanza of *Little House in Kolomna* can be found in Aleksandr S. Pushkin, *Polnoe sobranie sochinenii*, 10 vols., 4:392.

66. See Glen Worthy, "Gender Poetics and the Structure of Pushkin's 'Little House in Kolomna,'" *Elementa* 3 (1997): 271–90.

67. Stepanov, *Lirika Pushkina*, 317; Barkov, *Devich'ia igrushka*, 121.

68. Barkov, *Devich'ia igrushka*, 93, 46, 54.

69. Ibid., 54, 99, 46.

70. Ibid., 191.

71. Ibid., 54, 59, 115.

72. Ibid., 59, 153. Of course the Barkovian resonance of this key image, once again, is not its only association; on the contrary, the sexual and biblical subtexts of Pushkin's poem coexist and interpenetrate one another. A flaming coal is found not only in Isaiah 6:6, an important source for "The Prophet" as a whole, but also in Ezekiel 1:13, where the phrasing in the Old Church Slavonic version of the biblical text replicates Pushkin's peculiar phrasing almost exactly (see Berezkina, "'Prorok' Pushkina," 38).

73. Pushkin, *"Ten' Barkova": Teksty, Kommentarii, Ekskursy*, 33, 40.

74. Compare similar phrasing and imagery in these lines from the second stanza of *The Shade of Barkov*: "For the fourth time you inserted your glans / And again pushed apart the crevice, / For the fourth time—you drove it home, hammered it in. . . . / And pulled out your limp prick" (V chetvertyi raz ty plesh' vpustil / I snova shchel' razdvinul, / V chetvertyi—prignal, vkolotil. . . . / I khui povisshii vynul) (Pushkin, *"Ten' Barkova": Teksty, Kommentarii, Ekskursy*, 33).

75. Aleksandr S. Pushkin to Lev Pushkin, n.d. [12 January–early February] 1824, in Pushkin, *Polnoe sobranie sochinenii*, 10 vols., 10:66; Pushkin to Viazemsky, 29 November 1824, in Pushkin, *Polnoe sobranie sochinenii*, 10 vols., 10:88. In the first instance, Pushkin is expressing his disgust at Mikhail E. Lobanov's translation of Racine's *Phèdre*; in the second, he is alluding to the Latvian-born writer Evstafii I. Ol'dekop, who had angered him by publishing a German translation of *The Captive of the Caucasus* (*Kavkazskii plennik*) with parallel Russian original, thereby circumventing Pushkin's authorial rights and depriving him of the profits of his work. Pushkin flags his obscene substitutions in both cases by inserting the phrase "Blank the s.o.b.!" (Mat' ego v rifmu!), where the literal equivalent of "blank" is the word "rifma" (rhyme word), pointing to the unspoken "ebat'" (fuck).

76. Shapir, "Iz istorii russkogo 'Balladnogo stikha,'" 71.

77. It is not accidental that the sensual words "lobzat'" (to kiss) and "lobzanie" (kissing) come to the surface of Pushkin's 1836 poem "Imitation of the Italian" ("Podrazhanie Ital'ianskomu"), which, as Gasparov has noted, echoes so many of the themes, images, and vocabulary of "The Prophet" (and which also, incidentally, recapitulates the earlier poem's parodical practice, as indicated by the word "imitation" in its title) (Gasparov, *Poeticheskii iazyk Pushkina kak fakt istorii russkogo literaturnogo iazyka*, 249–50).

78. Kahn, *Pushkin's Lyric Intelligence*, 202, 204. Kahn's clear-sighted comments are focused on the poem's violent imagery; he does not consider its sexual connotations. My reading of "The Prophet" reveals it as a sort of inversion of the

phenomenon that Kahn analyzes in his chapter on *The Gabrieliad* in the present volume, according to which "a heretical message and seemingly innocent style" are ironically combined (264); in the case of "The Prophet," the message is seemingly innocent while the style is subversive.

79. Pushkin, *"Ten' Barkova": Teksty, Kommentarii, Ekskursy*, 35.

80. For a discussion of the theme of free will in Pushkin's works, see the essay titled "'Svoboda' i 'schast'e' v poezii Pushkina" in Sergei G. Bocharov's *Poetika Pushkina: Ocherki* (Moscow: Nauka, 1974), 3–25.

81. It should be noted that "vosstanie" is the term used in Russian for the Decembrist uprising.

82. Pushkin, *"Ten' Barkova": Teksty, Kommentarii, Ekskursy*, 36.

83. Pushkin's poem "I built myself a monument not made by human hands" ("Ia pamiatnik vozdvig sebe nerukotvornyi" [1836]) may be read as a reprise and continuation of the poet's ambassadorial mission at the end of "The Prophet": "News of me will travel through all of great Rus'" (Slukh obo mne proidet po vsei Rusi velikoi) (Pushkin, *Polnoe sobranie sochinenii*, 10 vols., 3:340).

84. For example, see the discussion in Ram, *The Imperial Sublime*, 164.

85. Ibid., 172.

86. For example, see Berezkina, "'Prorok' Pushkina," 35–36; and Surat, "'Ia veruiu v prorochestva piitov . . . ,'" 219.

87. Gasparov, *Poeticheskii iazyk Pushkina kak fakt istorii russkogo literaturnogo iazyka*, 237, 247. Given the (parodic) echoes Gasparov notes between "Imitation of the Italian" and "The Prophet," Judas may be seen as yet another hypostasis of Pushkin's poetic prophet. See p. 144 in the present volume for Proskurin's perceptive comment on the centrality of this figure across disparate contexts.

88. Pushkin, *Evgenii Onegin*, in his *Polnoe sobranie sochinenii*, 10 vols., 5:62.

89. Shapir, "Iz istorii russkogo 'balladnogo stikha,'" 69. Tsiavlovsky provides a typology of Pushkin's "impure" texts in his commentary to *The Shade of Barkov*; he includes those that have "immodest content expressed in a modest form," texts that "lack any degree of immodesty but contain crude vulgarisms," and texts that combine "immodest content with indecent words" ("Kommentarii, 228–29). The shimmering duality of meanings we have noted in "The Prophet" demonstrates that a fourth subtype should be added to Tsiavlovsky's list: namely, texts that lack both overt immodest content and lexical profanity yet still emerge from a poetics of obscenity through linguistic and parodic play.

90. Bethea, *Realizing Metaphors*, 187, 98n174.

91. This remark is recorded in Smirnova's memoirs and quoted in Tsiavlovskii, "Kommentarii," 231.

Resexing Literature

Tsar Nikita and His Forty Daughters

J. Douglas Clayton and
Natalia Vesselova

Pushkin's *Tsar Nikita and His Forty Daughters* (*Tsar' Nikita i sorok ego docherei*) is one of the most striking examples of the poet's "erotic poetry."[1] Although it was unprinted in his lifetime, references to it in Pushkin's letters make clear his authorship.[2] The poem relates the story of a certain Tsar Nikita who has forty beautiful daughters from different mothers. There is, however, a problem with the young princesses: they have no genitalia. This fact becomes a state secret, the betrayal of which, the tsar declares, will entail women having their tongue cut out and men "something worse." To resolve the situation, the tsar convokes his council; one venerable councilor tells of an old witch who will be able to solve the problem. The tsar thereupon sends emissaries to the four corners of his land to seek her out. The search is fruitless until one "eager fellow" (retivyi) enters a dark forest and finds the witch living in a hut. She promises in three days to have a "parcel" and an answer. She performs spells for three days, and a "demon" appears and brings her a casket "full of the sinful things." She picks forty of the best, locks them in the casket, and sends them off with the emissary. While resting on his journey back, he is tempted to unlock the casket, whereupon the "little birds" (ptichki) fly out, perch on branches, and wiggle their tails. The emissary tries to tempt them back into the casket, to no avail. He comes across an old crone and asks her for advice. Her reply is simple: she tells him just to show them his organ (although she does not explicitly refer to his genitalia), and they will all fly back no doubt. The ruse works; he entices them back into the casket and brings them to the princesses. The result is seven days of merriment.[3]

This poem was unprintable in Pushkin's lifetime because it broke a series of taboos. First, it referred to the sexual organs and the sexual act directly, albeit without mentioning names. The styles of eighteenth-century classical Russian literature prohibited such directness, although some eroticism was possible; by the time Pushkin wrote the poem, these prohibitions had been superseded by even stricter notions of decency that outlawed anything that would offend "the female reader." The author flouts this prohibition most flagrantly in his physiological reference to the "familiar smell" of the female genitalia when the emissary sniffs the casket. Second, the title of the poem, which includes the word "tsar," invites the reader to read into the poem subversive references to contemporary Russia; these are reinforced when the poet daringly apostrophizes the censorship—a shadowy presence that controls all publications but that ought not to be mentioned in a published literary text. In short, it challenged the interdictions surrounding such all-pervasive realia of life as sex and the political control of literature. We argue that *Tsar Nikita* brilliantly contrives to lampoon both reigning literary taboos and the political system that enforced them: ultimately its theme is the liberation of literature.

Until now, scholarly discussion of Pushkin's poem has focused principally on the potential "sources" of inspiration for the text.[4] The questions of the work's genre, the potential meanings that it contains, and its place in Pushkin's oeuvre have as yet remained unelucidated. Even a cursory glance at the range of source texts that scholars have proposed suggests that what we are dealing with here is a typical, for Pushkin, hybrid genre in which the poet brings together different generic traditions. It is in the interplay of these that we must seek the potential meanings generated by the poem. In the coda, the poet teases the reader with the "apparent simplicity" of the plot by imagining the reader's reaction: "Many will rebuke me and will now ask, perhaps: why do I make such a stupid joke?" (Mnogie menia ponosiat / I teper', pozhalui, sprosiat: / Glupo tak zachem shuchu?).[5] Such disingenuous hints direct the reader beyond a simple interpretation of the plot toward hidden layers of meaning.

First among the intertextual antecedents we find the Slavic "folkloric" aspect, a feature that superficially seems to relate the poem to the poet's folktales (skazki); they, however, were written much later and have a different purpose. The main difference lies in the fact that the folktales were designated in their titles as *skazki* and were intended to be printed, whereas it was clearly impossible that *Tsar Nikita* would be approved by the censor, so it circulated only in manuscript form in the poet's lifetime. On the formal level, the "folkloric" aspect is reduced to the use of the trochaic meter, rather than the dominant iambic, a conventional signal to the reader that this is a "folkloric" work.[6] The language is a stylized version of folk speech, simple and colloquial, with an abundance of diminutives. Finally, the action unfolds in an imagined folk time, although occasionally the curtain of convention slips and topical allusions appear, most notably to the "stupid censorship" and to Nerchinsk, a contemporary Siberian destination for dissidents, so that the authorial comments form a metapoetic frame resembling that in *Ruslan and Liudmila* (*Ruslan i Liudmila*). The folkloric plot elements in *Tsar Nikita* include the "little bird" (ptichka) as a metaphor for the female genitalia and such motifs as the loss of an organ and the enticing and capturing in a "casket" (larek) of a little bird that perches on a "branch" (suchok). According to Georgii Levinton and Nikita Okhotin, such motifs were particularly prevalent in Ukrainian, Transylvanian, and Serbian folk poetry and rituals, with which Pushkin came into contact during his exile in Kishinev.[7]

A second potential "source" for *Tsar Nikita* mentioned in the secondary literature is the poetry, whether real or apocryphal, of Ivan Barkov (1732–68), with which Pushkin was familiar, as is known from a number of references to the eighteenth-century poet in his unpublished poems—especially *The Shade of Barkov* (*Ten' Barkova* [1814–15]) but also the epigram written in Anna Kern's album:

Не смею вам стихи Баркова
Благопристойно перевесть,
И даже имени такого
Не смею громко произнесть![8]

[I don't dare translate Barkov's verse into decent language for you, and I don't even dare to say his name out loud!][9]

Indeed, in Barkov's poetry we find the motif of flying genitalia; for example, in his sonnet 1:

Если б так хуи летали,
Как летают птицы,
Их бы тот час поймали
Красные девицы,
Все расставили бы сетки,
Посадили б в нижни клетки.[10]

[If pricks could fly as birds do fly, fine wenches would catch them straightaway, would all set out nets, would imprison them in low cages.]

As Levinton and Okhotin point out, Barkov's poetry is clearly related to the folk tradition, with which it shares several elements, such as the flying genitalia and the need to capture them. Moreover, Barkov's poetry resembles the folk tradition in its unabashed use of so-called unprintable words.[11]

Unlike folk poetry and that of Barkov, and even Pushkin's own usage when writing to friends, *Tsar Nikita* is not driven by the need to use "unprintable" words; on the contrary, the refusal to name the organ in question is an important part of the authorial play in the text. We must therefore discount Barkov as a direct intertextual reference. On the other hand, the avoidance of words banished by the censor is a feature that *Tsar Nikita* has in common with another important generic tradition mentioned by scholars, namely French eighteenth-century "libertine" literature, which generally seeks to be daring without using obscene vocabulary. Both Boris Tomashevsky and Anthony Cross have suggested works by Claude-Henri de Fusée de Voisenon (1708–75), especially the "Histoire du Sultan Misapouf," and by Prosper Jolyot de Crébillon (1674–1762) as possible sources of motifs and plot elements for Pushkin's poem. Interestingly, Voisenon in the dedication to his conte promises the lady addressee a "conte de fée," that is, a *skazka*. Moreover, in the same dedication he points to the essential feature of the genre of the libertine conte: "I have nevertheless avoided all the words that might injure modest ears: all is veiled, but the gauze is so flimsy that even those with the weakest eyesight will lose none of the picture."[12]

Les Bijoux indiscrets (*The Indiscreet Jewels* [1747]), a salient example of the *conte libertin*, by Denis Diderot (1713–84), is an even more evident generic forebear of Pushkin's poem.[13] In Diderot's text, the fantastic personification of a part of the body produces an anthropomorphic image in the tradition of Swiftian satire: the sultan Mangogul acquires a ring that, when pointed at a woman, makes her genitalia speak. The term *bijoux indiscrets* (indiscreet jewels) is thus an elegant euphemism using the traditional jocular French term for the male and female genitalia. Pushkin was naturally familiar with this French euphemism and plays on it—but with reference to the male testes—in the poem "A violinist once came to a castrato" ("K kastratu raz prishel skrypach" [1835]).[14] In the case of Pushkin's *Tsar Nikita*, the image is a zoomorphic one: rather than "jewels" we find "little birds" (although notably Diderot, too, in one place compares the female genitalia to a bird, a magpie).[15] Even more important are the generic parallels between Pushkin's poem and Diderot's prose novel, for both authors place the action in an imaginary exotic place inhabited by strange creatures, through which the reader can clearly perceive the allegorical intent, since this was a common device of eighteenth-century philosophical and satirical literature. In the case of Diderot, the exotic locus is an imaginary Africa, whereas Pushkin evokes a fantastic world derived from Slavic folk poetry. Moreover, in Diderot's text we find a character deprived of an organ; in the "Vision de Mangogul" (chap. 16), a young woman appears "without an arse" (sans cul) and is pursued by a carpenter who wants to drill two holes in her. This absence of both vagina and anus in a woman suggests a satirical intent: to make fun of those who out of prurience would suppress all mention of physiological functions in literature. Pushkin too invites interpretation of his poem as an allegory, so that generically it can be seen as an amalgam of the French libertine conte, especially Diderot's novel, and native Russian folklore traditions.

In *Tsar Nikita* Pushkin's satirical reluctance to name the princesses' missing organ, the way he addresses the reader, making a game out of the issue of naming, and the hypocritical refusal of the censor to permit certain words suggest a deeper purpose than a mere literary joke. For Diderot the target of the allegory was social hypocrisy; in Pushkin's case the metapoetical elements suggest that the principal issue is literature itself, although it is true that the poem also encodes a carefully veiled critique of authority. If we take the references to contemporary realia as an invitation to see Tsar Nikita as representing the emperor, or, familiarly, tsar, Alexander, then the idea that the tsar had sired forty daughters with a variety of women is a daring comment quite in the vein of Diderot on the morals of Alexander, who had nine illegitimate children with six mistresses. This comment can be compared to Diderot's introductory remarks about the sultan Mangogul—a transparent depiction of Louis XV. This is not to suggest a revolutionary, "antimonarchical" intent in the poem (here one must agree with Levinton and Okhotin); rather it reflects Pushkin's personal animus toward Alexander (expressed, for example, in the tenth chapter of *Eugene Onegin* [*Evgenii Onegin*]).[16]

Just as Diderot's text (and the *conte libertin* in general) was a subversive response to the hypocrisy of the reign of Louis XV and the imposition of the *bienséances* (proprieties) in French literature, so too can Pushkin's text be read as a transparent allegory of the fate of literature in Russia during the Alexandrian period. The imposed silence at Tsar Nikita's court about his daughters' predicament parallels the reference in the poem to the censorship to which literature was subjected in Russia, which particularly irked Pushkin:

Как бы это объяснить,
Чтоб совсем не рассердить
Богомольной вашей дуры,
Слишком чопорной цензуры?[17]

[How could I explain it so as not to enrage your silly, sanctimonious frump, the overly fussy censorship?]

The personal, biographical subtext of the work receives greater force through the mention of exile to Nerchinsk in Siberia, a fate that Pushkin narrowly escaped when Alexander decided to punish him for his uncensored poetry and an obvious reference to the plight of the poet, who at the time of writing *Tsar Nikita* was in exile in Kishinev, Moldavia.

A key role in the text is fulfilled by the theme of castration and impotence. At the same time that those male courtiers who speak out about the daughters' problem are threatened with castration, the women are threatened with having their tongues cut out—a suppression of speech and also a symbolic form of castration, rendering powerless. Additionally, the tsar's daughters are born sexless, and thus they are deformed, less than perfect, beings, female eunuchs; that is to say, in a sense the theme of castration applies to them as well. The cutting out of tongues is an echo of *Boris Godunov* (*Boris Godunov*), where Tsar Boris cuts out the tongues of those who spread rumors, so that Tsar Nikita fits into a paradigm of impotent and incompetent rulers who, to maintain their power, mutilate their subjects either physically or, in the case of Alexander, metaphorically, by suppressing their speech through censorship. In several of Pushkin's works we find in opposition to the impotent ruler a young hero whose sexual virility gives him a kind of victory or revenge over the authority figure. In *The Gabrieliad* (*Gavriiliada* [1821]), for example, the young and handsome archangel Gabriel scores a double victory—over Joseph and the Almighty—by seducing Mary. Impotence in the most literal sense is derided in the description of the *senex* Joseph, the "patron saint of cuckolds":

Ленивый муж своею старой лейкой
В час утренний не орошал его [ее тайный цвет];
Он как отец с невинной жил еврейкой,
Её кормил—и больше ничего.[18]

[Her lazy husband did not water it [her secret flower] with his old watering can in the morning hour; he lived like a father with the innocent Jewish girl, he fed her—and nothing more.]

It should be noted that the nemesis may be short lived or incomplete: Satan beats Gabriel to Mary's bed, so that it is the devil who carries off her maidenhead, a typical piece of Pushkinian irony.

Thus, a plot matrix emerges in which a figure (or, as in *The Gabrieliad*, two figures—Gabriel and Satan!) whom the reader takes as a projection of the poet exacts revenge on the mighty by seducing their wives and daughters. This combination of virility and literary freedom comes together in the epigram "A Comparison" ("Sravnenie" [1813–17]), where the poet triumphantly writes:

Не хочешь ли узнать, моя драгая,
Какая разница между Буало и мной?
У Депрео была лишь ,
А у меня : с ,[19]

[Dost thou not wish to know, my dear one, what is the difference between Boileau and me? Despréaux had only a , whereas I have a : and a ,]

The poem *Art poétique* (1674)—by Nicolas Boileau-Despréaux (1636–1711), who, owing to an unfortunate accident, was a eunuch from childhood—had created a set of rules for poetry that included balance, harmony, and good taste; in Pushkin's perception he is another impotent (literally and metaphorically) authority inhibiting the free expression of the poet. The epigram underscores the parallel between sexual virility and the free untrammeled talent of the writer. The absence of all or part of a sexual organ—principally the castration of males—is clearly a significant motif for Pushkin.

Thus, the poem *Tsar Nikita* not only repeats the characteristic Pushkinian theme of the sexual impotence of older men versus the young poet's virility but also equates virility with free speech, the penis serving, as it were, as a metaphor for the tongue (and vice versa). In particular, the reference to the emissary's penis and its power to attract the "little birds" encodes the sexual power of the emissary (and by extension, of the poet) and stands in contrast with the eunuch-like impotence of the greybeards in power, including Tsar Nikita, whose own exploits in the sexual domain (siring forty daughters) are evidently at an end, since his daughters are themselves sexually mature (or would be, if they had the appropriate equipment). *Tsar Nikita*, this masterpiece of Pushkinian erotica, has to be read contextually as another expression of the youthful theme of the young poet "liberating," or sexing, young women. The function of the tsar's emissary parallels that of Gabriel in *The Gabrieliad* or the poet himself in the epigram on Boileau. That is to say, we read the emissary as a projection of the author's voice into the text, an ironic self-portrait. In character, he is a bit of a simpleton who gives in to his curiosity and opens the casket, releasing the *ptichki*. He is unable to entice them back into their container: like the *bijoux* in Diderot, they have a life and a will of their own. Having had recourse to a witch to provide him with the missing organs, the naive emissary now has to seek advice from an old crone passing by. By exposing his own organ, the hero of the poem entices and captures the escaped "little birds"; he thereby magically restores the sexuality of the tsar's daughters by removing their deformation.

Thus is the kingdom healed through the emissary's "exploit." The poet is not explicit about the mechanism: is the implication that the hero has sex with the female organs (however that can be imagined)? If so, his Herculean feat of resexing forty princesses can perhaps be taken as an ironic comment on Pushkin's own reputedly relentless sexual activity.[20] In any case, the poem is an interesting expression of Pushkin's view of female sexuality, since, whether or not it is the emissary who liberates (i.e., deflowers) the princesses (before they even get their genitalia back), the seven-day-long celebration that ensues when he returns to the palace, bringing the little *ptichki* in the casket, suggests that Pushkin believes women should not remain virgins and that they enjoy sex as much as men. From a metapoetic point of view, the work is a clear allegory of Pushkin's reinsertion of the erotic into literature, especially literature destined for the liberated female reader: he is not "castrated," nor is his tongue metaphorically cut out. His revenge is sexual; it is by the same token a literary revenge over the strictures of Boileau and those of the censor.[21]

In this light, it can be argued that the true focus of the poem is metapoetic. Sexual subversion finds its literary equivalent in the use of "forbidden" images and themes in literary works. Indeed, the equivalence of writing and the sexual act is a frequent object of Pushkin's literary games, as he declares with tongue in cheek that "I rarely, rarely sin with her [my muse]" (redko, redko s nei [muzoi] greshu).[22] The perceptive reader can see in the forty desexed daughters of the tsar the sentimental ideal, enforced by the censor, of the virginal female reader (going back to Richardson, Rousseau, and Karamzin), whose innocence must be protected from even the vaguest mention of sexuality: they have nothing between their legs, just as the woman in Diderot's novel has no arse.[23] *Tsar Nikita* can be read as an allegory of the young Pushkin liberating his muse from sentimental values of decorum, as well as the *bienséances* promoted by Boileau. It is a revolt that is played out on a number of levels in different works: thematic (the flouting of sexual and religious taboos), linguistic (the introduction of "archaisms" and "base" speech as opposed to the Karamzinian ideal of an anodyne middle style), and generic (the choice of anacreontic verse, folktale, or mock epic over the elegy, the favorite genre of sentimentalism).

Elsewhere (e.g., in *The Gabrieliad*) the erotic content is overtly combined with a flouting of religious taboos, but not in *Tsar Nikita*.[24] In *Tsar Nikita* we see Pushkin the "young archaist" breaking norms by reverting to eighteenth-century forms but with a new, romantic interest in the folkloric. *Tsar Nikita* has in common with Diderot's *Les bijoux indiscrets* the use of allegory, but the Russian poet was writing over seventy years later, in a new context. His revolt against Karamzinian norms was primarily aesthetic and personal, although to be sure the notion of the "female reader" and sentimental concepts of religious piety were enforced by the censor and thus a political fact; in this sense he differed from other "young archaist" poets and future Decembrists (such as Kiukhel'beker and Ryleev) whose revolt was mainly or wholly political in content. In other words, where the Decembrists were political,

Pushkin was subversive. The function of desire—both aesthetic and sexual—as a vital force for the renewal of literary forms and the self-expression of the poet is highlighted in the last word of *Tsar Nikita* (here, and almost always, the most important in Pushkin's work): "khochu" (I want). This is a bold declaration of the freedom of the poet to choose the subject matter he desires; it also expresses sexual desire. This last word is preceded by the question "What business is it of theirs?" (Chto za delo im?). Such a bold assertion of the poet's right to create freely—and indeed to procreate freely—although it sounds like an aside, lifts the poem to a new level of significance and sums up its deepest theme. That is to say, the emissary "revealing himself" to the little birds is an allegory of the resexing not only of the female reader but of contemporary literature itself.

This intent is underscored when the poem is read against other works of the poet. In particular, the fact has apparently gone unnoticed that *Tsar Nikita* and the poem "The Little Bird" ("Ptichka" [1823]), written by Pushkin in Kishinev at around the same time, are related works. Indeed, in general, the relationship between works written closely together in time is a relatively little explored aspect of Pushkin's oeuvre. Yet frequently a reading of one work in the context of another can yield new meanings that reverberate between the two. Such is the case with *Tsar Nikita* and "The Little Bird." Writing about the sources of *Tsar Nikita*, Levinton and Okhotin make an important observation: that analysis of the folk material underlying the poem yields a generalized plot, what they call a "single ritualistic complex—the rite of welcoming spring [*obriad vstrechi vesny*]." They continue:

> Its disparate elements . . . coalesce into a single entity only through the prism of Pushkin's folktale. The welcoming of spring is marked principally by the ritualistic baking of cookies in the form of little birds ("little larks") or so-called "infants" (shapes with an extended phallic form) . . . [that] are placed on roofs, elevated places, *or trees*. . . . Thus the plot of folktales about enticing down from a tree that which is most linked with fertility can be seen to have an extremely archaic mythological meaning.[25]

Levinton and Okhotin's observations apply with especial significance to the poem "The Little Bird":

В чужбине свято наблюдаю
Родной обычай старины:
На волю птичку выпускаю
При светлом празднике весны.

Я стал доступен утешенью;
За что на Бога мне роптать,
Когда хоть одному творенью
Я мог свободу даровать![26]

[In a foreign land I sacredly observe a custom of my native tradition: I set free a little bird during the bright festival of spring. I have become amenable to consolation; why should I grumble at God, when I have been able to give freedom to at least one creature!]

Mapping the plot elements of this poem onto *Tsar Nikita*, we can see that both poems have a "double bottom"—a concealed meaning beneath the ostensible one. *Tsar Nikita* is a daringly allegorical poem about the poet's problems with the censor, his persecution by Tsar Alexander, and his sexual revenge that at the same time contains a sacred, ritualistic meaning rooted in Slavic folklore and associated with the vernal celebration of fertility. In "The Little Bird" we find at first reading a description of a traditional Slavic pre-Christian and, later, Easter ritual commonly practiced in the spring season: setting free a little bird from a cage. On the other hand, viewing the poem in the light of *Tsar Nikita* and Levinton and Okhotin's observations, we can read the liberation of a *ptichka* as the poet's finding "consolation" in the sexual act in order to gain relief from his fate as an exile in a "foreign land."[27] Thus, the relationship between these two texts—*Tsar Nikita* and "The Little Bird"—suggests that the "pornographic" or risqué sexual content in Pushkin's writing is an inversion of the sacred.[28] Far from subverting and denying traditional values, it reinforces them by giving them richer meanings. It is perhaps this fact of the obscene as an inversion of the sacred, not its denial, that sets the Russian poet's texts apart from his Western counterparts such as Diderot: by transgressing taboos, Pushkin confirms their force.

NOTES

1. On the application of this term to Pushkin's poetry, see Sergei V. Denisenko, *Eroticheskie risunki Pushkina* (Moscow: Nezavisimaia gazeta, 1997), 13–66; and Sergei V. Denisenko, "'Ot vozderzhaniia muza chakhnet . . .': Erotika Pushkina," in Aleksandr S. Pushkin, *Chas nevinnogo dosuga*, ed. Sergei V. Denisenko (St. Petersburg: Azbuka, 2004), 5–20. See also Anthony Cross, "Pushkin's Bawdy; or, Notes from the Literary Underground," *Russian Literature Triquarterly* 10 (1974): 203–4.

2. The poem is dated by compilers of Pushkin's lyrics to 1822, that is to say, to the period of his administrative exile in Kishinev, a fact that we demonstrate is not without importance for its interpretation. For more on Pushkin's service in the south of Russia, see Irina Reyfman, "Pushkin the Titular Councilor," in the present volume.

3. The absence of a marriage ceremony to mark this "happy ending" is noteworthy, as researchers have pointed out: "It is precisely the marriage ceremony (or marriage ceremonies—forty of them?) which is a glaring omission in the finale of 'Tsar Nikita,' given that in the text Pushkin strictly observes the pattern of the magical folk tale (although there is a 'mighty feast')" (Georgii A. Levinton and Nikita G. Okhotin, "'Chto za delo im—khochu . . .': O literaturnykh i fol'klornykh istochnikakh skazki A. S. Pushkina 'Tsar' Nikita i 40 ego docherei,'" *Literaturnoe obozrenie* 11 (1991): 30. Other examples of the elision or displacement of the marriage ceremony in Pushkin include *Eugene Onegin* (*Evgenii Onegin*) and "The Snowstorm" ("Metel'" [1831]).

4. For exhaustive reviews of the research on the subject, see Levinton and Okhotin, "'Chto za delo im—khochu,'" 28–35; and Igor' A. Pil'shchikov, "'Nichego il' ochen' malo . . .' (Skazka Pushkina 'Tsar' Nikita i 40 ego docherei'): Dopolnenie k kommentariiu," in Aleksandr S. Pushkin, *Ten' Barkova: Teksty, Kommentarii, Ekskursy*, ed. Igor' A. Pil'shchikov and Maksim I. Shapir (Moscow: Iazyki slavianskoi kul'tury, 2002), 466–79.

5. Aleksandr S. Pushkin, *Tsar' Nikita i sorok ego docherei*, in his *Polnoe sobranie sochinenii*, 10 vols., ed. Boris V. Tomashevskii (Leningrad: Nauka, 1977–79), 2:131.

6. The trochee was also the preferred meter for the jocular poems Pushkin wrote while at the lyceum; for more on this topic, see Pil'shchikov, "'Nichego il' ochen' malo,'" 475.

7. Levinton and Okhotin, "'Chto za delo im—khochu,'" 32.

8. Pushkin, *Polnoe sobranie sochinenii*, 10 vols., 3:93.

9. On Pushkin's response to Barkov, see Igor Pilshchikov's "If Only Pushkin Had Not Written This Filth" in the present volume.

10. Ivan Barkov, *Luka Mudishchev i sramnye pesni* (Moscow: Eksmo, 2002), 324. The sonnet bears a striking resemblance to the poem "A Comical Desire" ("Shutochnoe zhelanie" [1802]) by Gavriil Derzhavin: "If fair maidens could fly like birds and sit on boughs, I would like to be a little bough, so that thousands of little girls could sit on my branches. O that they might sit and sing, weave their nests and whistle, and bring up their offspring; I would never bend down, would admire them ever, would be the happiest of all boughs" (Esli b milye devitsy / Tak mogli letat', kak ptisty, / I sadilis' na suchkakh,— / Ia zhelal by byt' suchochkom, / Chtoby tysiacham devochkam / Na moikh sidet' vetviakh. / Pust' sideli by i peli, / Vili gnezdy i svisteli, / Vyvodili i ptentsov; / Nikogda b ia ne sgibalsia,— / Vechno imi liubovalsia, / Byl schastlivei vsekh suchkov). On the poetic relationship between Barkov and Derzhavin in Pushkin's poetry, see Alyssa Dinega Gillespie's "Bawdy and Soul " in the present volume, esp. 189–91.

11. The sexual references to "little birds" in Barkov are echoed in a poem by Mikhail Kheraskov (1733–1807) titled "The Little Bird" ("Ptichka" [1796]): "If I were a little bird, I would fly to the one I loved and would land close to her; if I could, I would sing: 'Lina, you are beautiful, you are the soul of a little bird!' My little nose would touch her lips; each of her dear hairs would seem like a snare; I would like to trap my little foot in the snare, to be together with Lina and love Lina longer in sweet captivity" (Kogda b ia ptichkoi byl, / Ia k toi by poletel, / Kotoru poliubil, / I blizko k nei by sel; / Kol' mog by, ia zapel: / 'Ty, Lina, khorosha, / Ty ptichkina dusha!' / Moi malyi by nosok / Ustam ee kasalsia; / Mne b kazhdoi volosok / Silkom u nei kazalsia; / Ia b nozhku uviazit' / Khotel v silke po vole, / Chtob s Linoi vmeste byt' / I Linu by liubit' / Vo sladkom plene bole). The mentions of nose, lips, and snare are clear double entendres, but the "little bird" represents the poet's persona rather than the female genitalia. There is little to suggest that this poem was of importance for Pushkin, except perhaps for the title.

12. Claude-Henri de Fusée de Voisenon, *Contes de l'abbé de Voisenon et poésies fugitives du même auteur* (Paris: Librairie Garnier frères, n.d.), 4.

13. See Andrei D. Mikhailov, "Pushkin i Didro," in *Pushkin v XXI veke: Sbornik v chest' Valentina Semenovicha Nepomniashchego* (Moscow: Russkii mir, 2006), 56.

14. The full text of the poem is as follows: "A violinist once came to a castrato, the former was poor, the other rich. 'Look,' said the ball-less singer, 'at all my diamonds and emeralds: I was sorting them out of boredom. Oh, by the way, my friend,' he continued, 'when you are bored, what do you do, pray tell.' The poor man replied indifferently: 'Me? I scratch my balls'" (K kastratu raz prishel skrypach, / On byl bedniak, a tot bogach. / "Smotri,"—skazal pevets [bezmudyi],— / "Moi almazy, izumrudy— / Ia ikh ot skuki razbiral. / A! kstati, brat,"—on prodolzhal,— / "Kogda tebe byvaet skuchno, / Ty chto tvorish', skazat' proshu.'" / V otvet bedniaga ravnodushno: / "Ia? ia [mude] sebe cheshu") (Pushkin, *Polnoe sobranie sochinenii*, 10 vols., 3:322).

15. Denis Diderot, *Les bijoux indiscrets* (Paris: Gallimard, 1981), 60.

16. Levinton and Okhotin, "'Chto za delo im—khochu,'" 32.

17. Pushkin, *Tsar' Nikita i sorok ego docherei*, 2:126.

18. This last line is an interesting echo of the line "Nothing! . . . Nothing—or very little" (Nichego! . . . Nichego il' ochen' malo) in *Tsar Nikita*, referring to the female genitalia (Pushkin, *Tsar Nikita i sorok ego docherei*, 2:127). This emphasis on the word "nichego" (nothing) may well go back to Crébillon: "Rien du tout." See Levinton and Okhotin, "'Chto za delo im—khochu,'" 29.

19. Aleksandr S. Pushkin, "Sravnenie," in his *Polnoe sobranie sochinenii*, 10 vols., 1:262.

20. Such hyperbolic sexual prowess is reflected in the figure of Ebakov in Pushkin's *The Shade of Barkov*. See Gillespie, "Bawdy and Soul," in the present volume.

21. As Denisenko notes, the erotic theme in Pushkin's poetry—and hence the theme of the sexually active young rake/poet—was to diminish in importance in the later 1820s, as Pushkin "became more mature" (Denisenko, "'Ot vozderzhaniia muza chakhnet,'" 18).

22. Aleksandr S. Pushkin, "Del'vigu," in his *Polnoe sobranie sochinenii,* 10 vols., 2:32. "Pushkin's description of the creative process is highly reminiscent of the sexual act; this is understandable: the hand, the goose quill, the clean sheet of paper" (Denisenko, *Eroticheskie risunki Pushkina,* 42). For a detailed analysis of the writing-as-sex metaphor in late eighteenth- and early nineteenth-century Russian poetry, especially that of Batiushkov and Barkov, see Maksim I. Shapir, "Iz istorii parodicheskogo balladnogo stikha: 'Perom vladeet kak eldoj,'" *Russian Linguistics* 17.1 (1993): 65–69; and Gillespie, "Bawdy and Soul," in the present volume.

23. "Karamzin's literary and linguistic reform was based on well-known forms of artistic practice. Monumental oratorical genres were replaced by minor, seemingly extraliterary ones that were designed to correspond to the atmosphere of the salon. The literary evolution was accompanied by a change in the intended 'reader.' Karamzin's reader was feminine, a 'tender female'; the author was 'One who writes as he speaks, / Whom ladies read.' These salons were a bizarre literary fact that Pushkin found unacceptable. The 'female reader' was the justification and prism of a special system of aestheticized, 'pleasant' literary language" (Iurii N. Tynianov, "Arkhaisty i Pushkin," in his *Arkhaisty i novatory* [Munich: Fink, 1967], 148).

24. For more on this topic, see Mikhail Vaiskopf, "'Vot evkharistiia drugaia': Religioznaia erotika v tvorchestve Pushkina," *Novoe literaturnoe obozrenie* 37 (1999): 129–47.

25. Levinton and Okhotin, "'Chto za delo im—khochu,'" 31.

26. Aleksandr S. Pushkin, "Ptichka," in his *Polnoe sobranie sochinenii,* 10 vols., 2:134.

27. This reading of "The Little Bird" as part of a sacred-profane inversion may be extended to at least one other poem on an Easter theme with sexual content written during the Kishinev exile: "Christ is arisen" ("Khristos voskres" [1821]): "Christ is arisen, my Rebecca! Today, following in my soul the law of the God-man, I exchange kisses with you, my angel. And tomorrow, my Jewish girl, for a kiss I am ready without hesitation to go over to the faith of Moses and even place in your hand that by which one can distinguish a true Jew from Orthodox Christians" (Khristos voskres, moia Revveka! / Segodnia sleduia dushoi / Zakonu boga-cheloveka, / S toboi tseluius', angel moi. / A zavtra k vere Moiseia / Za potselui ia, ne robeia, / Gotov, evreika, pristupit'— / I dazhe to tebe vruchit', / Chem mozhno vernogo evreia / Ot pravoslavnykh otlichit') (Pushkin, *Polnoe sobranie sochinenii,* 10 vols., 2:71).

28. Vaiskopf's assertion that "Pushkin did not totally disagree with the romantic tendency to a direct identification of the sacred and the erotic series

(of motifs)" seems inadequate: for Pushkin they are, rather, in opposition to each other. Pushkin, in the space of a single poem, playfully transcodes from one set of motifs to another without making either the dominant ("'Vot evkharistiia drugaia,'" 141).

The Poetics of Dry Transgression in Pushkin's Necro-Erotic Verse

JONATHAN BROOKS PLATT

Among Pushkin's last love lyrics are two poems addressed to dead beloveds—"Incantation" ("Zaklinanie" [1830]) and "For the shores of your distant homeland" ("Dlia beregov otchizny dal'noi" [1830]). Both poems imagine, indeed demand, an erotic reunion with the dead woman in question, and both recall a particular moment of fascination with the beloved's death agony. "Incantation" summons the beloved back in any form, but ideally as she was on her last day, pale as winter and marred by her death throes. "For the shores of your distant homeland" waits for a promised kiss of reunion, even though it has turned to dust along with both the beloved's "beauty" and her "torments"—allowing no distinction between these mutually inextricable elements of her appeal.[1] Yet despite these poems' evident necro-eroticism, it is impossible to call them taboo in the reception of Pushkin. Unlike the bawdy *Gabrieliad* (*Gavriiliada* [1821]) or *The Shade of Barkov* (*Ten' Barkova* [1814 or 1815]), the dangers of pollution in Pushkin's (in fact quite numerous) necro-erotic works have generally proved easy to neutralize.[2] These two lyrics are usually read on a popular level as expressing the optimistic, morally admirable idea that love conquers all, and more sophisticated readings typically offer only subtle variations on this theme.[3] Oleg Zyrianov of Ural State University, for example, calls the demand for the promised kiss in "For the shores of your distant homeland" "utopian" and argues that "Incantation" is notable for its "conscious erasure" of the "motifs of vampirism and necrophilia" found in similar works by Pushkin's European and American contemporaries. The Russian poem's speaker summons his dead lover "not in order to learn the secrets of the grave, let alone to wallow in a perverted voluptuousness in the spirit of decadence, but to resurrect (in the full sense of the word) the beloved shade, in some sense anticipating Nikolai Fedorov's national variant of the philosophy of universal resurrection."[4] Zyrianov's failure to find an element of transgression in Pushkin's poems is not simply a result of blind denial. These poems' transgressive quality is indeed different from the more plainly macabre erotic tradition that runs from baroque theater to the gothic novel, through Byron and Poe to Baudelaire and decadence. Transgression in "Incantation" and "For the shores of your distant homeland" comes without the shudder of horror, disgust, or deviant bliss typical for this literary current. In other words, it is a transgression that does not recognize itself as such.

It is what I will call a *dry* transgression. To understand what this means requires an understanding of the dialectical logic at the heart of what Philippe Ariès referred to as "the age of the beautiful death" in European culture.[5] According to the French historian, the eighteenth century witnessed a dramatic change in dominant European views of death and dying. A new sense of hygiene (i.e., a shift in the taboos governing pollution) saw cemeteries relocated and mortal remains shifted away from city churches.[6] This distancing of the corporeal reality of putrefaction was accompanied by death's objectification by science—anatomical dissection became "a fashionable art"—and, with the emergence of sentimental and romantic aesthetics, its mystification by culture.[7] Weepy deathbed scenes in sentimental novels, forlorn lovers wandering in an elegiac mist, floating Ossianic shades, sublime reunions in eternity . . . Literature made death beautiful, fascinating, strangely desirable and warm, and thus further sanitized its polluted, entropic aspect. Decay was not excluded from culture as from the spaces of daily life, however. Rather, it was sublated within it—that is, negated and preserved in the Hegelian sense of *aufheben*.

The dialectical aspect of the beautiful death is most evident in its contradictory treatment of mortal finitude, making death at once the most absolute of limits and yet still somehow permeable. As any sentimental deathbed scene will testify, death is the defining moment and guarantor of meaning in a human life, redeeming all struggle with its consummated fullness.[8] But, at the same time, dead loved ones are not lost once they achieve this mystic meridian; their spirits remain among the living, preserved in loving memory, in the images of art or as haunting presences.[9] The reason the limit of death can serve as both the absolute end and the sublime "not-end" of life lies in its status as an unknowable quantity. As Ariès tells us, the beautiful death is also "the death of the other."[10] The dead do not perceive their own fullness, as only a still-living (and, thus, "lacking") observer can, but neither does the unconsummated observer know the full truth of death. This inaccessibility gives the other's mortal fullness an aura of warm desirability and beauty while at the same time disturbing it, making the dead linger and return. These spectral presences are all just surrogate images of the absent dead, projections of the observer's desire to know what must always remain beyond his grasp: the dead other's fullness, which even now the observer violates through the excess of representation.[11] A deathbed scene, a gloomy erotic elegy—any form of aesthetically fixing the other's death in the prism of a desirous gaze depends on this powerful dynamic of a phantom fullness flashing within the nonfullness of representation's simultaneous lack (as mere image) and excess (as supplement to the real). And here again dialectical logic manifests itself. The observer's faith in the fullness and beauty of death strives to negate the much more dangerous nonfullness of decomposition, where the fall of the cadaver into decay is also a fecund gushing of new, alien life. It is the negated materiality of decomposition that is subsequently preserved in an idealized form as the nonfullness of representation. The quavering aura of the beautiful specter is a purified image of the corpse's rot.

Desire for the consummated other is not only "theoretical," however. It also has a practical aspect, most commonly appearing as an erotic quality in the death of a female beloved. With this added element, the positing of an existential limit—the limit of mortal fullness—within representations of beautiful death is paired with an erotic limit as well: the limit of necro-erotic transgression. The dialectical character of transgression has long been recognized. Transgression "suspends a taboo without suppressing it," to quote Georges Bataille.[12] In other words, it negates the limit imposed by the taboo, crossing over to what lies beyond, but in doing so reaffirms the power of the taboo through its actualization. Transgression renews and purifies the taboo it violates, and anthropologists have long argued that ritually transgressive acts (sacrifice, war, royal incest, feast days, etc.) guard against the same threats of ambiguity and "boundary pollution" as taboos.[13] Thus, if the age of the beautiful death is understood as one of shifting taboos, it makes sense that the age would also exhibit a high incidence of transgression. However directly this transgressive element appears in the text, nearly all representations of beautiful death from the period invite such analysis. Any movement toward the necro-erotic taboo suggests the possibility of its violation, releasing a certain measure of force, emanating from the limit of transgression and transmitted to the reader as eroticism. It is this force that is strangely absent in the two necro-erotic poems of Pushkin's in which I am interested.

Both poems invoke a favorite theme of the poet's, one he explored rather extensively around the time they were written—the prolific autumn he spent stranded on his Boldino estate behind a cholera quarantine. This theme is that of appeals, toasts, and invitations addressed to the dead, usually accompanied by the superstitious fantasy that such appeals could be taken seriously, drawing the dead forth into the realm of the living.[14] In the love lyrics, this fantasy becomes the imagined erotic reunion with the dead beloved. A broader theme of holding nonliteral language accountable for its literal meaning is also pervasive in Pushkin's oeuvre. In general, a playful actualization of linguistic ambiguities—literalizing metaphors, canceling the negation in ironic statements, and so forth—was one of Pushkin's favorite devices, one that paralleled his preferences for the concrete and the diegetic over the vague and the contemplative.[15] This attitude to language naturally tends to evoke metaliterary concerns, and often Pushkin's actualized ambiguities seem primarily to serve defamiliarizing ends, destabilizing generic and stylistic forms, possibly in an effort to renew them. This fact is particularly significant for my discussion, since the logic of defamiliarization is also dialectical, in many ways recalling ritual transgression. Before considering the two Boldino lyrics, I will address this particular question in two necro-erotic poems from Pushkin's southern period.

One of Pushkin's earliest necro-erotic works is "A Youth's Grave" ("Grob iunoshi" [1821]), which works in the pastoral elegiac tradition, especially resembling its modern melancholic avatars.[16] The poem sticks fairly close to the generic model, indulging in gloomy elegiac intonations popular at the time. But it also departs from the tradition, particularly in its concluding images. The conventional generic frame of an elegy for a dead or dying youth—typically a poet or at least a "sensitive soul"—involves a beloved in mourning, a formulaic figure for the youth's survival in memory after his (usually amorous) death. The beloved in mourning traditionally expresses her sorrow with a symbolic whisper, a sigh, or at most a lonely tear shed upon the gravestone—a flicker of unspent, vaguely necro-erotic desire that is at once sublimated and controlled.[17] The conventionality of the image is quite important in this process, as it marks the deliverance of the youth from transient existence into the permanence of symbols and memory. Pushkin's penchant for destabilizing conventional formulae leads him to break this mold, however, and he fleshes out his beloved with sensual details:

Напрасно утром за малиной
К ручью красавица с корзиной
Идет и в холод ключевой
Пугливо ногу опускает:
Ничто его не вызывает
Из мирной сени гробовой.[18]

[In vain for raspberries in the morning / The beauty with her basket to the brook / Goes and into the cold water / Fearfully dips her foot: / Nothing will summon him / From the peaceful shade of the grave.]

The foot dipped into the cold stream powerfully concretizes the image of the beloved in mourning and significantly amplifies her unspent desire for the lost youth. Forcing the conventional image to take on real flesh, the poem effectively reverses the roles of lover and beloved, and the necro-erotic content of the scene is thrust to the fore. The sensuality of the girl's actions—which have no obvious connection to the death of her beloved—are isolated and emphasized by the contrastive word "naprasno" (in vain), suggesting that although resurrecting the dead youth is impossible, the girl would indeed like to entice him back with her erotic foot. The conventional resolution of similar works in the genre is thus rejected in favor of an open ending of uncertainty—the speaker claims the girl's testing of the waters of death is futile, but she is apparently not so sure.

A similar effect is produced by what is perhaps Pushkin's most necro-erotic work—the uncompleted sketch "The terrible hour will come . . . your heavenly eyes" ("Pridet uzhasnyi chas . . . tvoi nebesny ochi" [1823]). Oleg Proskurin has interpreted the poem as a direct attempt to bring the conventions and abstractions of elegiac narrative down to earth. As he writes, "The theme of love beyond the grave, usually developed in a spiritualist or Horatian-Tibullian key, is presented as *real* love for a dead person: the meeting with the dead beloved occurs not in the heavens but in the family crypt; the heroine is not an ethereal shade but a cold corpse."[19] After predicting his beloved's death, the speaker promises to remain beside her:

Но я, дотоле твой поклонник безот<радный>,
В обитель скорбную сойду [я] за тобой
И сяду близ тебя, печальный и немой,
У милых<?> ног твоих—себе их на колена
Сложу—и буду ждать [печаль<но>] . . . [но чего?]
Чтоб силою мечтанья моего[20]

[But I, still your joyless admirer, / I will follow you into the mournful cell / And sit near you, sad and mute, / At your dear feet—toward me onto my lap / I will draw them—and I will wait sadly . . . but for what? / So that through the power . . . of my fantasy]

This poem's defamiliarizing character is clearest when compared with one of the most well-known necro-erotic paintings of the period, Anne-Louis Girodet's 1808 *The Burial of Atala*, which takes its subject from François-René de Chateaubriand's immensely popular novel. Just before Pushkin's poem breaks off, a strange, seemingly superfluous—and quite revolting—detail is introduced in which the speaker puts the beloved's dead feet on his lap. The suggestion is that the lover has assumed a position identical to the one in which Chactas appears in Girodet's painting. Whether or not Pushkin intended this association, a comparison of the two very similar necro-erotic images reveals the way in which Pushkin's poem subtly deviates from the mainstream aesthetic currents of the time, again through the introduction of an excessively sensuous detail.[21]

Girodet's scene is immaculately chaste on the level of symbolism. To be safe, it includes not one but two crucifixes (three, if one includes the shovel), as if indicating the ascension of Atala's soul along the path

Anne-Louis Girodet, *The Burial of Atala* (1808). Musée du Louvre, Paris.

stretched between them. With an allegorical touch common to early romantic canvases, Chactas's feet in the grave suggest his eventual reunion with Atala's body in the earth (and question whether his heathen soul will join her in heaven). But on another, more purely sensory level, the painting exhibits more than a shade of necro-erotic suggestiveness. The light cascading over Atala's dead (but apparently excited) breasts is manifestly erotic, as is the muscled Chactas embracing her cold legs. One could even seek a hidden meaning in the corpse being nestled so bizarrely between Chactas's luxurious black hair and the hermit's wizened beard. Is this erotic expenditure's link to physical decay? The painting—like Chateaubriand's novel—depends on the tension between these delicate hints of transgressive desire and the immaculate image of a beautiful death. By contrast, Pushkin's poem seeks no such balance, forcing necro-erotic suggestiveness to the surface. The temporality of verse is a great advantage here: Chactas experiences a frozen moment of sublime love, whereas Pushkin's speaker must actively draw his beloved's cold feet toward him before he can clutch them against his body. It is notable that this grim reality comes across as a harsh rent in the linguistic fabric of the poem. The detail is presented in a syntactically awkward manner, breaking into the line as a parenthetical, while itself split across an enjambment. Just as in "A Youth's Grave," the text of "The terrible hour will come . . . your heavenly eyes" seems to be fully immersed in the codes and intonations of the beautiful death when, quite unexpectedly, a sensuous detail disturbs the necro-erotic waters, defeating expectations.

At first glance the defamiliarizing action of both poems seems fairly clear. Traditional images of beautiful death allow the suggestion of necro-erotic transgression, lingering voluptuously on the warmth and fullness of death's image, basking in the glow of death's sublime unknowability. But they do so in order to have two things at once. The limits of both transgression and death are simultaneously absolute and permeable. They can be suspended—the image hints tantalizingly—but if they are, the full weight of their power will fall upon you. So desire is sublimated, and the dream of fullness remains only a flash within the nonfullness of an image. When Pushkin's poems go that much further toward the edge of transgression, it would seem that they are postponing sublimation, suggesting that one *must* go further toward (the beyond of) the limit and that the corporeality of transience and desire—say, in the image of a fetishized foot amid sepulchral decay—must be experienced more fully before its sublation into art. In other words, the object of defamiliarization is not the beautiful death's dialectic of transgression; rather, it is this dialectic's abstemious dampening and masking. This reading would seem to fit the judgment of those critics who (pace Zyrianov) have found poems like "The terrible hour will come . . . your heavenly eyes" to be reminiscent of the more decadent works of Baudelaire.[22] However, there are a number of elements in these poems that suggest the need for a more nuanced understanding of their form of defamiliarization. First of all, although the limit of death and transgression is plainly present in both poems, it is treated as a kind of perplexing and unresolved question—might a dead beloved return? can a mourning lover's desire perform miracles?—rather than as a sublime threshold. The idea of crossing over this limit—answering the question in the affirmative—is also present, yet it appears not as the impossible beyond of transgression but as a fairly wholesome dream of resurrection in the flesh, recalling Zyrianov's Fedorovian parallel. The wry deviancy that paves the way for this idea—erotic feet and corpses—is not the harbinger of sublimity (as it typically is in Baudelaire) but a kind of obstinate ignorance of the very impossibility of the beyond of the limit. We remain the same, whether living or dead, and so our desire flows across this limit *as if it were not even there*. But, if that is the case, what precisely has been defamiliarized and renewed? In fact, the defamiliarizing action seems to be moving in the opposite direction. What at first appeared to be an intensification of the limit logic of beautiful death ends up as its more complete effacement, a drying out of the limit until (as in Zyrianov's readings) it is no longer perceptible at all.[23]

Turning now to the two Boldino lyrics, one finds that they are also in part metaliterary experiments, which defamiliarize stylistic and generic elements of the beautiful death and even engage specific precursor texts. As has long been established, the genesis of "Incantation" can be found in the collection of four minor English poets that Pushkin brought with him to Boldino, which served as an inspiration for several other lyrics as well as large parts of the *Little Tragedies* (*Malen'kie tragedii*).[24] In this case the source text is "An Invocation" by Barry Cornwall (the pseudonym of Bryan Waller Procter), first published in 1820. Aside from a few phrases and images, the elements Pushkin borrowed from Cornwall lie primarily in the poem's situation. Both poems revolve around a speaker who claims that if at night the dead return to haunt the living, he will have his beloved back, no matter what form she takes. This framework leads naturally to a focus on what may be called the metamorphoses of mourning—the transformations, both affective and ontological, endured by lover and beloved when divided by death. Cornwall's effort falls well within the sphere of the beautiful death in its treatment of the theme, though it is not as chaste as earlier works in the tradition. Most notable is its Byronic lingering over the macabre forms in which the beloved might return: "Or be thou like a daemon thing, / Or shadow hovering, / Or like the bloody shapes that come / With torch and sound of drum, / Scaring the warrior's slumbers, I / Will welcome thee, and wish thee nigh."[25] Nonetheless, by the end of the poem, it is clear that the speaker is merely indulging a moment of darkness in order to make the light that much brighter. The beloved does finally respond to his prayer, appearing not as a demonic shade but as a guiding star of consolation, testifying to the speaker's successful sublimation of his potentially transgressive desire: "But there thou art, a radiant spirit, / And dost inherit / Earlier than others thy blue home, / And art free to roam / Like a visiting beam, from star to star / And shed thy smiles from skies afar. // . . . And I will ever turn at night / Unto thy soothing light, / And fancy, while before thine eyes, / I am full in the smile of Paradise."[26]

Pushkin's "Incantation" is a very liberal imitation of Cornwall's poem, and it follows an entirely different trajectory:

О, если правда, что в ночи,
Когда покоятся живые,
И с неба лунные лучи
Скользят на камни гробовые
О, если правда, что тогда
Пустеют тихие могилы,—
Я тень зову, я жду Леилы:
Ко мне, мой друг, сюда, сюда!

Явись, возлюбленная тень,
Как ты была перед разлукой,
Бледна, хладна, как зимний день,
Искажена последней мукой.
Приди, как дальная звезда,
Как легкой звук иль дуновенье,
Иль как ужасное виденье,
Мне все равно, сюда! сюда! . . .

Зову тебя не для того,
Чтоб укорять людей, чья злоба
Убила друга моего,
Иль чтоб изведать тайны гроба,
Не для того, что иногда
Сомненьем мучусь . . . , но тоскуя,
Хочу сказать, что все люблю я,
Что все я твой: сюда, сюда![27]

[O, if it is true, that in the night / When the living are asleep / And the moonbeams fall from the sky / And slide across the gravestones, / O, if it is true that then / The quiet tombs are emptied— / I summon a shade, I wait for Leila: / Come to me, my friend, here, here! // Appear, beloved shade / As you were before our parting / Pale, cold, like a winter's day, / Marred by your final torment. / Come like a distant star, / Like a light sound or waft of air, / Or like a terrible vision / It is all the same to me, come here! here! . . . // I summon you not / To reproach the people whose spite / Killed my friend, / Or to learn the secrets of the grave, / Not because at times /

I am racked with doubt . . . but yearning, / I want to say that I still feel love, / That I am still yours: come here, here!]

The tendency to make images of beautiful death more corporeal, familiar from the earlier poems of Pushkin I have discussed, is apparent from the first stanza. If the dead in Cornwall's poem appear as ethereal ghosts "wandering from their homes of light," Pushkin's corpses emerge ghoulishly from their tombs. But, at the same time, Pushkin's poem can also be said to be more abstract, in that it exhibits a metaliterary dimension absent from Cornwall's. The list of forms the beloved may take in the second stanza—much broader than those listed by Cornwall—is usually read as a dense collection of allusions to other treatments of the dead beloved theme.[28] When a similar list of negated motivations for the speaker's desire (each with its own implicit narrative) is introduced in the third stanza, the metaliterary aspect of the poem becomes impossible to ignore. The second stanza thus presents its catalog of forms as choices not only for the dead beloved but also, by implication, for authors seeking to represent a dead beloved in literature. The star, the sound, the waft of air, the terrifying vision—these are some of the surrogate images made available by the limit logic of the beautiful death. Indeed, if one traces each of the different choices back to their likely sources, a range of attitudes to that logic also becomes available. There are texts like Cornwall's, for example, that depict the bereaved lover's unspent desire as a morbidity that must be overcome. Such texts offer the symbolic image as an appropriate surrogate for the beloved's lost body, one that allows the lover to go on living (perhaps even to love again).[29] But there are also gloomier works in which final consolation comes only with the lover's own death. Such narratives of mourning unto death depict a bereaved lover who finally accepts the corporeal absence of his beloved only by dissolving into eternity himself.[30] And then there is the alternative of a melancholic passion that cannot be sublimated. In this case, finding no symbolic surrogate, the lover summons his dead beloved as phenomenal form, no matter how ghastly, and is willing to die—often at her own hands—in order to remain beside her.[31]

Each of these variants allows the force of necro-erotic transgression (the inverse of mourning) to flood the text to a different degree. Each locates itself at a different distance away from the limit, raising or lowering the dialectical tension between fullness and nonfullness, beauty and rot, accordingly. It is therefore highly telling that Pushkin's speaker claims all these differences of degree are one and the same (vse ravno) to him. They are all the same because the limit that defines them is not actually present in Pushkin's text. Necro-eroticism takes an entirely different form in "Incantation" than it does in the poems to which it alludes, all of which invoke the erotic lushness of transgression to some degree. The first indication of this difference comes, once again, in the form of an unusual moment of sensuous excess in Pushkin's poem. The beloved in "Incantation" has practically no attributes; the poem consists almost entirely of the gloomy graveyard scene and the sundry negated (either directly, or indirectly through the claim that there is no difference between them) possibilities for populating it with a story. The one exception is the opening of the second stanza, where the speaker lingers over the image of the beloved on her last day. Although this image is still only one of the many options for the beloved's return, its rich descriptiveness marks it out from the others, suggesting that perhaps in this case they are not all the same. The culminating line, "Marred by your final torment," has a similar effect to the image of the speaker drawing his beloved's cold feet to him in "The terrible hour will come . . . your heavenly eyes," but now, any sense of a rupture in the text is gone. The image of the dying beloved's cool pallor—a common positive attribute of deathly beauty—is unexpectedly followed by the image of her death throes, and no shift in syntax or tone allows the reader to prevent his erotic attachment to the first image from following to the second.

Again we are dealing with a necro-erotic moment whose deviancy is not given its due, whose pleasure does not seem to be the pleasure of transgression. The fact of transgression is undeniably present but it remains dry, and in many ways it is ancillary to the general movement of the poem. What is this movement? The speaker casts off a veritable horde of potential narratives, rejecting one precedent model after another as he locates his desire for the dead beloved through a kind of intertextual apophasis. But, ineluctably, the movement of the poem continues on toward its object—"come here, here!"—namely, the expenditure of the speaker's unspent desire for the beloved. Her beauty is of a deathly kind, certainly—Pushkin was not immune to the tastes of the age—but the underlying metaphysical structure of that deathly beauty is somehow different. The limit of the text is not the limit of transgression, nor is it the sublation of putrescence in the quavering fullness of the other's beautiful death. What is the limit then, since all purposive movement must pass through a limit condition to reach its goal? Here the metaliterary dimension of "Incantation" is key. As I have already mentioned, the speaker's final cry in the third stanza—"I want to say that I still feel love"—follows the listing of three negated reasons for disturbing his beloved's eternal rest—he disturbs it not because he is anxious to reproach those who drove her to her death, not because he seeks to learn "secrets of the grave," and not because he is racked with doubts about her fidelity. The first two of these negations are typical of scenarios that involve a dead beloved. The third reason, however, does not recall such scenarios or indeed any images of beautiful death. Instead of the gloomy elegy's morbid desire for the dead, the idea of doubting a beloved's fidelity throws the reader back to another current of elegiac discourse: the strictly erotic elegy that describes the arduous pathways, at times quite crooked, that lead to a beloved's heart.

An erotic elegy makes use of limit logic in an entirely different way than an elegy for a dead beloved. Instead of taking a more or less perverse pleasure in the struggle to bind a morbidly unspent desire, standing face to face with the abyss of death, an erotic elegy works to outline an infinitesimal space of interruption, in which love is obstructed by norms of social propriety, physical or emotional distance, or the beloved's faithlessness—in other words, interruptions that, unlike death, can quite conceivably be overcome. The erotic elegy is thus a world of mediated desires, deflected gazes, and deferred promises—a world cut through with all manner of boundaries and limits, not just the one absolute limit that defines the elegy for a beloved who is dead. If that limit is present in an erotic elegy, it is invariably the death of the speaker, the lover, standing in as a metaphor for the "little death" of desire's final expenditure, a limit that must be forever pushed back as the pleasure of anticipation—and the fount of amorous language it provokes—is indefinitely prolonged.

The principle act of metaliterary deviancy in "Incantation" is the use of the traditional intonations and structures of the erotic elegy to treat a morbid theme. But, again, it is a strange kind of defamiliarization at work here. According to traditional formalist theory, defamiliarization violates a conventional form to reveal the means (or "device") of its functioning, a functioning that has become impaired through overuse and that must now be (dialectically) broken and reassembled in a new way if it is to be restored to working order. One certainly finds the inner workings of the beautiful death exposed and shown up for their conventionality in "Incantation." No force whatsoever emanates from the limit between purity and pollution in this text. But what is given in its place? The limit of a new form, emitting a new force? Not in the least. For the logic of the erotic elegy is also compromised quite destructively by its presence in the poem—and without the promise of redemptive sublation. However much the limit of the beloved's death is effaced, replaced with the deferred limit of a more plainly erotic pleasure, the actual death of the beloved remains inescapable. Because of Pushkin's necro-erotic concreteness, the reader never forgets that the object of this pleasure is a woman marked by the raw physical realities of death. If we desire the transgressive pleasure these realities might bring (as in a work by Baudelaire) we must take them outside the poem's internal movement. If we remain within it, we find that these realities make a mockery of the erotic deferral suggested by the stylistics of the poem. Both the erotic elegy—once Pushkin's favored genre—and the beautiful death suffer from the hybrid into which they are thrust in "Incantation," and the suffering is not productive. To make the beloved's death just another minute interruption in a game of erotic deferral is to bleed it of all its power. And to release a flood of amorous discourse at this desiccated limit is to expose that discourse as empty and artificial beyond repair.

"For the shores of your distant homeland," Pushkin's other Boldino lyric addressed to a dead beloved, also practices the poetics of dry transgression—both in its defamiliarization of existing literary norms and in its effacement of the necro-erotic limit at the heart of the beautiful death. Like "Incantation," this poem also depends on allusive reminiscence, in this case pointing to Vasilii Zhukovsky's "Malvina" ("Mal'vina" [1808]). A quick glance at the two poems reveals many echoes, beginning with their nearly identical structure:

"Malvina"	"For the Shores of Your Distant Homeland"
С тех пор, как ты пленен другою,	Для берегов отчизны дальной
Мальвина вянет в цвете лет;	Ты покидала край чужой;
Мне свет прелестен был тобою;	**В час** незабвенный, **в час** печальный
Теперь—прости, прелестный свет!	Я долго плакал пред тобой.
Ах! не отринь любви **моленья**:	Мои **хладеющие руки**
Приди . . . не сердце мне отдать,	Тебя старались удержать;
Но взор потухший мой принять	**Томленье страшное** разлуки
В минуту смертного **томленья**.	Мой стон **молил** не прерывать.
Спеши, спеши! близка кончина;	Но ты от горького лобзанья
Смотри, как **в час последний** свой	Свои уста оторвала;

Твоя терзается Мальвина
Стыдом, любовью и тоской;
Не смерти **страшной** содроганье,
Не тусклый, безответный взгляд
Тебе, о милый, возвестят,
Что жизни кончилось **страданье**.

Ах, нет! . . . когда ж Мальвины муку
Не услаждает твой приход;
Когда **хладеющую руку**
Она тебе не подает;
Когда забыт мой друг единый,
Мой взор престал его искать,
Душа престала обожать:
Тогда—тогда уж нет Мальвины![32]

Из края мрачного изгнанья
Ты в край иной меня звала.
Ты говорила: «В день свиданья
Под небом вечно голубым,
В тени олив, любви лобзанья
Мы вновь, мой друг, соединим».

Но там, увы, где неба своды
Сияют в блеске голубом,
Где тень олив легла на воды,
Заснула ты **последним** сном.
Твоя краса, твои **страданья**
Исчезли в урне гробовой—
А с ними поцелуй свиданья . . .
Но жду его; он за тобой.[33]

[Ever since you were captivated by another, / Malvina has withered in the bloom of her years; / Because of you the world delighted me; / Now—farewell, delightful world! / Ah! do not deny the **pleas** of love: / Come . . . not to give me your heart, / But to receive my extinguished gaze / In the minute of my mortal **anguish**. // Hurry, hurry! the end is near; / Look, how **in** her **final hour** / Your Malvina is devoured / By shame, love, and woe; / Not a **frightful** shudder of death, / Not a dull, unresponsive gaze / Will make known to you, O dear one, / That the **suffering** of my life has ended. // Ah, no! . . . when Malvina's torment / Is not sweetened by your arrival; / When she does not offer you / her **hand grown cold**; / When my one friend is forgotten, / And my gaze has ceased to seek him out, / My soul has ceased to adore him: / Then—then there will be no more Malvina!]

[For the shores of your distant homeland / You abandoned a foreign country; / **In** that unforgettable **hour**, **in** that sorrowful **hour** / I wept long before you. / My **hands grown cold** / Tried to hold you back; / **The frightful anguish** of parting / My moaning **pleaded** you not to interrupt. // But you tore your lips / From our bitter kiss; / And from the dark country of exile / You summoned me to another land. / You said: "On the day of our reunion / Under the ever-blue sky, / In the shade of olive trees, the kisses of love / We will unite again, my friend." // But there, alas, where the vaulted skies / Glimmer in blue splendor, / Where the shade of olive trees lies on the waters, / You succumbed to your **final** sleep. / Your beauty, your **sufferings**, / Disappeared in the funeral urn— / And with them the kiss of reunion . . . / But I am waiting for it; you owe it to me.]

Zhukovsky's poem oozes with the force of the limit projected by its theme of a desire unto death—in which the speaker begs her unfaithful beloved to return and "receive her gaze" once more before she dies. The poem pays close attention to the physical act of dying—the hands going cold, the dull eyes, the agonizing progress toward the final shudder—but in the end it rejects these attributes as mere secondary indications of death. Not these, but the lack of desirous gestures—the extended hand, the searching eyes—will signal the end of Malvina, who thus distils herself into her desiring subjectivity, leaving the body as only its vessel. This contrast of corporeal and social signs provides a fine example of the dialectics of the beautiful death. The movement from the dying body to the desiring subject parallels the sublation of Malvina's death throes into her final consummation—as a subject—with the full expenditure of her desire. Although it is not stated explicitly in Zhukovsky's poem, the Sophie Cottin novel on which it is based reveals that Malvina in fact cannot die until her desirous condition is resolved.[34] Waiting for her beloved to come and finish her off, she remains perched at the limit of her death, unable to reach the resolution of fullness and nonfullness that her death will enact. For the poem's reader, however, Malvina's imagined death has already achieved this resolution. The morbid, necro-erotically suggestive corporeality depicted in the second stanza is transcended and preserved in the final images of Malvina consummated, having become the still object of her beloved's gaze.

Much as "Incantation" departed from Cornwall, Pushkin's "For the shores of your distant homeland" significantly reorganizes the ready-made literary material it borrows from Zhukovsky. First of all, the very presence of "Malvina" in the semantic background of the poem is complicated by the difference in the two scenarios of separation and death. While Malvina dies an agonizing death because she is cut off from the object of her love, the death of the beloved in Pushkin's poem comes peacefully—like a sleep—and in no way reflects unspent passions. While Zhukovsky's poem focuses on the torments Malvina endures after separation, waiting for her beloved's return, Pushkin's poem focuses on the moment of separation itself and emphasizes the promised reunion's nonoccurrence. The effect of these differences is a marked displacement of the Zhukovskian material in Pushkin's poem, thereby endowing a scene of mere separation with the attributes of agonizing death. This shift has significant consequences for the necro-erotic content of the poem. If "Malvina" ends with the sublation of death into a sign of love, "For the shores of your distant homeland" lingers over a strangely eroticized moment of parting ("The frightful anguish of parting / My moaning pleaded you not to interrupt"), whose explanation can only be an associative link to the true erotic source: the sickly beloved's impending death.

It might seem—once again—that Pushkin's poem moves significantly closer to the limit of necro-erotic transgression than its source text in an effort to defamiliarize it. "Malvina" indulges in several flashes of necro-erotic suggestiveness in its description of death, but it does so only to take satisfaction in overcoming the impulse, preserving the force of the limit within the denial of what lies beyond it. By contrast, "For the shores of your distant homeland" seems intent on evoking an unmitigated eroticism of the limit, lingering at it, taking its pleasure directly there. It is notable how quickly the arc of passion in the poem dips once the beloved performs her sublimatory shift from real flesh to surrogate words, tearing her lips from the kiss of parting to speak of the kiss of reunion. Sublimation is clearly not the object here. This promised kiss arouses no ardor in the speaker, and he coldly repeats the paradisiacal scene of reunion, now marked—"alas"—as the scene of the beloved's death. But then it is here, in this lull produced by the speaker's failure to enjoy the beloved's death, that things become strange in a way quite different from the normal poetics of defamiliarization. The limit of the beloved's death—what seemed to be the source of all erotic power in the poem—is utterly dry, the lowest point of energy in the poem. The energy picks up again with the final quatrain, but these lines contain a bizarre ambiguity, actualizing an instability in the dialectics of necro-eroticism.

The instability begins with the lines "Your beauty, your sufferings, / Disappeared in the funeral urn." The lack of any syntactic or intonational division between the beloved's beauty and her sufferings has an effect similar to that of the lines about the beloved's last day in "Incantation." The reader finds himself caught in a moment of necro-erotic suggestiveness that does not announce itself in any way. This desiccation of the necro-erotic limit is followed by the final image of the speaker still waiting for the promised kiss, despite the beloved's death. On one level, this image reproduces the exceedingly common motif of reunion in the afterlife, a centerpiece of the beautiful death. However, the metaphoric language of these lines evokes strange physical images when taken literally: the promised kiss is lost in the funeral urn but could yet emerge (or be excavated?) from the beloved's mortal dust. One can even sense a slyly necro-erotic gag in the final phrase, "on za toboi." The final kiss beyond (or in) the grave could be read as originating from the speaker rather than the beloved: instead of the idiomatic "you owe it [the kiss] to me," the phrase could be read literally as "it [the kiss] is following after you." These moments of ambiguity develop the original flash of uncertainty in the beauty/sufferings line. But this bubbling up of corporeal putrescence does not reflect a movement further along the dialectic toward transgressive sublation of the taboo. Rather, it is a witness to that logic's unraveling.

"Incantation" seems to use this same uncertainty to destabilize (unproductively) two influential forms of amorous discourse—the erotic elegy and the beautiful death. "For the shores of your distant homeland," whose metaliterary aspect is much more subdued, reveals that there is more to this destabilization than genre. Now the focus falls upon the identity of the space of interruption that prolongs desire and on the space in which a still-desirous lover lingers after erotic death (big or little). The poem zeroes in on this space—which, in both variants, separates the desiring subject from the expenditure of his desire—as a moment in the existential dynamic of self and other. The central image of the poem is the kiss—first of parting, then of reunion in either a paradisiacal or sepulchral space. As a figure of erotic union, the kiss represents the dream of self and other joined in perfect synthesis, overcoming the divide between them. But, as any lover knows, this dream can never be realized; some remnant of the original contradiction always lingers, causing the endless repetitions and wanderings of desire.[35] The beautiful death is a fantasy structured around this remnant. Its different levels of tension reflect the different degrees of force the fantasy may apply—always in vain—toward the remnant's eradication. The goal in every case is to construct a support for the dream of two things at once: the pure, unreachable limit where dialectical tension is at its highest, where nonfullness and fullness, self and other meet in a union that does not destroy but in fact purifies their difference. In Pushkin's two poems, this limit is removed from the topology of the fantasy, leaving it uniform and homogeneous (with no different degrees of tension). The fantasy space extends across the desiccated furrow where the limit once was, now as a place in which desire is not torturous, but sustainable.

The transition from the kiss of erotic union to the bizarre kiss in the urn that lurks in the final lines of "For the shores of your distant homeland" characterizes this space, first of all, as one of radical ambiguity—the inverse of dialectical synthesis. The ambiguity of the phrase "on za toboi"—in which the moments of erotic union become confused, overlapping awkwardly—is already prepared for by the displacements enacted on "Malvina" in the first stanza. A dying beloved desperate for consummation in her lover's gaze becomes a lover desperate for his beloved to die in his arms. The two images would seem to complement each other perfectly, but the shift is incomplete—for some reason the imploring speaker of the poem is the one who inherits Malvina's cold hands (khladeiushchie ruki), not the dying beloved—a slip that suggests a strange confusion of bodies. Furthermore, the elision of the remnant's intractability has the effect of replacing the impossible beyond of transgression with an absurdist, irrational demand. This transition reveals the space's availability as a subject position, no longer a crucible of sublation in the other and/or in death. In other words, if the typical observer of beautiful death cries out, "It would be such bliss to love my beloved to/in death, but I know it is impossible," the speaker of Pushkin's poems obstinately says, "It is impossible to love my beloved after death, but that is the reality of my desire." Finally, it is important to recognize that the actual resurrection of the dead beloved is not a constituent moment in this space. Indeed, we may only follow Zyrianov and link these necro-erotic poems to the philosophy of Fedorov if we accept that Fedorov, too, was more interested in expectation than in the achievement of his great task. For such is the space that Pushkin's two Boldino poems define (like "A Youth's Grave" and "The terrible hour will come . . . your heavenly eyes" before them): a space in which no dialectical reconciliation—such as the reconciliation of life and death in resurrection—is possible. Instead of offering the blissful agonies of the dialectic, these poems efface divisions and limits though absurdist obstinacy, cultivating indistinction (even that of putrescence) as a more sustainable medium for desire.[36]

Notes

1. The addressee of both poems is typically understood to be Amalia Riznich, one of Pushkin's beloveds during his sojourn in Odessa in 1823–24, who died of tuberculosis in 1825. The poems are also often linked to a third elegy, "Parting" ("Proshchanie" [1830]), believed to be addressed to another of Pushkin's beloveds from the same period, Elizaveta Vorontsova. The biographical narrative

commonly associated with these three poems pertains to the poet's bidding farewell to the loves of his youth on the eve of his marriage.

2. See Dmitrii D. Blagoi, "Na rubezhe tridtsatykh godov: Boldinskaia osen'," in his *Sotsiologiia tvorchestva Pushkina: Etiudy* (Moscow: Federatsiia, 1929), 156–262.

3. In one online publication, a professor at Rostov University, summarizing the poetic fruits of Pushkin's relationship with Riznich, writes that both Boldino lyrics "erase that 'unbreachable boundary' . . . , revealing a triumphant eternity that suffuses the entire universe. The traditionally infernal, evil meaning is removed from the sepulchral ghost the poet summons [in 'Incantation']. . . . This is not a summons in the name of forgiveness or repentance but a living summons of love" (Nina Zababurova, "Iavis' vozliublennaia ten,'" *Rostovskaia elektronnaia gazeta*, 6 December 1999, http://www.relga.ru/Environ/WebObjects/tgu-www.woa/wa/Main?textid=1903&level1=main&level2=articles). One finds a similar reading in a recently published school textbook, in which the students are urged to interpret the poem "as an incantation by love in the name of love" (zaklinanie liubov'iu vo imia liubvi) (Valentin I. Korovin, ed., *Literatura, 10 klass: Uchebnik dlia obshcheobrazovatel'nykh ucherezhdenii*, vol. 1. [Moscow: Prosveshchenie, 2007], 149).

4. Oleg V. Zyrianov, *Evoliutsiia zhanrovogo soznaniia russkoi liriki: Fenomenologicheskii aspekt* (Ekaterinburg: Izdatel'stvo Ural'skogo universiteta, 2003), 163, 465.

5. Philippe Ariès, *The Hour of Our Death*, trans. Helen Weaver (New York: Knopf, 1981), chap. 10. In the discussion that follows, I do not use the term "dialectical" in the strict Hegelian sense but in a broader one more inclusive of the diverse trends of romantic thought.

6. Russia followed this trend, founding large public cemeteries beyond the city limits in Petersburg in 1710 and Moscow in 1758.

7. Ariès, *The Hour of Our Death*, 366. Peter I's fascination with dissection is well known. The Russian emperor established an anatomical theater in the Academy of Sciences in 1724.

8. See Elisabeth Bronfen, *Over Her Dead Body: Death, Femininity and the Aesthetic* (Manchester: Manchester University Press, 1992), chap. 5.

9. See Terry Castle, *The Female Thermometer: Eighteenth-Century Culture and the Invention of the Uncanny* (New York: Oxford University Press, 1995), chap. 8.

10. Philippe Ariès, *The Hour of Our Death*, pt. 4.

11. See Bronfen, *Over Her Dead Body*, 84–85.

12. Georges Bataille, *Erotism: Death and Sensuality*, trans. Mary Dalwood (San Francisco: City Lights Books, 1986), 36. See also René Girard, *Violence and the Sacred*, trans. Patrick Gregory (Baltimore: Johns Hopkins University Press, 1977).

13. The concept of boundary pollution is central to Mary Douglas's classic study of taboo in *Purity and Danger: An Analysis of the Concept of Pollution and Taboo* (New York: Routledge, 2002).

14. The most comprehensive treatment of the theme in Pushkin's oeuvre remains Mikhail O. Gershenzon, "Ten' Pushkina," in his *Stat'i o Pushkine* (Moscow: Academia, 1926), 69–95.

15. See Boris Gasparov, *Poeticheskii iazyk Pushkina kak fakt istorii russkogo literaturnogo iazyka* (St. Petersburg: Akademicheskii proekt, 1999), 113–16; and, more generally, Nadezhda N. Ivanova, "Poeticheskaia 'glagol'naia' perifraza u Pushkina," in *Poeticheskaia frazeologiia Pushkina*, ed. Viktor D. Levin (Moscow: Nauka, 1969), 293–372; and Vadim E. Vatsuro, "K istorii elegii 'Prostish' li mne revnivye mechty,'" in *Vremennik Pushkinskoi komissii, 1978* (Leningrad: Nauka, 1981), 5–21.

16. For a discussion of the poem's intertextual resonance, see Oleg Proskurin, *Poeziia Pushkina, ili Podvizhnyi palimpsest* (Moscow: Novoe literaturnoe obozrenie, 1999), 67–76.

17. Here I should note the difference between the Freudian term "sublimation" and the Hegelian "sublation," which can easily be confused in this essay, since images of beautiful death typically involve both processes. By "sublimation," I mean the suppressing or dampening of a transgressive impulse, replacing the taboo object of desire with a loftier surrogate. "Sublation," by contrast, refers to the dialectical synthesis of opposites—purity and impurity, fullness and nonfullness, the horizon of the self and the other's consummation.

18. Aleksandr S. Pushkin, "Grob iunoshi," in his *Polnoe sobranie sochinenii*, 17 vols., ed. Vladimir D. Bonch-Bruevich et al. (Moscow: AN SSSR, 1937–59), 2:210–11.

19. Oleg Proskurin, "Pomety Pushkina na poliakh 'Opytov v stikhakh' Batiushkova: Datirovka, funktsiia, rol' v literaturnoi evoliutsii," *Novoe literaturnoe obozrenie* 64 (2003): 272.

20. Aleksandr S. Pushkin, "Pridet uzhasnyi chas . . . tvoi nebesny ochi," in his *Polnoe sobranie sochinenii*, 17 vols., 2:296.

21. On this question it is interesting that an edition of engraved prints based on Girodet's painting was published by lithographer Hyacinthe Aubry-Lecomte in 1822, a year before Pushkin wrote his poem. See David Wakefield, "Chateaubriand's 'Atala' as a Source of Inspiration in Nineteenth Century Art," *Burlington Magazine* 120 (1978): 20.

22. Several of Baudelaire's early necro-erotic lyrics, such as "A Martyr" and "A Carrion," can be read as parodies of amatory discourse, "pétrarquisant sur l'horrible" (waxing Petrarchean about the horrible), as Sainte-Beuve famously remarked. On this topic, see William Olmsted, "Immortal Rot: A Reading of 'Une Charogne,'" in *Understanding Baudelaire*, ed. William J. Thomson (Nashville: Vanderbilt University Press, 1997), 60–71. The association of Pushkin's necroeroticism with Baudelaire can be found in Vikentii V. Veresaev, *V dvukh planakh* (Moscow: Zakharov, 2000), 32; and Blagoi, "Na rubezhe tridtsatykh godov," 209, 214. Ol'ga S. Murav'eva also focuses on the defamiliarizing power of transgression in her study of Pushkin's dead beloved theme ("Obraz 'mertvoi

vozliublennoi' v tvorchestve Pushkina," in *Vremennik Pushkinskoi komissii*, vol. 24 [Leningrad: Nauka, 1991]: 17–28).

23. One may recall in this context Olga Meerson's theory of "neostranenie" (refamiliarization) in her discussion of the prose of Platonov and its treatment of the strange and shocking as ordinary. See *Svobodnaia veshch': Poetika neostraneniia u Andreia Platonova* (Oakland, CA: Berkeley Slavic Specialities, 1997).

24. Nikolai V. Iakovlev, "Poslednii literaturnyi sobesednik Pushkina: Bari Kornuol'," *Pushkin i ego sovremenniki: Materialy i issledovaniia* 28 (1917): 5–28.

25. Barry Cornwall, *A Sicilian Story with Diego de Montilla and Other Poems* (London: John Warren, 1820), 140. The Byronic reminiscence is from *The Giaour*, which is also the source of the name Leila in Pushkin's imitation.

26. Ibid., 141.

27. Aleksandr S. Pushkin, "Zaklinanie," in his *Polnoe sobranie sochinenii*, 17 vols., 3:246.

28. For a summary of these allusions, see Nataliia I. Mikhailova, "Stikhotvorenie A. S. Pushkina 'Zaklinanie': Iz nabliudeniia nad tekstom," in *Vremennik Pushkinskoi komissii*, vol. 26 (St. Petersburg: Nauka, 1995): 95–100.

29. For another example, see also Gavriil Derzhavin's "The Invocation and Appearance of Plenira" ("Prizyvanie i iavlenie Pleniry" [1794]).

30. See Vasilii Zhukovsky's "Prisoner" ("Uznik" [1819]) and "Aeolian Harp" ("Eolova Arfa" [1814]).

31. See Byron's *Giaour* and the song in Nikolai Karamzin's "Bornholm Island" ("Ostrov Borngol'm" [1793]). Another possible allusion that fits this mold is Alphonse de Lamartine's "Recollection" ("Souvenir" [1819]).

32. Vasilii Zhukovskii, "Mal'vina," in his *Sobranie sochinenii*, 4 vols. (Moscow: Khudozhestvennaia literatura, 1959), 1:80–81.

33. Aleksandr S. Pushkin, "Dlia beregov otchizny dal'noi," in his *Polnoe sobranie sochinenii*, 17 vols., 3:257.

34. In Cottin's novel, Malvina, betrayed by her husband, Edmond, falls into a melancholy death-in-life limbo, wearing a veil and visiting a tomb she erects for herself nightly, referring to herself in the third person, and waiting patiently, insensible to all around, for separation from her beloved to become a final separation from life.

35. See Jacques Lacan, *The Seminar, Book 20, On Feminine Sexuality: The Limits of Love and Knowledge, 1972–1973 (Encore)*, trans. Bruce Fink (New York: Norton, 1998).

36. Much of my argument here derives from Alexei Yurchak's discussion of the necrorealist movement in late Soviet art and film as part of a broader practice of the "politics of indistinction." See his "Necro-Utopia: The Politics of Indistinction and the Aesthetics of the Non-Soviet," *Current Anthropology* 49.2 (2008): 199–224. It is not impossible that such practices form part of a discursive tradition that stretches back to Pushkin.

The Blasphemies of *The Gabrieliad*

Andrew Kahn

Pushkin's *The Gabrieliad* (*Gavriiliada* [1821]) violates taboos of a social, religious, and political kind, and these interrelated transgressions against the authorities of church and state made an ostensibly witty poem into a dangerous piece. The working definition of taboo that I draw on is that it is "a proscription of behaviour for a specifiable community of people, for a specified context, at a given place and time."[1] In the first instance, the poem's treatment of virginity, while falling far short of the French tradition of libertine pornography that Pushkin and his contemporaries enjoyed, undermined contemporary Russian attitudes about sexual license and female conduct. Secondly, the antibiblical narrative articulated by Satan, the first of Mary's three seducers including the archangel Gabriel and God, represented a sacrilegious attack on the symbolic purity of the Virgin and for that reason offended against church dogma. Finally, the very existence and circulation of the poem exploited the relative liberalness of legal statutes governing speech, taking advantage of the gap between the law and state control to send out a subversive message championing rationalism against religious obscurantism, laughter against seriousness, and poetic freedom against censorship. Influenced by free speech theorists like Judith Butler and the social anthropologist Mary Douglas, I argue that *The Gabrieliad* looks subversive, rather than merely rude, when we read its sacrilegious narrative symbolically as performative speech that challenges the limits of social tolerance and state censorship.

Violating Respectability

Let us briefly review the central and most subversive episode of the narrative on which this argument depends. The young Mary lives in an ostensibly sexless marriage with Joseph, who is mocked for his inertia and eventually ridiculed as a cuckold. Enticed by her youthful beauty, God alerts the archangel Gabriel, who is sent to reconnoiter on his behalf. An angel in heaven, he serves, as the narrator notes (l. 147), as a pimp on earth. But Satan is on the qui vive and beats Gabriel to the first interview with Mary. He applies his eloquence to a revisionist account of Eve and the Garden of Eden, exposing original sin as no more than a self-serving ruse on the part of God and justifying Eve's license and female sexuality as innocent pastimes. Such persuasion arouses Mary's awareness of her own body and the physical workings of desire and leads her to yield her virginity to Satan. The experience proves so enjoyable that the next day she finds it hard to resist the blandishments of Gabriel, who betrays his employer by seducing Mary. By this stage, Mary herself has become highly sexed. As she dreams of further pleasure, God appears to her in the form of a dove—in Christian iconography a standard symbol of the Holy Spirit—which violates and inseminates her. The birth of Jesus will be a virgin birth only in the sense that he is fathered by a bird rather than a man.[2] With each and every seduction, lust invades the Virgin's waking thoughts and dreams. With each episode, the narrator becomes even keener on desecrating her divine image. The Gospel story has been rewritten, the doctrinal miracle of the Virgin birth has been thoroughly dismantled, and, from a Christian viewpoint, Mary's reputation has been sullied. Even more radically, the text encourages the notion that Mary takes Christ's place in this reversal of the Fall, since she "dies" for our sins while the devil casts himself as the redeemer.

The plot of the poem centers on the deflowering of a virgin. That she happens to be *the* Virgin is a point about the poem's blasphemous content that I shall treat shortly. In the first instance, however, the significance of virginity can be helpfully understood with reference to its ethical meaning in the value system of Pushkin's readership and society.

Innocence is a tacit, defining feature of female virtue in literature from the eighteenth century to the 1820s.[3] While occasional references to chastity make it a desirable quality in a female, it is only an unspoken sine qua non of a good marriage. What mattered even more than being a virgin was acting like a virgin.[4] While the church maintained its traditional disapproval of nonprocreative sex as sinful, its real concern was to safeguard morality and public decency. Ecclesiastical law had little to say about innocence and sexual purity provided women made at least an outward show of modesty.[5] Legal texts suggest that greatest concern was reserved not for curbing sexual license but for preventing infringements of public decency, often as caused by drunkenness.[6] In general, the implicit view in the representation of female sexuality in literature from the 1770s to the 1830s is that female desire is acceptable, so long as it does not disturb social stability. By the 1820s, the social composition of the urban gentry was more stable than in the 1770s, and tastes were more conservative. The bourgeoisification of the reading public went hand in hand with the strict manners observed at the court of Nicholas I. The ideology of femininity displayed in conduct literature and in literary representations was taken seriously. Restraint and *pudeur* (decency) were seen as marks of good breeding and education as well as Christian virtue. By the 1820s, in Russia as well as in France, the ideal of the bourgeois lady who is domestic and not wanton had taken root and virginity had acquired greater symbolic importance in the description of respectability. For example, the censor Alexander Krasovsky was notorious for pouncing on any misuses of the word "deva" (maiden/virgen) that looked either irreligious or wanton.[7] As a burlesque performance in an eighteenth-century style, *The Gabrieliad* was not notably pornographic.[8] Works of greater explicitness had circulated during the reign of Cather-ine the Great without provoking the interest of the synod or the ruler. Had *The Gabrieliad* appeared forty years earlier, at a time when Barkov's priapic poetry circulated unofficially but unmolested, the act of deflowering and description of serial adultery would have been read as scabrous but not shocking (had the heroine been any other than the Virgin Mary).

Times and manners had changed. The license of an earlier age was not acceptable. Pushkin's treatment of virginity represented sexual matters in a way that was calculated to offend the civil authorities as much as the church.[9] In 1820 *Ruslan and Liudmila* (*Ruslan i Liudmila*) had earned Pushkin immediate popular and critical acclaim as a demonstration of the native Russian genius for storytelling, and the poem was praised as a great advance in the creation of a national Russian literature. In that romance tale, virginity and nationhood stand together as the two linchpins of the morality of a mythic ancient Russian state. By defending her virginity, the heroine comes to embody an ideal of feminine purity.[10] In *The Gabrieliad*, by contrast, Pushkin seized the chance to have fun by showing off his command of pastiche of eighteenth-century poetic style and by inverting the message of innocence rewarded that had been delivered by *Ruslan and Liudmila*. Acts of seduction in *The Gabrieliad* occur as a folkloric set of three because the plot and role of the heroine are the mirror image of their counterparts in *Ruslan and Liudmila*. The seductiveness of Pushkin's first great success lay in the perfect congruity of traditional style and plot; the discomfort of his most notorious work lay in the ironical combination of a heretical message and seemingly innocent style. In this respect, *The Gabrieliad*, had it circulated more widely, would certainly have shocked at least a large part of Pushkin's new readership who regarded him as charming, lightweight, and patriotic (despite the taint of disgrace his exile brought on him). In fact, the manner of *The Gabrieliad* retains his celebrated lightness of touch, but its message can be seen as a broadside against the respectable manners of a conservative readership (called the "middle classes" [gospoda srednei ruki] by Gogol). *The Gabrieliad* assails norms of propriety that were taking hold in the post-Napoleonic world of the Russian bourgeoisie at a moment late in Alexander's reign when both prudishness and mysticism set the moral tone.

It might be argued that the failure to prosecute Pushkin as the suspected anonymous author should be implicitly understood as proof that the poem's contents were perceived as no more than an inoffensive dirty joke. On its own terms, rather than as a rewriting of Genesis, the poem does look tame by comparison with the prurient norms of French erotic fiction and verse. In fact, the absence of government reprisal most likely reflects the slow circulation of a small number of manuscript copies. The history of a vibrant manuscript culture that existed outside publishing in the period remains to be written. Little is known about it—and especially little is known about the dissemination of Pushkin's works in these years. But by the time the authorities caught up with Pushkin in the second half of the 1820s and sought to prosecute him, his suspect morals as an atheist and seducer made the attribution all the more plausible and damning. It also made the circumstances of a legal case deeply embarrassing to Nicholas I, who had pardoned Pushkin in 1826 and was willing to accept Pushkin's alleged claim that the work was a "youthful indiscretion" and spare his own blushes. In the respectable circumstances of urban society, *The Gabrieliad* offended as an attack on manners and expectations of good behavior. The disrespect for chastity and female innocence was certainly not criminal, but it patently contravened gender expectations and the tone observed at court and in the good society from which Pushkin's readership was drawn.

Desanctifying the Virgin

Behind its attack on virginity as a female ideal lies a more radical message. *The Gabrieliad* radically rewrites the Old Testament account of the Garden of Eden and then assaults a cardinal tenet of Christianity by staging a series of seductions in which Mary, the mother of Jesus, emblem of virginity, and antidote to Augustinian original sin, willingly and happily indulges in sex. Sex that is, moreover, extramarital and even—in the final act of congress with the holy dove—bestial. These circumstances point to a further level at which *The Gabrieliad* operates as an instance of blasphemy. Religious narrative can represent a cultural category in which, to use the language of Mary Douglas, impiety acts as a secular defilement of a public or national value.[11] As Douglas has noted, largely if not exclusively with respect to primitive societies, sexuality is often associated with boundary pollution. Within Douglas's paradigm in which the demarcation of boundaries between the permissible and impermissible determines the meaning of pollution in a society, the blasphemy of Pushkin's text consists in its offending against spiritual powers embodied in the church and its sacraments.[12] The doctrinal importance of the Virgin's perpetual virginity, although perhaps understated when set alongside the importance of the Immaculate Conception in Byzantine theology, is clear. The virgin birth of the *theotokos*, her divine motherhood, and her virginity are articles of faith as declared by the early church.[13] Yet her ritual role is not as a model of virginity. Mariology in the Eastern Orthodox tradition makes the Virgin, above all, an intercessor for individuals and nations in times of trouble, a force for social cohesion and survival. By defiling the Virgin's iconic status, Pushkin breaches a taboo against disrespect of the Virgin. Just as the preservation of modesty in female decorum guarantees the social order, the violation of the Virgin's ritual purity symbolically threatens that order.

The corruption of the Virgin is dangerous because sexual chastity has an ancient association with the moral superiority and righteousness essential to the Virgin's position as defender of Orthodoxy and the Russian nation. Transgression of her iconic status taps into ideas about pollution and taboo that form a powerful cultural topos in Russian thinking from the early modern period through the Enlightenment. In these narratives, unchristian behavior or sin puts the safety of the state at risk. In such instances, prayers to the Virgin invoking her intercessionary powers against invaders have been one response. Once sin has been expiated, God's blessing will in theory be restored to a nation prepared to live according to the rituals and ceremonies of the Orthodox state as guaranteed by the tsar. While individual instances of blasphemy do not, of course, risk destabilizing an entire value system, they are seen as undermining holiness—holiness that attests God's blessing through which the nation and its citizens will prosper.[14] Anthropologically, blasphemy provokes divine punishment, and because it invites disorder and formlessness, it looks like a crime. Seen in Durkheimian terms, the protection of pious speech (for instance, through censorship) defends the sanctity of ritual, the purpose of which is to reinforce the state's ideology and self-image through a well-articulated religious system that will not tolerate blasphemy.

What Pushkin's poem assaults is the broader taboo of calling into question the *doxa* (common belief) of the state religion, which must not be subject to rational disbelief or mockery. The Virgin is the embodiment of the ideology of "collectivism" (sobornost'), and her worship constitutes the ritual form that is deemed to be essential to the preservation of the Christian status of the Russian state against impurity. Her watchful protection of the Orthodox Church guarantees the integrity of actual and metaphorical boundaries dividing the pure and impure, Christian and pagan, non-Orthodox and Orthodox, pious and diabolical. By definition, therefore, any violation of her ritual status undermines the belief on which the effectiveness of church and state depend. In the medieval and unreformed theory of kingship that still pertained in early nineteenth-century Russia, the tsar embodied both political authority and sanctity. Once scripture has been discredited, sacraments of the church and the charisma of the tsar become vulnerable. By disputing the authority of sacred scripture and divine revelation, the poet challenged the divine power of the lawgiver as a myth.

Yet desanctifying the Virgin is only one aspect of the poem's subversive discourse of religious and moral norms, since it more broadly attacks as taboo unspoken assumptions of the moral order guaranteed by church and state. God emerges no less compromised and scandalous than the Virgin Mary. In *The Gabrieliad* it is the God of the Old Testament who acts like an oriental lecher of the first order, determined to debauch the Virgin, whose youth and beauty make her a delectable conquest. Indifferent to worship, he behaves like a lovesick adolescent given to indulging his own hackneyed literary style. Pushkin's narrator lampoons God's literary disability as much as his lovesickness (ll. 122–31):

И ты пылал, о Боже, как и мы!
Создателю постыло все творенье,
Наскучило небесное моленье,
Он сочинял любовные псалмы
И громко пел: «Люблю, люблю Марию,
В унынии бессмертие влачу . . .
Где крылия? К Марии полечу
И на груди красавицы почию!»
И прочее . . . все, что придумать мог,—
Творец любил восточный, пестрый слог.[15]

[And you, Lord, burned with love like us! / All of creation became hateful to the creator, / Heavenly prayer bored him / He composed psalms of love / And loudly sang: "I love, I love Mary, / I drag through immortality in desolation . . . / Where are my wings? I shall fly to Mary / And rest on the breast of this beauty!" / And so on . . . everything that he could possible invent,— / The creator loved an Eastern, colorful style.]

Satan is the most active and vocal of all the poem's protagonists. Satan's narrative humanizes God the Father in the best tradition of mock epic by replacing theological doctrine with petty motivation and lust. While he marshals all his eloquence in order to beat God to the conquest, his intentions are broader because he expounds a view of human nature that rejects original sin and refutes any social curbs inhibiting pleasure. The spokesman for the most subversive ideology in the piece, Satan proceeds by rewriting the story of the expulsion of Adam and Eve from the Garden of Eden. Western Christianity made sex and passion the stigma and burden of exile from the Garden of Eden. The devil argues, on the contrary, that the imperative of chastity was the result of this anthropomorphized God's sexual jealousy and desire for Eve. For this reason, Satan champions a liberation theology of the sexual. By educating Eve in erotic pleasure, he takes credit for teaching men and women to enjoy their inborn desires and equates purity with permissibility rather than prohibition. By psychologizing God and unmasking his motives, Satan dismantles the divine authority that stands behind the taboo against recreational sex.

This counternarrative of sin takes aim at the basis of Christian morality. *The Gabrieliad* mocks the dogma of original sin and gives no suggestion that humanity can recapture purity through Pauline devotion. In a nutshell, the argument is that because the body is made to seek pleasure, there is no such thing as sin. The origin of Mary's downfall, as told by *The Gabrieliad*, lies in sexual frustration. This is why Pushkin presents the New Testament account as a story of an unhappy marriage, in which the sexually dormant Joseph deserves to be cuckolded for having failed to satisfy his bride. Mary's virginity is the result of unhappy accident rather than inherent saintliness. In this light, *The Gabrieliad* is a parable about the nature of the female libido, which is seen as highly active and attractive. In the proem to his mock epic, Pushkin begins by stating its mission of salvation—"Verily the salvation of the young Hebrew girl's soul is dear to me" (Voistinu evreiki molodoi / Mne dorogo dushevnoe spasen'e, ll. 1–2)—which he casts as a chance to rescue the body from unnecessary inhibition. Far from being an ideal of chastity, Mary is a model of female license and sexual gratification. If she is torn between uxorious guilt and adulterous desire, it is because she is, first and foremost, a bodily rather than a heavenly creature. In stripping away her mystery, Pushkin pays attention to the physiological origins of her desire.

He does so by providing a symptomology of love that uses classic signs of eighteenth-century biomechanical theories of sensibility in order to corroborate Satan's view. When Mary blushes and sighs, her desire expresses the bodily processes that stimulate the imagination to produce arousal-causing images and that lead to the suspension of moral choice and the elimination of a sense of shame. All awareness of sin and guilt retreat as the subject yields to the dictates of the body. The initial description of Mary applies the usual euphemisms of eighteenth-century erotic verse, citing her physical attributes (ll. 13–16):

Бровь темная, двух девственных холмов
Под полотном упругое движенье,
Нога любви, жемчужный ряд зубов.

[A dark brow, two maiden bumps' / Taut motion under the fabric, /
A leg made for love, a pearly row of teeth.]

From time to time the narrator comments on Mary's captivating smile, which is an involuntary signal of her sexual charisma. Attentive to a natural reticence that enhances her appeal (ll. 78–83), he never applies the vocabulary of sin and shame to her, for desire is driven by the unpredictable workings of the body. In this physiological model, which is prevalent in European materialist writing and pervades fiction and poetry of the period, desire is rarely voluntarist, that is, within the agency of the subject.[16] Blushes betray wishes of which the mind may be entirely ignorant.[17] Hence the narrator asks, "Why did you, Hebrew girl, smile / And why did a blush cross your face?" (Zachem zhe ty, evreika, ulybnulas' / I po litsu rumianets probezhal?, ll. 17–18). But once the body conditions the mind to respond to its impulses, the physical and psychological disposition to respond to desire increases. There is a surface titillation to the plot of *The Gabrieliad*, which emulates the hedonistic manner of eighteenth-century models.[18] The Virgin Mary, once debauched, grows to enjoy not only sexual satisfaction but also the erotic pleasures of flirtation, feigned modesty, teasing, and seduction.[19] The notion that the individual can actually sense blood being stirred—"We sense movement in the blood" (My chuvstvuem volnenie v krovi [l. 104])—is not merely a metaphorical expression. The narrator self-consciously informs us that the language of the passions is only a translation into terms we find intelligible for a secret process, and this process, as a chemical reaction unchained in the mind, has a real physiological existence; its impact on the soul is tangible because it, too, is physical in nature. Pushkin's lexical choices put an emphasis on the working of blood that makes the passage more than a statement of Epicurean reflexes, most especially by citing how desire weighs down the soul. By definition, the soul can only be so burdened if it is itself corporeal, a notion that smacks of materialism and implies atheism.

Pushkin spins out three variations on a single plot line not only because the triadic structure inverts the standard set of challenges posed to folkloric heroes but because they correspond to three types of stimulus that release Mary's desire: the gaze, memory, and eloquence. The blush that starts as a sign of having moved some increment beyond innocence mutates into a sign of attraction and ardor. All erotic initiative comes from the Virgin, and this is the inevitable result of the mind-body connection that Pushkin's narrator summarizes in his intervention (ll. 100–20). At the heart of the passage, the specific power of the "bashful glance" (vzor stydlivyi) evokes shame (styd). These lines explore how and why a look has the power to ignite the passions. Impressed even more by the archangel's splendid pinions and his handsome physique (his "tall figure, languid gaze" [vysokii stan, vzor tomnyi, l. 82]), Mary also registers in her dream the nature of his glance. The word "stydlivyi" connotes desire restrained by shame about less honorable intentions. Mary sees through Gabriel's eloquence to his true motivation because her unconscious mind conveys the longings of her body to her imagination. When she wakes the morning after her dream (l. 80), she is in a state of erotic hangover. She luxuriates in the recollection (l. 90), during which the images of the dream continue to fire her desire. Her hedonism grows in direct proportion to the pleasure she experiences. The splendor of the archangel has left its imprint on her soul and softened her up for Satan's blandishments. The capacity of the body to store in memory a precise recollection of pleasurable sensation is signaled at the end of the dream episode. Memory replays in the mind sensations that preempt moral judgment. These remembered desires "perverted her bashful beauty" (stydlivuiu sklonili krasotu, l. 116). Despite the Virgin's best judgment, memory undermines her self-restraint, most powerfully at the end of the poem, when desire overwhelms her.

By the time God decides to make his move, the Virgin has already succumbed twice. She applies her newfound knowledge to dissembling and projects glances full of desire that she conjures up based on her lascivious recollections of sex with Gabriel. Once again the erotic reaction is cast in the language of physiology (ll. 478–82):

Упоена живым воспоминаньем
В своем углу Мария в тишине
Покоилась на смятой простыне.
Душа горит и негой и желаньем,
Младую грудь волнует новый жар.

[Intoxicated with vivid memory / In her corner Mary quietly / rested on the rumpled bed-linen. / Her soul burns in desire and pleasure, / A new flame shakes her young breast.]

The poem does more than ridicule taboos on virginity. Consistent with its message about the incorrigible nature of sexuality, Mary's indoctrination in a new eroticism erodes her sense of guilt. It is part of the perverse humor of the poem to make her feel ashamed not because she has enjoyed sex but because she knows that the Almighty enjoys seigniorial rights and will be displeased that the Virgin is no longer a virgin. Characterization of desire displays gender equality, with male and female enjoying licentious parity. From a religious point of view the treatment is, of course, meant to be shocking. But from the viewpoint of the eighteenth-century rationalist, the aim in rewriting the myth of paradise is to alter radically the basis for sexual guilt.

As the new beginning for mankind, Christianity offered the promise of redemption through abstinence and repentance. Instead, Pushkin's Satan is a spokesman for Enlightenment values, proffering redemption through the acceptance of the body. The Virgin is given the chance to succeed Eve as the mother of all by enjoying sexual liberation and restoring to man a sense of guiltless pleasure. References to mankind are noteworthy here because Pushkin relates the status of myths to structures of power. Established religion, which is codified in the authority of scripture, is made an explicit target as the source of a repressive narrative. Revelation is not invoked as a source of textual authority. Instead, Pushkin makes of his devil an excellent reader who ably pits his account against the biblical version and uses all his charm and eloquence to prove to Mary that in following her body, she is being true to her own nature as a daughter of Eve.

From Irreverence to Blasphemy

A reading of the text framed in terms of its biblical revisionism and doctrinal subversion only adds substance to its brilliant levity as a performance. Yet it is blasphemous rather than merely a parodic prank. The perception of blasphemy as a religious or civil crime is very much a matter for local definition, but historians of the subject make it clear that, in general, acts of blasphemy occur and can be recognized without the existence of statutory definition and legal formulation. Over the course of the nineteenth century, particularly in France and Britain, blasphemy would come to be regarded as an offense against the social order and civil society because attacks on the church were seen as attacks on the state. Criminalized as a statutory violation, acts of heretical speech and hate speech fell in the jurisdiction of courts and were regulated by legislative bodies concerned to militate against offenses to public decorum. The definition of blasphemy (koshchunstvo or bogokhul'stvo) in the Russian context for this period is, however, still a matter of judgment more than explicit definition, since there is no formal description of crimes of blasphemy in canon law as defined by the Holy Synod, which in any case had more or less surrendered its censorship responsibilities by 1783. Blasphemy, like *lese-majesté*, is a crime of language that shows deliberate disrespect for the dogma of the church and its sacraments or for respectability.[20] The ecclesiastical authorities in Russia, as well as those abroad, gradually found themselves ceding the power to curtail and punish blasphemy to civil authorities.[21]

The distinction between blasphemy and irreverence is a matter of degree, and the prosecution of cultural delinquency by a given society is clearly a matter of sociological complexity. By way of contrasting illustration, we might consider that the obscene act depicted in Pushkin's poem "There lived a poor knight" ("Zhil na svete rytsar' bednyi"), in which the errant knight masturbates in front of an icon of the Virgin, is irreverent rather than technically blasphemous, since it does not call into question state religion or contradict dogma. The premise behind the charge of blasphemy is the "abuse of language to impugn the existence, nature or power of sacred beings, items or texts themselves."[22] We recognize the use of blasphemy when shock more than laughter is the reaction or when statements call into question the premises behind the authority of the state and church. Only a few contemporary responses to *The Gabrieliad* give an indication of how Pushkin's readers reacted. In a letter of 1825 to Petr Chaadaev, Ivan D. Iakushkin offers a probably typical response by citing the work's stylistic polish and regretting its sacrilege: "Recently I read his new poem *The Gabrieliad*. I think that it is the most respectable [*poriadochnyi*] of all his epic creations so that it is a pity that it is of a blasphemous-indecent kind [*sviatotatstvenno-pokhabnyi*]."[23]

Pushkin intimates how well he grasped the difference between parody and blasphemy in a letter of June 1823 to Alexander A. Bestuzhev. The letter treats a constellation of topics, including censorship (and the particular case of Radishchev—a first precocious sign of Pushkin's interest in Radishchev's radicalism), eroticism, and the attitude of his female readership. This document comes as close as Pushkin ever could to acknowledging authorship of *The Gabrieliad* until he allegedly made the confession to Nicholas I that led the tsar to end the investigation of him in 1828. The centerpiece of this letter, which is a bravura literary performance, is his analysis of humor in Maikov's mock epic *Elisei; or Bacchus Enraged* (*Elisei, ili razdrazhennyi Vakkh*), which he compares positively with Osipov's tedious parody of Virgil. Before moving on to complain of the censor's heavy-handedness over the publication of *The Captive of the Caucasus* (*Kavkazskii plennik*), he rebukes Bestuzhev for preferring *The Annunciation* (*Blagoveshchenie*) to *Elisei*, which he regards as more amusing. Commentators have rightly glossed this as a reference to *The Gabrieliad* but too hastily read Pushkin's statement about taste at face value.[24] The distinction he implies is between works of parody, like *Elisei*, which are merely humorous, and a work such as *The Gabrieliad*, which is not merely that. Bestuzhev is meant to understand that *Elisei* is more amusing than *The Gabrieliad* because its only point is literary parody, whereas *The Gabrieliad* is less amusing because its real purpose is actually quite serious.

Parody of the Bible constitutes profanity only when it fulfills certain conditions. The content of the poem invites a charge of blasphemy, but the cleverness of Pushkin's narrative structure creates an argument for the defense of the work as acceptable to Orthodoxy. There is a wicked irony in the way *The Gabrieliad* assigns its only truly blasphemous discourse to Satan. Despite its overt impiety, and despite the eventual charges that were instigated against him in 1828, *The Gabrieliad* may contain blasphemy from which Pushkin can be exonerated because of the way he manages his literary performance. Part of the poem's rebellious charge is that Satan turns out to be a much better writer than God, whose knowledge of human nature is shown to be fallible and whose style comes in for explicit criticism. Insofar as Satan is the only speaker to call into question dogmas of the church, the poem cannot be viewed as blasphemous, since Satan's role, after all, is to lure, deceive, and desecrate, and his performance in the text fulfills those expectations. To be sure, God and the archangel Gabriel are treated irreverently, but that disrespect is of a kind already familiar from Parny and Voltaire and associated with a type of Bakhtinian subversion typical of burlesque parody.[25] Satan's treatment of the Virgin should come as no surprise from the greatest of blasphemers. The characterization of Satan treats him as an enemy of religion, which is exactly the role he should take.

Yet because Satan's performance escapes the mockery meted out to all the other figures, Pushkin seems to endorse him and to stand with him against the church as an advocate of a new sexual theology. Accusations of blasphemy may refer to intention and perception rather than technical violation. From the perspective of the church, the gap between Satan and the Pushkinian narrator was far too close for comfort—Satan sounded like Pushkin and Pushkin sounded like Satan. Yet it would be disingenuous to argue that while technically innocent of breaking the law, Pushkin had innocent intentions. It was not until 1828 that Seraphim, metropolitan of St Petersburg and Novgorod, eventually rose up in outrage and incited the police to arrest Pushkin on charges of blasphemy (bogokhul'stvo).[26] He can hardly have been surprised, but the accusation came at a highly inconvenient time for the writer, who by then was hoping to consolidate his good relations with the tsar and stabilize his commercial standing.[27] Nor would a public acceptance that he was the author of *The Gabrieliad* bolster the authority of the poet who adopted the pose of the visionary genius in "The Prophet" ("Prorok" [1826]).[28]

Free Speech and Censorship Violation

Pushkin's aim in writing a subversive work cannot be separated from the extrasemantic significance that derives from its composition and circulation within its historical context. By celebrating sexual license through profane violation, and sacrilege through freedom of speech, Pushkin courted both danger and a clandestine success. In exiling Pushkin, the government aimed to attenuate his publishing prospects. Exile to the margins of empire was the best way of making him marginal as a writer.[29] The tsar decided that the duration of his sentence would be open to review, depending on Pushkin's behavior and expressions of contrition. Buoyed by the acclaim for *Ruslan and Liudmila* that accompanied him as he left metropolitan Russia, Pushkin found himself in the difficult position of trying to manage his reputation and literary career from a distance.[30] The readership for Pushkin's verse was exclusively metropolitan, and distance from centers of publishing hindered his publishing ambitions.

The strategy of isolating him was effective—but only up to a point. From the perspective of the government, it might in fact have been better to have kept him in town, anchored in the literary, political, and cultural institutions of St. Petersburg, where the authorities would have had a better chance of monitoring and regulating his conduct and the distribution of his writing. Unsurprisingly, almost as soon as Pushkin arrived in the south, stories began to circulate about mischievous behavior. Writing *The Gabrieliad* was not the way to win the hearts of the metropolitan readership or the authorities. Such an act of calculated defiance aimed at established institutions flouted his punishment with a statement of freethinking. His first commercial success with *Ruslan and Liudmila* had stimulated Pushkin to be businesslike about his publishing ventures and contracts. Now the state had put his career at risk by making it that much harder for him to negotiate contracts, and this cost him in commercial terms. Since it was unthinkable that *The Gabrieliad* could ever have been published for profit, its clandestine circulation cost Pushkin no future revenue. If anything, this act of an enfant terrible was consistent with his infatuation with the posture of the Byronic outcast or demon, although toning down his libertine energies would have better served his interests.

Beyond this desire to play the romantic, we can discern a less superficial strategy. It is plausible to surmise that Pushkin, having already forfeited his freedom, may have wished to retaliate by showing the state the limits on its power to regulate his thinking and curb the circulation of his thoughts. By using the clandestine manuscript culture to circumvent the suppression of unauthorized works, he embarrassed the state with the limitations of its own powers. Actual practices of oversight and punishment by the authorities for violating accepted standards were not bound by the legal definition of censorship as it existed in Russia from 1783 to the publication of the "Cast-Iron Statute" ("Chugunnyi ustav") of 1826. In broad terms, the laws on censorship were very loose and relied on self-policing, counting on institutions and individuals to exercise judgment and act in a manner sensitive to the interests of the ruler, the state, and, of course, their own self-interest.[31] Until the early 1820s, when the number of censors increased and individual censors became more interventionist, writers benefited from the decision to place the vetting of publications under the Ministry of Public Education. No one was under the illusion that the relative laxity of censorship permitted anything like complete freedom of print, but the 1804 university and censorship statutes encouraged a belief that tolerance would prevail, provided that writers exercised reasonable judgment, precisely what one contemporary called a "reasonable freedom of book publishing" (razumnaia svoboda knigopechataniia). Clause 21 of the censorship statute called for a "modest and sensible [*skromnoe i blagorazumnoe*] exploration of every truth relating to belief, mankind, the civic order [*grazhdanskoe sostoianie*], statutes [*zakonopolozheniia*], and the management of government in any of its branches." Provided such restraint was exercised, writers would not be subjected to strict censorship and would enjoy "total freedom to publish" with a view to fostering education or enlightenment (uspekh prosveshcheniia).

The standard for such reasonableness was measured by the reaction of the government of the day and was a matter of perception; it depended less on bureaucratic control than on the subjective judgments of individual ministers. In practice, this freedom was abused when the government deemed a violation to have occurred and reacted with hostility through the police (and not, of course, through the courts). By 1820, the liberal promise of Alexander I's reign was a fading memory. Censorship standards had become contaminated by the mysticism of Prince Golitsyn.[32] Pushkin noted this problem in a letter to Petr Viazemsky when he wrote that "our censorship is so idiosyncratic [*svoenravna*] that it is impossible to take the measure of its activities."[33] Compliance with the letter of the law was relatively easy, provided both sides agreed to this form of controlled transgression and regulation. This was all the more so if writers opted to circulate texts among a coterie rather than to publish where the legal intervention of the state was not clear-cut.

But testing the limits of the law, and gauging the limits on free speech, was much more unpredictable when the system was inefficient and an individual like Golitsyn determined what constituted criminal acts according to his own religious values. It would only be a few years before Nicholas I would consolidate the apparatus for investigation, and the effect of both random and systematic surveillance would be to create what has been called a "machinery of incitement."[34] Pushkin well understood that *The Gabrieliad* was more provocative and dangerous than an ordinary prank and fell far short of the "sensible exploration of every truth" stipulated by the 1804 censorship statute. In his letter from Kishinev of September 1822 to Viazemsky he mocked Golitsyn by saying that the poem he was sending was "in a mystical vein—I've become a courtier."[35] Given the spiritualist mode at court, blasphemy was the appropriate type of censorship violation for a writer determined to expose the hypocrisy of a government that was no longer committed to the spirit of tolerance once exercised by Catherine the Great and at least briefly adopted by Alexander I. Given the new prudishness of social custom, blasphemy that featured sexual outrageousness provided an even greater potency because it attacked the reciprocal reinforcement that obtained between conventional morality and church and state.

Although futile in real terms and personally counterproductive, the act of writing represented a symbolic attack against the control on speech and thought exercised by state and church. Although Pushkin was reported to be the author, *The Gabrieliad* was an anonymous work. Its power derived from its shocking irreverence, verbal polish, and insouciance as a piece of eighteenth-century pastiche rather than from his identity, though it also benefited from his notoriety. Although Pushkin would famously speak of himself as a "naughty child," his pranks almost always had a serious point. The Petersburg dandy who in April 1820 displayed a portrait of a French assassin in the theater understood how subversive it was to violate the highly ritualized space of the theater, where content is scripted and the behavior of the audience prescribed. The true danger of such an event lay not in the momentary reaction of the audience but in the way social networks fomented rumor and advertised such radicalism. The surveillance measures implemented by the Third Section (secret police) are an indication of the seriousness of the perceived threat. Like the episode in the theater, *The Gabrieliad* was explosive not only because its content was unacceptable but because its circumstances of production revealed the weakness of the state's authority. The circulation of a clandestine manuscript was a gesture of free speech in a society where free speech did not exist as a legal right. Yet nothing he did was in technical breach of the censorship law. Still, the violation of censorship codes and of norms dictating respect for Orthodoxy revealed how ineffective the system was in coercing Pushkin into repressing his thoughts and self-censoring. In fact, the extreme nature of his transgression here gives us the measure of his bold assertion of his right to think and write as he pleased, even at the cost of offending the authorities.

Freud remarked that "anyone who has violated a taboo becomes taboo himself because he possesses the dangerous quality of tempting others to follow his example: why should he be allowed to do what is forbidden to others? Thus he is truly contagious in that every example encourages imitation."[36] Freud's insight identifies precisely the anxiety about contagion that lies behind systems of control like censorship. As expressed in terms of speech act theory, we can say that *The Gabrieliad* is a performative or illocutionary discourse. Once the manuscript entered the public domain, even in the form of an unauthorized, clandestine text, it acquired an iterability and openness to signification well beyond the author's purview. Pushkin was well aware of the issue. In his first "Epistle to the Censor" ("Poslanie tsenzoru"), written shortly after *The Gabrieliad*, Pushkin teased the censor by suggesting that ultimately the censor was powerless to stop the discursive operation of writers intent on spreading subversive ideas. In her discussion of the politics of the performative, Judith Butler identifies the illocutionary force of textual acts in political systems determined to control acts of signification.[37] Certain texts are problematic when their "discursive performativity" becomes unfixed and unfixable and can no longer be related to their point of origin and the intentionality behind them. It is clear that the words of *The Gabrieliad* were always intended to be subversive. If the poem were read solely within the biographical context, it could be criticized as the tantrum of a disgruntled, exiled, upstart atheist. But outside that context, the authorities dreaded its capacity, like that of any subversive work, to foment discontent with the regime among future readers.

Religious and secular power was embodied in a single figure in the tsarist state. The boundary between political and religious subversion is uncertain in a system in which state and religious power are structurally parallel.[38] Because in an autocratic regime manifestations of legal authority emanate from the utterance of an unapproachable entity, the function of the ruler's absolute voice is to guarantee the stability of the state's social ideology. Analogously, in the religious sphere, the faceless voice of the divinity brings religion into being and sanctions its existence through its revelation. For Louis Althusser, whose theory of state power gives serious consideration to speech acts, it is precisely the voice of the ruler or the divinity in legal pronouncements that establishes and consolidates forms of power. When a voice outside the power structure, invested with a charismatic authority rather than legislated status, disputes the legal hegemony of the state, it commits what Althusser calls an interpellative act. When read from the state's viewpoint, *The Gabrieliad* has the force of interpellation, posing a challenge to bureaucratic state power. It looks like the equivalent of fighting fire with fire because the poet's text articulates its message with an anonymity equivalent to that of the state's apparatus.

What the authorities feared was precisely the contagion-like diffusion of a radical message.[39] This is why the censorship regime held writers responsible for exposing others and encouraging them to violate the law by reading these works. Writers were deemed responsible for all the contexts in which the taboo violation occurred. The work of Robert Darnton on the underground bestsellers of the Enlightenment has exploded the notion that pornographic literature is purely entertainment without a political component; its popular appeal was linked to republican undercurrents because the clandestine circulation of works condemned as obscene by ecclesiastical authorities encouraged resentment and resistance to authority. Pushkin was clearly aware of the rapidity with which texts were copied and spread, and he counted on this unofficial market to sustain his more dangerous ideas. A draft dedicatory set of verses for *The Gabrieliad* positions the poet as a corrupter of youth by touting the excitement of the subversive poem, which is praised as being far more entertaining than approved publications. In a notebook entry, glossed as a reference to this work, Pushkin admits that his muse has sacrificed spiritual activity for this dangerous game and that the danger of the text is offered as its pleasure to readers who, like Eve and the Virgin Mary, prefer clandestine pleasures, the "secret flowers" (tainye tsvety), to stultifying journalistic prose.

Butler's discussion of the perils of free speech reminds us that challenges of the most powerful symbolic kind to domination often happen on the margins of society, where the state's legal presence is weak and taboo has the force of a magical power rather than a legal constraint.[40] No less than its transgressive content, the composition and circulation of *The Gabrieliad* violated fundamental proscriptions of the Russian state. If we read *The Gabrieliad* as an attack on a mystique of control, we can see that behind the act of blasphemy stands a political gesture against a state in which the religious and political authority of the despot make and sanction the law. Taboo is irresistible because the magical power invested in the prohibitions articulated by such a political system tempts the skeptic to expose them as rules established by authoritarian decree of church and state rather than manifestations of natural law and reason defined in contractual terms. Peeved by the censorship and the restrictive print culture of the time, Pushkin played the state's own rule book on blasphemy and censorship. Writing from the limits of empire, Pushkin showed remarkable daring by turning his marginal position into one of strength. When he recorded in a notebook fragment that his chatty muse "risks a dangerous game" (opasnoi zhertvuet igroi) he wasn't joking—at least not entirely.

Notes

For their comments I wish to thank Sharon Achinstein, Alexander Etkind, Simon Franklin, Luba Golburt, Eric Naiman, Anne Nesbet, Catriona Kelly, and Caroline Warman.

1. Keith Allan and Kate Burridge, *Forbidden Words: Taboo and the Censoring of Language* (Cambridge: Cambridge University Press, 2006), 27.

2. The use of the bird to represent sexual insemination here is an instance of the manipulation of Christian iconography, given the status of the dove, and therefore somewhat different from the use of "birds" to represent genitalia, as discussed in J. Douglas Clayton and Natalia Vesselova's "Resexing Literature" in the present volume, which has its roots in folklore.

3. William Mills Todd III, *Fiction and Society in the Age of Pushkin: Ideology, Institutions, and Narrative* (Cambridge, MA: Harvard University Press, 1986), 327.

4. My conclusions are based partly on the treatment of the subject in a number of scholarly works, including Barbara Alpern Engel, *Women in Russia, 1700–2000* (Cambridge: Cambridge University Press, 2004); and David L. Ransel, *Mothers of Misery: Child Abandonment in Russia* (Princeton: Princeton University Press, 1988).

5. For an example of a discourse on chastity, see *Russian Women, 1698–1917: Experience and Expression*, ed. Robin Bisha et al. (Bloomington: Indiana University Press, 2002), 21.

6. For samples of regulations governing sexual conduct, see the documents in *Russian Women, 1698–1917*, 110–30, in which the emphasis falls on the prevention of indecency and coerced sex.

7. See Marianna Tax Choldin, *A Fence around the Empire* (Durham: Duke University Press, 1985), 40–43.

8. But Anthony G. Cross assumes that it was read as pornographic in his "Pushkin's Bawdy; or, Notes from the Literary Underground," *Russian Literature Triquaterly* 10 (1974): 203–36.

9. See Aleksandr S. Pushkin, "O noveishikh bliustiteliakh nravstvennosti," in his *Polnoe sobranie sochinenii*, 17 vols., ed. Vladimir D. Bonch-Bruevich et al. (Moscow: AN SSSR, 1937–59), 11:98–99. Pushkin would pour scorn on such bourgeois prudishness, seeing shame as the product of unconsidered compliance with thoughtless conformity. In commenting on profanity, Pushkin's essay takes a theatrical delight in violating good tone. The writer of *The Gabrieliad*, incorrigible and irrepressible, is recognizable here.

10. See Oleg Proskurin, *Poeziia Pushkina, ili Podvizhnyi palimpsest* (Moscow: Novoe literaturnoe obozrenie, 1999), 36–41.

11. Mary Douglas, *Purity and Danger: An Analysis of Concepts of Pollution and Taboo* (London: Routledge, 2002), esp. chap. 2.

12. Readers inclined to apply this Oedipal hermeneutic might see in Pushkin's poem an explanation of social paradigms of sexual restraint and coercion that are cognate with Freud's model. For one Freudian reading of a Pushkinian narrative, see Caryl Emerson, "Grinev's Dream: *The Captain's Daughter* and a Father's Blessing," *Slavic Review* 40.1 (1981): 60–76.

13. For an overview, see Marina Warner, *Alone of All Her Sex: The Myth and Cult of the Virgin Mary* (London: Picador, 1976), chap. 3. See also the article on the Virgin Mary in *The Oxford Dictionary of Byzantium*, 3 vols., ed. Alexander P. Kazhdan (New York: Oxford University Press, 1991), 3:2173–77.

14. The connection between political subversion and attacks on religious images is seen as a historical constant by the most prominent historian of the subject. See David Nash, *Blasphemy and the Christian World: A History* (Oxford: Oxford University Press, 2007).

15. Aleksandr S. Pushkin, *Gavriiliada*, in his *Polnoe sobranie sochinenii*, 17 vols., 4:119–36.

16. For an overview, see the relevant discussions in François Duchesneau, *La physiologie des lumières: Empirisme, modèles, et théories* (The Hague: Mouton, 1982).

17. See Mary Ann O'Farrell, *Telling Complexions: The Nineteenth-Century English Novel and the Blush* (Chapel Hill: Duke University Press, 1997), 1–12.

18. For an essay on fictional techniques of prurience, see Michel Delon, *L'invention du boudoir* (Paris: Zulma, 1999).

19. On the connection between erotic representation in Pushkin's works and materialist theories of sensibility, see my *Pushkin's Lyric Intelligence* (Oxford: Oxford University Press, 2008), esp. 292–316.

20. Joss Marsh, *Word Crimes: Blasphemy, Culture and Literature in Nineteenth-Century England* (Chicago: University of Chicago Press, 1998), 8.

21. The synod retained the right to censor only works published by its own press. See Aleksei N. Kotovich, "Razvitie ustava dukhovno-tsenzurnykh komitetov, s 1808 po 1828 god, v sviazi s sovremennymi pravitel'stvennymi techeniiami," in his *Dukhovnaia tsenzura v Rossii, 1799–1855 gg.* (St. Petersburg: Rodnik, 1909), 83–140.

22. David Nash, *Blasphemy in Modern Britain, 1789 to the Present* (Aldershot, UK: Ashgate, 1999), 44.

23. Ivan D. Iakushkin to Petr Ia. Chaadaev, 4 March 1825, in Petr Ia. Chaadaev, *Polnoe sobranie sochinenii i izbrannye pis'ma*, ed. Sergei G. Blinova (Moscow: Nauka, 1991), 2:421.

24. Aleksandr S. Pushkin to Aleksandr A. Bestuzhev, June 1823, in Aleksandr S. Pushkin, *Pis'ma*, 3 vols., ed. Boris L. Modzalevskii (Moscow: Gosudarstvennoe izdatel'stvo, 1926), 1:50–52. In response to accusations of blasphemy, in 1827 Pushkin unpersuasively claimed that the poem had been written by the satirist of Catherine's reign, Prince Dmitrii Petrovich Gorchakov (1758–1824), whose notorious libertine verse had circulated clandestinely.

25. The poem's principal sources have been identified as Voltaire's *La pucelle* (ca. 1760) and Parny's *La guerre des dieux* (1799), which have been well discussed. Boris Tomashevsky's exploration of Pushkin's verbal debts remains a reliable guide. See Aleksandr S. Pushkin, *Gavriiliada: Poema*, ed. Boris V. Tomashevskii (St. Petersburg: Gosudarstvennaia tipografiia, 1922).

26. On Seraphim, see Oleg Proskurin, "Pushkin and Metropolitan Philaret," in the present volume, esp. 125–26 and 144–46.

27. See my *Pushkin's Lyric Intelligence*, chap. 6; and Proskurin, "Pushkin and Metropolitan Philaret," in the present volume, 116–17 and 143–44.

28. On the tension between the poet's projected hieratic status and pornographic sedition, see Alyssa Dinega Gillespie, "Bawdy and Soul," in the present volume, esp. 196–99.

29. The specific juridical meaning of "exile" and its relation to service is examined in the present volume by Irina Reyfman ("Pushkin the Titular

Councilor," esp. 44–47), who engages in debate with Igor Nemirovsky's usage. My sense of how Pushkin perceived his removal from metropolitan Russia is in this instance closer to the view advocated by Nemirovsky. Certainly Pushkin's double identification with both Byron and Ovid, who both wrote about themselves as exiles, reinforces the traditional sense of "exile."

30. See Mikhail Gronas, "Pushkin and the Art of the Letter," in *The Cambridge Companion to Pushkin*, ed. Andrew Kahn (Cambridge: Cambridge University Press, 2006), 132–33.

31. See the survey and case studies in Vladimir A. Rozenberg and Viacheslav E. Iakushkin, *Russkaia pechat' i tsenzura v proshlom i nastoiashchem* (Moscow: M. and S. Sabashnikovykh, 1905), esp. with reference to Golitsyn (chap. 1); and S. I. Grigor'ev, *Pridvornaia tsenzura i obraz verkhovnoi vlasti, 1831–1917* (St. Petersburg: Aleteiia, 2007), 40–43.

32. See Aleksandr N. Pypin, *Religioznye dvizheniia pri Aleksandre I* (St. Petersburg: Akademicheskii proekt, 2000), chap. 3. Even unquestionably devout and conservative figures like Admiral Shishkov, his successor, fell afoul of Golitsyn's regime.

33. Without drawing the connection to *The Gabrieliad*, Modzalevsky in his commentary to Pushkin's letters suggests that the Pushkin of circa 1820 was critical of Golitsyn's mysticism. See Pushkin, *Pis'ma*, 1:192.

34. Nash, *Blasphemy and the Christian World*, 56.

35. Aleksandr S. Pushkin to Petr A. Viazemskii, September 1822, in Pushkin, *Polnoe sobranie sochinenii*, 17 vols., 13:44.

36. Sigmund Freud, *Totem and Taboo* (London: Routledge, 1999), 32.

37. Judith Butler, *Excitable Speech: A Politics of the Performative* (New York: Routledge, 1997), chap. 1.

38. Louis Althusser, "Ideology and Ideological State Apparatuses," in *Lenin and Philosophy*, trans. Ben Brewster (New York: Monthly Review Press, 1971), 170–86. My reading of Althusser follows Butler's emphasis on performative speech as the key feature of his schema.

39. In fact, in a number of incidents people who were overheard reading *The Gabrieliad* in private were reported. See, for instance, the account of an interrogation of a servant who denounced his master for reading the poem, in *Letopis' zhizni i tvorchestva Aleksandra Pushkina*, ed. Mstislav A. Tsiavlovskii et al., 4 vols. (Moscow: RAN Pushkinskaia komissia, 1999), 3:424.

40. Butler, *Excitable Speech*, 132.

Politics and Poetry

The "Anti-Polish" Poems and "I built myself a monument not made by human hands"

Katya Hokanson

Ye who dwell
Where Kosciusko dwelt, remembering yet
The unpaid amount of Catherine's bloody debt!
Poland! o'er which the avenging angel pass'd,
But left thee as he found thee, still a waste,
Forgetting all thy still enduring claim,
Thy lotted people and extinguish'd name,
Thy sigh for freedom, thy long-flowing tear,
That sound that crashes in the tyrant's ear—
Kosciusko! On—on—on—the thirst of war
Gasps for the gore of serfs and of their czar.
The half barbaric Moscow's minarets
Gleam in the sun, but 'tis a sun that sets.
    Byron, "The Age of Bronze" (1823)

Although surely *The Shade of Barkov* (*Ten' Barkova*) takes the prize among poems that many readers wish Pushkin had not written, there are other works that tend to be passed over in silence rather than denied or placed under overt taboo. Pushkin's so-called anti-Polish poems, "Before the Sacred Tomb" ("Pered grobnitseiu sviatoi"), "To the Slanderers of

Russia" ("Klevetnikam Rossii"), and "Anniversary of Borodino" ("Borodinskaia godovshchina"), often treated as a trilogy, have been labeled as an unfortunate result of Pushkin's attempt to curry favor with the tsar or merely dismissed as inferior and poorly written, although he himself was proud of these poems throughout his life.[1] Furthermore, the lack of scholarly attention, especially to "To the Slanderers of Russia" and "Anniversary of Borodino," has prevented a fully informed reading of a much more canonized and admired work, "I built myself a monument not made by human hands" ("Ia pamiatnik sebe vozdvig nerukotvornyi"). This chapter places the two main 1831 "anti-Polish" poems into their proper historical and political context and demonstrates what this added context can bring to a discussion of Pushkin's famous monument poem.

When "To the Slanderers of Russia" and "Anniversary of Borodino" are mentioned at all, they are usually not treated as aesthetic works; Hans Rothe points out that until 2006, there had been no published interpretation of "To the Slanderers of Russia" for seventy years.[2] The poem was commented on in journalistic terms during this time period but not treated as a work of poetry, as it had been prior to that period, especially in the third quarter of the nineteenth century. Rothe suggests that Western readers have seen the poem as primarily political; unlike the politics they welcomed, excused, or neglected to see in other works by Pushkin, they deemed that the politics of "To the Slanderers of Russia" made it unworthy of detailed investigation. Even when conceding, for example, that "technically it is one of Pushkin's maturest performances," John Bayley says that it "pays the penalty of good journalism" and calls it an "instinctive outburst."[3] He does not even mention "Anniversary of Borodino." Rothe writes of a divergence in the reception of "To the Slanderers of Russia": admired by monarchists and ideologists of the state, it is often despised and ignored by liberals and democrats. The history of its reception, he notes, has not yet been written.[4] Ardent Russian nationalists recite these poems—especially "To the Slanderers of Russia"—at times of perceived disrespect of Russia by other nations, eliciting powerful displays of Russian ressentiment. But during the Soviet period, when imperialism and aristocracy were frowned upon, attempts to publish essays on the two poems were blocked.[5]

Pushkin wrote his poems against the background of the 1830 November uprising in Poland. Few international relationships are as complex as the one between Russia and Poland; even for a scholar to enter into the territory of Russo-Polish relations is to risk resentment and misunderstanding. The November uprising was but one in a long series of conflicts between Poles and Russians, whose iterations had included the devastation wreaked on Moscow and surrounding areas in the 1598–1613 Time of Troubles, particularly in 1611–1612, the 1794 Warsaw uprising, and the War of 1812, in which Polish forces made up a significant part of Napoleon's Grande Armée. During the second decade of the nineteenth century in Europe, both a growing russophobia and polonophilia were in evidence among many politicians, intellectuals, writers, and artists. Having joined forces with Napoleon, who promised to restore Poland's independence, the Poles had made a reputation for themselves as fierce and valiant warriors. Although the outcome of the war precluded the reestablishment of an independent Polish state, Napoleon's offer to the Poles had in fact been calculated to begin with, designed only to gain their assistance. After the war, although distracted for a time by the cause célèbre of the Greek uprising, Europeans increasingly rallied to the Polish cause, in a sense transferring their feelings about the Greeks (and other peoples pushing for independence) to the Poles.[6] This sympathy allowed many orators to give voice to fine sentiments about freedom and independence while casting as the villain the increasingly powerful Russian Empire, which was almost uniformly depicted as Oriental and barbarous, frequent use being made of imagery of rapacious Cossacks, despotism, slavery, and Russia as a mighty colossus.[7] As John Bowring warned in 1824 in the *Westminster Review*:

> There was a country a century ago which excited neither interest, nor jealousy, nor anxiety; it was known and thought of only as the land of strange and distant barbarians, of whom some vague notions might indeed be gathered together by the curious, from the travels of a few adventurous wanderers. . . . But things are altered now; and Russia, barbarous still, has aspired to, and has obtained, a dictatorship over the states of Europe. She sits like a huge *incubus* upon the rest, disposing of kingdoms at her will, directing and controlling the fate of nations. . . . She overhangs Europe and Asia like an inverted pyramid, which threatens to fall and crush them at its will. . . . It is indeed time that Europe, and that England especially, should awake to the dangers with which the Russian empire threatens her independence and repose.[8]

The Polish quest for independence in 1830 resulted in an uprising that was, despite initial military success, put down by Russian forces in September 1831. What was perceived by many Europeans, especially the French, as Poland's quest for freedom was understood quite differently by the Russians, who remembered the Polish troops fighting for Napoleon and viewed the relative independence afforded by the Congress of Vienna as something the Poles should be grateful for. Russians from both ends of the political spectrum, Norman Davies points out, were incensed by the uprising—particularly by the wave of venomously anti-Russian, pro-Polish propaganda disseminated by the most respected thinkers and poets of France, such as Hugo, Jullien, Delavigne, Béranger, and many others.[9] Pushkin and his contemporaries followed the French press closely both in the original journals and through reports in the Russian press.[10] The ire of figures like Pushkin, Vasilii Zhukovsky, and Petr Chaadaev (Zhukovsky and Chaadaev both later praised Pushkin's 1831 poems) was provoked by the onslaught of anti-Russian invective. French poets wanted to make Warsaw their Missolonghi, a city celebrated because of its defense in poetry.[11]

In February 1831, the Franco-Polish Committee declared in its manifesto that Poland would protect Europe from Russia just as it had saved Vienna from the Turks in 1683. This equation of the Russians with the Turks orientalized the Russians, usurped their own sense of themselves as the barrier between the Mongols and Europe, and ignored their recent (1829) victory over the Ottoman Empire. The rhetoric of the manifesto was similar to many other political and poetic expressions of support for the Poles and vilification of Russia:

> Poles! One first time below the walls of Vienna, you preserved Europe from the invasion of the Barbarians and strengthened the thrones of Europe's kings; now you will be for Europe and its kings a rampart against the invasion of this formidable power, which brings the menace of death to a people raised to be independent. . . . What then is this colossal power that intends to destroy us? Everything boils and weakens around it: the ground trembles under its feet.[12]

It was against this russophobic background that Pushkin wrote his three "anti-Polish" odes, two of which have had a very mixed reception.

Pushkin's most controversial political positions relate to Russia's imperial power. To the south and east, Pushkin supported imperial expansion and the "civilizing mission."[13] One of his most fought-over texts in that regard is the odic epilogue to *The Captive of the Caucasus* (*Kavkazskii plennik*), which elicited horror from some of Pushkin's friends at the time he wrote it and has been the subject of many attempts to discount it or explain it away in criticism.[14] With regard to Russia's relationship to the West, Pushkin's most controversial works are his "anti-Polish" poems—or perhaps one might call them "anti-Polish supporter" poems, since they are aimed at Russia's European critics, particularly the French, although their true addressee is the Russian people. Pushkin's two views coincide: the two ends of empire are two sides of the same coin. He takes special pains, particularly in "To the Slanderers of Russia" and "Anniversary of Borodino," to link the eastern and western ends of the empire. Alexander Suvorov, for example, is alluded to in "To the Slanderers of Russia" as the taker of Ismail in Turkey and the Praga section of Warsaw. In "Before the Sacred Tomb," Kutuzov's many war standards are evoked, thus allowing the knowledgeable reader to make the connection to his campaigns in Turkey and Poland as well as his famous matchup against Napoleon. And Suvorov plays an important role in "Anniversary of Borodino," as does Ivan Paskevich, who is also linked to victories in both Turkey and Poland. This emphasis on equating the two ends of the empire is certainly not accidental; Pushkin uses his poems to assert that Russia's rarely questioned right to expand eastward is matched by her far more frequently questioned right to control her western territories. He makes clear that it is Russia that stands between East and West, not Poland, and it is Russia that has protected Europe from Asiatic forces.

Both the idea that there is a "trilogy" of poems and the casting of them as "anti-Polish" have been disputed. As Rothe notes, the idea that the three poems form a trilogy was first put forward only in 1915.[15] Furthermore, while "To the Slanderers of Russia" and "Anniversary of Borodino" are clearly linked thematically and were written in quick succession, the third member of the trilogy, while usually considered to be "Before the Sacred Tomb," has sometimes been thought to be "Echo" ("Ekho"), but this is a minority opinion.[16] "Before the Sacred Tomb" was written first, when Pushkin doubted whether the Russians would prevail in the conflict, and addresses Mikhail Kutuzov, expressing the desire that he somehow might rise from the grave and command the troops once again. Unlike the other two poems, it was not printed in the brochure published by Pushkin and Zhukovsky after the Russian victory.

It was Waclaw Lednicki who first declared the supposed trilogy to be "anti-Polish" in 1926. Rothe disputes this appellation, asserting that the poems are anti-French, not anti-Polish.[17] The judgment of whether they are anti-Polish, however, varies according to who is interpreting them. In "To the Slanderers of Russia," Pushkin angrily denounces those who slander Russia, telling them to stay out of a "domestic, ancient quarrel" (domashnii, staryi spor, l. 5) among the Slavs. He notes that the Russians and the Liakhs—an ancient name for Poles—have long battled each other and asks whether the Slavic streams will flow together into the Russian sea, warning that if they do not, they will dry up. He admonishes the Western Europeans, who have not read the "bloody tablets" (krovavye skryzhali, l. 16) describing past conflicts, and reminds them that Napoleon was defeated on Russian soil.[18] He asks rhetorically whether they think Russia is too old and feeble to battle them and cites Russia's huge distances, from the Kremlin all the way to the wall of China, tauntingly inviting the supporters of the Poles to come and lay their bones in Russian graves as Napoleon's soldiers had. These gleeful, nationalistic lines can be hard to reconcile with Pushkin's exalted image, yet they were undoubtedly his true views, and they accorded with his views of Russian conquest in the south.[19] "Anniversary of Borodino," written after the fall of Warsaw, celebrates the Russian victory, which occurred on the same date as the battle of Borodino, and returns to many of the same themes as "To the Slanderers of Russia."

The fact that Pushkin quickly published the two odes, along with Zhukovsky's "An Old Song to a New Tune" ("Staraia pesnia na novyi lad"), together in a brochure in September 1831 with the permission and to the great praise of the tsar has been taken as evidence that Pushkin was currying favor in order to improve his chances of getting permission to publish other works. Pushkin's most astute readers, however, read "To the Slanderers of Russia" and "Anniversary of Borodino" as sincere expressions of Pushkin's deeply felt patriotic views and wounded pride, particularly given that so many of Russia's detractors were poets.[20]

The reception of "To the Slanderers of Russia" and "Anniversary of Borodino" was uneven. Zhukovsky, Chaadaev, a teenaged Mikhail Bakunin, and others shared Pushkin's sentiments, but others of his contemporaries did not.[21] Petr Viazemsky, for example, was dismayed by "To the Slanderers of Russia" and "Anniversary of Borodino," just as he had deplored the odic and belligerent epilogue of *The Captive of the Caucasus*. On the other hand, the later nineteenth-century critic Vissarion Belinsky praised "To the Slanderers of Russia" multiple times during his career.[22] The poem was used to exemplify patriotic expression through the 1860s but began to be questioned in the 1880s as Pushkin's degree of feeling or lack of feeling for the Poles began to be debated in Polish and Russian scholarship.[23]

"To the Slanderers of Russia" and "Anniversary of Borodino" are in fact addressed primarily to the French and other European supporters of the Polish uprising, more so than to the Poles themselves—although Pushkin's casting of the conflict as a Slavic "family quarrel" (semeinaia vrazhda), and hence outside the purview of Europeans, cannot be considered a neutral evaluation.[24] Pushkin effectively matches his own tone to the harsh European invective addressed to Russia. Clearly, the meaning of the poems changes according to who reads them and what views and alliances they already have. To Russians like Pushkin, who experienced the excitement of 1812 as a boy too young to join the army, the thought that Europe could forget Napoleon's tyranny and Russia's extraordinary sacrifices in defeating the Grande Armée was insulting. Pushkin's famous youthful ode "Reminiscences at Tsarskoe Selo" ("Vospominaniia v Tsarskom Sele" [1814]) had long before decried the barbarism of the invading French and praised the restraint of the Russian conquest of Paris. For the Russians, the Polish demand that there be a return to the 1772 borders—a demand that remained even as the Russian army surrounded Warsaw and that would have entailed the return of a huge amount of territory—was the chief objection and obstacle to a nonmilitary resolution.

The European press, however, was focused primarily on Polish claims to independence and made little note of the territorial demands. Even some Russians who were sympathetic to the Poles did not support the return of the territory.[25] Pushkin begins his "To the Slanderers of Russia" by addressing the French (ll. 1–6):

О чем шумите вы, народные витии?
Зачем анафемой грозите вы России?
Что возмутило вас? волнения Литвы?
Оставьте: это спор славян между собою,
Домашний, старый спор, уж взвешенный судьбою,
Вопрос, которого не разрешите вы.

[What are you sounding off about, you orators of nations? / Why do you threaten Russia with anathema? / What has aroused your ire? Unrest in Lithuania? / Leave off: it is a battle of Slavs amongst themselves, / A domestic, ancient quarrel, already weighed by fate, / A question you will not decide.]

Even if Polish readers agree that the poem is addressed to the French and other European promoters of the uprising, it is at least doubly insulting—first because a Russian poet addresses the French in the manner of one parent speaking to another about a misbehaving child, and second because the poet relegates a quest for national independence to the status of a mere "domestic quarrel" to be settled by its Russian head of household. Pushkin continues (ll. 7–14):

> Уже давно между собою
> Враждуют эти племена;
> Не раз клонилась под грозою
> То их, то наша сторона.
> Кто устоит в неравном споре:
> Кичливый лях, иль верный росс?
> Славянские ль ручьи сольются в русском море?
> Оно ль иссякнет? вот вопрос.

[Already for a long time amongst themselves / These tribes have clashed; / More than once before the storm has bowed / Either their or our side. / Who will prevail in the uneven quarrel: / The arrogant Liakh, or faithful Russ? / Shall the Slavic streams flow together in a Russian sea? / Or will it dry up? That is the question.]

Pushkin's initial notations for this poem described the Slavic streams as almost insignificant, "disappearing into the Russian sea," while the final draft has the less insulting "flowing together."[26] Oleg Proskurin notes that this Russian sea vs. Slavic streams was in turn a response to Polish poet Adam Mickiewicz's imagery from the foreword to his 1828 narrative poem *Konrad Wallenrod,* hence representing, Proskurin believes, a kind of "war of poetic metaphors." Mickiewicz, speaking allegorically, discusses Lithuania as a much larger river that shrinks into a narrow channel, essentially suggesting that Russia will do the same. Pushkin thus responds by declaring Russia a sea into which the Slavic streams will flow.[27] In general, the imagery in "To the Slanderers of Russia," including the references to a "family quarrel," was influenced by the foreword to *Konrad Wallenrod*, which is thought to have been one of the texts that led to the 1830 rising.[28]

Clearly, Pushkin's placement of Russia at the top of the hierarchy of Slavic peoples would not sit well with the Poles. Even as Pushkin emphasizes the "bloody tablets" of the ongoing disputes between the Russians and Poles in "To the Slanderers of Russia," he tells it from the Russian point of view (ll. 15–19):[29]

Оставьте нас: вы не читали
Сии кровавые скрижали;
Вам непонятна, вам чужда
Сия семейная вражда;
Для вас безмолвны Кремль и Прага.

[Leave us alone: you have not read / These bloody tablets; / To you this family quarrel / Is unintelligible, alien; / For you the Kremlin and Praga are mute.)

Viewing the Polish uprising as a matter of national independence, the French have not taken it on themselves to read the "bloody tablets" of previous battles between the two peoples; "the Kremlin" and "Praga" refer in shorthand to the numerous battles between the Russians and the Poles going back hundreds of years. Praga, a section of Warsaw, was taken by the Russians in 1794, while the Poles burned Moscow in 1611–12 and again in 1812. Pushkin's references in the 1831 poems tying 1612 to Napoleon's invasion in 1812, portraying the two years as a historical "rhyme," were to become a topos in Russian nationalistic discourse. As Olga Maiorova notes, the linkage between Russia's wars against invaders in both 1612 and 1812 "simultaneously represented ancient Rus' and Russia's imperial past and therefore could serve as a mythical foundation for a union of the people with the regime."[30]

To the earlier assertion that the Europeans hate the Russians or indeed all Slavs, Pushkin asks why and suggests some possible answers (ll. 23–30):

   За что ж? ответствуйте: за то ли,
Что на развалинах пылающей Москвы
   Мы не признали наглой воли
   Того, под кем дрожали вы?
   За то ль, что в бездну повалили
Мы тяготеющий над царствами кумир
   И нашей кровью искупили
   Европы вольность, честь и мир?

[And why? Answer: is it because / On the ruins of smoking Moscow / We did not recognize the insolent will / Of the one before whom you quaked? / Because we hurled into the abyss / The idol heavily looming over kingdoms / And with our blood purchased / The freedom, honor, and peace of Europe?]

Pushkin asserts that it was the Russians who halted the scourge of the idol Napoleon and brought peace to Europe. Nor had the Russians forgotten that a hundred thousand Poles were part of the Grande Armée, and that thirty-five thousand of them were in the vanguard of Napoleon's march on Russia. As Norman Davies puts it, the Poles were

> the only national formation in the entire motley host. . . . They reached Smolensk in August. They fought at Borodino. In September they entered Moscow. Exactly two hundred years after Gosiewski had put the Russian capital to the torch, they watched as it burned again.[31]

The Russians, like the Poles (but unlike the French, who are ignorant of Slavic history), also think back not just to 1812 but to 1611, when the Poles entered Moscow and, as Nikolai Karamzin described quite vividly in his *History of the Russian State* (*Istoriia gosudarstva Rossiiskogo*), burned and looted the city, going so far as to relight any fires that went out.[32] The Poles had already brought Dmitrii the Pretender to Moscow, which allowed the Russians, two hundred years later, to see in Napoleon a similarly false idol.[33]

Byron had written extremely derogatory verses about Suvorov at Ismail in "Don Juan," calling him "Hero, buffoon, half demon and half dirt" while also maiming his name by varying its spelling and rhyme scheme.[34] Refuting Byron's insulting portrait of Suvorov in *Don Juan*, Pushkin purposely points to the battle of Ismail in "To the Slanderers of Russia" (ll. 31–33):

> Вы грозны на словах—попробуйте на деле!
> Иль старый богатырь, покойный на постеле,
> Не в силах завинтить свой измаильский штык?

[You are threatening in words—now try it in deeds! / Or is the old bogatyr, resting on his laurels, / Unable to mount his Ismail bayonet?]

In 1823, Byron also wrote the pro-Polish and anti-Russian political poem "The Age of Bronze" cited in this chapter's epigraph:

Kosciusko! On—on—on—the thirst of war
Gasps for the gore of serfs and of their czar.
The half barbaric Moscow's minarets
Gleam in the sun, but 'tis a sun that sets![35]

Tadeusz Kosciuszko, the famed leader of the Polish rising of 1794, had earlier been recruited by Benjamin Franklin and became a hero of the American revolutionary war. Suvorov, despite what is suggested by Byron's sarcasm, defeated the Turks quite decisively at Ismail, a place that Pushkin personally visited. It was also Suvorov who took Praga in 1794; thus, Pushkin's allusions to Praga and to the "Ismail bayonet" refer to Suvorov while also underlining Russia's eastern and western military prowess. In fact, it was Russia's victory at Ismail that allowed her to turn her attentions to Poland, so that the two places are linked not only in terms of the breadth of the Russian Empire but also in terms of historical continuity and military success. Many of the same officers fought in both Turkey and Poland.[36]

Pushkin then describes the far-flung borders of the Russian Empire, trumpeting not only its might and expanse but its spanning of east and west, north and south (ll. 37–42):

Иль мало нас? Или от Перми до Тавриды,
От финских хладных скал до пламенной Колхиды,
  От потрясенного Кремля
  До стен недвижного Китая,
  Стальной щетиною сверкая,
  Не встанет русская земля?

[Or are there too few of us? Or from Perm' to the Tauride, / From the cold cliffs of Finland to flaming Colchis, / From the shaken Kremlin / To the walls of unmoving China, / Sparkling in a bristle of steel, / Will not the Russian land rise up?]

The geographic descriptions in this passage, though certainly expressed using the typical odic formula "ot . . . k . . ." (from . . . to . . .), may be at least in part a response to Jean-François Casimir Delavigne's extremely popular "La Varsovienne" ("The Woman from Warsaw"), a hymn to the Polish independence seekers that declared in geographic terms the length and breadth of the many sacrifices the Polish soldiers had made across the map in the name of Napoleon:

For you, Poland, they will fight, your sons,
More fortunate than at the time when victory
Mixed their ashes in the sand of Memphis,
Or the Kremlin crumbled under their glory.
From the Alps to Thabor, from the Ebro to the Black Sea,
They have fallen, twenty years, on the foreign shore.[37]

Delavigne's point was that now, by fighting the Russians during the uprising, the Poles would die in Poland, not in Spain, Egypt, Russia, or elsewhere—an announcement that Pushkin seems to rebut in the most biting words of his poem. He juxtaposes Napoleon's vast theater of battle to Russia's own vast spaces and effectively invites the French, as symbolized by the "embittered sons" of the slanderers, to come and lay their bones among the "not unfamiliar" graves of 1812, where so many Poles and Frenchmen already lie. At the same time, he reminds his readers of the devastation the Russians inflicted on Napoleon's Grande Armée by emphasizing one of the reasons they prevailed—the huge spaces of Russia (ll. 43–46):

Так высылайте ж к нам, витии,
Своих озлобленных сынов:
Есть место им в полях России,
Среди нечуждых им гробов.

[Send to us, then, orators / Your embittered sons: / There is room for them in the fields of Russia, / Among not unfamiliar graves.]

Europe's lack of respect for Russia undoubtedly does not just take the form of a lack of respect for Russia's past military achievements; as Raymond McNally notes, "jealousy, as well as fear, intermingled in the French mind because of Russia's peculiar position as an arbitrator of European affairs. . . . The French felt that Russia was culturally inferior to France and they never accepted Russia as a European nation."[38]

Pushkin's audience, of course, really consists primarily of the Russians themselves, although rhetorically speaking it includes the "slanderers" in the French Chamber of Deputies and the Poles. Megan Dixon finds that Pushkin uses the poems to develop a national voice, an observation that was first made by Chaadaev.[39] Besides allowing Pushkin to write in an odic style, with its typical elevation of the nation, Pushkin's framing of the conflict as a national "family quarrel" in essence diminishes the Poles' complaint and denies them the opportunity to see themselves as strugglers for independence in the mode of the Greeks while leaving aside entirely the fact that the uprising was a protest directed against government oppression. All of these factors complicate any "factual" discussion of the poems.

"To the Slanderers of Russia," written during the conflict between Russian and Polish forces, strikes a defiant warning note against the Europeans; "Anniversary of Borodino," written upon Pushkin's receipt of the news that Paskevich had prevailed in taking Warsaw and had sent the grandson of Suvorov to Nicholas to inform him of the news, is written in a triumphant tone. Whereas "To the Slanderers of Russia" dared Europe to take Russia on again, promising renewed defeat, "Anniversary of Borodino" revels in the accomplishment of this defeat—on the anniversary of the Battle of Borodino, 26 August in the Julian calendar. This date fit Pushkin's scheme perfectly, since he had compared 1812 to 1612; now he could also compare the turning point of the battle against the French, Borodino, to the newest Russian victory over the Poles.[40] Treating the French threats as real (in general, it was clear to everyone that the French government did not intend to become involved militarily in the uprising), Pushkin claims in the first two stanzas of "Anniversary of Borodino" that, having blotted out of memory the difficulty of fighting on Russian terrain, the Europeans thought they could take the Russians on once again: "They forgot the Russian bayonet and snow, / That buried their glory in the wasteland" (Zabyli russkoi shtyk i sneg, / Pogrebshii slavu ikh v pustyne, ll. 13–14).[41] Just as in 1812, the Russians would prevail (ll. 18–20):

Но долог будет сон гостей
На тесном, хладном новоселье,
Под злаком северных полей!

[But the sleep of our guests will be long / In their cramped, cold new home, / Underneath the meadow grass of the northern fields!]

Pushkin, who ostensibly addresses primarily the French "slanderers" in the first poem, varies his rhetorical addressee in "Anniversary of Borodino," addressing in turn the French, the Poles, and Russia herself. In this poem he hastens to assure the Poles that the Russians will not denigrate them as the French have denigrated the Russians. Pushkin says that the Russians will not burn Warsaw as the Poles had burned Moscow, nor will they drag the Polish pennants on the ground. These assurances refer not only to the Polish attack on Moscow during the Time of Troubles but also to the bloody Russian attack on Praga in 1794, in which Suvorov allowed Russian soldiers to loot and commit mayhem in retaliation for the April 1794 Warsaw uprising, when the Poles had massacred two thousand Russian soldiers.[42] Pushkin refers as well to an unfinished poem he had written in 1824, "To Count Olizar" ("Grafu Olizaru"), in which he describes Russian brutality against the Poles but affirms the ability of poetry to rise above national feeling.[43] "Anniversary of Borodino" makes the claim that this time, Russians will not visit destruction on their defeated foes, nor will the Poles have to hear a "song of shame from the lyre of a Russian bard" (pesn' obidy / Ot liry russkogo pevtsa, ll. 39–40). This assurance by Pushkin points to a contrast between the Russians' present beneficence and the Europeans' eagerness to denigrate Russians in their poetry. The apparent contradictoriness of the poet's promises—given that he also says that should France attack again, she would have to do so over the bones of Poland—may stem from his declaration that the recent victory over Poland is so total and decisive that Russia henceforward will be merciful to her humbled foes.

Pushkin turns from addressing the Poles to focus again on the "slanderers" (klevetniki), the primarily French anti-Russian agitators (ll. 41–46):

Но вы, мутители палат,
Легкоязычные витии,
Вы, черни бедственный набат,
Клеветники, враги России!
Что взяли вы? . . . Еще ли росс
Больной, расслабленный колосс?

[But you, the rabble-rousers of the chambers, / Orators with wagging tongues, / You, the disastrous alarm of the rabble, / Slanderers, enemies of Russia! / To what avail? . . . Is the Russian still a / *Sick, weakened colossus?*]

The word "ross" (Russian), used in "To the Slanderers of Russia" to distinguish the "faithful Russian" (vernyi ross) from the "arrogant Pole" (kichlivyi liakh), returns. Pushkin underlines "sick, weakened colossus"—a reference, Lednicki believes, to the Franco-Polish Committee's manifesto that calls Russia a "puissance colossale" (colossal power).

In the next lines Pushkin mocks the Polish demand for land, asking how far the Polish territories should extend and going so far as to suggest derisively that perhaps even Kiev might ally itself with Poland once again (ll. 49–52, 57–60):

Скажите: скоро ль нам Варшава
Предпишет гордый свой закон?
Куда отдвинем строй твердынь?
За Буг, до Ворсклы, до Лимана?
. . . .
Наш Киев дряхлый, златоглавый,
Сей пращур русских городов,
Сроднит ли с буйною Варшавой
Святыню всех своих гробов?

[Say: Will Warsaw soon / Direct us with its proud law? / Whither will we remove our bastions? / Past the Bug, to the Vorskla, to the Liman? / . . . / Will our decrepit Kiev, golden-domed, / That ancestor of Russian cities, / Unite with stormy Warsaw / The relics of all its tombs?]

In fact, the two countries, Poland and Russia, each claimed as their own a swath of the very same territory, rendering their "idealized fatherlands" geographically overlapping and thus mutually exclusive of one another.[44] The mocking tone continues as Pushkin asks if the Russian tsar has been bothered by the calumniators' "tumultuous noise and raucous shout" (ll. 61–65):

Ваш бурный шум и хриплый крик
Смутили ль русского владыку?
Скажите, кто главой поник?
Кому венец: мечу иль крику?
Сильна ли Русь?

[Have your tumultuous noise and raucous shout / Dismayed the Russian Tsar? / Say, who bowed his head? / To whom the crown: to the sword or the shout? / Is Russia strong?]

After asserting that Russia has withstood cholera and political unrest but remained strong, echoing lines from "To the Slanderers of Russia," Pushkin turns to address the Russians themselves, speaking in full odic cry: "Victory! The heart's sweet hour! / Russia! Arise and be elevated!" (Pobeda! serdtsu sladkii chas! / Rossiia! vstan' i vozvyshaisia!, ll. 71–72). He then praises the wounded commander-in-chief Paskevich, who had taken over for Diebitsch, who had died of cholera (ll. 76–80):

Могучий мститель злых обид,
Кто покорил вершины Тавра,
Пред кем смирилась Эривань,
Кому суворовского лавра
Венок сплела тройная брань.

[The great avenger of cruel offenses, / Who subdued the peaks of Tauris, / Before whom Erevan was peaceful, / To whom a triple battle / Wove a crown from Suvorov's laurels.]

Pushkin himself, of course, was with Paskevich in 1829 when he took Arzrum; Paskevich, like Suvorov who is evoked next, was victorious both in Turkey and in Poland. The evocation of Suvorov brings the subject back to the contemplation of fallen Russian heroes in a way that is reminiscent of Pushkin's first poem written in response to the Polish uprising, "Before the Sacred Tomb." In that poem Pushkin had pleaded with Kutuzov to rise from the grave, but in "Anniversary of Borodino" he realizes the metaphor, making Suvorov actually rise from his grave (ll. 81–90):

Восстав из гроба своего,
Суворов видит плен Варшавы;
Вострепетала тень его
От блеска им начатой славы!
Благословляет он, герой,
Твое страданье, твой покой,
Твоих сподвижников отвагу,
И весть триумфа твоего,
И с ней летящего за Прагу
Младого внука своего.

[Having risen from his grave, / Suvorov sees the taking of Warsaw; / His shade trembled / From the brilliance of the glory he began! / He blesses, hero, / Your suffering, your calm, / The valor of your fellow warriors, / And the news of your triumph / And flying with it from Praga / His young grandson.]

Now Pushkin closes the odic circle; Suvorov looks on from above as his grandson is sent to Nicholas to deliver the news of the fall of Warsaw. The past is present once again, and Pushkin has reiterated the inevitability of Russia's victory and the superiority of its military leaders. Suvorov's grandson completes the link to the past victories against the Poles and the Turks and to the time period of the ascendancy of the imperial ode. Thus Pushkin elevates the Polish conflict to the highest historical and poetic levels. As Harsha Ram notes, although in other odes or in elegies that in some sense served as substitutes for odes, Pushkin tends to shift the tense or otherwise suggest a lack of complete identification with Russian conquest, "To the Slanderers of Russia" and "Anniversary of Borodino" not only contain "conventionally odic belligerency" but also "signal a new kind of politics," presaging a cultural gulf between Russia and the West.[45] And in fact, the perceived lack of respect for Russia and her history, culture, and military achievements brought out these baldly stated sentiments in many other Russians besides Pushkin.

If the 1831 poems helped develop for Pushkin the voice of a national poet, he claims this stature fully in "I built myself a monument not made by human hands." Though it is quite the opposite of a "tabooed" text, and one that has been discussed extensively in scholarly literature, critics have contested the interpretation of this poem. Some critics have found the poem too immodest to have been intended to be interpreted straightforwardly; they have also questioned whether Pushkin could truly have intended to compare his poetry to the Alexander Column in St. Petersburg, putting forward instead other potential monuments in Alexandria and elsewhere as the object of comparison.[46] Sergei Bondi, citing Pushkin's readers' and even closest friends' lack of confidence in his abilities toward the end of his life, argues that Pushkin wrote the poem for posthumous publication in order to affirm his poetic achievement and with the confidence that the worth of his later works would eventually come to be understood by the public.[47]

Reading "I built myself a monument not made by human hands" in conjunction with the 1831 poems, however, allows for some important insights, since this work in many ways continues the assertions about Russian imperial power and influence of the earlier poems. "I built myself a monument not made by human hands" is widely known to be based on Horace's ode 3.30, "Exegi monumentum" ("I built a monument"), and probably also his ode 2.20, or at least Derzhavin's translation of it, titled "The Swan" ("Lebed'"), as well as Lomonosov's and Derzhavin's rewritings of "Exegi monumentum." Horace's "Exegi monumentum," as well as ode 2.20, "Non usitata, nec tenui ferar penna" ("I will be borne on no common, no feeble wing"), addresses his relationship to the empire, his poetic status, and his poetic afterlife. In ode 3.30, his relationship to Augustus is also explicitly addressed. In both odes, Horace celebrates his ascent from humble origins. He is the first to bring his "Aeolian song" to the Italians; he has come from poor parents to be the friend of his wealthy patron Maecenas, and, it is intimated in the poem, the equal of Augustus. His "Exegi monumentum" celebrates his creation of a poetic sepulchre that will outlive and overpower even the pyramids and that will last as long as Rome:

I have wrought a monument more lasting than bronze
And loftier than the peaks of the regal pyramids,
Which neither the gluttonous rain, nor the blustering wind
May destroy, or the innumerable
Series of years and the flight of times.[48]

Ode 2.20 shows Horace having become a swan-poet, flying over diverse lands of the empire and beyond:

I shall visit
The shores of the moaning Bosphorus, I shall visit
Roman Africa and the plains of the Arctic.
The Colchian shall come to know me, and the Dacian,
Who conceals his dread of our Marsian cohorts,
And far Geloni; by reading me the Spaniard
Shall become learned, as well as the Rhone-drinkers.[49]

Horace emphasizes the geographic reach of the Roman Empire and declares that by reading his poetry, the barbarous tribes on the borders of the empire will become civilized, leading to the expansion of the empire and the creation of new Romans through the teaching of his poetry. As Ellen Oliensis points out, Horace's poetic authority derives from Caesar's elevation to "Augustus"—he owes his laurels to the emperor.[50] Hence Horace's poetry is used to imperial ends: to enlarge, tame, and bring order to the empire. The poet works hand in hand with the emperor, the latter winning territory, the former Romanizing the populace.

Pushkin, unlike Horace, begins as an aristocrat, not a pauper; his relationship to the emperor is primarily as a rival, a being with whom he feels equal but who has authority over him as an autocratic ruler and toward whom he has decidedly mixed emotions. However, in "I built myself a monument not made by human hands," Pushkin makes it clear that the poet is greater than the tsar. Horace proclaimed his lofty stature somewhat obliquely, comparing his own poetic monument to the pyramids—monuments to pharaohs of the distant past, in another country. Nonetheless, any reference to the pyramids necessarily also alluded to Augustus's victory at Actium and his annexation of Egypt to the Roman Empire.[51] Pushkin, on the other hand, compares his poetic legacy to a monument unveiled only two years before—the tallest such column in the world, dedicated to the most recent tsar, Tsar Alexander—and proclaims that his poetry exceeds it in importance (ll. 9–12):

Слух обо мне пройдет по всей Руси великой,
И назовет меня всяк сущий в ней язык,
И гордый внук славян, и финн, и ныне дикой
Тунгус, и друг степей калмык.[52]

[Rumors about me will extend through all of great Rus', / And every tongue that exists in her will name me, / The proud grandson of the Slavs, the Finn, the now wild / Tungus, and the Kalmyk, friend of the steppes.]

Like Horace's, Pushkin's name and poetry will spread throughout the Russian Empire, extending to "every tongue that exists in her" (vsiak sushchii v nei iazyk), from the western Slavs (arguably Poles) in the southwest, to the Finn in the northwest, to the Kalmyk in the southeast and the Tungus (Evenks) in the northeast. As Renate Lachmann points out, the use of the word "iazyk" for tribe/tongue is both archaic and also a reference to paganism (iazychestvo), underscoring the similarities to Horace's expansion of Roman culture to "uncivilized" tribes.[53] The references to the Finn, the Pole, the Kalmyk, and the Tungus in the poem indicate the four corners of the vast geographical expanse that Russia lays claim to. While Napoleon had menaced Russia and amassed vast swaths of Europe, Pushkin both evokes and counters his stature with claims for Russia's own military might and huge territory (in "To the Slanderers of Russia") and for Russian poetry (in "I built myself a monument not made by human hands").

Pushkin's poetic monument, composed of poetry and hence unable (as long as there is at least one poet in the world) to become overgrown with weeds and forgotten, stands in contrast both to earthly tombs, so often alluded to in the 1831 poems, and to physical monuments built by

Alexander Column, Palace Square, St. Petersburg. Photograph by Peter Uspensky, used with permission.

powerful people. The phrase "gordyi vnuk slavian" (proud grandson of the Slavs), though disputed, has generally been accepted as a reference to the Poles.[54] The word "vnuk" itself (grandson or, poetically, heir) is reminiscent of the end of "Anniversary of Borodino," when the grandson of Suvorov is sent to tell the tsar the news of the fall of Warsaw. The word "klevetniki" (slanderers), which is a hallmark of "To the Slanderers of Russia" and "Anniversary of Borodino," is echoed in slightly different form in the second-to-last line of "I built myself a monument not made by human hands": "Accept praise and slander indifferently" (Khvalu i klevetu priemli ravnodushno, l. 19).[55]

Place Vendôme Column, Paris. Photograph by Allan Platt, used with permission.

Trajan Column, Rome. Photograph by Eric Medvet, used with permission.

Base of the Alexander Column, St. Petersburg. Photograph by Stephen M. Norris, used with permission.

Montferrand's monument, the Alexander Column—unlike the pyramids, which were elaborate tombs—is a monument to imperial military accomplishment. It was built in imitation of previous such monuments, primarily the Vendôme Column, erected in honor of Napoleon's victory at Austerlitz, which was in turn an imitation of the Trajan Column in Rome. The Trajan Column, which showcases Trajan's defeat of the Dacians, incorporated seized Dacian armor into its construction. Likewise, captured cannons were used to create the Vendôme Column. In similar fashion, military hardware of various epochs and compass points, including armor belonging to Alexander Nevsky and Yermak, is illustrated in bronze relief tablets on the base of Montferrand's stone column.[56] While a statue of Napoleon is situated atop the Vendôme Column, the Alexander Column is topped with a statue of an angel crushing a serpent, and the angel's face is a likeness of Alexander's. As such, Richard Wortman argues, it was also the first public monument of the cult of the Romanov dynasty. It was built specifically to be taller than the Vendôme Column in Paris, and it papered over the discontinuities of the eighteenth century.[57] Pushkin, by comparing his poetry to a monument rather than a tomb, changes the terms of Horace's declaration, bringing the reader's attention to the monument itself and to the two tsars to whom it is most closely related, Alexander and his brother Nicholas.

The iconography of the Alexander Column, erected in 1834 to commemorate Alexander's defeat of Napoleon in 1812, also clearly referred to the defeat of the Poles in 1831. The depictions on the bronze tablets at the base of the column are of the Vistula and Nieman rivers, which link the monument not only to the War of 1812 (the peace treaty was signed on a raft in the Nieman) but also to the suppression of the 1830 uprising in Warsaw, which lies on the Vistula. As Wortman points out, the ceremonial celebration of the dedication of the Alexander Column was implicitly linked with the suppression of the Polish uprising: "The crushing of the Polish rebellion inaugurated a new era of triumphalism marked by great military displays recalling Alexander's victories and the spirit of Vertus. Massive maneuvers and parades celebrated Russia's invincibility at the unveiling of the Alexander column in 1834, the meeting of Russian and Prussian armies at Kalish in 1835, the twenty-fifth anniversary of the Napoleonic War at Voznesensk in Kherson Province in 1837, and the opening of the Borodino monument in 1839."[58] Pushkin himself took part in a ceremony marking the end of the Polish campaign on the Field of Mars in 1831 that was accompanied by a similarly immense military parade. There was even a commemorative painting commissioned on that occasion, for which Pushkin's measurements were taken.[59]

However, Pushkin pointedly did not take part in the huge, elaborate 1834 celebration of the Alexander Column, even leaving the city to avoid doing so. The reason seems primarily to have to do with his frustration with his status as *kammerjunker*, although he also had a strong dislike for Alexander.[60] Wortman describes the event as follows:

> As many as 120,000 troops gathered in the capital on August 30, 1834, Alexander's name day, for a ceremony that marked the Alexandrine Column as a votive object in the emerging cult of dynasty. . . . At 11:00 a.m. Nicholas appeared on the square, cannon salvos sounded, and, at the third blast, columns of troops marched toward him. They quickly covered the entire vast expanse. . . . The emperor, now standing at the side of his brother-in-law, Prince William of Prussia, bared his head, and prayed together with his entire army. . . . Nicholas fell to his knees, followed by the entire army. When the Protodeacon uttered the prayer of Eternal Memory, the cloth fell, baring the column to public view. Nicholas then took command of the guard, and saluted the monument to the

Grigorii G. Chernetsov, *Parade on Tsaritsyn Meadow, 6 October 1831* (1832–37). State Russian Museum, St. Petersburg.

strains of band music and with loud shouts of "Hoorah!" from the crowd. The thunderous 248-gun salute that followed, accompanied by blaring music, struck Butovskii as a "frightening dream."[61]

Vasilii Zhukovsky, unlike Pushkin, did take part in the celebration and published an article describing the occasion in the *Northern Bee* (*Severnaia pchela*) in which he declared the monument so astonishing that it made poetry speechless, while the nearness of the object worked to suppress the imagination. Using similar imagery to that found in Pushkin's 1831 poems, Zhukovsky wrote that the army of hundreds of thousands marched together under the same eagles and was composed of

> the Russian and the Pole, the Livonian and the Finn, the Tatar and the Kalmyk, the Cherkes and the Transcaucasian warrior; and this army walked from Torneo to Ararat, from Paris to Adrianople, and with a great *hoorah* the cannons answered it from the ships of Chesma and Navarino. . . . Isn't this all Russia? . . . Russia, created by the centuries, by woes, by victory? Russia, formerly an ugly crag, outlined slowly by time, little by little, under the thunder of ancient internecine battles, under the sound of the Polovetsk raids, under the weight of the Tatar yoke, in Lithuanian battles, united by autocracy, having flowed together and rough-hewn by the hand of Peter, and now become the shapely column, uniquely enormous on the face of the earth?[62]

The "ugly crag" is clearly a reference to the equestrian statue of Peter atop its crag; Zhukovsky declares that the crag now recarved, as it were, into the form of a column has become a shapely piece of stone. Wortman notes: "For Montferrand stone remained the symbol of Russia's progress and the medium whose transformation exemplified the force and the allure of art."[63]

Pushkin seems to have composed his poem partly in response to Zhukovsky's overgenerous praise of the spectacle on Palace Square. Zhukovsky, writing for public consumption, asserts that one's poetic voice is stilled before the monument, which implies that architecture created for the glory of the state is greater than poetry. In "I built myself a monument not made by human hands," written privately and not published during his lifetime, Pushkin disputes this assertion. Pushkin proclaims on the contrary that his own poetic monument will rise yet higher; since the column represents in Zhukovsky's eyes the vast multiplicity of peoples controlled by Russia united as one, Pushkin makes of this multiplicity not an army but a group of peoples ready to know the Russian word. In fact, the public spectacle of the dedication is surely a kind of peacetime war, the emperor and the assembled military on parade representing a celebratory and orderly version of what is in reality the chaos and destruction of war. Furthermore, if one reads "I built myself a monument not made by human hands" in conjunction with the 1831 poems, and if in fact Pushkin finds his voice as a national poet in those poems, then his poetic "I" may be understood as one that encompasses the nation as a whole. By necessity, then, the national poet, as representative of the people, is more important than an earthbound monument.

One may certainly see the substitution of the quite new Alexander Column as an ironic comparison to the ancient pyramids that appear in Horace's "Exegi monumentum" and Derzhavin's adaptation of it. By using a contemporary reference instead of an ancient one, Pushkin evokes the defeat of Napoleon and alludes to a potential comparison of Tsar Alexander to Emperor Augustus, since just as Augustus had defeated Antony and Cleopatra, Alexander had defeated Napoleon, who had famously conquered Egypt in 1798; his invasion included a battle fought near the pyramids. It was, however, Nicholas who ordered the raising of the monument to his brother, which emphasized his own importance as well, just as Catherine emphasized hers by constructing the statue of Peter the Great. Hence Pushkin evokes Nicholas as well as Alexander by choosing the column as his reference point.

The relationship between emperor and prized poet is a symbiotic one; Augustus gave his stamp of approval to Horace, but Horace, with his poetry, also made Augustus what he was. In an inverse fashion, the attention of and oppression by the tsar is part of what affords Pushkin his stature. Alexandra Smith notes that by choosing the column, Pushkin emphasizes the interdependence of poet and tsar.[64] Defying the tsar in this sense, by claiming that his own legacy outshines the tsar's monument, also links Pushkin to his character Evgenii in *The Bronze Horseman* (*Mednyi vsadnik*), as Smith points out, while the selection of the column as Pushkin's reference point in "I built myself a monument not made by human hands" locates Pushkin's legacy in the heart of St. Petersburg.[65] As Richard Wortman notes, the very practice of creating statues contradicted Orthodoxy's prohibition against graven images, lending a controversial quality to such an undertaking to begin with; Pushkin's use of the word "nerukotvornyi" (not made by hand—an attribute of icons in the Orthodox religious tradition), about which much ink has been spilled, points toward the controversy.[66] Bondi believes that the poem was meant for posthumous publication and that while Horace spoke to Romans and Derzhavin to Russians, Pushkin spoke to the whole world.[67] This sentiment may not be original to Pushkin, however, since for Horace, the Romans comprised the whole world or eventually would, and hence it was in fact Horace's role to make the whole world learned and to make the whole world Roman—no higher goal could be imagined.

One might argue that it is in fact the national voice Pushkin assumed in the 1831 poems that allows him to speak so "immodestly" in "I built myself a monument not made by human hands" Having become a voice that speaks for the nation, his is the only voice that is equal to the autocrat's, the only one that renders the vast spaces of the empire a place where freedom and magnanimity might also reign. Having spent so much effort invoking the heroes of 1812 (and of 1831) and those who preceded them, singing their praises in defense of the nation, he now has earned the right to depict his own legacy, one that is grand in proportion to the grandiosity of those very spaces he has claimed and that is dependent as well on those very military achievements that have assured the important status of Russia and Russia's literary culture. Hence he compares his poetic legacy with the Alexander Column, which is so richly evocative of the trappings of earthly power and also of Russia's military might. The column is also inevitably emblematic of the autocracy's excesses, since it creates an angel out of a tsar whose legacy may well have included complicity in killing his own father. Pushkin's own poetic legacy is greater than that of tsars past not only because he is patriotic without losing sight of the importance of freedom and magnanimity but also because his words, like Horace's for Rome, lend meaning and shape to those vast spaces controlled by Russia.

NOTES

1. Leonid Frizman notes that Pushkin's view of the Poles was seen as "mistaken" and not objective in "Pushkin i pol'skoe vosstanie 1830–1831 godov: Neskol'ko vstupitel'nykh slov," *Voprosy literatury* 3 (1992): 213. A. V. Kozyrev alludes without citation to the "incorrect treatments" of "To the Slanderers of Russia" in "Patriotizm Pushkina," in *Velikii russkii poet A. S. Pushkin 1799–1949: Sbornik statei k 150-letiiu so dnia rozhdeniia*, ed. Aleksandr Serafimovich (Stavropol': Kraevoe knizhnoe izdatel'stvo, 1949), 34. Iurii M. Lotman writes that Pushkin had an "illusory thought about the possibility of influencing the government," admitting however that Chaadaev admired "To the Slanderers of Russia" (*Pushkin: Biografiia pisatelia* [Leningrad: Prosveshchenie, 1983], 195). Chester Dunning, following Lotman, sees "To the Slanderers of Russia" as a counter-response to Bulgarin (see Chester Dunning with Caryl Emerson et al., *The Uncensored Boris Godunov: The Case for Pushkin's Original Comedy* [Madison: University of Wisconsin Press, 2006], 116). Or as *The Cambridge Companion to Pushkin* puts it in the chronology of Pushkin's life for August 1831: "Pushkin publishes the patriotic 'To the Slanderers of Russia,' highly regarded at court but deemed craven by others" (ed. Andrew Kahn [Cambridge: Cambridge University Press, 2006], xiii). In November 1836 Pushkin wrote to Nikolai B. Golitsyn (in French), thanking him for translating "To the Slanderers of Russia" into French and describing the poem as "a piece of verse thrown at the enemies of our country"; he also makes it clear the poem is addressed to the French (Aleksandr S. Pushkin, *Polnoe sobranie sochinenii*, 17 vols., ed. Vladimir D. Bonch-Bruevich et al. [Moscow: AN SSSR, 1937–59], 16:184).

2. Hans Rothe, "A. S. Puskins 'Klevetnikam Rossii,'" *Zeitschrift für Slawistik* 51.1 (2006): 16.

3. John Bayley, *Pushkin: A Comparative Commentary* (Cambridge: University Press, 1971), 142–43.

4. Rothe, "A. S. Puskins 'Klevetnikam Rossii,'" 3.

5. See, for example, Frizman, "Pushkin i pol'skoe vosstanie." Frizman includes an introduction describing and quoting the letters of refusal he got in the 1960s when he first sent his article to potential publishers.

6. See Mark Brown, "The Comité Franco-Polonais and the French Reaction to the Polish Uprising of November 1830," *English Historical Review* 93.369 (1978): 774–93.

7. For a description of much of the russophobic terminology used, see Raymond T. McNally, "The Origins of Russophobia in France, 1812–1830," *American Slavic and East European Review* 17.2 (1958): 173–89. See also *Pologne, l'insurrection de 1830–1831: Sa réception en Europe*, ed. Daniel Beauvois (Lille-Wroclaw: Université de Lille III, 1982); and Waclaw Lednicki, *Pouchkine et la Pologne: A propos de la trilogie antipolonaise de Pouchkine* (Paris: Librairie Ernest Leroux, 1928).

8. John Bowring, "Politics and Literature of Russia," *Westminster Review* 1 (January–April 1824): 80–82. John Howes Gleason notes that though unsigned, the article was by Bowring. See *The Genesis of Russophobia in Great Britain: A Study of the Interaction of Policy and Opinion* (Cambridge, MA: Harvard University Press, 1950), 68.

9. Norman Davies, *God's Playground: A History of Poland*, 2 vols. (New York: Columbia University Press, 2005), 2:239.

10. Mark K. Pushkarevich, "Pol'skaia revoliutsiia 1830–1 goda," in his *Putevoditel' po Pushkinu* (Moscow: Khudozhestvennaia literatura, 1931), 288–90, http://feb-web.ru/feb/pushkin/put-abc/put/put-2885.htm?cmd=0 (accessed 31 August 2010). Pushkarevich notes: "The sympathy of Europe was on the side of the Poles. The French press of the time was full of attacks on Russia. A series of compositions appeared in which strongly polonophilic tendencies were displayed. Hugo, Béranger, Delavigne in France, Grillparzer, Lenau, von Platen, Kerner, Uland in Germany and Austria wrote works mocking a coarse, barbarous Russia. 'To the Slanderers of Russia' is an answer to the anti-Russian campaign provoked in Europe by the Russo-Polish war in Western Europe, the second part of a patriotic trilogy. . . . This ode was given an enraptured reception in wide circles of contemporary Russian society" (289–90).

11. Lednicki, *Pouchkine et la Pologne*, 92. See *Pologne, l'insurrection de 1830–1831*, especially Maria Straszewska, "'La cause polonaise' de 1830 dans la poésie et le théâtre français," 67–82 (Missolonghi is mentioned on page 71); and Edmond Marek, "L'insurrection polonaise de 1830–1831 dans la chanson française," 135–57. Missolonghi, the stronghold of the Greek independence movement, was the town where Byron died in 1824.

12. Franco-Polish Committee, "Manifeste du Comité central Français en faveur des Polonais," *Revue Encyclopédique* (February 1831): 443–44. The siege of Vienna by the Turks in fact continues to be an important cultural image to this day; the Historical Museum of the City of Vienna still displays artifacts from the siege and notes on its website that the "defence of Vienna in 1683 was caught in many visual images which bear witness to the interest in this event throughout Europe; . . . almost all of them are represented. These sources are enriched by objects from the so-called 'Turkish spoils of war,' such as a turban with a pinned-on medal to symbolise courage, or four 'horsetails' which were carried as a sign of high-ranking Ottoman dignitaries" (see http://www.wienmuseum.at/en/collections/history-and-city-life/political-history-and-city-chronicle.html [accessed 5 September 2010]).

13. See, among others, Georgii P. Fedotov, "Pevets imperii i svobody," in *Pushkin v russkoi filosofskoi kritike*, ed. Renata A. Gal'tseva (Moscow: Kniga, 1990): 356–75; Oleg Proskurin, "Pushkin and Politics," in *The Cambridge Companion to Pushkin*, 105–17, and his "Pushkin and Metropolitan Philaret" in this volume, esp. 121–28; and Sergei Davydov, "The Evolution of Pushkin's Political Thought," in *The Pushkin Handbook*, ed. David M. Bethea (Madison: University of Wisconsin Press, 1995), 283–320.

14. For detailed discussions of the epilogue, see Harsha Ram, *The Imperial Sublime: A Russian Poetics of Empire* (Madison: University of Wisconsin Press, 2003), 192–98; Susan Layton, *Russian Literature and Empire: Conquest of the Caucasus from Pushkin to Tolstoy* (Cambridge: Cambridge University Press, 1994), 101–9; Adrian Wanner, "Imperialism as an Infectious Disease: The Theme of Death in 'Kavkazskii plennik,'" *Pushkin Review* 3 (2000): 133–50; and Katya Hokanson, *Writing at Russia's Border* (Toronto: University of Toronto Press, 2008), esp. chap. 1.

15. Rothe indicates that Nikolai O. Lerner first designated the poems as a trilogy, following Annenkov's noting that they had been written at the same time ("A. S. Puskins 'Klevetnikam Rossii,'" 6). See Nikolai O. Lerner, "Primechaniia k stikhotvoreniiam 1831, 1832, 1833, 1834, 1835 i 1836 gg.," in Aleksandr S. Pushkin, *Polnoe sobranie sochineniia*, 6 vols., ed. Sergei A. Vengerov (St. Petersburg: Brokgauz-Efron, 1904–15), 6:408b. Lerner refers to Pushkin, *Sochineniia*, ed. Pavel V. Annenkov, 7 vols. (St. Petersburg: Voennaia tipografiia, 1855–57), 7:45.

16. See Rothe, "A. S. Puskins 'Klevetnikam Rossii,'" 6. Rothe points out that "Before the Sacred Tomb" was written earlier than the other two poems (between May and June 1831, whereas "To the Slanderers of Russia" was written on 16 August 1831 and "Anniversary of Borodino" on 26 August) and was not linked to them by Pushkin; he did link them to "Echo" (probably written between August and September 1831). "Before the Sacred Tomb" is also linked to "The Commander" ("Polkovodets"), Pushkin's poem about Barclay de Tolly, the deliberately unsung hero of 1812, which was written in April 1835.

17. Ibid.

18. Aleksandr S. Pushkin, "Klevetnikam Rossii," in his *Polnoe sobranie sochinenii*, 17 vols., 3:269–70.

19. Such apparent contradictions were not unheard of. As Boris Tomashevsky notes, the Decembrist Pavel Pestel' enthusiastically upheld both the cause of the Greeks and the Russian conquest of the Caucasus (*Pushkin*, 2 vols. [Moscow: Nauka, 1956–61], 1:407).

20. A good summary of this view can be found in Timothy J. Binyon's *Pushkin: A Biography* (New York: Vintage, 2002), 362–67.

21. Frizman, "Pushkin i pol'skoe vosstanie," 235.

22. In a discussion of the third volume of Pushkin's poems, Belinsky lists a number of poems, among them "To the Slanderers of Russia" and "Anniversary of Borodino," and says they are among Pushkin's best minor pieces ("Sochineniia

Pushkina: Stat'ia piataia," in his *Sobranie sochinenii*, 9 vols. [Moscow: Khudozhestvennaia literatura, 1981], 6:296). In his essay "About Children's Books" ("O detskikh knigakh"), Belinsky recommends that older children be read these poems aloud so that they can hear the beauty and harmony of the Russian as well as discover the poems' historical aspects, proclaiming that "whoever does not belong to his fatherland does not belong to humanity" (3:57). See other examples of Belinsky's praise cited in Rothe, "A. S. Puskins 'Klevetnikam Rossii,'" 15.

23. Rothe, "A. S. Puskins 'Klevetnikam Rossii,'" 8–10. See also Aleksandr N. Pypin, "Pol'skii vopros v russkoi literature," *Vestnik Evropy* 2 (February 1880): 703–736, 4 (April 1880): 686–709, 5 (May 1880): 239–71, 10 (October 1880): 681–711, and 11 (November 1880): 281–307; and Vladimir D. Spasovich, "Pushkin i Mitskevich u pamiatnika Petra Velikago," *Vestnik Evropy* 4 (1887): 743–93.

24. As Megan Dixon notes, Pushkin speaks "right past" the Poles; see her "Repositioning Pushkin and Poems of the Polish Uprising," in *Polish Encounters, Russian Identity*, ed. David Ransel and Bozena Shallcross (Bloomington: Indiana University Press, 2005), 59.

25. Olga Murav'eva, "'Vrazhdy bessmyslennoi pozor': Oda 'Klevetnikam Rossii' v otsenkakh sovremennikov," in *Novyi mir* 6 (1994): 198–204; George Vernadsky, review of Vladimir A. Frantsev's *Pushkin i pol'skoe vosstanie 1830–31* (Praga: Tipografiia "Politika," 1929), *American Historical Review* 35.2 (1930): 401–2.

26. See the discussion in Rothe, "A. S. Puskins 'Klevetnikam Rossii,'" 25. The difference would be between "izch" for "izcheznut'" vs. "sol'iutsia" in the final draft. Rothe refers here to Iakushkin, *Pushkin i ego sovremenniki* 17–18 (1913): 1.

27. Proskurin, unpublished excerpt from draft of "Pushkin and Politics." Mickiewicz writes in the foreword to *Konrad Wallenrod* that Lithuania "presents the singular spectacle of a people which disappeared in the immensity of its conquests, as a brook sinks after an excessive overflow, and flows in a narrower bed than before" (*Konrad Wallenrod: An Historical Poem by Adam Mickiewicz*, trans. Maude Biggs [London: Trübner, 1882], iv). Thanks to Michael Wachtel for alerting me to and providing me with the Proskurin excerpt and for consultations on the meaning of the word "Liakh."

28. See "Adam Bernard Mickiewicz," in *Encyclopedia of the Romantic Era, 1760–1850*, 2 vols., ed. Christopher John Murray (New York: Fitzroy Dearborn, 2004), 2:740.

29. The Polish view of the same history, not surprisingly, is different. These differences are played out to some extent in Mickiewicz's response to Pushkin's poems in the "Digression" from his verse drama *Forefathers' Eve* (*Dziady*), which in turn led ultimately to Pushkin's great, and comparatively temperate, poem *The Bronze Horseman*. Here Pushkin responds to many of Mickiewicz's objections and criticisms of Russia, and the negative characteristics Mickiewicz points out

(the monotony of the massed troops, for example) are portrayed in a positive way. See Waclaw Lednicki, *Pushkin's "Bronze Horseman": The Story of a Masterpiece* (Berkeley: University of California Publications in Slavic Studies, 1955); and Dmitrii P. Ivinskii, *Pushkin i Mitskevich: Istoriia literaturnykh otnoshenii* (Moscow: Iazyki slavianskoi kul'tury, 2003).

30. Olga Maiorova, "War as Peace: The Trope of War in Russian Nationalist Discourse during the Polish Uprising of 1863," *Kritika* 6.3 (2005): 517.

31. Davies, *God's Playground*, 2:223.

32. Pushkin may have had in mind the following excerpt from Karamzin: "Empty Moscow burned for two full days. Where the fires went out, there Liakhs, leaving Kitaigorod, lit them anew, in Belyi Gorod, in the Dereviannyi [Gorod] and in the suburbs. Finally the flames died down everywhere, since everything had become cinders, among which only black walls, churches, and stone cellars were left standing. This mass of cinders, with a circumference of twenty versts or more, continued to smoke for a few more days, so that the Liakhs in Kitai and the Kremlin, breathing the stench, lived as if in a fog—but they rejoiced; they robbed the tsar's treasury: they took all the utensils of our ancient crowned heads, their crowns, their croziers, dishes, rich clothes, so as to send them to Sigismund or to use them in place of money for the salary of the troops; they carried away the plunder they had found in the shops, in the houses of the merchants and noble people, they removed the covers from the ikons; divided into equal parts the gold, the silver, the pearls, the stones, and valuable cloth, with disdain they threw out the copper, the pewter, linen, cloth; they dressed themselves in velvet and cloth; they drank from Hungarian barrels and malmsey. Everything luxurious was abundant, only the necessary was lacking: bread! They caroused, gambled with bones and played cards, were dissolute and drunk, cut each other with knives!" (*Istoriia gosudarstva Rossiiskogo*, vol. 12 [Moscow: Kniga, 1989], chap. 4, columns 173–74).

33. In 1825 Pushkin had written his *Comedy about Tsar Boris and Grishka Otrep'ev* (*Komediia o tsare Borise i o Grishke Otrep'eve*), in which he took a positive view of the pretender Dmitrii as a figure who wanted to restore freedom to the serfs. He was forced to revise it, however, into a rather different play, *Boris Godunov*, published soon after the November rebellion had gotten underway, that presented a more negative view of the pretender. Although it might at first glance be tempting to compare the two invaders of Moscow, Napoleon is quite a different figure from the pretender: a figure from outside the Slavic "family" who had affected the history of all of Europe. If anything, the connection between 1612 and 1812 made in Pushkin's poem is less about a pretender and more about the inter-Slavic quarrel: the Russians had learned from the Polish invasion during the Time of Troubles and recognized Napoleon's opportunism, his making use of a "family quarrel" for his own purposes. Hence the French support of the Polish uprising was problematic on several levels: it did not

recognize Slavic history, it did not recognize Napoleon's opportunism, and it did not recognize Russia's contribution to Europe by defeating Napoleon.

34. "Suwarrow chiefly was on the alert, / Surveying, drilling, ordering, jesting, pondering; / For the Man was, we safely may assert, / A thing to wonder at beyond most wondering; / Hero, buffoon, half demon and half dirt, / Praying, instructing, desolating, plundering; / Now Mars, now Momus, and when bent to storm / A Fortress, Harlequin in Uniform" (George Gordon Byron, *Don Juan*, 7.55, in his *The Major Works*, ed. Jerome McGann [Oxford: Oxford University Press, 1986], 634). Peter Cochran notes: "Byron manipulates names fearlessly: he does not hesitate to spell the general's name 'Souvaroff' if he wants to rhyme it with "lover of" (VII, 39, 7–8) or 'Suwarrow' if he wants to rhyme it with 'sorrow' (VII, 49, 7–8) with 'tomorrow' and 'harrow' (VII, 83, 2–4–6) or with 'marrow' (VII, 8, 7–8)" ("Byron's Version of Russia," 4, International Byron Society, http://www.internationalbyronsociety.org/images/stories/pdf_files/russia.pdf [accessed 6 September 2010]).

35. George Gordon Byron, "The Age of Bronze," in his *Poetical Works*, ed. Frederick Page and John Jump (New York: Oxford University Press, 1970), 171. Byron does not use the Polish spelling of Kosciuszko. See also Lednicki, *Pouchkine et la Pologne*, 57–62.

36. See Simon Sebag Montefiore, *Prince of Princes: The Life of Potemkin* (London: Weidenfeld and Nicolson, 2000), 454–55; Robert Nisbet Bain, "The Second Partition of Poland (1793)," *English Historical Review* 6.22 (1891): 331–40.

37. Casimir Delavigne, *Poésies de Casimir Delavigne de l'Académie française, nouvelle édition: Messéniennes, chants populaires, poésies diverses, dernier chants, poèmes, ballades sur l'Italie* (Paris: Didier, 1856), 141. The song was written on 1 March 1831 for a benefit concert for the Poles. See Marek, "L'insurrection polonaise de 1830–1831 dans la chanson française," 145. Delavigne (1793–1843) was an extremely popular French poet. Despite the name Casimir, he was apparently not of Polish extraction and wrote exclusively in French.

38. McNally, "The Origins of Russophobia in France, 1812–1830," 189.

39. Chaadaev wrote to Pushkin on 18 September 1831 (in French): "I have just seen your two pieces of verse. My friend, you have never given me so much pleasure. Finally you are a national poet; you have finally found your mission" (Pushkin, *Polnoe sobranie sochinenii*, 17 vols., 14:228). See Dixon, "Repositioning Pushkin and Poems of the Polish Uprising," 61.

40. Needless to say, the characterization of the outcome of the battle at Borodino is a huge topic in itself. Pushkin here treats Borodino as an effective victory, which is somewhat true: Russian losses were huge that day, as were French losses. Technically the Russians lost the battle, although Dominic Lieven characterizes it as an "almost drawn battle" (*Russia Against Napoleon: The True Story of the Campaigns of War and Peace* [New York: Viking, 2009], 206).

41. Aleksandr S. Pushkin, "Borodinskaia godovshchina," in his *Polnoe*

sobranie sochinenii, 17 vols., 3:273–75. Frizman discusses the distinction between the rhetoric and the political reality in "Pushkin i pol'skoe vosstanie," 224–25.

42. The November uprising of 1830 began with the murder of Russian officers by young Polish students in officer training (Rothe, "A. S. Puskins 'Klevetnikam Rossii,'" 13).

43. See Lednicki, *Pouchkine et la Pologne*, 125.

44. Maiorova, "War as Peace," 519.

45. Ram, *The Imperial Sublime*, 214.

46. See Mikhail P. Alekseev, *Stikhotvorenie Pushkina 'Ia Pamiatnik sebe vozdvig'* (Leningrad: Nauka, 1967), chaps. 4 and 5 (on the meaning of the phrase "aleksandriiskii stolp") and chaps. 9–10 (on the significance of the monument). These issues are also mentioned by Vladimir Nabokov in his commentary to *Eugene Onegin: A Novel in Verse*, 4 vols. (New York: Bollingen Foundation, 1964), 2:310. For an overview of arguments about the meaning of the phrase "aleksandriiskii stolp," see Oleg Proskurin, *Poeziia Pushkina, ili Podvizhnyi palimpsest* (Moscow: Novoe literaturnoe obozrenie, 1999), 275–84. My own view is that the phrase "aleksandriiskii stolp" refers to the Alexander Column in St. Petersburg.

47. Sergei M. Bondi, "Pamiatnik," in his *O Pushkine: Stat'i i issledovaniia* (Moscow: Khudozhestvennaia literatura, 1978), 442–76.

48. Translated by Babak T. Lotfinia; see http://www.estudiosirlandeses.org/Issue2/Issue%202/Articles/McCann%E2%80%99sSongdogsbyAndrzejGabinski.htm#_edn11 (accessed 15 September 2010).

49. Translated by Katherine Elkins; see her "Stalled Flight: Horatian Remains in Baudelaire's 'Le Cygne,'" *Comparative Literature Studies* 39.1 (2002): 2–3.

50. Ellen Oliensis, *Horace and the Rhetoric of Authority* (New York: Cambridge University Press, 1998), 105.

51. See Michele Lowrie, "Spleen and the Monumentum: Memory in Horace and Baudelaire," *Comparative Literature* 49.1 (1997): 48–49.

52. Aleksandr S. Pushkin, "Ia pamiatnik sebe vozdvig nerukotvornyi," in his *Polnoe sobranie sochinenii*, 17 vols., 3:424.

53. Renate Lachmann, "Imitatio und Intertextualität: Drei russische Versionen von Horaz' *Exegi Monumentum*," *Poetica* 19.3-4 (1987): 210. In Old Church Slavonic the word "iazyk" meant "people/tribe."

54. Oleg Proskurin points out in a personal communication that "M. Budberg was the first person who identified 'proud grandson of the Slavs' (gordyi vnuk slavian) not as a Russian, but as a Pole. However, he explained his opinion not in written form, but at the oral discussion of the first version of Waclaw Lednicki's well-known work about 'I built myself a monument. . . .' Lednicki accepted this insight." See also Waclaw Lednicki, "Pushkin's 'Monument,'" in his *Bits of Table Talk on Pushkin, Mickiewicz, Goethe, Turgenev and Sienkiewicz* (The Hague: Nijhoff, 1956), 107–8. In turn, Proskurin adds his own opinion and supporting evidence in *Poeziia Pushkina, ili Podvizhnyi palimpsest*, 294, 441–43n109.

Alekseev says Lednicki is wrong and that the reference is to the southern Slavs (*Stikhotvorenie Pushkina 'Ia Pamiatnik sebe vozdvig,'* 82).

55. Rothe remarks that "To the Slanderers of Russia" is instrumental to reading not only "I built myself a monument not made by human hands" but much of Pushkin's later poetry ("A. S. Puskins 'Klevetnikam Rossii,'" 39).

56. Yermak Timofeevich, surname unknown (ca. 1532–85), was a Cossack leader and explorer and military leader of Russian forces in Siberia.

57. Richard Wortman, "Statues of the Tsars," in *"Remove Not the Ancient Landmark": Public Monuments and Moral Values*, ed. Donald Reynolds (Amsterdam: Gordon and Breach, 1996), 115. Wortman notes that "the succession problems of the eighteenth century and the political crises of the nineteenth led to sharp discontinuities between reigns that hardly sustained the myth of a unified dynasty. The statues to the tsars helped to disguise these uncomfortable truths in imposing artistic forms that created the illusion of an ongoing historical process" (112).

58. Richard Wortman, *Scenarios of Power: Myth and Ceremony in Russian Monarchy*, 2 vols. (Princeton: Princeton University Press, 1995–2000), 1:316.

59. See Binyon, *Pushkin*, 367. The painting, completed by Grigorii Chernetsov in 1831, was called *Parade on Tsaritsyn Meadow* (*Parad na Tsaritsynom lugu*). Pushkin is pictured near Zhukovsky and other writers.

60. See Alexandra Smith, "Pushkin's Imperial Image of St. Petersburg Revisited," in *Alexander Pushkin: Myth and Monument*, ed. Robert Reid and Joe Andrew (Amsterdam: Rodopi, 2003), 131. On Pushkin's service career and *kammerjunker* status, see Irina Reyfman's "Pushkin the Titular Councilor" in the present volume.

61. Wortman, *Scenarios of Power*, 1:316–17.

62. Vasilii Zhukovskii, "Vospominanie o torzhestve 30 avgusta 1834 goda," in his *Proza poeta* (Moscow: Vagrius, 2001), 65–66. In "Before the Sacred Tomb," about Kutuzov, Pushkin describes the granite columns (stolby) in the Kazan Cathedral in St. Petersburg and praises Kutuzov as "the pacifier of all [Russia's] enemies" (smiritel' vsekh ee vragov), as well as one of "Catherine's eagles" (i.e., Catherine's foremost generals) who is asked to rise and save "the tsar and us." There is an implicit comparison between the columns that mark the grave of the great 1812 hero and the column that has been created for a tsar perhaps undeserving of the tribute.

63. Wortman, "Statues of the Tsars," 117.

64. Alexandra Smith, *Montaging Pushkin: Pushkin and Visions of Modernity in Russian Twentieth-Century Poetry* (Amsterdam: Rodopi, 2006), 133.

65. Smith, "Pushkin's Imperial Image of St. Petersburg Revisited," 131.

66. Wortman, "Statues of the Tsars," 112.

67. Bondi, "Pamiatnik," 465.

Part 3

Taboo Readings

Taboo and the Family Romance in *The Captain's Daughter*

David M. Bethea

It is a relatively easy matter to identify places in Pushkin's early works where taboos are being challenged and broken. After all, this is the adolescent who constantly got into hot water with his mates and the authorities at the lyceum for participating in pranks (the *gogol'-mogol'* episode) or saying something rude or provocative. It is not so surprising then, given this starting point, that Pushkin would come to pen works like "Liberty: An Ode" ("Vol'nost': Oda"), "Fairy Tales: Noël" ("Skazki: Noel'"), "The Countryside" ("Derevnia"), "The Dagger" ("Kinzhal"), and eventually the incredibly blasphemous *The Gabrieliad* (*Gavriiliada*), which took the sacred stories of annunciation and virgin birth to previously unexplored (because so drenched in taboo) realms. Thus, let us begin by admitting that Pushkin the brazen taboo traducer is more in evidence from his adolescent days up to his Mikhailovskoe confinement (1824–26) and watershed poem "The Prophet" (*Prorok* [1826]). That being said, however, I would like to argue that it is the later Pushkin, the Pushkin of the 1830s, who may provide more interesting, and more far-reaching, examples of how the taboos of Russian culture are to be negotiated if one is to grow as a historically self-aware consciousness.

Taboos by definition set boundaries; how does one experiment at those boundaries without becoming tainted?

Background

Broadly speaking, the post-romantic, familied Pushkin reengages the notion of taboo but does so by moving away from the generic realm of poetry, especially light verse in the form of salacious anecdote or anti-establishment political tease, and moving toward an attitude and a genre expectation (prose) that see Russia's historical tensions in terms of epochal turning points, moments when the sacred bonds holding the nation together are about to be violated and the future is threatened by that violation. To take the two most obvious examples, in *The Bronze Horseman* (*Mednyi vsadnik* [1833]) we have the taboo of a graven (pagan) image substituting for the spirit of a Christian God and, as awesome totem, claiming authority for a city's (and a new enlightened country's) creation myth, and in "The Queen of Spades" ("Pikovaia dama" [1833]) we have the "new man" with the "profile of Napoleon" who is willing to commit murder, and possibly incest—and who thereby cynically sidesteps the gamble of true love—to obtain the capital he covets. That underlying these two works are Pushkin's very complicated 1830s relations to Peter I and Catherine II and the meanings for Russia of their respective epochs gives the sacred prohibition aspect of their plots a broader significance.

As object of scholarly inquiry, *The Captain's Daughter* (*Kapitanskaia dochka* [1836]) has been no stranger to Freudian and quasi-Freudian readings.[1] In this respect the historical novel is a logical extension, within the same time frame (1833–36), of the violated prohibitions of *The Bronze Horseman* and "The Queen of Spades." Perhaps the main departure to be observed in this later work is Pushkin's now even more focused effort to work a broader sampling of popular verbal expression (and thus consciousness) into the novel's texture.[2] Now we find a narrative suffused with popular sayings (the most famous being "Look after your clothes while they're new; cherish your honor from a tender age" [Beregi plat'e snovu, a chest' smólodu], but there are countless others, beginning with Savel'ich's favorite "The horse is standing on all four feet and still stumbles" [Kon' o chetyrekh nogakh, da spotykaetsia]), folksongs (the haunting "plaintive bargemen's song" [zaunyvnaia burlatskaia pesnia]), folk symbols (wolf), folktales (the Kalmyk *skazka* about the eagle and the raven), substandard speech (reflective of speakers from various social classes, including in the first instance the peasantry), and so on. Nowhere in Pushkin's oeuvre do we encounter a more pointed attempt to bring a storyline closer to how the Russian people think at a certain historical moment.[3] That the author is retreating to an earlier, simpler era, one whose crude bluntness felt refreshing against the backdrop of contemporary polite society and the lacquered duplicity of the Romanov court, only reinforces the point.

This move toward the popular is also, I would like to suggest, a move toward the popular *unconscious*, toward what would become in a later century Freudian (and post-Freudian) models of explaining group behavior. While there is much to object to in the classic Freudian episteme with its grounding of cultural production in neurosis, to avoid that episteme altogether does not make sense for our own cultural moment (it is a trace we can't ignore, as Derrida would say), and so I propose to begin by revisiting the basic concepts in *Totem and Taboo* (1913).

Freud bases his arguments in *Totem and Taboo* on the research done by eminent contemporaries, such as the anthropologist James Frazer, the archaeologist and biblical scholar Robertson Smith, and the social theorist Emile Durkheim. Their forays into primitive or archaic people's thinking allow Freud to erect a conceptual bridge between their ideas and his case studies involving the new "science" of psychoanalysis and the recently discovered "disease" of neurosis. Thus, the four essays in *Totem and Taboo* become a kind of metanarrative that tells the story of why primitive clans or tribes act the way they do, the psychological motives ultimately displacing the strictly social ones, à la Durkheim (a totem is merely "a visual representation of a social religion"), on the one hand, or strictly anthropological ones, à la Frazer (exogamy is a clan's way of avoiding incestuous behavior by forcing its male members to find mates from other clans), on the other.[4] At the same time, the mental activities of the primitive peoples, such as linking a prohibition to a totemic representative (e.g., one is not allowed to eat the meat of the totem except on special, religiously tinged, or "sacrificial" occasions) mirror neurotic patients, mostly children in these cases, who displace their fear of the father onto the animal world and who do so because of some prohibition (e.g., masturbation) that mapped itself onto the neurotic psyche in a context involving the animal.

As suggested, in many ways *The Captain's Daughter* seems a text tailor-made for Freudian interventions. For starters, it revolves around the interactions between a typical, in-no-way-distinguished youth of minor noble blood, Grinev, and a peasant, who "just happens" to become a rebel leader and the hero's surrogate father (posazhenyi otets), all textual facts that lead us directly into Freudian thinking. Clearly Pushkin has written a Russian version of the bildungsroman and clearly he has given us a protagonist whose personal Oedipal challenge is to grow up and become a man. However, and this is a point that for reasons of space we cannot fully expand upon here but needs nevertheless to remain a continuous partner in our thinking, the concurrently told facts of *The History of Pugachev* (*Istoriia Pugacheva* [1834]) provide an alternative storyline to the family romance presented in the novel.[5] It is this shadow storyline, with its almost complete lack of individual viewpoint, its rapid-fire shifts in setting, and its meaningless (in the sense of random, excessive) violence that gives the verbal "consciousness raising" taking place in *The Captain's Daughter* its more than virtual reality. In *The Captain's Daughter* we have the principles of Freud's *Totem and Taboo* raised to an entirely different level. Here we don't have the reason why a primitive clan member observes a prohibition, but *why he does not*, and on a terrifying, grand scale. Here we have all the elements of Freud's text, but reshuffled into a picture of Russian history as group psychosis. Let us now take a closer look at what that means.

At the center of *Totem and Taboo* is, as one would expect, the basic Oedipal struggle. Taboos exist as the strongest possible prohibitions because there is inherent in them a secret (i.e., unconscious) desire to break them. "After all," writes Freud, "there is no need to prohibit something that no one desires to do, and a thing that is forbidden with the greatest emphasis must be a thing that is desired."[6] The chief of a primitive tribe, or the totem that gives the tribe its identity, should not be killed because that is the same as killing the father. But deep down, even while the son/tribal member admires and loves the father/father figure, he also wants to replace him, hence the ambiguity and the appearance of guilt and conscience. Taboo thus understood "is a command issued by conscience; any violation of it produces a fearful sense of guilt which follows as a matter of course and of which the origin is unknown."[7] For our purposes, the primary thematic links in Freud's text as we enter Pushkin's are: the idea of initiation as a prohibition-laden liminal experience; the "taint" that attaches to a person who has violated a taboo and the fear of contact that goes with that taint; sickness and contagion as a function of the uncanny; the totem and its relation to taboo; the dual and related prohibitions of killing the father and sleeping with the mother that are then transposed to group or tribal psychology (and, by association, to acts in history); and the role of oaths/blessings in the psychology of taboo and the "magic" of spoken words.

Two other points of background need to be borne in mind as we read Pushkin's text through Freud's. First, Pushkin's thoughts on Catherine II as female ruler. In 1822, during his stay in Kishinev, Pushkin wrote down some historical notes on eighteenth-century Russian history that supposedly were designed to serve as an introduction to his autobiography, which was destroyed in 1825 as a precaution in the wake of the Decembrist uprising. We recall that Pushkin's mood in Kishinev was particularly cynical and disenchanted. Still, the picture he paints of Catherine, especially after he has just described Peter I rather eulogistically in the same document, is shocking in its overall negativity; it is here that we find the famous phrase likening the empress to "a Tartuffe in skirts." One could argue that a decade later, in the 1830s, the poet's attitude toward Catherine might have mellowed somewhat, except that by then Pushkin was feeling particularly trapped by his relationship to the court (his demeaning *kammerjunker* status, the tsar's interest in Natalie, etc.) and was using all his vast intellectual powers to try to understand how the declining status of the hereditary nobility and that of the peasantry were interrelated and how the problems plaguing the country went back largely to the eighteenth century, and above all to Catherine. While not stated explicitly, the connection between Pushkin's description of the corruption of Catherine's reign in his 1822 historical notes and the cynical atmosphere of the countess's household in "The Queen of Spades" is obvious:

> The reign of Catherine II had a new and powerful influence on the political and moral condition of Russia. Raised to the throne through the plot of a few mutineers, she enriched them at the expense of the people and humiliated our anxious nobility. If to rule means one should know the weakness of the human soul and how to take advantage of it, then in this respect Catherine deserves the amazement of posterity. Her magnificence blinded, her amiability attracted, her generosity created attachments. The voluptuous nature [*slastoliubie*] of this sly woman confirmed her dominion. . . . In time history will evaluate the influence of her reign on morals and reveal the cruel activities of her despotism under the mask of modesty and tolerance. It will show how the people were oppressed by her deputies, the treasury plundered by her lovers, how significant mistakes [were made] in her political economy, how her legislation was worthless, and how the posing in her relations with the century's philosophers was revolting—and when that happens Voltaire's flattered voice will not save her glorious memory from Russia's curse. . . . Catherine knew how her lovers

cheated and robbed, but she remained silent. Encouraged by such weakness, they knew no bounds in their cupidity, and a favorite's most distant relatives greedily took advantage of his brief access to power. It was because of this that there appeared the gigantic estates of completely unknown families and the total lack of honor and honesty in the higher class of people. From chancellor to lowliest clerk everything was stolen and everything was for sale. Thus did a debauched ruler debauch her government.[8]

The fact that Pushkin is completely unguarded here and is not thinking about censorship (the only reason this piece of manuscript survived was because the poet had given it to Nikolai S. Alekseev while he was still in Kishinev) is telling.[9] In his judgment, Catherine has used her "feminine wiles" to advance her agenda, to take advantage of others, and to create a sense of "randomness" (who will be the next favorite [*vremenshchik*] is a mystery, depending only on her whims) that severely undermines Russia's social fabric and institutions and fosters a universal cynicism and insecurity. In this regard, the empress is what the psychologist Erich Neumann calls the "Terrible Mother," a woman with great power and inexhaustible sexual appetite but without nurturing or maternal instincts. Socially, she is the femme fatale-cum-head of state; psychologically, she is the witch-like folkloric grim reaper, the *vagina dentata*.[10] This picture should be included as part of the implicit textual record when we turn to look more closely at the "family romance" in *The Captain's Daughter*, especially the phrase about "the total lack of honor and honesty [*sovershennoe otsutstvie chesti i chestnosti*] in the higher class of people." When at a tense moment early in the novel, for example, Ivan Kuzmich (Captain Mironov) calls his troops "detushki" (kids, children) and asks them to prepare to sacrifice themselves for the sovereign, their "matushka" (mother), it is against this larger, and darker, background that the heroic words are uttered.[11]

Our second point has to do with Emel'ian Pugachev, Catherine's male foil from the people. Just as Pushkin had other views of Catherine when he was not fictionalizing her, so too did he understand very well the rebel chieftain as an actual historical figure. *The History of Pugachev* presents numerous facts that attach clay to the popular hero's feet, perhaps the most famous being Bibikov's comment to Fonvizin that the peasant pretender was "nothing more than a puppet" (ne chto inoe, kak chuchelo) in the hands of his lieutenants.[12] Pugachev may have been crafty and in his way charismatic, but his haphazard way of strategizing and his uneven, often drunken (literally and figuratively, as in drunk in the saddle and drunk on his own power) leadership doomed his enterprise. This Pushkin deftly picked up on and documented, arriving at the conclusion that Pugachev was the very essence of the *sluchainost'*, or randomness (from *sluchai*, a chance event), that ruled Russian history. At the same time, Pugachev was not simply a rogue. He was the rogue who appears at a certain time and place *because* Catherine's government has created a situation that could not but explode.

Chapter 1 of *The History of Pugachev* constitutes the necessary prehistory to the appearance of Pugachev. Among the facts supporting the Cossacks' grievances against an arrogant and, in the case of their immediate superiors at the time of the Pugachev uprising, corrupt government Pushkin includes the following: (1) in return for their initial decision to submit to his authority, Tsar Mikhail Fedorovich granted these Cossacks a deed (gramota) to the Iaik River allowing them to take up residence on its banks as "free people" (vol'nye liudi); (2) thereafter, during the successive reigns of Peter I, Anna Ivanovna, Elizaveta Petrovna, and Catherine II, an effort was made to bring the Cossacks increasingly under "the general system of state governance," an effort that was resisted, however, because it traduced local tradition and subverted the well-established (essentially democratic, nonbureaucratic, preliterary) forms of governance already in place; and (3) beginning in 1762, during the reign of Catherine, the situation became exacerbated when government functionaries imposed harsh new conditions on the Cossacks (withholding of wages, institution of arbitrary taxes, and, most important, infringement on essential fishing rights) that caused them, in 1771, to revolt in earnest.[13] This revolt was quickly put down and the instigators punished. But Pushkin, citing the Cossacks' "just complaints" (spravedlivye svoi zhaloby), which is to say, the as yet undissipated trajectory of their righteous anger, saw in retrospect that these feelings had to find some violent outlet.[14] The "stern and necessary measures" to reestablish order could not keep the peace. The clipped, dramatic conclusion to the first chapter shows that Pushkin's voice is now on the verge of entering the wild, energetic stream of *sluchai*-in-motion: "Everything portended a new mutiny. Only a leader was missing. A leader was soon found [*predvoditel' syskalsia*]."[15] Not fortuitously, this is also precisely where the extended version of the family romance in the novel picks up: the people's (children's) complaints are just, the empress (the Terrible Mother) has been neglectful of her charges, and all hell is about to break loose.

Taboo in *The Captain's Daughter*

The Captain's Daughter is firmly emplotted around the relational structures and rituals associated with family—but this is family writ large, beginning in the opening pages with the Grinevs' nuclear unit but soon morphing into issues of clan, class, nation. Petrusha's original leave-taking from his childhood home—the moment at which the young man (nedorosl' [minor, inexperienced youth]) is freed from the physical presence of parental authority and allowed for the first time to make decisions on his own—is a logical entry point for discussion, as many of the themes and verbal cues to be developed in subsequent action are already embedded here in rudimentary form:

My parents blessed [*blagoslovili*] me. Father [*batiushka*] said to me: "Goodbye, Petr. Serve faithfully the one [i.e., sovereign] to whom you swear an allegiance [*Sluzhi verno, komu prisiagnesh'*]; obey your superiors; don't curry favor with them; don't volunteer for duty, but don't shirk it either; and remember the proverb, 'Take care of your clothes while they're still new; cherish your honor from a tender age.' [*Beregi plat'e snovu, a chest' smolodu.*] My dear mother admonished me in tears to take care of my health and exhorted Savel'ich to look after her child. They helped me into a hareskin coat [*zaiachii tulup*] and fox overcoat. I got into the wagon with Savel'ich and set out on my journey, shedding floods of tears.[16]

The notion of parental blessing, or *blagoslovenie* (literally, "good wording"), is significant, as in time it will govern the children's (Petrusha's and Masha's) actions, especially when it comes to creating their own family. Masha will not agree to marriage until the son has sought and received the parental blessing, which originally is withheld by Grinev père, Andrei Petrovich. Thus the parental blessing withdrawn or denied grows to have the power of taboo (the opposite of blessing being curse) in the sense that if it is not granted the marriage, once consummated, attains outlaw status, status *beyond the law*. To go against this prohibition is to face an ostracism that the old-fashioned and duty-bound Masha cannot bear. The same concept of blessing will reach Grinev's subconscious again a little later, in his dream during the snowstorm, and will be tied to his ambiguous relations with Pugachev, the surrogate father.

In this early parting episode Petr refers to his father as *batiushka*, which as a colloquialism can mean one's biological father, one's spiritual father (e.g., a priest), or the symbolic father of one's country/homeland (tsar'-batiushka). Grinev will have to learn to negotiate the space between the first and third versions of father, without losing his honor and without forfeiting the necessary blessing. Alongside the blessing comes inevitably its conceptual sibling the oath (prisiaga): if the blessing is given by the parent (whether biological or ecclesiastical) to the child, then the oath is given by the subject to the sovereign, from lesser to greater, as it were. The one binds the relationship from the top down, the other from the bottom up; both are sacred, since one's honor can be lost and social banishment (or worse) can follow if one breaks the bond.

Grinev senior's final piece of advice, after telling his son the manner in which one can serve honorably, is the much commented-on proverb: *Beregi plat'e snovu, a chest' smólodu*. The rhymed endings to the two phrases, -ovu and -odu, with the conjunction "a" (a contrastive "and") setting the one against the other, immediately join the homely, the idea of preserving one's dress, with the psychological/moral, the idea of preserving one's honor.[17] Moreover, as Sergei Davydov first demonstrated, the concepts are embedded in each other through intricate sound patterning, the "semantic aureole" of their "p" + "l" + "t" phonemes playing off here and elsewhere the ideas of "payment" (**platit'**) and "dress" (**plat'e**).[18] As Pushkin the poet matures into Pushkin the prose writer, he illustrates again and again how the literal and figurative are tightly woven together (from the outside in as it were), how payment in human relations is not only about keeping one's garment intact but also, and more importantly, about *overpaying*, about making the spontaneous Christian gesture of giving the shirt off one's back. If the father, with his sternness, insists on what should be *preserved* (i.e., not lightly given away), in this case honor and dress, then the mother in the very next sentence urges Petrusha to "take care of his health" (berech' . . . zdorov'e), which would naturally be her, the mother's, first concern for him. In the same breath she then instructs Savel'ich, the surrogate parent, to look after her boy. Avdot'ia Vasil'evna obviously cares more about her son's physical well-being, his warmth and comfort, and so quickly there appears the hareskin coat that contains the same sound pattern as the proverb (**plat**it'/**plat**'e → **tulup**) and that will thereafter miraculously become the crucial item in the "paying it forward" transaction or potlatch scenario that brings Grinev and Pugachev together and changes their relations from class/clan animosity to mutual understanding ("one good turn deserves another" [dolg **plate**zhom krasen]).[19] The more important point to make about the popular advice of the proverb at this juncture is that Grinev will succeed *by not following it literally*: he will neither preserve his wardrobe intact nor his honor, at least not in the way his father imagines. We will return to this idea of a loss-versus-gain economy in due course.

The way that Petrusha begins to negotiate the potentially fraught space between blessing and oath, obedience to family and loyalty to monarch/nation, is through the opposing semantic fields of *dolg* (debt, obligation, responsibility) and *volia* (freedom, license).[20] The young pup's first experience off the leash results in disaster on a small comic scale: the old hand Zurin gets him drunk in a Simbirsk tavern, takes advantage of him at billiards, and then the next morning has a note presented to him asking that the 100 ruble debt be paid. Understanding that his fledgling honor is at stake, Petr goes to Savel'ich and demands that he produce the 100 rubles. But Savel'ich, who cares for the young man's welfare much more than his honor, and in this respect resembles more closely Avdot'ia Vasil'evna than Andrei Petrovich, suggests that Grinev write Zurin to tell him it was all a joke. Grinev however, now defensive, feels he must play by male rules, where honor trumps practical concerns, and so rudely demands the sum from Savel'ich and even threatens to throw him out if the old servant does not comply. Even though Savel'ich is supposed to act as guardian, Grinev petulantly switches roles and pulls rank, stating that "I am your master and you are my servant." "Savel'ich looked at me in deep sorrow and went to fetch my debt [*dolg*]. I felt sorry for the old man, but I wanted to break myself free [*ia khotel vyrvat'sia na voliu*] and prove that I was no longer a child."[21]

At the beginning of chapter 2 (titled "The Guide" ["Vozhatyi"]), Grinev and Savel'ich work out a truce wherein the old man will be in charge of the young man's money, but the young man will remain in control of his honor: the literal and figurative meanings of debt and repayment will have to be recalculated from this point forward, a sign that the boy is entering the ambiguous world of adults on a more conscious footing.[22] He retains some of his *volia* but must weigh his eagerness to do what he wants against his emerging awareness of responsibility, beginning with the master-serf relationship. Petrusha and Savel'ich are joined at the hip as it were: the one cannot be unhappy without the other feeling it. And Grinev learns his lesson in the nick of time, as the author has orchestrated this initiating comic debacle on the eve of far more ominous transactions—transactions with little or no margin for error.

As we eventually learn, the "guide" of chapter 2 is none other than Pugachev, but how he is introduced, within a tight web of now familiar acoustic and visual motifs, is a masterful stroke on the author's part. Once again, as Petrusha and Savel'ich continue their onward journey to Orenburg and the Belogorsk Fortress, the young man is faced with a binary choice: to move onward toward their destination when the weather begins to look threatening or to turn back. He should have learned his lesson from the results of his billiard play with Zurin: push forward into a new situation only if you know the context and the potential consequences. But of course Grinev does insist on pushing on, ignoring both the driver's and Savel'ich's admonitions, and the white cloud (beloe oblachko) in the distance quickly turns into a great, and potentially dangerous, blizzard (buran)—the snowstorm that Pushkin had imbued with overtones of fate and retribution in his 1830 Boldino works "The Snowstorm" ("Metel'") and "The Devils" ("Besy") and that now takes on the added connotations of the chaos and randomness of Russian history itself. The road disappears and there is darkness all around. Grinev has brought them to this pass and now it is his responsibility to act. The white cloud that heralds the snowstorm suddenly morphs into a "black something" (chto-to chernoe) in the distance. Petr is the first to notice it. He asks the driver what it could be and the driver replies: "Perhaps [it's] a cart, perhaps a tree; but it moves, I fancy: it must be either wolf or man [*dolzhno byt', ili volk, ili chelovek*]."[23] This is of course Pushkin's fictional version of his history's "everything portended a new mutiny. Only a leader was missing. A leader was soon found." The passive "a leader was found" of the history is replaced by the "black something," either a wolf or a man, that slowly creeps into the foreground. We don't know yet that this black form is Pugachev; again, he is left unnamed both because artistically this is a means for the *siuzhet* to generate interest and because ontologically the snowstorm and "black something" are extensions of each other, seemingly interchangeable, werewolf (oboroten')-like in their fluid status.[24] This "black something" will embody the historical id, both the grey wolf helper of Russian folklore, that is, the clan's totem, *and* the repressed anger of Catherine's state, where the inability (or unwillingness) to distinguish between wolf and man has translated into a *lupus est homo homini* attitude.[25]

As anticipated, our now slightly more experienced hero makes the first move in this crisis. He does so by trusting the stranger's instincts—wolflike, this man is able to smell a neighboring village's smoke before he can see it—and by "giving himself up to God's will" (predav sebia bozh'ei vole), which act is strangely not the same thing as expressing one's own free will (the earlier "break myself free" [vyrvat'sia na voliu]).[26] The young nobleman sees a value in the peasant that is specific, contingent, not tied to abstract ideas or principles: "His cleverness and his keen sense of smell amazed me" (the Russian word for "smell" here is *chut'e*, often used of animals when describing their ability to pick up a scent).[27] It is at this juncture that Grinev, rocked to sleep during the ride that follows, gets in touch with the alternative knowledge of his subconscious and has his famous "prophetic" dream.

Not only do aspects of Grinev's dream turn out to be foreordained, their "strange circumstances" somehow explaining life when looked back on from the future, but the very details of the dream's framing—its basis in superstition (sueverie) and its liminal status between waking and sleeping ("I was in that state of mind and feeling in which reality yields to reveries and merges with them in the nebulous vision of approaching sleep")—align it immediately with the Freudian uncanny.[28] Dreams that are remembered and then at some level come true after the fact are always edged with anxiety. In this case Petrusha imagines himself returning home (the homecoming being a virtual obsessive motif in the later Pushkin) but not as the son who has proven himself a worthy adult. Quite the opposite. His first reaction is fear (opasenie) because this return is unwilling (nevol'noe) and because the parent, grown angry, will certainly look on this act as "intentional disobedience" (umyshlennoe oslushanie). Hence, before the son even makes his first move in the dream, he is aware of his filial failure and of the fact he has *traduced* a prohibition: having received the parental blessing to go out in the world, the child should return home as a success story. To come back to Andrei Petrovich prematurely, as the prodigal son (Pushkin's favorite story from the Bible), means humiliation and dishonor.

But what happens next turns the prodigal son story around and resituates it as a fairy tale.[29] Petrusha's mother meets him at the entrance to the house with the news that his father is gravely ill and that it is fortunate the son has made it home in time to ask the patriarch's dying blessing. The anxiety associated with the sick parent's leaving this world for the next thus replaces the anxiety associated with leaving the parents' nest for the adult world. When the son enters the bedroom, however, it is the peasant from the snowstorm who is in the parental bed (i.e., Pugachev in the role of the wolf from "Little Red Riding Hood"), not the ailing *batiushka*.[30] What is the connection? How could

Petrusha's failure to act as a grown-up be related to a father's illness when it is actually not the father who is ill?

I tiptoe up to the bed; mother raises the bed curtain and says, "Andrei Petrovich, Petrusha has arrived: he's heard of your illness and come back home; give him your blessing." I go down on my knees and raise my eyes to the invalid. But what do I see? Instead of my father I behold a muzhik with a black beard, looking at me gaily. I turn to my mother in bewilderment, saying, "What's the meaning of this? This is not father. And why should I ask a muzhik for his blessing?" "It's all the same, Petrusha," answers mother, "this is your father by proxy [*posazhenyi otets*]: kiss his dear hand [*potselui u nego ruchku*] and let him bless you." I could not agree to that. The muzhik jumps off the bed, draws an ax from behind his back, and starts flourishing it in all directions. I want to run, but I can't; the room is filling with dead bodies; I stumble over the corpses and slip in pools of blood. The terrifying muzhik calls out to me kindly, "Don't be afraid [*Ne bois'*], come to receive my blessing."[31]

This passage, tapping as it does into unconscious desires, is drenched with ambiguity and the shadow of taboo. According to Freud, "The word 'taboo' denotes everything, whether a person or a place or a thing or a transitory condition, which is the vehicle or source of this mysterious attribute. It also denotes the prohibition arising from the same attribute."[32] Thus, young Grinev himself is in a transitional state (his rite of passage from child to man), as is the father (before he becomes the muzhik), who is supposedly near death. These conditions straddle the concepts of "'sacred' and 'above the ordinary,'" on the one hand, and "'dangerous,' 'unclean,' and 'uncanny,'" on the other, in Freud's terminology.[33] At the same time, the father's bed is occupied by the stranger, and yet the mother, presumably worried more about her offspring's well-being, does not seem to mind: she recognizes her new bedmate as a substitute father and, under the circumstances, is content for him to play his role as proxy, the one who, in the absence of the father, gives away the bride or groom at a wedding (the technical meaning of "posazhenyi otets"). And rather than moaning in his death throes, the new father glances back "gaily" (veselo) at his kneeling son, perhaps the way a fairy-tale wolf would who is about to eat its unsuspecting prey. Nothing is as it seems. When the son refuses to kiss the hand of the stranger and ask his paternal blessing, because to accede to such a request is tantamount to breaking the bond with his biological father, the result is mayhem and carnage. Yet even as Petrusha seems to have *caused* the bloodshed in the logic of the dream sequence, since the muzhik jumps out of bed and begins wielding his ax wildly once his blessing is refused, this same "terrifying" man continues to beckon the youth "affectionately" (laskovo) and to tell him, in substandard, peasant Russian, "Don't be afraid, come to receive my blessing."[34] This is the same sort of uncanny logic we find in Tatiana's dream in *Eugene Onegin* (*Evgenii Onegin*), when in order to find out who Onegin really is she joins forces with the dark side (again, she gives herself over to popular/pagan forces and superstition) and dreams a weird story that seems both to predict and simultaneously bring about the fatal duel: even as Onegin is furious with Lensky for drawing him into the awkward melodrama of the nameday party, he gives Tatiana a look that is "wondrously tender" (chudno nezhen).

To read *The Captain's Daughter* through the lens of *Totem and Taboo*, we need to see all these different transitional states in play with one another. The son still hasn't proven himself (hence the anxiety), while his refusal to ask the new father's parental blessing suggests he is still bound to the values of his upbringing and does not want to betray his family and lose his honor; the biological father's authority is about to be undermined in uncanny ways—hence the theme of his demise. The proxy father, who is by turns brutal and endearing, will be the source of a new authority, but what that authority is seems fraught with deadly consequences that in some mysterious way are tied to Grinev's refusal to bond with him, and so on. All three male figures, then, have strong ties to the notion of taboo in this dream. Through their different role-playing we see that what is sacred is also demonic, uncanny. Adult knowledge involves the threat of psychic and moral contagion. As Freud sums up,

> The strangest fact seems to be that anyone who has transgressed one of these prohibitions himself acquires the characteristic of being prohibited—as though the whole of the dangerous charge had been transferred over to him. This power is attached to all *special* individuals, such as kings, priests or newborn babies, to all *exceptional* states, such as the physical states of menstruation, puberty or birth, and to all *uncanny* things, such as sickness and death and what is associated with them through their power of infection and contagion.[35]

The remainder of the novel is the extended story of what exactly the "dangerous charge" of taboo means in this case, how it threatens to "transfer over" to Grinev (and, by association, others) from Pugachev at various moments, and whether the experience—personal as well as national, historical—that comes from living at the source of this fatal energy can in the end be translated into usable knowledge.

Grinev, Pugachev, and Knowledge as Contagion

The final piece of the puzzle with regard to Grinev's and Pugachev's initial relations involves the young *barin*'s payment to the peasant for services rendered the next morning. This is the point where the "contagion" begins, we might add, although no crime has been committed thus far, nor has anyone's honor been lost. In this respect, contagion simply means one has entered a taboo zone and there could be consequences.

Once the party has been rescued from the snowstorm by the unnamed guide and has arrived at a remote inn, they rest for the evening. Grinev learns that the stranger has gotten a chill because he was dressed too lightly, the result of having pawned his coat (tulup) when the weather was milder and now being forced to travel around in the cold only in his *armiak* (peasant coat of heavy cloth). Why he has pawned his coat is not explained, but the impression is that he has done it for drinking money. The expression on his face is "pleasant, but roguish" (priiatnoe, no plutovskoe)—that is, this individual plays outside the rules. The peasant stranger and the innkeeper, clearly involved in some sort of intrigue, appear to know each other and exchange remarks in a code of popular sayings, one of which is "Hide the ax behind your back—the [forest] ranger is making his rounds" (Zatkni topor za spinu: lesnichii khodit).[36] The saying is particularly apt, since it suggests that these two (and others, the *nashi* [ours]) are up to something, metaphorically hiding the ax that chops down trees illegally when the authorities (the ranger) aren't noticing. At the same time, and in conjunction with the link between the tool and mass death in Grinev's dream, the ax may be being hidden on a more literal level as a weapon to be used against the unsuspecting representatives of order.

Grinev chooses to compensate the stranger for rescuing them—a good deed that the skeptical Savel'ich interprets as merely catching a free ride—and requests that his servant give the man a half ruble for vodka. Once again, Savel'ich loudly objects, and this time he knows he is within his rights according to the recent agreement between master and servant. But Petrusha will not be denied his generosity. He insists instead that to repay his debt his servant should produce something from his wardrobe over which he does retain control: "'All right,' I said with full composure, 'if you don't want to give him a half ruble [*poltina*], pull something out from among my clothes [*iz moego plat'ia*]. He is dressed too lightly. Give him my hareskin coat [*tulup*].'"[37] Payment in coin is replaced by payment in kind (pawned coat → gifted coat). The "p"+"l"+"t" sound orchestration subtly points us away here from concerns with monetary compensation to larger issues of human interaction and decency ("he is dressed too lightly"). Grinev expresses his "nobleman's free will" (barskaia volia), which is the actual phrase Pugachev uses in the text to show his approval and which indicates a kind of extravagance that the peasant understands, by giving him the "coat off his own shoulders" (i.e., the shirt off his back): "His Honor's giving me a coat off his own shoulders; that's his pleasure as master."[38] It doesn't matter that the recipient may drink away the gift or that the coat is too small; what matters is that it is a *more than adequate* token of appreciation that sets the relationship between Grinev and Pugachev in motion, a relationship Pugachev promises he will never forget. More importantly for subsequent developments, Grinev keeps his honor in this instance by *not* keeping his dress intact. In effect, he goes against the literal meaning of his father's parting advice.

The Belogorsk Fortress featured in chapters 3 through 6 is a parodic version of Catherine II's matriarchal Russia. It is still peacetime, and Vasilisa Egorovna, the commandant's wife, has for all intents and purposes taken command of the fort. When Grinev enters the commandant's house and reports for duty, the commandant is not present and his wife answers, "He's visiting with Father Gerasim, but it's all the same, young man, I'm his wife [*ia ego khoziaika*]."[39] The phrase "ia ego khoziaika" can also be translated humorously as "I'm his boss." Wherever he looks Grinev sees his heroic, "macho" expectations dashed. Instead of an imposing bastion he finds a tiny village with a log palisade; instead of assorted artillery, an old cast-iron cannon; instead of well-trained, energetic soldiers, a ragtag band of broken-down veterans. As Caryl Emerson puts it, "Belogorskii Fortress is a place where one grows old, not where one grows up."[40] Everything reflects the fact that this is essentially Vasilisa Egorovna's realm: the first person Petrusha meets in the anteroom of the commandant's house is an old soldier sewing a patch on a uniform; when the young man initially catches sight of the commandant's wife she is winding a ball of yarn from the outstretched arms of the second in command, Ivan Ignat'ich, to whom she barks repeatedly to keep his arms straight; it is she who decides where Grinev should be billeted—at the home of one Semen Kuzov, the "scoundrel" who let his horse into her vegetable garden—and she chides Ivan Kuzmich, Captain Mironov himself, for letting his dinner get cold because he has been "drilling" his soldiers, an activity Vasilisa

Egorovna considers excessive. "Great glory," quips Vasilisa Egorovna, "drilling your soldiers, indeed; they aren't able to learn the routines, and you don't know the first thing about them, either. It'd be far better if you sat at home and prayed to God."[41] This introduction to fortress life, along with the description of the village Goriukhino in Pushkin's mock *History of Goriukhino Village* (*Istoriia sela Goriukhina*), may be one of the most comical passages ever penned by the poet.

The point, while handled lightly, is that this world of castrated male authority is sufficient unto itself as long as that male authority is not needed. Ivan Kuzmich "was under his wife's thumb, which suited his easy-going disposition. Vasilisa Egorovna regarded matters connected with the [military] service as belonging to the household and ran the fort like her own home."[42] Indeed, the good woman's rules seem to operate adequately even when she is faced with an individual case of potential male violence: Grinev's and Shvabrin's first attempt at a duel is forestalled precisely because she is able to wheedle the needed information from the simple Ivan Ignat'ich and stop the fight before it starts. The formal means a nobleman has to protect his and his family's honor has no place in a remote army fort; it is an affectation. Appropriately, the young men's swords are taken from them and placed, again ironically by Palashka the maid, in Vasilisa Egorovna's cupboard. Still, Grinev does manage to learn two important lessons related to his rite of passage into adulthood during his stay at the Belogorsk Fortress: first, that in avoiding the taboo of dishonor, he must think not only of himself but of Masha, who has been slandered by Shvabrin; and second, that a parent's blessing is not a formality and that in angering his father by injuring himself in the duel and then managing to fall in love when he should have been learning his duty as a soldier, he has ruined their (his and Masha's) chances—at least for now, though as far as they are concerned permanently—of making a life together. Masha naturally interprets this turn of events according to her lights: it is not their "fate" or "God's will" to get married. In her thinking there are certain moral categories that are not to be questioned or, to put it the other way around, *there are certain moral categories that to question is taboo*, and the fact that a parent refuses his blessing, for whatever reason, is understood as "fate" or "God's will." But all this is of course a prelude to the unrestrained group violence of *pugachevshchina* (the Pugachev uprising), over which Vasilisa Egorovna has no control and in the wake of which she and her husband will be brutally murdered. When the time finally comes for Ivan Kuzmich and his troops to defend the fort and fight

Pugachev and his rebels in earnest, the matriarchal structure disappears in a flash.

Significantly, the darker, id-like elements of the Russian family romance begin to make themselves felt *before* Pugachev actually mounts his assault on the Belogorsk Fortress. First, the Cossacks become restless, a sure sign that they have advance knowledge and are preparing to switch sides. Then an old Bashkir, who is captured distributing seditious pamphlets, refuses to divulge his sources and is about to be tortured by Ivan Kuzmich's people when it is learned that he was one of the ones punished in the wake of an earlier (1741) rebellion and is, on closer inspection, not only horribly disfigured—"his nose and ears were missing"—but has a stump for a tongue and therefore cannot be forced to talk.[43] Obviously, the brutality in these relations has always gone both ways, which is part of the problem. Vasilisa Egorovna, who has been in command of the fort up to now, leaves before the men begin physically to assault the Bashkir. Not unlike the august matriarch who is her parodic model, she is in favor of obtaining the needed results through any means available but would prefer for the men to do the dirty work, saying euphemistically, "To tell the truth, I am not fond of searches/interrogations" (Ia, pravdu skazat', ne okhotitsa do rozyska).[44] Next, the news arrives that another neighboring fort, Nizhne-Ozernaia, has fallen to Pugachev, and that the commandant and all his officers have been hanged, his soldiers taken prisoner.

Here Pushkin again draws the shadow of *The History of Pugachev* into the novel by citing (understatedly) the actual horrific fates of Nizhne-Ozernaia's Major Kharlov and his wife Lizaveta (in chapter 3 of the *History*) and by having Grinev, who has only recently met them, express shock and dismay at their deaths. Our last picture of Major Kharlov before he is hanged in the *History* is of a half-mad warrior who is fighting virtually alone (his Cossack troops have deserted and those remaining are too old to defend themselves effectively) against an overwhelming enemy and who is bleeding profusely from multiple wounds. One of his eyes, which is dangling over his cheek, has been poked out by a lance. Lizaveta, whom Kharlov manages to send to her father Colonel Elagin at Tatishcheva before the battle at Nizhne-Ozernaia begins, is forced to become Pugachev's concubine (the fate continuously threatening Masha in the novel) when Tatishcheva also falls. She is eventually savagely killed by the peasant tsar's jealous lieutenants, and Colonel Elagin is skinned alive by the rebels, who use the fat from his corpulent body as salve for their wounds.

For anyone with even the slightest knowledge of the Pugachev uprising, it is clear we are in the process of crossing the threshold into a terrifyingly different realm, one where notions of "enlightenment" (Catherine's mask) are totally absent and where barbaric cruelty reigns supreme. Unable to smuggle Masha out to a safe haven, Ivan Kuzmich blesses his wife and daughter, says his last goodbyes, and then tells Vasilisa Egorovna to take Masha away, as "this is no place for women" (zdes' ne bab'e delo).[45] When Pugachev and his troops overrun the Belogorsk Fortress, everything is turned upside down in an atmosphere of carnival savagery. What was stable is fluid, what safe, dangerous. Now the sacred and the demonic overlap in a zone magnetized by taboo. Those loyal to the crown who refuse to swear an oath to the new sovereign, like Ivan Kuzmich and Ivan Ignat'ich, are summarily hanged. Vasilisa Egorovna, stripped naked and presumably raped, sees her murdered husband, screams out in despair, and is struck dead with a single blow by a rebel's saber. The woman's padded jacket, or *dushegreika* (literally, "soul warmer") that was her trademark is now seen being worn by one of the strutting Cossacks.[46] Her uncovered body will lie where it was struck down indefinitely. On threat of death, the impostor forces all the men to swear allegiance and have their hair cut in a circular bob, Cossack-style.

It is at this point that Grinev's dream plays out in reality. As the folkloric third (a magic number) about to be hanged after Ivan Kuzmich and Ivan Ignat'ich, Grinev prepares to accept his fate, especially in light of the fact that the traitor Shvabrin has just whispered some presumably damning evidence in Pugachev's ear. Phrases from the dream—the substandard "Ne bos', ne bos'" (Don't be afraid, don't be afraid) spoken to Grinev as he is being led to the gallows and the command "Tselui ruku, tselui ruku" (Kiss his hand, kiss his hand) after he has been granted mercy—now resurface as a test of manhood and honor, which he passes by not begging for his life and not kissing the impostor's hand. Shvabrin, on the other hand, who comes from St. Petersburg society and has already behaved dishonorably in his previous actions, demonstrates no qualms about changing sides; indeed, as the text suggests, he had been planning to do so all along. His Cossack haircut shows his survival-at-all-costs instincts and his disrespect for his own roots.[47]

But the larger point about Grinev's exposure to the rebel camp (chaps. 8 and 11) is that the "contagion" that should rub off on him from his interactions with the wolflike impostor (the taboo) does not in any essential way. Yes, he will be arrested for treason toward the end of the novel (again, Shvabrin's doing), but through it all his conscience remains clear. His extravagant gift of the *tulup* to the stranger on his initial trip to the Belogorsk Fortress turns out to be the lucky charm (the *sluchai*, the "random" good deed) that saves him at the gallows. For Pugachev recognizes the meddlesome Savel'ich, who emerges from the crowd right before Grinev is strung up and pleads before the "father" (otets rodnoi) that he, an old man, be taken in place of the "child" (the folksy "ditia"). And in this instance Pugachev *does* act like the merciful father. This same reference to "rodnoi otets" (one's very own father) is repeated ironically a little later in the novel when Petr appeals to the general in Orenburg to provide him with a detachment so that he can return to Belogorsk Fortress to save Masha. There Shvabrin has taken charge as Pugachev's man and is pressuring Masha to marry him. Grinev implores the general: "'Your excellency,' I said to him, "I am turning to you as I would to my own father [*kak k ottsu rodnomu*]; for the love of God, please do not refuse my request."[48] But this father figure (representing the state) declines the request, which means that Grinev, if he wants to save Masha and protect her honor, must play by outside rules—that is, he must act in the realm of taboo.

In an impulsive act, but one that has no hint of immaturity about it, Grinev sets off for the Belogorsk Fortress in hopes that somehow he will be able to free Masha on his own. The loyal but dawdling Savel'ich accompanies him, and the two are recaptured by Pugachev's forces. When he is brought before the peasant leader, the hero seizes the opportunity with an inspired idea, another proof that he is no longer simply a *nedorosl'*: "A strange thought entered my mind: it seemed to me that providence, bringing me face to face with Pugachev a second time, was presenting me with an opportunity [*sluchai*] to execute my plans. I resolved to take advantage of it."[49] Despite his advisers' objections, Pugachev is won over by the very same logic that started the two men's relationship in the first place: "'One good turn deserves another [*Dolg platezhom krasen*], he said with a wink and a twinkle in his eye."[50] It is during this exchange, when technically Grinev is violating the prohibition of his officer's oath of allegiance by consorting with the enemy (and in this respect *not* "preserving his honor from a tender age"), that Pugachev agrees to be the proxy father: the one who arranges for Grinev's safe return to the Belogorsk Fortress and who, after the confrontation with Shvabrin, "gives away" the orphan in marriage. Even when Shvabrin, who shamelessly begs Pugachev's forgiveness for having taken advantage of an orphan, exposes the fact that Masha is the daughter of Captain Mironov, Pugachev does not reverse his decision: "'Oh, well, let it be as you say,' he said. 'Hang him or spare him [*kaznit' tak kaznit', zhalovat' tak zhalovat'*]: don't do things by halves.'"[51]

In writing *The Captain's Daughter* Pushkin was clearly trying to return to an older set of precepts and values, ones determined in the harsh, often wartime conditions of the eighteenth century, that (as he perceived it) didn't allow space for nuance and interpretation. In his compromised situation in the last years of his life it was this old-fashioned clarity, especially when defending the honor of one's family and name, for which he yearned. The essence of this clarity is the ability of a gesture to be beautiful in its own right, to possess both a moral and aesthetic dimension, to stand alone as something proving nobility of character at a moment when that character is most severely challenged. In *The History of Pugachev* the most impressive example of such a gesture is when the Muslim Bikbai, preparing to be executed by Pugachev's forces, crosses himself and puts his own head into the noose.[52] By giving the fictional Pugachev the ability to recognize the beauty in a deed and to show generosity, that is, to repay beauty with more beauty, Pushkin was improving on the reality of the uprising in two ways. First, he was showing that, despite the ancient class distrust and the factors that led to the uprising in the first place, both peasant and nobleman could share a sense of honor.[53] Second, he was showing that this "paying it forward" has a way of breaking through class enmity and establishing relations in more human terms, which is Iurii Lotman's point in his celebrated piece on the "ideational structure" of *The Captain's Daughter*.[54] When Pugachev learns that Shvabrin is holding an orphan hostage and possibly abusing her, he is moved to act. The weak should not be taken advantage of by the strong. Likewise, when it becomes clear that Masha is the daughter of his sworn enemy and Pugachev still decides to continue in his role as matchmaker/surrogate father and to release the young couple, the result is similar: the moral and the aesthetic come together in an extravagantly beautiful gesture of being big enough as a person (lichnost') not to keep score.

To return to our opening comments, it is this idea of honor that Catherine's matriarchy has corrupted and that now has come back to haunt the monarch as a broad-based, frenzied male id that wreaks havoc because it has been too long denied and insulted. The taboo knowledge that Grinev acquires as his story of maturation merges with his country's trials is precisely the humanity that resides in the fictional

Pugachev, the imagined Pugachev, the Pugachev who can, through luck or chance, be approached and engaged with:

"Listen," I continued, seeing his favorable mood. "I don't know what to call you, and I don't wish to know. . . . But God is my witness, I'd be glad to repay you with my life for what you've done for me. Only don't demand of me anything that is against my honor and my Christian conscience. You are my benefactor. Please conclude the matter as you began it: let me and the poor orphan go free, wherever God will guide us. And wherever you may be, whatever may happen to you, we will pray to God every day to save your sinful soul."[55]

This is a humanity that, whatever its sins and outrages, deserves compassion ("we will pray to God every day to save your soul"), but that also needs existential bracketing ("don't demand of me anything that is against my honor and my Christian conscience"). One can try to understand the human incarnation. However, one can not, must not, give oneself wholly to it.

To sum up, the forbidden knowledge Grinev takes away from his time with the man who is the archenemy of the realm, the ghost of the husband Catherine had deposed, is essentially the following. First, this man acts as a father by exposing Petr to, but also in an uncanny way protecting him from, a world he would not have known otherwise—a world where men have been turned into wolves not only by their blood-thirsty and brute nature but more importantly by other men. Grinev was allowed to witness life in the wolf pack without becoming a wolf himself. Life as a werewolf (oboroten'), half man, half wolf, is better lived on the monster's terms: it is more honorable, according to the dark Kalmyk fairy tale Pugachev tells to Grinev as a way of explaining his behavior, to be an eagle and drink once-living blood than to be a raven and survive three hundred years on carrion.[56] And knowing this, even if the knowledge is vicarious through Pugachev, is the same as being *inspired,* since inspiration for Pushkin is always about risk and about playing at the edges of taboo.

Second, with this taboo knowledge the son is now able to address the new father figure accurately and appropriately: he is neither tsar, nor *batiushka,* nor runaway convict (katorzhnik) but is in a category of his own, the unnamable: "I don't know what to call you, and I don't wish to know." "Only God knows." In other words, Petr is searching in his mind for a word that does not imply judgment, either from the viewpoint of the rebels ("tsar") or from that of the crown ("impostor").

Pugachev's true relation to Grinev is that of *benefactor* ("good deed doer"). *Dolia* (lot, fate) and *dolg* (debt, obligation) are existentially interrelated for Pushkin: the obligation one feels to one's past, roots, tribal way of looking at things, is virtually coextensive with one's fate, with the hand one has been dealt by life. Shvabrin has no sense of *dolg*, no constraints of *dolia* that limit his ability to change disguises and camps, and in this respect he possesses a kind of total *volia* whose only requirement is survival at all costs.[57] But Grinev and Pugachev have different perceptions of the *volia* within their *dolia/dolg*: Pugachev knows he will be captured and executed without mercy—"My path is narrow: I've little freedom [*voli mne malo*]."[58] Likewise, as the grateful son, Petr is willing to repay his debt to Pugachev with his life, just as he is willing to pray for the rebel's sinful soul, but what he can't do is sacrifice to the benefactor his honor or his Christian conscience.

Third, chief among this wolf-man's benefactions to the hero is his patriarchal role in saving Masha and her honor. In the end it is as if the wolf is giving away Red Riding Hood at her own wedding. Here the taboo lurking in the background is not incest, the prohibition against marrying within the clan and the concomitant requirement of exogamy, but that of rape. It is never stated explicitly in the text that Shvabrin forces himself on Masha, although she looks "disheveled" (s rastrepannymi volosami) when Pugachev and Grinev finally demand that Shvabrin unlock the door into the room where she is being held prisoner. This is also the aspect of the unbridled male id that is always threatening to break through the surface as Pugachev's forces overrun Catherine's matriarchy. Our last picture of Vasilisa Egorovna is of a naked female body left to rot in plain sight; if Masha does not succumb to Shvabrin's demands that she marry him and give him the sexual access he has been after all along, her fate will be the same as that of Lizaveta Kharlova—that is, she will become the sex slave of the man who murdered her parents.

The taboo knowledge that Grinev acquires through his adventures with Pugachev the "proxy father" indeed saves Masha from the dishonor of becoming Shvabrin's wife. But this same knowledge is not enough to save Grinev from the dishonor of his own arrest and trial. Once again Shvabrin is given the opportunity to denounce his former friend by telling the authorities that Grinev had conspired with Pugachev. Ironically yet also appropriately, Grinev will not attempt to defend his own honor because to do so would mean to enter into the details of Masha's captivity at the hands of Shvabrin. Even to mention that situation would require a testimony on her part, one that would go into the deaths of her parents and her abuse by Shvabrin, that Petr, who is now her only protector and her *batiushka*, won't allow.[59] In his mind, her sense of honor trumps his own; he has given away the honor he promised to preserve in his first parting from his father in order to protect the honor of someone he now considers family.

This is of course the climactic moment in the novel, when Masha ceases to be a victim of *pugachevshchina* and becomes an historical actor (or more accurately, a fictional representative of an historical actor) in her own right. She must, à la Jeanie Deans, find a way to see the empress and make her case for her unfairly sentenced loved one.[60] Just as Pugachev dressed up to be the peasant tsar, wearing a red kaftan with tassels and riding a white charger, so now does Catherine, in her "chance" encounter with Masha in the garden, dress down for the occasion. When the two women come upon each other Catherine is wearing a simple padded coat, a *dushegreika* ("soul warmer") like the one that Vasilisa Egorovna was often seen in during her days at Belogorsk Fortress and that the Cossack paraded around in on the day Masha's mother was killed and her body left on the porch of the commandant's home. This is the poetic justice and the poetic symmetry Pushkin creates as a counterweight to the unrestrained brutality and senselessness of the Pugachev rebellion. If Pugachev can be refashioned by fiction from a wolf into a man with his own simple yet genuine code of honor, then Catherine can also be refashioned by the same fiction from the Terrible Mother of the 1822 historical notes to the Good Mother who is convinced by Masha's story and publicly acknowledges, through a letter that becomes a family heirloom, Grinev's innocence.

Masha, the young woman orphaned by her parents' service to the state, has come to ask not for court justice (pravosudie) but mercy (milost'), the generosity of spirit that Pugachev had himself shown toward Grinev ("kaznit' tak kaznit', milovat' tak milovat'"). And just as Pugachev's "stern soul" had been "touched" (tronuta) by Grinev's sincerity, so now is the good lady, in what had been in the earlier document her corrupt and corrupting soul, also "moved" (tronuta) by the visitor's tale.[61] Soon after Masha has reprised her story, she is called to the court to see the empress and is asked to come as she is, in "her traveling dress" (v dorozhnom plat'e)—a lovely concluding situational rhyme to the *dushegreika*. Catherine's final words to Masha acknowledge her "debt before the daughter of Captain Mironov" (ia v dolgu pered docher'iu kapitana Mironova).[62] The equilibrium in Russia's family romance has been restored (momentarily) through fiction, if not through history. In the final analysis, the forbidden knowledge about Pugachev and his uprising that Pushkin's novel imparts to the reader is not simply that they existed (if Catherine had had her way, all evidence of this tragic episode would have been expunged from historical memory) but that their existence at some level, despite the horrific carnage, is understandable.[63] They were the return of the repressed on a mass level, the haunting of Russian history by memories impossible to forget.

Notes

1. See, e.g., Caryl Emerson, "Grinev's Dream: *The Captain's Daughter* and a Father's Blessing," *Slavic Review* 40.1 (Spring 1981): 60–76.

2. With regard to the use of different forms of popular speech in *The Captain's Daughter*, see Wolf Schmid, *Proza Pushkina v poeticheskom prochtenii: "Povesti Belkina"* (St. Petersburg: Izdatel'stvo Sankt-Peterburgskogo universiteta, 1996), 226–37.

3. *Boris Godunov*, written in 1824–25 and published in 1831, is an obvious close competitor, but it is still "Shakespearean" and the conscious product of its blank verse form.

4. Sigmund Freud, *Totem and Taboo: Some Points of Agreement Between the Mental Lives of Savages and Neurotics*, trans. and ed. James Strachey (New York: Norton, 1950), 141, 132–33.

5. I use the term "family romance" in this chapter in the classical Freudian sense of the child who begins to question the authority of the parent (usually the one that is the same sex as the child) and tries to find his proper place in the larger social world. As Freud writes, "The freeing of an individual, as he grows up, from the authority of his parents is one of the most necessary though one of the most painful results brought about by the course of his development" ("Family Romances," *Collected Papers*, vol. 5, ed. James Strachey [New York: Basic Books, 1959], 74).

6. Ibid., 87.

7. Ibid., 86.

8. Aleksandr S. Pushkin, "Zametki po russkoi istorii XVIII veka," in his *Polnoe sobranie sochinenii*, 17 vols., ed. Vladimir D. Bonch-Bruevich et al. (Moscow: AN SSSR, 1937–59), 11:15–16.

9. See Tomashevsky's editorial comment in Aleksandr S. Pushkin, *Polnoe sobranie sochinenii*, 10 vols., ed. Boris V. Tomashevskii (Leningrad: Nauka, 1977–79), 8:388.

10. See Erich Neumann, *The Great Mother: An Analysis of the Archetype*, trans. Ralph Manheim, 2nd ed. (Princeton: Princeton University Press, 1963), 168.

11. Aleksandr S. Pushkin, *Kapitanskaia dochka,* in his *Polnoe sobranie sochinenii,* 17 vols., 8:322.

12. Aleksandr S. Pushkin, *Istoriia Pugacheva,* in his *Polnoe sobranie sochinenii,* 17 vols., 9:45.

13. Ibid., 9:9.

14. Ibid., 9:10. The Cossacks had been divided into two factions early in the eighteenth century: the "Ataman" (from Ataman Merkur'ev) and the "Longinov" (from Lieutenant-Colonel Longinov), or "popular" (narodnaia). It was the Longinov faction that was the more unruly, so that eventually, by the time of the 1770s uprisings, the two were generally referred to as the "obedient" (poslushnaia) and "disobedient" (neposlushnaia).

15. Pushkin, *Istoriia Pugacheva,* 9:12; Alexander Pushkin, *A History of Pugachev,* in *Complete Prose Fiction,* trans. Paul Debreczeny (Stanford: Stanford University Press, 1983), 368.

16. Pushkin, *Kapitanskaia dochka,* 8:282; Alexander Pushkin, *The Captain's Daughter,* in *Complete Prose Fiction,* 269.

17. Technically speaking, of course, *-odu* and *-ovu* cannot be called a rhyme pair because the consonants and stresses are different, but it is clear that Pushkin is playing with a version of internal rhyme here.

18. Sergei Davydov, "The Sound and Theme in the Prose of A. S. Puskin: A Logo-Semantic Study of Paromomasia," *Slavic and East European Journal* 27.1 (1983): 1–18, esp. 13. See also Wolf Schmid's excellent studies in a similar vein: *Proza Pushkina v poeticheskom prochtenii,* esp. 88–92, 226–37; and "Sud'ba i kharakter: O motivirovke v *Kapitanskoi dochke,*" in his *Proza kak poeziia* (St. Petersburg: Inapress, 1998), 89–102.

19. See David Bethea, "Slavic Gift-Giving, the Poet in History, and Pushkin's *The Captain's Daughter,*" in *Russian Subjects: Nation, Empire, and the Culture of the Golden Age,* ed. Monika Greenleaf and Stephen Moeller-Sally (Evanston: Northwestern University Press, 1998), 259–73, 422–29. Davydov discusses in depth the ***platit'/plat'e/tulup*** sound play and the latter's relation to plot in his "The Sound and Theme in the Prose of A. S. Puskin," 9–15.

20. Although apparently not related etymologically (see Maks Fasmer, *Etimologicheskii slovar' russkogo iazyka v chetyrekh tomakh,* ed. Boris A. Larin, 3rd ed. [St. Petersburg: Azbuka, 1996], 1:524, 526), *dolg* and *dolia* play similar roles in the narrative of *The Captain's Daughter* through the notion of "that part" of one's personal situation in the world that is given, not negotiable, the same as one's "fate."

21. Pushkin, *Kapitanskaia dochka,* 8:285; *The Captain's Daughter,* 272. I have modified the translation slightly here to allow the proper emphasis on "volia" (liberty, will, license).

22. Pushkin borrows a line from Fonvizin—the "zealous guardian of all my cash and linen, indeed of all my business" (i deneg, i bel'ia, i del moikh rachitel')—to describe Savel'ich's role (*Kapitanskaia dochka,* 8:284). The quotation is from Fonvizin's "Epistle to My Servants Shumilov, Van'ka and Petrushka"

("Poslanie k slugam moim: Shumilovu, Van'ke i Petrushke" [1770]). The description applies to Shumilov (Pushkin, *Polnoe sobranie sochinenii,* 10 vols., 8:537).

23. Pushkin, *Kapitanskaia dochka,* 8:288; *The Captain's Daughter,* 275.

24. "The wolf, according to tradition, is the most amiable and by nature most closely related [*rodnoe*] incarnation of the werewolf, and indeed many wolves are in actuality werewolves" (Abram Terts [Andrei Siniavskii], "Puteshestvie na Chernuiu rechku," *Syntaxis* 34 [1994]: 29).

25. On Pugachev's wolf-like character, see Terts, "Puteshestvie na Chernuiu rechku," 30. Elsewhere Terts quotes from the Russian folk tradition (Pushkin's *skazka*-like *Ruslan and Liudmila*) to show how the wolf (Pugachev) comes to the aid of the imprisoned tsarevna (Mar'ia Ivanovna): "There in the dungeon the tsarevna pines, while the brown wolf serves her faithfully" (V temnitse tam tsarevna tuzhit, / A buryi volk ei verno sluzhit) (28).

26. As part of his inheritance from Pushkin, Grinev received a secret trust in fate. In other words, in fateful situations he relies on chance, "giving himself over to God's will" (Terts, "Puteshestvie na Chernuiu rechku," 16).

27. Pushkin, *Kapitanskaia dochka,* 8:288; *The Captain's Daughter,* 275.

28. Pushkin, *Kapitanskaia dochka,* 8:289; *The Captain's Daughter,* 276.

29. The importance of fairy-tale plot dynamics in *The Captain's Daughter* was first noted by Igor P. Smirnov, "Ot skazki k romanu," in *Istoriia zhanrov v russkoi literature X–XVII vv.,* ed. Aleksandr M. Panchenko (Leningrad: Nauka, 1973), 284–320, esp. 310. The prodigal son motif becomes prominent in Pushkin's mature period, particularly in works like *The Blackamoor of Peter the Great* (*Arap Petra Velikogo* [1827]), where Gannibal returns to his godfather the tsar to help him build a new Russia after leading a frivolous life in Paris, and "The Stationmaster" ("Stantsionnyi smotritel'" [1830]), where the presumably "prodigal daughter" Dunia, who is actually not prodigal, returns to pay respects at her father's grave at the end of the story after Vyrin has himself acted "prodigally" and drunk himself to ruin. Indeed, on an autobiographical note, the story of the prodigal son seems to have been one of Pushkin's favorites because he hoped through his own work he would one day be forgiven for his rash youthful behavior and be restored to a position of dignity next to the "father" (whether that father was God or a far-seeing, merciful tsar). Obviously with regard to his own life, Pushkin was sorely disappointed in the "wise" and "merciful" behavior of the tsars he knew.

30. For the connection between "Little Red Riding Hood" and Grinev's dream, see Iurii Shcheglov, "Zagadki i nakhodki 'Stantsionnogo smotritelia,'" in *Etkindovskie chteniia II–III: Sbornik statei po materialam Chtenii pamiati E. G. Etkinda* (St. Petersburg: Izdatel'stvo Evropeiskogo universiteta, 2006), 32.

31. Pushkin, *Kapitanskaia dochka,* 8:289; *The Captain's Daughter,* 276.

32. Freud, *Totem and Taboo,* 29.

33. Ibid.

34. Pushkin, *Kapitanskaia dochka*, 8:289; *The Captain's Daughter*, 276.

35. Freud, *Totem and Taboo*, 29.

36. Pushkin, *Kapitanskaia dochka*, 8:290; *The Captain's Daughter*, 278.

37. Pushkin, *Kapitanskaia dochka*, 8:291; *The Captain's Daughter*, 278.

38. Pushkin, *Kapitanskaia dochka*, 8:291; *The Captain's Daughter*, 279.

39. Pushkin, *Kapitanskaia dochka*, 8:295; *The Captain's Daughter*, 282.

40. Emerson, "Grinev's Dream," 66.

41. Pushkin, *Kapitanskaia dochka*, 8:297; *The Captain's Daughter*, 284–85.

42. Pushkin, *Kapitanskaia dochka*, 8:299; *The Captain's Daughter*, 286. I have slightly modified the translation here to reflect more accurately Pushkin's syntax.

43. Pushkin, *Kapitanskaia dochka*, 8:318; *The Captain's Daughter*, 304.

44. Pushkin, *Kapitanskaia dochka*, 8:317; *The Captain's Daughter*, 304. Again, I have modified the translation to suggest a more literal reading: "rozysk" not as "torture" but as the less threatening, more neutral "search/interrogation."

45. Pushkin, *Kapitanskaia dochka*, 8:323; *The Captain's Daughter*, 309. Compare Kharlov's strategy of relocating Elizaveta with her father at Tatishcheva in the *History of Pugachev* with Kuzmich's inability to smuggle Masha out.

46. The *dushegreika* is an important leitmotif that reappears at the end of the novel.

47. Intriguingly, Pushkin seems to give Shvabrin his own physical attributes, and in the earlier drafts of the text Grinev and Shvabrin had been one person: "The next morning I had only begun to dress when the door opened and a young officer, not very tall, with a swarthy face that was strikingly unattractive, but exceptionally lively [*molodoi ofitser nevysokogo rosta, s litsom smuglym i otmenno nekrasivym, no chrezvychaino zhivym*], came into the room" (*Kapitanskaia dochka*, 8:296; *The Captain's Daughter*, 283). The physical description of Shvabrin's person as "a young officer, not very tall, with a swarthy face that was strikingly unattractive but exceptionally lively" is an obvious self-portrait. The connection is made in Emerson, "Grinev's Dream," 67n29. As Tomashevsky notes in his commentary: "The core of the novel's conception is the story of M. Shvanvich. He alone was supposed to be the hero of the novel. The division of one hero into two—the positive Grinev and the negative Shvabrin—took place in the last phase of Pushkin's work. All the drafts speak about one hero" (Pushkin, *Polnoe sobranie sochinenii*, 10 vols., 6:534).

48. Pushkin, *Kapitanskaia dochka*, 8:342–43; *The Captain's Daughter*, 328.

49. Pushkin, *Kapitanskaia dochka*, 8:348; *The Captain's Daughter*, 332.

50. Pushkin, *Kapitanskaia dochka*, 8:350; *The Captain's Daughter*, 334.

51. Pushkin, *Kapitanskaia dochka*, 8:356; *The Captain's Daughter*, 340.

52. Pushkin, *Istoriia Pugacheva*, 9:19.

53. See, for example, the fine discussion in Terts, "Puteshestvie na Chernuiu rechku," 40–51, esp. 44–45.

54. Iurii D. Lotman, "Ideinaia struktura *Kapitanskoi dochki*," in *Pushkinskii sbornik*, ed. M. T. Efimova et al. (Pskov: Pskovskii gosudarstvennyi pedagogicheskii institut im. S. M. Kirova, 1962), 3–20.

55. Pushkin, *Kapitanskaia dochka*, 8: 356; *The Captain's Daughter*, 340.

56. See Terts, "Puteshestvie na Chernuiu rechku," 29.

57. It could be argued of course that it is Shvabrin who is the ultimate taboo figure, the one whose behavior is the most tainting, and literally, from Grinev's viewpoint, this is true. However, because Shvabrin has no honor and is willing to do anything to save himself, he cannot be the *transitional* (i.e., totemic) authority figure, the figure who straddles the sacred and the demonic, that Pugachev can.

58. Pushkin, *Kapitanskaia dochka*, 8:352; *The Captain's Daughter*, 336.

59. This term, patriarchal and old fashioned, would obviously be inappropriate for a wife to use when referring to her husband in today's Western pluralistic culture(s). However, in the eighteenth-century context Pushkin is attempting to re-create it would not be far-fetched.

60. In Walter Scott's novel *Heart of Midlothian*, heroine Jeanie Deans walks to London to request a pardon for her sister, who has been unjustly accused of infanticide. On the *Heart of Midlothian* subtext see Melissa Frazier, "*Kapitanskaia dochka* and the Creativity of Borrowing," *Slavic and East European Journal* 37.4 (1993): 472–89.

61. Cf. Pushkin, *Kapitanskaia dochka*, 8:356 and 372.

62. Pushkin, *Kapitanskaia dochka*, 8:374; *The Captain's Daughter*, 356. I have again slightly modified the translation to render the phrasing (and syntax) more accurately.

63. Cf. Pushkin's famous phrase in the so-called omitted chapter of *The Captain's Daughter*: "May the Lord save us from another such senseless and ruthless Russian rebellion" (Ne privedi bog videt' russkii bunt—bessmyslennyi i besposhchadnyi) (Pushkin, *Kapitanskaia dochka*, 8:383; *The Captain's Daughter*, 450).

Through the Lens of Soviet Psychoanalysis and Utopian Dreams of the 1920s

Ivan Ermakov's Readings of Pushkin's Poetry

ALEXANDRA SMITH

The collapse of the Soviet Union in 1991 led to the revival of several approaches to literature that were previously treated as taboo subjects, including psychoanalysis. One example is the legacy of Ivan Dmitrievich Ermakov (1875–1942), a psychiatrist, artist, translator, and literary critic, whose previously published and unpublished essays on Pushkin, Gogol, and Dostoevsky appeared in Russia in book form in 1999.[1]

Ermakov was a major force in the advancement of the psychoanalytic approach to fine arts and literature in the Soviet Union: he was the first president of the Russian Psychoanalytic Society and one of the founders of the State Psychoanalytic Institute in Moscow in 1921 (it was closed in 1925), as well as an editor of the nine-volume series of Freud's work in Russian translation—the only officially approved translation of Freud during the Soviet period.[2] His books on Pushkin, Gogol, and Dostoevsky (published in 1919, 1923, and 1924, respectively) testify to the popularity of Freud's ideas in Russian literary criticism in the 1910s and 1920s. In the 1930s, when the psychoanalytic approach to literature was suppressed in favor of the socialist realist aesthetic, Ermakov had to work as a private consultant. He was arrested in 1941, and in 1942 he died in prison in Saratov. Although Ermakov was rehabilitated posthumously in 1959, his works were republished in Russia only in the post-Soviet period. The present chapter assesses Ermakov's contribution to the formation of the Pushkin myth in 1920s Soviet Russia, focusing on Ermakov's eclectic approach to Pushkin's life and works that incorporates both Marxist and Freudian ideas. Ermakov, I argue, subordinates his psychoanalytic method to his aim of promoting a notion of "culturedness" (kul'turnost') and the role of the irrational in literature.[3] Clearly, Ermakov had in mind a new Soviet reader capable of responding creatively to historical developments in the style of Pushkin. Although Ermakov's interpretation of Pushkin's works sounds too utilitarian in places, it sheds light on the rich interaction between art and life during the radical remaking of Soviet society in the 1920s.[4]

Ermakov in his 1923 volume on Pushkin describes his approach as an "organic" method of literary analysis that considers the form and content of a poem as well as the psyche of its author.[5] Such a conception of art has its roots in European romanticism and promotes a dialectical and symbolist view of poetry.[6] Ermakov deals primarily with *The Little House in Kolomna* (*Domik v Kolomne*) and the *Little Tragedies* (*Malen'kie tragedii*). In a nutshell, Ermakov argues that *Little House in Kolomna* reflects Pushkin's conflicting emotions on the eve of his marriage to Natalia Goncharova. In Ermakov's opinion, Pushkin wanted to marry Goncharova but at the same time feared the marriage and wished to escape it. The unresolved tension is translated into the unresolved plot of *Little House in Kolomna*. Ermakov's analysis of three poems included in the volume—"The Rabble" ("Chern'"), "I built myself a monument not made by human hands ("Ia pamiatnik sebe vozdvig nerukotvornyi"), and "Desire" ("Zhelanie")—reinforces his thesis that Pushkin in his self and his art is a poet of contradictions and conflicting emotions. Ermakov sees the inner emotional struggle expressed in Pushkin's writings as a manifestation of his "dynamic unconscious," which is inseparable from his creative process.[7] Ermakov's survey of contrasting aspects of Pushkin's creative psychology provides insight into Pushkin's "artistic laboratory" and presents the Russian national poet as a craftsman who values labor, introspection, and self-control.

By promoting Pushkin as an enlightened poet who could master his emotions and attain a higher consciousness through his creative activity,

Ermakov casts himself as an active participant in the cultural revolution, which might be seen as a two-stage process that took place in the 1920s and 1930s.[8] During its first, New Economic Policy period, such notions as "culturedness" and "self-enlightenment" were promoted widely as part of Bolshevik attempts to bring consciousness to the masses—despite the fact that many Bolshevik theoreticians could not agree on what culture was and what it should be.[9] Nevertheless, Lenin's notion of cultural revolution that focused on the habits of "civilized" societies and on the twin goals of overcoming "barbarism" and mastering science and technology inspired Soviet utopian thinkers to broaden the vision of proletarian culture offered by Proletkult activists.[10] Many Soviet critics, including Laborsh Kalmanson (pseudonym G. Lelevich), talked about the construction of new forms of life that would replace the old notion of everyday life, and many publications produced for educational purposes in the 1920s listed the qualities expected from those who were involved in cultural activities, propaganda, and education: acquisition of knowledge, "culturedness," self-governance, good time management, and moral principles that were subordinated to the new methods of regulating everyday life.[11]

In the 1920s the artistic avant-garde contributed to this formulation of ideologically correct forms of everyday behavior in response to Marxists' theoretical statements linking cultural revolution to reworking nature and reconfiguring people's personality characteristics, everyday habits, and feelings in the new Soviet context.[12] Ermakov's discussion of Pushkin's ability to rationalize his emotions might be seen as an expression of his utopian desire to present Pushkin as a model figure that could be used for the formation of a new Soviet man in the style of utopian experiment and speculation (these would become taboo subjects during the 1930s). In light of the ongoing drive to create "cultured" behaviors, Ermakov's effort to bring together literature, science, and psychoanalysis does not look coincidental: to a great extent in the 1920s, revolutionary self-fashioning and the transformation of others were interconnected.

Indeed, Ermakov's essays on Pushkin provide us with useful insights into a period of important cultural and social change that triggered many debates about the usefulness of Freud's works for Soviet literature, education, and Marxist thought. For example, Alexander Voronsky, one of the advocates of Freudian approaches to literature and an editor of the influential literary journal *Krasnaia nov'* (*Red Virgin Soil*), expressed his positive view of the significance of the unconscious to writers and critics on several occasions throughout the 1920s. Voronsky suggested that Soviet literary critics should possess a special sensitivity to the unconscious so as to be able to evaluate "the extent to which the various deeds of a hero are internally motivated and consistent with his nature."[13] In his 1925 article ""Psychoanalysis as a Method of Investigating Imaginative Literature" ("Psikhoanaliz kak metod issledovaniia khudozhestvennoi literatury"), I. A. Grigor'ev welcomes Ermakov's exploration of the unconscious while rejecting Freud's interpretation of sexuality.[14]

In contrast to Ermakov, Isai D. Sapir, a member of the Communist Academy in Moscow, makes a distinction between the sociological dimension of Freud's work and the psychological core of his theory in his 1926 article "Freudism and Marxism" ("Freidizm i marksizm"). Sapir's article highlights the inadequacies and contradictions of Freud's major concepts, including the idea of the reality of the unconscious. In Sapir's opinion, psychological mechanisms by themselves cannot explain the existence of ideology and other social phenomena. Sapir asserts that Freud's belief that the unconscious can be analyzed on the individual level, separate from these collective realities, is a serious methodological error.[15] Sapir's criticism of Freud can be easily extended to Ermakov's analysis of Pushkin's and Gogol's works. In a similar way, Roman Jakobson and Dmitrii Mirsky dismissed Ermakov's writings as an expression of "vulgar Freudianism" (vul'garnyi freidizm) and extravagant nonsense.[16] In his 1927 speech "Culture and Socialism," Trotsky (a former member of various Freudian associations organized by Adolf Joffe and Alfred Adler in Vienna) also expressed doubt that the philosophical underpinnings of Freud's ideas were truly materialist. Trotsky saw the Freudian theoretical approach to literature as a hypothesis that supported only some findings of materialist psychology.[17] Valentin N. Voloshinov, an associate of the linguistic philosopher and literary critic Mikhail Bakhtin around whom a circle of artists and scholars gathered in Leningrad during the early 1920s, also directed his efforts against the rising influence of psychoanalysis. Voloshinov's 1927 book *Freudianism: A Critical Essay* (*Freidizm: Kriticheskii ocherk*), which dismisses the doctrines of Henri Bergson for their emphasis on intuition and Freudian theory for its preoccupation with sexuality, might be seen as the last substantial examination of Freudianism in the Soviet Union.[18] Voloshinov suggests that Soviet readers' view of Freud's writings is highly reductionist; this view can be characterized by such statements as "the human psyche belongs to the realm of nature" and "human psychic life is part of elemental life."[19]

Furthermore, Freud's unified model of subjectivity—the combination of scientific and literary visions of selves as natural objects and conscious subjects—was seen by the Bolshevik leaders as a model that could undermine their attempt to organize an integrated worldview privileging a politically dominant minority. Ermakov's failure to produce a Marxist theory of literature based on combined psychoanalytic and physiological assessments of selves is comparable to the failure of many formalist critics to construct a Marxist theory of literature during the first Soviet decade. Both the psychoanalytic and formalist approaches were meant to merge literary analysis with science. Yet the theorization of the relationship between the conditions of life and literature that is found in the works of Ermakov and the Russian formalists (both of whom focus on the pragmatic links between literary speech and the contexts it describes and on the nature of literary material) was eliminated from the canon of Marxist theory, as outlined in Lev Trotsky's 1924 book *Literature and Revolution*. As Trotsky puts it, "only Marxism is capable of explaining why and from where a given direction in art has arisen in any given epoch, i.e. who has demanded certain artistic forms and not others, and why."[20] Since Trotsky dismisses many tenets of formalist theory and asserts that art should always be seen as a social servant and as historically utilitarian, neither Ermakov nor the Russian formalists would ultimately be able to subordinate entirely their theoretical approaches to literature to this core principle of dialectical materialism. Viktor Shklovsky's 1929 observation that "Marxists are not to be found" reveals his frustration with the formalists' inability to resolve the difficulties of adapting Marxist social and economic theory to issues of aesthetics.[21] Similar contradictions can be found among those Soviet critics who aspired to merge psychoanalysis and Marxism.

Wilhelm Reich's statement that "psychoanalysis has a future only under socialism because it undermines bourgeois ideology" sheds some light on Ermakov's attempt to reinvent Russian classical authors in accordance with Soviet psychologists' and psychoanalysts' efforts to create a Marxist psychology of mankind.[22] Owing to the absence of any concrete guidance from the founding fathers of communist theory, these efforts were eclectic and often contradictory. The eclectic nature of this utopian project is also felt in Ermakov's Freudian engagement with the Pushkin myth, which can be linked to the aspiration of some

Russian medical professionals (including Vikentii Veresaev) to use literature to shape a healthy outlook on the part of Soviet citizens and provide them with an opportunity to use literary works as models for the creation of new forms of everyday life.[23] Toward the end of the 1920s, the cultural policies of the New Economic Policy period were subjected to severe criticism and eventual suppression. Given the fact that in the Soviet Union, Freud's ideas became taboo beginning in this period, Ermakov's examination of inner conflict and the effects of violence on the human psyche, together with his interest in the therapeutic effects of reading, also came to be deemed unsuitable for the construction of the myth of a happy childhood and the ideology of a "new Soviet man."

Ermakov's writing on Pushkin offers insight into the early stages of the construction of the notion of "culturedness," which is entwined with the principle of self-control and the aesthetic appreciation of labor and craftsmanship.[24] Although Ermakov does not go so far as to present Pushkin as a Soviet writer (often defined in Soviet literature as an "engineer of the human soul"), he demonstrates that Pushkin's life was permeated with the rhetoric of labor and that it was subordinated to the poet's desire to turn his own life into a work of art.[25] Ermakov's analysis also created a mode of reading Pushkin's poetry as an internalized manifestation of the conflict between the poet and his oppressors, especially the bureaucracy and its censors—as did the 1921–22 commemorations of the eighty-fourth anniversary of Pushkin's death, which laid the ground for similar celebrations both in Soviet Russia and in emigration.[26]

Despite all the weaknesses and inconsistencies in Ermakov's readings of Pushkin's works, Ermakov engages with the formalist notion of the autonomy of literature in interesting ways; he is not, however, concerned with the notion of style. Ermakov sees any process of writing, reading, or performing as being essential for the formation of self. He ascribes to Pushkin's art the cathartic potential to help readers transcend contradictory influences and master emotions associated with traumatic experiences and the dark side of human consciousness. Yet his discussion of Pushkin contains a veiled allusion to the cultural and political demand of the Soviet government that was imposed on the average citizen to reconcile life as it was with life as it should be. Ermakov uses his analysis of Pushkin's works as an allegorical attempt to persuade his readers that both sides of life must be acknowledged and that life's contradictions can only be resolved through artistic experiences.

Ermakov's view of Pushkin as a director-like poet who created his own theatrical space in his works enabled such poets and composers as Anna Akhmatova, Marina Tsvetaeva, and Dmitrii Shostakovich to explore the role of the irrational in Pushkin's art.[27] Although we do not find any direct references to Ermakov's volume in their works, their interpretations of Pushkin's creative self and of their own childhood memories display their familiarity with Freud's ideas. For example, Catriona Kelly describes autobiographical narratives of the 1920s–1940s as follows: "In post-revolutionary memoirs, the world of the nursery has often become a darker and bleaker place, closer to the nightmare milieu imagined by Freud. Both in Bely's *Kotik Letaev* (1920) and in the memoir-essays written by Tsvetaeva in Paris (notably, *The House at Old Pimen*, 1934), the inspiration of the future artist was seen to proceed as much out of fear and trauma as out of the spellbinding sensual wonder of early experience. (Zoshchenko's agonized psychoanalytical memoir *Before Sunrise* [1943], searching for the psychic wound in ever earlier layers of the memory, is a belated exercise in the same vein.)"[28]

It is difficult to understand the popular trend of the 1920s of exploring the role of the irrational in literature, a trend that is seen, for example, in the works of Nikolai Osipov on Lev Tolstoi, without Ermakov's analysis of Pushkin's works.[29] Ermakov's pioneering explorations of the dynamic unconscious in Pushkin's works, which suggest that these works might be read as a form of psychodrama, also evoke Alexander Gabrichevsky's notion of space and Nikolai Evreinov's principle of the theatricality of life.[30] It is not coincidental that, in a Ermakov-like manner, Akhmatova later considered the image of Don Juan to be a dramatic embodiment of Pushkin's inner self.[31] It seems that both Ermakov and Akhmatova were influenced by the neo-romantic and Freudian discussions undertaken by Russian and European modernists in the early twentieth century—epitomized in Alfred Adler's 1918 lecture on Dostoevsky—that correlated illness with creativity.[32] Ermakov's interest in signs of neurosis found in Pushkin's writings is likewise in line with Russian and European psychiatrists' model of genius—a model based on specific intellectual assumptions regarding creative individuals that the romantics had appropriated from Greek antiquity, the Italian Renaissance, and the Enlightenment. During the modernist period these ideas were transformed into a system of beliefs that precluded the possibility of total mental health on the part of the creative genius.[33] Yet in the 1920s various Soviet psychiatrists, writers, and critics saw psychoanalysis as a tool that could contribute to the creation of a Marxist creative psychology and a new aesthetics.

The popularity of pathographies in this period testifies to the fact that medical practitioners wanted to influence major cultural developments by analyzing the rich interaction between art and life.[34] Ermakov's reading of Pushkin's *Little Tragedies*, too, invokes the genre of medical biography that had been used by the Russian "Victorians" in the prerevolutionary period as a forum for discussion of social issues related to the creative process. It is clear that Ermakov's interest in Pushkin's personal fears and emotional turmoil resembles his contemporaries' attempts to interpret literary works as expressions of personal anxieties, thereby blurring the boundary between biographical and literary accounts of a writer's life. For example, Russian writer and playwright Ivan Leont'ev-Shcheglov's article "Immodest Conjectures" ("Neskromnye dogadki") invites us to consider Pushkin's images of Mozart and Salieri as a true account of Pushkin's friendship with poet Evgenii Boratynsky; Vasilii Rozanov's essay "Something New on Pushkin" ("Koe-chto novoe o Pushkine") reinforces Shcheglov's interest in Pushkin's subjectivity and interprets Pushkin's Don Juan as an alter ego of the author; Vladislav Khodasevich's article on Pushkin's verse drama *The Water Nymph* (*Rusalka*) offers an autobiographical reading of the text, linking it to Pushkin's affair with a peasant girl who might have committed suicide.[35] All these works raise important questions about the ethics of representation and the interrelationship between art and life; they highlight Pushkin's interest in taboo subjects related to violence and the transgression of social conventions and seek a biographical explanation for that interest.

In a similar vein, Ermakov's principle of the empirical aesthetic implies that the value of any literary analysis can be measured by its correspondence to empirical verification. Such a belief stems from Ermakov's fascination with Dmitrii Pisarev, a Russian critic in the utilitarian mold, whose ideas Ermakov struggled to overcome all his life.[36] Ermakov explains his eclectic combination of psychoanalysis with organicist and formalist criticism in a Pisarev-like utilitarian manner: "At the present time we notice, on the one hand, a great enthusiasm for formalist research which divides the living body of a work of art into separate, lifeless atoms from which it is dreamt that in the distant future, it will be possible again to unite and restore the whole, undivided work."[37] Ermakov's interpretation of Pushkin's identity is closely associated with his belief that the creative process is based on perception and cognition that recognize the importance of the person who senses, knows, or remembers and is capable of transcending his sense of alienation from society. His suggestion that, during the Boldino period,

Pushkin's creative process was a healing tool that enabled him to overcome his anxieties and "get on the right track" illustrates well the utilitarian overtones of Freudian literary criticism.[38] Furthermore, Ermakov's analysis of Pushkin supports the use of the Freudian model as a theory of the normal personality, an approach that was increasingly condemned by Marxist critics.

Dissatisfied with formalist theoretical approaches that limit themselves to exploring only the *materiality* of speech acts, Ermakov goes further than the Russian formalists and pays close attention to the *semantics* of sensual images, expressive gestures, and even phonetic patterns. For example, Ermakov claims that while some lines in Pushkin's poems are abundant in consonants in their first half, expressing a romantic longing for escape and creating a sense of open-endedness, other lines tend to be saturated with consonants in their second part, conveying an impression of a self-contained space and a sense of closure. Moreover, Ermakov juxtaposes paintings and verse to argue that the phonetic organization of verse, alternating the use of vowels and consonants, corresponds to the organization of space found in paintings. He suggests, for example, that the use of the sounds *t, k, p, o,* and *s* in such lines of the poem "The Prophet" ("Prorok") as "na pereput'e mne iavilsia" (on the crossroads there appeared to me) and "i gad morskikh podvodnyi khod" (sea reptiles' underwater crawl) represents the lower realm of being, associated with organic matter.[39] By contrast, excessive use of the vowels *a* and *i* in such lines of the poem as "i gornii angelov polet" (and the celestial flight of angels) and "i shestikrylyi serafim" (and a six-winged seraph) create the impression of an ascending movement.[40] These examples demonstrate Ermakov's strong interest in Pushkin's gifts as a craftsman and as an effective communicator capable of painting with words. Ermakov's analysis suggests that Pushkin's skill at bringing together visual and verbal images could be highly relevant to Soviet educators and writers concerned with the materiality of signs.

Ermakov appears to be fully aware of the research on child language acquisition undertaken by many psychologists in the 1920s, including Lev Vygotsky and Sabina Spielrein (who in 1923 returned from Switzerland to Russia to participate in Ermakov's institute).[41] In his discussion of Pushkin's versification, Ermakov compares metrical patterns found in Pushkin's poetry to the use of iambic and trochaic meter in a child's speech. He claims, for example, that while in a child's speech the iambic meter represents helplessness, sadness, and a disoriented state of mind, the trochaic meter is associated with confidence and self-assurance.[42] Ermakov's observations point to the fact that he reads Pushkin's poetry through the prism of the 1920s debates about the effective use of language and literature for propaganda and educational purposes. Analysis of the childlike qualities of Pushkin's verse was useful to Ermakov and his associates because they were searching for a new form of expression of revolutionary feelings through myth, symbol, ritual, and community.

As Spielrein's findings demonstrate, the pleasure principle and the reality principle could be bridged by analysis of the several stages of language acquisition, including the transitional stage that she defines as the "magical" stage. In other words, a child acquires language thanks to a biological drive, but this "autistic" stage of child development rapidly becomes connected to social necessity following a transitional (magical) state of development.[43] Spielrein's work on child development in the early 1920s emphasizes the role of prosody and talks about the magical stage as being motivated by a force that binds words and deeds. Ermakov interweaves Spielrein's notion of the magical into his reading of Pushkin's poetry and states that every poem has three aspects that correspond to the three drives of self-expression, defined in terms of the three different stages of mythologized self-representation: the first stage is based on the desire to reproduce and repeat, a desire that is especially evident in rhythmical and phonetic patterns of poetic speech; the second stage is associated with the poet's desire to visualize his emotions with the help of visual and sound images; the third stage is related to symbolic language invested with universal appeal. Ermakov sees Pushkin's ability to transcend reality through poetry as an essential part of a ritual-like activity that links performance and imagination.

Ermakov's discussion of Pushkin's 1821 poem "Desire," which speaks of lost love and paradise, develops Spielrein's and Jung's belief that complexes do not belong only to personal experience but are also a product of ancestral experience.[44] In his analysis of this poem, as in his work on Pushkin's *Little Tragedies*, Ermakov surveys the expression of Pushkin's artistic psychology based on the Jungian vision of the self as a composite of several identities and links it to ritualistic aspects of poetic performance.[45] Ermakov's interpretation of "Desire" focuses on the poem's expression of an imaginary timeless space imbued with sensual images that the lyric hero reconstructs from his past. Ermakov uncovers in the poem some expressions of femininity "oriented toward the Mother Earth image," a source of life and creativity.[46] His analysis also turns on the notion of rewriting the texts produced by predecessors, a notion found in Harold Bloom's thesis that "a poem is not writing but *rewriting*."[47] Through his engagement with Pushkin's expressions of femininity and acts of rewriting/reproduction, Ermakov invokes the cyclicality of nature and culture, thereby affirming the ultimate value of both cyclicality and linearity for the creative process at a time when Marxist critics exclusively privileged the forward movement of historical time. Ermakov suggests that the reinvention of self in different contexts through the appropriation of different stylistic masks is a key to the survival of one's creative powers.

Ermakov's analysis of "Desire" highlights the importance of metaphysics to Pushkin's works. But his intention here is to demonstrate that Pushkin was able to overcome his hedonistic self by embracing the principles of materialist psychology. Similarly, he sees the Don Juan of Pushkin's play *The Stone Guest* (*Kamennyi gost'*) as an embodiment of neuroticism: "He is totally ruled by his anxieties and moods; he is preoccupied with understanding his own doubts; and he is prepared to sacrifice his own life and risk himself in order to escape from his tormented, doubting state of mind. Don Juan is not courageous, but paradoxically he gives an impression of a brave and reckless person, in spite of the fact that he is naïve and superficial. The impression he gives to others stems from the fact that he is self-centered and ignores others, since his main purpose in life is to assert himself."[48] Ermakov compares Pushkin's Don Juan to one of his patients who had developed a pathological fear of the battle trenches during the Russo-Japanese War. One day the patient overcame this fear by recklessly walking in front of the trench during a heavy exchange of fire, and as a result of his heroism he was awarded the St. George Cross. In spite of his analysis of Don Juan's anxieties and the analogy he draws between Pushkin's fictional character and his own patient, Ermakov sees Pushkin's character as a carefree hedonist who lacks spiritual values. He concludes that Pushkin's play portrays a psychologically stable and healthy person who displays abnormal tendencies related to his exaggerated fear of commitment and responsibility. In Ermakov's view, Don Juan's anxieties and risk-taking behavior reveal traits of Pushkin's own personality. Yet at the same time he implies that Pushkin used his creative self in order to overcome his fears.[49]

By linking Pushkin's works to traumatic events, Ermakov demonstrates that the Russian model of psycho-physiological suffering contains a high degree of empathy; this model is connected to the holistic idea that men afflicted with war neuroses have somatic wounds in both mind and body. Ermakov fuses the psychologically oriented model of trauma developed in Russia in the 1910s with literary analysis and Freudianism, thus legitimizing ideas about mind-body responses to the environment.[50] In the late 1920s, however, the Soviet Marxists' merger of experimental psychology and physiology, based on the belief in universal patterns of conditioned reflexes, overshadowed the notion of subjectivity that was of particular interest to Ermakov.

Ermakov's concern with the representation of attitudes to death and trauma in Pushkin's works stems from his awareness of the Russian population's exposure to violence and traumatic events during the Russo-Japanese War and the 1905 revolution. Ermakov's perception that, as a result of these conflicts, fear had become the dominant emotion in Russian culture explains why he is especially interested in how individuals overcome their anxieties.[51] By the same token, Ermakov's analysis of Pushkin's works might be seen as a veiled attempt to convey his concerns about the state of the mental health of the Soviet populace (which had been traumatized by World War I, the Civil War, and the Red Terror)—concerns that were overlooked by Soviet officials, who were primarily preoccupied in the 1920s with developing literacy.

In his discussion of Pushkin's play *The Miserly Knight* (*Skupoi rytsar'*), Ermakov alludes to contemporary mental health concerns allegorically through his reference to the traumatic discontinuity between the old and the new. Thus, he links *The Miserly Knight* to the poem *The Bandit Brothers* (*Brat'ia-razboiniki*) and argues that both works feature the motif of a struggle between the old and new orders in Freudian terms—as an expression of the "father complex." Such references to a guilty conscience and acts of murder must have been unwelcome to Soviet officials, who no doubt worried they might invoke parallels with the Red Terror and the Civil War. It is unclear whether Ermakov hints at unexplained irrational aspects of Pushkin's psychology expressed in *The Bandit Brothers* because he wanted to suggest that such criminal thoughts resisted articulation or because he wanted to draw attention to examples of Pushkin's self-censorship. For example, Ermakov links murder to envy: "For some unknown reason the accidental murder of an old man keeps haunting one of the brothers, who goes mad . . . and whose guilty conscience reveals the fact that he had killed—in the form of this old man—his own envy complex toward his father."[52]

Ermakov's discussion of Pushkin's *A Feast in the Time of Plague* (*Pir vo vremia chumy*) also touches on the inability of survivors of tragic events to repress their fear of death. Ermakov writes: "While trying to escape from the plague and from their thoughts about it, all characters of Pushkin's play do nothing but constantly think about the plague, unable to free themselves from these thoughts even during their sleep and even when fainting."[53] On receiving a request to sing about the carefree life ("let me summon you to sing a song, a song of reckless life[,] . . . some wild bacchantic strain / Such as the overflowing glass inspires"), Walsingham appears incapable of disengaging his mind from his melancholy.[54] Ermakov thus interprets Walsingham's hymn as an act of despair that enables him to verbalize his fear of death. Yet Walsingham cannot overcome his anxieties, owing to his failure to transgress.[55] Ermakov reads Pushkin's play as a form of parable imbued with the hope that one day the readers who empathize with the characters described in *A Feast in the Time of Plague* will come to terms with their loss. He also ponders the question of aesthetic response to the horror embedded in Pushkin's text: "Despair, thanks to the terrifying memories (Walsingham is deceiving himself), transforms danger into a means of healing [*perezhivanie*] and creates a hymn."[56] In Ermakov's opinion, Walsingham's delusional mind seeks protection from the winter and the plague, leading to his indulgence in irresponsible behavior as a substitution for fear of death. Ermakov's rendering of Pushkin's tragedy, which portrays the participants of the blasphemous feast as nihilists, poses a question about the healing aspects of creativity exemplified by Pushkin's artistic psychology that might help to build Soviet society. Ermakov identifies some strategies for survival in Pushkin's text that could be relevant in his own day and suggests that Pushkin's legacy is important to the formation of cultural unity.

By grounding Pushkin's *A Feast in the Time of Plague* in the tradition of melancholic poetry, Ermakov downplays the symbolist fascination with Walsingham's demonic traits. Instead, he links the mystical traits discussed by Dmitrii Merezhkovsky and Iulii Aikhenval'd to the realm of everyday life.[57] Ermakov is more interested in the internalized conflict between individual and society, claiming that Walsingham's mind "represents a battlefield between the two drives that determine his personality: his love for himself and his love for others."[58] According to this logic, Walsingham should have developed a conscious view of reality that could have enabled him to conquer his fear of death, but instead he is a weak person who makes excuses for his own passivity. Ermakov argues that Walsingham is incapable of rationalizing his emotions or of self-sacrifice: instead of responding to the priest's call to overcome his isolation and lead a collective response to the plague that haunts the whole community, he becomes completely withdrawn and silent. Ermakov's criticism of Walsingham's behavior reveals his negative attitude toward the glorification of anarchy and chaos as a metaphysical principle that was prevalent in the early 1920s and offers a new perspective on the formation of the collective self through art.[59] Ermakov ascribes to art the power to transcend a sense of estrangement from oneself and the community, thereby alluding to the possibility of constructing ideal societies in both the present and the future. According to Ermakov's vision, such societies should integrate past experiences into present life.

In light of his utopian aspirations, it is not surprising that Ermakov is especially keen to discuss the theme of painful memories as a recurring motif in Pushkin's works. According to Ermakov, the protagonists of all four *Little Tragedies* are incapable of changing their self-centered outlook. Nor does Walsingham reconcile his fantasy with reality: the virtual reality that he creates in his mind as a substitute for his tragic existence provides him with a temporary escape and leads to a repetitive melodramatic reenactment of his suffering. In Ermakov's opinion, Walsingham "becomes more conscious of his weakness and his spiritual emptiness" as the play progresses.[60] Having such a weak mind entrenches Walsingham more firmly in his fictional reality. Thus, Ermakov interprets the poetic statement in Walsingham's hymn that "there is wild delight in battle and at the edge of a dark abyss" (est' upoenie v boiu i bezdny mrachnoi na kraiu) not as an expression of the flight of imagination but as a description of the traumatized state of mind: "Thus, having entered the vicious circle of his gloomy thoughts, Walsingham is incapable of breaking free from it."[61]

Ermakov's analysis of Pushkin's play replaces the autonomous thinking self found in idealist philosophy with the existentialist notion of a "tacit cogito" who becomes involved in the world through language. According to the French philosopher Maurice Merleau-Ponty, "The consciousness which conditions language is merely a comprehensive and inarticulate grasp upon the world, like that of an infant at his first breath"; it becomes explicit through perceptual exploration of speech, but "silent consciousness grasps itself only as a generalised 'I think' in the face of a confused world 'to be thought about.'"[62] Ermakov's statement that Walsingham chooses to display his suffering self to others reflects the belief that an individual's behavior comprises both free choice and creative strategies that Merleau-Ponty articulates. Such a pioneering approach to Pushkin's artistic psychology emphasizes the poet's ability to shift from one point of view to another, thereby revealing his fluid and creative self. Ermakov sees Walsingham, for example, as the embodiment of Pushkin's vulnerable self: "Walsingham is weak and miserable, he does not confront the situation and he runs away from his painful memories. His actions manifest only the one side of personality that is selfish and narrow-minded. There is another side of self that is beautiful and valuable. Pushkin expressed it well in his poem 'Parting.' In this poem we come across an act of separation of two people, but it is described not as a completed event but as a continuous moment that transcends the poet's love."[63] Ermakov observes that, by contrast with Walsingham who suppresses his memories of Matilda, Pushkin's lyric hero in the poem "Parting" ("Proshchanie") uses his creative imagination to bring his beloved back to life.

In spite of Ermakov's interest in Pushkin's biography, paradoxically, his focus on the inner emotional battle of the poet's creative self (Pushkin's dynamic unconscious) leads to the innovative presentation of Pushkin's art as a single semiotic space or hypertext. By suggesting that Pushkin in "Parting" successfully expresses his healthy and life-asserting self better than he conveys it in *A Feast in the Time of Plague*, Ermakov dismisses the old-fashioned metaphysical inquiry into the soul and presents the whole of a person as the sum of his different selves. This approach implies the importance of the reinvention of the self in different contexts. For Ermakov, art affects the personality of the individual artist, not society as a whole. Ermakov believes that creative work enables the artist to experience catharsis that evokes similar responses in audience and readers: "Borrowing directly from Freud's theory of day-dreaming, he argues that art can provide the audience with an opportunity to indulge their own fantasies and to experience a catharsis similar to that of the artist. Since the fantasy content of art is believed to be derived from instinctual drives common to all mankind, this content will, at the deepest level, have a universal appeal."[64]

Ermakov brings together two different poetic responses to adverse circumstances, suggesting thereby that the life-asserting and creative use of melancholy manifested in Pushkin's "Parting" is superior to the exteriorization of Walsingham's suffering that leads him to madness. Ermakov detects a healing vision of simultaneity in Pushkin's poem "Parting" and in Mary's song in *A Feast in the Time of Plague*: "The poet thinks that the beloved one believes that he is dead and therefore that she is a widow. Although the poet assumes that in the eyes of his beloved he is a dead person, his imagination cannot allow death to prevail in spite of his melancholy: he continues to live and the image of his beloved continues to inspire his imagination; it is as if his heart accepts his separation as a form of exile, in the same manner as Mary accepts her fate."[65] Such an interpretation draws on Bergsonian notions of psychological time and simultaneity and brings Pushkin closer to the reader of the 1920s—the reader who struggles to reconcile his memories of the past with his present life. One can see in Ermakov's understanding of memory and bodily experiences of emotions the suggestion of a belief similar to Merleau-Ponty's that bodily experience cannot be fully understood objectively through the mechanisms of empirical physiology or self-analysis alone.[66] Ermakov's assumption that Pushkin's writings on fear and loss derive from the poet's personal feelings reveals Ermakov's search for a similarly combined approach to explaining human emotion and artistic expression.

In spite of the references to realism throughout his book on Pushkin, Ermakov's discussion of Pushkin's mythologized self reinforces the view of Pushkin as a romantic poet. It is not a coincidence that Ermakov's book is subtitled "An Attempt at an Organicist Understanding" ("Opyt organicheskogo ponimaniia"). For Ermakov, Pushkin's soul represents the fiery element that brings everything to life and purifies the manifestations of chaos. Ermakov links Pushkin's creativity to the cult of Eros and the sublimation of erotic desire: "The task of the poet is to preserve the fiery aspect of life, maintaining it throughout his entire life. The fiery aspect of Pushkin's works represents the divine forces of Eros, the god of love. This love for others unites the poet with the world and people. Pushkin finds his inspiration in the fiery aspects of reality."[67] Ermakov's belief in the organic nature of art is central to his aesthetic viewpoint, which derives both from early psychoanalytic literature and the organicist criticism that had developed in Russia out of German romantic idealist philosophy after the 1820s.

Ermakov dismisses Pushkin's Salieri, the miserly knight, and Walsingham as self-centered individuals whose irrational, obsessive behavior prevents them from living meaningful lives. In particular, he suggests that Walsingham's mode of suffering "does not lead to the establishment of a healthy life associated with the element of fire."[68] He also argues that Pushkin views a work of art as part of nature and produced like nature, thereby molding Pushkin into a Russian Goethe. However, even though critics and poets perceive Goethe as the father of organicist aesthetics, Goethe in fact dismissed excessive use of biological metaphor in literature. Thus, in 1772 he wrote about aspects of nature that have no regard for the individual and so destroy him, unlike art that "emerges from the efforts of the individual to maintain itself against the destructive power of the whole."[69] According to Goethe, nature organizes life that has no meaning, but the artist creates a dead artifact and bestows meaning on it.

Tsvetaeva's analysis of Pushkin's *A Feast in the Time of Plague*, like Ermakov's, reinstates Goethe's belief that art invests life with meaning and so saves it from complete oblivion. In her discussion of Pushkin and Walsingham, Tsvetaeva compares Pushkin to Goethe, suggesting that both of them preserved their sanity through writing. Tsvetaeva's statement that "Pushkin saved himself from the plague, just as Goethe saved himself from destruction through writing his book *The Sorrows of Young Werther*" echoes Ermakov's reading of Walsingham's hymn to the plague as a manifestation of internal conflict.[70] Being interested in subjectivity, she claims that Pushkin, the lyric poet, reveals himself through Walsingham's song. Tsvetaeva, like Ermakov, describes Pushkin's Mary as an embodiment of the empathy to which Pushkin aspires in and through his works, and she denounces Walsingham's hymn as a manifestation of self-destruction.[71] Both Tsvetaeva's and Ermakov's interpretations of Pushkin's play allude to the notion of the revolutionary state that was incorporated into Lenin's vision of a new order founded upon suppression of the Russian trait defined as spontaneity (stikhiinost').[72]

Ermakov's employment of Freudian analysis—which advances the hypothesis that art derives from an unconscious fantasy linked to primitive instincts (the id)—in relation to Pushkin's works is subordinated to his conviction (shaped by the symbolist principle of life creation [zhiznetvorchestvo]) that the ultimate task of the artist is to reconcile his fantasies with reality. Thus, Ermakov sees Pushkin's Mozart and Salieri in a dialectical manner as two competing selves of the poet's personality, pointing to a protomodernist split in Pushkin himself. Ermakov talks about Salieri's inner fear of losing his fame, and he similarly views Pushkin's protagonist from the play *The Miserly Knight* as a person who is afraid of losing his wealth and power. Likewise, Ermakov depicts Pushkin's Don Juan both as a character scared of his memories and as an alter ego of the author who sublimates his emotions, while Pushkin's Walsingham reveals the suffering self of the poet who responds to melancholy in a creative manner.[73] These interpretations point to Ermakov's search for the tools of mastery of human emotions.

Ermakov valued Freud's article "Creative Writers and Day-Dreaming," which argues that art is a means of controlling dreams that is rooted in a hidden infantile desire.[74] In Freud's opinion, "A strong experience in the present awakens in the creative writer a memory of an early experience (usually belonging to childhood) from which there proceeds a wish which finds fulfilment in creative work. The work itself exhibits elements of the recent provoking occasion as well as the old memory."[75] Ermakov develops the Freudian notion of a "usable past" into his own concept of "catharsis" when he compares Freud's theory of day-dreaming to the act of reading Pushkin's poetry: "Catharsis does not exist for its own sake but for the sake of creating new spiritual values, objective values. The literary artist cannot merely limit himself by seeking self-satisfaction, but, by working and laboring over his material, he is 'compelled' and obliged to create certain values."[76] Ermakov's survey of Pushkin's works written in Boldino before the poet's marriage implies that the internal emotional struggle Pushkin experienced over a possible postmarital loss of his independence resulted in his act of "coming into being." Ermakov states that during his time spent in Boldino, Pushkin overcame his child-related anxieties in order to surpass his ego-centered self.[77] Ermakov's discussion of Pushkin's anxieties invokes Spielrein's thesis on love. Spielrein's work on the death instinct highlights the fact that erotic attraction, which merges the images of two persons into one, can both inspire—by allowing one to transcend the limits of the ego—and threaten the ego's independence. The ego risks delving either into the archetypal depths of the collective unconscious or into feelings of depression and annihilation.

Although most psychoanalytic criticism has tended to focus on the relation between a literary text and the psy-chology of its creator, Ermakov incorporates the notion of readership into the analysis of literary texts. He thus prefigures Norman Holland's understanding of reading as fundamentally a re-creation of identity through a transactive interaction between reader and text.[78] Curiously, Ermakov implies that the process of reading dangerous texts exploring the dark sides of personality might have a therapeutic effect on the reader, enabling the reader to embrace the notion of the theatricality of everyday life as well as "culturedness."

The concept of estrangement (ostranenie), the renewal of perception of familiar objects as described by the Russian formalists, is key to Ermakov's interpretation of *The Miserly Knight*. Thus, he explains the baron's actions as the result of estrangement from his criminal self, suggesting that the baron finds pleasure in his thoughts about a certain medical condition that help him to forget his own crimes: "Doctors tell us that there are some people who find murder pleasurable" (Nas uveriaiut mediki: est' liudi, / V ubiistve nakhodiashchie priiatnost').[79] Ermakov also thinks that Pushkin's use of the word "playboy" (povesa) in relation to the old scrooge makes the play's readers more aware that the baron's attitude toward his wealth has overtones of erotic desire as well as a theatrical aspect. Ermakov sees a split in the baron's identity: "The baron does not really characterize himself as a playboy; he just defines his attitude toward his wealth as comparable to the playboy's relation with women who are either deceived, or stupid, or carnal."[80] Instead of focusing on the aesthetic function of the baron's estrangement, however, Ermakov describes the baron's behavior in terms similar to those used in Spielrein's study "Destruction as the Cause of Coming into Being" (1912), in which she talks about the defensive nature of psychotic regression from personal conflict into a universal experience. Ermakov's survey of Pushkin's *Little Tragedies* suggests the transformative potential of such universal images.

Ermakov's interpretation of *The Stone Guest* is particularly indebted to Spielrein's work on love and death. Ermakov is interested in Don Juan's potential to overcome his anxieties, but he concludes that Don Juan dies from his inability to address his complexes rationally. In Ermakov's view, Don Juan deludes himself: it is not the environment but his own complexes and his passivity that ruin him.[81] Such a line of thought echoes Spielrein's statement that "when one is in love, the blending of the ego in the beloved is the strongest affirmation of self, a new ego existence in the beloved. If love fails, the image becomes one of destruction or death."[82] Akhmatova dismisses Ermakov's interpretation and presents Pushkin's Don Juan as a true poet.[83] Caryl Emerson also suggests that Pushkin poeticizes and purifies the sensuous aspects of Don Juan's personality: "Pushkin awards his Don Juan lofty poetic dimensions that undercut the covetous physical aspect of his pursuit and add aesthetic luster to it."[84] Furthermore, as Jenny Stelleman rightly argues, what makes the play innovative is the presence of the implied author who is negated by the character. She points out that Pushkin's Don Juan uses both the stone statue and Donna Anna to turn himself into a legend: "This is what makes his last conquest unique. His magical, life-giving words enable the poet Don Juan, who here almost acts as co-author, to correct the implied author and allow, fully aware of the consequences, the sujet to resume its conventional course."[85] Instead of engaging with Pushkin's creative appropriation of the Don Juan legend as do these other commentators, Ermakov interprets Don Juan's death in Freudian terms: as the punishing hand of the father presenting Donna Anna's kiss as the kiss of the mother.

Yet Ermakov's pioneering efforts to view Pushkin's themes in the light of Spielrein's work reinforce his belief that creativity and affectivity serve as a source of energy that influences the dynamic formation of language and thought. All the flaws in his analysis of Pushkin's poetry notwithstanding, Ermakov demonstrates that the classical transparency that has often been attributed to Pushkin's poetry should be seen as deceptive given the complex interaction between mind and feeling that formed Pushkin's poetic personality. Ermakov thus develops Dmitrii Merezhkovsky's vision of Pushkin as a profound thinker for whom inspiration presupposes the power of reason, enabling the poet and his readers to comprehend the whole through the perception of its parts. In the final analysis, Ermakov's book on Pushkin constitutes an attempt at using psychoanalytic tools to support and reinforce Merezhkovsky's view that Pushkin is comparable to Goethe: that is, that Pushkin eventually overcame the disharmony of the Byronic creative impulse and embraced the principle of emotional self-control.[86] Ermakov also develops Merezhkovsky's idea that one of the fundamental themes embedded in Pushkin's poetry is the tension between civilized and elemental selves, and he presents this thesis as being useful for the construction of a Marxist aesthetic theory.

In the context of the process of systematizing Pushkin's legacy in Soviet Russia in the 1920s and 1930s, Ermakov's book on Pushkin appears to be at odds with the tendency to create an all-powerful myth of Pushkin as a national poet around which cultural and scholarly institutions could be organized. Critics usually portray the 1937 celebration of the centenary of Pushkin's death as a literary festival of unprecedented scale that was meant to display national, social, and cultural unity. It is difficult not to agree with Boris Gasparov, who describes the national celebration of the 1937 jubilee as a "definitive cultural watershed" that "marks the culmination of the evolution of the Pushkin myth in the age of Modernism."[87] Many stern Soviet critics and censors at the time would have defined Ermakov's book as an exploration of taboo subjects such as the metaphysical aspects of Pushkin's thought, the representation of violence and madness, the role of the irrational in literature, and the creative sublimation of sexuality. Yet Ermakov's 1923 book can nevertheless be seen, from several different perspectives, as having contributed to the formation of the Pushkin myth.

As Stephanie Sandler rightly observes, although in the 1920s Pushkin was not yet the favorite of Russia's newly literate readers, as early as 1924 some influential cultural figures, including Anatolii Lunacharsky, predicted that Pushkin's star would rise in the near future.[88] In anticipation of this event, Ermakov's analysis of Pushkin's creative psychology might have been understood by Soviet psychoanalytical critics as an allegorical reading—a fictionalized creative biography that takes account of the dual temporality of Pushkin's legacy, acknowledging both the Russian past and the Soviet present.[89] The allegorical sign has a dual function and points to something other than itself, making the reader aware of the seeming near impossibility of reconciling present and past or self and other. In a didactic sense, then, Ermakov's discussion of Pushkin's inner emotional struggle offered some useful insights into his creative process, enabling the reader of the 1920s to overcome his own traumatic experiences.

Sandler's juxtaposition of 1920s Soviet scholarship on Pushkin's life and works with the concurrent transformation of his ancestral home of Mikhailovskoe into a monument reveals the mechanism of substitution that would contribute to the monumentalization of Pushkin in subsequent decades. According to Sandler, Soviet-era Mikhailovskoe can be read allegorically as an imaginary space that makes visible the labor of preserving and points "a visitor's attention to what has been preserved, by whom, with whose help and in what circumstances"; "as allegory, Mikhailovskoe consists of no mere trees, hills, river or edifices, but of natural views described in Pushkin's writings or presumed to have provided inspiration for his greatness"; "it seems to convey a full sense of Pushkin's biography."[90] So, too, Ermakov's book might be seen as an allegorical representation of Pushkin's artistic "laboratory" comprising a culturally constructed landscape permeated with the rhetoric of labor.

At the same time, Ermakov's analysis of Pushkin's works can be read as a veiled reference to an effort in the literary and scholarly world of 1920s Soviet Russia to reverse the predictions about the twilight of culture articulated in poet Vladislav Khodasevich's 1921 speech "The Shaken Tripod" ("Koleblemyi trenozhnik"). Khodasevich claimed that the twentieth century's wars and revolutions had altered Russian readers' sensibilities irrevocably. Hence Ermakov's reading of

Pushkin's works as psychodrama may be construed as an attempt to reach out to Soviet readers who had been barbarized by the experiences of wars and revolutions and had thus become estranged from Pushkin's authentic language. As Khodasevich pointed out, such readers, affected by the wild dramatic scenes cultivated in contemporary films, were conditioned to translate Pushkin's emotion into the language of their own sensual experiences.[91] In the end, it is difficult to assess whether Ermakov's animated account of Pushkin's creative psychology was meant to compete with the increased influence of visual culture in 1920s Soviet Russia or whether Ermakov envisaged his model of the organic reading of literature as the basis for a new form of life writing that blends Marxist and Freudian approaches to the production of cultural artifacts.

Notes

I would like to express my gratitude to Caryl Emerson for her encouragement, suggestions, and criticisms of an early version of this chapter. I also would like to thank Alyssa Dinega Gillespie for her helpful suggestions.

1. Ivan D. Ermakov, *Psikhoanaliz literatury: Pushkin, Gogol', Dostoevskii* (Moscow: Novoe literaturnoe obrozrenie, 1999).

2. Ermakov's contribution to the development of psychoanalysis in Russia is discussed in Martin A. Miller, "Freudian Theory under Bolshevik Rule: The Theoretical Controversy during the 1920s," *Slavic Review* 44.4 (1985): 625–46; see esp. 625–26.

3. Several essays and books published in the early 1920s by Bolshevik moralists, including Leon Trotsky's 1923 book *Problems of Everyday Life: Creating the Foundations for a New Society in Revolutionary Russia*, were opposed to young militants' rebellious behavior based on the legacy of the Civil War. They advocated instead the importance of cultured behavior that comprised hygiene, punctuality, sobriety, self-discipline, respectful attitudes toward women, wearing clean clothes, and reading books. See the detailed discussion of the notion of civilized behavior in Anne E. Gorsuch, "NEP Be Damned! Young Militants and the Culture of Civil War," *Russian Review* 56.4 (1997): 564–80.

4. Ermakov's utopian vision of a new society might be seen as part of the process defined by Richard Stites as revolutionary performance. See his *Revolutionary Dreams: Utopian Vision and Experimental Life in the Russian Revolution* (New York: Oxford University Press, 1989), 7.

5. Ivan D. Ermakov, *Etiudy po psikhologii tvorchestva A. S. Pushkina: Opyt organicheskogo ponimaniia "Domika v Kolomne," "Proroka" i malen'kikh tragedii* (Moscow: Gosudarstvennoe izdatel'stvo, 1923), 5. Ermakov's understanding of art as a creative activity entwined with the cognition of life stems from an organic

conception of art advocated by Hegel. This conception links logic, the philosophy of nature, ethics, and aesthetics to the notion of organic life, suggesting that ideas are objectively living. Victor Terras discusses the importance of an organic vision of art for socialist realism and links it with the organicist aesthetics advocated by various representatives of German romanticism: "Socialist Realism shares with the whole organic tradition the notion that art has far more than a mimetic or emotive function. In arguments, rather common in Soviet aesthetic literature, as to whether art is creative activity or cognition, a majority of authors will take the position that it is both" ("Phenomenological Observations on the Aesthetics of Socialist Realism," *Slavic and East European Journal* 23.4 [1979]: 446). He also notes that socialist realist theory never abandoned the central positions of organicist aesthetics. For a broader discussion of the organicist tradition in the Russian history of ideas, see Amy Mandelker, "Semiotizing the Sphere: Organicist Theory in Lotman, Bakhtin, and Vernadsky," *PMLA* 109.3 (1994): 385–96.

6. According to René Wellek, "It grows out of the organic analogy, developed by Herder and Goethe, but proceeds beyond it to a view of poetry as a union of opposites, a system of symbols" (*A History of Modern Criticism, 1750–1950*, vol. 2, *The Romantic Age* [Cambridge: Cambridge University Press, 1981], 3).

7. Although Ermakov does not provide a clear definition of his term "dynamic unconscious," his analysis of Pushkin's poetry emphasizes the unconscious roots of symbolism and all cognitive processes. Ermakov's notion of self presupposes a fluid process of identity formation associated with competing emotions and inner struggle.

8. Peter Kenez defines the 1920s as a period of mass mobilization and suggests that without the preparatory work of the decade, a fully totalitarian society could not have emerged in the 1930s (*The Birth of the Propaganda State: Soviet Methods of Mass Mobilization* [Cambridge: Cambridge University Press, 1985], 12).

9. See Gorsuch, "NEP Be Damned!," 573–77; Michael David-Fox, "What is Cultural Revolution?," *Russian Review* 58.2 (1999): 190–97.

10. According to Lynn Mally, Lenin's references to such words as "culture" and "culturedness" were not consistent: sometimes he equated these terms with the accumulated knowledge of educated elites, but at other times he linked them to cleanliness and punctuality. Mally suggests that Lenin and his Bolshevik colleagues realized the necessity of a cultural transformation of Soviet society but "the blueprints for building a socialist culture were no clearer than those for a socialist polity" (*Culture of the Future: The Proletkult Movement in Revolutionary Russia* [Berkeley: University of California Press, 1992], xvi). See also Mally's discussion of the legacy of the Proletkult after 1921 (245–46).

11. David-Fox, "What is Cultural Revolution?," 193, 199. G. Lelevich was a pseudonym of Labori Gilelevich Kalmanson (1901–37), one of the leading Russian Association of Proletarian Writers critics and editor of the literary journal *On Literary Guard* (*Na literaturnom postu*).

12. David-Fox, "What is Cultural Revolution?," 195.

13. Aleksandr K. Voronsky, "Freudianism and Art," in his *Art as the Cognition of Life: Selected Writings, 1911–1936*, trans. and ed. Frederick S. Choate (Oak Park, MI: Mehring Books, 1998), 188.

14. I. A. Grigor'ev, "Psikhoanaliz kak metod issledovaniia khudozhestvennoi literatury," *Krasnaia nov'* 7 (1925): 221–36.

15. Isai D. Sapir, "Freidizm i marksizm," *Pod znamenem marksizma* 1 (1926): 70.

16. Roman Jakobson, "Socha v symbolice Puškinově," *Slovo a slovesnost* 3 (1937): 2–24; for the Russian version of the article, see Roman Iakobson, "Statuia v poeticheskoi mifologii Pushkina," in his *Raboty po poetike* (Moscow: Progress, 1987), 145–80 (quote on 157). See also Mirsky's dismissal of Ermakov's analysis in his review of Janko Lavrin's *Gogol* in *Slavonic Review* 5.13 (1926): 223.

17. Leon D. Trotsky, "Culture and Socialism," in Voronsky, *Art as the Cognition of Life*, 468.

18. Valentin N. Voloshinov, *Freidizm: Kriticheskii ocherk* (Moscow: Gosizdat, 1927).

19. Valentin N. Voloshinov, "Freudianism: A Critical Sketch," in *The Bakhtin Reader: Selected Writings of Bakhtin, Medvedev and Voloshinov*, ed. Pam Morris (London: Arnold, 1994), 39.

20. Leon D. Trotsky, *Literature and Revolution* (Ann Arbor: University of Michigan Press, 1960), 179.

21. Shklovsky quoted in Alastair Renfrew, *Toward a New Material Aesthetics: Bakhtin, Genre and the Fates of Literary Theory* (London: Legenda, 2006), 11. As Renfrew notes, "The Formalists—some with utter deliberation, others at least partly unwittingly—abandon[ed] the possibility of theoretical 'reunification' in favor of pretensions of occupying the very ground previously assumed to be the natural province of some form of Marxism" (*Toward a New Material Aesthetics*, 12).

22. Reich quoted in Miller, "Freudian Theory under Bolshevik Rule," 625.

23. In spite of the fact that Veresaev had chaired the cultural and education commission of the Moscow Soviet since 1917, his 1924 article "What Is Needed to Be a Writer" ("Chto nuzhno dlia togo, chtoby byt' pisatelem") was criticized by some leftist writers for ignoring the social basis of human activities. In her article on the use of Pushkin in everyday life during the Silver Age period, Irina Paperno discusses Veresaev's evolution as a biographer of Pushkin. She claims that Veresaev's 1929 book *On Two Planes* (*V dvukh planakh*) offers a scientific examination of Pushkin's personality and abandons the symbolist myth about the unity between Pushkin the man and Pushkin the poet ("Pushkin v zhizni cheloveka serebrianogo veka," in *Cultural Mythologies of Russian Modernism: From the Golden Age to the Silver Age*, ed. Boris Gasparov, Robert P. Hughes, and Irina Paperno [Berkeley: University of California Press, 1992], 27–28).

24. See Sheila Fitzpatrick, *The Cultural Front: Power and Culture in Revolutionary Russia* (Ithaca: Cornell University Press, 1992), 1–2.

25. This phrase was first coined by the writer Iurii Olesha and then used by Joseph Stalin in connection with the development of the doctrine of socialist realism.

26. Pushkin's oppressors were described in Alexander Blok's 1921 speech "The Poet's Role" ("O naznachenii poeta") as enemies of the poet who snatch away the peace and freedom that are prerequisite to the poet's activity. See Alexander Blok, "The Poet's Role," in David J. R. Richards and C. Roger Cockrell, eds., *Russian Views of Pushkin* (Oxford, UK: Willem A. Meeuws, 1976), 127–34.

27. Shostakovich composed an introspective vocal cycle, *Four Romances to Words by A. Pushkin* (*Chetyre romansa na slova A. Pushkina* [1936–37]), op. 46, which, like Ermakov's book, highlights the poet's inner conflicts and anxieties. For a brief discussion of the cycle and its relation to the imperative of "culturedness," see Philip Ross Bullock, "The Pushkin Anniversary of 1937 and Russian Art-Song in the Soviet Union," *Slavonica* 13.1 (2007): 4–5.

28. Catriona Kelly, *Children's World: Growing Up in Russia, 1890–1991* (New Haven: Yale University Press, 2007), 86.

29. Nikolai E. Osipov, *Psikhoanaliticheskie i filosofskie etiudy*, ed. Dmitrii Petrovich Brylev (Moscow: Akademicheskii proekt, 2000).

30. In his article on Tintoretto (1518–94), an Italian painter famous for his dramatic depiction of perspectival space, Gabrichevsky asserts that Tintoretto's landscapes represent the chaos of organic life imbued with meaning and permeated with allusions to the artist's inner emotional struggle ("Prostranstvo i kompozitsiia v iskusstve Tintoretto," *Soobshcheniia gosudarstvennogo muzeia izobrazitel'nogo iskusstva im. A. S. Pushkina* 9 [1991]: 286–87). On Evreinov's notion of the theatricality of life and his use of Freud's ideas in his 1912 play *The Theater of the Soul* (*V kulisakh dushi*), see Alexandra Smith, "Nikolai Evreinov and Edith Craig as Mediums of Modernist Sensibility," *New Theatre Quarterly* 26.3 (2010): 203–16.

31. Anna A. Akhmatova, *O Pushkine: Stat'i i zametki* (Leningrad: Sovetskii pisatel', 1977), 108.

32. Alfred Adler, "Dostoevsky," in his *The Practice and Theory of Individual Psychology*, trans. Paul Radin (London: Paul, Trench, Trubner, 1924), 280–90.

33. The notion of mad genius is discussed by George Becker in *The Mad Genius Controversy: A Study in the Sociology of Deviance* (Beverly Hills, CA: Sage Publications, 1978).

34. See Irina Sirotkina, *Diagnosing Literary Genius: A Cultural History of Psychiatry in Russia, 1880–1930* (Baltimore: Johns Hopkins University Press, 2002), 4.

35. Ivan L. Shcheglov [Ivan L. Leont'ev], "Neskromnye dogadki," in his *Novoe o Pushkine* (St. Petersburg, 1902), 132–47; Vasilii V. Rozanov, "Koe-chto novoe o Pushkine," *Novoe vremia*, 21 July 1900, 2. Rozanov's essay is reprinted in *Pushkin v russkoi filosofskoi kritike: Konets XIX–pervaia polovina XX v.*, compiled by Renata A. Gal'tseva (Moscow: Kniga, 1990), 182–91. There were several

publications of this article in 1924. In 1928 Khodasevich attacked Shcheglov's presentation of Pushkin as a criminal who could be punished under Soviet law in relation to the 1826 incident involving a peasant girl. See Vladislav Khodasevich, "V sporakh o Pushkine," in *Stat'i, retsenzii, zametki, 1925–1934 gg.*, vol. 2 of *Pushkin i poety ego vremeni*, 3 vols., ed. Robert Hughes (Stanford, CA: Berkley Slavic Specialties, 2001), 132–53.

36. Ermakov, *Psikhoanaliz literatury*, 15–18.

37. Ermakov quoted in English in Donald Young, "Ermakov and Psychoanalytic Criticism in Russia," *Slavic and East European Journal* 23.1 (1979): 79.

38. Ermakov, *Etiudy po psikhologii tvorchestva A. S. Pushkina*, 174.

39. Aleksandr S. Pushkin, "Prorok," in his *Polnoe sobranie sochinenii*, 10 vols., ed. Boris V. Tomashevskii (Leningrad: Nauka, 1977–79), 2:304.

40. Ermakov, *Etiudy po psikhologii tvorchestva A. S. Pushkina*, 187.

41. In 1923 Spielrein worked as a researcher at the State Institute of Psychoanalysis and as director of the Department of Child Psychology at the University of Moscow. See Marie J. Santiago-Delefrosse and J.-M. Oderic Delefrosse, "Spielrein, Piaget and Vygotsky: Three Positions on Child Thought and Language," *Theory and Psychology* 6.12 (2002): 723–47.

42. Tsvetaeva's 1937 essay "My Pushkin" ("Moi Pushkin") juxtaposes children's creativity and Pushkin's artistic psychology in a similar manner.

43. See Sabina Spielrein, "On the Development and Origin of Speech," *International Journal of Psychoanalysis* 1 (1920): 359–61; and Sabina Spielrein, "Quelques analogies entre la pensée de l'enfant, celle de l'aphasique et la pensée subconsciente," *Archives de Psychologie* 72 (1923): 305–22.

44. Spielrein identifies the importance of the mother in the formation of children's selves through the act of reading in her essay "Destruction as the Cause of Coming into Being," *Journal of Analytical Psychology* 39.2 (1994): 157.

45. Spielrein explains: "According to [Jung], we do not possess an undivided ego, but rather various complexes that struggle with each other for priority" ("Destruction as the Cause of Coming into Being," 160).

46. Ermakov, *Etiudy po psikhologii tvorchestva A. S. Pushkina*, 183.

47. Harold Bloom, "Poetry, Revisionism, and Repression," in his *Poetry and Repression: Revisionism from Blake to Stevens* (New Haven: Yale University Press, 1976), 1–26.

48. Ermakov, *Etiudy po psikhologii tvorchestva A. S. Pushkina*, 120.

49. Ibid., 121.

50. See Jacqueline Lee Friedlander, "Psychiatrists and Crisis in Russia, 1880–1917" (PhD diss., University of California, Berkeley, 2007), 422.

51. According to Jacqueline Friedlander, the events of this period broadened medical specialists' understanding of the traumatic event, compelling them "to come into direct contact with the battlefield" ("Psychiatrists and Crisis in Russia, 1880–1917," 262–64).

52. Ermakov, *Etiudy po psikhologii tvorchestva A. S. Pushkina*, 92.

53. Ibid., 138.

54. Alexander Pushkin, *A Feast in the City of the Plague*, trans. Alexander Werth, *Slavonic Review* 6.16 (1927): 181.

55. Lotman interprets Walsingham's hymn in a different way: he sees it as an act of victory (*Pushkin: Ocherk tvorchestva* [St. Petersburg: Prosveshchenie, 1997], 202).

56. Ermakov, *Etiudy po psikhologii tvorchestva A. S. Pushkina*, 139.

57. See Dmitrii S. Merezhkovskii, *Pushkin: Vechnye sputniki* (St. Petersburg: Tipografiia M. Merkusheva, 1897); and Iulii I. Aikhenval'd, *Pushkin* (Moscow: Kushnerev, 1916).

58. Ermakov, *Etiudy po psikhologii tvorchestva A. S. Pushkina*, 142.

59. Evgenii Steiner discusses the notions of chaos and dynamism in Soviet books for children in *Avangard i postroenie novogo cheloveka: Iskusstvo sovetskoi knigi 1920-kh godov* (Moscow: Novoe literaturnoe obozrenie, 2002).

60. Ermakov, *Etiudy po psikhologii tvorchestva A. S. Pushkina*, 145.

61. Ibid.,149.

62. Maurice Merleau-Ponty, *The Phenomenology of Perception*, trans. Colin Smith (London: Routledge, 2002), 404.

63. Ermakov, *Etiudy po psikhologii tvorchestva A. S. Pushkina*, 150.

64. Young, "Ermakov and Psychoanalytic Criticism in Russia," 74.

65. Ermakov, *Etiudy po psikhologii tvorchestva A. S. Pushkina*, 150.

66. Merleau-Ponty's distinctive method of combining phenomenological description with analysis of the result of empirical scientific inquiry is illustrated by his reference to the phenomenon of the phantom limb, which serves as a paradigm of bodily self-perception, wherein individuals who have lost an arm or a leg may continue to have experiences related to the lost limb (*The Phenomenology of Perception*, 76).

67. Ermakov, *Etiudy po psikhologii tvorchestva A. S. Pushkina*, 153.

68. Ibid., 155.

69. Quoted by John Neubauer, "Organicist Poetics as Romantic Heritage?," in Angela Esterhammer, *Romantic Poetry* (Amsterdam: John Benjamins, 2002), 493.

70. Marina I. Tsvetaeva, "Iskusstvo pri svete sovesti," in her *Sochineniia*, 2 vols. (Moscow: Khudozhestvennaia literatura, 1988), 2:378.

71. Ermakov, *Etiudy po psikhologii tvorchestva A. S. Pushkina*, 379.

72. Ermakov's interest in relieving the pain of rediscovered past emotions through reading and acting is linked to some experiments of Soviet filmmakers and theater directors of the 1920s that were concerned with the art of mastering spontaneous emotions through repetition. Amy Sargeant describes their fascination with manual labor and a machine aesthetic thus: "It was something of a contemporary commonplace to celebrate in manual labour an aesthetic as much as a social value. . . . The repetition of a given activity reduces the movement to an essential and typical standard denominator, to the least expenditure of

physical effort required to accomplish the task" (*Vsevolod Pudovkin: Classic Films of the Soviet Avant-garde* [London: I. B. Tauris, 2000], 14).

73. Ermakov, *Etiudy po psikhologii tvorchestva A. S. Pushkina*, 173.

74. See Young, "Ermakov and Psychoanalytic Criticism," 74.

75. Sigmund Freud, "Creative Writers and Day-Dreaming," in *The Complete Psychological Works of Sigmund Freud*, 24 vols. (London: Hogarth Press, 1973), 9:151. Quoted in Young, "Ermakov and Psychoanalytic Criticism," 74.

76. Ivan D. Ermakov, *Ocherki po analizu tvorchestva N. V. Gogolia* (Moscow: Gosizdat, 1924), 164.

77. Ermakov, *Etiudy po psikhologii tvorchestva A. S. Pushkina*, 175.

78. Norman Holland, "The Miller's Wife and the Professors: Questions about the Transactive Theory of Reading," *New Literary History* 17.34 (1986): 423–47.

79. See Ermakov, *Etiudy po psikhologii tvorchestva A. S. Pushkina*, 47.

80. Ibid., 45.

81. Ibid., 130.

82. Spielrein, "Destruction as the Cause of Coming into Being," 174.

83. Akhmatova, *O Pushkine*, 100–101. In spite of some polemical disagreements with Ermakov, Akhmatova, like Ermakov, focuses her analysis on Pushkin's creative psychology.

84. Caryl Emerson, *The Cambridge Introduction to Russian Literature* (Cambridge: Cambridge University Press, 2008), 50.

85. Jenny Stelleman, "The Stone Guest and Don Guan," *Russian Literature* 52 (2002): 508.

86. See Dmitrii S. Merezhkovskii, "Pushkin," in *Pushkin v russkoi filosofskoi kritike*, 103.

87. Boris Gasparov, "The 'Golden Age' and Its Role in the Cultural Mythology of Russian Modernism," in *Cultural Mythologies of Russian Modernism*, 15–16.

88. Stephanie Sandler, "Remembrance in Mikhailovskoe," in *Cultural Mythologies of Russian Modernism*, 237.

89. For a discussion of the function of this dual temporality in the speeches of the 1937 Pushkin plenum of the Soviet Writers' Union, see Carol Any's "The Red Pushkin and the Writers' Union in 1937" in the present volume.

90. Sandler, "Remembrance in Mikhailovskoe," 246, 244–45.

91. Vladislav Khodasevich, "Koleblemyi trenozhnik," in his *Sobranie sochinenii*, 4 vols. (Moscow: Soglasie, 1996), 2:81.

The Red Pushkin and the Writers' Union in 1937
Prescription and Taboo

CAROL ANY

Amid the ideological shifts of the early and mid-1930s, Pushkin went from being a landowning member of the oppressor class to a near-revolutionary comrade-in-arms of the Decembrists, training his art against the throne. The public unveiling of this new, quasi-Soviet Pushkin took place in the oxymoronic year of 1937, which paired mass slaughter with staged public jubilee over the new constitution, the triumphal twentieth anniversary of the revolution, and the Pushkin centennial. The Stalinized Pushkin became a ubiquitous cliché rendering all other interpretations of Pushkin taboo; yet we should not imagine that it was simply handed down from above in ready-made form at a certain point in time and immediately internalized by the public. Even as the regime positioned Pushkin in support of Soviet ideological premises, writers and intellectuals expressed alternative interpretations. Stephanie Sandler has shown that writers like Mikhail Bulgakov and Daniil Kharms wrote works that invoked the official Pushkin while simultaneously undercutting the overt, "safe" message with veiled allusions to the Great Terror.[1] These works failed to pass censorship in

1937, but not all taboo interpretations were kept safely out of the public arena. This chapter argues that such interpretations found their way into published articles about Pushkin, as well as into high-profile speeches at one of the culminating events of the jubilee, the fourth plenum of the Writers' Union, known as the Pushkin plenum, held in February 1937. Writers used their remarks about Pushkin to express their objections to socialist realist aesthetics and to allude to their own literary and moral captivity.

After the revolution and throughout the 1920s, Bolshevik officials had regarded Pushkin as a member of the oppressor class and downplayed his significance. The chief literary censor in the 1920s, Pavel I. Lebedev-Poliansky, excluded Pushkin from the list of approved literary classics.[2] Even the old intelligentsia, eager to find in Pushkin and other nineteenth-century intellectuals a model of heroic behavior that they could emulate, often found that Pushkin fell short.[3] The eminent and influential Pushkin scholar Vikentii Veresaev, in the preface to his 1929 book *V dvukh planakh* (*On Two Planes*), hinted at his disappointment in Pushkin as a failed hero. He wrote that in Pushkin,

> I thought I would find the highest, most radiantly illuminated bearer of "the living life," the most authentic crowning of that rare ability among humans—to transform life in his consciousness into beauty and gladness. In the course of my work on Pushkin I became convinced that my approach to him was thoroughly wrong, that I would not find in him what I sought. What I did find will be told in this book.[4]

In the end, Veresaev's book drew a stark line between the "perfect" artist and the deeply flawed man. Despite Veresaev's initial intention, his book turned out to be very much a product of the 1920s, an era that viewed Pushkin with suspicion if not scorn.

Sometime around 1930, Stalin began to consider what uses might be made of the Russian past, and he reimagined Pushkin as a political progressive who paved the way for revolution.[5] For reasons of his own, he, too, now required a heroic Pushkin. An emphasis on Pushkin's ties to the Decembrists and his conflict with the monarchy could allow Russia's national poet to function as a kind of Old Testament patriarch, a symbol of Soviet social ideals rooted in a heroic past. Publicly, however, the assessment of Pushkin remained what it had been in the twenties until July 1934, when a Politburo resolution called for the creation of an All-Union Pushkin Committee charged with memorializing and popularizing Pushkin's work.[6]

The resolution provided a clue to the new Pushkin by declaring that he had "perished by the bullet of a foreign adventurer doing the will of the landowning aristocracy"; but even then, awareness of Pushkin's new status was not widespread. The anointed poet-bard Dem'ian Bednyi and the prominent theater director Alexander I. Tairov, both so well-connected that one would expect them to have been in the know, picked that very time to commence work on their fateful production of Alexander Borodin's comic opera *Epic Heroes* (*Bogatyri*). This satire of the legendary figures of the Russian past was completely at odds with the new thinking that would co-opt Russia's heroic mythology for Soviet purposes. Bednyi and Tairov's timing could not have been worse. Immediately following the premiere in November 1936, *Epic Heroes* was banned, and Bednyi underwent a campaign of public disgrace that effectively retired him from the official pantheon of revolutionary literature.[7]

Given strict literary censorship and institutionalized controls over writers, how could the *Epic Heroes* debacle have occurred? It is a truism that the party line on numerous matters from foreign affairs to the arts was rigid and authoritative; it is a conundrum that this same rigid and authoritative party line could change frequently and sometimes dramatically. Reconciling the absolutist nature of the party line with its tendency to lurch unpredictably was highly problematic. Turnabouts in the party line caused widespread confusion among mid-level officials, minor bureaucrats, the creative intelligentsia, and the general public. Sometimes, as in the browbeating of composer Dmitrii Shostakovich in 1936, the new line was clear, but the apparent lack of a reason for it caused perplexity and even consternation.[8] At other times, as Alexander M. Dubrovsky has shown, Stalin simply did not give his emergent thought clear and public articulation.[9]

Under these conditions, taboo interpretations could and did find their way into the public arena due to misconceptions and gray areas. These included (1) lag time between officials' adoption of a new line and public awareness of it; (2) confusion over what the official interpretation was; (3) seepage of recently acceptable ideas into the new taboo regimen, infecting it with possibility and questioning; and (4) attempts by the creative intelligentsia to push the envelope when they perceived a gray area. We should be careful, then, in our treatment of statements like "One couldn't say X" under Stalin. As time went by and the new party line with its attendant taboos became clear, some taboo interpretations vanished completely from public discourse; others, as we shall see, fluttered beneath the surface in double-voiced statements, suggestions, and hints.

Epic Heroes was not the only case of taboo material receiving flagrant publicity by mistake. An article by Dmitrii S. Mirsky, written at about the same time as the Politburo resolution on Pushkin was passed, slipped through during the lag time between preparations for a change in party line and its proclamation. Mirsky's article was written for the 1934 volume of *Literary Heritage* (*Literaturnoe nasledstvo*); however, the volume's publication was delayed, and it appeared only in the middle of 1935.[10] Mirsky disparaged Pushkin's behavior and social views through the prism of Marxist class analysis even as the official portrayal of Pushkin was about to do a volte face. Like Veresaev, Mirsky drew a sharp distinction between the poetic genius and the unlikeable man. Mirsky's Pushkin placed self-interest over principle, showed servility to the monarch, and exhibited "immoderate social snobbery."[11] This was still the Pushkin of the 1920s, and Mirsky probably believed he was following the party line. This did not stop him, however, from posing pointed and even risky questions. Could great literature be created by a member of a declining reactionary class? What was the relationship between great art and social progress? Mirsky answered these questions in a way that was unacceptable to both the 1920s and the 1937 party lines, concluding that the imperialist bourgeoisie creates great art that proletarian writers could learn from, art that would survive in a classless society.[12] By exalting Pushkin's poetry, Mirsky transgressed the "old" Pushkin. By identifying the root of Pushkin's art as its class grounding instead of his politically progressive outlook, he fell afoul of the "new" Pushkin.

Most importantly for our purposes, Mirsky's analysis of Pushkin's poetry emphasized its ambiguity and double-voicedness, a view that was thoroughly incompatible with the accessible-art doctrine that Stalin promulgated in December 1935. In Mirsky's reading of *The Bronze Horseman* (*Mednyi vsadnik* [1833]), Petersburg signifies both absolutism and revolution in a constantly shifting symbolism that dodges any comfortably grounded ideological interpretation. The poem for Mirsky is double voiced and unresolved. Mirsky saw this ambiguity as a reflection of Pushkin's literary role in a Russia where the breakneck pace of social development meant that Pushkin's art encompassed the whole trajectory from privileged nobility to people's revolution, a process that in Europe had taken half a millennium. This made it impossible to separate the "nobleman who is already emitting a stench from the great poet of bourgeois liberation."[13] Mirsky's Pushkin—the poet's character weaknesses and his toadying to the tsar, the idea that a socially retrograde mind could produce great art, the interpretation of *The Bronze Horseman* as ambivalent, and the very suggestion that ambiguity resides in great literature—was antithetical to the heroic Pushkin in the making.

The laconic formulation of the Politburo resolution—"perished by the bullet of a foreign adventurer doing the will of the landowning aristocracy"—signaled a new conception of Pushkin and provided a clue as to what it should be. The newly heroic Pushkin emerged in two important books of 1935 and 1936, one by Valerii Kirpotin (director of the Communist Academy's Institute of Literature and Language and, until 1936, head of the Central Committee's literature section) and the other by the independent nonparty scholar Iurii Tynianov. If Tynianov's book skirted taboos, Kirpotin was to discover, much to his surprise, that his most orthodox efforts could not prevent him from blundering into the Stalinist trap of ex post facto taboo.

Kirpotin fleshed out the new Pushkin in a book intended for the mass reader. It was published as a monograph in 1936 and reprinted in the January 1937 issue of the literary monthly *October* (*Oktiabr'*).[14] This book became the basis for the new official image of Pushkin: a courageous visionary, almost a revolutionary, who dreamed of liberty and justice for all Russia and dared to confront the autocracy, not just once or twice but repeatedly and without fail, and whose "simple" verse reflects his love for "the people," emitting an infectious joie de vivre. This image rested upon five main traits attributed to the poet: (1) social and political progressivism, (2) personal courage, (3) love of the simple people, (4) joie de vivre (optimism), and (5) an aesthetics of simplicity.

Each of these five elements in the new image of Pushkin linked him to the self-proclaimed achievements of the Communist Party. Pushkin's vaunted political "progressivism" realized its potential in the Soviet Union's claim to be "the most advanced country in the world." His "love for the people" implied his embrace of the revolution that made the people its beneficiary. His proclaimed personal courage linked him to mythologized Bolshevik commissars like Vasilii Chapaev, as well as fictional heroes like Gleb Chumalov and Pavel Korchagin (from Fedor Gladkov's novel *Cement* [*Tsement*] and Nikolai Ostrovsky's *How the Steel Was Tempered* [*Kak zakalialas' stal'*], respectively). Pushkin's widely acknowledged joie de vivre (zhizneradostnost') became the counterpart and reinforcement of Stalin's dictum "Life has become better, comrades, life has become more fun." The admirable "simplicity" of his writing made him the ultimate arbiter of Soviet literature (through the intermediacy of orthodox party critics who claimed to speak for him) with its self-imposed standard of accessibility. Meanwhile, the packaging of these elements together made it easy to see Pushkin's death at the hands of the courtier Georges d'Anthès as self-sacrifice for the people's cause, which thus became an implied sixth element of the cliché—the piece that had already been supplied by the Politburo resolution. Pushkin conferred the legitimacy of honored tradition on the Soviet successor state, which in turn revalidated Pushkin by bringing his presumed sociopolitical program to fruition through its radical application of his ideas.

Kirpotin also introduced the cliché's lexicon, taking the standard self-congratulatory epithets from Soviet agitprop and now applying them to Pushkin as well. Words like "svoboda" (freedom), "svobodoliubivyi" (freedom loving), "volia" (liberty), "vol'noliubivyi" (liberty loving), "progressivnyi" (progressive), "peredovoi" (vanguard), "demokraticheskii" (democratic), "revoliutsionnyi" (revolutionary), "zhizneradostnost'" (joie de vivre), "reaktsionnye sily" (reactionary forces), and "bichevat'" (to scourge), which pointed simultaneously toward Pushkin and Soviet achievement, were part of the emotionally charged "projective language" (to use Boris Groys's term) of official Soviet mythology.[15] Kirpotin's reference to Pushkin's "furious attack" (iarostnoe napadenie) on the autocracy corresponded to modern-day Soviet "furious attacks" on fascism and imagined saboteurs; with that single phrase, Kirpotin drew Pushkin into the linguasphere of *Pravda*'s sanctimonious shrieking. Phrases like this one acquired overtones from the official language of self-righteous outrage that sounded alongside it in linguistic counterpoint.

Kirpotin's book provided a knowledge base for newly literate, less sophisticated readers, giving them a way to imagine Pushkin and a vocabulary for speaking about him. It sprinkled Pushkin's biography with short poems and manageable excerpts from longer poems that could be memorized or at least recognized. The overused words of the cliché's lexicon cluttered every page but derived at least some legitimacy from Pushkin's own use of them in poems such as "Liberty" ("Vol'nost'" [1817]), "To Chaadaev" ("K Chedaevu" [1818]), and "The Countryside" ("Derevnia" [1819]). These early political poems, besides expressing antipathy to autocracy and serfdom, also could be read as predictions that were now triumphantly realized in the Soviet state, as in "To

Chaadaev," where the word "tovarishch" (comrade) even points to the revolution:

Товарищ, верь: взойдет она,
Звезда пленительного счастья,
Россия вспрянет ото сна,
И на обломках самовластья
Напишут наши имена.[16]

[Comrade, believe: it will rise, / The star of captivating happiness, / Russia will rise up from its sleep / And on the shards of autocracy / They will write our names.]

Read in the context of socialist realism, this poem, which opens with a farewell to youthful, private hopes for love and fortune, even seems to trace a path to consciousness similar to that found in socialist realist exemplars like Gladkov's *Cement* and Ostrovsky's *How the Steel Was Tempered*.[17]

Notably, however, Kirpotin's book offers a more rounded and human Pushkin than does the version of the cliché adopted by the press, and not long after its publication, certain of its statements were declared to be wrong. Advance excerpts that had appeared in the *Literary Gazette* (*Literaturnaia gazeta*) and *Young Communist Truth* (*Komsomol'skaia pravda*) in 1936 were greeted by objections that Kirpotin had made Pushkin too revolutionary, but by 1937 the criticism was that he had not made him revolutionary enough. The frustrated Kirpotin defended himself: "I cannot say [that Pushkin was the ideologue of the peasant revolution], because it isn't true."[18]

While making Pushkin into a political and social progressive of firm character, Kirpotin nonetheless described the poet's evolving political conservatism (also offering personal and historical justification for it). Acknowledging that Pushkin thought the Jacobins no better than the Russian autocracy and that he "was not initiated into the secrets of the Decembrist societies," Kirpotin attempts to compensate for this disappointing outsider status by assuring his readers that Pushkin "greedily drank in the atmosphere of gentry revolutionary circles" and by schooling them to understand that what was most important was Pushkin's "furious attack" on the autocracy.[19]

Perhaps the most interesting thing in Kirpotin's book is that, in an unsuspectingly innocent way, it, too (like Mirsky's interpretation of

The Bronze Horseman), opened the door to double-voiced readings of Pushkin. Kirpotin explains that in "To Licinius" ("Litsiniiu" [1815]), ostensibly addressed to the Roman dictator, "Pushkin furiously attacked autocracy, Alexander I, and Arakcheev," and he provides an excerpt so the reader can see how a single text can generate two meanings.[20] Similarly, he excerpts from Pushkin's poem "Liberty" to show that the Decembrists willfully read the lines about Napoleon as a description of the Russian tsar:

Самовластительный злодей!
Тебя, твой трон я ненавижу.
Твою погибель, смерть детей
С жестокой радостию вижу.
Читают на твоем челе
Печать проклятия народы,
Ты ужас мира, стыд природы,
Упрек ты Богу на земле.[21]

[Vile autocrat! / I abhor you and your throne. / With cruel joy I see / Your ruin and your children's death. / The people's curse / Is stamped upon your brow. / You are the world's horror, nature's shame, / A reproach to God on earth.]

That these readings-by-analogy were safe and fed the Stalinist view does not undo their potential as a subversive lesson to the mass reader in allegorical and Aesopian interpretation.

In its April 1937 issue, *October* published responses to Kirpotin's book from several writers and critics under the rubric of "discussion." Just as Kirpotin had given a fuller and more objective description of Pushkin than the cliché that was finally adopted, so did nearly all of those who contributed to *October*'s discussion pages. Communist writers and critics, though making much of Pushkin's historical role in bringing about the revolution, did not shy away from raising troublesome issues such as Pushkin's pride in his noble birth, his obedience to Nicholas I, and his handful of poems praising the monarch.[22] All of these difficulties were soon to be swept under the rug, but as late as April 1937, party critics acknowledged them and generally sought mitigating or exculpatory explanations. Political wavering was understandable in a man standing practically alone against his society; his poems supporting the tsar were written under pressure and did not reflect his true feelings;

he "always" resolved his hesitations in favor of progressivism and rebellion.[23] Communists felt that acknowledging Pushkin's weaknesses did not prevent them from feeling a strong sense of kinship with him.

Behind the question of what the mass reader should know about Pushkin, however, lurked another question that no Communist critic dared voice (although Mirsky in his 1934 article came close): could the mass reader even understand Pushkin? And would Pushkin studies now be separated from Pushkin for the masses, entailing a different level of literary and perhaps even ideological sophistication? This fearful question was injected into the debate by the elder litterateur Sergei Sergeev-Tsensky in his response for the *October* discussion on Kirpotin's book. How should the masses understand Pushkin? They won't understand him, wrote Tsensky, because critics teach them to decipher Pushkin's verse as prose messages. No present critics understand poetry as poetry, Tsensky argued, and with a quotation from Derzhavin, he pointed to poetry's fundamental ambiguity:

Я телом в прахе истлеваю,
Умом громам повелеваю,
Я царь, я раб, я червь, я бог.[24]

[In body I decay in dust, / In mind I command the thunderbolts, / I'm a tsar, I'm a slave, I'm a worm, I'm God.]

One need look no further than the Russian Academy of Sciences edition of Pushkin's complete works, whose first volumes appeared in 1937, to see that Tsensky had hit the bull's-eye. The publication of an elite scholarly edition could only make manifest the absurd disjunction between academic Pushkin scholarship and the falsified popularization. To avoid this embarrassment, and also to block sensitive information and interpretations that might dangerously contradict the cliché, the edition was published without its most valuable asset—the scholarly commentary.[25] By its very omnipresence, the cliché wrested Pushkin from the domain of academic scholars. If the formalists had made Pushkin into a "difficult" writer, Stalin's 1935 pronouncements on "accessibility" in art guaranteed that he would be oversimplified.

The launching of the cliché in Kirpotin's book, however, did not prevent the simultaneous publication of a novel that, arguably, presented a very different Pushkin. Tynianov's novel *Pushkin*, which appeared in installments from 1935 to 1937, reflected the intelligentsia's increasing fascination through the 1930s with personal behavior in the face of pressure to betray personal beliefs and principles.[26] Even the Russian formalists, whose work of the 1910s and 1920s bracketed biography as "extraliterary," became part of the 1930s quest for behavioral analogues and models.[27] Sifting through history for models by which to live, the old intelligentsia continued to be disappointed, as Angela Brintlinger has shown, in its craving for a heroic Pushkin who could serve as such a model—a moral giant with the courage to match his literary genius.[28] Pushkin had, under the influence of a misplaced hope in the tsar, written in praise of the monarch's harsh nationalist policies, and on the coattails of a brilliant society wife, he had risen to a position of political favor, which only turned out to be the setup for his demise. Seen in this way, Pushkin's biography, instead of offering an ethical model for writers of the 1930s, served depressingly as its antithesis.

Tynianov's novel countered this discouraging conclusion, reflecting the need in the 1930s for a hero and serving as an antidote to the weak-willed Pushkin of Veresaev.[29] Pushkin emerges as a teenage gadfly aiming his poison pen at lyceum officials who served the monarch; his personal behavior, while rash, is also courageous. Even his sexual trysting, unmannerliness, and unbridled behavior, rather than appearing as character flaws walled off from his artistic genius, find their echo in the literary erotica filched from his father's library that fed his poetic inspiration.

Tynianov describes a culture of informers in Pushkin's milieu, where literary factions curried favor by allying themselves with political officials. This toxic environment breeds a cast of characters common to both 1812 and 1937: a high-minded, idealistic school principal so frustrated by the political establishment that he succumbs to alcoholism; an erudite writer, having finally pulled enough strings to get his magnum opus published, left with a feeling not of triumph but of humiliation; a playwright who commits suicide when his play is pointedly rejected by the reigning literary doyen. At the lyceum, where a number of the students try their hand at creative writing, Tynianov shows the different treatments accorded to the gifted writer (Pushkin) and the officially approved writer (Illichevsky).

Intrepid challenger of the tsarist court, Tynianov's adolescent Pushkin also points in another direction, for he leads a secret inner life that implicitly connects him to the endangered species of the Soviet intelligentsia. He shares his thoughts with no one. He reads forbidden books;

he writes secret verse and hides or even burns it. Beleaguered members of the old intelligentsia seeking a Pushkin for 1937 might have discerned among their contemporaries a surprising literary counterpart to Pushkin. In his unruly behavior as a budding poet, in his brilliant verse and satiric epigrams, in his closeness to secret societies from which his friends barred him entry fearing he would blurt out their secrets, Pushkin was, unexpectedly, a version of the poet-ruffian Pavel Vasil'ev. Vasil'ev, who wrote an anti-Stalin epigram predating Mandel'shtam's and who engaged in street scandals as a form of protest against the literary establishment, was expelled from the Writers' Union for antisocial conduct in 1935 and was arrested four times.[30] His final arrest occurred on 6 February 1937, two weeks before the plenum opened, and he was shot on 16 July.[31]

Not everyone read Tynianov's novel as a double-voiced analogy. The novelist Konstantin Fedin, already an authoritative voice in Soviet literary politics, praised it as Marxist in approach, and it was taken as evidence that Tynianov had overcome his formalist errors.[32] Tynianov, recognized as the preeminent scholar working on Pushkin, was selected to be a keynote speaker at the Writers' Union's fourth plenum, held from 22 to 26 February 1937.

By now, nearly everyone, from orthodox Stalinists to closet resisters, agreed on the centrality of one fundamental point: Pushkin was in conflict with the autocrat and therefore was "with us" (Pushkin s nami). Both loyalists and the disaffected based their identification with Pushkin on this axiom. Even as Communists proclaimed Pushkin to be "with us," disaffected writers had their own idea of who was meant by "us." Pushkin, too, had suffered under a tyrannical autocrat and perhaps could provide a model for behavior in Stalin's Soviet Union. For loyalists, Pushkin was a link in the chain of events that led to the revolution and the destruction of the monarchy. For the disaffected, he was a symbol of resistance not only to an autocratic tsar but also to Stalin's dictatorship. The image of Pushkin pointed simultaneously in two opposite directions.

The five days of the Pushkin plenum were packed with speeches and informal reflections about Pushkin and his significance for Soviet literature. Since 1937 marked both Pushkin's centennial and the twentieth anniversary of the revolution, the plenum provided a natural opportunity for the regime to identify Pushkin with its claims and policies.[33] The events surrounding the Pushkin plenum remind us of just how thoroughly Stalinist celebration culture was interwoven with the culture of terror.[34] The preceding six months had been a whirlwind of political publicity stunts: the Zinov'ev-Kamenev trial, the pomp and circumstance surrounding the Stalin Constitution, the Piatakov-Radek trial, and the Pushkin celebrations.[35] The Pushkin plenum was thus firmly placed within the carefully structured alternation of festivity and fear, reward and punishment. Even within the few days of the plenum itself, the familiar alternation of celebration and terror made its mark. The Writers' Union plenum overlapped with the Central Committee plenum of the Communist Party of the Soviet Union (CPSU), where Nikolai Bukharin was desperately struggling to defend himself against Stalin's accusations of antiparty activity. The five days of tributes to Pushkin were bookended by Stalin's crushing of the opposition: the Pushkin plenum began one month after the trial of Piatakov, Radek, and their fifteen codefendants, and it ended on the day of Bukharin's and Aleksei Rykov's arrest.[36]

The regime symbolically tied Pushkin to the show trials of the old Bolsheviks by holding the plenum in the Hall of Columns, still fresh from the Piatakov-Radek trial. Vladimir Stavsky, who was running the Writers' Union, even postponed the plenum so that it could be held in that venue: the state funeral on 21 February of Politburo member Sergo Ordzhonikidze, whose sudden death, likely by suicide, just days after the conviction of his protégé Iurii Piatakov, temporarily preempted the Pushkin plenum from the Hall of Columns.[37]

The Writers' Union held plenums annually from 1934, when it began its formal existence, led by party bureaucrat Alexander S. Shcherbakov acting in consultation with Maksim Gorky, who served as the union's nominal chairman until his death in June 1936. That September, its leadership passed to Stavsky, a minor writer of wooden, predictable short fiction about collectivization and sabotage, whose rise through the party ranks had brought him into the inner circle of literary power. Stavsky's tenure as head of the Writers' Union coincided exactly with the Great Terror, and his hot-headed nature and ideological naïveté made him the perfect person to conduct a hunt for "enemies" in the writers' community.

About one hundred writers were selected to be delegates to the Pushkin plenum, which featured five keynote addresses, two by officials and three by writers. Stavsky and Andrei S. Bubnov, the commissar of education and culture, gave speeches connecting Pushkin to Soviet ideology; the poet Nikolai Tikhonov gave the major address on Pushkin's poetry; Tynianov spoke on Pushkin's prose; and the Communist theater critic and scholar Iogann Al'tman spoke on Pushkin's drama. All the scheduled addresses were submitted beforehand for vetting and editing, although after the speakers had finished, delegates had a chance to offer their own spoken comments without prior approval. The first day of the plenum began with Stavsky's and Bubnov's speeches, thus establishing the primacy of ideology over art. Only then was it the writers' turn, with Tikhonov speaking that afternoon and Tynianov and Al'tman the next morning.

Stavsky in his opening address kept current events in the foreground, sounding the alarm on domestic sabotage and foreign enemies: "Fascism has turned into a brutal beast. The cannibals of the twentieth century are tearing the remnants of bourgeois democracy to shreds."[38] He then turned to Pushkin, foreshortening and indeed eliminating the chronological distance between 1837 and 1937 with the claim that Pushkin "would approve" of the Old Bolshevik show trials. He invoked the newly formed Pushkin cliché, linking it piece by piece to the Soviet state: Pushkin was a friend of the Decembrists who dreamed of a distant day that had now arrived, a fighter against tyranny who provided an example for the Soviet Union's struggle against fascism in Europe, the first Russian writer to consider literature a national cause (implying a socially engaged aesthetic), and a writer whose work was always accessible (echoing Stalin's call for accessibility in art).[39] Many writers followed Stavsky's lead, making reference to Bukharin, Radek, and other "traitors" in their own remarks to the plenum.[40] Communist loyalist writers at the plenum all but invoked the ghost of a Red Pushkin hovering over the proceedings; the party poet Aleksei Surkov envisioned a reproachful Pushkin asking the assembled writers, "What have [you] done to show the progressive working class?"[41] Emotional assertions that Pushkin had "fought alongside us" in the Civil War brought Pushkin into Soviet discourse and appealed to a widely shared sense that Pushkin had entered the collective Soviet psyche.[42]

The three writers' keynote addresses, however, departed from Stavsky's line and attempted to restore parts of Pushkin that had been lost in the selective official reading of him. As surprising as it may seem given the high-profile nature of the plenum, all three of these speeches are marbled with taboo messages. All used Pushkin to critique Soviet literary policy, to deplore the poor quality of new literary works, and to argue against the Soviet practice of interpreting writers selectively by highlighting certain of their works while ignoring others.

With the official ideological addresses by Stavsky and Bubnov out of the way, it was Tikhonov's turn. It is easy to read his remarks as double voiced, and it is clear from the archival record that the audience received them that way. Tikhonov remarked upon the failings of Soviet poetry, and he quoted lines from Pushkin's "Severe Judge of French Rhymesters" ("Frantsuzskikh rifmachei surovyi sudiia" [1833]) that could also describe the false Soviet poets of the 1930s:

О вы. которые восчувствовав отвагу
Хватаете, мараете бумагу—
Тисненью предавать труды свои спеша,
Постойте наперед—узнайте, чем душа
У вас наполнена—прямым ли вдохновеньем
Иль необузданным одним поползновеньем
И чешется у вас рука по пустякам.
Иль вам не верят в долг, и деньги нужны вам?[43]

[O you who, feeling valor, / Seize and soil a sheet of paper— / Hastening to give your labors to the printed page, / Stop a moment—find out what fills your soul— / Unmediated inspiration or only unbridled crawling forth, / And do you itch to write at every trifle, / Or do you just need money for your debts?]

At this point, the archival record notes that applause interrupted Tikhonov's recitation, a reaction that strongly suggests that the audience appreciated Pushkin's lines for their applicability to 1937—as a reprimand to Stalin's pet poets.[44] When the applause subsided, Tikhonov completed the passage:

Не лучше ль стало б вам с надеждою смиренной
Заняться службою гражданской иль военной?

[Shouldn't you rather, in submissive hope, / Take a civil or military post?]

This final couplet elicited another round of applause. The distinction between "rhymesters" and poets was not lost on this gathering. Those present would also have recalled other lines from this poem, even though Tikhonov did not read them:

Новейшие врали вралей старинных стоят—
И слишком уж меня их бредни беспокоят.
Ужели всё молчать, да слушать? О беда! . . .
Нет, всё им выскажу однажды завсегда.

[The liars of today merit the liars of yesterday— / And their chatter disturbs me far too much. / Must I really hold my peace and listen? Oh grief! . . . / No, I'll tell them off once and for all.)

Tikhonov (and his sympathetic listeners) received a rebuke from Surkov, who took the floor to express his displeasure: "I didn't like Tikhonov's address," said Surkov. "He didn't relate Pushkin to issues that are important for us today."[45]

It may seem surprising that this section of Tikhonov's address passed the review process, until one considers that the person vetting the reports would have been Stavsky, whose rabid enthusiasm for hunting down saboteurs was matched only by his astonishing political and literary naïveté. Stavsky was not the man to perceive double-voicedness or analogy. He did, however, censor passages that he considered to be against party interests, and he is probably responsible for the excision of a large portion of Tikhonov's speech that is crossed out in the draft preserved in the Writers' Union archive. In the excised portion of his address, Tikhonov identified a number of Soviet poets who, in his opinion, showed a strong Pushkinian influence, including Boris Pasternak, Nikolai Zabolotsky, Boris Kornilov, and Nikolai Aseev, to whom he had devoted a substantial portion of his address.[46] The whole section on Aseev is crossed out, as are Tikhonov's briefer remarks on Zabolotsky and Kornilov and most of the section on Pasternak.

Aseev, whose early experiments with *zaum'* ("trans-sense" language) had led to charges of formalism, had also written many smooth, "accessible" poems, and he even helped to create popular cultural icons (one of his poems became a popular song about the cavalry general Marshal Budennyi, and he collaborated on the subtitles for Eisenstein's celebrated film *The Battleship Potemkin* [*Bronenosets Potemkin*]). In the excised portion of his speech, Tikhonov insisted that Aseev needed to be read in his entirety, and he complained that many of his poems were unjustly ignored or frowned upon.[47] We can understand this statement both as a defense of Aseev's futurist poetry and as a sidelong jab at the Pushkin cliché as the ultimate sound bite. Tikhonov also quoted from Aseev's poem "The Bull" ("Byk"), which compares Pushkin to a bull who, although killed in a bullfight, never gave in to his enemies.[48] "Aseev is a restless poet," wrote Tikhonov in the draft of his address. "He knows that poetry is a dangerous craft, because it needs to be approached with the same intelligence as explosives, or else it will blow the person who treats it carelessly to bits."[49] It is impossible to say whether Tikhonov intended this statement as an allusion to writers' vulnerability to arrest, but it certainly seems safe to say that some of his listeners would have made that connection.

Tynianov's address began on safe ground, linking Pushkin to Soviet values, making the point that Pushkin sided with the disenfranchised and the "new man," and quoting a passage from *The Blackamoor of Peter the Great* (*Arap Petra Velikogo* [1828]) that had a surprisingly Soviet sound to it: "To Ibrahim, Russia was like a gigantic workshop . . . where machines were in motion and where every worker was part of a mechanism that had been set in motion and was busy with his job. Ibrahim considered himself obligated to labor at his own lathe as well."[50] The "new man" fighting alongside the ruler sounds very much like the Soviet "new man" fighting alongside Stalin, and Tynianov seemed to adduce this similarity with approval, commenting: "This excerpt is surprising for 1828; it sounds like an excerpt from our prose, so deeply did Pushkin understand the Petrine epoch. . . . The pathos of this piece lies in the new man [Ibrahim Gannibal], who fights alongside Peter for reform and who masters a new, high culture."[51]

After this auspicious beginning, however, Tynianov went on to describe Pushkin's aesthetics in a way that implied a critique of socialist realism. Pushkin's language and style were diverse, said Tynianov, and offered wide latitude for reader interpretation.[52] Characters like Sil'vio and the stationmaster in *Tales of the Late Ivan Petrovich Belkin* (*Povesti pokoinogo Ivana Petrovicha Belkina* [1830]) are barely sketched out, so that readers have a great deal of interpretive freedom to fill in the details. Pushkin's narrative is only a half narrative—it is his half of a dialogue with his reader, who fills in the rest. Tynianov supports his argument by pointing to the ending of the story "Kirdzhali" ("Kirdzhali" [1834]), when Pushkin turns to his readers and asks their opinion.[53] This sort of freedom of interpretation was thoroughly incompatible with socialist realism's insistence on positive heroes and irredeemable villains; it further transgressed Soviet literary aesthetics in its preference for readers' doing the work of interpretation rather than passively receiving an "accessible" text.[54]

Tynianov continued his indirect polemic with socialist realism by noting Pushkin's criticism of literary *odnoobraznost'* (monotony, sameness of manner).[55] Into the monotonous sameness deplored by Pushkin, it was easy to read a latter-day version of it: socialist realism's monolithic poetics of solemn glorification and tendentiousness, prescribed by Zhdanov in his keynote speech at the Writers' Union's first congress.[56] In that context, Tynianov's observation that Pushkin battled the prevailing, restrictive notions of literary taste and fought back when critics attacked his work reflected on writers' conditions in 1937.

Al'tman's speech continued the implicit argument against socialist realism's monolithic aesthetics: "Pushkin shows us that the comic, the tragic, the lyric, and the intimate can all be mixed without detriment."[57] Both Tynianov and Al'tman were in effect continuing Mirsky's line of thought in his 1934 article: Pushkin's aesthetics are "open," allowing contradictory interpretations that, far from diminishing his art, make it more profound. All three critics saw in Pushkin's aesthetics a multilayered ambiguity that implied an actively interpreting reader, not the passive recipient of the univalent, pro-Soviet text.

Al'tman identified Pushkin's main themes as freedom, dignity, the "conflict between [an individual's] personal will and the needs of the state," and the spread of personal immorality under tyrannical regimes.[58] This characterization conforms to the official cliché, and it is fair to say that Al'tman intended it this way; but its Aesopian possibilities would certainly have occurred to many in the audience. Taking Pushkin's characters Germann, Aleko, and Onegin as his examples, Al'tman argued that under more benevolent circumstances these characters would not have been so villainous. In *Mozart and Salieri* (*Motsart i Sal'eri* [1830]), Al'tman said, Salieri's crime "is the fruit of a tortuous struggle within himself. He remains alive, but morally he has perished."[59]

Similarly, Al'tman discussed *A Feast in the Time of Plague* (*Pir vo vremia chumy* [1830]) in terms that conformed to the cliché: "Pushkin seems to say, 'Fight to the end.' The tragedy is not that the feasters may die the next day but that their leader is in despair and is not a fighter."[60] Al'tman's comment brings to mind the Soviet Union as a nation willing to offer the ultimate sacrifice of its own as long as they are led honorably by the fighter Stalin. But Al'tman went on to offer a quotation from the play *The Water Nymph* (*Rusalka* [1829–32]) that resonated in Stalin's direction in an opposite way. The miller's daughter, referring to the prince who has had his fun with her only to abandon her with a shrug, laments, "I loved him so much . . . or is he a beast?"[61]

The taboo messages contained in the keynote speeches were reinforced and supplemented by other writers who took the floor. The poet Vera Inber alluded humorously to the dullness of Soviet literature, relaying a librarian's remark that Soviet poets were in trouble, because readers were asking only for Pushkin. The real problem, offered Inber, will come if, after reading Pushkin, people then read Soviet poets. The archival record notes laughter from the audience.[62]

The first four days of the plenum were infiltrated with taboo messages by analogy and implication. At the same time, most of the speeches had impeccable deniability, because they could also be understood as referring simply to Pushkin's personal and literary behavior as an opponent of the retrograde autocrat Nicholas I. None of the speakers could be faulted for quoting Pushkin; yet Pushkin's verse acquired a double-voicedness in the context of Soviet speeches addressing the question of "Pushkin for our time."

On the final day of the plenum, however, the poet Il'ia Sel'vinsky broke the taboos wide open with a speech blasting Soviet literary criticism and *Pravda* itself. Sel'vinsky was one of several poets who essentially boycotted the plenum, including—not surprisingly—Aseev and Bednyi and also Alexander Bezymensky, Semen Kirsanov, Pasternak, Mikhail Svetlov, Iosif Utkin, and Alexander Zharov. The very act of staying away was taboo. Articles in *Pravda* and *Izvestiia* attacking Sel'vinsky, published on the last two days of the plenum, goaded him into showing up for the final session.[63]

Sel'vinsky took the floor and explained why he had skipped the first four days: "It is difficult and painful for me to be at the plenum after being spat on, covered with garbage, and kicked into the dirt. I've been getting kicked into the dirt for many years."[64] No less a luminary than Lev Tolstoi had skipped the 1880 Pushkin celebration without being made a spectacle of public indignation; so why, Sel'vinsky wanted to know, were Soviet writers considered guilty if they skipped this Pushkin plenum?[65] Sel'vinsky exposed the technique of defining poets through skewed, selective readings that excerpted "four lines out of a thousand."[66] He reminded his audience that Maiakovsky, recently ordained by Stalin as "the best and most talented Soviet poet," had at one time denigrated Pushkin. Maiakovsky, argued Sel'vinsky, was simply expressing the dialectical relationship between any master and his forebears. Look at Stalin's biography, Sel'vinsky continued, and you'll see that he continues Lenin's cause by pushing away from him—something that is normal and necessary.[67]

Sel'vinsky exposed the spurious methods used to hound Soviet writers. He complained about the abusive treatment of writers in the press, including smear tactics such as identifying the author's beliefs with those of one of his fictional characters. The mass reader, said Sel'vinsky, has no time to check; he takes the critic at his word, and the critic has no business deceiving the masses. Critics of low literary standing published widely read articles dismissing gifted writers. "Let someone better than I say that I'm a bad writer," said Sel'vinsky. "Then I'll take the criticism seriously." The delegates applauded him at the end of his speech.[68]

The official Pushkin of 1937 emerged amid taboo undercurrents that rippled through published discussions and highly publicized events like the Pushkin plenum. Not only nonparty writers but even as orthodox a party official as Kirpotin, in promoting a Pushkin for the masses, gave a more objective description of Pushkin than did the official Soviet cliché. Other Communist critics, too, preferred to humanize Pushkin, acknowledging and excusing his compromises with the autocracy. Even in the spotlight of the plenum, writers offered one another Aesopian readings over the head of the dull-witted Stavsky and invoked Pushkin to imply their rejection of socialist realism in favor of a more open, multilayered aesthetics of ambiguity. The writers understood, too, that their literary critique veered uncomfortably close to a moral imperative. Sergeev-Tsensky summed it up after the plenum was over: the poet of Pushkin's day possessed an unanswerable authority. Writing as part of *October*'s "discussion" forum in response to Kirpotin's book, Tsensky cites (inaccurately) Pushkin's "The Echo" ("Ekho" [1831]):

Поёт ли дева за холмом,
Гремит ли гром,
На всякий звук ты должен отзываться.
Тебе же нет ответа.
Таков и ты, поэт.[69]

[If a young girl sings beyond the hillside, / If thunder rumbles, / You must respond to each and every sound. / To you, however, there can be no response. / That's what it means to be a poet.]

A poet, in other words, has an obligation to his world; and the poet who fulfills that obligation gains an authority, whether aesthetic or moral, that is absolute and therefore unanswerable. Tsensky added his own comment: "This unanswerability on the part of the poet was keenly felt *in those times*."[70] Without saying so overtly, Tsensky implied a contrast with his own day, when writers and poets deferred to the unanswerable authority of the state.

Notes

1. See Stephanie Sandler, "The Pushkin Myth in Russia," in *The Pushkin Handbook*, ed. David M. Bethea (Madison: University of Wisconsin Press, 2005), 410; and Stephanie Sandler, "The 1937 Pushkin Jubilee as Epic Trauma," in *Epic Revisionism: Russian History and Literature as Stalinist Propaganda*, ed. Kevin M. F. Platt and David Brandenberger (Madison: University of Wisconsin Press, 2006), 200, 206–7. Sandler argues persuasively that the story of Pushkin's death—which was often retold as part of the 1937 Pushkin celebrations, containing as it did elements of conspiracy and the authorities' desire to eliminate him—came to be seen as a variant of the deaths of Stalin's victims.

2. Konstantin A. Zalesskii, *Imperiia Stalina: Biograficheskii i entsiklopedicheskii slovar'* (Moscow: Veche, 2000), 272.

3. Angela Brintlinger, *Writing a Usable Past: Russian Literary Culture, 1917–1937* (Evanston: Northwestern University Press, 2000), 148.

4. Vikentii V. Veresaev, *V dvukh planakh: Stat'i o Pushkine* (Moscow: Izdatel'skoe tovarishchestvo Nedra, 1929), [5].

5. Alexander M. Dubrovsky, "Chronicle of a Poet's Downfall: Dem'ian Bednyi, Russian History, and *The Epic Heroes*," in Platt and Brandenberger, *Epic Revisionism*, 84.

6. *Vlast' i khudozhestvennaia intelligentsia* (Moscow: Mezhdunarodnyi fond Demokratiia, 2002), 218. The Politburo resolution on memorializing Pushkin was passed on 27 July 1934; it was reinforced by two subsequent resolutions, on 15 December 1935 and 29 December 1936 (*Vlast' i khudozhestvennaia intelligentsia*, 280, 344–46).

7. Dubrovsky, "Chronicle of a Poet's Downfall," 88.

8. *Pravda*'s notorious attack on Shostakovich can be found in "Sumbur vmesto muzyki," *Pravda*, 28 January 1936, 3. For an excellent analysis, see Leonid Maksimenkov, *Sumbur vmesto muzyki: Stalinskaia kul'turnaia revoliutsiia, 1936–1938* (Moscow: Iuridicheskaia kniga, 1997). For a reaction to the attack on Shostakovich, see Iurii Olesha in *Soviet Culture and Power: A History in Documents, 1917–1953*, ed. Katerina Clark and Evgeny Dobrenko (New Haven: Yale University Press, 2007), 231; as well as Vladimir V. Ermilov's letter to Alexander A. Fadeev of 11 February 1936, Russian State Archive for Literature and Art, Moscow [RGALI], f. 1628, op. 2, ed. khr. 712, ll. 131–32).

9. Dubrovsky, "Chronicle of a Poet's Downfall," 82. Even as savvy a Stalin watcher as Lev Mekhlis, *Pravda*'s editor in chief, did not always immediately sense the shifts in Stalin's thinking; see Iurii Rubtsov, *Alter ego Stalina: Stranitsy*

politicheskoi biografii L. Z. Mekhlisa (Moscow: Zvonnitsa-MG, 1999), 72. From time to time newspapers would print op-ed pieces on literature under the rubric of "discussion," allowing the expression of views that did not have party approval (although sometimes such articles would be counterbalanced or "corrected" by a more authoritative article appearing on the same page).

10. See Jonathan Brooks Platt, "Feast in the Time of Terror: Stalinist Temporal Paradox and the 1937 Pushkin Jubilee" (PhD diss., Columbia University, 2008), 126.

11. Dmitrii S. Mirskii, "Problema Pushkina," *Literaturnoe nasledstvo* 16–18 (1934): 101.

12. Ibid., 96.

13. Ibid., 101–2.

14. Valerii Ia. Kirpotin, "Aleksandr Sergeevich Pushkin," *Oktiabr'* 1 (1937): 5–65.

15. On projective language, see Boris Groys, *The Total Art of Stalinism: Avant-Garde, Aesthetic Dictatorship, and Beyond* (Princeton: Princeton University Press, 1992), 112.

16. Aleksandr S. Pushkin, "K Chedaevu," in his *Polnoe sobranie sochinenii*, 17 vols., ed. Vladimir D. Bonch-Bruevich et al. (Moscow: AN SSSR, 1937–59), 2:72.

17. On the path to consciousness, see Katerina Clark, *The Soviet Novel: History as Ritual* (Chicago: University of Chicago Press, 1984), 84–86.

18. Valerii Ia. Kirpotin, "Aleksandr Sergeevich Pushkin," *Oktiabr'* 4 (1937): 198. For a discussion of how Kirpotin came to abandon his scholarly standards, see David Powelstock, "Fashioning 'Our Lermontov': Canonization and Conflict in the Stalinist 1930s," in Platt and Brandenberger, *Epic Revisionism*, 296–300.

19. Kirpotin, "Aleksandr Sergeevich Pushkin," 16–17.

20. Ibid., 16.

21. Aleksandr S. Pushkin, "Vol'nost'," in his *Polnoe sobranie sochinenii*, 17 vols., 2:45.

22. A tiny minority of diehards continued to insist that Pushkin did not belong in the pantheon of classics. See, for example, the comments of Liia M. Myshkovskaia in "Nasledie Pushkina i kommunizm," *Oktiabr'* 4 (1937): 195–96.

23. See the remarks of Nikolai Nakoriakov in "Nasledie Pushkina i kommunizm," 194.

24. Ibid., 191–92.

25. Sergei Fomichev, "Pushkinskaia tekstologiia: Akademicheskoe izdanie polnogo sobranie sochinenii Pushkina," in *The Pushkin Handbook*, ed. David M. Bethea (Madison: University of Wisconsin Press, 2005), 26.

26. The first two parts of Tynianov's novel were published in *Literaturnyi sovremennik* (*The Literary Contemporary*) from 1935 to 1937 and reprinted in 1937 and 1938. A third installment appeared in the *Standard* (*Znamia*) in 1943.

27. Boris Eikhenbaum's *Lev Tolstoi: 50-ye gody* (Leningrad: Priboi, 1928) and *Lev Tolstoi: 60-ye gody* (Leningrad: Khudozhestvennaia literatura, 1931) adopt this approach. See Carol Any, *Boris Eikhenbaum: Voices of a Russian Formalist* (Stanford: Stanford University Press, 1994), 127.

28. Brintlinger, *Writing a Usable Past*, 58.

29. Alexandra Smith writes that Tynianov "presents the poet's biography as that of a hero" ("Conformist by Circumstance v. Formalist at Heart: Some Observations on Tynianov's Novel *Pushkin*," in *Neo-Formalist Papers*, ed. Joe Andrew and Robert Reid [Amsterdam: Rodopi, 1998], 301). Smith also hints that in this case, formalist suppositions and Stalinist aesthetics unexpectedly led to the same end—Pushkin as hero.

30. See Valentina A. Antipina, *Povsednevnaia zhizn' sovetskikh pisatelei, 1930–1950-e* (Moscow: Molodaia gvardiia, 2005), 183–91.

31. See Stanislav Kuniaev and Sergei Kuniaev, comps., *Rassterzannye teni* (Moscow: Golos, 1995), 264–304.

32. Konstantin Fedin, "Virtuoznyi master," in *Vospominaniia o Iu. Tynianove: Portrety i vstrechi* (Moscow: Sovetskii pisatel', 1983), 309, cited in Smith, "Conformist by Circumstance v. Formalist at Heart," 296.

33. See Karen Petrone, *Life Has Become More Joyous, Comrades: Celebrations in the Time of Stalin* (Bloomington: Indiana University Press, 2000), 122.

34. See Sandler, "The 1937 Pushkin Jubilee as Epic Trauma," 199; and Arlen V. Blium, *Sovetskaia tsenzura v epokhe total'nogo terrora 1929–1953* (St. Petersburg: Akademicheskii proekt, 2000), 169, cited in Sandler, "The 1937 Pushkin Jubilee as Epic Trauma," 199.

35. The six-day trial of Grigorii Zinov'ev, Lev Kamenev, and fourteen other defendants that began on 19 August 1936 and the trial of Iurii Piatakov, Karl Radek, and seventeen others that opened on 23 January 1937 were the first two of the three showcase trials of the Great Terror and signified Stalin's success in eliminating the Old Bolsheviks who had been key figures in the Russian revolution.

36. A transcript of many of the speeches at the CPSU plenum can be found online at http://www.memo.ru/history/1937/index.htm (accessed 15 November 2007).

37. RGALI, f. 631, op. 15, ed. khr. 169, l. 7.

38. RGALI, f. 631, op. 15, ed. khr. 179, 22 February 1937, l. 10.

39. RGALI, f. 631, op. 15, ed. khr. 179, ll. 17–19.

40. RGALI, f. 631, op. 15, ed. khr. 179, ll. 9–12; ed. khr., 187, ll. 134–58.

41. RGALI, f. 631, op. 15, ed. khr. 180, l. 93.

42. RGALI, f. 631, op. 15, ed. khr. 179, l. 67.

43. Aleksandr S. Pushkin, "Frantsuzskikh rifmachei surovyi sudiia," in his *Polnoe sobranie sochinenii*, 17 vols., 3:305–6. Tikhonov quotes from a pre-1937 edition of the poem that was based on a manuscript misreading; modern editions have "neobdumannym" (thoughtless) in place of "neobuzdannym" (unbridled).

44. RGALI, f. 631, op. 15, ed. khr. 179, l. 59.

45. RGALI, f. 631, op. 15, ed. khr. 181, l. 83ff.

46. RGALI, f. 631, op. 15, ed. khr. 179; most of the text on sheets 60–66 is crossed out.

47. RGALI, f. 631, op. 15, ed. khr. 179, l. 59.

48. RGALI, f. 631, op. 15, ed. khr. 179, l. 61. The poem appears to be unpublished.

49. Ibid.

50. RGALI, f. 631, op. 15, ed. khr. 180, l. 18; Aleksandr S. Pushkin, *Arap Petra Velikogo*, in his *Polnoe sobranie sochinenii*, 17 vols., 8:13. On the practice of selective quotation from Pushkin's works in Soviet and post-Soviet times, see Alyssa Gillespie's introduction to the present volume ("Beyond Pushkin as Dogma," 18–19).

51. RGALI, f. 631, op. 15, ed. khr. 180, l. 18. On Stalin's redefinition of Peter the Great as a state builder and part of a "usable past" for the Soviet Union, see David Brandenburger, *National Bolshevism: Stalinist Mass Culture and the Formation of Modern Russian National Identity, 1931–1936* (Cambridge, MA: Harvard University Press, 2002), 47–58.

52. A similar point is made in Alexandra Smith, "The Reach of Modern Life: Tynianov's Pushkin, Melancholy and the Critique of Modernity," *Wiener Slawistischer Almanach* 61 (2008): 90.

53. RGALI, f. 631, op. 15, ed. khr. 180, l. 25.

54. Tynianov's reference to Pushkin's "barely sketched-out" characters suggests the formalist interest in fragmentation and interruption, and his invitation to the reader to contribute meaning through the act of interpretation implies what Monika Greeenleaf has aptly called "the addressee's unforeseeable contribution to the generation of meaning" ("Tynianov, Pushkin, and the Fragment: Through the Lens of Montage," in *Cultural Mythologies of Russian Modernism: From the Golden Age to the Silver Age*, ed. Boris Gasparov, Robert P. Hughes, and Irina Paperno [Berkeley: University of California Press, 1992], 281).

55. RGALI, f. 631, op. 15, ed. khr. 180, l. 8.

56. *Pervyi vsesoiuznyi s"ezd sovetskikh pisatelei 1934: Stenograficheskii otchet* (Moscow: Gosudarstvennoe izdatel'stvo khudozhestvennaia literatura, 1934), 4.

57. RGALI, f. 631, op. 15, ed. khr. 179, l. 65.

58. RGALI, f. 631, op. 15, ed. khr. 180, ll. 44–45.

59. RGALI, f. 631, op. 15, ed. khr. 180, l. 56. On Soviet writers' use of historical analogy to come to terms with the Stalin era, see Katerina Clark, *Petersburg: Crucible of Cultural Revolution* (Cambridge, MA: Harvard University Press, 1995), 192; Smith, "The Reach of Modern Life," 93; Ludmilla Trigos, "An Exploration of the Dynamics of Mythmaking: Tynianov's *Kiukhlia*," *Slavic and East European Journal* 46.2 (2002): 283–300; and Oksana Bulgakova, "Pushkinskie motivy u Eizenshteina," in *Pushkinskaia konferentsiia v Stenforde, 1999: Materialy i issledovaniia*, ed. David Bethea et al. (Moscow: OGI, 2001), 472–84.

60. RGALI, f. 631, op. 15, ed. khr. 180, l. 63.

61. Ibid.; Aleksandr S. Pushkin, *Rusalka,* in his *Polnoe sobranie sochinenii,* 17 vols., 7:193–94.

62. RGALI, f. 631, op. 15, ed. khr. 183, l. 35.

63. RGALI, f. 631, op. 15, ed. khr. 186, l. 35.

64. RGALI, f. 631, op. 15, ed. khr. 186, l. 34.

65. Ibid.

66. RGALI, f. 631, op. 15, ed. khr. 186, l. 41.

67. RGALI, f. 631, op. 15, ed. khr. 186, l. 39.

68. RGALI, f. 631, op. 15, ed. khr. 186, l. 43. As far as I can determine, Sel'vinsky's blunt and courageous speech did not result in adverse consequences for him, nor should this necessarily be surprising. Many other factors, such as class background, accusations of foreign involvement, and association with high-profile figures accused of state crimes, were more important in determining who got arrested and who did not.

69. Tsensky misquotes the lines. See Aleksandr S. Pushkin, "Ekho," in his *Polnoe sobranie sochinenii,* 17 vols., 3:276.

70. "Nasledie Pushkina i kommunizm," 192 (emphasis added).

Krzhizhanovsky's Pushkin in the 1930s

The Cleopatra Myth from Femme Fatale to Roman Farce

Caryl Emerson

On 2 January 1936, as part of the upcoming Pushkin jubilee, the State Moscow Chamber Theater commissioned a stage adaptation of Pushkin's *Eugene Onegin* (*Evgenii Onegin*) from one of its longtime lecturers in the Experimental Acting Studio, Sigizmund Krzhizhanovsky.[1] Incidental music was to be provided by Sergei Prokofiev, then in the process of repatriating with his family from Paris to Moscow. The musical score was composed, costumes were even sketched, but the play script, several times revised, never passed theatrical censorship. In the opinion of party watchdogs and official Pushkinists, Krzhizhanovsky had intervened too radically in the canonical text. While retaining the torso of the Onegin stanza, he had removed Pushkin's narrator, reassigned lines, shifted major events to deep winter, changed the order of some crucial episodes, and enriched the speaking parts with fairy tales and other poetry by Pushkin. The centennial event itself—the death of a poet in a duel—was staged only as a stub: in a howling blizzard,

Onegin mutters remorsefully over the dead body of his friend. This postmortem scene grows directly out of Tatiana's terrifying, gratifying dream.[2]

The stalled *Onegin* project was canceled abruptly in December 1936, in the panicked aftermath of an unrelated crisis at the Chamber Theater: the Politburo's sudden attack on a production of Borodin's operatic farce *Epic Heroes* (*Bogatyri*), with libretto by Dem'ian Bednyi (see Carol Any in the present volume).[3] The theater's director, Alexander Tairov, hastened to cleanse his jubilee-year repertory of all controversial projects. The dramatized *Onegin* disappeared. For Krzhizhanovsky, this collapse was the latest (but not the last) in a decade of failures to realize his creative work in press, film, or on stage. A gifted adaptor for the theater, he was also a writer of phantasmagorical prose and a provocative, although "unofficial," student of Pushkin, Shakespeare, and George Bernard Shaw. The focus of the present chapter is a second Pushkin-centered project undertaken by Krzhizhanovsky in the 1930s, in its own way as noncanonical as his dramatic variations on the inner life of Tatiana Larina: the staging and then satirizing of the symbolist-era Cleopatra myth. But first, a word about this little-known Russian writer.

Krzhizhanovsky, Quasi-Person

Sigizmund Krzhizhanovsky (1887–1950), russophone modernist of Polish descent, was born near Kiev and died in his beloved adopted city Moscow, almost wholly unpublished and unperformed. His tall thin person with pince-nez was a familiar figure in the literary salons of Kiev and, after 1922, among avant-garde circles of the capital. Over a period of thirty years Krzhizhanovsky authored 150 short prose works, ranging in length from novellas to one-paragraph miniatures. As a literary critic, however, he specialized in drama, devising the term "realist-experimenter" for Shakespeare (and for himself) and constructing his own work on the boundary between fantasy, shadows, and things.[4] By the early 1920s, his long-term interests in Kantian philosophy, dream psychology, and cutting-edge theories of time-space perception had inspired him to see in theatrical art an analogue for human thought more generally.[5] He adapted works by Pushkin, Tolstoi, Shakespeare, Swift, and G. K. Chesterton for stage, radio, screen—all the while authoring hilarious comedies of his own (ten have survived), filled with punning wordplay and philosophical allusion. During World War II, Krzhizhanovsky tried to fit his literary gifts to socialist realist priorities, turning to patriotic libretti, military-historical drama, and pious (although still impressionistic) sketches of Moscow under siege. But during his lifetime, no collection of his prose ever made it through to print, nor any of his original plays to opening night. Only nine short stories, one stage adaptation in 1923, a 1942–43 libretto on the legendary General Suvorov, and a handful of critical articles, largely on drama, saw official light of day.[6]

This invisibility was largely due to Krzhizhanovsky's nonmaterialist neo-Kantian (or "idealist") aesthetics. But he was dogged as well by bad luck, bad timing, personal stubbornness, and lack of influential patrons. In 1932, Maksim Gorky casually assessed several of his meta-philosophical stories and found them too intellectual, "better suited to the late nineteenth century" and irrelevant to the struggles of the working class.[7] This unfortunate verdict stuck to the author up to and beyond his death. When, in 1939, he was finally voted into the Soviet Writers' Union, one of his sponsors explained the delay by noting that comrade Krzhizhanovsky, an erudite polyglot and critic, was known for being "very modest and impractical, unable to do anything for himself."[8] More to the point, he refused to revise on command, whether for censors or for well-meaning collaborators. So Krzhizhanovsky free-lanced for a living—hiring himself out for editorial work, public lectures, translations, encyclopedia entries, academic backup for radio shows. He was known as a specialist on the English classics and on the poetics of "literary parts": titles, stage directions, and epigraphs. For six years, from 1925 to 1931, he worked as head proofreader (kontrol'nyi redaktor) for the *Great Soviet Encyclopedia*. Surely his most satisfying part-time job was as pedagogue, lecturer, and adapter of plays at the Moscow Chamber Theater, where he was on the roster of employees from 1922 until 1949.

In 1957, seven years after Krzhizhanovsky's death, his widow Anna Bovshek (1887–1971) appealed to the Writers' Union for her husband's literary "immortalization" (uvekovechenie pamiati), an official ritual that posthumously commemorated union members. A commission chaired by the Shakespeare scholar Alexander Anikst was appointed to review all published and unpublished work. Its report a year later argued forcefully that the candidate's meager profile in print "gave absolutely no idea of the originality of his talent or the meaning of his creative work for Soviet literature"—and thus a thirteen-hundred-page, two-volume edition of his writings was "absolutely indispensable."[9] The union voted in favor. But in 1959 the project ran afoul of institutional inertia and a hostile reader's report. The manuscripts remained in Bovshek's clothes closet until 1965, when, after some reluctance, the Russian State Archive for Literature and Art agreed to make room for them. In the late 1960s, the poet Vadim Perel'muter began to examine these files. He ushered into print the first collection of Krzhizhanovsky's prose tales at the height of glasnost (1989). Another twenty years passed, and a fully annotated five-volume *Collected Works* appeared under Perel'muter's editorship. A mini-boom developed in Russia around Krzhizhanovsky's tales, which soon spread to France and Poland; his English-language profile was launched with seven stories in 2007, several more in 2009, and his best novella in 2011.[10] But his literary criticism and drama have yet to find a market outside Russian academic scholarship. In the projects resuscitated here—Krzhizhanovsky's part in the crowning and then decrowning of the symbolist-era Cleopatra myth—the forces of tradition, censorship, satire, farce, and taboo operate on several levels, as an unrecognized writer pulls a canonical jubilee Pushkin into ever more illicit zones.

There were two "Cleopatra dramas" in Krzhizhanovsky's creative life. The first was arguably the most opulent example of her myth on the Stalinist-era stage. In December 1934, to mark the twentieth anniversary of the Moscow Chamber Theater, Tairov premiered a hybrid extravaganza, *Egyptian Nights* (*Egipetskie nochi*), with music by Sergei Prokofiev. Letters exchanged between director (in Moscow) and composer (still in Paris) suggest that the spectacle was designed for a gala European-American tour to celebrate Soviet cultural internationalism while showcasing Tairov's wife, Alisa Koonen, a talented tragedienne and the theater's leading actress.[11] The foreign tour never came to pass; the production, however, enjoyed a successful two-year domestic run.[12] Beyond its title, it owed little to Pushkin's unfinished prose-verse sketch from 1837. The opening scenes were adapted from George Bernard Shaw's 1898 history play *Caesar and Cleopatra*; the rest was from Shakespeare's 1607 tragedy *Antony and Cleopatra*. Pushkin's contribution was modest. His 1828 "Cleopatra" poem ("The palace gleamed" ["Chertog siial"]), declaimed to Prokofiev's music, served to connect the two English plays and the two halves of the queen's amorous career. Most certainly Krzhizhanovsky (known as a specialist on these two English playwrights) was a consultant for this curious, cobbled-together script.

The second Cleopatra drama, *That Third One* (*Tot tretii*), is indisputably the work of Krzhizhanovsky himself and still largely unknown (written in 1937, it was published in Russian only in 2010).[13] Here Pushkin's "Cleopatra" poem serves not as a bridge between two pre-existing dramatic treatments but as stimulus for an entirely new plot. Krzhizhanovsky re-motivates Pushkin's poem, supplies a supporting cast, and then spins out an adventure sequel featuring the final of the three infatuated men who respond to the queen's challenge of certain death for a single night of love. In Pushkin, we recall, the first two volunteers have proper names and professions: Flavius, "brave Roman warrior" (Flavii, voin smelyi) and Criton, "youthful sage" (Kriton, mladoi mudrets). The third, however, "did not bequeath his name to the ages" (Poslednii imeni vekam / ne peredal).[14] Picking up on Pushkin's last-minute cue that the queen might have taken pity on this timid final volunteer, Krzhizhanovsky spares and then tracks the "third" in Alexandria, against a backdrop of the crumbling Second Triumvirate and bumbling Roman secret police.

Lada Panova, world authority on the literary theme of Russia and Egypt, considers *That Third One* the most original and ambitious of all twentieth-century attempts to complete Pushkin's Cleopatra fragments.[15] As a completion, however, it goes against the conventional grain. In contrast to serious melodramatic resolutions by Valerii Briusov (1916) and Modest Gofman (1935) and also to Anna Akhmatova's exalted self-fashioning in her own "Cleopatra" lyric of 1940, Krzhizhanovsky's play is a travesty, most uncommon for Russian "Cleopatrimony."[16] As Panova everywhere emphasizes, the authority of Pushkin's sultry femme fatale portrait of Egypt's queen was overwhelming for Russian poets—even though the sadomasochistic wager it describes is almost certainly apocryphal, the product of unscrupulous Roman propaganda and a very minor part of Cleopatra's image worldwide.[17] Tairov too had reasons to mute that Pushkinian subtext. The remainder of this chapter explores these two dramatic projects, Tairov's musicalized spectacle of 1934 and Krzhizhanovsky's barely audible farce of 1937, as mirror images of Cleopatra's potential for the Stalinist stage.

Fitting the Sun of Russian Poetry into Tairov's *Egyptian Nights*

In 1933, Tairov published an essay in the newspaper *Izvestiia* on adapting literary classics to the stage.[18] There he urged directors of new productions to identify "social nodes" (sotsial'nye uzly) in familiar repertory that spoke to contemporary problems. In April 1934, in a climate of rising fascism abroad, Tairov counseled the Communist Academy that any new staging of Shakespeare's *Antony and Cleopatra* must emphasize not its erotic but its political aspect. A proper politics would be two tiered: first a "political struggle among the triumvirate—Antony, Lepidus, and Octavius"—and then "the struggle of Egypt with Rome, the struggle of Cleopatra for the independence of Egypt."[19] The appropriate "social node," then, was to be Mark Antony against Octavius, with the renegade Roman soldier Antony cast as the protector of a threatened "colony" against the brutal intentions of imperial Rome. This battle line must be made explicit, Tairov wrote, since today "Mussolini, Hitler, and a whole series of big and small 'Caesars' . . . repeat or try to repeat, under different historical conditions, the experience of Octavius."[20] It would appear that Cleopatra as femme fatale and lover of Roman warriors had been sidelined by the times, replaced by a defiant patriot willing to sacrifice herself for her nation's honor.

Such an image can indeed be teased out of Shakespeare's tragedy. But no path leads to it from Pushkin's death-for-love wager, nor from Bernard Shaw's kittenish heroine.[21] The first four scenes of Shaw's *Caesar and Cleopatra*, which would come to serve as the basis for Tairov's part 1, are full of witty Shavian repartee between Julius Caesar (in his fifties) and the child queen (who is sixteen). The action peaks when Caesar, having coached his protégée on how to govern without cruelty or coquettishness, promises to send her a boyfriend more her own age, Mark Antony, "a beautiful young man with strong round arms" (the girl shrieks with delight).[22] Although the queen pouts and flirts to get Caesar's attention, he is immune to it. Whether he spends his nights with her is unclear; a busy Roman military ruler would not consider such details of his domestic comfort anyone's business on or off stage, nor would Shaw consider this issue a worthy pivot for a serious history play. The plot ends on the same affectionately avuncular note on which it opens: Caesar confirms his promise to send Mark Antony to Egypt and sails away for Rome. There are no sultry embraces, no baby son Caesarion. What Shaw gives us is the symmetrical arc of festive historical comedy—and neither Tairov nor Koonen could have possibly warmed to it. Nevertheless, Tairov wrote Shaw in July 1932, asking permission to use a bit of *Caesar and Cleopatra* for a new Chamber Theater project involving Shakespeare. He pointed out to Shaw that his 1898 Rome-and-Egypt play "objectively" could be considered "the first part of

Antony and Cleopatra"—because the two heroines share an "organic interconnection" and the two plays together display "a unified line of development."[23]

Shaw's response to this outrageous theatrical misjudgment is unknown, and even Tairov (who went ahead with his plans to use Shaw's play) soon backed off from it. As rehearsals wore on, a great deal of Shavian banter fell away from these scenes or was expressed through pantomime.[24] Also trimmed back was the role of Julius Caesar, Shaw's alter ego and intellectual voice. Shaw the dramatist sorely tried Tairov's patience. In an off-the-record talk with his company on 2 March 1934 (nine months before opening night), Tairov was already speaking of "Shaw's main failings as a playwright," noting the "unbridled lack of discipline in his speeches [*bezuderzhnost' rechi*]," which, Tairov remarked, "I am paring back in a most serious fashion, and I think to B. Shaw's benefit."[25] The director entered his native element only with Pushkin's poem and then with part 2 of the spectacle, basically acts 2–5 of Shakespeare's *Antony and Cleopatra* in a new translation by the Soviet literary bureaucrat Vladimir Lugovskoi. Cleopatra still pouted and raged, but her reputation as harlot, gypsy, strumpet, and Egypt's dish was now greatly downplayed.

Recalling the Chamber Theater's *Egyptian Nights* in later years, neither Krzhizhanovsky nor Prokofiev considered the pastiche successful as serious drama.[26] Each sensed that Shakespeare's tragedy was too monumental and authoritative to be fused with the playful, prosy, militantly antimelodramatic Shaw, who risked sounding trivial as prologue to it. The transition from Julius Caesar to Mark Antony—and Cleopatra's maturation from sixteen-year-old flirt to matron and captivating mistress of a Roman triumvir—rested wholly on Pushkin's slender poem. And although the poem's lurid plot did lend the prestige of Russia's greatest poet to the production, that plot bore no discernible relation to events in Cleopatra's biography as depicted on stage, in either the Shavian or the Shakespearean portions.

Reviews of Tairov's *Egyptian Nights* were mixed. Prokofiev's music was highly praised; the gold-plumed costumes and symmetrical choreography were sumptuously set off by Vadim Ryndin's faintly fascist-looking pyramidal set. The problem was the story. On 5 April 1935, theater critic Osaf Litovsky opened his review in *Soviet Art* (*Sovetskoe iskusstvo*) by citing a letter he had received from one spectator after the show, asking why Caesar got younger in the second act. Litovsky explained that these were two different Caesars, the elderly Julius

Maquette by Vadim Ryndin for the set "Rome and Egypt" that opened the Moscow Chamber Theater's production of *Egyptian Nights*, 1934. Courtesy of the Russian State Archive of Literature and Art, Moscow.

in part 1 and his adopted son Octavius in part 2. But the error was natural, he notes, because "absolutely nothing . . . unites Shaw and Shakespeare except the biography of the woman they shared, Cleopatra."[27] Overall, the male leads received little sustained attention; party critics, alert to contemporary Italian strongmen, did not approve of the Caesaro-centric, Caesaro-philic "Shavian half" of the show.[28]

The best defense we have for the cohesion of the play comes from Koonen's memoirs, which profoundly re-accent her husband's party-minded attempts to politicize the story. The Egyptian queen, in her view, is Everywoman in search of love. Koonen credits the Chamber Theater production for clarifying Cleopatra's quasi-legendary life, of which Shaw, Shakespeare, and Pushkin each recount one phase.[29] In part 1, Shaw gives us the little girl hiding scared within the Sphinx's paw, looking on the conqueror Julius Caesar as a *dedushka*, or grandfather (in Shaw, "old man"). This is the good, mentoring Caesar who promises her a grown-up love. In part 2, that love reaches its hungriest point. After Antony's death, the queen's erotic energy is transfigured into pure Egyptian patriotism, enabling her to trick Octavius, the second and despised Caesar, out of his Roman triumph. Koonen adroitly finesses Pushkin's contribution to this heroic trajectory. His entr'acte poem, delivered by a "wandering improvisator" (brodiachii improvizator), sings of that stretch of time between Julius Caesar and Mark Antony, years "filled with numerous legends about Cleopatra's dissolute life, her many lovers" and reflecting "the atmosphere of the Palace at Alexandria during that time."[30] Koonen insists that Pushkin, for all his focus on the lethal wager, showed us the queen "not so much as a sensuous enchantress but as a woman tormented by dissatisfaction and longing who only later will find joy in her great love for Antony."[31] The decadent appetites of Pushkin's Cleopatra neither debase her majesty nor interrupt the wholesome biographical arc of her onstage life. The purpose of the poetic insert, Koonen argues, was to amplify her legend—emphasizing, as ballads often do, some violent, colorful event attributed to a heroic or mythic protagonist.

The several partial *Egyptian Nights* playscripts in Tairov's archive suggest that the director deployed Pushkin's mythopoetic, deeply familiar text as a Russian banner or "binder" to domesticate the two flanking non-Russian sources.[32] The poem, chanted against a vague nocturnal backdrop of Sicilian harbors and pubs, served as the conduit out of Shaw into Shakespeare. It is overheard by Roman soldiers, among whose number is Enobarbus. Over wine, he is inspired to deliver his celebrated monologue on the ravishing queen on her golden barge that "burned on the water" like a "burnished throne" with its purple, perfumed, lovesick sails (*Antony and Cleopatra*, 2.2.201–3). This reminiscence by Enobarbus is the most wantonly seductive portrait of the Egyptian queen in all of Shakespeare's play (although there it is delivered, of course, in Rome). Its details provide plausible biographical motivation for the caprice of Pushkin's Cleopatra. But in Tairov's production, both the barge and the wager were distanced, mythologized, secondhand accounts, cast in ballad time and no-man's space. Pushkin's lines were recited by two voices simultaneously: a male voice (the wandering singer) chanted on stage while a female voice (Cleopatra's) doubled the text in the wings.[33]

Koonen's retrospective on her own role is a curious addendum to the Cleopatra myth. It turns the incompatibility of the play's three source texts—everyone's complaint about the theatrical *Egyptian Nights*—into a device to tame the queen's "infinite variety." Tairov was committed to cleansing the behavior of his heroine on stage. "As the show wore on," one critic notes, Koonen's tantrums and fits of jealousy "retreated to the background and then disappeared altogether."[34] This distinctly one-way moral trajectory suggests a larger Russian context for the Egyptian queen. Celebration of the strong sacrificial woman, purified through confronting and then disciplining her own illicit passions, has a lengthy history on Russian page and stage. It migrates from Pushkin's Tatiana to Lermontov's Tamara (*The Demon* [*Demon*]), from the heroines of Turgenev and Goncharov up through Ostrovsky's Katerina in *The Storm* (*Groza*) and Shostakovich's (not Leskov's) *Lady Macbeth of Mtsensk* (*Ledi Makbet Mtsenskogo uezda*). In 1933, it surfaced in Tairov's socialist realist triumph still fresh in everyone's mind, Vsevolod Vishnevsky's *Optimistic Tragedy* (*Optimisticheskaia tragediia*), featuring Koonen as a female Bolshevik commissar embracing death in the line of duty.[35] To showcase this prototypical Russian heroine, all Shavian intonations had to be toned down. In his many dozens of plays, with the possible exception of his 1923 history play *Saint Joan*, Shaw had little use for such simplified heroines (or heroes) thirsting for virtue, and he polemicized tirelessly against their falseness.

In the winter of 1935, the British theater critic André van Gyseghem interviewed Tairov before a performance of *Egyptian Nights*. He learned that Tairov had indeed been vexed by "Shaw's strong satirical note" but had resolved the contradiction by taking the prologue of the Shaw play, with its rebuke to British imperialism, more seriously than the play itself.[36] Gyseghem's account makes it clear that Tairov, who had almost no English, was hopelessly at sea in topical Shavian humor. The director also evinced no interest in Shaw's intricate polemic with Shakespeare. These details should be kept in mind while considering our second Cleopatra play, which was a product of the second, far more stressful half of the 1930s. Krzhizhanovsky's temperament (as well as his diligent study of the English language and anglophone comedy) qualified him in precisely those areas where his loyal friend Tairov fell short. In 1934, staging yet another inventive Russian Shakespeare was not controversial. But why, we might ask, had Tairov bothered to borrow from Bernard Shaw at all?

The Russian Shakespeare and Russian Shaw Help Shape "Cleopatrimony"

By producing an *Egyptian Nights* that stitched Pushkin's canonic Cleopatra into the work of two celebrated English-language playwrights,

Tairov was responding judiciously to high-profile publicity campaigns launched early in the Stalinist period that asserted Soviet Russia's right to assimilate the best literature of the bourgeois West. At the first Congress of Soviet Writers (1934), Shakespeare was presented to the Russian public as a class ally, "ours" (nash) on a par with Pushkin, a writer whose expansive, life-affirming genius now spoke more truly to progressive Soviet audiences than to the (literally) bankrupt cultures and economies of America and Europe.[37] The All-Union Theatrical Society set up a Shakespeare section to consult with theaters about properly party-minded productions. Shakespeare's path to canonization was peculiar, however. The Bolshevik 1920s had not fetishized the Bard. In 1932, at the Vakhtangov Theater, Nikolai Akimov had mounted a racy vaudeville-style *Hamlet* to a disjointed score by Dmitrii Shostakovich, during which (among other indignities) Horatio produces the ghost's voice by bellowing into a clay pot, a rosy robust Ophelia drowns herself while drunk, and the decadent sounds of waltz, tango, and can-can replace the usual Elizabethan period music.[38] It was a sign of revolutionary vigor that the bourgeois legacy could be treated with such impiety. By the mid-1930s, however, a more elevated presentation of Shakespeare's tragedies was preferred. This shift toward conservative norms suited the exquisite stage discipline of Tairov's "synthetic theater." Although the Chamber Theater was not a humorless place, it had always been most successful with high-minded, stylized productions.

Also in high favor, in addition to Shakespeare, was the most famous living writer of social comedy in English, George Bernard Shaw. The triumphant visit of this Fabian socialist to Moscow in July 1931, to celebrate his seventy-fifth birthday in the land of the Soviets, had been impeccably choreographed with cheering crowds, festive dinners, and a two-hour audience with Stalin.[39] Shaw knew Tairov's directorial work. In 1926 the Chamber Theater had staged Shaw's *Saint Joan* as an anticlerical burlesque, more in the spirit of Shakespeare's lampoon of the maid in *1 Henry VI* than of Shaw's probing, earnest portrait constructed against that caricature. Koonen had been uncomfortable in the title role. She would have chafed even more, however, in an orthodox Shavian interpretation of the play. A tragic actress in the rhythmic declamatory style of Racine, Koonen excelled at Phèdre and at Oscar Wilde's Salomé. In 1934 she was a credible sultry Cleopatra in *Egyptian Nights*. In her memoirs, however, she confessed that she had never liked "plays on such a conversational plane" as Bernard Shaw's, for their endless witticisms exhausted her.[40]

Tairov's decision to combine Shakespeare and Shaw in a single Cleopatra play yoked together by Pushkin's sensational verse anecdote might have been politically shrewd, but it was still an artistic risk. The incompatibility of its parts was exacerbated by Shaw's complex attitude toward Shakespeare—his deep knowledge of the plays and reverence for them alongside his campaign against "Bardolotry."[41] Shaw's position here recalls Pushkin's ambivalent Shakespearism, especially the poet's naughty "Voltairean" fantasy, while working on *Boris Godunov*, of creating a drama devoid of erotic love. In his 1901 preface to *Three Plays for Puritans* (the second was *Caesar and Cleopatra: A History*), Shaw notes how his own Egypt play would set right all the things he disliked in Shakespeare's *Antony and Cleopatra*. Prominent among those flaws is its "stage sensuousness," so very boring to watch. What begins in Alexandria as vigorous realistic dialogue, Shaw wrote, decays by the final act into an absurdly botched (and debauched) finale of suicides, made all the more ridiculous by the "theatrical sublimity" routinely accorded it. Furthermore, Shakespeare misrepresents and insults successful builders of empires like Caesar and Mark Antony, whose hard political work is shown to dissolve helplessly before "the typical wanton in whose arms such men perish." About this last point Shaw was adamant. "I have a technical objection to making sexual infatuation a tragic theme," he wrote. "Experience proves that it is only effective in the comic spirit. We can bear to see Mrs. Quickly pawning her plate for love of Falstaff, but not Antony running away from the Battle of Actium for love of Cleopatra."[42] Neither Tairov nor Koonen, both at heart sentimental modernists, could have sympathized with the debunking, deromanticizing side of Shaw. But Krzhizhanovsky would prove a close student of Shaw in his own Rome-and-Egypt project, adjusting Cleopatra and her lovers to Shaw's cerebral, acidic spirit.

Krzhizhanovsky's "Applied Poetics"

My hypothesis so far has two parts. First, that Krzhizhanovsky advised Tairov on his *Egyptian Nights* production—but the final results could only have disappointed him. Second, that the spirit (or taint) of Shaw so carefully muted in the Chamber Theater's 1934 *Egyptian Nights* reappeared three years later in Krzhizhanovsky's own hidden, forbidden satyr play *That Third One*, a covert response (or supplement) to Tairov's tragic-melodramatic spectacle. This shift in theatrical sympathies provides some insight into alternative interpretations of Pushkin that were possible even well into the Stalinist 1930s. During an idolatrous jubilee, Krzhizhanovsky pitted the playful, mocking, mock-epic side of the youthful Pushkin against the sacrificial life-and-death seriousness of the Egyptian queen's wager, a product of Pushkin's more mature years. It was a bold move. By the symbolist era, the cult of Pushkin as perfect but persecuted poet had fused with the myth of Cleopatra as seductive but punishing muse. In that spirit, Tairov—a state-favored director with a good feel for box office success—had linked his three sources mechanically through their conventional tragic climaxes. Krzhizhanovsky, student of Shakespeare and Shaw and a writer without a theater to protect (or even a reputation to risk), dared to connect them using the far richer, more ambivalent resources of comedy: festive, philosophical, and black.

That Third One was more than a farce composed against the political current, however. Krzhizhanovsky's philosophy of performance art also played a role. In his essay "Stanza by Stanza through *Onegin*," generated in 1936 while working on his jubilee adaptation of Pushkin's novel-in-verse, he expressed dissatisfaction with the two dominant approaches in Pushkin studies of his time.[43] One school favored subjective-ecstatic studies in the style of "My Pushkin"; the other, fact-obsessed sleuthing over every detail of the biography or text. Krzhizhanovsky preferred "a blend of formalist analysis and creative visual imagination," what he called "applied poetics" (prikladnaia poetika), to guide us in grasping "the infiltration of the image into the word."[44] Fascinated by the eye and inspired by the potential of cinema, he often subtitled his own "infiltrations" for the stage "scenic projections."

Pushkinistics as a creative teasing-out of potential images was also in keeping with Krzhizhanovsky's larger theater aesthetic, which valued highly those plays composed in what he called the "as-if" (kak by) mode.[45] "As-if" theater is nonillusionist. It believes in stylization, fantasy, footlights, walls. It even "strives to reinforce all these boundaries, doubling and tripling the line that separates its world from the world, the actor from the spectator."[46] By taking pride in artifice, it opposes itself to Stanislavskian realism as well as to the interactive Soviet-era mass spectacle and the Dionysian participative ritual of symbolist drama. "As-if" space is militantly its own world. It obeys its own rules and speaks its own languages; only by cultivating an agile linguistic consciousness alert to phonemic associations and multiple meanings can it construct a believable (internally consistent, "stage-real") environment that permits the playwright to experiment. As critic and creative writer, Krzhizhanovsky's priorities were the same: wit, rhythm, pacing, condensed wordplay, and the dynamic between word and thing.[47] As his own work went unpublished and unstaged, he became ever more insistently the commentator, seeking out values precious to him in the work of revered and more famous others: Shakespeare, Shaw, Pushkin. This commentary usually took the shape of critical essays, but it also turned up in his plays.

Krzhizhanovsky wrote *That Third One* at the crest of the Pushkin centennial, in March–April 1937. He read it aloud only once, in 1938 in Moscow, at a literary evening at Konstantin Stanislavsky's house.[48] Present at that reading was a distracted Vsevolod Meyerhold, already publicly disgraced. The great director liked the play but thought it most unlikely to be staged. Meyerhold, consummate theatrical insider, was correct. The time for spoofs and travesties had passed. But this illicit comedy—taken together with the 1934 Chamber Theater spectacle, a musically spare but otherwise overripe expression of the Cleopatra myth—contributes to three topics of enduring fascination even today. First is the legendary queen of Egypt. Second is the vulnerability of all mythic representation to the double-voiced genre of tragifarce, an energetic category of Russian revolutionary theater that combines vaudeville, circus, commedia dell'arte, and moments of intense tragic lyricism with desperate sides of the absurd.[49] Finally, and closest to the boundary of Russian cultural taboo, *That Third One* explicitly carnivalizes the symbiosis of great beauty and great poetry—a creative, mutually immortalizing relationship that Pushkin took with the utmost seriousness.

Filling Out Pushkin's Verse for the Stage

In his 1936 dramatic *Eugene Onegin*, Krzhizhanovsky had interpolated additional poetic works, mostly by Pushkin—as thematic subtext and as compensation for the deleted narrator. Vladimir Lensky stumbles through Pushkin's discarded drafts to arrive at a better lyric in the opening scene. Idle youths at a Petersburg ball exchange gossip in the form of a Pushkinian epigram. Tatiana becomes for a while the enchanted tsarevna in Pushkin's poeticized Russian version of *Snow White* (*Tale of the Dead Tsarevna and Seven Bogatyrs* [*Skazka o mertvoi tsarevne i o semi bogatyriakh*]). Near the end of the play, drunken students at dawn on the Neva waterfront sing the poet's early anacreontic verse. Such a notion of fidelity (to a writer's entire creative mind rather than a single base text) was familiar to Russian theatrical adaptation, especially when the literary source was thin on spoken dialogue. In expanding the text and context of Pushkin's poem "Cleopatra"—a single inconclusive episode in the queen's life—into a full-length play, Krzhizhanovsky had to interpolate a great deal. Remaining within Pushkin's zone meant turning first to the poet's related fictive worlds. But those worlds, too, were open ended and speculative; all of Pushkin's Roman-Egyptian writings are fragmentary.

Consider the poem's most famous physical gesture pertaining to the fate of the Third: "And the proud queen / rested her sad gaze on him" (I grustnyi vzor ostanovila / Tsaritsa gordaia na nem).[50] Pushkin struggled over Cleopatra's reaction to this final nameless volunteer. In some versions she reacts with "tenderness" (umilenie), in others with a "sad gaze" (pechal'nyi vzor), "mournful gaze" (grustnyi vzor), "languid gaze" (tomnyi vzor), "attentive gaze" (vzor vnimatel'nyi), even "a ray of pity" (luch' zhalosti).[51] The relative kindness or cruelty of this imperial glance has fostered an entire critical industry around Cleopatra's personality, from Pavel Annenkov and an enraged Dostoevsky in the nineteenth century to Mikhail Gershenzon, Valerii Briusov, and Boris Tomashevsky in the twentieth.[52] Cleopatra, it seems, could embody almost anything: the marriage of eros and power tempered by mercy; the tension between human pity and an oath sworn before the gods; the casual violence of the East acting on men's appetites; even opulent Alexandria as cultural analogue to decadent imperial Petersburg. In the nobler context of Pushkin's 1833 "Tale from Roman Life" ("Povest' iz rimskoi zhizni"), a fragment adapted from Tacitus, the Cleopatrian moment is resolved by a doomed Petronius meditating on the courage necessary to die by one's own hand. Krzhizhanovsky, however, made no attempt to decode the poet's intent. He devised a "scenic projection" of Pushkin's 1828 "Cleopatra" poem, an extension of one of its intonations or plot lines—and then subjected every pious cliché within that plot to comic inversion and decay. Only at the last moment, when *That Third One* had become a galloping farce and was at risk of dissolving into wholly arbitrary mischief, is comedy itself inverted and a serious note sounded. The play then ends on another life-and-death wager, one that addresses not beauty but poetry, a wager less capricious and more poignant than Cleopatra's. But first Krzhizhanovsky had to find a context for this word-image experiment in Pushkin.

He found this context, it would appear, in Pushkin's 1835 prose fragment "We were spending the evening at the dacha" ("My provodili vecher na dache"). The guests at Princess D.'s dacha are discussing Cleopatra's wager. Was such a challenge exclusive to the cruelty of the ancient world, or could volunteers be found today? How would such a test be conducted? A legal contract was unthinkable. Cleopatra "had the necessary means to make her debtors pay" (imela vsevozmozhnye sposoby zastavit' dolzhnikov rasplatit'sia)—torture, secret police, spies—but we of the nineteenth century have only a man's word of honor that he would shoot himself the following day. "But on the following day he could leave for foreign lands, making a fool of his lady" (A on na drugoi den' uedet v chuzhie kraia—a ona v durakh). Yes he could, came the response, if he were willing "to remain forever dishonored in the eyes of the woman he loves" (ostat'sia navek beschestnym v glazakh toi, kotoruiu liubit).[53]

This society conversation, like so many in Pushkin, begins trivially and then suddenly turns serious before breaking off. Serious here is the comparison of the Cleopatrian wager (and the possibility of pulling out of it) to a duel of honor. Would a man in love "hesitate even for a moment"? But what if the woman does not return your love—as is likely from a person pleased to proffer such a bestial contract? Is saving one's own life after committing to an impulsive wager any stupider than allowing some hothead to insult you, after which your honor obliges you to "expose your forehead to his bullet"? Is such a reaction really honor and courage or simply foolish posturing, a throwing away of one's life? Pushkin's prose fragment allowed Krzhizhanovsky to open up the Cleopatra myth beyond the surface titillation of sex and certain death, beyond the "stage sensuousness" that Shaw found so boring in treatments of great eros as great tragedy, into genuine moral provocation. Like the rumination on duels in chapter 6 of *Eugene Onegin*, this casual bit of society conversation develops into a challenge to societal convention at its deepest, most wasteful core.

Such ethical dimensions were altogether muted in Russia's symbolist-decadent readings of Pushkin's poem. As exemplified by choreographer Michel Fokine (whose ballet *A Night in Egypt* [*Noch' v Egipte*] premiered in St. Petersburg in 1908), Cleopatra and her twinned temptress Salomé were interesting on stage solely in their sensuous and lethal aspect.[54] By the 1930s, however, the aphrodisiac Egyptian queen of Pushkin's "Cleopatra" was an exhausted image. Thus Krzhizhanovsky, preparing to expand the poem into a comedy, returned to Pushkin's prose fragment, this time to focus on the "debtor who got away," the recipient of the queen's favors who escaped "to foreign lands, making a fool of his lady." In keeping with this new antic genre, the escapee, too, plays the fool. Krzhizhanovsky treats themes of seduction and male honor frivolously, as would commedia dell'arte, carnival, or Sir John Falstaff on a medieval English battlefield. But then he proceeds to supply his own serious, even sinister, backdrop to the story, more blasphemous and closer to home than any "social node" Tairov could ever have condoned.

We recall that to justify his *Egyptian Nights*, Tairov had likened Octavius (later Caesar Augustus) to his Roman successor Mussolini. Krzhizhanovsky moves the subtext from fascist Italy back to Soviet Russia. This shift was fraught, for the wedge of Roman history between the assassination of Julius Caesar in 44 BC and the consolidation of power by Octavius over the next three decades shows distinct parallels with Russia's reconstitution of itself in the mid-twentieth century as a "Third Rome"—or, more properly, a fourth.[55] When Julius Caesar adopted Octavius as his heir, Rome was still a republic. When Caesar Augustus died in AD 14, Rome was an empire. The Roman Senate would declare Augustus a god and ordain the rise of a new world order. In the 1930s, this imperial precedent came together for Russia in a "social node" of some grandeur—but did a Stalinist-era playwright dare touch it?

Fortune's Fool, or Krzhizhanovsky's *Third*

That Third One, a comedy in four acts and fourteen scenes, originated in 1929 as a prose fragment laden with folk and classical legends, including one on the Cleopatrian theme of a snake.[56] These stories find a minor place in act 3, but the main action of the play, properly for this jubilee year, is governed by Pushkin's "Cleopatra." The curtain rises on a Mediterranean harbor, Alexandria, recalling the nocturnal Sicilian harbor in Tairov's entr'acte. A Roman ship has just docked; Flavius, Criton, and a nameless "skinny youth" disembark. We are now in the prehistory of Pushkin's poem. The two named Romans banter with each other to establish their Pushkinian identities as warrior and sage.[57] The scrawny Third strikes a pose and interrupts them with a poem. Enter our first blow against the myth: he is a hopelessly bad poet.

Everywhere the Third tries to find an audience for his poetry, but whenever he begins to recite, people drift away. After hearing out six lines of the Third's naïvely obscene love rhetoric cast in a clumsy antique meter, Criton mutters "Tedious!" and melts away into the crowd. "It's always like this," says the Third. "You start to recite—and everything empties out. What's one to do?" (Vot i vsegda tak. Nachnesh' chitat'—i vokrug pusto. Chto delat'?).[58] What the Third ends up doing to secure an audience for his wretched poetry will drive the rest of the play and save his life.

"But why should the ages need your name?"

Krzhizhanovsky began his writing career as a poet but considered himself a poor one. He came to believe that his own verses, with their weaknesses exaggerated, fared better as comic inserts into his dramas than as freestanding poems from his own pen. The figure of the bad and pushy poet as hero, the poet who puts you to sleep with his verse or is pelted with rocks until he falls silent, is an ancient comic theme. Eumolpus in the *Satyricon* of Petronius—the writer featured in Pushkin's "A Tale from Roman Life"—is one such miserable poet, and as Lada Panova suggests, Eumolpus, a native resident of Roman satire, is one likely source for the Third; another probable inspiration is the fabricated nineteenth-century poet Koz'ma Prutkov, one of Krzhizhanovsky's favorites.[59] The major difference between these pompous and self-confident poets and our Pushkin-derived hero is that the Third knows he is bad. So awful does he feel about his lack of talent that he will seek fame some other way. "You know," he confesses to his metrics teacher Nigidius in the Alexandrian square, "this thought has been dogging my footsteps like a shadow: what if suddenly I don't bequeath my name to the ages? That would be terrible." To which Nigidius replies: "For the ages it wouldn't be so terrible. Why should the ages need your name?"[60] Pushkin's plot—about the Third, whose name history forgot—is launched.

In scene 2, the Roman visitors drop by the palace. Cleopatra reclines on her throne, with half a dozen suitors in the first circle and her spies closer to the door. This is Pushkin's heroine but taken out of legend and comically aged in real time—a device familiar from Voltaire's Cunégonde and Pushkin's own Naina in *Ruslan and Liudmila* (*Ruslan i Liudmila*). Several men pay court to the bored queen, but she is not stirred. The Third then leaps up and begins to recite his hexameters. Inexplicably inspired, he feeds her a prompt from Pushkin's poem: "In your love is bliss for us" (V tvoei liubvi dlia nas blazhenstvo).[61] This unexpected, electric proximity to Pushkin's actual text drags into play Pushkin's next line, thus precipitating the wager. Cleopatra rises from the couch and declaims: "You can purchase this bliss" (Blazhenstvo mozhno vam kupit'): your life for a night of love. The other suitors ignore the challenge. But Pushkin's three Romans agree to it: Flavius the warrior to display his bravery, Criton the philosopher because "logical consistency" demands it, and the Third because it promises him a "moment of glory."[62]

As soon as he commits, however, the Third is aghast and wants to pull out. But it is too late. Soldiers surround him, congratulate him, offer him all sorts of pleasure to fill his final days and nights. He is picked up by the local courtesan Kreseida, who considers him too skinny for the task and takes him under her wing to nourish and coach. In part to forestall the Third from declaiming a dreadful poem (dedicated to a woman's navel), the guests begin to discuss Cleopatra. But these are not Shakespeare's dissatisfied courtiers, nor are they Pushkin's guests at Princess D's. The discussion is far more clinical. *The Third can't take it. The queen can't stimulate it.* "I'm speaking as a medical man," says Egidius. "Three nights in a row. Can the third night really be worth as much as the first? Weariness, hypersaturation, the two nights of no sleep that precede the third; blue circles under the eyes, limp embraces."[63]

Act 2 opens on the third day. Seeing Criton's head on a stake outside the palace, the closely watched poet is now desperate to flee. But if he bolts, he will be considered "a fugitive, deserting the Tsaritsa's embraces." The queen's chief perfumer arrives to prepare him, and Kreseida starts to mourn. At this point Shaw—ever the debunker of seduction scenes—leaves a potent trace. At the beginning of Shaw's *Caesar and Cleopatra,* the teenage queen is still in thrall to the tyrannical Ftatateeta, her chief nurse, whom Caesar eventually tames but whose name he never learns to pronounce (it comes out "Teetatota"). The disempowerment of this bullying battle-axe nurse was one Shavian episode that Tairov preserved in his *Egyptian Nights.* In his own scene 5, Krzhizhanovsky, master of the punning name, introduces one "Tatifata," handmaiden to the queen and obsequious singer of Cleopatra's diminished charms (she resurfaces years later, in scene 11, as nanny for Cleopatra's child with Antony). Tatifata's job is to talk up the queen. But Shaw's threatening nurse has now become an old, flattering courtier, and when Cleopatra peers anxiously in the mirror and sees blue circles under her eyes or a telltale wrinkle, the nurse insists this is "the blue of the sky in spring" or "a ray of the sun."[64]

By the third night the queen is capricious and out of temper. Flavius, she reports, was a "crude beast" (gruboe zhivotnoe); "let his head be taken out to the trash heap with the garbage." She is exhausted. "These men are swine—even Criton . . . and his philosophy is repellent: suicide as an act of wisdom. In my view it's a lot cleverer to kill others. Before they manage to kill you. . . . And it's all so boring, so boring: first here behind the forehead, then in the heart, then in the loins."[65] From his quarters the Third reports in sick—a stomachache—but the queen won't hear of it. Playing for time, he offers to tell the queen the story of his life. But Cleopatra insists he perform: "I have a rule, if you come to a woman for the sake of Venus, do your deed and leave . . . but hurry up, I'm falling asleep."[66] Suddenly the Third sees a ray of hope. He offers to recite one of his poems. The queen is pleased; verses can wake you up. He begins to declaim a paean to his beloved's neck—and sure enough, Cleopatra is soon sound asleep. The Third dons her clothes and jewels and slips out of the palace.[67]

The remainder of act 2 incorporates a bit of Shakespeare's *Merchant of Venice* with a detective-pursuit scenario, which recalls Krzhizhanovsky's stage adaptation of a Chesterton spoof on spy novels for the Moscow Chamber Theater in 1923.[68] The chief executioner is astonished that the queen is still dallying with her new lover long past dawn. Tatifata then arrives with the news that Cleopatra has ordered the execution of her negligent guards and centurions. The Third, meanwhile, surfaces in the Jewish Quarter, where he promises the pawnbroker Khanebi all his royal garments and jewelry "as a gift for his daughter," the lovely Judith, in exchange for a night's hiding.[69] This pawnbroker is no embittered Shylock. Nor is he the caricatured Solomon from Pushkin's little tragedy *The Miserly Knight* (*Skupoi rytsar'*). He's a professional trader, willing to provide safe haven even for a pagan Roman, until the Third can sneak aboard a ship and escape. Our Pushkinian subtext has now expanded beyond the 1828 poem to encompass that skeptical guest at Princess D.'s dacha, who had assured the company that today's young man, faced with Cleopatra's wager, might well choose—and choose wisely—to flee the country and "make a fool of his lady" (a ona v durakh), not caring one whit for his word of honor.

At this point halfway through the play, the Cleopatra story is joined to two larger topics precious to Pushkin. The first is the poet and power (poet i vlast'); the second is the poet and immortality (poet i bessmertie).

Briusov had coupled these two themes with the Cleopatra myth in his 1899 sonnet "Cleopatra," with its ringing final lines spoken by the queen:

Бессмертен ты искусства дивной властью,
А я бессмертна прелестью и страстью:
Вся жизнь моя—в веках звенящий стих.

[You are immortal through the magic power of art, / I am immortal through my seductive charm and passion: / My entire life is a line of verse ringing across centuries.]

Lada Panova assesses this symbiotic "Briusovian" phase of the myth thus: "To enter eternity, Cleopatra needs to be immortalized in a poem, while a poet for the same reason needs to describe an immortal figure, such as Cleopatra."[70] But what if the poet is a bad one and Cleopatra no longer fascinates—that is, if genius, beauty, and time fail us? As the Cleopatra theme in *That Third One* becomes ever more hackneyed, de-eroticized, sunk in crude matter, the themes of power and immortality become more serious and (for all the comic levity of their treatment) compelling.

Act 3 opens on a moonlit shore: the campfire scene in Krzhizhanovsky's 1929 prose fragment. Merchants and the Third are swapping fables when two secret agents suddenly appear in search of the "thief of the Tsaritsa's Night."[71] What follows resembles Grigorii Otrep'ev's flight across the Lithuanian border in Pushkin's *Boris Godunov*: inept gendarmes interrogate; the Third pulls out a knife, wounds an agent, and disappears into the dark. But since the Empire is everywhere, destinations are unclear and boundaries arbitrary. By the second half of the act, the emaciated Third has turned up at the walls of the city among a group of exiled philosophers, spinning a theory of life. He is being pursued by his own poetry teacher in disguise, who was recruited by Egyptian intelligence (Nigidius is in fact a double agent).

Act 4 returns us to Cleopatra, several years later. At this point, *That Third One* shifts definitively from a parody of Pushkin's poem (and its celebration of the immortal bond between beauty and poetry) to a parody of Shakespeare's tragedy. As if in a crooked mirror, the tragic Cleopatra story is now recast on her lovers' home ground, as Roman satire in the style of Petronius—or perhaps as a Swiftian parody on such satire. A close student of the history of comedy, Krzhizhanovsky must have been inspired by the *Satyricon*, "parasitic on almost every known literary form" of its day, featuring its own hungry, under-recognized poet (Petronius's Eumolpus), who accompanies Encolpius and his rival Ascyltos on their hair-raising wanderings throughout the corrupt Neronian empire.[72] But *That Third One* remains mired in Rome's eastern provinces. Mark Antony is again attending on the Egyptian queen. He is still recognizably Shakespeare's hero—impulsive, swaggering, a Roman general reduced to a "strumpet's fool"—but he is no longer a dashing lover. Instead he is tied to a nagging, jealous all-but-spouse with a squalling infant (that ancient comedic scenario), a fading woman whose vanity can be mollified, or diverted, only by a full-scale secret police operation against the man who slighted her beauty. While Tatifata fusses over their infant son, Cleopatra cannot stop fretting about the Third who got away. How can his head still be on his shoulders and not on a pike? "In the Jewish Quarter," she mutters, "everyone said that Cleopatra could be had for free."[73] Assuring her "that the arm of a Roman is long" and that the miscreant will be grabbed "by the heels even at the edge of the world," Antony offers to restore her honor.[74] This honor, however, is not of the sort that agitated the guests at Princess D.'s dacha in Pushkin's prose fragment—a sensibility defined by the duels of the romantic period. It is also not the honor of an ancient Roman who, when defeated in battle (like Shakespeare's Brutus or Mark Antony), falls on his own sword or who, when shamed by his own betrayal (like Enobarbus), mysteriously perishes in a ditch. Nor is it Cleopatra's honor in act 5 of Shakespeare's *Antony and Cleopatra*, where any death is better than being hoisted up to "the shouting varletry / Of censuring Rome" (5.2.56–57). We are now in twentieth-century space, where successful politicians think in more corporate fashion, imperially, and survive. The modern devices for preserving personal and national honor are fabricating your enemies, manipulating your insults for political gain, and scapegoating.

It occurs to Mark Antony that this foolish Third, whom Cleopatra can neither forget nor forgive, might serve as a convenient pretext for a general purge. To his security chief Rufus Septimus he declares: "I am surrounded by thieves encroaching on my kingdoms, on my honor, trying to steal the sword from my sheath"—but "before one strikes a knife into a heart, we must uncover the thoughts that live there."[75] For a task of this magnitude, the present security forces are insufficient. "Who are our eyes that see through the dark, the ears that hear through the silence? Three or four dozen pitiable dilettantes." So divide the empire into four quadrants, Antony tells Rufus, cast a wide net, and begin "Case no. 1 on some Third [*Delo nomer odin o nekotorom Tret'em*], for that's what he is called here in Alexandria." Cleopatra is pleased. Echoing a familiar Silver-Age conflation of femme fatale plots, she can now move against the man who spurned her, just as Salomé had moved against Jokanaan. Both Antony and Rufus assure her: "We will have his head on a platter."[76]

By scene 12, the Third thinks he is safe. He is back with Kreseida, living off her earnings and entertaining (or putting to sleep) her clients with his poetry. Krzhizhanovsky lovingly allows Pushkin's verse to continue gestating under the surface of his play, at times welling up in the mouths of incompetents. For three years now the Third has "been thinking of writing a poem about my encounter with Cleopatra."[77] Nigidius, amid much wine and many false starts, coaches him through to several clumsy variants on Pushkin's opening line before settling on its precise wording, "The palace gleamed." Finally Nigidius, discouraged by his pupil's slow progress, suggests that he try his hand at "ordinary despised prose" (obyknovennoi prezrennoi prozoi).[78] The Third is pondering this possibility when his courtesan rushes in and urges him to flee: Septimus Rufus is on his trail. His case has been transferred from the inept Egyptian secret service to the far more efficient, unsentimental Romans. In a panic, the Third vows that no poet will ever finish a poem about his night with Cleopatra.

The final two scenes are rapid-fire slapstick. The Third has fled to the Temple of Mars and hides himself near the foot of the statue, in the drainage gutter for sacrificial blood. A priest is preparing a slaughtered goat. Rufus Septimus runs into the Temple—and the terrorized Third, splattered with blood, immediately gives himself up: "Blood! Blood! Cleopatra, take my head! I, the Third, am paying for your third night!"[79] But to his astonishment, Rufus begs his forgiveness and requests the Third's protection. He wants to *serve* the Third, not arrest him. There's been a regime change: Antony has fallen, Cleopatra too is dead, and Rufus pleads with the fugitive to intercede for him with Octavius. For who will pity a police agent of the accursed Antony? The dazed Third realizes that he has become a patriot, a victim, and a hero.

The last scene opens on a new and secure imperial order. Octavius, now Caesar Augustus, is holding court like Pushkin's Pretender in the first Polish scene of *Boris Godunov*: receiving, pardoning, gathering in bribes and gifts. Rufus Septimus, despite his poor judgment earlier, has retained his post as head of the security police. He is advised not to fuss over his list of suspects but simply to reverse it: "On the Friends list write 'Enemies'; on the Enemies list write 'Friends.' Get it?"[80] Then the new tsar requests to see that curious fugitive, the Third, the late "Cleopatra's debtor." The poet enters declaiming a sycophantic ode. But Octavius is a Roman in the mold of Shaw's sensible, empire-building Julius Caesar; he has no time for verses. He interrupts with the terse advice that it is indecent for a man to run away—from the field of battle, the bed of love, or the bier of death. And he pronounces the Third's punishment: his head can stay in place, but "I will cut off his name. Let it sink into darkness" (Tak ia otrubliu emu imia. Pust' ono kanet v t'mu).[81] The Third will be exiled without country or identity. Rufus, experienced in rooting out rumor and conspiracy, does not think the strategy will work. "Killing the name, it is impossible to kill the legend," he warns Octavius. "Let this poet dissolve in the ages like salt in water, but others will come."[82]

"Let this poet dissolve": here, at the end of this Roman tragifarce, we sense a bittersweet personal subtext. Among Krzhizhanovsky's fragments on Shakespeare from 1934 is one titled "The Sacrificial Goat That Got Away" ("Sbezhavshii 'tragos'").[83] It develops the idea that the "goat song" (tragos + odu) of tragedy—a hymn to Dionysius sung by a pagan priest as he slits the throat of the sacrificial animal—is the origin of the comedic impulse in Shakespeare. If we turn from Shakespeare's tragedies to his comic cycles, Krzhizhanovsky muses, "hasn't the poor goat managed to slip out from under the very knife and save himself in the closed little world of Shakespearean comedy?"[84] In *That Third One*, everything had indeed "slipped out from under the knife": the tragedy of *Antony and Cleopatra*, relegated to the sidelines; the death wager of Pushkin's poem, dwindling out through a comic loophole. But the cost of comedic survival is high: the name of the poet was lost.

By 1937, Krzhizhanovsky must have seen a bit of his own fate in the Third. So far his head had been spared, but his literary legacy would surely sink into darkness. The plot through which he expressed this anxiety in his comic play—the juxtaposition of a persecuted or unpublished writer against the tyrants of imperial Rome—enjoyed some currency in the Stalinist period. Mikhail Kuzmin's 1929 play *The Death of Nero* (*Smert' Nerona*) is one variant; another is Mikhail Bulgakov's great Rome-Jerusalem-Moscow novel *The Master and Margarita* (*Master i Margarita*).[85] While sharing the antic qualities of those works, *That Third One* stands apart from them by its utter absence of a slowed-down space for poetic contemplation and its wholly debased hopes for transcendence. Krzhizhanovsky's Third is not only comedy, he is farce. In keeping with the norms of that genre, his spindly body is forever forced to speed up, to appear ridiculous and inarticulate. His role in the world is not ordained but improvised. But effective farce is more than a string of stunts. As Eric Bentley puts it, for the hero of farce, "aggression and flippancy," "hostility and lightness of heart" must always be in balance so that violence, while awful, is never wholly arbitrary.[86]

"The inscrutable underside of an icon": Satire, Farce, Taboo

In her introduction to the present volume, Alyssa Gillespie remarks that in Russia's complex reception of Pushkin, "the taboo functions as the photographic negative of the myth . . . the inscrutable underside of the shining cultural icon" that the poet has become. An underside is both a clue and a trap. Adore something excessively and its perfection becomes untouchable. What is off limits to us will invite our curiosity and whet our appetite, stimulate our desire to prove it is merely human and fallible. Tragedy has ancient means—strict rules, even—for exploring tabooed areas while retaining the dignity of all participants. The violations of comedy have always been more devastating. This chapter closes with some thoughts on satire, farce, and taboo as they relate to Krzhizhanovsky's *That Third One*, a play designed to make us laugh but in which no target of the parody—neither hero, nor audience, nor author—is slated to survive. No one except Alexander Pushkin.

Some theorists of farce, like Eric Bentley, connect its creative pleasures directly with an indulgence in the forbidden ("bedroom farces" do this), with our illicit or impious "wishes to damage the family, to desecrate the household gods." Nothing is expected from the desecrators except humor and havoc, for the "farceur is a heretic: he does not believe that man was made in God's image." The Roman or Atellan farces, Bentley reminds us, worked with four character types only, three fools and one knave: the blockhead, the braggart, the silly old man, and the trickster.[87] Northrop Frye supplies a more diverse and ethically responsible cast. In his *Anatomy of Criticism*, he links irony and satire to the parody of all romance (and all romantic fixation on perfect form) that sits at the center of the mythos of winter; of his six phases, the third, "satire of the high norm," is the mode most likely to come into conflict with adored, tabooed objects and take pleasure at trying to bring a lofty thing down.[88] But the Russian folklorist and formalist Vladimir Propp

(1895–1970), in his posthumously published notes *On the Comic and Laughter* (*Problemy komizma i smekha*), probably comes closest to defining the specific force of satire as Krzhizhanovsky employs it.[89] The task in *That Third One* is to travesty every person or political structure on stage while still protecting a taboo—that is, to target the blockheads, braggarts, silly old men, and tricksters while still preserving intact at the play's core a precious and untouchable value. That value is Pushkin. But can the poet be exempt? Propp would say yes: drawing on authored literature as well as on a vast store of traditional folkloric texts, he notes that what often looks like "a parody of literary forms for satirical purposes" is "directed not against their authors." During the riots and retributions of 1905, he recalls, a travesty of Pushkin's "Exegi monumentum" poem ("I built myself a monument not made by human hands" ["Ia pamiatnik sebe vozdvig nerukotvornyi"]) was circulated in St. Petersburg. Its targets were the dedicatee, addressee, audience, the whole awful surrounding world during that disruptive year—but at no point the source poet.[90] Pushkin simply could not be reached by those means. At the end of *That Third One*, Rufus Septimus argues with Octavius Caesar over the efficacy of cutting off the name of a man destined to play a role—however episodic and anonymous—in a greater poet's future work. Eventually, to compensate him for the expense of his traumatic involvement with "that Egyptian woman," Octavius awards the homeless, exiled Third a pension for life.[91] And thus the cohesion of culture is guaranteed, passing from poetic subject to creative poet, even as it is fiercely parodied in newly corrupted contexts. Because taboo both traps and protects the sacred qualities of its object, no poet will ever wholly dissolve.

Notes

1. 2 January 1936, Russian State Archive for Literature and Art, Moscow [RGALI], f. 2280, op. 1, ed. khr. 98.

2. See Caryl Emerson, "The Krzhizhanovsky-Prokofiev Collaboration on *Eugene Onegin*, 1936 (A Lesser-Known Casualty of the Pushkin Death Jubilee)," in *Sergey Prokofiev and His World*, ed. Simon Morrison (Princeton: Princeton University Press, 2008), 60–189.

3. For this story see Alexander M. Dubrovsky, "Chronicle of a Poet's Downfall: Dem'ian Bednyi, Russian History, and *The Epic Heroes*," in *Epic Revisionism: Russian History and Literature as Stalinist Propaganda*, ed. Kevin M. F. Platt and David Brandenberger (Madison: University of Wisconsin Press, 2006), 77–114.

4. Sigizmund Krzhizhanovskii, "Shekspir—realist-eksperimentor . . . ," in

"Komediografiia Shekspira," in Sigizmund Krzhizhanovskii, *Sobranie sochinenii*, 5 vols., ed. Vadim Perel'muter (St. Petersburg: Symposium, 2001–10), 4:172.

5. See his discussion of Hans Vaihinger's *Die Philosophie des Als Ob* and "truth itself as a collision of two opposing fictions" in the 1924 "Teatralizatsiia mysli," in Krzhizhanovskii, *Sobranie sochinenii*, 4:636–37.

6. For a brief (and to date the only) overview of the writer's life and works in English, see the excellent monograph by Karen Link Rosenflanz, *Hunter of Themes: The Interplay of Word and Thing in the Works of Sigizmund Kržižanovskij* (New York: Peter Lang, 2005). The biography appears on pages 1–21.

7. Vadim A. Perel'muter summarizes and comments savagely on Gorky's letter in "Posle katastrofy," in Krzhizhanovskii, *Sobranie sochinenii*, 1:25–31.

8. The remark was made by the playwright and drama theorist Vladimir Vol'kenshtein (1883–1974) on 13 February 1939 at a meeting of the Dramaturgs' Section of the Union of Soviet Writers of the USSR; see "Stenogramma Rasshirennogo zasedaniia Biuro sektsii dramaturgov ot 13-ogo fevralia 1939. g.," RGALI, f. 631, op. 2, ed. khr. 355, l. 48. Stenographer's typographical error "Vol'penshtein" in transcript corrected.

9. See the request of Evgenii Lann, chair of the Commission for the Literary Legacy of Sigizmund D. Krzhizhanovsky, dated 31 May 1958, to the publishing house Sovetskii pisatel', in "Materialy Komissii po literaturnomu naslediiu S. D. Krzhizhanovskogo (1957–59)," RGALI, f. 2280, op.1, ed. khr. 117, "V izdatel'stvo Sovetskii pisatel'," entry 2, page 1.

10. Sigizmund Krzhizhanovsky, *7 Stories*, trans. Joanne Turnbull (Moscow: GLAS Publishers, 2006), won the Rossica Translation Prize in 2007. *Memories of the Future* followed in 2009 and *The Letter Killers Club* in 2011.

11. See letter from Aleksandr Ia. Tairov to Sergei S. Prokofiev, 24 February 1934, where the director assures the composer (then Paris representative for VOKS [Soviet Russia's All-Union Society for Cultural Ties Abroad]) that such a tour "will doubtless take place," since "several clippings from American newspapers" already indicate "enormous interest in the spectacle" (RGALI, f. 1929, op. 4, ed. khr. 368, page 2 of typescript letter).

12. The production ran from 14 December 1934 until April 1937, with over one hundred performances. See Ludmilla Petchenina and Gérard Abensour, "Egyptian Nights: In Search of the 'New Simplicity,'" *Love for Three Oranges* 7 (May 2004): 11–20; and Nick Worrall, *Modernism to Realism on the Soviet Stage: Tairov—Vakhtangov—Okhlopkov* (Cambridge: Cambridge University Press, 1989), 61–65.

13. Perel'muter claims in a headnote to his 2007 publication of a fragment from *That Third One* that the theme of Cleopatra was "already on Krzhizhanovsky's desk" in the early 1930s, "although not, to be sure, in prose but in theatrical form: together with Tairov's [assistant] director L. L. Luk'ianov, he had been thinking through [*obdumyval*] a composition from works by Pushkin, Shakespeare, and Shaw for the Chamber Theater spectacle *Egyptian Nights*."

See Sigizmund Krzhizhanovskii, "Dva fragmenta: K 'Istorii nenapisannoi literatury,'" ed. Vadim A. Perel'muter, *Toronto Slavic Quarterly* 20 (Spring 2007): 3. *That Third One* was finally published in Russian in 2010, in Krzhizhanovskii, *Sobranie sochinenii*, 5:75–142. I thank Joanne Turnbull and Maksim Amelin, editor of Symposium Publishers, for sharing the prepublication galley proofs. In Krzhizhanovsky's typescripts the title is sometimes written as "Tot, tretii" ("That One, the Third").

14. Aleksandr S. Pushkin, "Chertog siial," in his *Polnoe sobranie sochinenii*, 17 vols., ed. Vladimir D. Bonch-Bruevich et al. [Moscow: AN SSSR, 1937–59], 3:130–32. This poem is reproduced in the improvisator's Cleopatra poem at the end of "Egyptian Nights," in Pushkin, *Polnoe sobranie sochinenii*, 17 vols., 8:275.

15. Lada G. Panova, "Final, kotorogo ne bylo: Modernistskie razviazki k 'Egipetskim nocham' A. S. Pushkina," in *Poetika finala: Mezhvuzovskii sbornik nauchnykh trudov*, ed. Tat'iana I. Pecherskaia (Novosibirsk: Novosibirskii gosudarstvennyi pedagogicheskii universitet, 2009), 68–94. *That Third One* is discussed on pages 80–84.

16. See Lada G. Panova, "Anna Achmatova's 'Cleopatra': A Study in Self-Portraiture," in *Russian Literature* 95 (2009): 507–38. Her essay contains a good survey of "Cleopatrimony" among Russian poets beginning with Pushkin.

17. Lada G. Panova, *Russkii Egipet* (Moscow: Progress-Pleiada, 2006), 228, sections 2, 2.1. See also her "Egipetskii tekst russkoi literatury," *Zvezda* 5 (2006): 192–206; and, in English, "Russian Cleopatrimony: From Pushkin's 'Egyptian Nights' to the Silver Age," in *Pushkinskii vestnik/Pushkin Review* 11 (2008): 103–27. The elegiac Roman poet Sextus Propertius (d. 15 BC) was among the first to call Cleopatra a "whore queen"; see the discussion in Stacy Schiff, *Cleopatra: A Life* (New York: Little, Brown, 2010), 298–99.

18. Aleksandr Ia. Tairov, "Kak ia rabotaiu s klassikami," *Izvestiia*, 29 July 1933, reprinted in Aleksandr Ia. Tairov, *Zapiski rezhissera: Stat'i, Besedy, Rechi, Pis'ma* (Moscow: Vserossiskoe teatral'noe obshchestvo, 1970): 240–42.

19. Aleksandr Ia. Tairov, "Egipetskie nochi," address to the Communist Academy, April 1934, in Tairov, *Zapiski rezhissera*, 369, 370.

20. Ibid., 370.

21. Although Shaw was an outspoken opponent of musical settings of his plays, at the age of eighty he did advise and help produce a screenplay for the brilliantly successful 1946 film version of *Caesar and Cleopatra* (directed by Gabriel Pascal), with Claude Rains as Caesar and Vivien Leigh—looking authentically sixteen—as Cleopatra.

22. For Tairov's scenic plan as reconstructed from his notes by the musicologist Elizaveta Dattel', see Aleksandr Ia. Tairov, "Plan stsenicheskoi kompozitsii," in Sergei Prokofiev, *Egipetskie nochi: Muzyka k stsenicheskoi kompozitsii*, ed. Elizaveta Dattel' (Moscow: Sovetskii kompozitor, 1963), 176–79, esp. 177. Dattel' integrates Prokofiev's musical cues into Tairov's plot summary of the twenty-two scenes.

23. Aleksandr Ia. Tairov, "B. Shou (Iiul' 1932)," *Pis'ma*, in Tairov, *Zapiski rezhissera*, 486.

24. Judging by two surviving (undated) English-language variants of the theater program, it appears that the length of the spectacle varied (between twenty-two and twenty-eight scenes) throughout its two-year run—and the variable was always Shaw. See Production History Files, Henry Wadsforth Longfellow Dana Collection of Russian Theatrical Scripts and Papers, Harvard Theater Collection, Houghton Library, Harvard University, Cambridge, MA; Alexsansdr Ia. Tairov, *Egipetskie nochi/Egyptian Nights*, 1935, box 15, folder 30. According to Dattel' "several scenes were abbreviated in the course of rehearsals" (Tairov, "Plan stsenicheskoi kompozitsii," 177n3; see also 178n1). In her preface to *Egipetskie nochi*, she further notes that "a large number of instrumental pieces were destined for pantomime, which was abundant in the production. What in Shaw and Shakespeare was hidden in the stage directions appeared on stage as pantomime" ("O muzyke S. Prokof'eva k spektakliu 'Egipetskie nochi,'" 6).

25. "Stenogramma 1-oi besedy A. Ia. Tairova k postanovke 'Egipetskie nochi', 2 Marta 1934," RGALI, f. 2328, op.1, ed. khr. 495, l. 42.

26. See Sigizmund Krzhizhanovskii, "Zabytyi Shekspir," in his *Sobranie sochinenii*, 4:320: "The Chamber Theater mounted a spectacle-amalgam, *Antony and Cleopatra*, having wedged into Shakespeare's play fragments from Shaw and from *Egyptian Nights*. But . . . the inclusion of any alien [*inorodnye*] elements in a text of Shakespeare's was, of course, a mistake." For Prokofiev's opinion, see his *Autobiography, Articles, Reminiscences*, ed. S. Shlifstein, trans. Rose Prokofieva (Honolulu: University Press of the Pacific, 2000): "However, notwithstanding the delightful humour of Bernard Shaw, old Shakespeare turned out to be so much of a titan by comparison that he willy-nilly crowded out poor Shaw; who as a result dwindled down to one brief, unimportant episode tacked on at the beginning of the play" (84).

27. Urizl' [Osaf Litovskii], "O 'Egipetskikh nochakh': Shekspirovskii spektakl' v Kamernom Teatre," *Sovetskoe iskusstvo*, 5 April 1935. He notes curiously that Enobarbus was played "on a Falstaffian plane," suggesting Krzhizhanovsky's hand in the Shakespearean portions of the playscript.

28. One negative review by the German communist-in-exile Bernhard Reich singling out the heroes expressed irritation at Shaw's admiration of the successful, stoic "Caesar type" (exemplified by both Julius and Octavius) for his "purposefulness and disdain of empty phrases"—even though Reich hastened to add (with Hitler in mind) that such Caesars always hide their true motives; "the real heroes to be presented" are the ones who "shed blood openly, freely, truthfully, out of historical necessity." See Bernhard Reich, "Der Cäsarentypus," RGALI, f. 1397, op. 5. ed. khr. 26. This German-language typescript, destined for the Stalinist journal *International Literature* (*Internatsional'naia literatura*), is marked "Return to author."

29. Alisa Koonen, *Stranitsy zhizni* (Moscow: Moi 20-yi vek, 2003), 17, 461–70. This book was approved for publication by Iskusstvo in 1975, one year after Koonen died, at age 84.

30. Ibid., 464, 462.

31. Ibid., 462.

32. Pushkin's Cleopatra poem occupies all of part two, scene 1, of *Egyptian Nights*. Scene 2 ("in a little pub" in the same port) opens on Maecenas's line "You stayed well by't in Egypt" from *Antony and Cleopatra* (2.2.186), which is given as "Khorosho li vam zhivetsia v Egipte?" in Lugovskoi's translation. Roman soldiers, drinking wine and discussing their Egyptian tour of duty, ask Enobarbus to share his first impressions of Cleopatra. See the director's assistant's playscript (dated 1934–35) "Egipetskie nochi," in RGALI, f. 2328, op. 1, ed. khr. 494, l. 14–18.

33. Tairov, "Plan stsenicheskoi kompozitsii," 178n1.

34. Iurii A. Golovashenko, *Rezhisserskoe iskusstvo Tairova* (Moscow: Iskusstvo, 1970), 149.

35. Ibid., 156–61, esp. 161. The commissar dies of wounds in full view, which had not been the playwright's ending. At first Vishnevsky was not pleased, but he came around after the box office success. Tairov's version, which also cleansed the play of sexual innuendo and of its local polemics with other playwrights, eventually became the official text.

36. André van Gyseghem, *Theatre in Soviet Russia* (London: Faber and Faber, 1943), 89–90. The report of the interview is untrustworthy, however; in Gyseghem's summary, Tairov gets a great deal wrong that he could not have made errors about, including the content of Pushkin's poem. Gyseghem does admit to feasting heavily and talking "a lot of very bad French" (88) during the evening.

37. Arkady Ostrovsky, "Shakespeare as a Founding Father of Socialist Realism: The Soviet Affair with Shakespeare," in *Shakespeare in the Worlds of Communism and Socialism*, ed. Irena R. Makaryk and Joseph G. Price (Toronto: University of Toronto Press, 2006), 56–83.

38. See Alma H. Law, "*Hamlet* at the Vakhtangov," *Drama Review* 21.4 (1977): 100–109. Also thanks to Simon Morrison, "Russian Musical Interpretations of *Hamlet*," lecture delivered at Lincoln Center, New York City, March 2006.

39. For this story, see T. F. Evans, "Myopia or Utopia? Shaw in Russia," in *Shaw Abroad*, ed. Rodelle Weintraub (University Park: Pennsylvania State University Press, 1985), 125–45, esp. 131–41.

40. See Koonen, *Stranitsy zhizni*, 392–93.

41. Shaw lays out his case against Bardolotry in his preface to his 1910 play *The Dark Lady of the Sonnets* (Bernard Shaw, *Complete Plays with Prefaces*, 6 vols. [New York: Dodd, Mead, 1962], 2:630–38). Shaw reviewed productions of Shakespeare for the *Saturday Review* from 1895 to 1898; see also his criticism of the overly melodramatic Janet Achurch ("with all the stops pulled out") in a

Manchester production of *Antony and Cleopatra* in a 20 March 1897 review, reprinted in *Shaw on Shakespeare: An Anthology of Bernard Shaw's Writings on the Plays and Productions of Shakespeare*, ed. Edwin Wilson (New York: E. P. Dutton, 1961), 15–22.

42. Bernard Shaw, preface, *Three Plays for Puritans*, in Bernard Shaw, *Complete Plays with Prefaces*, 6 vols. (New York: Dodd Mead and Company, 1963), 3:xxxvii, liii, liv.

43. Sigizmund Krzhizhanovskii, "Po strofam 'Onegina,'" in his *Sobranie sochinenii*, 4:416–17. The essay was first published in 2006.

44. Ibid., 417.

45. In 1923, Krzhizhanovsky worked out a "philosopheme of the theater" in his lectures to the Actors' Studio on stage psychology. He coined the triad "being, everyday life, as-if" (bytie, byt, by) to represent three types of theater: mystery plays and liturgy (static and undramatic), the naturalistic/illusionist stage (dynamic but in captivity to the visual and palpable world), and theater as projective states of consciousness ("Filosofema o teatre," in Krzhizhanovskii, *Sobranie sochinenii*, 4:43–88, esp. 55–56).

46. Ibid., 56.

47. See Rosenflanz, *Hunter of Themes*, chap. 2, esp. the sections "Kržižanovskij's Theoretical Stance on Wordplay" and "Wordplay in Kržižanovskij's Prose," 32–55.

48. See Nina M. Moleva's memoirs in "Legenda o Zigmunte pervom," included in *Vospominaniia o Krzhizhanovskom*, ed. Vadim Perel'muter (forthcoming), http://az.lib.ru/k/krzhizhanowskij_s_d/text_0320.shtml, 37–42, esp. 37 (accessed 7 October 2007).

49. See the analysis of this genre in Julia Listengarten, *Russian Tragifarce: Its Cultural and Political Roots* (Selinsgrove: Susquehanna University Press, 2000), especially her distinction between satire and tragifarce in chap. 5.

50. Pushkin, "Chertog siial," 3:131.

51. For the most authoritative of these variations see Aleksandr S. Pushkin, *Polnoe sobranie sochinenii*, 17 vols., 3:692.

52. For a survey of this reception, see Leslie O'Bell, *Pushkin's "Egyptian Nights": The Biography of a Work* (Ann Arbor, MI: Ardis, 1984), 24–33.

53. Aleksandr S. Pushkin, "My provodili vecher na dache," in his *Polnoe sobranie sochinenii*, 17 vols., 8:424.

54. For more on the Russian-Egyptian ballets of this period, see Lada G. Panova, *Russkii Egipet* (Moscow: Vodolei Publishers, 2006), 91–92; and Mikhail N. Fokin, *Protiv techeniia* (Moscow: Iskusstvo, 1962), 195–99.

55. On the competition during the 1930s "among ambitious European states—Stalin's Russia, Germany, and Mussolini's Italy"—for the mantel of Rome, see Katerina Clark, *Moscow the Fourth Rome: Stalinism, Cosmopolitanism, and the Evolution of Soviet Culture, 1931–1941* (Cambridge, MA: Harvard University Press, 2011), 20–27, esp. 21.

56. In that earlier context, three wanderers huddle around a campfire at night on the edges of the Roman world and tell legends. Only in passing does someone mention "the fugitive by the name of Third . . . There's three of us: which of us is the Third? . . . That poet from Rome, the one the queen's spies are searching for." Evoking Pushkin's fugitive Grishka Otrep'ev in disguise, this episode with its legends is embedded in act 3, scene 8, of Krzhizhanovsky's play. See "Fragmenty k romanu 'Tot Tretii,'" in Krzhizhanovskii, *Sobranie sochinenii*, 5:234–56, esp. 237.

57. Sigizmund Krzhizhanovskii, *Tot tretii: Komediia*, in his *Sobranie sochinenii*, 5:75–142. In act 1, scene 1, Criton remarks to Flavius that "You, Flavius, fight with a sword, I with a thought" (Ty, Flavii, b'esh'sia mechom, ia—mysl'iu), to which Flavius retorts: "Excuse me, my wise friend Criton, but the blows of thought against thought are not as intelligible as blade against blade" (Prosti, moi mudryi drug Kriton, udary mysl'iu v mysl' ne tak vniatny, kak udar klinkom v klinok [78]).

58. Krzhizhanovskii, *Tot tretii*, 5:79.

59. See Panova, "Final, kotorogo ne bylo," 83, for plot similarities with Eumolpus from Petronius's *Satyricon*, as well as the most obvious Koz'ma Prutkov parody on poems to female body parts (a weakness of the Third): his lyric "The Neck" ("Sheia"), dedicated to the poet Vladimir Benediktov, Pushkin's younger contemporary. Other bad-poetry connections to Cleopatra can be found in Prutkov; see the parody subtitled "Imitation of Catullus" ("Podrazhanie Katullu").

60. Krzhizhanovskii, *Tot tretii*, 5:81.

61. The Pushkin original is "In my love is bliss for you" (V moei liubvi dlia vas blazhenstvo); see Pushkin, "Chertog siial," 3:130.

62. Krzhizhanovskii, *Tot tretii*, 5:86.

63. Ibid., 5:95.

64. Ibid., 5:100.

65. Ibid., 5:101.

66. Ibid., 5:103.

67. This transvestite detail, an ancient comic motif, has its own parodied Pushkinian subtext: the "cook" Mavrusha's escape, or escapade, in Pushkin's 1830 poem *Little House in Kolomna* (*Domik v Kolomne*).

68. Act 2 as well as scenes 8 and 9 of act 3 bear resemblances to G. K. Chesterton's 1908 novel *The Man Who Was Thursday*, a spoof on double agents and the revolutionary fantasies of the European political underground (as in *That Third One*, virtually every anarchist and spy in Chesterton's novel turns out to be a disguised double agent, paid by and loyal to the government).

69. Krzhizhanovskii, *Tot tretii*, 5:111.

70. Panova, "Russian Cleopatrimony," 113; see 113–14 for the text of Briusov's sonnet.

71. Krzhizhanovskii, *Tot tretii*, 5:116.

72. Victoria Rimell, "The Satiric Maze: Petronius, Satire, and the Novel," in *The Cambridge Companion to Roman Satire*, ed. Kirk Freudenburg (Cambridge: Cambridge University Press, 2005), 160–73, esp. 160. On Eumolpus as a double-voiced "Roman" source for the Third, consider these two segments from the Eumolpus chapter in the *Satyricon*: "As Eumolpus recited his verse, some of those strolling through the arcade started throwing stones at him. But he took this as a tribute to his genius" and "'Yes, my young friends,' said Eumolpus, 'poetry has led many of us astray. For as soon as someone has managed to write a line of verse that scans, and woven some sense into a moderately subtle turn of phrase, he thinks he's set foot on the top of Helicon!'" (*Satyrica*, trans. R. Bracht Branham and Daniel Kinney [Berkeley: University of California Press, 1997], 86, 117).

73. Krzhizhanovskii, *Tot tretii*, 5:126.

74. Ibid.

75. Ibid., 5:127.

76. Ibid., 5:128.

77. Ibid., 5:131.

78. Ibid., 5:133. To "lower himself to despised [or humble (*smirennaia*)] prose" is an option considered by Pushkin's narrator in *Eugene Onegin* (chap. 3, stanza 13). Pushkin also uses the phrase in the second stanza of his comic poem *Count Zero* (*Graf Nulin* [1825]) to describe the rural setting of this irreverent seduction spoof: "speaking in despised prose" (prezrennoi prozoi govoria). Closer to playwriting, Pushkin mentions "prezrennaia proza" in his drafts of a 1827–28 letter to the *Moscow Herald* (*Moskovskii vestnik*) on *Boris Godunov*, where he claims to have exchanged the respected alexandrine for blank pentameter verse and even in certain scenes for despised prose (see Pushkin, *Polnoe sobranie sochinenii*, 17 vols., 11:66–69).

79. Krzhizhanovskii, *Tot tretii*, 5:135.

80. Ibid., 5:140.

81. Ibid.

82. Ibid., 5:141.

83. Sigizmund Krzhizhanovskii, "Komediografiia Shekspira," in Krzhizhanovskii, *Sobranie sochinenii*, 4:153–237; for "Sbezhavskii 'tragos,'" see 204–10.

84. Ibid., 205.

85. For discussions of these two works in the Stalinist context, see Judith E. Kalb, *Russia's Rome: Imperial Visions, Messianic Dreams, 1890–1940* (Madison: University of Wisconsin Press, 2008), chaps. 5 and 6.

86. See Eric Bentley, *The Life of the Drama* (New York: Atheneum, 1964), 244–48, pairs quoted from 244. Krzhizhanovsky's Third is, in the end, creatively aligned with the improvisator of Pushkin's *Egyptian Nights*, who is, like him, a poetic wanderer and a fugitive, not to mention an Italian, and also something of a tragic clown.

87. Ibid., 226, 248, 249.

88. Northrop Frye, *Anatomy of Criticism: Four Essays* (Princeton: Princeton University Press, 1957), 223–39.

89. Vladimir Propp, *On the Comic and Laughter*, ed. and trans. Jean-Patrick Debbèche and Paul Perron (Toronto: University of Toronto Press, 2009), 62–63.

90. Ibid., 63.

91. Krzhizhanovskii, *Tot tretii*, 5:141.

Selected Bibliography

Allan, Keith, and Kate Burridge. *Forbidden Words: Taboo and the Censoring of Language*. Cambridge: Cambridge University Press, 2006.

Bessmertnykh, Leonid V. "O nekotorykh izdaniiakh eroticheskikh proizvedenii A. S. Pushkina i M. Iu. Lermontova." *Novoe literaturnoe obozrenie* 6 (1993–94): 289–305.

Bethea, David M., ed. *The Pushkin Handbook*. Madison: University of Wisconsin Press, 2005.

———. *Realizing Metaphors: Alexander Pushkin and the Life of the Poet*. Madison: University of Wisconsin Press, 1998.

Bogomolov, Nikolai A., ed. *Anti-mir russkoi kul'tury: Iazyk, Fol'klor, Literatura*. Moscow: Ladomir, 1996.

Brintlinger, Angela. *Writing a Usable Past: Russian Literary Culture, 1917–1937*. Evanston: Northwestern University Press, 2000.

Choldin, Marianna Tax. *A Fence around the Empire*. Durham: Duke University Press, 1985.

Cooke, Brett. *Pushkin and the Creative Process*. Gainesville: University Press of Florida, 1998.

Cross, Anthony G. "Pushkin's Bawdy; or, Notes from the Literary Underground." *Russian Literature Triquarterly* 10 (1974): 203–36.

Debreczeny, Paul. *Social Functions of Literature: Alexander Pushkin and Russian Culture*. Stanford: Stanford University Press, 1997.

———. "Zhitie Aleksandra Boldinskogo: Pushkin's Elevation to Sainthood in Soviet Culture." In *Late Soviet Culture from Perestroika to Novostroika*, ed. Thomas Lahusen with Gene Kuperman, 47–68. Durham: Duke University Press, 1993.

Denisenko, Sergei V. "'Ot vozderzhaniia muza chakhnet': Erotika Pushkina." In Aleksandr S. Pushkin, *Chas nevinnogo dosuga*, ed. Sergei V. Denisenko, 5–20. St. Petersburg: Azbuka, 2004.

Douglas, Mary. *Purity and Danger: An Analysis of Concepts of Pollution and Taboo.* London: Routledge, 2002.

Dunning, Chester, with Caryl Emerson et al. *The Uncensored Boris Godunov: The Case for Pushkin's Original Comedy.* Madison: University of Wisconsin Press, 2006.

Eidel'man, Natan Ia. *Pushkin i dekabristy.* Moscow: Khudozhestvennaia literatura, 1979.

Emerson, Caryl. "Grinev's Dream: *The Captain's Daughter* and a Father's Blessing." *Slavic Review* 40.1 (1981): 60–76.

Fedetov, Georgii. "Pevets imperii i svobody." In *Pushkin v russkoi filosofskoi kritike: Konets XIX–pervaia polovina XX v.*, ed. Renata A. Gal'tseva, 356–75. Moscow: Kniga, 1990.

Freud, Sigmund. *Totem and Taboo: Some Points of Agreement Between the Mental Lives of Savages and Neurotics.* Trans. James Strachey. New York: Norton, 1950.

Frizman, Leonid. "Pushkin i pol'skoe vosstanie 1830–1831 godov: Neskol'ko vstupitel'nykh slov." *Voprosy literatury* 3 (1992): 209–37.

Gasparov, Boris. *Poeticheskii iazyk Pushkina kak fakt istorii russkogo literaturnogo iazyka.* St. Petersburg: Akademicheskii proekt, 1999.

Gasparov, Boris, Robert P. Hughes, and Irina Paperno, eds. *Cultural Mythologies of Russian Modernism: From the Golden Age to the Silver Age.* Berkeley: University of California Press, 1992.

Grigor'ev, Sergei I. *Pridvornaia tsenzura i obraz verkhovnoi vlasti, 1831–1917.* St. Petersburg: Aleteiia, 2007.

Guseinov, Gasan. *DSP: Sovetskie ideologemy v russkom diskurse 1990-kh.* Moscow: Tri kvadrata, 2003.

Hopkins, William Hugh. "The Development of 'Pornographic' Literature in Eighteenth- and Early Nineteenth-Century Russia." PhD diss., University of Michigan, 1977.

Kahn, Andrew, ed. *The Cambridge Companion to Pushkin.* Cambridge: Cambridge University Press, 2006.

———. *Pushkin's Lyric Intelligence.* Oxford: Oxford University Press, 2008.

Knox, Zoe. *Russian Society and the Orthodox Church: Religion in Russia after Communism.* London: RoutledgeCurzon, 2005.

Kon, Igor S. *The Sexual Revolution in Russia: From the Age of the Czars to Today.* Trans. James Riordan. New York: Free Press, 1995.

Kotovich, Aleksei. *Dukhovnaia tsenzura v Rossii, 1799–1855 gg.* St. Petersburg: Rodnik, 1909.

Levitt, Marcus C. *Russian Literary Politics and the Pushkin Celebration of 1880.* Ithaca: Cornell University Press, 1989.

Levitt, Marcus C., and Andrei L. Toporkov, eds. *Eros and Pornography in Russian Culture/Eros i pornografiia v russkoi kul'ture*. Moscow: Ladomir, 1999.

Liapunov, Vadim. "Not in Vain and Not by Chance: Pushkin and Philaret (Drozdov), Metropolitan of Moscow." In *Philaret, Metropolitan of Moscow, 1782–1867: Perspectives on the Man, His Works, and His Times*, ed. Vladimir Tsurikov, 36–40. Jordanville, NY: Variable Press, 2003.

Literaturnoe obozrenie 11 (1991). Special issue of the journal dedicated to the erotic tradition in Russian literature.

Lotman, Iurii M. "Dekabrist v povsednevnoi zhizni." In his *Besedy o russkoi kul'ture*, 331–84. St. Petersburg: Iskusstvo-SPB, 1994.

———. *Pushkin: Biografiia pisatelia; Stat'i i zametki, 1960–1990; "Evgenii Onegin," Kommentarii*. St. Petersburg: Iskusstvo-STB, 1995.

Maiofis, Mariia. *Vozzvanie k Evrope: Literaturnoe obshchestvo "Arzamas" i rossiiskii modernizatsionnyi proekt 1815–1818 godov*. Moscow: Novoe literaturnoe obozrenie, 2008.

Murav'eva, Ol'ga S. "Obraz 'mertvoi vozliublennoi' v tvorchestve Pushkina." In *Vremennik Pushkinskoi komissii*, vol. 24 (Lenigrad: Nauka, 1991), 17–28.

Nash, David. *Blasphemy and the Christian World: A History*. Oxford: Oxford University Press, 2007.

Nemirovskii, Igor' V. *Tvorchestvo Pushkina i problema publichnogo povedeniia poeta*. St. Petersburg: Giperion, 2002.

Nepomnyashchy, Catharine Theimer, Nicole Svobodny, and Ludmilla A. Trigos, eds. *Under the Sky of My Africa: Alexander Pushkin and Blackness*. Evanston: Northwestern University Press, 2006.

Novikov, Vladimir. "Dvadtsat' dva mifa o Pushkine." *Vremia i my* 143 (1999): 178–93.

Peschio, Joe. *The Poetics of Impudence and Intimacy in the Age of Pushkin*. Madison: University of Wisconsin Press, 2012.

Pil'shchikov, Igor' A., and Maksim I. Shapir. "Tekstologiia vs aksiologiia: Eshche raz ob avtorstve ballady Pushkina *Ten' Barkova*." *Antropologiia kul'tury* 3 (2005): 219–48.

Platt, Kevin M. F., and David Brandenberger. *Epic Revisionism: Russian History and Literature as Stalinist Propaganda*. Madison: University of Wisconsin Press, 2006.

Proskurin, Oleg. *Literaturnye skandaly pushkinskoi epokhi*. Moscow: OGI, 2000.

———. *Poeziia Pushkina, ili podvizhnyi palimpsest*. Moscow: Novoe literaturnoe obozrenie, 1999.

Pushkin, Aleksandr S. *"Ten' Barkova": Teksty, Kommentarii, Ekskursy*. Edited by Igor' A. Pil'shchikov and Maksim I. Shapir. Moscow: Iazyki slavianskoi kul'tury, 2002.

Ram, Harsha. *The Imperial Sublime: A Russian Poetics of Empire*. Madison: University of Wisconsin Press, 2003.

Raskolnikov, Felix. "Pushkin and Religion." *Russian Studies in Literature* 42.1 (2005–6): 7–35.

Reid, Robert, and Joe Andrew, eds. *Alexander Pushkin: Myth and Monument*. Vol. 2 of *Two Hundred Years of Pushkin*. Amsterdam: Rodopi, 2003.

Reyfman, Irina. *Ritualized Violence Russian Style: The Duel in Russian Culture and Literature*. Stanford: Stanford University Press, 1999.

Rozenberg, Vladimir, and Viacheslav Iakushkin. *Russkaia pechat' i tsenzura v proshlom i nastoiashchem*. Moscow: M. and S. Sabashnikovykh, 1905.

Sandler, Stephanie. *Commemorating Pushkin: Russia's Myth of a National Poet*. Stanford: Stanford University Press, 2004.

———. "Sex, Death and Nation in the *Strolls with Pushkin* Controversy." *Slavic Review* 51.2 (1992): 294–308.

Shapir, Maksim I. "Iz istorii russkogo 'balladnogo stikha': *Perom vladeet kak eldoi*." *Russian Linguistics* 17.1 (1993): 57–84.

———. *Stat'i o Pushkine*. Edited by I. A. Pil'shchikov. Moscow: Iazyki slavianskikh kul'tur, 2009.

———. *Universum versus: Iazyk, stikh, smysl v russkoi poezii XVIII–XX vekov*. Moscow: Iazyki russkoi kul'tury, 2000.

Slater, Wendy. "The Patriots' Pushkin." *Slavic Review* 58.2 (1999): 407–39.

Tertz, Abram [Andrei Siniavsky]. *Strolls with Pushkin*. Trans. Catharine Theimer Nepomnyashchy and Slava I. Yastremski. New Haven: Yale University Press, 1993.

Todd, William Mills, III. *Fiction and Society in the Age of Pushkin: Ideology, Institutions, and Narrative*. Cambridge, MA: Harvard University Press, 1986.

Tomashevskii, Boris V. *Pushkin*. 2 vols. Leningrad: AN SSSR, 1956–61.

Vaiskopf, Mikhail. "'Vot evkharistiia drugaia': Religioznaia erotika v tvorchestve Pushkina." *Novoe literaturnoe obozrenie* 37 (1999): 129–47.

Veresaev, Vikentii V. *V dvukh planakh: Stat'i o Pushkine*. Moscow: Zakharov, 2000.

Virolainen, Mariia N., ed. *Legendy i mify o Pushkine*. St. Petersburg: Akademicheskii proekt, 1999.

Vishlenkova, Elena A. *Religioznaia politika: Ofitsial'nyi kurs i "obshchee mnenie" Rossii Aleksandrovskoi epokhi*. Kazan: Izdatel'stvo Kazanskogo universiteta, 1997.

Wachtel, Michael. *A Commentary to Pushkin's Lyric Poetry, 1826–1836*. Madison: University of Wisconsin Press, 2011.

Contributors

Carol Any is working on a study of the Soviet Writers' Union in the Stalin years. She is the author of *Boris Eikhenbaum: Voices of a Russian Formalist* and teaches at Trinity College in Connecticut.

David M. Bethea is Vilas Research Professor of Slavic languages at the University of Wisconsin–Madison and professor emeritus of Russian studies at the University of Oxford. He is the author of various books on classical and modern Russian poetry, including *Realizing Metaphors: Alexander Pushkin and the Life of the Poet* and *The Superstitious Muse: Thinking Russian Literature Mythopoetically*. At present he is working on a creative biography of Pushkin.

J. Douglas Clayton is professor of Russian at the University of Ottawa, Canada. His research interests include the poetry of Alexander Pushkin, Russian modernist theater, the plays and prose of Anton Chekhov, and Franco-Russian cultural relations. His publications include *Ice and Flame: Aleksandr Pushkin's "Eugene Onegin"*; *Pierrot in Petrograd: Commedia dell'arte/Balagan in Twentieth-Century Russian Theatre and Drama*; and *Dimitry's Shade: a Reading of Alexander Pushkin's "Boris Godunov."*

Caryl Emerson is A. Watson Armour III University Professor of Slavic Languages and Literatures at Princeton University. Research interests include Mikhail Bakhtin, nineteenth-century Russian literary classics (Pushkin, Tolstoi, Dostoevsky), and Russian opera and vocal music. Among her current projects are Tolstoi and Bernard Shaw on Shakespeare; the modernist Sigizmund

Krzhizhanovsky; and the adaptation of the Russian literary tradition to the Stalinist-era stage.

ALYSSA DINEGA GILLESPIE is associate professor of Russian at the University of Notre Dame. She is the author of *A Russian Psyche: The Poetic Mind of Marina Tsvetaeva,* which is forthcoming in a Russian-language edition from Pushkin House, St. Petersburg; and editor of *Russian Literature in the Age of Realism* in the Dictionary of Literary Biography series. Her research interests center on the psychology of poetic genius and the myths poets create around their poetic calling. She is currently writing a book on Pushkin's poetic ethics.

KATYA HOKANSON is associate professor of Russian and comparative literature at the University of Oregon. Her research interests include orientalism and imperialism in Russian nineteenth-century literature and culture. She is the author of *Writing at Russia's Border*. She has published articles on Pushkin and on Russian women travelers in Central Asia and India. Her current project is a monograph on nineteenth-century Russian women travelers in the Caucasus and Central Asia.

ANDREW KAHN is professor of Russian literature at the University of Oxford and fellow and tutor, St. Edmund Hall, Oxford. He has written widely about the literature and ideas of the Russian and European Enlightenments. His books include *Pushkin's "The Bronze Horseman"* and *Pushkin's Lyric Intelligence*. He is the editor of *The Cambridge Companion to Pushkin*.

IGOR NEMIROVSKY completed his undergraduate studies at Tartu University, where he studied under Iurii Lotman and Boris Gasparov. His graduate studies at the Institute of Russian Literature (Pushkin House) in St. Petersburg led to his focus on Russian literature of the eighteenth and early nineteenth centuries, as well as the Decembrist movement. Nemirovsky worked as a researcher at Pushkin House from 1988 to 2006. He was a fellow at Harvard University's Davis Center for Russian and East European Studies in 2004–5 and has taught at Harvard, Boston College, and Tufts University. Since 2007 he has served as the director of Academic Studies Press in Boston. He is the author of *Tvorchestvo Pushkina i problema publichnogo povedeniia poeta* (*Pushkin's Literary Art and the Problem of the Poet's Public Behavior*) and articles on Pushkin, Karamzin, Radishchev, and the Decembrists.

JOE PESCHIO received his PhD in Russian literature from the University of Michigan. Since 2004, he has headed the Slavic languages program at the University of Wisconsin–Milwaukee. His first book, *The Poetics of Impudence and Intimacy in the Age of Pushkin*, is forthcoming from the University of Wisconsin Press. As part of the team at the Fundamental Digital Library of Russian Literature and Folklore (FEB-web.ru) since 2003, he has worked toward philologically responsible digitization of the Russian canon, and he established in Milwaukee the first FEB-web digitization lab outside of Russia. The entirety of the Green Lamp archive described in his article for this volume is to form the basis for a Russian-language digital scholarly edition of the papers of the Green Lamp funded by the National Endowment for the Humanities, with a projected online publication date of 2012.

IGOR PILSHCHIKOV is a leading researcher at the Institute for World Culture at M. V. Lomonosov Moscow State University and a senior researcher at the Estonian Institute for Humanities of Tallinn University. He completed undergraduate studies at Tartu University in Estonia, received his PhD equivalent in Russian and European literatures from Moscow State University, and earned a habilitation degree in general linguistics and literary theory from the Institute of Linguistics of the Russian Academy of Sciences in Moscow. He is the author of *Batiushkov i literatura Italii* (*Batiushkov and Italian Literature*) and *Leksika i frazeologiia "Evgeniia Onegina"* (*The Lexicon and Phraseology of "Eugene Onegin"*) and coeditor of Alexander Pushkin's *"Ten' Barkova": Teksty, Kommentarii, Ekskursy* (*"The Shade of Barkov": Texts, Commentaries, Discussions*), Boris Iarkho's *Metodologiia tochnogo literaturovedeniia* (*The Methodology of a Precise Science of Literature*), and volume 1 of Evgenii Boratynskii's *Polnoe sobranie sochinenii i pisem* (*Complete Collected Works and Letters*). He has contributed numerous articles on Pushkin and his epoch to academic periodicals and yearbooks.

JONATHAN BROOKS PLATT is an assistant professor in the Department of Slavic Languages and Literatures at the University of Pittsburgh. He received his PhD from Columbia University and is currently completing a book on Stalinist attitudes to time in the 1937 Pushkin jubilee. His next project deals with the problematic legacy of Pushkin's "nondialectical" aesthetics in nineteenth-century Russian culture.

OLEG PROSKURIN graduated from Moscow State University and has taught at the Moscow State Pedagogical University, the University of Illinois at Chicago, Northwestern University, and Middlebury College. He has been a research fellow at the Institute for European Studies at Cornell University and at the Davis Center for Russian and Eurasian Studies at Harvard University. He is currently a visiting professor in the Department of Russian and East Asian Languages and Cultures at Emory University. His publications include *Poeziia Pushkina, ili Podvizhnyi Palimpsest* (*Pushkin's Poetry, or A Dynamic Palimpsest*), *Literaturnye skandaly pushkinskoi epokhi* (*Literary Scandals of the Pushkin Era*), and a book-length commentary on Alexander Pushkin's narrative poems in vol. 1 of Push-kin's *Sochineniia: Kommentirovannoe izdanie* (*Works: An Edition with Commentary*).

IRINA REYFMAN is professor of Russian literature at Columbia University. She received her MA degree equivalent from Tartu University in Estonia and her PhD degree from Stanford University. In her studies, Reyfman focuses on the interaction between literature and culture, examining both how literature reacts to cultural phenomena and how it contributes to the formation of cultural biases and forms of behavior. Reyfman is the author of *Vasilii Trediakovsky: The Fool of the "New" Russian Literature* and *Ritualized Violence Russian Style: The Duel in Russian Culture and Literature*. She is also a coeditor of *Mapping the Feminine: Russian Women and Cultural Difference*. Her current projects include a book that will examine how obligatory state service and the existence of the Table of Ranks shaped Russian writers' views of themselves as professionals. It will also consider whether the prominence of the rank system prompted the development of specifically Russian types of literary discourse.

ALEXANDRA SMITH is reader in Russian studies at the University of Edinburgh and the author of *The Song of the Mockingbird: Pushkin in the Works of Marina Tsvetaeva* and *Montaging Pushkin: Pushkin and Visions of Modernity in Russian Twentieth-Century Poetry*, as well as numerous articles on Russian literature and culture. Currently she is working on several publications related to the project "Reconfiguring the Canon of Russian Twentieth-Century Poetry, 1991–2008," funded by the AHRC (Arts and Humanities Research Council).

NATALIA VESSELOVA is a PhD candidate in English at the University of Ottawa, Canada. She holds a PhD equivalent degree in literary theory from Tver State University in Tver, Russia. Her professional experience includes teaching poetics and Western literatures as well as the publication of over forty articles on comparative literature. Vesselova's current scholarly interests are focused on eighteenth-century European culture and Canadian literature.

Index

Notes: All works are indexed under the English translation of the title (followed by the Russian title, unless it is very close to the English), as well as under the type of work (e.g., prose). Page numbers in italics indicate illustrations.

Publications of the Wisconsin Center for Pushkin Studies

Realizing Metaphors: Alexander Pushkin and the Life of the Poet
David M. Bethea

The Pushkin Handbook
Edited by David M. Bethea

The Uncensored Boris Godunov: The Case for Pushkin's Original Comedy, with Annotated Text and Translation
Chester Dunning with Caryl Emerson, Sergei Fomichev, Lidiia Lotman, and Antony Wood

Alexander Pushkin's Little Tragedies: The Poetics of Brevity
Edited by Svetlana Evdokimova

Taboo Pushkin: Topics, Texts, Interpretations
Edited by Alyssa Dinega Gillespie

Pushkin's Tatiana
Olga Hasty

Derzhavin: A Biography
Vladislav Khodasevich; Translated and with an introduction by Angela Brintlinger

The Imperial Sublime: A Russian Poetics of Empire
Harsha Ram

Pushkin and the Genres of Madness: The Masterpieces of 1833
Gary Rosenshield

Pushkin's Rhyming: A Comparative Study
J. Thomas Shaw

A Commentary to Pushkin's Lyric Poetry, 1826–1836
Michael Wachtel